Charity Governance

Charity Governance

Con Alexander

Jos Moule

JORDANS

Published by
Jordan Publishing Limited
21 St Thomas Street
Bristol BS1 6JS

Whilst the publishers and the author have taken every care in preparing the material included in this work, any statements made as to the legal or other implications of particular transactions are made in good faith purely for general guidance and cannot be regarded as a substitute for professional advice. Consequently, no liability can be accepted for loss or expense incurred as a result of relying in particular circumstances on statements made in this work.

Crown Copyright material is reproduced with kind permission of the Controller of Her Majesty's Stationery Office.

British Library Cataloguing-in-Publication Data

A catalogue record for this book is available from the British Library.

ISBN 978 1 84661 048 6

Typeset by Letterpart Ltd, Reigate, Surrey

Printed in Great Britain by Antony Rowe Limited

PREFACE

Governance has been a significant feature on the corporate landscape of the UK and other developed economies for more than a decade. Starting with the Cadbury Report in 1992 and culminating in the more recent Higgs Report in 2003, a series of high profile committee reports have been commissioned to look at particular aspects of the way in which companies are run. These have all served to highlight different aspects of the governance agenda, and have resulted notably in the evolution over time of the Combined Code for UK listed companies. This voluntary code of best practice has been supplemented more recently by various legislative developments. In particular, the publication of the Company Law Reform White Paper in 2005 marked the end of a huge consultative process relating to the governance of companies and the modernisation of company law generally.

Although there have been no equivalent reports or consultation exercises of this kind in relation to charities, they have not been immune from developments in good governance. Charity trustees are spending more time considering the range of issues that can loosely be described as 'charity governance'. In other words, all of the issues which determine how a charity is operated and controlled by its trustees.

This book attempts to summarise and explain the most significant aspects of good governance for charities. It deals with the framework of company, trusts, charity and other branches of law that regulate how charities are formed, the powers they have, how they are operated and controlled and the way in which they are made accountable. We have, though, also tried to build on the legal framework by dealing with many of the practical issues that arise and, in particular, the approach taken by the sector's regulator, the Charity Commission, and also by HM Revenue & Customs.

Where relevant, we have used and quoted from the helpful guidance produced by both the Charity Commission and HM Revenue & Customs in relation to charities. This is an excellent resource and is all available online (at www.charity-commission.gov.uk and www.hmrc.gov.uk respectively). All of this material is subject to Crown copyright protection.

We have been writing this book during a period when two very significant pieces of legislation in relation to charities have become law. Both the Charities Act 2006 and the Companies Act 2006 received Royal Assent on 8 November 2006. When this book is published, neither Act will be fully in force, although implementation timetables have been published for both by the Office of the

Third Sector and the DTI respectively. They are available online at www.cabinetoffice.gov.uk (for the Charities Act 2006) and www.dti.gov.uk (for the Companies Act 2006). In order to make this book as useful as possible, we have tried to look forward to the new law. We have therefore commented on provisions in both the new Acts which are not yet in force but have sought to make it clear in the text and footnotes where particular provisions should be confirmed to be in force before being relied upon. The coming into force of both Acts can be checked online at the addresses mentioned above.

In writing this book, we have drawn upon our own practical experience of the sort of issues faced by charities ranging from grant makers to service providers. And we have dealt with the differing legal positions of charitable companies, corporations, trusts and associations in as much detail as we can in the space available. On the principle that we should look forward, we have also dealt with charitable incorporated organisations. Having said all this, the two forms of charity most commonly encountered as things stand (the charitable company limited by guarantee and the charitable trust) are the main focus of this book.

We hope this book will be useful to lawyers, accountants and other professionals advising charities, particularly those who may not regard themselves as charities specialists. We also hope that it will be useful to charity trustees themselves and those employed by charities.

With this in mind, the book breaks down in the following way:

- The first four chapters are intended to provide a framework for the rest of the book, with much reference material that we hope will be useful in the context of other chapters.

'What is a charity?' explains the legal definition of charities.

'Types of charity' looks at the distinguishing characteristics of the various different types of incorporated and unincorporated charity.

'Modern legal framework' explains the different legal regimes to which charities are subject.

'The Charity Commission' explains the role of the Charity Commission as the regulator of charities.

- The next four chapters look at core governance issues:

'Governance structures' explains the relationship between the members and trustees of charities.

'Trustees' duties and liabilities' looks at the potential personal liability of trustees in relation to their charities.

'Trustees' powers' discusses the position of a charity's trustees in relation to the exercise of any power, whether it is express, implied or statutory.

'Trustee governance' looks at the nuts and bolts of acting as a trustee and discusses issues ranging from how they are appointed and retire to delegation.

- The remaining chapters look at seven areas that, in practice, often raise issues of governance for a charity's trustees:

'Charity assets' explains the different ways in which charities hold and can deal with their assets, including permanent endowment and land.

'Investment' examines all of the issues raised by the exploitation of assets by way of investment, including the appropriate use of an investment policy and delegation of investment management.

'Taxation' summarises the key tax implications of particular activities that may be carried out by a charity, but looks in particular detail at the activities that can give rise to non-charitable expenditure and associated tax liabilities.

'Borrowing' explains all of the issues that are likely to be encountered by a charity's trustees in relation to commercial borrowing, including the restrictions on the mortgage of a charity's land.

'Trading' looks at the governance issues raised by trading by charities and their trading subsidiaries.

'Reporting and accounting' looks at the accounting framework and the way in which charity trustees report to their stakeholders and the wider public.

'Restructuring' explains the different ways in which a charity's trustees can respond to change by altering the way in which the charity is structured and deals with issues ranging from straightforward constitutional changes through to dissolutions.

- The full text of the Charities Act 1993, as amended by the Charities Act 2006, is in the Appendix.

Disclaimer

This material in this book is provided for general purposes only and does not constitute legal or other professional advice. It should not be acted upon without seeking appropriate independent professional advice.

Neither the publisher nor the authors accept any responsibility for loss occasioned to any person however caused or arising as a result of or in consequence of action taken (or not taken) in reliance on the material in this book.

Thanks

The authors would like to thank:

Lois Bradburn for all of her good work on this book over and above the call of duty over the past six months.

Chris White, Mark Woodward, Anna Keeling, Iain Evans, Claire Bundy, Sam Boundy, Vicki Carr and Mark Womersley of Osborne Clarke and James Potts of Erskine Chambers for their help in preparing this book.

Con Alexander would like to thank:

Hugh Craig of Bates, Wells & Braithwaite and Nigel Reid of Linklaters for their advice and guidance in the past.

Tamsin James for her love, friendship and good advice. Con's contribution to this book is dedicated to Tamsin, Olivia, Kitty and Ivor, with love.

Jos Moule would like to thank:

His wife, Joanna and children, Charlotte, Georgina and Henry for their love and patience.

Abbreviations

There are a number of words and phrases we have used throughout this book and which have the following meanings:

- 'Advice' is advice given by the Charity Commission in accordance with the Charities Act 1993, s 29 (see **4.16**).

- 'Charities Acts' means the Charities Acts 1993 and 2006.

- The 'Charity Commission' is the Charity Commission for England and Wales (see **4.1**).

- A 'CIC' is a community interest company (see **2.75**).

- A 'CIO' is a charitable incorporated organisation (see **2.31**).

- 'Companies Acts' means the Companies Acts 1985 and 2006.

- An 'Inquiry' is an inquiry into a charity instituted by the Charity Commission (see **4.35**).

- An 'Order' is an order of the Charity Commission made in accordance with the Charities Act 1993, s 16 (see **4.19**).

- A 'Scheme' is a scheme made by the Charity Commission in accordance with the Charities Act 1993, s 16 (see **4.26**).

- 'Terms of Reference' are explained at **8.35**.

Our main aim in writing this book has been to prepare what we hope is a practically orientated guide to charity governance. Any comments will be gratefully received.

We have tried to state the law in force in England and Wales as at 1 March 2007.

Con Alexander

Jos Moule

Bristol, March 2007

CONTENTS

TABLE OF STATUTES

References are to paragraph numbers.

TABLE OF STATUTORY INSTRUMENTS

References are to paragraph numbers.

TABLE OF CASES

References are to paragraph numbers.

1

WHAT IS A CHARITY?

1.1 There is no single way of identifying a charity. Most will be on the register of charities maintained by the Charity Commission, but many will not. And different legal definitions determine what a charity is for different purposes. When one adds to that the very wide range of activities carried out by charities in the 21st century, the task becomes more difficult.

CHARITY LAW

1.2 Having said this, the starting point for most purposes will be what constitutes a charity for the purposes of charity law. A statutory definition will be introduced by the Charities Act 2006.[1] There is a different (but very similar) definition for tax purposes. This is explained in more detail at **11.5**. The Charities Act 2006 definition is ostensibly straightforward. A charity is any institution which:

'(a)   is established for charitable purposes only, and
(b)   falls to be subject to the control of the High Court in the exercise of its jurisdiction with respect to charities.'[2]

1.3 The definition therefore requires three things:

*   an 'institution';

*   that it is established only for charitable purposes; and

*   that it is subject to the control of the High Court in the exercise of its jurisdiction with respect to charities.

1.4 Each of these component parts needs to be looked at in more detail, because each of them has aspects that are not immediately obvious to anyone looking to apply the definition in practice.

INSTITUTION

1.5 There is a limited definition of what an 'institution' is.[3] The Charities Act 1993 states simply that an institution 'includes any trust or undertaking'.In practice,

---

[1]   Expected to come into force in early 2008.
[2]   Charities Act 2006, s 1(2).
[3]   Charities Act 1993, s 97.

charitable institutions can take almost any legal form. The most obvious examples include companies, trusts and unincorporated associations. The position is explained in more detail in **Chapter 2**.

CHARITABLE PURPOSE

1.6 'Charitable purpose' is defined by s 2 of the Charities Act 2006. It is any purpose that falls within a number of 'descriptions' of purposes set out in the Act and is also for the 'public benefit'. Both requirements must be met.

Statutory descriptions

1.7 The list of descriptions set out in s 2 of the CA 2006 is long and includes:

• the prevention or relief of poverty;

• the advancement of education;

• the advancement of religion (including a religion which involves belief in more than one god and a religion which does not involve belief in a god);

• the advancement of health or the saving of lives (including the prevention or relief of sickness, disease or human suffering);

• the advancement of citizenship or community development (including rural or urban regeneration and the promotion of civic responsibility, volunteering, the voluntary sector and the effectiveness or efficiency of charities);

• the advancement of the arts, culture, heritage or science;

• the advancement of amateur sport;

• the advancement of human rights, conflict resolution or reconciliation or the promotion of religious or racial harmony or equality and diversity;

• the advancement of environmental protection or improvement;

• the relief of those in need by reason of youth, age, ill-health, disability, financial hardship or other disadvantage;

• the advancement of animal welfare; and

• the promotion of the efficiency of the armed forces of the Crown, or of the efficiency of the police, fire and rescue services or ambulance services.

1.8 This list reflects the way in which the law of charitable purposes has developed prior to the passing of the Charities Act 2006, which will make[4] some significant

---

4 Expected to come in force in early 2008.

changes to both the Charities Act 1993 and the general law of charities. Perhaps the most significant change will be the introduction of a statutory definition of charitable purposes.

1.9   In order to understand the statutory definition fully, it helps to look at a little history. Before the passing of the Charities Act 2006, the categories of charitable purposes were defined by the courts in the cases that came before them. Over the centuries, four accepted heads of charitable purpose emerged. These are:

- the relief of poverty;

- the advancement of education;

- the advancement of religion; and

- any other purpose regarded as 'beneficial to the community'.

1.10   The last category (purposes beneficial to the community) was used by the courts, and subsequently the Charity Commission under the overall control of the courts, to develop the scope of charitable purposes generally, subject to a test of 'public benefit' which itself evolved over time. Many of the charitable purposes recognised within this category (such as animal welfare and the advancement of human rights) are now expressly recognised by the Charities Act 2006, subject to a statutory test of public benefit.

1.11   The definition of charitable purpose in the Charities Act 2006 does not close the door on the development of new purposes that can be recognised as charitable. There is a statutory provision for new purposes which are analogous to or 'within the spirit of' the purposes listed in the Act.[5] The Act also ensures that any purpose not mentioned in the Act that was charitable under the law that applied previously will not lose that status.

1.12   A detailed discussion of charitable purposes is outside the scope of this book. For practical purposes, the important points to bear in mind are:

- Because an institution must be 'established for' charitable purposes, its constitution must state those purposes clearly and precisely. Where that is done will depend upon how the institution in question is set up. There is more information about this in **Chapter 2**.

- Because the institution must be established 'for charitable purposes only' it must also be clear that the purposes are limited to those that are charitable. If an institution has some purposes that are charitable and some that, while philanthropic, are not, then the institution will not qualify as a charity.

- It must also be clear that the assets of the institution can only ever be applied for its charitable purposes. An institution's constitution should not contain any 'default' provisions which could apply surplus assets for any non-charitable purpose. Usually, a charity's constitution will set out expressly what will happen to the institution's surplus assets in the event that it is wound-up.

---

5   Charities Act 2006, s 2(4)(b).

- The charitable purposes for which an institution is established are the single most important part of its constitution because their scope will determine what the institution can do and often how it can do it. The widest objects that an institution can have are 'such purposes as are exclusively charitable under the law of England and Wales'.

- Charities established before the implementation of the changes to be made to charity law by the Charities Act 2006 are much more likely to have purposes which reflect the four heads of charity that were used by the courts and the Charity Commission before then. Charities established after the changes take effect are more likely to have purposes that reflect the descriptions set out in the statutory definition.

Public benefit

1.13 The second component of the statutory definition of what constitutes a charitable purpose is the requirement that it must be for the public benefit. The Charities Act 2006 states expressly that public benefit must be tested using the criteria developed by the courts.[6] And while the courts will remain the ultimate arbiters of whether a particular purpose is for the public benefit, the Act also provides for the Charity Commission to issue guidance on the public benefit requirement[7] which must be taken into account by charity trustees when they exercise any of their powers or duties to which the guidance is relevant.

1.14 The Charity Commission has a statutory duty to issue guidance on the requirement of public benefit and it is also obliged to carry out whatever consultation it considers appropriate before issuing or revising that guidance.[8] The guidance available at present is set out in the Commission's publication 'The Public Character of Charity'.[9] It is understood that the Commission is reviewing this guidance to take account of the impact of the Charities Act 2006 and that the Commission's draft revised guidance ('Public Benefit – the legal principles') will be formally consulted on by the Commission in accordance with s 4 of the Charities Act 2006 during the first half of 2007.

1.15 For practical purposes, the most important points to bear in mind are:

- There is no legal presumption that charitable purposes falling within the descriptions set out in s 2 of the Charities Act 2006 are for the public benefit. In practice, this means that the public benefit of all charitable purposes must be demonstrated and cannot be assumed. This has altered the position of charities whose purposes are to relieve poverty, or to advance education or religion (such charities are assumed to be for the benefit of the public prior to the coming into force of the Charities Act 2006).[10]

- The Commission's existing guidance states that:

  '"Benefit" in this context means the net benefit to the public. It is not simply a question of showing that some benefit may result. For example, it may be that the achievement of a given aim would provide some degree of benefit, but would for other

---

6   Charities Act 2006, s 3(3).
7   Charities Act 2006, s 4 which came into force on 27 February 2007 (SI 2007/309).
8   Charities Act 2006, s 4(1).
9   Charity Commission publication RR8.
10 Charities Act 2006, s 3(2).

reasons cause great harm so on balance it would be to the public's disadvantage. If the harm outweighs the benefits, the purpose would not be charitable.'

- The Commission's guidance goes on to identify the three key questions in relation to public benefit. First, what is meant by 'the public'? Second to what extent may individuals benefit privately? Third, to what extent is public benefit affected by charging?

- The first requirement is that a charity must be able to show that its activities will benefit 'the community' (in other words the public at large) or at least a 'sufficient section of the community'. As the Commission points out, 'this is not a simple matter of numbers'. What constitutes a 'sufficient' section of the community will vary from charity to charity depending upon the benefits provided and the people to whom they are made available.

- It is not enough to show that an institution has been established for charitable purposes which are for the benefit of the community or a sufficient section of the community. An intrinsic part of this test is that any private benefit to an individual made available by an institution arises either directly as a consequence of the pursuit of the charity's purposes or is properly incidental to the pursuit of those purposes.

- There are many ways in which too great a degree of private benefit could arise. A grant made to a beneficiary for the relief of poverty may do more than relieve their poverty and enrich them to too great an extent. While paying employees is properly incidental to the pursuit of a charity's purposes, salaries which are too high in the context of the charity's own income or market rates generally may also confer too great a degree of private benefit. A grant made to a 'for profit' business with the aim of generating work for impoverished beneficiaries of a charity may confer too great a degree of private benefit on the owners of the business.

- In practice, most questions in relation to private benefit depend upon whether individuals have benefited privately in a way which is (in the Commission's words) 'legitimately incidental' to the pursuit of the charity's charitable purposes. The Commission's guidance makes it clear that every question of this kind must be considered on its own facts but, in general, the Commission takes the approach that:

  'A private benefit is legitimately incidental if it arises as a necessary but incidental consequence of a decision by the trustees which is directed only at furthering the organisation's charitable purposes (as opposed to a separate purpose in effect providing private benefit), and the amount of benefit is reasonable'.[11]

- An institution will not be charitable if its main aim is to generate profit for individuals or for the institution itself. This is most likely to be an issue in the context of charities that charge fees for the services they provide. The examples usually given are independent schools and private hospitals, but many charities charge for what they do and operate in much the same way as commercial entities do in seeking to produce surpluses with which to enhance the services they provide. This is increasingly true of charities providing services under contracts with Government.

---

[11] Charity Commission publication RR8.

•   The Commission's guidance on charities that do charge fees for their services is
     helpful. While the Commission would only ever look at the position of the charity
     on an individual basis, the principles it is likely to apply are as follows:

> 'Charges should be reasonable.
>
> Charges may, if appropriate to the overall purposes of the charity, be set at a rate that
> generates a surplus to help fund the charity's other current or future activities.
> Looking at the overall purposes of the charity includes taking general account of the
> circumstances of its intended beneficiaries.
>
> Any charge should not be set at a level which deters or excludes a substantial
> proportion of the beneficiary class since this would be contrary to the purposes of the
> charity. The service provided should not cater only for those who are financially
> well-off. It should in principle be open to all potential beneficiaries (as opposed to the
> entire exclusion of those with limited financial means).
>
> It should be clear that there is a sufficient general benefit to the community directly or
> indirectly from the existence of the service.'[12]

1.16   It is important to remember that the Charity Commission regards the
descriptions of charitable purposes in s 2 of the Charities Act 2006 as no more than
descriptions. An institution which has charitable purposes modelled on the descriptions
on the 2006 Act will not necessarily be accepted by the Commission as established for
charitable purposes only. For example, an institution established for the 'relief of those
in need by reason of youth, age, ill-health, disability, financial hardship or other
disadvantage' is likely to need to specify the 'other disadvantage' that it has in mind in
order to be accepted for registration by the Commission.

JUDICIAL CONTROL

1.17   The third and final requirement imposed by the Charities Act 2006 is that the
institution is 'subject to the control of the High Court in the exercise of its jurisdiction
with respect to charities'. This fairly inaccessible phrase is aimed at ensuring that any
institution claiming charitable status (and the UK tax and other advantages that come
with it) is subject to the overall authority of the courts of England and Wales.

1.18   The way in which this requirement applies has been the subject of a number of
Court decisions.[13] From a practical point of view, it is helpful to look at the criteria that
the Charity Commission uses when it is considering an application for registration as a
charity. These are not definitive (because only the courts can interpret the requirement
definitively) but reflect the decisions taken by the courts in the past and are a useful
guide to their likely approach in the future.

1.19   The Commission's criteria differ depending upon how an institution is set up. It
draws a distinction between companies and every other sort of institution. The position
in relation to a company is straightforward. Only a company incorporated in England

---

[12]   Charity Commission publication RR8.
[13]   *Camille and Henry Dreyfus Foundation, Inc v IRC* [1954] 2 All ER 466; *Gaudiya Mission v Brahmachary*
[1997] All ER 1957; *His Beatitude Archbishop Torkom Manoogian, Armenian Patriarch of Jerusalem v
Yolande Sonsino & Others* [2002] EWHC 1304 Ch.

and Wales (under the Companies Acts) can qualify. The position for other sorts of institution is more complicated. The Commission looks first at whether the institution is governed by the law of England and Wales. If not, it cannot qualify. If English law does apply, the Commission looks for at least three of the following criteria to be satisfied:

- The institution is administered in England or Wales.

- A majority of the people responsible for its management and administration are resident in England and Wales.

- All or most of the institution's assets are in England or Wales.

- All or most of the institution's activities will take place in England or Wales.

CHARITY REGISTRATION

1.20 If it is a company incorporated in England and Wales or otherwise meets at least three of the criteria mentioned above, an institution will qualify as a charity for the purposes of charity law. This brings with it an obligation (under s 3B of the Charities Act 1993) to apply to the Charity Commission to have its name and certain other details added to the register of charities maintained by the Commission unless the institution falls within certain categories of exempt and excepted charities. These exceptions are explained in **Chapter 4**.

1.21 Once an institution is registered as a charity, it is conclusively presumed to be a charity. This is stated to be 'for all purposes' but does not include tax purposes and is subject in any event to any later decision by the Charity Commission to remove it from the register. There is a wide discretion for the Commission to remove any charity from the register which 'it no longer considers is a charity'.[14] This may be because, eg the charity's purposes are no longer charitable as a result of a change in the law or in society.

CHARITY TRUSTEES

1.22 While it is not part of the Charities Act 2006 definition, almost every charity will in practice also have one or more 'charity trustees'. These are defined by the Charities Act 1993 as:

> 'the persons having the general control and management of the administration of a charity'.[15]

1.23 Knowing who the trustees of a charity are is essential because it is the trustees who are responsible for ensuring that the charity fulfils its purposes in line with its constitution and within the legal framework imposed on charities in England and Wales. And from their own perspective, it is the trustees who will be personally liable for any failure to meet these responsibilities. Even a brief review of the Charities Act 1993 will show the range of duties owed by charity trustees.

---

[14] Charities Act 1993, s 3(4).
[15] Charities Act 1993, s 97.

1.24   There is no simple rule of thumb that determines who the charity trustees of any given charity are, mainly because of the diversity of different forms of charitable institution. There is more about charity trusteeship in the context of specific forms of charity within **Chapter 2**. Essentially, however, the charity trustees of a charity are those who are responsible for what it does and how it does it at the highest level. They are sometimes referred to as those who take 'strategic' decisions. This implies that the activities of the charity will be sufficiently complex to require others to implement those decisions, but as a practical guide this applies in the same way to smaller charities where the trustees will both take and implement strategic decisions.

1.25   The key point from a practical point of view is that the law applies a 'de facto' test to charity trusteeship. It looks at what a person actually does rather than what he is described as or the post that he holds. If the decisions that a person takes are the sort of decisions about general management and control that would or should ordinarily be taken by the trustees then it does not matter that he or she has not been formally appointed as a trustee because the law will treat him or her in the same way as any person who has.

1.26   For this reason, it is important to ensure that charity trustees are distinguished from:

- the people who set the charity up (usually referred to as the 'founders') or have made donations to it ('donors');

- the people employed by the charity or who volunteer to do work for it; and

- the members or other stakeholders in the charity.

1.27   This does not mean that people within one of these categories cannot also be charity trustees and, in many cases, the trustees are also founders, donors or members, but these roles are in principle separate and distinct. Where the boundaries between the different roles become blurred, problems are more likely to arise. This is essentially a governance issue. There is more about this in **Chapter 5** and **Chapter 8**.

2

TYPES OF CHARITY

INTRODUCTION

2.1   As explained in **Chapter 1**, the Charities Act 1993 definition of a charitable 'institution' says no more than that it is an institution whether incorporated or not and includes any 'trust or undertaking'. This means that, in principle at least, almost any legal form can be used to set-up a charity provided that the other requirements of the Act (exclusively charitable purposes and judicial control) are satisfied. Partnerships and Limited Liability Partnerships (both of which must be established for profit) cannot be established as charities.

2.2   In practice, charitable institutions take one of a number of different forms. Before we look at this in more detail, it is helpful to understand that there is a significant distinction between those forms of institution that are incorporated and those that are not.

2.3   An incorporated institution is one that has a legal existence (usually referred to as a legal personality) that is separate from the legal personality of the people who are its members or who control its activities or who were responsible for its incorporation in the first place. In other words, an incorporated institution is capable of interacting with the outside world in its own right, rather than via the people who control it. This has several important consequences:

- An incorporated institution can own property in its own name (in what is usually referred to as 'perpetual succession') and deal with that property using the powers it has in its constitution.

- It can enter into agreements with third parties (and sue and be sued on those agreements) in its own name.

- Because it can incur its own liabilities, its members and the other people interested in it will not usually have any liability for them.

2.4   These are essentially the hallmarks of incorporation. It follows that the consequences of unincorporated status are:

- An unincorporated institution can only own property via other people. When those people change, the property must be transferred to their successors.

- It can only enter into agreements (and sue and be sued) in the names of other people.

- The people who enter into agreements or own property for or on behalf of an unincorporated institution are personally liable as a consequence.

2.5   There are a number of different incorporated and unincorporated institutions that operate in the charitable context:

Incorporated	Unincorporated
Companies limited by guarantee	Trusts
Companies limited by shares	Associations
Charitable Incorporated Organisations[1]	
Industrial and Provident Societies	
Friendly Societies	
Corporations	

2.6   The key features of each of these forms of institution are as follows:

COMPANIES LIMITED BY GUARANTEE

2.7   A company limited by guarantee is incorporated under the legislation that governs companies (the Companies Acts). It is the most commonly used form of incorporated charitable institution, but is also often used for a wide range of other non-charitable purposes usually characterised as 'not for profit'; in other words, for purposes which are not aimed at private gain or enrichment (or at least not directly). These include trade associations, clubs and societies, registered social landlords and scientific research associations.

2.8   A company limited by guarantee has a 'two tier' governance structure. It will have one or more 'members' and one or more 'directors'. Because the company is limited by guarantee, the members have no shares in its capital and no entitlement to the dividends and other distributions of its profits and assets to which the members of a company limited by shares are entitled, including any surplus assets on a winding-up. But they do give a 'guarantee' of the company's liabilities in the event that the company is wound up and has insufficient assets to pay its debts. The guarantee is a requirement of the Companies Act 2006,[2] but the guarantee is usually only nominal (typically limited to £1). In other words, the members' liability is limited to this amount if the company is insolvent.

2.9   Membership confers important rights to vote on certain fundamental matters, including:

• altering the company's constitution;

• the appointment and removal of its directors; and

• winding the company up.

---

[1]   Charities Act 1993, s 69, sch 5B (expected to come into force in early 2008). See **2.31**.

[2]   Companies Act 1985, s 1(2)(b); Companies Act 2006, s 3(3).

2.10   The directors are responsible for the day-to-day management and control of the company. For that reason, they will be its 'charity trustees' under the Charities Act 1993 as well as its directors under the Companies Acts. This dual role is explained in more detail in **Chapter 5**. A charitable company will usually have a minimum of two directors. The directors are usually referred to collectively as the 'board'.

2.11   The company will also usually have a secretary (although, following the coming into force of the Companies Act 2006 this will no longer be a requirement for a private company).[3] The secretary is responsible for assisting the directors to ensure that the company complies with its obligations under the Companies Acts.

2.12   The constitution of a company limited by guarantee is set out in its memorandum and articles of association. Technically, these are two separate documents although in practice they are almost always referred to and treated as one. The Companies Act 2006 has made some significant changes to the way in which a company's constitution is structured. Once the provisions have come into force, the memorandum of association will be no more than a document stating that the first members of the company (usually referred to as the 'subscribers') wish to form, and have agreed to become members of, the company.[4]

2.13   All of the other provisions of a company's constitution are set out in its articles of association (as supplemented by any resolution passed by members or agreement made between the members of the company). The existence of any resolutions or agreements can be checked on by carrying out a search with Companies House, because there will be an obligation to ensure that a written memorandum of their terms is filed within 15 days of being made.[5]

2.14   Every company must have articles of association. If none are registered when the company is incorporated, the Companies Act 2006 provides that a set of 'model articles' prescribed for limited companies (with different model articles for different types of company) will apply.[6] A company can also chose to adopt some or all of the provisions of the model articles or to adopt a set of articles that expressly exclude the model articles. A similar set of provisions applies to companies incorporated before the coming into force of the Companies Act 2006.

2.15   Because the articles will, following the coming into force of the Companies Act 2006, set out the purposes for which a company is established (often referred to it as its 'objects'), a company that wishes to establish itself as a charity will need to adopt articles which expressly confirm its charitable purposes and the powers which it can use to achieve those purposes. As far as a company's objects are concerned, the Companies Act 2006 provides[7] that, unless the company's articles specifically restrict the objects, they are unrestricted. Clearly, in order to qualify as a charity, a company's objects will need to be restricted to charitable purposes only.

2.16   The articles regulate how the company is managed and administered by the members and the directors. They will specify:

---

[3]   Companies Act 2006 s 270 (expected to come into force in April 2008).
[4]   Companies Act 2006 s 8 (expected to come into force in October 2008).
[5]   Companies Act 2006 s 30 (expected to come into force in October 2008).
[6]   Companies Act 2006 s 20 (expected to come into force in October 2008).
[7]   Section 31.

- how new members of the company will be appointed and the circumstances in which they will stop being members;

- whether the members have to pay a subscription to the company;

- whether the company will have different kinds of member with different kinds of rights in relation to the company;

- provisions for members' general meetings and the way in which they can vote and count in the quorum;

- how the directors are appointed by the members (and often also by the directors themselves) and the circumstances in which they will stop being directors;

- provisions governing directors' meetings and the way in which they vote and count in the quorum; and

- provisions designed to assist the directors to run the company effectively, including by appointing committees and advisory boards.

2.17   Before the coming into force of the Companies Act 2006, a charitable company's memorandum is more significant. In particular, it will spell out the purposes for which the company is established, its powers to achieve those purposes and the fact that the liability of its members is limited. Its articles will spell out how the company is to be managed and administered by the members and directors (as in **2.16** above). A company incorporated before the coming into force of the Companies Act 2006 will continue to have memorandum and articles of association in this form. The fact that the Companies Act 2006 prescribes a different procedure for incorporating companies does not affect the validity of the constitutions of charitable companies incorporated before the new provisions come into force.

2.18   The relationship between a charitable company's members and its directors, and the way in which the constitution regulates that relationship, is one of the most important aspects of good governance. See **Chapter 5**.

2.19   Not every company limited by guarantee will be a charity. That depends upon whether certain key parts of the constitution are adapted so that it will qualify as an 'institution ... established for charitable purposes only'. In practice, the key provisions are:

- The objects of the company must be charitable (see **Chapter 1**).

- They must also be exclusively charitable. It is not possible to have non-charitable objects that are ancillary to charitable objects; they must either be expressed as powers or left out altogether if a company is to qualify as a charity.

- The constitution prevents any of the members or directors from benefiting from the company's assets in any way at any time. In this context, 'benefit' means financial or monetary benefit. This is because a company capable of conferring benefits on its members or directors would not be able to satisfy the public benefit requirement now given statutory force by the Charities Act 2006. There are some permitted exceptions from this for members and directors but these are small in scale. Benefits for the directors of a charitable company are explained in **Chapter 6**.

* The constitution also includes a provision that obliges any surplus assets on a winding up of a charitable company to be applied for similar charitable purposes rather than passing to the company's members. This is another aspect of the requirement that members should not benefit from a charitable company's assets but it should be expressly stated.

2.20 A company limited by guarantee is incorporated and regulated by the Registrar of Companies (usually referred to as 'Companies House'). In practice, a charitable company limited by guarantee is regulated by both Companies House (under the Companies Acts) and the Charity Commission (under the Charities Acts) and must generally submit an annual report and accounts to both bodies.

COMPANIES LIMITED BY SHARES

2.21 A company limited by shares is also incorporated under the Companies Acts and is the usual legal form adopted by those undertaking trading and other commercial activities in the UK.

2.22 A company limited by shares has an authorised capital in respect of which it will issue one or more shares. In a commercial context, the shares entitle their holder to a proportion of its profits and its assets in the event that it is wound up and are often issued in order to raise funds for the company from those subscribing for the shares. The shareholders themselves are recorded in a register and the company will usually issue certificates to them in respect of each holding. If a shareholder wishes to transfer their shares, they must complete a form and submit it to the company, which will update its register and issue a new certificate to the new shareholder.

2.23 Companies limited by shares also have a 'two tier' structure. Every company will have at least one shareholder (sometimes referred to as a 'member') and at least one director. In addition to an entitlement to a share in the company's profits and assets, shares confer the same rights on shareholders as the rights exercisable by members of a company limited by guarantee.

2.24 The directors are responsible for the day-to-day management and administration of the company in exactly the same way as the directors of a company limited by guarantee. The relationship between the members and the trustees will also be key to the governance of the company. See **Chapter 5**.

2.25 The constitution of a company limited by shares is also set out in its memorandum and articles of association. They will contain provisions very similar to those in the memorandum and articles of a company limited by guarantee, except that there will be provisions for the company's share capital, including the rights of shareholders to transfer shares and the rights of directors to issue new shares.

2.26 The articles of association will be in the model form specified by the Companies Act 2006 (or, in the case of companies incorporated before that Act comes into force, the form specified by the Companies Act 1985) unless some other provision is made.

2.27   Not every company limited by shares will be a charity. In fact, there are relatively few charitable companies limited by shares. This is primarily because the existence of share capital is a complication that most charities neither want nor need. Shareholders will not in any event be entitled to any dividend or other kind of distribution on their shares and, because shareholders are actually entitled to shares in the company, they must transfer them whenever they wish to resign as members of the company and the company must update its register. These are generally unnecessary complications.

2.28   The members of a company limited by guarantee, on the other hand, are able to join or resign as members without any significant complications. So where there is a choice between using a company limited by shares and a company limited by guarantee, it will usually be most straightforward to use a guarantee company except where there is some other compelling reason for using a share company. This is the approach taken by the Charity Commission to new charities in any event.

2.29   If a charitable company is to be limited by shares, its constitution will need to be adapted in much the same way as the constitution of a company limited by guarantee. In particular, there will need to be an express prohibition on any dividend or other distribution on shares. Like a company limited by shares, it will be subject to regulation by both Companies House and the Charity Commission.

Terminology

2.30   The terms used to describe the members and directors in the context of a charitable company are often confusing. The directors of a charitable company are often referred to as its 'trustees' and that is the approach we have adopted in this book. However, there are no hard and fast rules about this. Many charitable companies may refer to their directors as 'directors'. The company's constitution will usually define its directors in a particular way although they may sometimes be referred to in practice using a different description from the one set out in the constitution. Some of the more common terms that may come up in practice are as follows:

Word	Meaning
Director	A director of a company under the legislation which governs companies
Member	A member of a company limited by guarantee or a shareholder
Shareholder	A member of a company limited by shares
Subscriber	A member of a company when it was first set up
Trustee	Another way of describing a director of a charitable company
Board	One of the ways in which the directors can be described collectively
Council	Another one of the ways in which the board of directors can be described collectively

Secretary	The company secretary under the legislation that applies to companies
Treasurer	A director who has been given primary responsibility for a charitable company's finances. This is not a post required by law, but the articles of some companies provide for it
Chairman	The chairman of the board of directors (who will often also be the chairman at general meetings of members)
Company	The company itself but references in the articles to 'resolutions of the company' are actually to resolutions of the members
Patron	Usually an honorary position which confers no rights and obligations and does not make an individual a trustee
President	Another way of describing a patron

CHARITABLE INCORPORATED ORGANISATIONS

2.31   A charitable incorporated organisation (usually referred to as a 'CIO') will (once the relevant provisions of the Charities Act 2006 are in force) be able to be set up under the Charities Act 1993.[8] The provision for CIOs was introduced into the 1993 Act by the Charities Act 2006 with the aim of providing a form of incorporated entity specifically designed for charitable activities.

2.32   Before the introduction of the CIO, anyone wishing to set-up an incorporated charity would usually use a company limited by guarantee, but adapted to ensure that it could qualify as a charity. Adaptation was required because limited companies were originally designed for commercial use, rather than charitable activities.

2.33   As a consequence, charitable companies are subject to regulation by both Companies House and the Charity Commission. The CIO is an attempt to create a new entity bringing with it the advantages of incorporation but without the burden of dual regulation and with the flexibility to create a constitution aimed specifically at charitable activities and governance.

2.34   The key features of a CIO will be:

• It is incorporated.

• It has a 'two tier' structure made up of one or more members and one or more charity trustees (although the trustees and the members can be identical; see Charities Act 1993, s 69B(6)).

• The liability of the members for the CIO's debts can be limited to a maximum specified amount (which can be a nominal amount of £1) or excluded altogether.

---

[8]   Charities Act 1993, Part 8A, Sch 5B; Charities Act 2006, s 34, Sch 7 (expected to come into force in early 2008).

- It has a single constitution that must comply with certain requirements set out in Regulations (yet to be made). The constitution must also be as similar to a statutory form set out in regulations made by the Charity Commission or as near to their form as the 'circumstances admit'. In other words, if the statutory form is unsuitable, it does not need to be used provided that the general scheme of the statutory form is followed.

- The constitution of a CIO will need to provide that none of its income or property can be paid or transferred, directly or indirectly, by way of dividend or otherwise by profit to any of the CIO's members and that no charity trustee of a CIO should obtain any form of financial benefit from his or her position, unless that benefit is authorised by the CIO's constitution, or by a statutory provision, or by the court or the Charity Commission.

2.35   The final form of the Regulations is not yet available[9] but it is anticipated that they will apply many of the provisions of the Companies Act 2006 and the Insolvency Act 1986 in relation to companies to CIOs. This would include, for example, provisions in relation to wrongful and fraudulent trading and the execution of documents.

2.36   The Government intends to review the usefulness of CIOs within 5 years of the passing of the Charities Act 2006. If they have proved to be useful, the longer-term aim may be to convert all other forms of incorporated charity into CIOs.

INDUSTRIAL AND PROVIDENT SOCIETIES

2.37   A charity may be set up as an industrial and provident society intended to be conducted for the 'benefit of the community' under the Industrial and Provident Societies Act 1965.[10] There is another form of Industrial and Provident Society which can be incorporated under the 1965 Act (which is intended to trade on a co-operative basis) but this cannot be used to establish a charity.

2.38   An industrial and provident society is an incorporated body. Like a company, it has a 'two tier' structure of members and trustees. Its members and trustees have limited liability and the society can hold assets, and sue and be sued, in its own name. Many of the provisions of the Industrial and Provident Societies Acts 1965, 1967, 1975, 1979 and 2002 (together with the Co-operatives and Community Benefit Societies Act 2003) (which regulate societies) incorporate provisions in a very similar form to the provisions of the companies legislation.

2.39   Industrial and provident societies have traditionally been used to set up charitable housing associations (registered as 'social landlords' under the Housing Act 1996). Any society which is registered as a social landlord under the Housing Act 1996 is an exempt charity (they are regulated by the Financial Services Authority and, in so far as their status as a 'social landlord' is concerned, the Housing Corporation) rather than the Charity Commission. Before the coming into force of the

---

9   Draft Regulations are expected in 2007.
10   Section 1.

Charities Act 2006, all industrial and provident societies were exempt charities. This will no longer be the case, with the consequence that some societies will be required to register with the Charity Commission.[11]

FRIENDLY SOCIETIES

2.40 A friendly society is a 'mutual assurance' association of individual members who, in order to qualify as members, must be poor. A friendly society has corporate status under the Friendly Societies Act 1992 and can hold property in its own name. Charitable friendly societies are exempt charities and are regulated by the Financial Services Authority rather than the Charity Commission.

CORPORATIONS

2.41 A 'corporation' is any other incorporated institution that can own property, and enter into agreements and sue and be sued on those agreements, in its own name. A charitable corporation may be established by Royal Charter or by Act of Parliament. Other corporations (such as local authorities) may hold property on charitable trusts, although they will not themselves be charitable because not all of their purposes will be charitable purposes. The constitution of a corporation will depend upon the way in which it has been established and will in any event vary from corporation to corporation. A corporation established by a Royal Charter will, for example, have all of the powers and capacity of a natural person.[12] A detailed analysis of the law in relation to corporations is outside the scope of this book.

TRUSTS

2.42 Trusts were originally developed as a way of protecting assets, usually in a family context, by separating their 'legal' ownership from their 'beneficial' ownership. The legal owners ('trustees') hold and control trust assets for the benefit of other people ('beneficiaries'). The trustees are under a duty to safeguard the assets. If they do not, the beneficiaries can seek compensation from them for any losses that they suffer.

2.43 The beneficiaries of a charitable trust are its charitable purposes. Because there is no way in which a purpose can enforce a trustee's duties, this role is taken by the Attorney General and the Charity Commission. See **Chapter 4**.

2.44 A charitable trust is easy to establish, requiring only a single trust deed to set it up, and is regulated only by the Charity Commission. A trust can also be established by a will. The trust deed or will need not be in any particular form, but will ideally address certain fundamental points:

- it will specify the charitable objects of the trust;

- it will also identify the first trustees;

---

[11] This requirement is expected to come into force in 2008.
[12] *Pearce v University of Aston (No 2)* [1991] 2 All ER 469.

- the trustees' entitlement to benefit personally from the trust will be limited, with any exceptions clearly spelled out;

- the trustees' powers to apply the trust's assets (and to invest, insure them etc) will be specified; and

- it will explain how the trustees must take decisions, how often they must meet, the quorum required in order to pass resolutions etc.

2.45 Not every charitable trust will be established by a clearly drafted trust deed or will. This is because all that is required in order to establish a valid charitable trust is a sufficient degree of certainty about three things. First, the charitable purposes of the trust must be certain. Secondly, that the assets which are subject to the trust are certain. Thirdly, that there is sufficient certainty that the creation of a charitable trust was intended.

2.46 Subject to the requirement that a declaration of trust over land or any interest in land must be in writing,[13] there are no technical words that must be used in order to establish a trust provided the three certainties mentioned in **2.45** are present. In principle, therefore, a charitable trust over assets other than land could be declared orally provided there is sufficient evidence of the position. Equally, charitable trusts may be established by documents other than trust deeds and wills. Many charities are established by a conveyance or transfer of assets to be held by the transferees for particular charitable purposes. Provided the three certainties are present, a charitable trust will be established in such cases, although a Scheme of the Charity Commission is often required to supplement the powers given to the charity trustees to deal with the assets (see **Chapter 4**).

2.47 It is open to anyone who wishes to establish a charitable trust to specify terms on which the relevant assets are to be held. Charitable trusts can (and often do) state that the trustees have a power to hold and invest assets with a view to applying the investment income that is produced but with an obligation to retain the capital of the assets in perpetuity. Other trusts will specify that trustees have a power (or perhaps an obligation) to apply both the capital and income of the charitable trust's assets. The terms of a charitable trust will differ from case to case and a detailed examination of the provisions of the trust's constitution will always be required in order to determine the powers and obligations of the trustees in relation to the charity's assets. There is more about this at **Chapter 9**.

2.48 There are a number of legal rules which govern the way in which gifts for charitable purposes will take effect in the event that they should fail. A detailed discussion of this area is outside the scope of this book.[14]

2.49 Most charitable trusts will have a 'single tier' governance structure simply made up of the trustees. But it would be perfectly possible to write a trust deed so that it has members who appoint and remove the trustees or exercise other powers (there are a number of charitable trusts that include provisions along these lines). See **Chapter 5**.

2.50 Because a trust is unincorporated, it can only interact with the outside world via its trustees. This means that:

---

[13] Law of Property Act 1925, s 53(1)(b).
[14] For further information see, for example, *Tudor on Charities*, Sweet & Maxwell, 9th edn.

- The trustees must hold all of the trust's assets in their own names or the name of a nominee on their behalf. If the assets are held in the trustees' names they must be transferred whenever a trustee is appointed or retires.

- The trustees must enter into all contracts that relate to the trust personally. They will remain liable even after they have retired as trustees, unless there is a provision for them to be released from their obligations.

ASSOCIATIONS

2.51 A charitable unincorporated association will exist where two or more people (usually individuals) make a legally binding agreement between themselves to act together to advance particular charitable purposes. There are no statutory formalities which must be observed in order to set up an association but the terms of the agreement between the members will usually be set out in a body of rules. The rules will vary from association to association, but will usually contain provisions relating to the admission of new members, the retirement of existing members, the way in which assets are held and who will have day-to-day management and control of the association's activities.

2.52 In many cases (although not all) an association's rules will provide for the appointment of a committee of members who are responsible for the management and control of the association's activities. They will be the association's charity trustees. An association set up in this way will have a 'two tier' governance structure which is broadly similar to the structure of a company or a CIO. However, an association is not an incorporated body, cannot hold assets or enter into contracts on its own and does not confer any limited liability on its members or its trustees. Because the assets of an association cannot be held in its own name, they must be held by individuals on trust for it. The rules will usually identify the people who are to act as trustees. This may be the members of a committee, although some rules will provide that assets must be held by a separate group of trustees from the trustees who make up the committee. Generally, the trustees who hold the association's assets will act only on the direction of the committee and not on their own initiative.

2.53 Because an association is not able to enter into contracts in its own name, contracts must be entered into on behalf of all of the members of the association, usually by the members of the committee. In order to ensure that contracts can properly be entered into by committee members, the rules will usually need to contain an express power of delegation (or there must be an appropriate statutory power). There is more about delegation in relation to charitable unincorporated associations in **Chapter 8**.

SCHEMES

2.54 A Scheme is the legal mechanism by which the Charity Commission can alter the provisions of a charity's constitution in certain circumstances. A Scheme will not usually be made where a charity has an existing power to amend its own constitution. Incorporated charities will generally have an appropriate power of amendment, so Schemes are invariably made in relation to existing charitable trusts and other unincorporated charities. The making of a Scheme will not alter the fundamental legal structure of a charitable trust or any other unincorporated charity, but it will often become a charity's constitutional document. While a charity cannot be established, therefore, by way of a Scheme, it may regulate the charity's governance arrangements.

NEW CHARITIES

2.55   Anyone looking to set up a new charity will need to choose which of the forms of charitable institution will best serve their purposes. It is difficult to give any definitive guidance on how to approach this question because a lot depends on what a new charity is intended to do, but there are certain fundamental questions that often help to make the process easier.

2.56   The fundamental question is whether to use an incorporated or unincorporated body. This depends on a number of things.

2.57   Is liability likely to be an issue because of what the charity will do (eg provide services or undertake a particular project) or because of the assets it will own (eg land that may be contaminated)? If the answer to this question is 'yes', then using an incorporated body will confer limited liability for members and trustees in most circumstances. The trustees (and, in certain circumstances, the members) of an unincorporated body will almost inevitably be personally liable in respect of what their charity does and how it does it. That liability may be limited in other ways but these are all less certain than the limited liability of an incorporated body. See **Chapters 5** and **6**.

2.58   An incorporated body can hold assets in its own name. While the trustees of an unincorporated body can in most circumstances use a nominee to hold assets on their behalf, arrangements must be made for title to pass from trustee to trustee as they are appointed and retire. This is not difficult but adds to the burden of administering the charity properly and can cause problems if it is not done. The appointment and retirement of trustees of an incorporated body has no impact on the assets held in its name.

2.59   An incorporated body can enter into contracts in its own name. The trustees of an unincorporated body must enter into contracts that relate to it personally. Again, this is not in itself a particular problem but it adds to the burden of administering the charity and the risk that it is not done properly.

2.60   The position in relation to asset holding and entering into contracts for unincorporated charities is sometimes solved by appointing a corporate trustee or by incorporating the charity trustees under Part VII of the Charities Act 1993 (see **Chapter 6**). While this may simplify the position in relation to asset holding and entering into contracts (and using a corporate trustee may improve the liability position of the individual trustees), creating additional incorporated bodies may add to the burden of administering the charity (although not usually significantly).

2.61   Some take the view that an unincorporated body is easier to administer than an incorporated body, partly because they are not subject to formal legal administrative requirements and partly because they are regulated with a 'lighter touch'. It is certainly true that the Charity Commission alone regulates most unincorporated bodies, whereas both the Commission and Companies House regulate companies. It is also true that most unincorporated bodies can operate fairly informally within the terms of their constitutions.

2.62   Having said this, the filing and reporting requirements of the Commission tend to match those of Companies House and, more generally, there is a strong argument that the precisely formulated and comprehensive requirements of the legislation that applies to companies actually provides a good and easily understood framework for effective administration, whereas an unincorporated body's constitution may not be particularly clear or easily understood. In practice, a lot will depend upon how complex the charity's affairs (and therefore its administration) are likely to be.

2.63   Some also take the view that an unincorporated body can be established more easily and cheaply than an incorporated body. This is probably true of the most simply constituted unincorporated body but the availability of good precedent documents and online advice from the Charity Commission and other sources in relation to companies makes the difference marginal in the majority of cases.

2.64   Incorporated bodies (and companies in particular) are almost inevitably more familiar to commercial entities (particularly banks and other financial institutions) that the charity may wish to engage with than unincorporated bodies. So, for example, a bank will find it easier to lend to a charitable company than a charitable trust because it routinely lends to companies and the charitable component does not fundamentally alter the way in which a company looks and behaves. This is not an insurmountable problem for unincorporated bodies, but may be an issue depending on what the charity wishes to do. So most banks will be able to open an account for a charitable trust as easily as an account for a charitable company, but may find it more difficult (and therefore more time consuming and costly) to enter into a syndicated loan facility with it. In particular, an unincorporated body is not able to grant a 'floating charge' over its assets as security for borrowings. There is more about borrowing at **Chapter 12**.

2.65   The table below summarises the position:

Issue	*Incorporated*	*Unincorporated*
Liability	Limited liability in most circumstances	Personal liability for trustees
Asset holding	Assets held in body's own name	Assets held in names of trustees (except where trustee body incorporated)[15]
Contracts	Body contracts in own name	Trustees contract in their own names
Administration	Greater degree of regulation/well-established administrative framework	Lesser degree of regulation/less well-established administrative framework
Set-up	Arguably more complicated documents and set-up process	Arguably less complicated documents and set-up process

---

[15]   See **6.26**.

Recognition	Greater degree of third party recognition	Less recognisable by third parties

2.66   On balance, incorporated status is likely to be an advantage for any charity that plans to do things that may involve liability, that will own assets that are either complex or used operationally or carry with them some associated liabilities. The most obvious examples of this are:

- taking a lease or buying the freehold of a property;

- raising finance by e g taking a bank loan, particularly where a floating charge is to be given as security for the loan;

- employing people;

- giving advice or entering into contracts to provide goods or services; and

- organising events involving members of the public.

CHOOSING AN UNINCORPORATED BODY

2.67   That is not to say that unincorporated charities do not have their place. They are likely to be most appropriate in the following circumstances:

- Charities that do no more than hold and invest their assets with a view to making straightforward grants and donations to other charities or for other charitable purposes, usually referred to as 'grant making trusts' or 'foundations'.

- Charities established by groups of individuals for a particular purpose that does not involve any significant liability or potential liability, e g a league of friends that organises hospital visits or a charity that promotes a particular religion.

- A charity established to do no more than raise funds for a particular purpose, e g an appeal to raise funds for new hospital equipment or facilities or the 'friends of' a university, college or school looking to raise funds from alumni or parents.

2.68   Which form of unincorporated body should be used will depend upon what it is intended to do. It will be most appropriate to set up a grant making trust or foundation or an appeal as a trust, whereas a league of friends or other body involving participation by a group of members will generally be an association. A Scheme will only be relevant to existing charities and is not an option in relation to new charities.[16]

2.69   If an incorporated body is required, the choice will usually be between a company limited by guarantee and, subject to the relevant provisions of the Charities Act 2006 coming into force (expected to be in early 2008), a CIO, unless there are particular reasons for using some other form. For example, historically many housing associations have been set up as industrial and provident societies in order to ensure that they are exempt charities, regulated only by the Financial Services Authority and the

---

[16]   See further at **4.26**.

Housing Corporation and not also by the Charity Commission.[17] Or an existing charity may petition for incorporation by Royal Charter in recognition of the particular value of its work.

2.70 The main advantage of using a CIO is likely to be that it is specifically designed to be used as a vehicle for charitable activities and will be regulated only by the Charity Commission. The main advantage of using a company limited by guarantee as against a CIO is that a company is a long established legal form governed by a well-developed and comprehensive body of statute and case law. There are very few questions about the way in which such companies function that cannot be answered by reference to that body of law. By contrast, a CIO is the creation of a relatively recently enacted statute (the Charities Act 2006) which describes what it is and how it functions in, at least by comparison to the Companies Acts, a few brief provisions and which is not presently the subject of any decided case law which might supplement the statutory provisions.

2.71 The chief disadvantage of using a CIO, therefore, is likely to be that there is presently not the same degree of certainty about how it will function in most circumstances as there is about a company limited by guarantee. This may mean that, in practice, there will be a degree of caution about using a CIO rather than a company. Lawyers in particular may be reluctant to recommend the use of a CIO to their clients while it remains a relatively 'new' legal form.

2.72 In our view, this would be an overly cautious approach to an entity specifically designed for carrying out charitable activities, particularly when the Charities Act 1993 will (subject to the relevant provisions of the Charities Act 2006 coming into force) contain a range of provisions which are aimed at ensuring that CIOs will function in a certain and reliable way and many of the provisions intended to regulate CIOs are based upon the framework of the Companies Acts and the Insolvency Act 1986. For example:

- Subject to anything in its constitution, a CIO has power to do anything which is 'calculated to further its purposes or is conducive or incidental to doing so' (Sch 5B, para 1(1)).

- In favour of a person who deals with a CIO in good faith and has given consideration in money or money's worth, the validity of any act done by the CIO, and the power of the charity trustees of the CIO to act to bind it, cannot be called into question on the ground that the CIO either lacked the relevant powers in its constitution or because of any constitutional limitation on those powers unless the third party actually knew that the act was beyond the CIO's powers or contravened any limitation in the constitution (Sch 5B, para 5(2) and (3)).

- A party to an arrangement or transaction with a CIO is not bound to enquire whether it is within the CIO's constitutional capacity or the powers of its charity trustees (Sch 5B, para 5(5)).

- Section 69Q of the Charities Act 1993 gives the Secretary of State a wide power to make regulations governing how CIOs operate. This power is likely to be used to plug any gaps in the CIO regime as they appear.

2.73 A better reason for remaining cautious about using a CIO while it remains reasonably unusual is that it is likely to be less recognisable to third parties than a

---

[17] But see **2.39**.

company limited by guarantee. This may cause practical difficulties, although the position may well change as more CIOs are incorporated and registered as charities.

2.74   Section 69 of the Charities Act 1993 (which is expected to come into force in early 2008) contains a number of provisions aimed at enabling charitable companies, industrial and provident societies and unincorporated charities to become CIOs. This legislation is aimed at facilitating the long-term goal of the CIO legislation: the consistent use of CIOs as the legal entity for charities. But it will also enable anyone who wishes to establish a new charity, but who is cautious about the workability of the CIO legislation, to opt for one of the more traditional approaches in the knowledge that there is a statutory provision for its conversion into a CIO should that, with the benefit of hindsight, turn out to be the best approach.

COMMUNITY INTEREST COMPANIES

2.75   Community Interest Companies (or 'CICs', as they are usually referred to) were introduced by the Companies (Audit, Investigations and Community Enterprise) Act 2004. They are intended to be a legal form earmarked specifically for those who wish to pursue some sort of enterprise in the interests of the public (or 'community') rather than their own personal economic interests. In other words a CIC is an entity which can only function on a 'not for profit' basis. The hope is that CICs will develop as a 'brand' for developing community interest in much the same way as the 'charity' brand.

2.76   CICs can be incorporated under the Companies Acts as a company limited by shares or by guarantee. The provisions of the Companies Acts apply to a CIC in the same way as they apply to any other company limited by shares or by guarantee, except to the extent that they are modified by The Community Interest Company Regulations 2005 (SI 2005/1788). The most significant modification is the introduction of an 'asset lock'. Essentially, a CIC's assets must be held for its community interest objects and any distributions to any of its members (other than another CIC or charity) must be on 'arms' length' terms. In other words, the CIC must receive value in return for any payment it makes to a member for goods or services supplied to it. There are also specific provisions that limit the amount of any dividend that can be paid by a CIC to its members.

2.77   Prior to the introduction of the CIC, the usual way in which to establish an entity with community interests as its object rather than personal profit was to use a company (usually limited by guarantee) with a specific provision in its memorandum precluding any distribution of its profits for any purpose other than its public or community interest objects. While the constitution of a 'not for profit' company could provide that none of its assets should be distributed to its members, this could not override the fundamental principle of company law that, subject to any agreement between them requiring unanimity, 75% or more of the members of the company could at any time resolve to alter those provisions. CICs were intended to solve this potential problem by creating the 'asset lock' we have described.

2.78   Section 22 of the Companies Act 2006 will (once it has come into force)[18] introduce statutory provisions for the 'entrenchment' of specific provisions of a

---

[18]   Expected to be in October 2008.

company's articles, so that they can provide that they can be altered only if particular conditions are met or procedures are complied with. This could include, for example, a condition that the company's assets cannot be distributed to its members without their unanimous agreement. These provisions may undermine the use of CICs to an extent, except in very limited circumstances, although no provision for entrenchment can ever prevent all of the members of a company from agreeing to alter its constitution.[19] The asset lock provided for by the provisions governing CICs goes further than this.

2.79 A CIC cannot be registered as a charity. CICs are regulated by the CIC Regulator rather than the Charity Commission. They do not qualify for the exemptions and reliefs from tax which can be claimed by charities but are subject to a 'lighter touch' regulatory regime. It is possible that what a CIC could be established to do may be charitable. In deciding whether or not to establish a CIC or a charity, the decision to set up a charity will usually be driven by the desire to obtain the exemptions and reliefs from tax available to charities and the degree of public recognition given to the 'charity' brand (particularly where funds are to be raised from donors who will wish to see a high degree of regulation and accountability).

2.80 A CIC is likely to be more appropriate where tax is not a particular concern or where there is a desire to make limited distributions to its members (which will not be possible in relation to activity) and the potential disadvantage of the lower degree of public recognition likely to be given to the 'CIC' brand is outweighed by the desire for a lighter touch regulatory regime.

---

[19] Companies Act 1985, s 17(2)(b); Society for Promoting Employment of Women [1927] WN 145.

3

MODERN LEGAL FRAMEWORK

3.1   Charities are subject to a number of different legal regimes. The position can be summarised as follows:

- All charities are subject to charity law.

- All charities are also subject to tax law.

- Every charity will be subject to the legal regime that applies to its particular legal form.

- Every charity will also be subject to the legal regimes that apply as a consequence of what it does.

CHARITY LAW

3.2   The law that applies to all charities, irrespective of the legal form that they take, is set out in the Charities Acts 1992, 1993 and 2006 and in a number of statutory instruments made under those Acts. The 1992 Act relates to certain forms of fundraising and public collections by charities. The 1993 Act (as amended by the Charities Act 2006) is a much more comprehensive piece of legislation aimed at the regulation of charities and which, among other things, governs:

- the status of the Charity Commission and its regulatory powers;

- the disposition of land owned by charities;

- charity accounts, reports and returns; and

- 'small' and 'local' charities.

3.3   Certain 'exempt charities' are not subject to some of the provisions of the 1993 Act. Other 'excepted charities' are not obliged to register with the Charity Commission. There is more information about exempt and excepted charities in **Chapter 4**.

3.4   Part VIII of the Charities Act 1993 relates specifically to charitable companies. It regulates certain aspects of the relationship between charity and company law as they apply to charitable companies. Part 8A of the Charities Act 1993 relates specifically to CIOs.

3.5   The 1992, 1993 and 2006 Acts are by no means comprehensive and are essentially additions to a body of Court decisions that deal with the aspects of charity law not dealt with by the Acts themselves.

TAX LAW

3.6   Every charity will be subject to tax law. Tax law is governed by a number of different statutes governing different taxes. This is dealt with in more detail in **Chapter 11**.

REGIMES THAT APPLY TO DIFFERENT LEGAL FORMS

Companies

3.7   Charities established as companies are subject to the provisions of the legislation that governs all companies established in England and Wales, the Companies Act 1985 (as amended by the Companies Act 2006 as and when it comes into force). This is complex legislation, some of which is not relevant to charitable companies, but much of which is. In particular:

- provisions relating to a company's capacity and the execution of documents (Companies Act 2006, Part 4) (see **Chapter 8**);

- provisions regulating the information about the company that must be made available on a company's letterhead and other documents (Companies Act 2006, Part 5, Chapter 2);

- provisions dealing with the duties of the company's directors (Companies Act 2006, Part 10, Chapter 2) (see **Chapter 6**);

- provisions in relation to members' meetings (Companies Act 2006, Part 13) (see **Chapter 5**); and

- provisions in relation to accounts and reports (Part 15 Companies Act 2006) (see **Chapter 14**).

3.8   The Companies Acts are supplemented by a large and comprehensive body of case law that regulate those aspects of the legal position of companies which the Acts do not cater for.

3.9   The Companies Acts regulate the rights and duties of all company directors, including directors of charitable companies. Directors are also subject to a body of case law that supplements the provisions of the 2006 Act, as well as the Companies Directors Disqualification Act 1986 which, as the name suggests, deals with the disqualification of directors from office where they are convicted of offences or carry out certain other acts which make them unfit to hold office. See **Chapter 8**.

Charitable incorporated organisations

3.10 Subject to the coming into force of the relevant provisions of the Charities Act 2006 (expected in early 2008), CIOs will be governed by the provisions of the Charities Act 1993, as supplemented by Regulations. These will deal with, amongst other things, how CIOs are constituted, the conversion of other legal entities into CIOs, amalgamations of CIOs, their winding up and insolvency and the powers and duties of their members and trustees.

3.11 Because there are no CIOs in existence yet, there is obviously no existing case law that relates to them (although, as charities, they are obviously subject to charity law).

Trusts

3.12 Charities established as trusts are subject to the patchwork of statute and case law that make up the English law of trusts. Perhaps the most important point to appreciate is that the law of trusts was developed by the courts as part of their 'equitable' jurisdiction in order to protect the interests of those often incapable of looking after their own interests. As a consequence, the statutes that apply to them are very much laid over a well-developed and reasonably complex body of case law that is much more accessible to the lawyer than the layman. This is obviously important in understanding how trusts operate, but it is equally important to the charity trustees of all charities (whichever legal form that they take) because very many of their most significant rights and duties are governed by the law of trusts rather than the law that related to charities generally or to charities established as, say, companies.

3.13 The most significant statutes that form part of the law of trusts are:

- Trustee Act 1925

- Trusts of Land and Appointment of Trustees Act 1996

- Trustee Delegation Act 1999

- Trustee Act 2000.

3.14 Not every part of each of these statutes applies to a charity established as a trust, nor to the trustees of every charity. The most significant aspects of each of them as they apply in practice are identified in this book.

Unincorporated associations

3.15 There are no statutes that relate specifically to unincorporated associations. An association is created by a contract between its members. The law of contract is made up of a body of case law supplemented by statutes that deal with specific aspects of contracts.

3.16 The law of trusts will often also be relevant to charitable associations because their assets are often held on trust for their charitable objects. This is dependent on the terms of their constitutional documents and often also on the terms on which assets are donated to them, but the law of trusts will usually be relevant.

REGIMES THAT APPLY BECAUSE OF WHAT CHARITIES DO

3.17   There are many different legal regimes that can apply to a charity as a consequence of what it does. Some examples may help to illustrate this:

- A charity that educates children (say, an independent school) will be affected by the Education Acts (in relation to the standards of education it provides), the Protection of Children Act 1999 (in relation to ensuring the safety of pupils), the Data Protection Act 1998 (in relation to the confidentiality and security of personal data) and employment and health and safety legislation.

- A charity that raises funds from the public to assist those in poverty overseas is likely to be affected by the law on fundraising (in the Charities Act 1992), the VAT law that applies to certain fundraising activities, the law that relates to commercial contracts and trademark licences, the law that applies to it overseas in the places it is active, the law relating to advertising and employment and health and safety legislation as it applies to its employees and volunteers.

3.18   Neither of these lists is in any sense exhaustive and a full analysis and explanation of all of the different legal regimes that might apply to charities is outside the scope of this book. In this sense, a charity is in much the same position as any commercial entity operating in a particular area.

4

THE CHARITY COMMISSION

INTRODUCTION

4.1   The Charity Commission for England and Wales (the Comisiwyn Elusennau Cymru a Lloegr in Welsh) regulates all charities in England and Wales (although its regulatory role in relation to exempt charities is circumscribed (see **4.55**). It is a statutory corporation established under the Charities Act 1993 to perform its functions on behalf of the Crown. The Commission replaced the former regulator (the Charity Commissioners for England and Wales) and is free of any control by the Government, except for any particular statutory controls and any administrative controls the Treasury imposes in relation to its spending.

4.2   The governance framework for the Commission is set out in the Charities Act 1993.[1] It consists of a chairperson and between four and eight other members, at least two of whom must be legally qualified and at least one of whom is familiar with conditions in Wales and is appointed after consultation with the National Assembly for Wales. The Commission also has a Chief Executive.

4.3   The Commission is established in line with the reforms introduced by the Charities Act 2006. The 2006 Act also introduced a number of statutory objectives, general functions and duties.[2]

OBJECTIVES

4.4   The Commission's objectives are:

- public confidence – to increase public trust and confidence in charities

- public benefit – to promote awareness and understanding of the public benefit requirement (see **Chapter 1** for more detail on this)

- compliance – compliance by charity trustees with their legal obligations in exercising control and management and administration of their charities

- charitable resources – to promote the effective use of charitable resources

- accountability – to enhance the accountability of charities to donors, beneficiaries and the general public.

---

[1]   Charities Act 1993, s 1A, Sch 1A.
[2]   Charities Act 1993, s 1B.

GENERAL FUNCTIONS

4.5   In addition to these objectives, the Commission has a number of general functions:[3]

- determining whether institutions are or are not charities

- encouraging and facilitating the better administration of charities

- identifying and investigating apparent misconduct or mismanagement in the administration of charities and taking remedial or protective action in connection with misconduct or mismanagement therein

- determining whether public collections certificates should be issued, and remain in force, in respect of public charitable collections

- obtaining, evaluating and disseminating information in connection with the performance of any of the Commission's functions or meeting any of its objectives

- giving information or advice, or making proposals, to any Minister of the Crown on matters relating to any of the Commission's functions or meeting any of its objectives.

4.6   These general functions are effectively the broad headings under which the Charity Commission discharges the specific powers vested in it by Charities Act 1993. There is more about these at **4.10**.

GENERAL DUTIES

4.7   The Charity Commission also has a number of general duties.[4] These are:

- So far as is reasonably practicable, it must, in performing its functions, act in a way which is compatible with its objectives and which it considers most appropriate for the purpose of meeting those objectives.

- It must, on the same basis, also act in a way that is compatible with the encouragement of all forms of charitable giving and voluntary participation in charity work.

- In performing its functions it must have regard to the need to use its resources in the most efficient, effective and economic way.

- In performing its functions, it must, so far as relevant, have regard to the best regulatory practice (including the principles under which regulatory activities should be proportionate, accountable, consistent, transparent and targeted only at cases in which action is needed).

---

3   Charities Act 1993, s 1C.
4   Charities Act 1993, s 1D.

- In performing its functions it must, in appropriate cases, have regard to the desirability of facilitating innovation by or on behalf of charities.

- In managing its affairs, the Commission must have regard to such generally accepted principles of good corporate governance as it is reasonable to regard as applicable to it.

4.8   These duties are obviously sensible duties for any regulator to own although their generality and the extent to which they are hedged by 'so far as reasonably practicable', 'so far as relevant', and 'in appropriate cases' makes their enforceability against the Commission reasonably doubtful. The ability of third parties to challenge the Commission in respect of its acts and omissions as regulator is explained in more detail at **4.60**.

INCIDENTAL POWERS

4.9   The Commission also has a statutory power to do anything which is calculated to facilitate, or is incidental or conducive to, the performance of its functions. But this does not give them any power to act in the place of any charity trustee, to substitute its own views for those of a trustee nor to do anything else that means it will become directly involved in administering a charity.[5]

SIGNIFICANT SPECIFIC POWERS

4.10   The most significant of the Commission's regulatory powers are conferred on it by the Charities Act 1993.

Register of charities

4.11   The Commission maintains the register of charities.[6] It includes the names and other details of all charities other than those that are exempt or excepted (there is more information about these charities at **4.55** and **4.58**). Every other charity is obliged to apply for registration by the Commission, and the Commission is obliged to register every such charity. It is also obliged to review existing registrations in order to ensure that every institution that is registered continues to be a charity or whether the Commission should exercise its discretion to remove from the register any institution which the Commission no longer considers to be a charity or which has ceased to exist or operate.[7] Maintaining an accurate and up-to-date register is part of the Commission's general function of obtaining, evaluating and disseminating information in connection with the performance of any of its functions or meeting any of its objectives.[8]

4.12   The Charities Act 2006 introduced new provisions into the 1993 Act that oblige a charity's trustees to apply for its registration and also to notify the Commission if the charity ceases to exist or there is any change to its details in the register or to its 'trusts'.

---

[5]   Charities Act 1993, s 1E.
[6]   Charities Act 1993, s 3.
[7]   Charities Act 1993, s 3.
[8]   Charities Act 1993, s 1C(3).

'Trusts' means the constitutional document (or documents) which establish and govern the charity (and which will vary depending on the charity's legal form).[9]

4.13 The register is undoubtedly central to the Commission's ability to regulate charities properly. Now that it is available online, it is an invaluable source of information for both the public and those involved with the sector. The information available is not detailed, but will usually identify the charity's objects, how it is established, who its trustees are, its 'area of benefit' (which is the Commission's way of identifying any geographical area that the charity is intended to benefit) and its annual income. Copies of the constitutional documents for some charities are also available on-line. Copies of all charities' constitutional documents are maintained by the Charity Commission.[10]

Reports, accounts and returns

4.14 The accuracy of the register maintained by the Commission depends upon the extent to which charities comply with their obligations to supply information to the Charity Commission and, in particular, to submit the reports and accounts and annual return required by the Charities Act 1993.

4.15 The accounting and reporting obligations of charities are an essential part of governance. The requirements are explained in detail in **Chapter 14**.

Advice

4.16 The Commission has the power to advise any charity trustee on anything that relates to the performance of his or her duties as a trustee or the proper administration of the charity. If the trustee acts in accordance with that Advice, he is presumed to have acted in accordance with his duties as trustee. This is part of the Commission's general function of encouraging and facilitating the better administration of charities.[11]

4.17 There are some restrictions on this. The Advice cannot be relied on if the trustee knows or has reasonable cause to suspect that the Commission has not been told all of the facts that are material to the Advice, nor if there is a Court decision on the point in question or one pending.

4.18 The Commission will not use this power where they think that the trustee proposes to do something he or she has no power to do (this will usually require an Order) (see **4.19** for more on Orders). The Commission will also refuse to advise on anything that might affect the rights of any third party.[12] In practice, Advice is often sought on, for example, whether something the charity proposes to do is within its charitable objects.

Orders

4.19 The Commission has power to make Orders under the Charities Act 1993[13] where they conclude that:

---

9   Charities Act 1993, s 3B, 97(1).
10   Charities Act 1993, s 3(10).
11   Charities Act 1993, s 29.
12   Charity Commission Report 1982, paras 24–26.
13   Charities Act 1993, s 26.

'...any action proposed or contemplated in the administration of a charity is expedient in the interests of the charity....'

Once made, an Order authorises the charity's trustees to do whatever it is they are proposing or contemplating notwithstanding that they do not have, or may not have, power to do so. This is achieved by deeming anything done by trustees under an Order to fall within their powers.

4.20 The scope of this power is limited to things associated with the administration of a charity. In practice, an Order cannot be used where:

- It will authorise the trustees to do something that is 'expressly prohibited' by the 'trusts' of the charity.
  'Trusts' means the constitutional document (or documents) which establish and govern the charity (and which will vary depending on the charity's legal form).[14] There is no statutory definition of 'expressly prohibited' but the Charity Commission will look at the constitutional documents to decide whether 'the founder of the charity has made it clear in the governing document that some particular power or type of power is not available to the trustees'.[15]

- It will authorise the trustees to do something that is expressly prohibited by any Act of Parliament.[16]
  This provision may catch any charity whose constitution is (in whole or part) regulated by an Act of Parliament. Certain Acts (relating to ecclesiastical leases) can be disregarded.[17]

- It will 'extend or alter the purposes of the charity'.[18]

- It imposes duties or directions on the charity trustees that do not relate to the powers they are given by the Order itself.

- If the trustees already have a power to amend the constitutional documents of the charity to give themselves the power that they need.
  Where the trustees do have a power of amendment which is sufficiently wide, the Commission will expect them to use it unless what they proposed to do requires something more than an amendment, eg authority for a trustee to act with a conflict of interest.

- If the trustees already have the power they need, either in the charity's constitutional documents or under statute.
  Except in certain specific circumstances,[19] the Commission does not make 'comfort' Orders for trustees where the extent of their powers are clear. They may, though, consider giving Advice under CA 1993, s 29 in order to confirm the position.[20]

---

[14] Charities Act 1993, s 97(1).
[15] Charity Commission Operational Guidance OG1 A1 6.1.
[16] Charities Act 1993, s 26(5).
[17] Charities Act 1993, s 26(6).
[18] Charities Act 1993, s 26(5).
[19] See **12.25**.
[20] See section on Advice at **4.16** and also OG1 A1 7.

- As a matter of policy, the Commission will not make an Order if it concludes that the grant of the authority sought should be subject to a right of appeal.[21]
  This will usually be the case where what is proposed will have some effect on a third party's rights under a charity's constitution, eg to appoint trustees.

- An Order cannot be used in relation to certain consecrated buildings.[22]

4.21   In all of these cases, the Commission's policy is that it will consider making a Scheme rather than an Order (with the implications explained at **4.26**). This is because an Order can be made more quickly and easily than a Scheme.

4.22   An Order can only be used to give charity trustees the power to do something. It cannot direct them to act in a particular way, although any power that is given can be (and often is) made subject to conditions and directions which the trustees must observe when they exercise the power.

4.23   An Order can be used to give authority for both general and specific transactions. The Commission's policy is to try to give trustees a sufficiently wide power of amendment to enable them to give themselves the authority they need for both general and particular transactions.[23] This is obviously a sensible approach aimed at allowing trustees to act with discretion to take the steps they think are in the best interests of their charities without a requirement to refer to the Commission for authority on more than one occasion. Amendments to constitutional documents are explained in **Chapter 15**.

4.24   Some of the most common applications for orders are:

General authority	More detail:
Power of amendment	**Chapter 15**
Power to adopt a total return policy to investment	**Chapter 10**
Specific authority	
Trustees' conflicts	**Chapter 6**
Power to spend capital	**Chapter 9**
Constitutional changes	**Chapter 15**
Transfer of assets to another charity	**Chapter 15**
Borrowing	**Chapter 12**

---

[21]   OG1 A1 2.
[22]   Charities Act 1993, s 26(7).
[23]   OG1 B1 3.2.

4.25 The procedure for obtaining an Order is straightforward:

- The trustees (or someone authorised by them) should write to the Commission explaining what is required and all of the relevant circumstances. It is important that the position is explained as fully as possible and all relevant circumstances disclosed, partly because the Commission have a power to discharge an order which they consider they were misled into making[24] and partly because this is more likely to help speed up the process. Knowingly or recklessly providing the Commission with false or misleading information is in any event an offence.[25]

- The trustees will need to resolve to apply for an Order in accordance with the provisions of the charity's constitution.

- The Commission will generally draft the order using their own precedents, but the trustees and their advisors will usually be given an opportunity to comment on the draft.

- There is no statutory requirement for an Order to be publicised before it is made but the Commission can ask trustees to publicise the proposal to make an order.[26] They also have the power to publicise an Order once it has been made.[27] The Commission's view on this is that '... we may wish to give publicity to orders where the potential for wider public involvement may enhance the quality of a particular decision or help to dispel fears or possible criticism of the trustees or ourselves'.[28] Where an Order is sought in relation to a particularly contentious matter, it may be that publicity for the draft leads the Commission to conclude that it would be better for a scheme (with an associated right of appeal) to be made.

- there is no right of appeal in relation to an Order made by the Commission. The only option for someone who objects to the making of an order is to complain to the Commission (see **4.60** for more on this).

Schemes

4.26 A Scheme is the legal mechanism by which the Commission can change a charity's constitutional provisions. Once made, it takes effect as part of the constitution and will be either:

- a 'fully regulating' Scheme which deals with all aspects of a charity's purposes and administration and becomes the charity's governing document; or

- a Scheme that changes a distinct part of a charity's governing document.

4.27 The Commission's policy is not to make a Scheme where there is any other way of making a change to a charity's constitutional documents. So a Scheme will not be available where:

---

[24] Charities Act 1993, s 89(3).
[25] Charities Act 1993, s 11(1)(b).
[26] Charities Act 1993, s 89(2).
[27] Charities Act 1993, s 89(2).
[28] OG1 A1 8.2.

- An Order under CA 1993, s 26 can be made giving the charity's trustees a power to amend the charity's constitutional documents to give them the power that they need (see **4.19** for more detail in relation to this).

- The trustees already have a power to amend the constitutional documents of the charity to give them the power that they need.

  Powers of amendment of this kind will enable trustees to alter the way in which their charity's purposes are worded without changing their substance. Sometimes the power is clearly not capable of altering the actual words that are used (typically because there is a restriction on any change to the 'objects clause' as opposed to the charitable objects or purposes themselves).

  In the case of a charitable company, its members can exercise the power they have under the Companies Acts to alter its constitution, although the Commission's prior written consent is required in certain circumstances under the Charities Act 1993, s 64 (see **Chapter 15** for more detail on this).

- The trustees already have the power they need, either in the charity's constitution or under statute.

- The charity can take advantage of the provisions of the Charities Act 1993, s 74C and 74D, which, once in force, will allow certain unincorporated charities to alter their constitutional documents by resolution, including both their charitable purposes and their administrative powers and procedures (s 74D came into force on 27 February 2007; s 74C expected to come into force in early 2008).

  There is more detail about the charities that can utilise these provisions at **15.9** and **15.12**.

4.28   The Charity Commission's most significant Scheme-making power is contained in the Charities Act 1993, s 16. Section 16 gives the Commission jurisdiction to make Schemes concurrently with the High Court (which has an inherent jurisdiction to make Schemes for charities). This means that, in most cases, a Scheme will be made by the Commission rather than the Court, except where an application is contentious or involves difficult questions of fact or law.[29] In those circumstances, or if the Commission thinks that there are other good reasons for doing so, the Commission has a discretion to decide not to exercise its jurisdiction.

4.29   The Schemes that the Commission can make under the Charities Act 1993, s 16 relate to:

- The cy-près application of gifts to a charity where its purposes have failed.[30]

- The cy-près application of gift to a charity where the donors are unknown or have disclaimed.[31]

- The administration of a charity.[32]

---

[29]   Charities Act 1993, s 16(10).
[30]   Charities Act 1993, ss 13(1), 14(7).
[31]   Charities Act 1993, s 14.
[32]   Charities Act 1993, s 16(1)(a).

- The appointment, discharge, or removal of any charity trustee or any officer or employee of a charity.[33]

- Vesting or transferring property or requiring others to vest or transfer property.[34]

4.30 The Commission's jurisdiction under s 16 is exercisable where:

- The Court makes an order directing it to do so, in which case the Commission will 'settle' the Scheme; in other words draft the provisions of the Scheme so as to give effect to the directions the Court gives.[35]

- An application for a Scheme is made by a charity or by the Attorney General.

- The Commission concludes that a charity's trustees ought to have applied for a Scheme but have unreasonably failed to do so and the trustees have been given an opportunity to make representations to the Commission; in these circumstances, the Commission can proceed as if they had received an application for a Scheme from the charity.

4.31 Charities established by Royal Charter or statute are not within the Charity Commission's Scheme-making jurisdiction. Because the authority of the Crown and Parliament is higher than the authority of the Court, they are only within the jurisdiction of the Court as a consequence of the express provisions of the Charities Act 1993, s 15 and the Commission's concurrent jurisdiction does not extend to them. However, the Charities 1993, s 17 does give the Commission the ability to 'settle' a Scheme for a charity which is established or regulated by any Act of Parliament.

4.32 There are certain questions that cannot be determined by the Commission using its Scheme-making power and which may, therefore prevent it from making a Scheme for a charity. These are:

- Any question about the ownership of property where there is a dispute between a charity and a third party claiming an interest in it. This is a question that only the Courts are in a position to answer.

- Any question about 'the existence or extent of any charge or trust'. This is aimed at other kinds of third party claims over assets. Again, only the Courts are in a position to answer this question.

The Commission also has discretion to refuse to make a Scheme where it concludes that it is more appropriate for the Courts to consider an application. This is usually where the application is particularly contentious or involves difficult questions of fact or law. See **4.28** for more on this.

4.33 In practice, most Schemes made by the Commission will be aimed at the following:

---

[33] Charities Act 1993, s 16(1)(b).
[34] Charities Act 1993, s 16(1)(c).
[35] CA 1993, s 16(2).

- To give an unincorporated charity a new 'fully regulating' constitution where what is proposed involves alterations to its charitable purposes (and therefore goes beyond what can be achieved using an Order).

- To make changes to an unincorporated charity's constitution which are likely to be contentious. This is often where the charity's constitution gives third parties certain rights in relation to it, eg to appoint trustees or exercise powers of veto, and there is a dispute between the charity and the third parties or perhaps between the third parties themselves.

- To alter a charity's purposes to allow the cy-près application of its assets.

- Where an unincorporated charity's trustees wish to make changes to its constitution that will override an express prohibition (so that an Order cannot be made). This would include, eg an application to include a provision for trustee remuneration where there is a prohibition on trustee benefits.

- Where the trustees are to be directed to do something required by the Commission properly to regulate the charity.

4.34   In summary, the procedure for obtaining a Scheme is as follows:

- The Commission prefers applications to be made using its standard forms. Using them is not obligatory but there is no sensible reason not to. They include a certificate to the effect that the application has been properly authorised by the charity's trustees in accordance with its constitution. The trustees will need to ensure that an appropriate resolution is passed. The Commission are unlikely to ask for evidence of this where the certificate has been completed, but proper authorisation will be required in any event.

- The forms do not explain any of the background to the application. This will need to be explained in a covering letter disclosing all relevant information and, where relevant, explaining the more important provisions that the trustees wish to see included in the Scheme. Again it is important that the position is explained as fully as possible and all relevant circumstances disclosed, partly because the Commission have a power to discharge a Scheme which they consider they were misled into making[36] and partly because this is more likely to help speed up the process. Knowingly or recklessly providing the Commission with false or misleading information is in any event an offence.[37]

- In straightforward cases, the application form can be submitted to the Commission with a covering letter. Where the issues are more complex or there any doubts about the Commission's jurisdiction to make a Scheme, it is often helpful to write to the Commission to confirm the position before submitting the application form.

- Applicants should not prepare their own draft Schemes. The Commission will prepare a draft based upon the information available to them using their own precedents and model form Schemes. The Commission has a discretion to add to the draft any incidental or supplementary provisions it thinks are expedient to give

---

[36]   Charities Act 1993, s 89(3).
[37]   Charities Act 1993, s 11(1)(b).

effect to the Scheme and they will usually take the opportunity to add provisions from their own model form schemes. The Commission will invariably send the Scheme in draft to the applicant with a view to obtaining their comments on it and agreeing the final form.[38]

- Any Scheme for the administration of a charity or the appointment, removal or discharge of a charity trustee must be publicised by the Commission in draft before it is made unless the Commission concludes that publication is not necessary. Where the Scheme will remove any trustee against his or her will, at least one month's notice must be given to them personally (the Commission has no discretion not to give this notice). The aim of publication is to solicit representations in relation to the Scheme from those who have some interest in it. The Commission are obliged to take any representations that are made into account in deciding whether to make the Scheme, but they have a discretion whether or not to modify the draft Scheme as a consequence. The Commission will determine how the draft Scheme is publicised, but every draft Scheme is usually posted on the Commission's website, together with an invitation to make representations by email.[39]

- The Commission will add its seal to a Scheme in order to make it. Once a Scheme relating to the administration of a charity has been made it must be made available at the Commission's offices for at least one month. Schemes are usually posted on the Commission's website.[40]

An appeal against any Scheme in respect of a charity made by the Commission using its Charities Act 1993, s 16 jurisdiction can be made using the appeals procedure summarised at **4.67** to **4.77**.

Inquiries

4.35   The Commission has the power to institute an Inquiry into any charity (including an exempt charity in certain circumstances). There are no statutory grounds for this but it must be seen as an important part of the Commission's general function of 'identifying and investigating apparent misconduct or mismanagement in the administration of charities and taking remedial or protective action ...'.[41]

4.36   The Commission can either carry out an Inquiry itself or appoint a third party to do it for them (usually an accountant or solicitor). Whoever conducts the Inquiry has wide powers to gather the information that they need, including directing any person to supply accounts and statements, provide copy documents and give evidence on oath.[42] The Commission may (and usually does) decide to publish a report into an Inquiry on its website, generally with some guidance on the wider lessons to be learned from the Inquiry.

4.37   Opening an Inquiry brings into play a number of other important powers aimed at allowing the Commission to take the remedial or protective action that forms part of their general function.

---

[38]   OG1 B3.
[39]   Charities Act 1993, s 20.
[40]   Charities Act 1993, s 20(5), (6).
[41]   Charities Act 1993, s 1C(2).
[42]   Charities Act 1993, s 9.

4.38   Where the Commission is satisfied that there has been any misconduct or mismanagement in the administration of a charity or that it should act to protect the charity's property, it can:

- Suspend any charity trustee, officer, agent or employee of the charity (and, subject to the coming into force of the Charities Act 2006, if they are also a member of the charity, suspend that membership[43]).

- Appoint additional trustees.[44]

- Vest any of the charity's property in the official custodian for charities.[45]

- Order anyone holding any property for the charity not to dispose of it without the Commission's approval.[46]

- Order anyone who owes the charity any liability not to discharge it without the Commission's approval.[47]

- Restrict the transactions that the charity can enter into or the payments it can make without the Commission' approval.[48]

- Obtain a warrant to enter premises and seize documents, computer files etc where there are reasonable grounds for believing that an order to produce them will not be complied with or that they will be destroyed or tampered with.[49]

4.39   These powers are likely to be exercised at an early stage in any Inquiry in order to protect the charity's position pending the outcome of the Inquiry. The Commission may also decide to appoint an 'interim manager' (previously referred to as a 'receiver and manager') of the charity under s 18(1)(vii) Charities Act 1993. This is an individual (usually an accountant or solicitor but not an employee of the Commission itself) appointed to take control of a charity where there is a concern that its assets are at risk.[50] The interim manager has three months from his appointment to investigate the affairs of the charity and report to the Commission on the position and the proposals for rectifying the position. This may include the winding-up of the charity.[51]

4.40   Another significant protective power that will be introduced to the Charities Act 2006 (expected to be in early 2008) will apply where the Commission is satisfied that there has been any misconduct or mismanagement in the administration of a charity or that it should act to protect the charity's property. In those circumstances, it can direct any charity trustee, any officer or employee or the charity itself (where it is a body corporate) to take any action the Commission thinks is expedient in the charity's interests. This includes directing the relevant person to do something outside his or her powers (which is deemed to have been done within his or her powers) but not anything which is prohibited by any Act of Parliament or 'expressly prohibited' by the charity's

---

[43]   Charities Act 1993, s 18; s 18A expected to come into force in early 2008.
[44]   Charities Act 1993, s 18(1)(ii).
[45]   Charities Act 1993, s 18(1)(iii).
[46]   Charities Act 1993, s 18(1)(iv).
[47]   Charities Act 1993, s 18(1)(v).
[48]   Charities Act 1993, s 18(1)(vi).
[49]   Charities Act 1993, s 31A.
[50]   Charity Commission Report 1997 paras 116 to 122.
[51]   SI 1992/2355.

constitutional documents or otherwise inconsistent with its purposes. Nothing done as a consequence of any direction affects any contractual or other rights.[52]

4.41 Once the Inquiry into a charity (or an interim manager's report) has helped to clarify the position, the Charities Act 2006 will (once it comes into effect, which is expected in early 2008) authorize the Commission to exercise the powers it has to make a scheme for the administration of the charity and to remove any charity trustee, officer, agent or employee of the charity (and, if they are also a member of the charity, terminate that membership[53]). These powers can be used to make any necessary change to the charity's constitution and, in conjunction with its power to appoint trustees, put it under the control of a new body of trustees. The exercise of these powers depends on the Commission satisfying itself that there has been some misconduct or mismanagement in the administration of a charity and that it should act to protect the charity's property.

4.42 'Misconduct and mismanagement' is not defined by the Charities Act 1993 and is essentially a question of fact to be decided upon by the Commission. However, the Charities Act 1993, s 18(3) specifically refers to arrangements for any person to be paid by a charity for services which are excessive in relation to the value of the charity's assets. This is one of the circumstances the Commission often pick up in their review of a charity's annual report and accounts. It is worth reading the reports into completed Inquiries posted on the Commission's website, partly because they illustrate the sort of governance failings that charities can succumb to but also because they offer an insight into the kind of activities the Commission is likely to regard as mismanagement and misconduct.

OTHER PROTECTIVE POWERS

4.43 The Commission has a number of other powers it can exercise to protect charities and which are not dependent on the opening of an Inquiry. These are:

- Power to remove charity trustees in certain specified circumstances, including a trustee who has stopped acting as a trustee and will not confirm whether he or she is willing to act or not.[54]

- Power to appoint charity trustees in certain specified circumstances, including where there are no trustees able to act because of death and incapacity.[55]

- Power to vest a charity's property in new trustees where the Commission removes or appoints trustees.[56]

- Power to determine who the members of a charity are if, as sometimes happens, the charity itself is no longer capable of determining who its members are.[57]

---

[52]   Charities Act 1993, s 19A.
[53]   Charities Act 1993, ss 18, 18A; expected to come into force in early 2008.
[54]   Charities Act 1993, s 18(4).
[55]   Charities Act 1993, s 18(5).
[56]   Charities Act 1993, s 18(6).
[57]   Charities Act 1993, s 29A.

- A new power introduced by the Charities Act 2006 to direct any person who holds or controls a charity's assets whom the Commission is satisfied is unwilling to apply them properly for the charity's purposes to deal with the assets in any way the Commission determines. The Commission must also conclude that making an order to this effect is desirable in order to ensure that the charity's assets are properly applied. The Commission can direct the relevant person to do something outside their powers (which is deemed to have been done within their powers) but not anything which is prohibited by any Act or Parliament or 'expressly prohibited' by the charity's constitutional documents or otherwise inconsistent with its purposes. Nothing done as a consequence of any direction affects any contractual or other rights.[58]

REVIEWS

4.44 The Commission has a rolling programme of review visits to charities. These are aimed at encouraging best practice in charity governance as part of the Commission's general function of encouraging and facilitating the better administration of charities. A charity is generally selected for review because a particular issue relating to it has come to the Commission's attention, or there are issues arising out of its accounts or because it operates in an area that the Commission are interested in.

4.45 Reviews take place in three stages. Once a review visit has been arranged, the Commission will ask the charity to supply it with a range of information, including minutes of trustees' meetings, policy documents and other internal governance documents. The Commission will consider this information alongside the information it holds on the charity (its governing document, accounts and annual return) in order to identify the issues for discussion during the visit. After the visit, the Commission will produce a draft report that it will share with the charity before it is finalised. The report will identify those areas where the Commission believe the charity can improve its administration and those areas that are working well. The Commission does not presently publish review reports.

4.46 Because there is no specific statutory power to carry out reviews, a charity is not obliged to agree to a review visit by the Commission. Having said that, there is clearly no objection to engaging with the Commission and anecdotal evidence suggests that many charities find reviews very useful in identifying areas that need improvement. If a review turns up evidence of 'deliberate malpractice or fraud', the Commission is likely to consider instituting an Inquiry.[59] In other cases of mismanagement, the Commission may conclude that it is better to work with the charity's trustees to resolve any issues.

GUIDANCE

4.47 The Commission has no specific power under the Charities Act 1993 to issue general information and guidance to charities, so the wide range of material they do produce must form part of their general function of encouraging and facilitating the better administration of charities and disseminating information in connection with its functions or objectives. The material the Commission produce is available on-line and is

---

[58] Charities Act 1993, s 19B; expected to come into force in early 2008.
[59] See Charity Commission guidance on review visits; FAQs.

generally very helpful, and often invaluable, in assisting charity trustees and their advisors. It falls into a number of different categories.

Publications

4.48 The Commission produce a very wide range of publications (these are numbered and prefixed 'CC'). They range in scope from guidance on issues of general significance such as, eg the public character of charity and the independence of charities from the state to more specific advice in relation to, eg the sale of alcohol on charity premises.

4.49 Different publications are aimed at different audiences. Some are intended to assist the public generally and the trustees of smaller charities, while others are aimed at charity sector professionals and the trustees and employees of larger charities. They are all available on the Commission's website.

Operational guidance

4.50 In addition to their publications for public consumption, the Commission also publishes its internal guidance to its own staff on its website (under the heading 'operational guidance' and numbered and prefixed 'OG'). This is a very useful resource for anyone who wants to understand how the Commission approach particular aspects of charity law and regulation and highlights their policies and expectations as well as including examples of the sort of model documents that the Commission produces (eg model Orders and Schemes). Understandably, the guidance assumes a reasonably high degree of knowledge about charity law and regulation, but it is a recommended starting point for anyone looking in detail at a particular issue.

Guidance

4.51 The Commission also publishes a range of guidance on particular issues, often those that are particularly topical. The issues covered are diverse, including operating overseas, social investment, the implications of pension scheme deficits, child protection and campaigning in relation to elections. There is a full list of the guidance on the Commission's website.

Decisions

4.52 The Commission publishes some of the decisions it takes in relation to charities on its website, particularly where they relate to novel areas of charity law or are of wider interest. Most relate to applications for registration as a charity and deal with what can constitute a charitable purpose.

Regulatory reports

4.53 The Commission prepares regulatory reports into aspects of charity governance and finance annually. The reports are available on the website and are prefixed 'RR' or 'RS'. They cover a wide range of areas, including collaborative working, reserves, membership issues and transparency and accountability. Reports are not strictly guidance, but they are a useful summary of the research that the Commission does and the likely developments in policy in particular areas.

OTHER SPECIFIC POWERS

4.54   The Commission has a number of other specific powers. The more significant of these are:

- power to require a charity's name to be changed[60]

- power to make Schemes to establish common investment and common deposit funds[61]

- power to authorise ex gratia payments[62]

- power to give directions about dormant bank accounts[63]

- power to order taxation of a solicitor's bill[64]

- power to relieve trustees and auditors from liability for breach of trust.[65]

EXEMPT CHARITIES

4.55   Exempt charities are not fully regulated by the Charity Commission, although in most other respects they are subject to charity law in the same way as charities that are not exempt. The rationale for exempting some charities is that some other body or Government department already regulates them. The full list of exempt charities is set out in Schedule 2 to the 1993 Act. Subject to the coming into force of the changes made in relation to exempt charities in the Charities Act 2006 (expected in 2008), some of the more important exempt charities will be:

- Universities and university colleges[66]

- Higher and Further Education Corporations

- any Industrial and Provident Society which is a registered social landlord under Part 1 of the Housing Act 1996

- any other institution administered by any exempt charity and established for any general or special purpose of that charity (excluding students unions).

4.56   The Charities Act 1993 (as amended by the Charities Act 2006) puts the body or Government Department who is the 'principal regulator' of an exempt charity under a statutory duty to do all that it reasonably can to promote compliance by the charity trustees with their legal obligations.

---

[60]   Charities Act 1993, s 6.
[61]   Charities Act 1993, ss 24, 25.
[62]   Charities Act 1993, s 27.
[63]   Charities Act 1993, s 28.
[64]   Charities Act 1993, s 31.
[65]   Charities Act 1993, ss 73D, 73E.
[66]   As specified by the Charities Act 1993, Sch 2.

4.57   The Commission's powers in relation to an exempt charity are limited. Following the coming into force of the Charities Act 2006, the most significant powers exercisable by the Commission will to:

- institute an Inquiry into an exempt charity provided it is asked to do so by the charity's principal regulator

- require an exempt charity to change its name[67]

- require an exempt charity to produce documents and search records[68]

- exercise its Scheme-making jurisdiction[69] (see **4.26–4.34** for more detail)

- exercise its powers to take remedial or protective action in relation to an exempt charity following an Inquiry[70]

- give its prior consent to Court proceedings taken in relation to any exempt charity.[71]

EXCEPTED CHARITIES

4.58   Subject to the coming into force of the changes made in relation to exempt charities in the Charities Act 2006 (expected in 2008), certain charities (usually referred to as 'excepted charities') will continue to be free of requirement to be registered by the Charity Commission and are also exempt from the requirement to file annual reports and accounts.[72] There will be four categories of excepted charity:

- exempt charities

- any charity that complies with the conditions set by an order of the Commission and whose gross income in its financial year is £100,000 or less

- any charity which complies with the conditions set out in regulations made by the Secretary of State and whose gross income in its financial year is £100,000 or less

- any charity whose gross income in its financial year is £5,000 or less.

4.59   Any charity within the first three categories is entitled to be registered if it wishes.

COMPLAINTS AND APPEALS

4.60   There are a number of options open to charity trustees who wish to complain about, or challenge, decisions taken by the Charity Commission. Those who wish to make a complaint about the way in which the Commission has dealt with a particular

---

[67]   Charities Act 1993, s 6.
[68]   Charities Act 1993, s 9.
[69]   Charities Act 1993, s 16.
[70]   Charities Act 1993, s 18.
[71]   Charities Act 1993, s 33.
[72]   Charities Act 1993, s 46.

issue can use the Commission's own internal complaints procedure. If they are still not satisfied, the complaint can be taken to the Independent Complaints Reviewer or the Parliamentary Ombudsman.

4.61   Where a charity's trustees wish to challenge a formal decision taken by the Commission (rather than making complaints about the way in which the issue has been handled) they can appeal the decision to the Court or (once it has been set up), the Charity Tribunal provided for by the Charities Act 2006.[73] It is expected that the Tribunal will not start to hear appeals until 2008, but the framework within which it will operate is set out in the 2006 Act and is explained below.

Internal complaints procedure

4.62   The Charity Commission operates an internal complaints procedure in relation to both its formal decisions and its quality of service. Complaints about formal decisions are dealt with by the Commission's Head of Customer Service but may finally be reviewed by the Charity Commissioners. Complaints about quality of service are dealt differently, with an ultimate right of appeal to the Head of Customer Service. There is much more information about the Commission's Internal Complaints Procedures in the Commission's Operational Guidance.[74]

4.63   If a charity's trustees do not consider their complaint will be dealt with satisfactorily using the Commission's own internal procedures, they can take the complaint to the Independent Complaints Reviewer or the Parliamentary Ombudsman.

Independent Complaints Reviewer

4.64   The Independent Complaints Reviewer deals only with complaints about maladministration by the Commission and not its formal legal decisions. The sort of complaints usually considered by the Reviewer relate to unreasonable delay by the Commission or allegations of unreasonable or discriminatory behaviour.

4.65   The Reviewer will carry out an investigation into the complaint and compile a report which is sent to both the complainant and the Commission. The Reviewer's powers if he or she upholds the complaint are relatively limited. The Reviewer will generally make a recommendation to the Commission about the action it should take to remedy the position. This may include a recommendation that the complainant receives some sort of financial compensation. In practice, it appears that the Commission will generally act in accordance with the Reviewer's recommendation.

Parliamentary Ombudsman

4.66   Like the Independent Complaints Reviewer, the Parliamentary Ombudsman deals with any complaint that the Commission has failed to act properly (eg because of an unreasonable delay). The Ombudsman has no power to review formal legal decisions taken by the Commission. The Ombudsman also has limited powers to recompense a complainant. He or she can make recommendations to the Commission (including a recommendation that financial compensation should be paid). In practice, the Commission appears to comply with the Ombudsman's recommendations.

---

[73]   Charities Act 2006, s 8, Schs 3, 4.
[74]   OG 93.

Appeals to the High Court

4.67 A charity's trustees can bring an appeal to the High Court against decisions of the Charity Commission in relation to the registration of a charity and Schemes and Orders made by the Commission. Appeals on these issues can also be bought in the High Court by the Attorney-General in his capacity as the protector of charities.

4.68 In practice, very few appeals are made by charity trustees to the High Courts. This is generally considered to be because the cost of Court proceedings can be high and those who wish to appeal may often have limited financial resources at their disposal. The setting up of a Charity Tribunal is intended to provide a more cost effective avenue for appeal. Once the Tribunal has been set up, the scope of appeals directly to the Court will be more restricted.

Charity Tribunal

4.69 As we have mentioned, the Charity Tribunal will be set up in order to provide an avenue specifically for appeals against decisions by the Commission to exercise (or, as the case may be, not to exercise) its statutory powers in relation to a charity.

4.70 The Tribunal's jurisdiction does not extend to the exercise of all of the Commission's statutory powers,[75] but many of the Commission's most significant powers are subject to a right of appeal to the Tribunal. These include a decision to register, or not to register, a particular entity as a charity, a decision to remove, or not to remove, a charity from the register of charities maintained by the Commission and a decision to institute an Inquiry. A decision to make an Order or Scheme (or not to make them, as the case may be) are also subject to the right of appeal. The most significant omission from the Tribunal's jurisdiction is a decision by the Commission to give, or not to give, advice.

4.71 The Tribunal considers only the formal legal decisions of the Commission in relation to the exercise of its statutory powers. It does not consider complaints in relation to maladministration (due, for example, to delay). Where the Tribunal upholds an appeal against a decision of the Commission, it will generally have a number of options open to it. These include quashing the decision taken by the Commission, remitting the decision to the Commission (with or without a direction to Commission about the decision it should reach), to substitute the Tribunal's own decision or to add to the Commission's decision in some way. Which of these options is available to the Tribunal will depend upon the decision of the Commission that is being appealed against.

4.72 Some decisions of the Commission are subject to a review by the Tribunal rather than an appeal. This means that the Tribunal will look only at the way in which the Commission reached the decision (in other words, whether it followed a proper decision-making process) rather than looking at all of the facts which were available to the Commission in relation to the original decision.

4.73 Different appeals can be brought by different people but will generally include a charity's trustees and the charity itself (where it is incorporated).

---

[75] There are detailed provisions in relation to this which are set out in Charities Act 1993, Sch 1C.

4.74   Where a charity brings an appeal to the Tribunal, it is responsible for paying its own legal and other costs. The same will be true of the Charity Commission. There are limited circumstances in which the Tribunal will have a power to order that the Commission or the appellant must pay the other's costs. An order can be made where the Tribunal considers that either party has acted 'vexatiously, frivolously or unreasonably'. The Tribunal can also award costs against the Charity Commission if it considers that the Commission's decision which is subject to the appeal was unreasonable in the first place.

4.75   The costs of the appellant may be reduced where the Attorney-General exercises his right to intervene in cases brought before the Tribunal (which would generally only be the case particularly where an important legal issue is being considered by the Tribunal). Where the Attorney-General intervenes in relation to a charity's appeal, the charity's trustees can expect him to argue the appeal in full, which may mean that the appellant charity can limit its own legal and other professional costs.

4.76   The Tribunal has no power to compensate a successful appellant for any loss it has suffered as a result of a decision by the Commission.

4.77   There is a right of appeal from any decision of the Tribunal to the High Court.[76]

---

[76]   Charities Act 1993, s 2C.

5

GOVERNANCE STRUCTURES

5.1 The way in which a charity is constituted is fundamental to its governance. A charity's legal form will determine a great deal about the way in which it operates. It will also determine a great deal about who the charity's trustees are and the powers they can exercise and the duties that they are under.

5.2 There is more about the way in which trustees can ensure that they exercise good governance of their charity in **Chapter 8**. This chapter is concerned with the impact on governance of the relationship between the trustees of a charity and its members. By 'members' we mean anyone who has some relationship with a charity that enables them to exercise some right or power in relation to it. The nature of that relationship will vary from charity to charity depending on the way in which it is constituted and the specific constitutional provisions that govern membership. Some of the more obvious relationships are:

- Where the beneficiaries of a charity are also its members because they are intended to have some say or involvement in the way in which the charity is run. So, for example, the tenants of a charitable housing association are often also its members.

- Where donors to a charity are also its members because of the significance of their donations to funding its operations. This would include, for example, a charity that conserves historic sites and relies upon a wide membership of individuals interested in such sites to fund a significant part of its work.

- Where a wide membership of individuals gives a charity a certain status or legitimacy that it requires in order to carry out its work. This could include, for example, a charity providing advocacy or services for people with disabilities which has disabled people among its members.

- Where a charity relies upon volunteers for its work and wishes to encourage their continued participation by giving them some say in the way in which it operates.

- Where a charity may draw some or all of its trustees from its members.

- Where a charity is established by stakeholders who have an interest in continuing to have some say in which it operates. This would include, for example, a charity established by individual donors or a charity established by one or more other charities to advance particular charitable purposes.

5.3 Many charities will have individual members but there are no legal restrictions on a charity having corporate members. Many charities do have corporate stakeholders as members, including companies, local authorities and other public bodies and other charities. There is more about stakeholders of this kind acting as members at **5.84–5.92**.

5.4   Not every charity will have members. Charitable companies and CIOs will inevitably have them because this is one of the requirements of the legislation under which they are incorporated. Charitable unincorporated associations will also inevitably have members because they are essentially true 'membership organisations', ie they consist of a group of individuals who wish to act together with some common charitable purpose. Charitable trusts, on the other hand, have no legal requirement for members and, in practice, most do not have them.

5.5   The kind of rights that members may have as part of their membership relationship will also vary from charity to charity.

- Some members may exercise a number of important rights in relation to a charity. These can include rights to:
    - alter the charity's constitution
    - appoint and remove its charity trustees
    - wind the charity up and distribute its surplus assets for similar charitable purposes.

- These rights may derive from the legal form that the charity takes. So, for example, the members of a charitable company will have these rights under the Companies Acts. The members of other charities may have them because of provisions in the charity's constitution (for example, a charitable unincorporated association).

- Other rights conferred upon members may be much less significant from a legal point of view but are as important in governance terms. Members may not have rights to vote on the issues mentioned above, but may be entitled to receive newsletters and other information from a charity, or a right of reduced admission to its properties or facilities or the right to attend an annual meeting to discuss, but not vote on, the way in which the charity is operating.

- In some cases, the members of a charity may be entitled to both voting and other rights.

5.6   The rights that the members exercise will generally reflect the balance of power between the members and trustees intended by the people who set the charity up or who last amended its constitution. In this sense, members can play an important constitutional role in acting as a check and balance on the powers of the trustees.

5.7   Like other terms used in relation to charities, 'member' can mean different things in different contexts. In the context of charitable companies, 'member' usually means the members of a company under company law, as identified in its register of members. However, it can also refer to individuals who, while they are not company law members of the company, exercise certain rights in relation to the company. There is more about membership of charitable companies in **Chapter 2**.

5.8   While the relationship between trustees and members will vary from charity to charity there are certain models that are used more often than others.

'FLAT' MODEL

5.9   The key feature of this model (sometimes referred to as an 'oligarchical' model) is that the members are the same people as the trustees. The aim is to give the trustees an absolute discretion to control the charity. The simplest and most common forms are the charitable trust (which has no members) and the charitable company whose trustees are also its members (and whose articles will include provisions which mean that a trustee will be a member for only so long as he or she is a trustee and vice versa). A charitable company set up in this way is often used in preference to a charitable trust because of liability issues but where, in contrast to the membership model, there is no need or desire to involve any third party in the governance arrangements going forward. The Charities Act 1993 will, subject to the coming into force of the Charities Act 2006,[1] expressly provide that the trustees of a CIO may also act as its members (and vice versa), although there is no obligation to arrange things in this way.

5.10   This is a reasonably straightforward governance structure and one that reflects the fact that it is the trustees who are ultimately responsible for managing a charity's operations and will be liable if they fail to do so properly. However, it may not work for a charity that needs to include beneficiaries or other stakeholders as members in order to ensure that it can operate effectively. In those circumstances, the 'hybrid' model may meet its requirements without exposing it to some of the potential problems inherent in the 'membership' model (see **15.18–15.21**).

5.11   There are a number of considerations that need to be taken into account in relation to a model of this kind. These are explained in more detail at **5.25**.

'MEMBERSHIP' MODEL

5.12   At the other extreme, the key feature of the 'membership' model is a group of members capable of exercising some oversight and control over the activities of the charity trustees.

5.13   The advantage of this model is that it undoubtedly gives the members a say in the governance of the charity and allows them, for example, to take action in respect of anything proposed by the charity trustees which the members consider will not be for the benefit of the charity's purposes. In that sense, the members may be the custodians of a particular ethos or approach inherent in the way that the charity operates, subject of course to the overriding requirements of charity law.

5.14   The disadvantage of this approach is that it may give the members a degree of control over a charity which may actually impede its effective operation in circumstances where:

- The members may not appreciate or understand operational circumstances to which the charity trustees are responding.

- The members may be motivated by 'personal' beliefs or aims rather than concern for the charity's purposes.

---

[1]   Charities Act 1993, s 69B(6); expected to come into force in early 2008.

- Some members may disagree with other members about the way in which the charity should operate and use their membership powers to try to win the argument.

5.15 These are all real possibilities. Recent court cases have seen a group of scientologists acting to establish control over a mental health organisation whose psychiatric practice they disagreed with and members of the National Trust seeking to review the Trust's policy on allowing deer hunting on its land. The cost to both charities in terms of management time and legal and other expenses is likely to have been high.

5.16 The position is complicated by the lack of clarity about the legal duties of the members of most charities. There is more about this at **5.22**.

5.17 The Charity Commission have published a Regulatory Report into membership charities[2] which confirms that in the region of 50% of disputes considered by the Commission relate to the sort of membership issues mentioned above. There is more about the particular problems that arise at **5.28**.

'HYBRID' MODEL

5.18 The key feature of this model is that it gives the control of a charity to its trustees while allowing others to become members with limited rights. So members would have an entitlement to, say, attend an annual meeting, to receive information about the charity's operations or have privileged rights of admission to property but would have no legal right to control any aspect of the charity's governance.

5.19 In the context of a charitable company, the charity trustees would act as its company law members, but its constitution will provide for a wider class of members with rights specified in the constitution, or perhaps by the trustees using a power given them by the constitution. The same effect can be achieved in relation to any other charity by vesting legal rights of control in the charity trustees and vesting other rights in a class of members.

5.20 This approach can be (and often is) used to create different categories and classes of membership. So, for example, a charity can create classes of 'full' members able to vote and other members with no, or restricted voting rights but other entitlements. It is often preferable to give the charity trustees the power to create different classes of member and to determine the rights that they should have. This gives them the flexibility to alter the rights exercisable by different classes without altering the charity's constitution.

5.21 Using a hybrid model raises many of the issues raised by both the flat and membership models depending on the arrangements that are actually adopted. There is more information about this at **5.25** and **5.28**.

---

[2]   RS7.

MEMBERS' DUTIES

5.22 With one important exception, the legal duties of the members of a charity are not clear. This is due to the lack of any clear case law in this area. While there are many cases dealing with the duties of shareholders in commercial companies, they do not clearly establish that a shareholder's powers must be exercised for the benefit of a company as a whole, and there are in addition no clear precedents in the context of charitable companies. The position in relation to charitable unincorporated associations is just as unclear.

5.23 The exception will be CIOs. Under new provisions of the Charities Act (and subject to the coming into force of the Charities Act 2006, which is expected in early 2008), the members of a CIO will be obliged to exercise their powers in the way that they decide, in good faith, would be most likely to further the purposes of the CIO.[3] The legislation does not specify what will happen as a result of any failure to comply with this duty, but a breach is likely to allow a claim to be made to the courts for an appropriate order.

5.24 While the position in relation to the members of other forms of charity is unclear, the courts are likely to impose a duty on members. Many charities do have corporate stakeholders as members, including companies, local authorities and other public bodies and other charities. This is consistent with the approach taken by the courts in relation to charities generally (often as part of its equitable jurisdiction) and also with the statutory duty that will be imposed in relation to CIOs by the 1993 Act (which the courts may well refer to in making a decision).

FLAT MODEL ISSUES

5.25 One practical problem posed by this model in practice is that trustees often do not appreciate that they are acting in two capacities, ie as trustees and as members. So, for example, decisions may be taken by members and trustees in different ways, with different notice, quorum and voting requirements for meetings. This can cause problems where, for example, the charity's powers are not properly exercised as a consequence. Trustees sometimes regard this dual capacity as no more than a technicality invented by lawyers to generate fees. It is certainly a technical requirement (trustees are unlikely to take a different decision in their different capacities) but one that is inevitable where a model of this kind is used. In practice, the key to this issue is ensuring that trustees receive a proper induction when they are appointed.

5.26 Another problem that can arise in relation to this model is that, unless properly drafted, the charity's constitution may not ensure that the trustees from time to time are also the members from time to time (and vice versa). Problems can arise in practice where a trustee ceases to act as a trustee but remains a member and is perhaps unwilling to relinquish his or her membership.

5.27 A further issue can arise where there is no limit on the number of members of a charity, with the result that there is no limit on the number of trustees. In general, a charity with too many trustees is likely to experience problems in decision-making and effective governance generally.

---

[3]   Charities Act 1993, Sch 8A; expected to come into force in early 2008.

MEMBERSHIP MODEL ISSUES

5.28   The Charity Commission's Regulatory Report RS7 says this about the governance issues faced by membership charities:

> 'Membership charities, like all charities, can run into difficulties if proper attention is not paid to their governance arrangements. The scope for problems is greater in membership charities, however, because the number of people involved can make the governance arrangements more complex to manage. Differences of opinion sometimes arise which, if not well managed, can disrupt the smooth running of the charity and result in charitable resources being wasted. Analysis of a sample of Charity Commission casework showed that more cases are opened for membership charities than other organisations, including a greater proportion of cases related to internal disputes.
>
> Our findings show that membership charities receive wide-ranging benefits from their members, and these benefits include:
>
> - enhancing the trustee board's transparency and accountability;
> - providing a greater appreciation of the needs of beneficiaries;
> - improving a charity's influence within the charity sector, giving weight to an advocacy role;
> - providing fundraising opportunities; and
> - providing a consistent source of trustees.
>
> However, Charity Commission experience indicates that those few charities that do run into problems with their membership are likely to have one or more of the following features:
>
> - Trustees are not clear about their role and their legal responsibilities toward their charity's members.
> - Charity members are not clear about their role and responsibilities towards the charity.
> - There are insufficient or inadequate governance structures in place to manage the charity's relationship with its members.
> - The trustee body puts up barriers to membership involvement, either deliberately or inadvertently.
> - The charity's membership lacks diversity so the trustee board is self-perpetuating or change-resistant and unrepresentative of its potential beneficiaries.
> - Members or trustees deliberately abuse voting procedures and rights.
> - There are weak administrative arrangements in place leading to problems such as accusations of elections being held on the basis of inaccurate membership lists or problems with organising quorate meetings.'

5.29   There are a number of key points that will need to be addressed if a membership charity wishes to manage its relationship with its members effectively. These are set out below.

5.30   If a charity is to manage its relationship with its members well, it has to know who they are. This is often a problem in practice. While company law obliges the trustees of a charitable company to maintain a register of its members, this is a requirement that is often not observed in practice. Without the discipline of making an annual return of members and issuing them with share certificates that is available to share companies, a charitable company limited by guarantee may well have records that do not show definitively who its members are. And while other charities (such as unincorporated associations) may have a constitutional requirement for a register of members to be kept, information is often out of date.

5.31 The Charities Act 1993 gives the Charity Commission the power to determine who are the members of a charity, either on the application of the charity itself or at any time after an Inquiry (see **4.35**) has been instituted.[4] This is obviously a useful fallback provision in the event that there is uncertainty or dispute about the identity of a charity's members. But the key points will be that:

- The charity's constitution clearly sets out the mechanism for members to become, and cease to be, members.

- Records of membership are kept up to date.

- If possible, there is a provision in the charity's constitution for the trustees to determine conclusively whether a person is or is not a member of the charity where the position is uncertain.

5.32 The charity trustees must understand the legal relationship between the charity and its members, the members' rights and duties in relation to the charity and the trustees' own duties to the members. It will be the trustees' responsibility to interpret the constitution in relation to members and they must understand how it is intended to work. The key points will be that:

- where relevant, the trustees understand the differences in status between different categories of member

- a clear explanation of the position is provided to new trustees as part of their induction (see **Chapter 8**).

5.33 The charity's constitution must set out the provisions governing membership clearly and, in line with the general principle that the constitution should be a living document and fit for its purpose, must reflect what happens, or is intended to happen, in practice. The key points are:

- Ensure that the constitutional provisions in relation to members are up to date and, if not, revise them.

- Consider setting out the framework for the membership arrangements in the constitution but setting out the detail in a set of rules or subsidiary handbook for members that can be altered by the trustees from time to time without the need for a change to the constitution itself.

- Irrespective of where the membership arrangements are set out, ensure that, as a minimum, they cover:
  - who is eligible to be a member of the charity and, where relevant, the eligibility criteria for different types of member;
  - how membership can be terminated or suspended and any grievance procedure that can be invoked by a member in these circumstances;
  - how voting rights are to be distributed;
  - conditions and rules regarding attending and voting at the annual general meeting, including the voting and quorum provisions;
  - provisions for calling an extraordinary general meeting and the voting and quorum provisions; and

---

4   Charities Act 1993, s 29A.

    –   how alterations to the constitution or dissolution of the charity can be decided on.

5.34 Members must be given the tools to understand their rights and duties in relation to the charity. The key points are:

- The constitutional provisions in relation to membership must be explained, with an emphasis on the rights of members to vote on, say, the appointment of trustees. A handbook or set of rules is often the best way of explaining the position in a way that will be easily understood by a wide range of members.

- The charity should communicate with the members regularly and effectively in order to keep them informed about its operations and, in particular, issues which affect them as members.

- Trustees should consider whether a charity's constitution should include an express provision governing members' duties to the charity. This will obviously not be strictly necessary in relation to a CIO (whose members will have a statutory duty to act in good faith and in a way which is most likely to further the interests of the charity), but a similar provision might usefully be added to the constitution of any charity.

5.35 Where members have voting rights, the arrangements for those rights to be exercised must be clearly formulated and explained. The key points are:

- The periods of notice for annual and extraordinary general meetings must be clear and notices must be given on time and set out the business which is to be discussed at a particular meeting.

- The arrangements for giving notice must be clear and adhered to. Giving notice electronically is likely to be the most cost effective method but this must be expressly authorised by the charity's constitution.

- The voting and quorum requirements at a meeting must be observed but must also be workable. A provision which requires a quorum of not less than one-third of the members may make sense in the context of a charity with 30 members, but much less sense for a charity with 300 members. The same is true of majority voting requirements. A requirement for two-thirds of the members at the meeting to vote for a particular resolution may be workable whereas a requirement for a vote of two-thirds of all of the members may not.

- Provisions for proxy voting may help to ensure that meetings are quorate and that resolutions can be passed, but the charity's constitution must provide for them expressly and the relevant provisions must be clearly explained to members.

There is more about members' meetings at **5.38**.

5.36 A charity may wish to adopt a mediation procedure in relation to disputes with members. This should be set out in writing and made available to all members, perhaps as part of a set of rules or a handbook.

5.37 The consequences of allowing disputes with members to arise are potentially serious. The courts have considered a number of cases relating to membership disputes.

In addition, the Charity Commission may well consider intervening in disputes in certain circumstances and using its powers in relation to Schemes, Orders and Inquiries accordingly (see **Chapter 4** for more on this). The Commission's own guidance on this is that:

'The Charity Commission may intervene:

- where concerns are expressed about serious mismanagement, for example involving a failure to observe the requirements of charity law;
- where there is clear evidence of deliberate abuse;
- where trustees are not acting in accordance with the provisions of the governing document;
- where the administration of the charity has broken down to such an extent that the charity is not working effectively;
- where there is a clear danger of the name of charity being brought into disrepute; or
- where honest errors have resulted in problems (such as decisions of inquorate meetings being acted upon) that require us to authorise actions necessary to remedy the situation; and
- where the use of the Charity Commission's powers are proportionate to it.

Sincerely held but differing views are of no concern to the Charity Commission if trustees are acting properly. Matters of policy or administration may be disputed within the trusteeship or within the membership but they must be settled within and in accordance with the terms of the charity's governing document. Members who disagree with the direction of the charity to which they belong can make a change by exercising their right to vote, either at the AGM or by calling an EGM (which requires a sufficient number of members agreeing to it), or by putting themselves in a position to be elected on to the committee. Where none of these courses of action result in a satisfactory conclusion for a disaffected member, they should accept the majority opinion or consider leaving. A complaint to the Charity Commission should only be made where there are well-founded suspicions or evidence of malpractice.'[5]

MEETINGS

5.38 Except in relation to charitable companies, there is no general legal requirement that a charity need hold meetings of its members. The position will be determined by a charity's constitution, which will usually require meetings to be held and, if so, will generally spell out in some detail the way in which they are convened, the business that should be transacted at them and the voting and quorum requirements. The most important aspects of meetings are summarised below, but we should emphasise that the position will depend upon the specific provisions of every charity's constitution and will, therefore, vary from charity to charity.

5.39 As we have mentioned, there are specific legal requirements in relation to meetings of a charitable company's members. We have summarised the main considerations below at **5.62**.

5.40 The Charity Commission has published some helpful guidance on meetings in conjunction with the Institute of Chartered Secretaries and Administrators.[6] This is a useful summary and, as the Commission points out:

---

5   RS 7.
6   CC 48.

'Where business is transacted at meetings, it is essential for the good governance of charities that the meetings should be effective. Meetings provide an environment for informed decision making, clarification of responsibilities and monitoring the implementation of decisions.'

Frequency

5.41　There are no legal restrictions on the frequency with which members' meetings should be held except where the provisions of a charity's constitution specify a particular number. While there is a formal legal requirement in relation to an 'annual general meeting' (or 'AGM') in relation to a charitable company, any other charity need hold an AGM only if it is required to do so by its constitution.

5.42　If a charity's constitution does require the holding of an AGM, it will often spell out the business that needs to be transacted at it. This will generally include the approval of the charity's accounts for the previous financial year and the election or re-election of the charity's trustees by the members. The position will, however, vary from charity to charity.

Notice

5.43　There are no legal rules that govern the periods of notice that are required at members' meetings. The notice period is governed solely by the provisions of the charity's constitution. The key points are:

- The charity's constitution will often identify who is able to call a meeting. The charity's trustees will generally be able to do so, but the constitution may also provide for one or more of the members to do so.

- The charity's constitution will often specify the number of days' notice that need to be given to members. Any reference to 'clear days' excludes the day on which the notice is received by the member and the day of the meeting itself. The same is true of references to 'days' where there is nothing else in the constitution which provides that the days on which notice is received and the meeting is held are to be counted within the notice period.

- The notice must be sent to everyone entitled to receive it under the charity's constitution.

- The charity's constitution may specify how notice should be given (eg by post, fax or email). It may also specify when notice is deemed to be given (eg by specifying that notices sent by first class post are deemed to have been served on the following day). The Charities Act 1993, s 81 provides specifically for notices to be given to a charity's members by post, in which case they are deemed to have been delivered 'in the ordinary course of post'.

- The charity's constitution will also generally state the address to which a member's notice should be given. Again, the Charities Act 1993, s 81 allows the charity's trustees to send the notice to the last address given to the charity by a member.

- The notice must, as a minimum, confirm the date, time and place of the meeting and state its purpose sufficiently clearly. The key point is whether the notice contains sufficient information about the matters that will be considered to enable members to decide whether or not to attend the meeting.

- The notice must not contravene any rules and regulations in relation to the charity. There is more about this at **5.46** below.

5.44 Where a notice is not properly given, any decisions taken at the meeting will be invalid. There are a number of ways in which decisions may still validly be taken notwithstanding that notice has not been properly given:

- It may be possible to rectify an invalid notice by sending out a further notice clarifying the position, but the second notice would need to be sent within the time limits which apply to the giving of the original notice of the meeting.

- The charity's constitution may include an express provision that an accidental omission to give notice of a meeting to someone entitled to receive it (or their failure to receive it because, for example, it has been lost in the post) will not invalidate the meeting that is held subsequently.

- If all of the people who are entitled to receive notice of a meeting waive the requirement to receive a valid notice, the meeting can still proceed. Some charities' constitutions may lower this requirement so that, for example, a specified percentage of members can agree to waive the entitlement to a valid notice.

5.45 Some charities' constitutions may not provide for express periods of notice. Those convening a meeting in the absence of such provision will need to give reasonable notice. The periods of notice that apply to the meetings of a charitable company's members (21 clear days' notice for an AGM and 14 clear days' notice for any other meeting) would be a reasonable starting point. The trustees of a charity which is in this position may well wish to amend its constitution to include specified periods of notice. There is more about constitutional changes at **Chapter 15**.

Rules and regulations

5.46 A charity's constitution will often give its trustees power to make rules and regulations in relation to the way in which they convene and hold members' meetings in order to give them flexibility to work in the most effective way. This is the approach usually taken by the constitution of a charitable company (and reflects the approach taken by companies generally) but any charity can adopt a similar approach with an appropriate constitutional provision. Any rules and regulations that are made should preferably be in writing and reviewed by the trustees from time to time. This should not conflict with the provisions of the constitution itself (on the basis that the constitution can only properly be altered in accordance with whatever mechanism applies to it). Any notice given by the charity's trustees must comply with any relevant rules and regulations.

Electronic meetings

5.47 A valid meeting can only usually be held where the participants can see and hear each other (which will include meetings held by way of video conference or web camera). However, a charity's constitution can expressly widen the definition of 'meeting'. An appropriate provision could authorise meetings to be held by way of telephone conference.

Voting

5.48   Voting at members' meetings will be in accordance with the charity's constitution but, if the constitution is silent, a 'simple' majority can pass resolutions. A 'simple' majority exists where more members vote for a particular resolution than against it. A charity's constitution may also provide that a higher or 'special' majority is required in relation to a particular resolution. So, for example, a resolution to dissolve a charity will often require a two-thirds majority vote in order to pass it.

5.49   The majority generally required is a majority of the charity's members present at the relevant meeting. The charity's constitution may alter this in relation to certain resolutions. So, for example, a resolution to exercise the sort of power of dissolution we have mentioned in the previous paragraph may only be passed by a two-thirds majority of *all* of the charity's members rather than a two-thirds majority of the members who actually attend the meetings.

5.50   Detailed requirements in relation to the majority required in respect of particular resolutions are often dealt with in a charity's rules and regulations rather than its constitution. There is more about rules and regulations at **5.46**.

5.51   The charity's constitution (or any rules and regulations made under it) govern the way in which members' votes are cast and counted. If the charity's constitution is silent, voting will be on a 'show of hands'. This means that the chairman of the meeting will ask the members present to indicate how they vote by holding up their hands. This is often a quick and effective way of passing resolutions, but it does not allow for voting by members who may have different voting rights. This may be because, for example, a particular class of members is able to cast more votes on a particular issue than another class of members. The 'show of hands' method is also potentially imprecise given that the chairman must count the votes cast and may make a mistake in doing so.

5.52   For these reasons, a vote may also be taken using a 'poll'. The purpose of a vote by poll is to ensure that votes cast are recorded in writing and are counted in an accurate way which, if appropriate, reflects any weighted voting rights. There is the common law right for any member to demand a poll on a particular resolution, although this can generally be limited or excluded by express provisions in the charity's constitution.[7]

5.53   The charity's constitution or rules and regulations relating to meetings may specify who should act as chairman of a member's meeting (this will often be the chairman of the board of trustees acting in another capacity) and whether he or she should exercise a 'casting' or 'second' vote in the event of deadlock. If there is no express provision for the chairman to exercise a casting or second vote, he or she cannot exercise such a vote.

Written resolutions

5.54   If a charity cannot hold a meeting to consider a resolution, the alternative is for all of the members to sign a written resolution. As a general principle, all of the members can agree to do in writing what only a majority of them could resolve to do at a meeting. A charity's constitution may contain an express provision for a written resolution of all of the members of the charity but, where the constitution is silent, the members can still sign a written resolution unless there is something in the charity's

---

[7]   *R v Wimbledon Local Board* [1882] 8 QBD 459.

constitution which conflicts with, or prohibits, this approach. A charity's constitution may provide for a minimum number of members to sign a written resolution, in which case it will be valid provided their signatures can be obtained.

Quorum

5.55 A charity's constitution will usually specify the quorum that applies at a meeting. In other cases, the quorum may be set out in rules or regulations in relation to the conduct of meetings. Different quorums may apply to different meetings or to different resolutions. The quorum required will often vary from charity to charity. A charity with a significant number of individual members will wish to avoid a quorum based upon a percentage of their number which may mean that, in practice, members' meetings can never be quorate. The quorum will often be the 'lower of' or 'greater of' a fixed number or proportion of members, so that they can keep pace with changing numbers of members.

5.56 The number of members necessary for a quorum must be present 'in person'. An authorised representative of a corporate member will be present 'in person' for the purposes of this rule. Proxies, however, will not count unless the charity's constitution or rules and regulations in relation to meetings expressly provide that they should count.

5.57 In general, a meeting must be quorate from start to finish. However, a charity's constitution (or rules and regulations relating to the conduct of meetings) may provide a meeting has only to be quorate at the start of the meeting. If so, all of the resolutions passed at the meeting will be valid notwithstanding that it may have become inquorate part of the way through.

Other attendees

5.58 There are a number of people who may attend member's meetings in addition to the members themselves. Who can or should attend will depend generally upon the charity's constitution or the rules and regulations relating to the conduct of its meetings, but will often include:

- the secretary (if there is one);

- professional advisers to the charity;

- the charity's trustees (including the chairman of the board, who will often act as the chairman of the members' meeting); and

- senior employees (if any).

5.59 Clearly, attendance at a members' meeting does not mean that any of these people are entitled to vote on any of the business being considered by the members at the meeting, although the chairman of a meeting may sometimes consider it helpful for some attendees to speak at the meeting, perhaps in order to explain particular issues for the members.

Minutes

5.60 Whether there is an express legal requirement on a charity to maintain minutes of its member's meetings will depend upon the terms of its constitution, but the obligation to maintain good records is in any event a part of the trustees' duty to safeguard its assets. For this reason, all charities should maintain, comprehensive and accurate records of the business transacted at their members' meetings. The Charity Commission's guidance states that:

> 'Whatever may be the legal requirement, we recommend that accurate minutes are kept of all meetings. Minutes do not need to be a word for word record, but need to record information that is important to the charity. We recommend that each set of minutes give:
>
> - the name of the charity.
> - the type of meeting.
> - the date and time the meetings was held.
> - apologies for absence.
> - the names of those present, including
>   - in what capacity they attended e.g. trustee, advisor etc; and
>   - for what items on the agenda
> - the precise wording of any resolution together with the name of the proposer and (optionally) the seconder of the motion.
> - a summary of the discussion on each item of business.
> - information upon which the decision was based.
> - details of the decision, i.e. who voted and how and, in the event of an equality of votes, if the chair used a casting vote.
> - the action required.
> - the names of the people who are responsible for implementing the decision.
> - the date, time and venue of the next meeting.'[8]

5.61 The Charity Commission's guidance also emphasises the importance of preparing and approving accurate minutes. It states as follows:

> 'It should be noted that the formal minutes, once approved and signed as an accurate record by the chairman, form the only legal record of the business at the meeting.'[9]

COMPANY MEETINGS

5.62 As we have indicated earlier in this chapter, there is a specific body of rules derived from companies legislation and case law which governs the way in which meetings of the members of a charitable company must be conducted. We summarise the main consideration below. These comments should be read in conjunction with our comments on meetings generally at **5.38–5.61**.

Frequency

5.63 The Companies Act 2006 will (once it has come into force) abolish the requirement for private companies to hold an 'annual general meeting' (or 'AGM'). Subject to this, every charitable company is presently obliged to hold an AGM in each calendar year (and not more than 15 months must have elapsed since the last AGM) unless the company's members have passed an 'elective resolution' to dispense with the holding of AGMs.[10] When no elective resolution is in place, the main purpose of the

---

[8]   CC 48.
[9]   CC 48.
[10] Companies Act 1985, s 366A.

AGM is to lay the company's accounts before the members, re-appoint the company's auditors (and fix their remuneration) and deal with any retirement by rotation of the trustees.

5.64 Although, as we have said, the Companies Act 2006 will abolish the requirement for a charitable company to hold an AGM, one can still be held and many charitable companies may wish to do so or may be obliged to do so by their constitutions.

5.65 Any meeting of the members of a charitable company other than an AGM is an 'extraordinary general meeting' or 'EGM'. There is no requirement that an EGM should ever be held, but both the directors and members have the power to call one. This is explained at **5.66**.

Notice

5.66 The Companies Acts spells out in detail the procedures for convening, and giving notice of, meetings of members. Broadly:

- The charitable company's trustees have the power to convene an EGM whenever they think it appropriate in the interests of the charity. Most charitable companies' constitutions will give trustees an express power to convene an EGM in any event.

- The trustees of a charitable company must also convene an EGM on a 'members' requisition'. This is a demand by those members representing not less than one-tenth of the total voting rights of all of the members at the date of the requisition who are able to vote at general meetings.[11]

- Notice of any meeting must be sent to anyone who is entitled, under the terms of the company's constitution, to receive notice. In general, this will be all of the members of the charitable company. The charitable company's auditors are also entitled to receive notice of any meeting.[12]

- A charitable company's constitution will usually specify that notice of a meeting must be given to its members in writing. This includes giving notice electronically, either to an email address or via a website.[13]

- The charitable company's constitution will also usually specify when notice is deemed to be given. Notices should be sent to the address recorded for a particular member in the register of members. This includes an electronic address.

- The notice must confirm the date, time and place of the meeting and state its purpose sufficiently clearly. The key point is that the notice must contain sufficient information about the matters that will be considered to enable members to decide whether or not to attend the meetings.

- The periods of notice required for a particular meeting are specified by section 369 of the Companies Act 1985. In the case of an AGM, 21 days' notice in writing is required. In the case of an EGM 14 days' notice in writing is required. The Companies Act 2006 (once it has come into force) will lower the period of notice

---

[11] Companies Act 1985, s 368.
[12] Companies Act 1985, s 390.
[13] Companies Act 1985 (Electronic Communications) Order 2000.

to 14 days for any general meeting.[14] The period of notice required excludes both the day on which the notice is received by the member and the day on which the meeting is held.

- There are certain provisions for 'special notice' to be given for particular resolutions, including any resolution to remove a trustee by ordinary resolution.[15] The period of special notice is not less than 28 days before the meeting at which the relevant resolution is to be proposed.

5.67 Where the notice is not properly given, any decisions taken at the meeting will be invalid. There are a number of ways in which decisions may still validly be taken notwithstanding that notice has not been properly given:

- It may be possible to rectify an invalid notice by sending out a further notice clarifying the position, but the second notice would need to be sent within the time limits which apply to the giving of the original notice of the meeting.

- The charitable company's constitution may include an express provision that an accidental omission to give notice of a meeting to someone entitled to receive it (or their failure to receive it because, for example, it has been lost in the post) will not invalidate the meeting that is held subsequently.

- The Companies Act 1985 contains a provision for a majority of members to consent to the giving of a short notice. The 'requisite majority' for this purpose is all of those members who together hold not less than 95% of the total voting rights exercisable at the meeting. In the case of an AGM, all of the members entitled to attend and vote must consent to short notice. The position will be altered by the Companies Act 2006, which applies a single 'requisite percentage' to every general meeting.[16] This will be 90% unless the charitable company's constitution sets a higher percentage.

5.68 Where a decision is taken by the members of a charitable company at a meeting which has not been validly called, the decision can effectively be ratified by a subsequent resolution of the members at a properly called meeting.

Rules and regulations

5.69 A charitable company's constitution will often give its trustees power to make rules and regulations in relation to the way in which they convene and hold members' meetings. The new rules and regulations that are made should preferably be in writing and be reviewed by the trustees from time to time. These should not conflict with the provisions of the charity's constitution. Any notice given by the charity's trustees must comply with any relevant rules and regulations.

Electronic meetings

5.70 A valid meeting can only usually be held where the participants can see and hear each other (which will include meetings held by way of video conference or web

---

[14] Companies Act 2006, s 307.
[15] Companies Act 1985, s 303.
[16] Companies Act 2006, s 307.

camera). However a charity's constitution can expressly widen the definition of 'meeting'. An appropriate provision could authorise meetings to be held by way of telephone conference.

Voting

5.71   Voting at the meetings of members of a charitable company will be in accordance with the charity's constitution. The majority required in respect of certain resolutions will be determined by company law.

5.72   Resolutions passed by a simple majority are usually referred to as 'ordinary resolutions' in the context of charitable companies. References to 'resolutions' in the Companies Acts should be interpreted as references to 'ordinary resolutions'. A 'special resolution' of the members means a resolution passed by a majority of not less than 75%. This will include, for example, a resolution to alter a charitable company's constitution.

5.73   A charitable company's constitution will determine how members' votes are cast and counted. In general, voting will be by way of a 'show of hands'. However, there is both a common law and statutory right for members to demand that voting should be way of a 'poll'.[17] This right cannot be excluded by the terms of the charitable company's constitution. The statutory right enables five or more members or members holding not less than one tenth of the total voting right to demand a poll.

5.74   The purpose of a vote by poll is to ensure that votes cast are recorded in writing and are counted in an accurate way which reflects any weighted voting rights.

5.75   The charitable company's constitution may specify that the chairman of the members' meeting should exercise a 'casting' or 'second' vote in the event of deadlock. In the absence of a provision of this kind, the chairman has no second or casting vote in addition to any other vote he or she may have.

Written resolutions

5.76   The Companies Act 1985, ss 381A, 381B, 381C and 382A gives statutory effect to the common law principle that all of the members can agree to do in writing what only a majority of them could resolve to do at a meeting. An express provision of this kind will also often be found in the constitution of a charitable company.

5.77   The Companies Act 2006 will deregulate the position in relation to written resolutions.[18] Essentially, the 2006 Act provides that a written resolution is passed when the 'required majority' of members have signed it. The required majority is the number of members who would be required to vote for a particular ordinary or special resolution at a meeting. The ability to pass written resolutions of this kind is subject to a number of detailed requirements in relation to the circulation of written resolutions to all members but, provided these restrictions are observed, the ability to pass written resolutions in this way is likely to be broadly helpful.

---

[17]   Companies Act 1985, s 373.
[18]   Companies Act 2006, Chap 2.

Quorum

5.78   A charitable company's constitution will usually specify the quorum that applies at a meeting but, if no quorum is specified, the quorum is two members personally present.[19] In the case of a single-member charitable company, the quorum is reduced to one person.

5.79   The quorum required by a charitable company's constitution may vary depending upon the resolution that is proposed. Typically, the quorum will be the 'lower of' or 'greater of' a fixed number or proportion of members, so that they can keep pace with a changing number of members.

5.80   The number of members necessary for the quorum must be present at the meeting 'in person'. An authorised representative of a corporate member will be present 'in person' for the purposes of this rule.[20] A proxy will not be personally present, unless the charitable company's constitution expressly provides for it to count.

5.81   In general, a meeting must be quorate from start to finish. However, a charitable company's constitution may often provide that a quorum must be present 'at the time when the meeting is called to order'. This means that the quorum must be satisfied at the start of the meeting but is not necessary for the quorum to be maintained until the finish.

Other attendees

5.82   A charitable company's auditors have a right to attend general meetings.[21] Who else can or should attend will generally depend upon the terms of the charity's constitution. The position is broadly similar to the position in relation to charities that are not set up as companies.

Minutes

5.83   The Companies Act 1985, s 382(1) obliges every charitable company to keep minutes of all of the proceedings of its general meetings. Subsection 382(2) provides that any minute which is signed by the chairman of the meeting, or by the chairman of the next succeeding meeting, is evidence of the proceedings. The Charity Commission's guidance in relation to minutes is in CC 48.

STAKEHOLDER MEMBERS

5.84   Charities with stakeholder members face a series of particular issues that will need to be addressed. By 'stakeholder members' we mean corporate members of charities who are members because they have some interest in what the charity does. These can include companies, local authorities and other public bodies and other charities. So, for example, a charity established to provide sports and leisure services under a contract with a local authority may admit the local authority as a member.

---

[19]   Companies Act 1985, s 370(4).
[20]   Companies Act 1985, s 375.
[21]   Companies Act 1985, s 390.

5.85 A stakeholder member will often appoint an individual (usually referred to as an 'authorised representative') to act on its behalf. The charity's constitution should provide expressly for this and set out the mechanism by which such individuals are appointed and removed.

5.86 A stakeholder member may also have the right to appoint a trustee of the charity in order to give it more direct influence over the way in which the charity operates. Again, the mechanism by which such individual trustees are appointed and removed should be clearly set out in the charity's constitution.

5.87 Giving a stakeholder the right to be a member of a charity can cause problems where there is a conflict between the interests of the stakeholder and the interests of the charity. The stakeholder member's authorised representative may wish to give priority to the stakeholder's own interests over the interests of the charity. As explained at **5.22**, the duty owed by a member to a charity is unclear, except in relation to a CIO or where there is an express duty incorporated into the constitution. Having said that, it is possible that the court will conclude that any member should act in good faith in the interests of the charity. Both the stakeholder and the charity should be made aware of the position in cases of conflict.

5.88 The problems caused by conflicts of interest are more acute where a stakeholder is able to appoint or nominate a trustee of the charity. Again, the trustee may be faced with a decision where he or she would prefer to give priority to the interests of the stakeholder over the interests of the charity. The position is likely to be particularly difficult where the appointee or nominee is an officer or employee of the stakeholder or, where the stakeholder is itself a charity, is one of its trustees. The duty of a charity trustee to act only for the benefit of his or her charity and to avoid conflicts of interest is absolutely clear, so that any decision by a trustee which is motivated by a desire to prefer the stakeholder's interests will be a breach of trust.

5.89 There are some steps that can be taken to avoid problems arising out of conflict of this kind:

- Where a charity is being set up by one or more stakeholders, some thought should be given to whether stakeholders should have an express right to appoint or nominate trustees in addition to acting as members. The alternative would be to give the stakeholder member a right to appoint an 'Observer' with a right to attend and speak at trustees' meetings with a view to explaining the stakeholder's views and reporting back to the stakeholder on the trustees' thinking in relation to the charity. An Observer has no voting rights and is not therefore a charity trustee (unless he or she actually participates in the management and control of the charity), so that there is no scope for any conflict of interest to arise. The disadvantage of this approach is that the stakeholder will generally have less influence over the charity's activities than if it were able to appoint a trustee directly.

- As part of their induction, trustees appointed or nominated by stakeholders should understand that, while they have been appointed to represent the views of the stakeholders in relation to the charity, their duty is to act in the best interests of the charity alone.

- The charity's constitution should include a mechanism for dealing with conflicts of interest that will allow trustees to declare their interests and/or not to participate in particular potentially conflicted decisions. There is more about trustees' conflicts of interests in **Chapter 8**.

5.90   The charity's constitution should clearly distinguish between a stakeholder's right to appoint a trustee of the charity and the right to nominate a person for appointment as a trustee by the charity's own trustees. Giving a stakeholder a direct right to appoint a trustee may mean that the person appointed does not match the criteria set by the charity's trustees for appointments. This issue should be addressed in the following way:

- If the stakeholder has a right to appoint trustees, the trustees should have the power to set clear criteria for appointees as part of their identification of the skills required for trustees generally.

- The trustees could also have the power to appoint additional trustees to fill any skills gap. These are usually referred to as 'co-opted' trustees. There is more information about this in **Chapter 8**.

- Stakeholders could be given the right to nominate trustees for appointment by the trustees instead of a direct right of appointment. This will allow the trustees to control the composition of the board and the skill set of the trustees.

5.91   Stakeholder involvement should be reviewed on a regular basis. As time passes and a charity develops, its stakeholders may change with the consequence that its stakeholder members should change. Those establishing new charities should consider including a mechanism for adding new stakeholder members, perhaps with the consent of a majority of existing stakeholder members. The possibility of stakeholder members ceasing to exist or changing their legal form by way of restructuring or merger should also be dealt with expressly so that it is clear in which circumstances membership rights will cease or transfer to a successor.

5.92   Stakeholders will need to consider whether there are restrictions on their own ability to become stakeholder members:

- Every stakeholder should ensure that its own constitution authorises it to act as a stakeholder in a charity.

- Company stakeholders should consider whether becoming a stakeholder member will have any implications for them under the accounting rules and practice that require the consolidation of accounts.

- Local authority stakeholders should consider the implications of the Local Government Finance Act 1988. The 1988 Act imposes restrictions on the ability of local authorities to become members of charities without consolidating their accounts with its own.

'FEDERAL' AND 'BRANCH' ARRANGEMENTS

5.93   Charities are sometimes set up as part of a 'federation' of other charities, generally operating in different localities. The aim is usually to carry out the work of the charity in particular geographical areas but under the influence of a national 'headquarters' charity which may provide support and assistance to the local charity (perhaps in the form of a standard constitution, assistance with governance arrangements etc).

5.94 The degree of affiliation between the local and the national charities will vary from case to case. From the point of view of good governance, it is obviously essential that the relationship between the two entities is clearly established. In practice, this will mean ensuring that there is clarity in relation to the degree of control that the national charity can exercise over the local charity.

5.95 In contrast to this 'federal' approach, some national charities operate using a 'branch' structure. There is no legal definition of a 'branch' for this purpose. The key point is that the activities carried out locally are the activities of the national charity, but are carried out by individuals on the charity's behalf, usually on the basis of delegated authority. Typically, a local 'sub-committee' of the board of trustees of the main charity will have delegated authority to carry out all of the charity's activities in a particular area. Typically, the delegation will impose a number of restrictions on their ability to operate, including, for example, their ability to spend the charity's funds or to incur significant liabilities.

5.96 Clearly, if a branch structure of this kind is to operate effectively it is essential that the terms on which the sub-committee is authorised to operate are very clear. In exercising authority delegated by the charity's trustees, the delegates themselves will be subject to the same liabilities as charity trustees. They will need to understand the implications of this for them personally.

5.97 The position in relation to the branches is made more complicated by the definition of 'branch' used by the Charities SORP 2005 for accounting purposes. A detailed discussion of this area is outside the scope of this book, but it is important to appreciate that the definition for accounting purposes is wider than the legal interpretation. See the Charity Commission's operational guidance OG 34 for more detail in relation to the reporting and accounting obligations of branches.

6

TRUSTEES' DUTIES AND LIABILITIES

6.1   The trustees of any charity, regardless of how it is constituted, owe the same duties under the law relating to charities, trusts and trustees. So, for example, the trustees of a charitable company will owe the same duties as the trustees of a charitable trust.[1] There are obviously specific duties imposed by the Charities Act 1993 (eg to register their charity, to apply for a Scheme in certain circumstances etc), but of greater importance are the duties that underpin all of their acts as trustees. The most important duties are:

- to ensure that the charity's assets are applied only for its particular charitable purposes;

- to act within the powers they have as trustees of the charity;

- to exercise those powers only in the best interests of the charity and only for the purposes for which they have been given;

- to avoid any conflict between the charity's interests and the personal interests of the trustee or the duties he or she may owe in some other capacity;

- to act unpaid and avoid any arrangement which may result in the trustee taking any personal benefit directly or indirectly; and

- to exercise their powers personally, without delegating responsibility for decisions to anyone else.

6.2   In discharging these duties, charity trustees are under an obligation to exercise due care and skill. The trustees of an unincorporated charity are under a statutory obligation[2] to exercise such care and skill as is reasonable in the circumstances in excising a range of powers, including power of investment and delegation. The level of care and skill required is assessed having regard to:

- any special knowledge or expertise that the trustee has or holds him or herself out as having; and

- where a trustee acts in the course of a business or profession, to any special knowledge or expertise that it is reasonable to expect of a person acting in the course of that kind of business or profession.

In principle, this duty applies only to the exercise of the powers conferred on the trustees of unincorporated charities by the Trustee Act 2000, but the courts are likely to apply a

---

[1]   *Re The French Protestant Hospital* [1951] Ch 567.

[2]   Trustee Act 2000, s 1.

similar /duty of care to the exercise of other powers exercised by trustees. This is also the approach taken by the Charity Commission.[3]

6.3   The trustees of a charitable company will owe a statutory duty as company directors to exercise reasonable care, skill and diligence under the Companies Act 2006 (once the relevant provisions come into force) but the assumption should be that in assessing whether a trustee has discharged his or her duty as a charity trustee, the court will look at the higher standard imposed on trustees by the Trustee Act 2000. That is consistent with the approach taken to the trustees of incorporated charities in the past. It is also consistent with the Charity Commission's approach.[4]

6.4   It is important to appreciate that, while this test does not require a charity trustee to meet wholly objective standards of skill and experience, it does not impose a wholly subjective test (which would only require the trustee to meet his own standards of skill and experience).

6.5   In addition to the duties summarised above, the trustees of a charitable company will owe other duties under the Companies Acts and the Insolvency Act 1986. These provisions will apply to the trustees of a charitable company in exactly the same way as the directors of any commercial company.

CHARITABLE COMPANIES – COMPANIES ACT 2006

6.6   The Companies Act 2006 will impose a number of specific statutory duties on company directors[5]. These are:

• to act within their powers;

• to exercise independent skill and judgement;

• to exercise reasonable care, skill and diligence;

• to avoid conflict of interest;

• to declare interests;

• not to accept benefits from third parties; and

• to promote the success of the company.

6.7   Some of these duties derive from the existing common law as it related to the fiduciary duties of company directors and the expectation is that the courts will apply the common law principles previously established in interpreting these statutory provisions. Others re-express statutory duties imposed by the Companies Act 1985. Significantly, however, these duties are also consistent with the duties imposed upon charity trustees generally (as summarised above). So, for example, a director of a

---

[3]   CC 3.

[4]   CC 3.

[5]   Companies Act 2006, ss 171–177; expected to come into force in October 2007, (except for s 175, expected to come into force on 1 October 2008).

charitable company will owe a duty to avoid conflicts of interest under both the common law rules relating to trustees and the statutory rules imposed by the Companies Acts.

6.8   One possible exception to this is the duty to promote the success of the company, which replaces the common law principle of acting in a company's best interests that applied previously. The duty on every director is that he 'should act in a way he considers, in good faith, would be most likely to promote the success of the company for the benefit of the members as a whole' and that, in doing so, he or she must consider:

- the likely long term consequences of the decision;

- the interests of the employees;

- the need to foster business relationships with suppliers, customers and others;

- the impact of the company's operations on the community and the environment;

- the desirability of maintaining the company's reputation for high standards of business conduct; and

- the need to act fairly between the members of the company.

6.9   The duty to promote the success of the company is driven by a desire to use the Companies Act 2006 to put directors' duties in a wider social, ethical and environmental framework than had previously applied. This reflects the principle identified by the Company Law Reform Final Report (and endorsed by the Government) of 'enlightened shareholder value'. This is a new principle and one that is as yet untested in the courts. For that reason, there is a degree of uncertainty about the way in which it will apply to directors.

6.10   The Companies Act 2006 does not modify the duty to promote the success of the company as it applies to charitable companies. Clearly, not all of the matters specified by the Companies Act 2006 will be relevant to charitable companies. There will, for example, be no practical requirement to act fairly between the members of a charitable company in the same way as the shareholders in a commercial company, because the members have no personal financial interest in the charity.

6.11   The list of matters specified by the Companies Act 2006 is not exhaustive, so there is some scope for the directors of a charitable company to modify them so that they are relevant to the charity's own particular circumstances. Having said that, there may be circumstances in which this duty could conflict with the duties imposed on charity trustees generally. The duty to take into account the impact of the charity's activities on the community generally may, for example, conflict with the duty to act only in the best interests of the charity where its charitable purposes focus only on a particular section of the community. Whether conflicts such as this will arise in practice is uncertain.

6.12   In addition to these statutory duties, the Companies Acts impose a number of more administrative duties on company directors. These include duties to:

- maintain the company's statutory books and records;

- file resolutions and other corporate documents with Companies House;

- keep accounting records; and

- prepare and file an annual report and accounts.

6.13   There are more than 150 criminal offences in the Companies Act 2006 which may be committed by a company and for which a director in default may be prosecuted. The penalties range from imprisonment for up to two years to fines. Experience suggests that criminal prosecutions are rare. The more usual sanction for default is a financial penalty imposed by Companies House or disqualification as a director (see **6.16**).

CHARITABLE COMPANIES – INSOLVENCY ACT 1986

6.14   Where a charitable company has financial problems, its trustees will be faced with difficult judgements about the best way of managing them. In those circumstances, there are two provisions of the Insolvency Act 1986 (IA 1986) that can impose personal liability on the directors of a charitable company for 'wrongful' and 'fraudulent' trading.

Wrongful trading (IA 1986, s 214)	Where, before the start of an insolvent liquidation of the company, a director knew or ought to have known that there was no reasonable prospect that the company would avoid insolvent liquidation, its liquidator can apply to the court for an order obliging the director to contribute to the company's assets out of his or her own personal assets. The director can avoid liability to make a personal contribution if he or she can show that, once they had concluded, or ought to have concluded, that there was no reasonable prospect that the company would avoid insolvent liquidation, he or she took every step with a view to minimising the potential loss to creditors.
Fraudulent trading (IA 1986, s 213)	Where, in the course of the insolvent liquidation of a company, it appears that any business of the company has been carried on with intent to defraud its creditors, the liquidator can apply to the court for an order obliging anyone who was knowingly a party to carrying on the business in that way (including the directors) to contribute to the company's assets out of his or her own personal assets. The liquidator must show (beyond reasonable doubt given that fraudulent trading involves dishonesty) that the director took positive steps to continue to trade and incur debts when he or she knew that there was no reasonable prospect of repaying them.

6.15   The liquidator of any insolvent charitable company will assess whether there are claims against the trustees for wrongful or fraudulent trading. Liability extends to any 'shadow director'; in other words, to anyone not formally appointed as a director but in accordance with whose directions or instructions the appointed directors were accustomed to act.

6.16 The liquidator can also bring other claims against the trustees of a charitable company under the Insolvency Act 1986. These include claims for misconduct in the course of winding-up,[6] false representations to creditors,[7] material omissions from statements relating to the charitable company's affairs[8] and misfeasance or breach of statutory duty.[9] The liquidator will also make a report to the DTI on the conduct of the directors and any shadow directors of the company. That report may form the basis of proceedings to issue disqualification orders under the Company Directors Disqualification Act 1986.

6.17 In practice, and in the absence of any dishonesty, the trustees of a charitable company in financial difficulty will be most concerned about liability for wrongful trading. The key steps in relation to managing this risk are:

- taking legal and financial advice at an early stage;

- ensuring that the financial information required to make judgements about the charitable company's finances is up to date and accurate; and

- assessing the situation regularly and ensuring that all deliberations and decisions are properly recorded.

LIABILITY

6.18 What are the consequences of a breach by a charity trustee of any of the duties outlined above? The short answer is 'personal liability'. In other words, that the trustee is personally liable to compensate the charity out of his or her own assets for the losses that would not have been suffered if the breach of duty had not occurred. This is the starting point, but the position will vary depending on the legal form that the charity takes.

6.19 A charity trustee of any charity (however it is constituted) is potentially personally liable to compensate the charity for any losses that would not have been suffered but for his or her breach of trust. Liability would be determined by the court, which will look at all relevant circumstance, in deciding how far the liability should extend. In practice, no liability will arise where:

- The court exercises its discretion to relieve any trustee from personal liability where the trustee can show that he or she acted honestly and reasonably and ought fairly to be excused for the breach;[10] or

---

[6]   IA 1986, s 208.
[7]   IA 1986, s 211.
[8]   IA 1986, s 210.
[9]   IA 1986, s 212.
[10]   Trustee Act 1925, s 61; Companies Act 1985, s 727.

- The Charity Commission exercises the discretion to relieve any trustee from personal liability under the Charities Act 2006.[11]

Other instances of personal liability can arise, depending on how a charity is constituted.

Charitable companies

6.20 The Companies Act 2006 will introduce a statutory 'derivative action'.[12] A member of a charitable company can bring a common law claim on behalf of or for the benefit of the company in respect of some wrong done to it (this is usually known as a 'derivative' action because the member's right to claim derives from the company's right to claim). The common law claim can be bought even if the company, its trustees and the majority of other members do not wish to pursue it. The ability to pursue a derivative claim at common law is generally restricted to cases of fraud or the illegality of failure to pass an appropriate resolution. The Companies Act 2006 extends the existing derivative action and will make it much easier for members to sue trustees for a broader range of conduct than under the existing common law. These include any actual proposed act or omission involving negligence, default, breach of duty or breach of trust.

6.21 A member's ability to bring a derivative action under the 2006 Act may be a concern for the trustees in certain circumstances. There is a safeguard against 'frivolous' claims, which is that the courts must be satisfied that a claim bought by a member discloses a '*prima facie*' case before the claim is allowed to proceed. The courts will look at whether or not the member is acting in good faith, the importance a trustee promoting the success of the company would attach to it, whether the conduct complained of is likely to be authorised or ratified by the company and whether the company itself has decided not to pursue the claim. It remains to be seen whether or not the 2006 Act will, once it comes into force, stimulate a greater number of claims by the members of charitable companies.

Unincorporated charities

6.22 Where a charity is unincorporated, a liability that is incurred by a trustee in breach of trust is likely to be his or her personal liability. This is because an unincorporated charity has no legal personality of its own and can only interact with third parties via its trustees. This means that the trustees themselves take on liabilities to third parties personally; in other words, they are potentially personally liable to meet the liabilities in question. This could be, for example, rent due under a lease taken out in the names of the trustees for the purposes of the charity.

6.23 Generally speaking, the trustees will not have to meet the liabilities out of their own assets (if they did, there would obviously be very few people willing to act as trustees) because they can indemnify themselves in respect of properly incurred liabilities out of the charity's assets. Many charities' constitutions will provide for an express indemnity. Failing that, there is a statutory indemnity under the Trustee Act 2000 in respect of properly incurred liabilities.[13]

---

[11]   Charities Act 1993, s 73D.
[12]   Companies Act 2006, ss 260–269; expected to come into force in October 2007.
[13]   Trustee Act 2000, s 31.

6.24 This means that there are two circumstances in which the trustees of an unincorporated charity may have personal liability:

- Where the charity's assets are not sufficient to meet the liabilities due to a third party.

- Where the trustees do not properly incur the liability in the first place, so that the trustees cannot indemnify themselves out of the charity's assets.

Trustees may seek expressly to limit their contractual liabilities to a third party by agreeing that the third party's only recourse is to the assets of the charity from time to time. This must be expressly agreed (it is not enough to state simply that the trustees are contracting in their capacity as trustees. The trustees may also be able to insure themselves against the risk of any shortfall in the charity's assets (see **6.33**).

6.25 Where a liability is incurred in breach of trust (eg because the trustees had no power to incur it, perhaps by taking a loan when they have no power to borrow), the liability is unlikely to have been properly incurred, so that the trustees remain personally liable for it with no recourse to the charity's assets (and notwithstanding that the exercise of the power may actually have been in good faith and for the charity's benefit).

6.26 In certain circumstances, the trustees of an unincorporated charity may wish to consider whether appointing a corporate trustee or arranging for their own incorporation under the Charities 1993, Pt VII may help to limit their liabilities. Each of these possibilities is explained in a little more detail below.

Corporate trustees

An unincorporated charity may have a body corporate acting as its sole charity trustee. This could be, for example, a professional trust company or bank appointed to act on a paid basis or a local authority. In other cases a charity may wish to appoint a sole corporate trustee in order to simplify the way in which its assets can be held or contracts can be entered into. Using a sole corporate trustee will also help to avoid exposing individuals who might otherwise act as trustees to personal liability to third parties in respect of, for example, liabilities in excess of the charity's assets available to pay them.

Where a corporate trustee is appointed, it will have all of the usual duties and liabilities of a charity trustee. Its directors (who might otherwise act as individual trustees of the charity) will not be charity trustees, although they will owe fiduciary duties to the corporate trustee in directing the way in which it functions as a charity trustee.

In the event that the corporate trustee is in breach of its duties as charity trustee, only the trustee itself will be directly personally liable (to the extent of its corporate assets) as a result. However, that is not to say that the corporate directors will not also have some indirect liability as a consequence. If the corporate trustee's breach of trust is due to breaches of duty by its directors then the corporate trustee may have claims against the directors personally in respect of the losses it has suffered as a consequence. ➡

The individual directors' potential liability will be indirect but, for all practical purposes, they should assume that they owe the same duties to the charity as the corporate trustee. In other words, that they should regard themselves as charity trustees. This is confirmed by the Charity Commission in OG 38 B4.

The liability position of trustees who opt for incorporation under Charities Act 1993, ss 50–62 is different (see below).

Incorporation of charity trustees

Part VII (ss 50–62) of the Charities Act 1993 provides a mechanism for the individual trustees of an unincorporated charity to opt to become a incorporated body. The effect of their incorporation is to:

- vest all of the charity's assets (and all associated rights and liabilities) in the incorporated body;

- allow the trustees to sue and be sued in the name of the incorporated body;

- allow the trustees to execute documents in the name of the incorporated body; and

- give the incorporated body all of the powers (subject to the same restrictions) of the individual trustees.

Incorporation solves many of the problems posed by unincorporated status, by allowing the charity to hold assets, enter into contracts and act generally in the name of a single incorporated body rather than the names of the individual trustees from time to time.

However, incorporation does not affect the liability of the individual trustees for any breaches of trust they are responsible for (this is expressly provided for by the Charities Act 1993, s 54). The effect of incorporation on the individual trustees' liability to third parties in respect of contracts and other liabilities incurred to others is not absolutely clear, but the general view is that it does not confer limited liability in the same way as, say, the limited liability status of a company and takes effect only for the specific purposes of holding assets etc mentioned in the Charities Act 1993.

Trustees' liabilities for breach of trust and to third parties may be affected by appointing a corporate trustee to act in their place (see above).

INDEMNITY INSURANCE

6.27 Many charity trustees (and particularly prospective trustees) will want to consider whether the risk of personal liability can be managed using indemnity insurance. The key point in relation to trustee indemnity insurance is that the premiums paid by a charity are benefits to the trustees personally and, as such, are subject to all of the usual prohibitions on trustee benefits (there is more detail about this at **6.35**).

6.28   If a charity is to take out indemnity insurance for the benefit of its trustees, it must have a power to do so. The position is:

- The charity's constitution may expressly authorise it to take out indemnity insurance. This will usually be an express exception from the prohibition on the trustees benefiting personally from the charity's assets.

- If there is no express power to insure the trustees, the charity may be able to use the statutory power conferred by the Charities Act 1993, s 73F to insure its trustees against personal liability in respect of:
  - any breach of trust or duty committed by the trustees in their capacity as charity trustees
  - any negligence, default, breach of trust or duty committed by them in their capacity as directors or officers of any incorporated charity or any 'body corporate carrying on any activities on behalf of the charity' (this provision is therefore arguably wide enough to cover the directors or officers of a trading subsidiary of the charity).

  The statutory power applies only where the trustees are satisfied that it is in the best interests of the charity to purchase the insurance and that there is nothing in the charity's constitution that expressly prohibits it, but the sort of general prohibition on trustee benefits found in most charity constitutions is not an express prohibition for this purpose.

- If there is no express authority in the charity's constitution and the statutory power cannot be used (because the constitution expressly prohibits the purchase of indemnity insurance) then the trustees can apply to the Commission for consent to the inclusion of a power. The Commission operate a 'self-certification' system that puts the onus on the trustees to consider whether the purchase of the insurance is for the charity's benefit. Often this may be because it is difficult to recruit new trustees without the comfort of indemnity cover. Provided the trustees provide the relevant self-certificate, the Commission will give its consent (by way of Scheme in respect of an unincorporated charity and under the Charities Act 1993, s 64 for a change to the memorandum of a charitable company). There is more detail about this procedure in the Commission's Operational Guidance.[14] Given the statutory power to insure, it is only likely to be relevant to charities that have an express prohibition on the purchase of indemnity insurance.

6.29   The statutory power cannot be used to pay for insurance which covers any of the following liabilities:

- a fine imposed in criminal proceedings or a penalty payable to any regulatory authority;

- any liability arising out of criminal proceedings in which the trustee is convicted of any offence arising out of any fraud or dishonesty or wilful or reckless misconduct by him or her; or

- any liability incurred by the trustee to the charity that arises out of any conduct that he or she knew (or must reasonably be assumed to have known) was not in the interests of the charity or where he or she did not care whether it was in the charity's interest or not.

---

[14]   OG 100 A1.

6.30 The net effect of this is that a charity cannot insure its trustees against their own breaches of trust unless they are as a result of negligent acts or omissions that the trustee did not know about and cannot reasonably be assumed to have known about.

6.31 Most express powers to purchase indemnity insurance will be subject to similar restrictions. They would not otherwise have been accepted by the Charity Commission on an application for registration or a subsequent application for an express power. The Commission's view is:

'Trustee indemnity insurance *cannot* as a matter of public policy provide an indemnity to a trustee for his or her personal liability for:

- fines;
- the costs of unsuccessfully defending criminal prosecutions for offences arising out of the fraud or dishonesty or wilful or reckless misconduct of a trustee;
- liabilities to the charity which result from conduct which the trustee knew, or must be assumed to have known, was not in the interests of the charity or which the trustee did not care whether it was in the best interests of the charity or not. Any authority which we provide in order to facilitate the purchase of trustee indemnity insurance will be conditional on the inclusion in the policy of provisions which suitably reflect these public policy restrictions.'[15]

6.32 This view is reflected in the Commission's Operational Guidance on express authorisation to purchase indemnity insurance and the model form of power recommended by them.[16]

6.33 Even where a charity has an express power to purchase indemnity insurance, trustees should consider carefully whether it will actually improve their position and be for the benefit of their charity, particularly given the restrictions on the liabilities that it can cover:

- Many of the liabilities which concern trustees can often be insured by the charity itself, e g loss to the charity's assets giving rise to a shortfall as against the trustees' liabilities. The Charity Commission recognises that, even in the context of an unincorporated charity, a distinction should be drawn between liabilities which are primarily those of the charity and those which are primarily liabilities of the trustees. On that basis, the Commission does not treat trustee reimbursement insurance to cover any shortfall in assets against liabilities as trustee indemnity insurance notwithstanding that they will benefit personally as a consequence.

- The main advantage of indemnity insurance will be to cover negligent breaches of trust. In the context of a charitable company, the most significant example of that would be liability for wrongful trading. But there is a question mark over the extent to which cover for wrongful trading can be obtained given the prohibition on insuring liabilities arising out of conduct that a trustee knew or must be assumed to have known was not in the charity's best interests. Given that the test for wrongful trading is that the trustee must have known or ought to have known that there was no reasonable prospect of the charity avoiding insolvent liquidation, it is possible that cover for wrongful trading cannot be provided.

---

[15] CC 49.
[16] OG 100.

6.34   The Charity Commission's guidance acknowledges that indemnity insurance may often be provided under a policy which covers other aspects of a charity's activities. If indemnity cover is included, authorisation by the Commission will be required even where the indemnity element of the policy is stated by the insurer to be provided at no extra cost.

TRUSTEE BENEFITS

6.35   As part of the requirement that all charities must be for the public benefit, charity law prohibits the provision of benefits by a charity to its trustees without express authority to do so. This is a very important aspect of every charity trustee's duty to act voluntarily and gratuitously, which is itself part of the duty to avoid any conflict between a trustee's duties to a charity and his or her own personal interests. Put simply, the concern is that a trustee cannot act in good faith and bring independence of mind to a charity's affairs if he or she is also concerned about its ability to pay him or her or provide them with other benefits.

6.36   That is not to say that a charity cannot in certain circumstances pay its trustees, but this can only happen where there is an appropriate authority in its constitution. Without that authority, it does not matter whether the charity has received value for money for services provided by its trustees, or would not have been able to obtain the services anywhere else or only on much worse terms. The trustees will be in breach of trust for making the unauthorised payments and the trustee who has received the payments will be liable to repay them in full to the charity, with an obligation on the trustees of the charity to consider enforcing that liability.

6.37   Subject to the coming into force of s 73B of the Charities Act 1993[17], the 1993 Act will define a trustee benefit as 'a direct or indrect benefit of any nature'. In practice, the benefits that are usually relevant are:

- payments for services provided to a charity by a trustee;

- payments by a charity to an employee (often the chief executive) who is also a trustee; and

- payments by a charity to a trustee for acting as a trustee.

Reimbursement of expenses

6.38   Benefits do not include the reimbursement of expenses incurred by a trustee in acting as trustee. These can be reimbursed by the charity without any authority in its constitution (although an express authority is often included). However, expenses do not include any sort of compensation for loss of earnings or profit suffered by a trustee in spending time acting as trustee. Benefits freely enjoyed by a trustee alongside the public or as a beneficiary of the charity are also excluded from the general prohibition.

---

[17]   Expected to come into force in early 2008.

'Shared purse' arrangements

6.39 It is important to appreciate that the restrictions on the provision of benefits to trustees apply in the same way to benefits made available to anyone closely associated with them. The Charity Commission's guidance on payments to trustees refers expressly to what they call 'shared purse' arrangements:

> 'The legal concept of the 'shared purse' means that if a trustee is a party to appointing his or her spouse or partner to a paid post within the charity, or to contracting with that person to provide a paid service to the charity, or in any way to assist in securing payment for that person from the charity's funds, then the trustee could be said to profit indirectly from the arrangement. If there is any financial interdependence between the parties, such payments can be a trustee benefit requiring explicit authority – in just the same way as a direct payment to the trustee.
>
> If a payment of this nature is made without an express authority, the trustee concerned is liable to make good any payment made to the spouse or partner in just the same way as if the trustee had received the payment directly. In practice, the actual recipient of the payment is jointly liable.
>
> In the case of a more distant relative being employed by a charity, issues of self-interest or adverse influence by a trustee are less likely to arise, unless there is any direct evidence to the contrary. But trustees still need to manage the issue in a way that does not expose the charity to outside criticism. For this reason, any arrangement with a related party should be transparent, so that it can be seen that it has been made in the charity's interests, and that the potential conflict of interest has been declared'.[18]

6.40 There is a statutory definition of who should be considered to be 'connected' to a trustee in the context of payments to trustees. This applies only to the statutory power referred to at **6.46** below, but best practice will be to assume that a similar test applies in relation to all proposed payments to trustees. The categories of connected person[19] are:

(a)   a child, parent, grandchild, grandparent or sibling of the trustee;

(b)   a spouse or civil partner of the trustee or anyone within (a);

(c)   anyone in partnership with the trustee or anyone within (a) or (b);

(d)   any 'institution' controlled by the trustee or anyone within (a), (b) or (c) (whether acting alone or together). 'Control' means that the relevant person can secure that the affairs of the 'institution' are conducted in accordance with his wishes;

(e)   any 'body corporate' in which the trustee or anyone within (a), (b) or (c) has a 'substantial interest' (whether alone or taken together). A substantial interest is more than 20% of the share capital or voting rights in the relevant 'body corporate'.

6.41 It is open to anyone establishing a charity to decide that its trustees should receive benefits of this kind, usually on the basis that they think it will help the charity to function more effectively. So, for example, someone establishing a charity may decide to appoint a bank as one of its trustees in order to ensure a degree of professional

---

[18]   CC 11.
[19]   Charities Act 1993, s 73B, Sch 5.

expertise and continuity in its administration and that, in order to secure the bank's services, it should be paid for doing so. The Charity Commission accept that this is possible, subject only to ensuring that the charity can continue to meet the public benefit requirement. The test applied by the Commission is whether the benefits that can be provided are in excess of what might be considered reasonable payment for the services actually provided. The Commission will expect there to be other restrictions on the power to pay a trustee where that power is included. These are summarised at **6.43** below.

Express authorisation

6.42 Where an existing charity wishes to provide benefits to its trustees, it can only do so if it has the relevant authority. The starting point will be its constitution, which may include the relevant authority, often as an exception to a general prohibition on trustees benefiting from their trusteeship. The position will vary from charity to charity but the following benefits will typically be provided for:

- a reasonable rate of interest on money loaned to the charity by a trustee (usually capped at a percentage rate below a bank base rate);

- a reasonable rent on property leased to the charity by a trustee;

- reimbursement of expenses;

- payments to companies for services where the trustee owns less than 1% of the share capital (this is intended to avoid the need for authorisation where payments are made to listed companies or companies in which the trustee has only a 'de minimis' interest); and

- premiums in respect of trustee indemnity insurance.

Payment for goods and services

6.43 More modern charity constitutions may also contain provisions for the payment of trustees for goods or services provided to the charity. Powers of this kind will usually be subject to a number of conditions which require that:

- the payment for the goods or services which are supplied is reasonable;

- the trustee providing the goods or services is not involved in taking any decision in relation to their supply;

- only a minority of trustees provide goods and services to the charity at any time; and

- the trustees conclude that paying the trustee for the goods and services is in the best interests of the charity.

6.44 If there is no express power of this kind in the charity's constitution and the trustees wish to pay one of their number for providing goods and services, there are four options open to them:

- If the charity wishes to pay its trustee less than £1,000 in aggregate for services provided during the charity's financial year, and a majority of trustees will be unpaid, the trustees can self-certify the position under the Charity Commission's 'de minimis' policy in relation to small charities.[20]

- If the charity wishes to pay trustees more than £1,000 in aggregate in its financial year and its annual income is less than £20,000, the trustees can use a 'fast track' procedure which involves submitting a declaration to the Charity Commission.[21]

- Subject to the coming into force of the Charities Act 2006 (expected in early 2008), the trustees may be able to use the statutory power conferred by CA 1993, s 73A to pay a trustee for services.

- The trustees may be able to apply to the Charity Commission for an express power to make payments.

6.45 Both the 'de minimis' and 'fast track' applications are subject to certain conditions designed to ensure that the payments are reasonable, that the paid trustees are in a minority and that the payments are disclosed in the charity's accounts. See OG 205 for more detail on the application process.

Statutory powers

6.46 The statutory power to pay a trustee for services will (once it is in force)[22] subject to a number of conditions:

- The payment due to the trustee is specified in a written agreement. This is good practice in any event.

- The payment must not be more than what is reasonable in the circumstances. This is a judgment for the trustees to make taking into account the terms of the proposed agreement. In most cases, they are likely to need comparators in order to enable to decide what level of payment is reasonable. Again, this is good practice in any event in order to ensure that the charity is getting value for money.

- The trustees must decide, before they enter into the agreement, that it is in the best interests of the charity to pay the trustee for the relevant services.

- If there is more than one paid trustee (whether under the statutory power or some other power), they must be a minority of the trustees.

- The constitution of the charity must not contain any express provision that prohibits the trustee from receiving payment. The Charities Act 1993, s 73A does not define what constitutes an 'express provision', but there is a clear argument that the sort of general prohibition on benefits to trustees found in many charity constitutions will be caught. If this is right, then some charities will not be in a position to take advantage of the statutory power unless they are first able to amend their constitutions.

---

[20]   OG 205 B1.
[21]   OG 205 B2.
[22]   Expected to be in early 2008.

- The trustees are subject to the statutory duties of care imposed by the Trustee Act 2000.

- The trustees must take into account the guidance given by the Charity Commission in relation to such agreements. The Commission's existing guidance is summarised at **6.49**.

- The rules apply to anyone 'connected' to a trustee in the same way as to a trustee him or herself.

6.47 The statutory power applies only to services (and specifically excludes payments for acting as trustee or to employees who are also trustees). Payments can be made for goods but only if they are supplied in connection with the provision of services. If, therefore, the trustees of a charity wish to pay a trustee for the supply of goods or the charity's constitution prohibits the use of the statutory power, they will need to consider applying to the Charity Commission for an appropriate power.

Charity Commission authorisation

6.48 The Charity Commission's guidance in relation to the payment of trustees by a charity without an existing power is as follows:

> 'When we consider providing authority for payments to trustees in relation to an existing charity without a power to pay trustees, we take into account the fact that the founder or promoter decided to establish the charity without such a power. However, we are primarily looking to see whether providing the authority will be in the interests of the charity in the light of its current circumstances.

> Practically, this means that we will only authorise payment provisions (either for a general power or a 'one-off' authority) where the trustees can show there will be a clear benefit to the charity, in terms of cost or otherwise, that will outweigh the disadvantages. These can include the need to manage any potential conflict of interest, and loss of expertise of the paid trustee when the trustee body is discussing matters in relation to the service provided by that trustee.

> In a situation where there is no favourable cost comparison with an outside agent or firm and no special expertise or knowledge possessed by the trustee concerned, there is unlikely to be any clear advantage to the charity, and the trustees would be expected to look outside the trustee body for the provision of the service.'[23]

6.49 The Commission will expect the trustees to have considered a number of different questions as part of their assessment of what is in the interests of the charity. These are spelled out in CC 11 and provide a helpful basis for the trustees' decision making:

- What procedures will the remaining unpaid trustees put in place to manage the conflict of interest that will arise as a consequence of the payment?

> 'We expect trustees to recognise that a conflict of interest exists (which may also include conflicts with outside commitments, eg other trusteeships, business interests), and take adequate steps to minimise its effects. We recommend that trustees develop a written policy on how they deal with the issue.'

---

[23]   CC 11.

- Have arrangements been made to disclose any payments to trustees in the charity's annual report and accounts?

  'The trustees should be aware of the requirements of the Charities SORP (Accounting and Reporting by Charities: Statement of Recommended Practice (SORP 2000)) in this area.'

- Do the trustees have appropriate budget provisions and financial forecast systems in place?

- Have the trustees consulted the charity's stakeholders (ie major funders, members, beneficiaries, donors)? If they have done so, what was the response?

  'Trustees need to consider the impact their decision to pay a trustee might have on those with an interest in the charity.'

- Are the number of trustees to be paid in the minority on the trustee body?

  'Depending on the size and constitution of the trustee body, we generally recommend that no more than one or two trustees should be employed and paid. The higher the proportion of paid trustees, the greater the risk of potentially damaging conflict of interest.'

- Should independent advice be taken before deciding the level of payment?

  'The trustees may wish to consider taking impartial and independent advice to help them decide on pay arrangements. This is particularly important if a majority of the trustees are to be employed and paid.'

- Have the trustees obtained quotes for the work to be done, and drawn up a shortlist of individuals or companies which should be asked to tender for the work?

  'As a matter of good practice, we would expect trustees to obtain a number of quotes so they can ensure (and demonstrate) that they are obtaining value for money.'

- Does the contract contain features to protect the charity's interests?

- Do the trustees have any arrangements for testing or challenging invoices which might be disputed?

  'If trustees are in doubt about the validity of an invoice, they may wish to have procedures in place to verify it, possibly including independent scrutiny.'

- Was the affected trustee prevented from seeing confidential information about the tender process?

  'We recommend that trustees who are tendering for work should absent themselves from the meeting or part of the meeting at which related matters are discussed, even if that is not actually a condition of the trustee payment authority. This includes discussions leading up to the decision to go to tender.'

6.50 Any application to the Charity Commission will need to spell out the trustees' views on these points and the work they have done to satisfy themselves that payments will be for the benefit of their charity. The trustees will also need to satisfy themselves that the services in question are not services that form part of the trustee's duties as trustee. That will obviously require an analysis of the services in question, but trustees should be aware that the Charity Commission may take the view that certain services are intrinsically trustee duties. There is unlikely to be much doubt that, for example, professional legal or accounting services fall outside a trustee's duties, but the provision of, say, business planning services might be seen by the Commission as no more than part of the trustees' role in planning the charity's strategy.

6.51　If the Charity Commission agree to the grant of a power this will be by way of an Order or a Scheme (see **4.19–4.34**). In the case of an unincorporated charity, a Scheme will be required if there is an express prohibition on such payments in the charity's constitution or, in the case of a charitable company, by way of consent under the Charities Act 1993, s 64 consent to a resolution to alter the articles of association of the charity. The power granted will be subject to the sort of restrictions that apply to the exercise of the statutory power (see **6.46**).

Other payments

6.52　Payments to trustees for acting as trustees or to a trustee who is also an employee are more contentious than payments to trustees for discrete services. There is no statutory power to make payments of this kind, so any charity that wishes to be able to do this and does not already have authority in its own constitution, will need to make an application to the Charity Commission for authority. The Charity Commission will expect the trustees to have considered all of the points mentioned in the first six bullet points in **6.49** together with the following points in relation to payments for acting as trustees:

- What evidence do the trustees have to show a lack of willing volunteers with the required skills?

  'The trustees should be able to demonstrate the steps they have taken to recruit an unpaid trustee, eg by advertising the vacancy and approaching individuals and organisations. Trustees may, however, wish to attract trustees from social and economic backgrounds who cannot afford to act as a trustee unless paid. We appreciate there may be good reasons for recruiting trustees on lower incomes, and that employing and paying them for carrying out the duties of a trustee may be more in the interests of the charity than the use of volunteers.'

- Could the duties for which the trustee is to be paid be shared amongst the whole trustee body, or could the number of trustees be increased to spread the workload?

  'Trustees should consider what other options there are apart from paying a trustee'.

- Are all the duties to be undertaken appropriate to a trustee or could they properly be delegated to an agent or employee?

- How will the charity ensure the payment represents value for money?

  'We recommend that paid trustees are in the minority. The trustees may wish to consider taking impartial and independent advice to help them decide on the pay arrangements, and to check that the charity is obtaining value for money.'

- What arrangements are in place for reviewing performance and for assessing whether there is a continuing need for paid trusteeship?

  'The trustees may wish to set a time limit for the paid arrangements to continue. This will enable the trustees to review the situation at the end of the period and to extend the period of payment, if necessary.'

- What arrangements are in place for bringing payment to an end, and how will this affect the trusteeship of the individual in question?

- Has the impact on the degree of personal liability been discussed with the trustee in question?

  'A higher standard of care is expected of a paid trustee'

6.53   The Commission will also expect the following additional points to have been considered in relation to a trustee who proposes to become a paid employee:

- Is the position of paid employment to be advertised on the basis of fair and open competition, and if not, why not?

  'If the trustees consider that one of their number would be particularly suited to the job, they would need to say why, in relation to the abilities of that individual.'

- How has the payment package been determined?

  'Trustees should take steps to compare rates with similar employment elsewhere, take independent advice where appropriate, and ensure that there is a system of periodic review.'

- Why is it desirable for employment to be combined with trusteeship, and what special dimension will this bring to decision-making?

  'Where is nothing to prevent employees or advisers attending trustee meetings to give advice and guidance on relevant matters. Trustees would need to demonstrate why the roles of employee and trustee should be combined.'

- Does the need to employ a trustee apply to the individual or the post?

  'The trustees should consider whether the person holding that particular post (for example, an artistic director or chief executive) should always be a trustee, or whether an exceptional person who currently happens to occupy that post would bring vital skills to the trustee body.'

- Is there clear segregation between the duties performed as a trustee and those carried out as an employee of the charity?

- How will performance be measured?

  'The trustees should ensure there is an objective and independent performance appraisal system in place.'

- What arrangements are in place for bringing employment to an end, and how will this affect the trusteeship of the individual in question?

'The trustees should give particular attention in the contract of employment to any performance element in the pay, commissions or compensation for loss of earnings.'

7

TRUSTEES' POWERS

7.1   In order to discharge their duties to the standard required by law, the trustees of every charity must:

- act within the powers they have as trustees;

- exercise those powers only in the best interests of the charity and only for the purposes for which they have been given; and

- exercise their powers personally, without delegating responsibility for decisions to anyone else.

7.2   An incorporated charity will have powers in its own right. These will be exercisable by its trustees (usually by an express provision in its constitution). We refer to them as 'trustees' powers' because, in practice, they are exercised by the trustees rather than by the charity.

7.3   In discharging these duties, charity trustees are under an obligation to exercise such care and skill as is reasonable in the circumstances having regard to:

- any special knowledge or expertise that the trustee has or holds him or herself out as having; and

- where a trustee acts in the course of a business or profession, to any special knowledge or expertise that it is reasonable to expect of a person acting in the course of that kind of business or profession.

There is more about this statutory duty of care at **6.2**. However, in order to ensure that they discharge it, trustees will need to ensure that they understand the sources and scope of their powers and the restrictions on, and other considerations in relation to, their exercise.

7.4   There are two reasons why this is important:

- If the trustees fail to act within their powers, or exercise them in the wrong way, they will be acting in breach of trust. There is more about the consequences of that at **6.18**.

- If the trustees purport to exercise a power that they do not have or exercise a power in the wrong way, the charity will be acting *ultra vires* (in other words, outside its capacity). The effect of that will depend upon the way in which the power was purportedly exercised, but in general the effect will be to make any agreement entered into or liability incurred by the charity on the strength of the power void or, in some cases, voidable. Clearly, this may expose the charity to claims and its trustees to personal liability for any losses suffered by the charity as a consequence.

7.5 Before identifying the sources of charity trustees' powers, it is helpful to understand that, as a general principle, the powers conferred upon all charity trustees can only ever be exercised in order to promote the charity's charitable purposes. There is a fundamental difference between those purposes (the charity's ultimate objectives) and the powers (which are no more than the means by which the purposes can be achieved). So, for example, an express power for a charity to give a guarantee must be interpreted as a power to give guarantees that advance its purposes, perhaps by guaranteeing the liabilities of impoverished beneficiaries.

7.6 Charity constitutions will generally draw a clear distinction between the purposes and powers, usually by expressly stating that the powers are only exercisable in order to advance the purposes (the format of a modern charitable company's constitution is a good example of this). But even if this is not expressly spelled out, the position is the same, irrespective of whether the powers are said to be exercisable at the discretion of the trustees or not.

SOURCES OF POWERS

7.7 The powers available to charity trustees have three potential sources:

- express powers conferred by the charity's constitution;

- powers that can be implied into the charity's constitution; and

- powers conferred by law, primarily by statute.

7.8 The specific powers available to any particular charity under any of these three heads will depend upon its legal form. The position of companies, CIOs and unincorporated charities is examined below.

7.9 The powers available to a charity's trustees in relation to its assets will also vary depending upon whether they are 'trust assets'. All of the assets of an unincorporated charity will be trust assets. In general, the assets of a charitable company will not be held on trust (and will constitute its 'corporate assets'), but there are exceptions to this. There is more detail about this at **Chapter 9**.

EXPRESS POWERS

7.10 Most modern charity constitutions will spell out the charity's powers in reasonable detail. There is obviously a judgement to be made in drafting provisions of this kind because, in practice, including very detailed provisions may mean that a third party seeking to rely upon a particular power becomes concerned that the detail included does not deal sufficiently precisely with the particular issue they are considering. The best approach will be to ensure that the powers included are drafted with this possibility in mind. Using an appropriate standard form document may also give some comfort that the scope of the powers is sufficient.

Companies

7.11 Following the coming into force of the Companies Act 2006, a charitable company's purposes and powers will be set out in its articles of association. Companies incorporated before the coming into force of the 2006 Act will have their purposes and powers set out in their memorandum of association.

7.12 The Companies Acts prevent the validity of any act done by a company being called into question by reason of anything in the company's constitution.[1] The Acts also provides that, in favour of a person dealing with a company in good faith, the power of its directors to bind the company is deemed to be free of any limitation in the memorandum and articles. In other words, no third party acting in good faith need have any concern that any act is ultra vires and outside a company's capacity because it has no power to do it or because it does have a power but the restrictions on its exercise have not been observed. However, this rule applies to the acts of charitable companies in a modified form. It can only be relied upon by a person who:

- gives full consideration in money or money's worth in relation to the act in question and does not know that the act is not permitted by the company's constitution or is beyond the trustees' powers; or

- who does not know at the time the act is done that the company is a charity.

7.13 Clearly, therefore, anyone who does not meet these criteria (and many third parties who deal with charities are likely to ask for confirmation of its powers so that they will have actual or constructive notice that a charity lacks a power or that it is subject to restrictions) cannot rely upon the protection conferred by the Companies Acts. Having said that, there is an additional protection for anyone who subsequently acquires an asset originally transferred by a charity without an appropriate power. Provided that they acquire the asset without actual notice of the circumstances that affect the validity of the transfer and give full consideration for the asset, they will get good title to it.[2]

7.14 The *ultra vires* rule that applies to charitable companies does not affect the duty of its charity trustees to comply with the provisions of its constitution in relation to the exercise of its powers and does not restrict their liability for failing to comply with that duty. In addition, it does not prevent any member of the company from taking action to restrain the directors from taking action that is outside the company's powers.

7.15 From the point of view of both the charity trustees and third parties, therefore, it will be essential that a charity has the express powers required to operate it in the way the trustees wish.

7.16 If there is no express power, it will usually be possible to add one or to modify any restrictions on an existing power. This requires a members' resolution and is dealt with in more detail in **Chapter 15**.

---

[1]   Companies Acts 1985, s 35; Charities Act 1993, s 65; Companies Act 2006, s 42.
[2]   Companies Acts 1985, s 65.

CIOs

7.17 The Charities Act 1993 gives a CIO the power to do anything that is 'calculated to further its purposes'. This power is subject to any restriction in the CIO's constitution. It remains to be seen whether CIO constitutions will generally include the range of express powers usually seen in a company's memorandum or articles. In practice, third parties may insist on an express power.

7.18 CIO's are subject to an *ultra vires* rule that is modelled on the rule that applies in relation to companies. See **7.12** for further detail on this.

7.19 The charity trustees of a CIO are in the same position as the trustees of a charitable company in relation to liability for breach of trust in acting outside their powers.

7.20 If there is no express power, it will usually be possible to add one or to modify any restrictions on an existing power. This requires a members' resolution and is dealt with in more detail in **Chapter 15**.

Unincorporated charities

7.21 The express powers of any unincorporated charity will be set out in its constitution. They will need to be construed in context. There is no statutory provision similar to the *ultra vires* provisions in relation to companies and CIOs.

7.22 If there is no express power, the trustees may have a sufficiently wide power of amendment to add a new power or modify an existing one. This will usually be exercisable by the trustees but the position will depend upon the constitutional provisions as they vary from charity to charity. There is more about amendments in **Chapter 15**.

7.23 If there is no existing power of amendment available to the trustees, they may be able to apply for an Order or a Scheme of the Charity Commission to give them the necessary authority. There is more about this in **Chapters 4** and **15**.

IMPLIED POWERS

7.24 If there are no express powers that authorise something a charity proposes to do, it may be possible to imply a power into its constitution. Whether this is possible will depend upon how the charity is constituted, what its constitution says and the approach taken by its trustees and any third party with whom the charity wishes to engage.

Companies

7.25 The possibility of implying powers into a charitable company's constitution usually turns on the 'sweep-up' provision often included. This usually states that the company has power to do 'such other lawful things as are necessary to achieve its objects'. 'Necessary' might sometimes read 'conducive' or 'expedient' or 'incidental', but the meaning is essentially the same.

7.26 Essentially, the powers that can be implied using a provision of this kind will be limited to carrying out the charity's purposes. This is in line with the general principle of construction of the powers of charities explained at **7.5**. The powers that can be implied have been fairly restrictively construed by the courts in the past (albeit in the context of an Industrial and Provident Society, although the same principle is likely to apply).[3]

7.27 Perhaps the most one can say about the approach that can be taken to implied powers is that the position can never be determined with sufficient certainty without a decision of the court. In practice, most third parties dealing with charities will want to see an express power authorising whatever is proposed and will not be interested in debating the possibility of implying a power. The same may be true of the charity's trustees, albeit that they may often be reluctant to incur the delay and expense involved in obtaining an express power.

CIOs

7.28 CIOs have a statutory power to do anything which is 'conducive or incidental' to their purposes. The courts are likely to take the same approach to powers implied under this provision as they do in relation to companies. So too are third parties.

Unincorporated charities

7.29 Whether powers can be implied into the constitution of an unincorporated charity will depend upon what is in the constitution. Often, there will be a provision in a similar form to the sort of 'sweep-up' clause found in a company's memorandum or articles or a CIO's statutory power to the same effect.

7.30 The courts are likely to take a very similar approach to implied powers of this kind for unincorporated charities as they do for companies and CIOs. So too are third parties.

STATUTORY POWERS

7.31 All charities have certain powers conferred by the Charities Act 1993. These are:

- power to co-operate with local authorities and other charities;[4]

- power to make ex gratia payments (with the consent of the Charity Commission);[5] and

- power to waive entitlement to property (with the consent of the Charity Commission).[6]

7.32 Particular types of charity have other powers conferred by the Charities Act 1993:

---

[3] *Rosemary Simmons Memorial Housing Association Ltd v United Dominions Trust Ltd* [1987] 1 All ER 281.
[4] Charities Act 1993, s 78.
[5] Charities Act 1993, s 27(1)(a).
[6] Charities Act 1993, s 27(1)(b).

- power to spend the capital of an unincorporated charity;[7]

- power to transfer the property of an unincorporated charity;[8]

- power to replace the purposes of an unincorporated charity;[9] and

- power to modify the powers and procedures of an unincorporated charity.[10]

These powers have been altered by the Charities Act 2006 and will come into force in early 2008 (with the exception of the power to modify powers and procedures, which came into force on 27 February 2007).

Companies

7.33   Companies have no additional statutory powers conferred specifically by the Charities Acts over and above those mentioned in **7.31**.

CIOs

7.34   CIOs have no additional statutory powers conferred specifically by the Charities Acts over and above those mentioned in **7.31**.

Unincorporated charities

7.35   In addition to the powers conferred by the Charities Act 1993 mentioned in **7.31**, the trustees of most unincorporated charities will be able to rely upon a range of statutory powers available to trustees generally. The more important of these powers are:

- Power to insure the charity's assets (including power to insure the charity against the consequences of breach of trust by its trustees, but not insurance indemnifying trustees against the consequences of their own breaches).[11]

- Power to deal with land. There is more about this in **Chapter 9**.

- Power to delegate trustees' powers.[12] There is more about this in **Chapter 8**.

- A limited power to borrow money in connection with land.[13] There is more about this in **Chapter 12**.

- Power to invest the charity's assets.[14] There is more about this in **Chapter 10**.

---

[7]   Charities Act 1993, ss 75, 75A and 75B.
[8]   Charities Act 1993, s 74.
[9]   Charities Act 1993, s 74C.
[10]   Charities Act 1993, s 74D.
[11]   Trustee Act 1925, s 19.
[12]   Trustee Act 2000, s 11.
[13]   Trusts of Land and Appointment of Trustees Act 1996, s 6.
[14]   Trustee Act 2000, s 3.

7.36 The statutory powers available to the trustees of an unincorporated charity are by no means comprehensive. In general, its trustees will wish to ensure that, where possible, they have express powers. Where that is not possible, the statutory powers will be a useful fallback.

ADVICE

7.37 Where the charity trustees do not have a particular power to do something that they wish to do, the Charity Commission will not issue them with Advice that would deem them to have acted in accordance with their duties as trustees. Where a third party is involved, it is unlikely to want to reply on Advice in any event.

RESTRICTIONS

7.38 There are a number of things that may restrict the exercise of charity trustees' powers. These are:

• restrictions imposed by the charity's own constitution;

• restrictions imposed by the Charities Acts and other statutes; and

• restrictions imposed by the law generally.

Constitutional restrictions

7.39 Any restrictions on the exercise of express powers conferred by a charity's constitution should be observed. These could include, for example, obtaining any third party consent to a sale of an asset, borrowing only up to a specified limit or buying only particular types of investment.

Statutory restrictions

7.40 There are a number of restrictions on the exercise of powers conferred by the Charities Act 1993, but the two most significant provisions are:

• The requirements of the Charities Act 1993, ss 36 and 37 in relation to the disposal of land owned by a charity. There is more about this in **Chapter 9**.

• The requirements of the Charities Act 1993, ss 38 ad 39 in relation to mortgages of charity land. There is more about this in **Chapter 12**.

7.41 In addition, significant restrictions are imposed in relation to powers conferred by other statutes. The most important are:

• the restrictions on the power of investment conferred by the Trustee Act 2000. There is more about this in **Chapter 10**; and

• the restrictions on the power of delegation conferred by the Trustee Act 2000. There is more about this at **7.48**.

Other restrictions

7.42   Charity trustees must exercise the powers conferred upon them honestly and after giving proper consideration to everything relevant to the decision that they take. The courts have indicated that trustees must act in good faith and reasonably and it is the standard of the 'reasonable trustee' that they will look for in assessing whether a decision was properly taken or not.[15]

7.43   In making that assessment, the courts will look at whether the trustees armed themselves with all relevant information, whether they took (or should have taken) advice from an expert and whether they considered the right question and properly applied their minds to it. Another essential aspect of this is that the power in question is being exercised for the purpose for which it is given.

7.44   Most decisions will not, of course, ever be reviewed by the courts and they are in general very reluctant to interfere with trustees' decisions but the benchmark set by them is the obvious starting point for trustees in exercising their powers.

ADVICE

7.45   In exercising their powers trustees must consider whether they first need to take advice on the issue that they are considering. Some statutory powers impose an express statutory obligation to take advice or at least to consider taking it. The most obvious example is the power of investment conferred upon the charity trustee of an unincorporated charity (see **Chapter 10** for more on this). Obligations may also be imposed by statute (eg the Charities Act 1993 obliges charity trustees to take advice before mortgaging or disposing of land) or by the charity's constitution (eg the constitution of a charitable company may oblige its trustee to consider taking advice on investment).

7.46   Regardless of the obligations imposed on charity trustees, the key point is that many trustees will not be in a position to take a proper decision about particular issues without taking advice. This could include, for example, issues raised by the funding requirements of a charity's final salary pension scheme, where the legal and actuarial position can be complex. Advice will obviously not be required in every case but charity trustees will need to consider whether it is necessary in relation to most substantive decisions.

7.47   There is no objection to charity trustees taking advice on areas outside their own areas of competence. The cost of that advice is a properly incurred expense payable out of the charity's funds.

DELEGATION

7.48   In addition to identifying the source and scope of their powers, charity trustees will need to ensure that they understand who is responsible for their exercise. In the majority of cases, powers will be vested in the charity trustees themselves although there are other possibilities:

---

[15]   *Scott v National Trust* [1998] 2 All ER 705.

- a charity's constitution may vest certain powers in its members or other third parties; and

- a charity's constitution may vest powers in the charity trustees but make their exercise subject to the consent of third parties, e g the settlor of a charitable trust or the Charity Commission.

7.49 Where a power is vested in the charity trustees themselves, they must exercise it personally in accordance with the provisions of the charity's constitution. In general, this will require a decision by the charity trustees themselves unless there is authority in the constitution for the decision to be delegated. This reflects the overriding duty on all charity trustees to act personally unless they are authorised to delegate any of their functions to someone else.

7.50 There is more about delegation in **Chapter 8**. The key point is that charity trustees must identify in whom a particular power is vested before a decision is taken. In practice, it is reasonably easy for a decision to be taken by the wrong people if the position is not clearly established at the outset. A decision taken on this basis will be invalid.

PROCESS

7.51 In exercising their power, the charity trustees must ensure that they follow the process set out in their charity's constitution. At its most straightforward, this may mean no more than ensuring that the relevant decision is taken at a properly convened and quorate meeting where the trustees have available to them all of the advice and other information that they need to consider the position.

7.52 In other cases, the process may be more complicated. Where, for example, a members' decision is required, the constitution's requirements in relation to notice, quorum and voting must be observed. There is more about members' meetings in **Chapter 5**.

RECORD-KEEPING

7.53 There are several reasons for keeping clear and comprehensive written records of the exercise of trustees' powers. The first is that any well-governed charity will wish to have proper records of all of the most important aspects of its operations. The second is that changes in trustees and employees may mean that the reasons for decisions taken in the past may not be clear to later generations unless there is a clear written record of the position. Third, if the exercise of the trustees' power is ever challenged, the trustees will want to be able to show that it was properly exercised. Without a clear written record (including copies of any advice taken and full minutes of discussion), that may be difficult to do. In the very worst case, the courts will wish to assess whether the trustees acted reasonably and their position is likely to be very much stronger if they have written evidence to support this.

CHECKLIST

7.54   In exercising their powers, charity trustees should ensure that they have dealt with the following points:

- Do the charity trustees have an express power under the charity's constitution to do whatever it is they want to do?

- If there is no express power, can the charity trustees exercise a power in their charity's constitution to add an express power? Or can they apply to the Charity Commission for an Order or Scheme giving them the necessary express power?

- If there is no express power, can the trustees rely upon an implied or statutory power?

- Whatever form the power takes, what are the restrictions on its exercise?

- Are the charity trustees obliged to take advice in relation to the exercise of the power in question?

- Even if they are not obliged to do so, should they take advice on the issue they are considering?

- Is the power vested in the charity trustees or in a third party?

- If the power is vested in the charity trustees, do they propose to take the decision or is it to be delegated? If it is to be delegated, is there a power of delegation and has this been exercised in accordance with the charity's constitution?

- Are there any third party consents that are required in relation to the exercise of the power?

- Has the decision-making process set out in the charity's constitution been observed?

- Have the charity trustees' deliberations in relation to the exercise of the power been properly recorded in writing?

8

TRUSTEE GOVERNANCE

INTRODUCTION

8.1 It is generally recognised that the key to the effective governance of a charity is its trustees and the way in which they discharge their statutory responsibility for controlling and managing it. In the view of the Charity Commission:[1]

> 'Trustees matter a great deal. It is very important for any charity to have trustees committed to their task and with the skills, knowledge and experience that the charity needs.
>
> Trustees play an essential role in the governance of charities. They also have a lot to contribute to their success. For example they can:
>
> - serve as a means of communication with communities that a charity exists to serve;
> - bring valuable professional or other experience to charities; and
> - help to ensure that charities are well-managed through the appointment of senior executive staff.'

8.2 With the exception of a sole corporate trustee, every charity should have more than one trustee. While there is no legal objection to a sole trustee acting (except in certain limited circumstances[2]), the capacity for debate and discussion in relation to the management of a charity is an intrinsic part of trusteeship. This is also true of a sole corporate trustee, which will invariably be under the control of more than one individual.

8.3 Trustees can be described collectively in a number of different ways; common references are to a 'committee', 'council' or 'board' of trustees, but there are no legal restrictions on describing them in other ways. A charity's constitution will usually define the trustees as a group in a particular way and it is usually preferable to use this definition in practice where possible. For the sake of simplicity, we use the terms 'board of trustees' or 'board'.

OTHER POSTS

8.4 There are a number of other posts commonly found within charities that do not mean that the post holder is a trustee. It is important to understand the distinction between trusteeship and the role and responsibilities of the holders of other posts. This can only be determined definitively on the basis of a charity's constitution, but some of the more common posts are:

---

[1] CC 30.
[2] Only a sole trustee which is a trust corporation can give a valid receipt for the proceeds of sale of land under the Law of Property Act 1925, s 27.

Post	Meaning
Patron	Usually an honorary position which confers no rights or obligations on the holder (who is often a member of the 'great and good' whose association with, and support for, the charity is intended to enhance its public perception).
President	Usually another way of describing a Patron and, often a 'Patron in chief'. The past Chairman of a charity may sometimes become a president of the charity after he or she has ceased to be a trustee. Again, this is usually an honorary position with no rights or obligations in relation to the charity.
Observer	Usually an individual nominated by a stakeholder member of a charity to attend trustees' meetings on its behalf in order to advise the charity on the stakeholder's views and to report proceedings to the stakeholder. Generally, an Observer will have no more than a right to attend and speak at trustees' meetings. He or she will have no voting rights in relation to the charity. See **5.84** for more on Observers.
Secretary	Usually the person responsible for administering the trustees as a group by giving notice of meetings, keeping minutes, registers and other records etc and also for ensuring that all documents required by the Charity Commission and any other regulator are properly filed. In the context of a charitable company, the Secretary will be the company secretary appointed under the Companies Acts. The Secretary may also be a trustee, but will act in a different capacity in relation to each post.

8.5   Not every charity will have posts of this kind. The position will depend upon the provisions of a charity's constitution.

COMPOSITION OF THE BOARD OF TRUSTEES

8.6   A number of different provisions will determine the composition of the board of trustees. These are as follows.

8.7   While there are no legal restrictions on the minimum or maximum number of trustees who may act, most charities' constitutions will set limits. There is obviously a balance to be struck between deploying a sufficiently wide range of skills and experience on the board and ensuring that it remains sufficiently compact to operate effectively. In practice, a board may prove to be too large to allow decisions to be taken effectively, particularly where not all of the members of a large board are actually able to attend meetings on a regular basis. Where a wide range of skills and experience are required but there is a desire to keep the board reasonably small, the solution will generally be for the trustees to delegate some of their powers and discretions to committees of the board. This is explained in more detail at **8.112**.

8.8   It is essential that the board of trustees can bring the right sort of skills and experience to the charity. What is required will depend upon what the charity does, but there will often be a requirement for trustees with experience of finance, accounting and law. One way of helping to ensure that the right skills and experience is available is for the trustees to identify the skill sets they consider are necessary for the charity's health and development. This can be used as the basis for the charity's policy on trustee recruitment.

8.9   In order to ensure that the mix of skills and experience on the board is continually refreshed, most charities will wish to set limits on the terms for which trustees hold office. There is no legal requirement that trustees should only act for a particular term and, if no term is specified, the rule is that a trustee will continue to act until he or she retires, is removed, dies, becomes incapable of acting or is otherwise disqualified from acting as a charity trustee (there is more about this at **8.29**). Many charities do adopt this approach and rely upon the good sense and discretion of their trustees in deciding when to call time. The disadvantage of this approach is that trustees can remain in office in circumstances where they have very little to offer to the charity because of changes in their own lives or changes in the way that the charity operates. This is generally bad for the charity because it may not have trustees equipped to deal with changes in the environment in which it operates.

8.10   There is obviously a balance to be struck between bringing new trustees (with new skills, experience and ideas) to the board and preserving the continuity and collective experience of the board. Using terms of office fixed by the constitution is the usual way of striking this balance. The key provisions are generally:

- Setting a fixed term of office for every trustee. The recent trend in relation to terms of office appears to be between 3 and 5 years (on the basis that this strikes a balance between continuity and refreshment).

- A trustee who has come to the end of his or her term of office may be eligible for re-appointment for a further term, but the maximum number of terms may be specified. Popular choices are 2 and 3 terms.

- A 'cooling-off' period (often of a year) during which a retiring trustee cannot act may be included either between each term or, more usually, at the end of a specified number of terms. The aim is obviously to give both the retiring trustee and the charity a chance to see how they get on without each other.

- An 'override' provision which will allow the board to resolve that a trustee's term of office should continue beyond the term for which he or she is appointed where they are doing particularly valuable work on a particular project or aspect of the charity's operations and need to be able to continue to act while that work continues.

- Provisions that allow the retirement and appointment and re-appointment of trustees to be staggered, so that trustees who have acted for similar periods of time do not all retire en masse leaving a board of new trustees to start work without the benefit of their collective knowledge and experience. There is more about this at **8.11**.

Staggered retirement

8.11   Staggering the retirement of trustees can be done in a number of different ways.

- Many charitable companies will use a form of 'retirement by rotation' based upon the provisions of the Companies Acts that apply to private companies limited by shares. The idea is that a proportion of the trustees (often, but not necessarily, one-third) should retire every year, with those who have acted for the longest retiring before those appointed after them (and any trustees who have acted for the same period being identified by drawing lots). This has the effect of staggering trustee retirements and the appointment of other trustees to take their places.

- The retirement usually takes place with effect from the end of the annual general meeting ('AGM') that all companies have to hold except where they have an 'elective resolution' in place to dispense with this requirement. This approach ensures that there will be one event that takes place annually at which trustees can retire (and perhaps be re-appointed) and new trustees can be appointed. This does assume that the power to appoint and re-appoint lies with the members attending the AGM, but the appointments can as easily be dealt with at a board meeting held after the AGM if the power to appoint trustees lies with the trustees themselves.

- The Companies Act 2006 will (once it is in force) abolish the requirement for private companies to hold an AGM altogether. However, an AGM can still be held and many charitable companies may wish to do so, if only to deal with the retirement and appointment of trustees. And the articles of many charitable companies will assume that an AGM will be held for this purpose. If the no AGM is to be held, then another way of dealing with trustee appointments and retirements will need to be identified in the constitution.

- There is no legal objection to charities other than companies holding AGMs and many may wish to do so in order to deal with the retirement and appointment of trustees. The provisions dealing with the AGM will need to be spelled out in the charity's constitution because there is no legal regime equivalent to the Companies Acts that provides a framework for the holding of meetings by other forms of charity.

- If no AGM is held, retirements can be dealt with using the same basic principle but by reference to another date. The obvious choice is a trustees' meeting, perhaps the first or last to be held in the year, although this assumes that the appointment of new trustees can take place at the same time (whether by the trustees or the members or anyone else with the right to appoint trustees). It will generally be preferable to deal with the retirement and appointment or re-appointment of trustees at the same time in order to ensure that the board retains a full complement of trustees. This may not always be practicable, but is less likely to present a problem than, say, retiring a third of a charity's trustees on 1 January in every year when there may then be an interval until they can be re-appointed or others appointed in their place.

- Good records of trustees' terms of office are essential.

CHAIRMAN

8.12   Every board of trustees needs a chairman to oversee board meetings, to provide leadership to the trustees and, where the charity has employees, often to act as the main point of contact at board level for the chief executive and other senior employees.

8.13   The chairman will inevitably be one of the trustees. Although there is no legal restriction on someone who is not already a trustee being appointed as chairman, he or she will play a very active part in the management and control of the charity at the highest level. In practice, therefore, the chairman is often already a trustee of the charity, having had an opportunity to demonstrate that he or she has the skills and experience required to perform the role well. For the same reason, the trustees themselves will almost invariably appoint the chairman. While the chairman could in principle be appointed by the members of a charity, it is the trustees who are likely to be best placed to make a judgement about who would best meet the requirements of the role.

8.14   The mechanism for appointing the chairman (if there is one) should be specified in the charity's constitution. The chairman's term of office should also be specified and will be co-extensive with his or term of office as trustee. If he or she ceases to be a trustee, they will also cease to be chairman unless the charity's constitution provides to the contrary. In practice, this would be an unusual provision.

8.15   There are no legal rules that govern how long the chairman may hold office for. The position will normally be determined by the charity's constitution, which may provide that the trustees should determine the term when they make the appointment. An alternative will be for the constitution to specify a term of office in the same way as it will spell out the trustees' terms of office. In practice, the term of office of the chairman needs to strike a balance between allowing the chairman to establish him or herself in the role and ensuring that a chairman who is not performing in what is likely to be the most important role at board level does not continue over the longer term. This may mean that the emphasis is on appointment for shorter periods than the trustees (perhaps on annual basis), but with no restriction on the number of times an effective chairman can be re-appointed while they remain a trustee.

8.16   Many charities will wish to make Terms of Reference (see **8.35** for more on this) for their chairman. The terms made will vary from charity to charity, but may look something like this:

Chairman

Terms of Reference

The board (the **'Board'**) of trustees (the **'Trustees'**) of the [Charity] (the **'Charity'**) has adopted the following terms of reference in respect of the Charity's Chairman.

Role

In addition to complying with his general duties as a Trustee of the Charity, the Chairman's role is to provide overall leadership to the Charity in a manner which ➡

---

maximises the contributions of Trustees and employees and ensures that all remain focused on achieving the aims set out in the Charity's vision and mission statements.

The Chairman is primarily responsible for the three key aspects of the Charity's governance:

- How the Trustees work together as an effective Board

- How the Board sets and achieves the Charity's aims

- The relationship between the Board and the Charity's senior executives.

Effective working

In order to encourage effective working, the Chairman is expected to:

- Help identify the skills and experience required on the Board.

- Ensure that there is a plan for Trustee succession and help to seek new Trustees from diverse sources.

- Arrange comprehensive Trustee induction and training programmes.

- Chair meetings effectively by using carefully structured agendas and briefing papers and encouraging participation by all Trustees.

- Ensure that the Trustees review both the performance of the Board and their own individual contribution annually.

- Establish and keep under review an appropriate governance model for the Charity, including the use of Committees of the Board.

- Ensure that terms of reference are in place for Trustees, the Treasurer and Committees of the Board.

Achieving the Charity's aims

In order to achieve the Charity's aims, the Chairman is expected to:

- Ensure that those aims are clearly identified and set out in its vision and mission statements and its guiding principles and that they are kept under review.

- Ensure that the Charity's aims reflect its legal charitable objects.

- Ensure that a business plan and budget are set annually and are properly monitored in the light of the Charity's aims and the Board's assessment of its strengths and weaknesses and the threats and opportunities to and for it.

- Work closely with the Chief Executive to ensure that there is clarity about the Charity's aims at all levels within the organisation.

➡

- Ensure that the efforts of the senior executives and other members of management are effectively directed within a framework of clearly structured strategies.

- Ensure that there is an effective risk management policy in place.

- Ensure that the Charity has appropriate policies on investment and reserves.

- Promote the Charity to its beneficiaries and other stakeholders, the media and the public at large, where this assists the senior executives' public relations strategy.

Effective delegation

In so far as the relationship between the Board and the senior executives is concerned, the Chairman is expected to:

- Ensure that both he and the Chief Executive understand each other's roles.

- Act as the main point of contact on the Board for the Chief Executive.

- Ensure that terms of reference are in place for the Chief Executive and other senior executives.

- Ensure that a process for evaluating the performance of the Chief Executive and other senior executives is established and adhered to.

- Ensure that the Chief Executive is clear about the key performance indicators that the Board wishes to use to monitor the performance of the senior executives and by which the Chief Executive will be held accountable.

- Appraise the Chief Executive annually (with another member of the Board).

Conflicts of interest

The Chairman is expected to pay particular attention to the possibility of any conflict arising in relation to any aspect of the Charity's operations.

This will include any conflict for members of the Board or any senior executive.

TREASURER

8.17 Although there is no legal obligation to do so, many charities do appoint a treasurer to oversee their finances. This is entirely dependent upon the provisions in a charity's constitution. The treasurer will usually be a trustee appointed by the board. The charity's constitution should spell out the mechanism for the treasurer's appointment, his or her term of office, and the basis on which he or she can be removed.

8.18 Many larger charities will prefer to delegate the consideration of financial matters to an audit committee rather than appointing an individual trustee as treasurer (although the two things are not mutually exclusive). Where a charity does have a treasurer, it is important to recognise that he or she does not become solely responsible for a charity's finances as a consequence (unless there is an express delegation of responsibility in the charity's constitution to this effect, which would be unusual). All of the trustees remain collectively responsible for understanding, and taking decisions in relation to, the charity's finances. The treasurer's role is usually to act as the first port of call for employees in relation to financial matters and to provide other members of the board with guidance in relation to the charity's financial affairs.

8.19 The treasurer is often an accountant or someone else with financial experience, but there is no legal requirement that they should have any particular qualifications. The charity's constitution will often set criteria.

8.20 Charities may wish to make Terms of Reference in relation to the treasurer's role. The Terms made will vary from charity to charity, but may look something like the Terms set out below (which include an option for the Treasurer to serve on an Audit Committee):

Treasurer

Terms of Reference

The board (the **'Board'**) of trustees (the **'Trustees'**) of the [Charity] (the **'Charity'**) has adopted the following terms of reference in respect of the Charity's Treasurer.

Role

In addition to complying with his general duties as a Trustee of the Charity, the Treasurer's role is:

- To provide advice, information and comfort to the other Trustees on the Board on their responsibilities in respect of the financial aspects of the Charity's operations.

- To act as the main point of contact on the Board for the Finance Director, head of internal audit and any other member of management concerned with the financial aspects of the Charity's operations.

- To serve as a member of the Audit Committee.

Each of these roles is dealt with in more detail below.

Because of the wide-ranging scope of the Treasurer's role, he or she will not usually be expected to serve on any Committee of the Board other than the Audit Committee.

Because of the requirements of the role of the Treasurer he or she will usually be a qualified accountant or some other person whom the Board considers to have a high degree of financial and commercial expertise and acumen. ➡

Board

As part of his or her duty to advise the Board in relation to its financial responsibilities, the Treasurer is expected to do the following things:

- Ensure that, in close co-operation with the Finance Director, an appropriate financial policy framework is in place to guide the Board's financial decision-making (including recommending to the Finance Director how management accounts and other financial information is best presented to the Board).

- Develop a close understanding of the most important financial and other assumptions in the Charity's business plan and the annual budgetary proposals put forward by the Charity's management with a view to advising the Board on them.

- Advise the Board in relation to the budget, management accounts and the Charity's financial statements and the financial aspects of the business plan.

- Advise the Board on significant financial issues that arise and are outside the scope of the authority delegated to the Charity's management.

- Develop a close understanding of the Charity's internal financial controls with a view to ensuring that they operate effectively.

- Act as the initial point of contact for any Trustee in relation to any question they may have on any of the financial aspects of the Charity's operations.

- Recommend to the Board when they may wish to consider taking professional advice on any financial aspect of the Charity's operations.

The Treasurer is also expected to advise the Board on the relationship between the financial aspects of the Charity's operations and the Board's policies on investment and reserves.

Management

The Treasurer is the day-to-day contact at Board level in relation to any financial aspect of the Charity's operations for the Finance Director and must provide support and advice to both of them. In order to facilitate this, the Treasurer is expected to arrange meetings with the Finance Director on a regular or ad hoc basis, as he or she considers appropriate.

The Treasurer is also the point of contact at Board level for the head of internal audit and external auditor in relation to any financial aspect of the Charity's operations. The Treasurer is expected to arrange meetings with the head of internal audit and the external auditor on a regular or an ad hoc basis, as he or she considers appropriate.

The Chief Executive may also discuss any financial aspect of the Charity's operations with the Treasurer. ➡

The Treasurer is expected to ensure that a record is kept of the matters discussed with the Chief Executive and the Finance Director, the head of internal audit and the external auditor and will report to the Board and/or the Audit Committee (as appropriate) at every Board and/or Committee meeting on the matters so discussed.

Audit Committee

In fulfilling his role as a member of the Audit Committee (and subject always to the terms of reference for that Committee), the Treasurer is expected to:

- Provide financial acumen and expertise to the Audit Committee.

- Plan (in conjunction with the external and internal auditors) an annual cycle of meetings of the Audit Committee and recommend the agenda of each such meeting for consideration by the Committee.

- Plan who to invite to each meeting of the Audit Committee (eg the head of internal audit, the external auditor, the Finance Director, any other employee of the Charity with responsibility for its finances) and make appropriate recommendations to the Committee.

- Recommend to the Finance Director how management accounts and other financial data relating to the Charity's operations should best be presented to the Audit Committee.

- Recommend to the Audit Committee when they may wish to consider taking professional advice on any of the matters within the Audit Committee's terms of reference.

- Make recommendations to the Committee in relation to the Charity's internal audit function.

The Treasurer is also expected to make recommendations to the Audit Committee in relation to the performance, constitution and terms of reference of the Committee with a view to ensuring that it operates at maximum effectiveness.

Conflicts of interest

The Treasurer is expected to pay particular attention to the possibility of any conflict arising in relation to any financial aspect of the Charity's operations.

This will include any conflict for the external auditor in addition to the members of the Board or any member of management.

SECRETARY

8.21   As a result of the de-regulation of company administration implemented by the Companies Act 2006, private companies will (once the relevant provisions of the 2006 Act are in force) no longer be required to have a company secretary responsible for administering the board and members' meeting and dealing with other administrative matters, including filing information with Companies House.[3]

8.22 However, it will still be open to any charitable company to opt to have a secretary and many charities will (regardless of whether they are set up as companies or not) wish to have some provision in their constitution for the appointment of a Secretary with primary responsibility for administrative matters.

8.23 The mechanism for the appointment of the secretary will be set out in the charity's constitution (with certain aspects of a charitable company secretary's appointment dealt with in the Companies Acts). There are no legal restrictions that will prevent one of the trustees also acting as secretary, although the post could as easily be given to a non-trustee, including one of the senior executives of the charity or perhaps a professional adviser. The charity's constitution should clearly set out the mechanism for the secretary's appointment and removal, any requirement that he or she should be a trustee and should provide for the board to determine the scope of their duties. In the context of a charitable company, of course, the secretary's duties will be regulated to a degree by the Companies Acts.

8.24 Many charities may wish to make Terms of Reference for their secretary. The Terms made will vary from charity to charity, but may look something like this (provisions relating to a charitable company are in square brackets):

Secretary

Terms of Reference

The board (the **'Board'**) of trustees (the **'Trustees'**) of [Charity] (the **'Charity'**) has adopted the following terms of reference in respect of the Charity's Secretary.

Role

The Company Secretary's role is to:

- Ensure the smooth running of the Board and Board Committees' activities by assisting the Chairman to set agendas and prepare papers and distribute them to the Board and to advise on Board procedures and ensure that they are adhered to.

- Advise and assist the Board with respect to their duties and responsibilities.

- Ensure that the Charity complies with its constitution.

- Keep under review all legislative, regulatory and corporate governance developments that might affect the Charity's operations and helping to ensure that the Board is fully briefed on those issues and that it has regard to them when taking decisions.

- Act as a primary point of contact for Trustees as regards information and advice in relation to proceedings of the Board. ➡

---

[3] Companies Act 2006, s 270; expected to be in force in April 2008.

- Ensure that every new Trustee is properly inducted into the Charity's operations and their roles and responsibilities.

- Ensure that the Charity complies with all statutory requirements of the relevant [companies and] charities legislation, including in particular:
  — [Filing forms 288, annual returns, annual reports and accounts, resolutions adopted at any AGM and new articles of association with Companies House.]
  — Filing annual returns, trustees' details forms and annual reports and accounts with the Charity Commission.

- Ensure that the Charity's [statutory] registers (in particular the registers of trustees, trustees' interests and members) are kept up to date and held at the registered office.

- Make arrangements for and manage the process of the AGM and establish, with the Board's agreement, the items to be considered at the AGM, including resolutions dealing with governance matters.

- Co-ordinate the publication and distribution of the Charity's annual report and accounts.

- Keep accurate and comprehensive minutes of all meetings of the Board and AGMs and other meetings of the Charity's members.

- Ensure that all business letters, notices and other official publications show the information required by the [companies and] charities legislation.

- Ensure that procedures are in place for the proper administration of the Charity's subsidiary companies.

- Arrange indemnity insurance cover for the trustees in accordance with the instructions of the Board.

- Ensure that the concept of stakeholders (including employees) is in the Board's mind when important operational decisions are taken.

- Act as an additional enquiring voice in relation to Board decisions which particularly affect the Charity, drawing on his or her experience and knowledge of the practical aspects of management including law, tax and business finance.

- Act as a confidential sounding board to the Chairman and other trustees on points that may concern them.

Reporting

The Company Secretary is responsible to the Board and should be accountable to the Board through the Chairman on all matters relating to his duties as a company officer.

➡

> Where the Company Secretary has other executive or administrative duties in addition to those as Secretary, he or she reports to the Chief Executive (or any other member of management to whom responsibility for that matter has been delegated by the Board).

'EX-OFFICIO' AND 'CO-OPTED' TRUSTEES

8.25   Some charities may have 'ex-officio' or 'co-opted' trustees. These terms are really no more than a reference to the way in which particular trustees are appointed.

8.26   An 'ex-officio' trustee becomes a trustee because he or she has been appointed to some other post or office that carries with it the right to become a trustee of the charity in question. The post or office could be with the charity itself (for example, the chief executive) or with some other organisation (for example, the Dean of a Cathedral may be an ex-officio trustee of a school associated with the Cathedral).

8.27   A 'co-opted' trustee is usually appointed by the board either to fill a trustee vacancy or as an additional trustee to fill a gap in the skill set of the board. They will typically be appointed for a shorter period than trustees appointed by the charity's members or trustees in the usual way, although this will depend upon the terms of the charity's constitution.

8.28   The most important thing to appreciate about co-opted and ex-officio trustees is that they are as much trustees of the charity as trustees appointed in any other way. The fact that they may, for example, hold office for a shorter period does not affect the nature or extent of the duties that they owe to the charity. It is only the mechanism by which they are appointed that differs.

DISQUALIFICATION

8.29   There are a number of provisions that may disqualify an individual from acting as a charity trustee.

8.30   The Charities Act 1993[4] disqualifies anyone from acting as a charity trustee if they:

- have been convicted of any offence involving dishonesty or deception;

- are subject to an undischarged bankruptcy order or have made a composition with their creditors which has not been discharged;

- have already been removed as a charity trustee by the Charity Commission or by the courts on the grounds of misconduct or mismanagement of the administration of a charity; or

---

[4]   Charities Act 1993, s 72.

- are subject to a disqualification order or a disqualification undertaking under the Company Directors Disqualification Act 1986 (this provision applies to a person seeking to become a trustee of any charity regardless of whether it is constituted as a company or not).

8.31 The Charity Commission has a discretion to waive certain of these requirements. Acting as a charity trustee while disqualified is a criminal offence under the Charities Act 1993.[5]

8.32 The courts can make disqualification orders against directors of companies under the Company Directors Disqualification Act 1986 in a variety of circumstances, including:

- on conviction of an indictable offence;

- for any fraud committed in the winding-up of a company; or

- following an investigation into the company's affairs by the Department of Trade and Industry or on an application in respect of wrongful trading or fraudulent trading (there is more about this in **Chapter 6**).

8.33 Disqualification as a director of a company will mean that the person who has been disqualified cannot act as a trustee of any charity, whether set up as a company or not, unless the Charity Commission is willing and able to exercise its discretion to allow him or her to act.

8.34 In addition to the statutory provisions, the constitution of most charities will set out a number of circumstances in which a charity trustee is disqualified from acting. This will have the effect of removing an existing trustee or disqualifying a prospective trustee. Typically, the express provisions will mirror the provisions of the Charities Act 1993.

TERMS OF REFERENCE

8.35 'Terms of Reference' are usually made by the board as part of their governance arrangements for three purposes:

- to define the scope of the role of particular members of the board or other post holders within the charity, eg the chairman, treasurer or secretary;

- to define the scope of the duties delegated to committees of the board relating to particular aspects of the charity's operations; and

- to define the scope of the roles and duties of senior employees.

8.36 Terms of Reference for committees are usually made pursuant to the exercise by the board of an express power to delegate some or all of its functions to a committee. The Terms themselves must reflect the requirements in the charity's constitution in relation to delegation on this basis. There is more about this at **8.87**.

---

[5] Charities Act 1993, s 73.

8.37 Terms of reference for individual trustees and post holders are more like to be made on an 'informal' basis; in other words, without a particular requirement or provision for them in the charity's constitution. Having said that, many charities' constitutions will provide for the board to determine, for example, the scope of the role of the chairman or secretary, in which case creating Terms of Reference is usually an effective way of achieving this.

8.38 Terms of Reference are usually written in a more informal way than the provisions of a charity's constitution. The intention is to put flesh on the bones of the legal structure in a way that will be intelligible to the charity's trustees, any employees and others.

BOARD MEETINGS

8.39 The main focus of trustees' attention and effort will be their meetings. Because charity trustees will generally act on an unpaid basis, they may not spend a great deal of time acting as trustees other than at meetings, although certain posts which trustees may hold (e g chairman or treasurer) are likely to involve more day-to-day work.

Frequency

8.40 There are no legal restrictions on the frequency with which board meetings should be held except where the provisions of a charity's constitution specify a minimum number. The Charity Commission's preference appears to be for a minimum of two meetings to be held every year, but the number of meetings that are required in practice will generally be determined by the scale and complexity of the charity's operations.

Board papers

8.41 One of the keys to effective discussion and decision-making at board meetings is distribution of information beforehand. There are no hard and fast rules about what charity trustees should and should not see, but the following things are likely to be relevant:

- Regular financial information, particularly where a charity's income is derived largely from operational activities rather than, say, investment income and gains. This could include, for example, management accounts.

- Where the charity's operations mean that it has employees, the trustees may wish to see short reports from the chief executive and other senior employees on particular aspects of the charity's operations.

- The trustees should see draft minutes of the previous meeting for their approval.

- Reports and papers relating to particular projects under consideration should be circulated.

8.42 In order to ensure that trustees have sufficient time to read and digest information made available before a meeting, all papers should be distributed in good time. They should be sent with a formal notice of the meeting, although information can be sent subsequently without invalidating the notice provided that the notice contains sufficient information about the matters that will be considered to enable the trustees to decide whether or not to attend the meeting.

Notice

8.43   There are no legal rules that govern the periods of notice that are required for trustees' meetings except that the notice given must be reasonable in the circumstances (eg short notice in an emergency is likely to be reasonable). The notice period is governed solely by the provisions of the charity's constitution. This may specify a particular period of time or it may simply provide that meetings can be called on notice determined by the trustees from time to time.

8.44   Where a charity's constitution specifies that notice must be given in a particular way, these provisions must be adhered to. Notices can be given by email or using some other electronic means provided the charity's constitution provides for this. As we have indicated, the notice must provide sufficient information to the trustees about what will be discussed to enable them to decide whether or not to attend. The charity's constitution should ideally specify who is able to give notice of a meeting. As regards board meetings this is typically any trustee, but notice is sometimes required to be given via the Secretary (if there is one).

Rules and regulations

8.45   The charity's constitution will often give trustees a power to make rules and regulations in relation to the way in which their board meetings are convened and held in order to give them flexibility to work in the most effective way. This is the approach usually taken by the articles of charitable companies (and reflects the approach taken by companies generally) but any charity can adopt a similar approach. Any rules or regulations that are made should preferably be in writing and reviewed by the trustees from time to time. They should not conflict with the provisions of the constitution itself (on the basis that the constitution can only properly be altered in accordance with whatever mechanism applies to it). This will often be expressly spelled out in the provisions of the constitution dealing with rule making.

Electronic meetings

8.46   The general rule is that a meeting can only validly be held where the participants can both see and hear each other. This means that, unless a charity's constitution expressly prohibits it, trustees can hold meetings by electronic means, including by way of video conference or web camera. Because a telephone conference call does not allow trustees to see each other, it cannot constitute a 'meeting' unless the charity's constitution expressly provides for meetings to be held on this basis. If there is no specific power to conduct trustees' meetings by telephone conference call, some trustees may still be able to phone into a physical meeting of trustees provided that (disregarding the trustees who are on the telephone) they can form a valid quorum for the meeting.

Voting

8.47   Voting at meetings will be in accordance with the charity's constitution but, if the constitution is silent, then a simple majority can pass resolutions. The trustees of private trusts are obliged to pass resolutions unanimously unless there are provisions in their constitution to the contrary. This is not true of charity trustees, who act by majority. In some cases, a constitution may specify a higher majority in relation to particular decisions, or may specify that certain resolutions can only be passed with the consent of particular trustees (for example, a trustee appointed by a particular stakeholder or an ex-officio trustee). In practice, most chairmen will seek consensus in relation to trustees' resolutions but where this is not possible, the majority will rule.

8.48 The constitution should ideally specify whether or not the chairman should exercise a 'casting' or 'second' vote in the event of deadlock. If there is no express provision for the chairman to exercise a casting or second vote, he will have only one vote as a trustee.

Written resolutions

8.49 If a meeting cannot be held to consider a resolution, the alternative is for the trustees to sign a written resolution. Whether a written resolution needs to be signed by all of the trustees in a charity in order to be valid will depend upon the provisions of its constitution. If the constitution is silent then all of the trustees must sign. If the constitution provides for a minimum number of trustees to sign then it will be valid provided their signatures can be obtained. Careful consideration should be given to including a provision in a charity's constitution that will allow the majority of trustees to pass resolutions in writing. The requirement for unanimity is usually intended to reflect the fact that the trustees do not have an opportunity to debate the resolution before it is proposed and allowing resolutions to pass by majority may mean that there is no opportunity for that kind of debate to be had.

8.50 In practice, trustees are often keen to make decisions by way of email exchange confirming that a particular decision is approved. Again, resolutions can only be validly passed in this way if the charity's constitution expressly provides for this to happen.

Quorum

8.51 The charity's constitution will usually specify the quorum requirements of board meetings. The quorum will often be a 'lower of' or 'greater of' fixed number proportion of the trustees so that the quorum can keep pace with a fluctuating number of trustees. If there is no quorum present in accordance with a charity's constitution, resolutions cannot be validly passed at the meeting. If obtaining a quorum proves difficult in practice, the approach often taken is to provide in the constitution for a lower quorum after, say, two previous inquorate meetings.

Other attendees

8.52 There are a number of people who may attend board meetings in addition to the trustees themselves:

- the Secretary (if there is one);

- any Observers;

- professional advisers; and

- senior employees (if any).

8.53   Where other people routinely attend trustees' meetings, the board may wish to make part of the meeting 'closed' to non-trustees in order to allow debate and discussion amongst the trustees alone.

Minutes

8.54   Charitable companies are obliged to maintain minutes of all trustees' meetings (once the Companies Act 2006 is in force, this will be for at least 10 years from the date of the relevant meeting). Failure to do so is a criminal offence by the trustees and any company secretary.[6] Minutes are deemed to be evidence that the relevant meeting was properly convened and held and that any appointment made at it was valid (in the absence of any evidence to the contrary).

8.55   There are no equivalent legal provisions which apply to charities that are not set up as companies, but the obligation to maintain good records is a part of the trustees' duty to safeguard their charity's assets. In that sense, the obligation on charitable companies should be regarded as the benchmark for unincorporated charities.

8.56   The Charity Commission's guidance states that:

'Whatever may be the legal requirements, we recommend that accurate minutes are kept of all meetings. The minutes do not need to be a word for word record, but need to record information that is important to the charity. We recommend that each of the minutes give:

- the name of the charity.
- the type of meeting.
- the date and time the meetings was held.
- apologies for absence.
- the names of those present, including:
    - in what capacity they attended e.g. trustee, advisor etc; and
    - for what items on the agenda.
- precise wording of any resolution together with the name of the proposer and (optionally) the seconder of the motion.
- a summary of the discussion on each item of business.
- information upon which the decision was based.
- details of the decision, i.e. who voted and how and, in the event of an equality of votes, if the chair used a casting vote.
- the action required.
- the names of the people who are responsible for implementing the decision.
- the date, time and venue of the next meeting.'[7]

8.57   The Charity Commission's guidance also emphasises the importance of ensuring that the minutes are an accurate record of the business that is transacted:

'It should be noted that the formal minutes, once approved and signed as an accurate record by the chairman, form the only legal record of the business at the meeting. Clearly, trustees can take notes of meetings for their own purposes; these should not however be used as an afterthought to the official minutes. It is important that, if a trustee is unable to agree that the draft minutes are an accurate record of the meeting, then he or she should draw the matter to the attention of the chairman before they are approved and signed.'[8]

---

6   Companies Act 2006, ss 248, 249; Companies Act 1985, s 382.
7   CC 48.
8   CC 48.

8.58   For this reason, it is very important that draft minutes are circulated to all of the trustees in order to ensure that they have an opportunity to review and, if necessary, suggest any changes to them. If a trustee cannot agree that minutes are accurate, then the Commission's view is that 'his or her dissention should be formally noted and recorded as a postscript to the minutes before they are signed'.

APPOINTMENT

8.59   For most charities, identifying potential new trustees will be essential in order to maintain the right mix of skills and experience on the board as existing trustees retire. Many charities plan for trustee succession in order to ensure continuity on the board. New trustees may be drawn from a number of different sources, including the charity's members and beneficiaries.

8.60   Every new charity trustee must be properly appointed in accordance with the mechanism set out in the charity's constitution. This will vary from charity to charity, but there will usually be a number of key points:

- The charity's constitution should identify who is responsible for the appointment. Is it the charity's members (if it has members)? Is it the board of trustees? Or is some third party responsible?

- There are some specific rules that apply to unincorporated charities (see **8.64**).

- Regardless of who is responsible for making the appointment, is there any nominations procedure that must first be observed (for example, does the board or a third party have to nominate people for appointment by the members) and are any third party consents required?

- If the trustee is to be appointed at a meeting of the members or the trustees, has proper notice been given of the proposal in accordance with the charity's constitution?

- Have the prospective trustees agreed to act as trustees of the charity? There is more about this issue at **8.77**.

8.61   Newly appointed trustees of charitable companies must have their appointment notified to Companies House on form 288a. The new trustee has to sign his or her consent to act and the form has to be countersigned by an existing trustee or the company secretary. The charity's register of directors should also be updated to reflect the appointment.

8.62   Formal requirements for the appointment of new trustees of other charities will depend upon the provisions of their constitution. This may include requirements in relation to consent or the entry of their name in a register of trustees. For charities other than companies, there are no legal requirements obliging the maintenance of a register of trustees; this is obviously a sensible approach from the point of view of best practice.

8.63   The appointment of new trustees of a charity need not be notified to the Charity Commission. Changes will be notified using the annual return (see 14.18 for more on this). That information will then be made available online on the Commission's website.

Unincorporated charities

8.64   There are some specific considerations that must be taken in account in relation to the appointment of new trustees of charitable trusts and other unincorporated charities.

8.65   Often the constitution of an unincorporated charity will state expressly who is entitled to appoint new trustees. However, if there is no express power, the trustees of a charitable trust or unincorporated association can exercise the powers conferred by the Trustee Act 1925, s 36. Essentially, s 36 provides that:

- In default of the express nomination of a person with the power to appoint new trustees by a charity's constitution, the existing trustees (or the personal representatives of the last surviving trustee) can appoint new trustees both in place of an outgoing trustee and as an additional trustee, where all the existing trustees are continuing in office.

- This is a power and not a duty. The trustees cannot be compelled to exercise it.

- The power to replace an outgoing trustee applies where a trustee is dead, remains out of the UK for more than 12 months, wishes to retire, is unfit, refuses to act or is mentally or physically incapable of acting.

- The power to appoint an additional trustee can be used at any time but only if the total number of trustees after the appointment is no more than four or (unless the charity trustees hold land) such higher number as may be specified by the charity's constitution.

8.66   Where there is no express power to appoint new trustees (and the power conferred by s 36 of the Trustee Act 1925 in relation to unincorporated charities is not capable of being exercised) a charity may be able to seek an order from the Charity Commission under the Charities Act 1993, s 18(5). This section gives the Commission the power to appoint a new charity trustee:

- in place of a charity trustee who has been removed by them under their s 18 powers following the opening of an Inquiry (see **4.35** for more on this);

- where there are no charity trustees at all, or where, because of any vacancy in the board or the absence or incapacity of any of the trustees, the charity cannot apply for their appointment; or

- where the Commission concludes that it is necessary for the proper administration of the charity to have an additional charity trustee because one of the existing charity trustees (who ought nevertheless to remain a charity trustee) either cannot be found or does not act or is outside England and Wales.

8.67   In addition, the Charities Act 1993, s 18(5)(c) gives the Charity Commission the power to appoint additional trustees of a charity which is presently being administered by a single charity trustee (other than a 'corporation aggregate') where the Commission is of the opinion that it is necessary to increase the number of trustees for the proper administration of the charity.

8.68 The Charity Commission also has jurisdiction (under the Charities Act 1993, s 16) to exercise the same jurisdiction and powers that are exercisable by the High Court. The court has an inherent jurisdiction to appoint new trustees to charities, even when there are no vacancies on the trustee board and where there is a power of appointment in existence and people capable of exercising it.

8.69 Alternatively, an application could be made to the court itself to exercise its inherent jurisdiction to appoint new trustees. Whenever it is desirable that a new trustee should be appointed and it is 'inexpedient, difficult or impractical to do so without the assistance of the Court', the court can also appoint a new trustee, either as an additional trustee or in substitution for an existing trustee, under the jurisdiction confirmed by the Trustee Act 1925, s 41. The court will not usually exercise this power unless it is satisfied that there is no provision in the charity's constitution which provides for the appointment of trustees and the power under the Trustee Act 1925, s 36 is not available.

8.70 Unincorporated charities have no legal personality separate from their trustees and the charity's assets can only be owned and held by the trustees themselves (or some of them) unless there is a provision for them to be held by a nominee.

8.71 The difficulty posed by the appointment of new trustees of charities of this kind is that legal title to the charity's assets must be vested in its trustees from time to time. This is in order to ensure that the individuals who are a charity's trustees at any particular time can deal with the assets effectively and have full control over them. This is an intrinsic part of every charity trustee's duty to safeguard the assets of a charity.

8.72 One way of dealing with this would be for title to the charity's assets to be transferred out of the name of any retiring trustee and into the names of the continuing and any newly appointed trustee. This would mean executing transfers in relation to land and shares and other securities, assignments of debts and all other individual assets. Clearly, where a charity's trustees change fairly frequently, transferring the assets in this way can become a fairly onerous burden. In practice, it is not often done.

8.73 Transfers of this kind can generally be avoided by ensuring that every charity trustee is appointed, or retired, by signing a document that constitutes a 'deed'. A deed is a document like any other but is executed in a particular way. The person making the deed must have his or her signature witnessed and intend it to be delivered as a deed.[9]

8.74 Where trustees' appointments and retirements are done by way of deed, s 40 of the Trustee Act 1925 provides that, unless the deed contains a provision to the contrary, it will automatically vest all of the charity's assets in the new or continuing trustees. Section 40 does not apply to every asset (for example, mortgages of land or transfers of shares or securities where a form of transfer has to be registered by the company). In addition, registered land will only be transferred on production of the deed to the Land Registry so that the proprietorship register can be brought up to date.[10]

8.75 Where no deed is used, the same effect can be achieved by appointing or retiring charity trustees by resolution of a meeting of the trustees, members or other people exercising the relevant power. A memorandum recording the appointment or retirement of the trustees will bring the provisions of s 40 of the Trustee Act 1925 into play provided that the memorandum has been signed either at the meeting by the chairman

---

9   The document should also state that it is intended to be executed as a deed.
10   Land Registration Act 2002, s 27.

or in some other way directed by those present at the meeting and it is witnessed by two people who were present at the meeting. Clearly, the execution of the memorandum in this way is intended to replicate the formalities for execution of a deed.[11]

8.76   The constitutions of many charitable trusts and other unincorporated charities will sometimes expressly require new trustees to be appointed (and old trustees to retire) by way of deed. Sometimes they refer simply to appointment by 'resolution of' the members or trustees or 'by the members'. Notwithstanding that there is no reference to a deed, the trustees should ensure that every appointment is dealt with either by deed or by memorandum. Ideally, every unincorporated charity's constitution should provide expressly for appointments to be by way of deed.

Consent to act

8.77   The Charity Commission recommends that all new charity trustees should sign a declaration confirming that they are willing to act as a trustee. A similar declaration is required from the trustees of any charity that is applying for registration by the Commission. It may seem to be obvious that anyone who has agreed to become a charity trustee and has signed the necessary documents and complied with the necessary formalities is willing to act. But the Commission's point is really that no-one should become a charity trustee unless they have taken the time and trouble to understand the scope of their role, their powers and, most importantly, their duties.

8.78   This is an important governance issue in practice. Essentially, a trustee is only worth the skills and experience he or she is willing and able to bring to a charity. If a new trustee does not appreciate that, say, they will be required to attend four meetings a year and end up attending only one, the other trustees may wonder (quite rightly) whether they should have appointed someone more willing to make a real contribution to the charity's work.

8.79   Obtaining the formal consent of a new charity trustee to act is one step that charity trustees can take in order to ensure that new trustees brought on board will add value to the charity. An example of the kind of undertaking that could be sought is as follows:

Trustee's undertaking

I confirm my willingness to accept the appointment and responsibility of a trustee of the [charity]. I have read and understood the following:

- The [charity's] constitution.

- The [charity's] Terms of Reference for trustees.

- 'Responsibilities of charity trustees' (CC 3) published by the Charity Commission.

I understand that, together with my fellow trustees, it is my duty to act within the [charity's] constitution and by its code of practice to ensure that the [charity] fulfils its charitable purposes, which are:

➡

---

11   Charities Act 1993, s 83.

To promote the [charitable purposes].

With utmost faith, I will be diligent and exercise reasonable care in carrying out my duties as a trustee of the [charity].

Signed: ....

Name: .... Date: ....

8.80 This undertaking helps to ensure that the new trustee has taken steps to understand what it is that he or she is taking on. However, it really only makes sense in the context of a wide-ranging induction process.

Induction

8.81 A charity trustee cannot expect to understand the nature and extent of his or her role and responsibilities without an induction. And all charity trustees are in any event under a legal duty to ensure that they familiarise themselves with the charitable purposes and assets of their charity and the provisions of its constitution. As a minimum, a new charity trustee should be given the following items:

- a copy of the charity's constitution and, if appropriate, a summary of its charitable purposes;

- an explanation of how it operates to achieve its charitable purposes, with particular attention to the core areas of its operations;

- a copy of the charity's latest report and accounts;

- a copy of any Terms of Reference for the charity's trustees adopted by the board;

- any trustee policies. This would include, for example, policies on expenses and conflicts of interest;

- an explanation of the charity's relationship with any trading subsidiary (if there is one). There is more about this in **Chapter 13**;

- details of the charity's key employees and their respective roles and lines of reporting;

- details of the place and date of trustees' meetings and the information which will be made available for meetings; and

- a summary of the charity's internal financial controls.

8.82 As part of a new trustee's induction, it is likely to be sensible to set out some Terms of Reference for the charity's trustees generally. This will obviously also be an important document as regards the existing trustees. As with all Terms of Reference, any Terms that are set should be reviewed by the charity trustees from time to time. Terms will obviously vary from charity to charity, but an example of the sort of provisions one might expect to see is as follows:

Trustees

Terms of reference

The board (the **'Board'**) of trustees (the **'Trustees'**) of the [Charity] (the **'Charity'**) has approved these Terms of Reference for Trustees.

Board meetings

Trustees are expected:

- To attend meetings of the Board having carefully read and considered the agenda and briefing papers.

- To participate in Board meetings in a reasonable, objective and prudent manner, not allowing prejudice to impinge on the debate and decision-making process.

- To contribute actively to the Board in giving firm strategic direction to the Charity, setting overall policy, defining goals and setting targets and evaluating performance against agreed targets.

- To monitor the Charity's financial position and ensure total accountability.

- To assist in the formulation of budgets and strategic plans.

- To approve the Charity's annual report and accounts.

Trustees' responsibilities

Trustees' responsibilities are:

- To ensure that legal, financial and management duties comply with the Charity's constitution and charitable objects.

- To safeguard the good name and ethos of the Charity by ensuring that all activities are conducted with probity and propriety.

- To ensure the effective and efficient administration of the Charity as well as its financial stability.

- To ensure protection and conscientious management of the property and assets of the Charity and to ensure the proper investment of its funds.

- To act in the interests of all, rather than any local or sectional interest.

- To act collectively with the other Trustees, not as an individual.

- To disclose any conflict of interest.

- To maintain appropriate confidentiality.   ➡

- To honour the collective responsibility for decisions properly taken, channelling concerns or disagreements through the chairman.

- To review annually the performance of the Trustees.

- To approve the annual appraisal of the Chief Executive.

- To ensure that an annual general meeting is held every calendar year and the annual return, accounts, report and all other relevant documents and resolutions are filed within the appropriate time limit.

What trustees may also be able to offer

Trustees must be able to offer:

- An informative/educational/ambassadorial role at a local and regional level.

- Availability to serve on committees of the Board or working groups where relevant.

- Willingness to take part in induction and training as appropriate.

- Specific skills and contacts.

- Willingness to offer advice to other Trustees and staff drawn from personal experience.

- Responsibilities to employees.

Trustees' responsibilities to be the charity's employees are:

- To ensure compliance with current employment and equal opportunities legislation as well as good practice and the Charity's current policy on these and related matters.

- To ensure the establishment of procedures for the recruitment, support, appraisal and remuneration of employees.

- To ensure that disciplinary and complaints procedures are in place.

- To work in close co-operation with the Chief Executive and other senior executives.

Object drift

8.83 A good example of a failure by charity trustees to appreciate the scope of their role, the nature of their powers and duties and the legal framework within which their charity operates is 'object drift'. This means no more than follows. A charity may be established for the relief of poverty but starts to operate programmes which help people in poverty as a consequence of ill health. The charity operates successfully and its activities develop to the extent that it starts to help anyone in ill health regardless of their economic circumstances. Over time, the charity's activities in relation to health become more important than its activities in relation to poverty. The work it does in relation to health is very valuable but it is not work that falls within the charity's legal purposes. In principle, the charity's trustees are in breach of trust for allowing the charity to operate in this way.

8.84 In many cases, 'object drift' of this kind is due to changes in the composition of the board of trustees over time. As old trustees retire and new trustees are appointed, there is always a danger that new trustees do not properly understand what the charity does or the legal framework within which it operates and will agree (with the best of intentions) to something that the charity is legally incapable of doing, or at least not without giving rise to a breach of trust.

8.85 Avoiding this sort of problem depends upon a number of factors, but a comprehensive and effective induction of a new trustee is obviously an essential starting point.

CRB checks

8.86 There is a raft of legislation aimed at ensuring that any organisation that works with children or vulnerable adults carries out checks on the various different lists of individuals who may pose a risk to them. The statutes in question are the Protection of Children Act 1999, the Criminal Justice and Court Services Act 2000, the Care Standards Act 2000 and the Education Act 2002. A detailed analysis of these provisions is outside the scope of this book, but the trustees of any charity that works with children or vulnerable adults must ensure that they familiarise themselves with the framework of the legislation. This is aimed at ensuring that every individual who will work with children or vulnerable adults is the subject of a criminal records check with the Criminal Records Bureau ('CRB'). The CRB maintains lists of individuals who have been convicted of criminal offences associated with children and vulnerable adults. There is much more information available at www.crb.gov.uk. Charities whose main beneficiaries are children or vulnerable adults may also wish to consider developing protection policies in relation to their beneficiaries.

DELEGATION

8.87 The delegation of charity trustees' powers is an area that often seems to cause problems in practice. It helps if one understands that the starting point is that every charity trustee should exercise his or her powers personally unless they are expressly authorised to allow someone else to exercise them. That is essentially what delegation amounts to; a charity trustee authorising some other person to exercise his or her powers.

8.88 Powers of delegation are important because they affect many aspects of many charities' operations. These range from the trustees of a charitable trust authorising someone to sign documents on their behalf to the trustees of a charitable company delegating consideration of a complex transaction to a specially constituted committee of the board.

8.89 Without an appropriate power of delegation that is exercised properly by the relevant charity trustees, decisions taken and acts carried out by people to whom the trustees' powers have purportedly been delegated will have no legal effect. The consequences of that will vary from case to case but the scope for potential liability for a breach of trust by the charity trustees is obvious, with some potential personal liability for the people to whom powers were purportedly delegated.

8.90 Before we look in more detail at the powers of delegation available to the trustees of charities it is important to appreciate that, as a general rule, delegation of a power does not involve the delegation of responsibility. While the court may in certain circumstances conclude that a delegate should be liable for any failure to exercise a delegated power properly in much the same way as the charity trustees by whom the power is delegated to him or her, the charity trustees will, as a general rule, remain personally liable for the acts and defaults of the delegate. For this reason, there are three fundamental issues that should ideally be addressed in any power of delegation.

8.91 These are:

- A clear indication of whether the delegate has the authority to take decisions and carry out acts which will bind the charity trustees or whether the delegate is authorised only to advise the charity trustees, to take decisions that must be ratified by the trustees or to carry out basic administrative or ministerial functions that do no more than give effect to the trustees' decisions.

- An express provision for any delegate to report back to the charity trustees so that they understand exactly how the delegated powers are being exercised and can take steps to prevent acts and decisions which may, for example, be a breach of trust.

- The power of delegation could be made subject to a requirement that at least one of the delegates must be a trustee. This is with a view to ensuring that the trustee-delegate can monitor what his or her co-delegates are doing, report back to his or her co-trustees and take steps to prevent any acts or decisions that may, for example, be a breach of trust.

8.92 There is no strict legal requirement for provisions of this kind to be included in powers of delegation, but they make good practical sense as safeguards of the trustees' position and the position of the charity generally. The Charity Commission's preference is for powers of delegation to include at least one trustee as a delegate. In principle, this should not be necessary provided a provision for monitoring and reporting back is included and works effectively, but one can see that including at least one trustee-delegate is likely to give the trustees a more direct line of reporting.

8.93 In principle, it would be possible to construct a power of delegation in such a way that the delegate take on not only the powers but the duties of the charity trustees whose powers they are exercising. A provision to this effect would need to be very clear indeed and would result in the delegates becoming charity trustees in their own right. For this reason alone, it is generally better to assume that charity trustees will remain responsible for the acts and decisions of their delegates.

8.94 The powers of delegation available to charity trustees will depend primarily upon the way in which their charity has been set up.

Charitable companies

8.95 The constitution of a charitable company will generally contain an express provision to the effect that the business of the charity will be managed by the trustees who may exercise all of its powers.[12] The articles will also usually include an express power to delegate any of the trustees' powers to any committee consisting of one or more persons, at least one of whom must be a trustee.

8.96 The Companies Acts and Charities Act 1993 provide that, in favour of a person dealing with a company in good faith, the directors' power to bind the company, or to authorise others to do so, is deemed to be free of any limitation under the company's constitution (see also **7.12**).[13]

8.97 This power does not apply to charitable companies except in favour of a person who does not know that the company is a charity or gives full consideration in money on moneys worth and does not know that the act in question is not permitted by the company's constitution or that it is beyond the powers of the charitable company's trustees. Clearly, therefore, it is essential that the trustees of a charitable company understand their powers of delegation and exercise them properly. Failing to do so is likely to make the acts and decisions of the delegate void.

8.98 The only other power of delegation available to the trustees of the charitable company is the ability to appoint 'alternate directors'. An alternate director is any person appointed by a charity trustee to act in his place and can only be appointed if there is an express provision for this in the charitable company's constitution. This will set out the basis on which the alternate is appointed and the scope of his or her powers. The relevant provisions will normally provide for the alternate to act in the place of the trustee who has appointed him or her where the trustee is absent. The alternate will usually cease to be an alternate director if the person ceases to be a trustee.

8.99 The power to appoint an alternate director is useful in practice where a trustee is likely to be absent for a period of time and wishes to appoint someone to act in his or her place while they are away. The power will not usually be used to delegate particular trustee powers or functions. Alternate directors are an exception to the usual rule that those appointing delegates will remain responsible for the delegate's acts and decisions. A charitable company's constitution will usually expressly provide that an alternate director is solely responsible for his or her own acts and defaults to the exclusion of any liability for the trustee who has appointed him or her.[14]

8.100 A trustee of a charitable company cannot delegate any of his or her powers or functions to another person using a trustee power of attorney under s 25 of the Trustees Act 1925 (see also **8.109**).

Unincorporated charities

8.101 Many unincorporated charities will have an express power in their constitution authorising the delegation of trustees' powers and functions to other people. Where there is an express power, its provisions must be properly observed, particularly in relation to any conditions that apply (for example, that a majority of delegates must

---

[12] See e g Companies Act 1985, Table A, regulation 70.
[13] Companies Act 1985, s 35; Companies Act 2006, s 42; Charities Act 1993, s 65.
[14] See e g Companies Act 1985, Table A, reg 69.

themselves be trustees or that any act or decision taken by the delegates must be ratified by the trustees in order to become effective). A power of delegation contained in the constitution of an unincorporated charity will often be expressed as a power to employ and appoint agents.

8.102 In addition to any express powers conferred on charity trustees by the constitution of their charity, s 11 of the Trustee Act 2000 confers a general authority on trustees (acting collectively) to delegate certain of their functions. The general authority conferred by the 2000 Act is in addition to any other powers to appoint agents and delegates exercised by the trustees but is also subject to any restrictions or exclusions imposed by the charity's constitution.

8.103 Section 11(3) of the Trustee Act 2000 provides that charity trustees may delegate the following functions:

- any function consisting of carrying out a decision that the trustees have taken (in other words, acts of a purely administrative or ministerial nature);

- any function relating to the investments of the charity's assets (there is more about this in **Chapter 10**);

- any function relating to raising funds for the charity, except by carrying out a 'primary purpose trade' (there is more about primary purpose trades generally in **Chapter 13**); and

- any other function prescribed by an order made by the Secretary of State.

8.104 Clearly, except where the function relates to investment (usually discretionary investment management) or fundraising, the general authority is limited in its scope. It cannot (subject to these exceptions) be used to delegate the power to take substantive decisions about the charity or any aspect of its operations.

8.105 The general authority can appoint any person as a delegate, including any of the trustees themselves. Two or more delegates can be appointed provided that they exercise the same function jointly. The general authority is also subject to a number of restrictions. The charity trustees have a discretion to determine the terms on which any delegate should be appointed but cannot, unless it is reasonably necessary, agree to terms which:

- permit the delegate to appoint a substitute;

- include any exemption clause restricting the delegate's liability; or

- permit the delegate to act in circumstances which give rise to potential conflicts of interest.

8.106 Charity trustees must exercise the general authority in accordance with their statutory duty of care (as to which see **Chapter 6**), particularly in relation to the selection of the delegate and the terms on which he or she is to act.

8.107 Provided the charity trustees comply with their statutory duty of care[15] in selecting the delegate and determining the basis on which he or she should act, the Trustee Act 2000 provides that they will not be liable for any of the delegate's acts or defaults.[16] This is an exception to the general rule that a charity trustee will remain liable for the acts and defaults of his or her delegate.

8.108 The general authority to delegate conferred by the Trustee Act 2000 relates to collective delegation by charity trustees. In other words, the board of trustees exercise the power conferred upon them collectively to delegate particular powers and functions to one or more other people. However, there are other powers of delegation that can be exercised by a trustee individually which may sometimes be relevant.

8.109 Section 25 of the Trustee Act 1925 gives any charity trustee the ability to delegate all or any of the powers and discretions invested in him or her as a trustee using a power of attorney. Any person can be appointed as an attorney, including any co-trustee. However, the delegation cannot be for more than 12 months (although that period does not have to start on the day on which the power of attorney is actually executed). And the charity trustee making the power of attorney must (within seven days of granting it) give written notice of the delegation to each of his co-trustees and any other person who has the power to appoint new trustees.

8.110 A charity trustee will remain liable for every act or default of the delegate appointed pursuant to a power of attorney. This is in contrast to the provisions of the Trustee Act 2000, where a charity trustee will only be liable for the acts and defaults of a delegate if he or she has failed to comply with the statutory duty of care in selecting the delegate in the first place.

8.111 A trustee power of attorney of this kind can be useful in certain circumstances. Where a trustee is required to execute a document but will not be available at the relevant time, a power of attorney is likely to be the most effective way of dealing with the position. However, powers can be used to delegate all or any trustee functions, not just administrative or ministerial acts and could also be used, for example, to delegate all of a trustee's powers and discretions to an attorney during a period of absence. The scope of the attorney's authority will depend entirely upon the terms of the power set by the trustee.

Committees

8.112 Larger charities with more complex operational requirements are likely to use delegation as a governance tool. By creating committees of the board with non-trustees as members, the board may be able to harness the skills and experience of a wider range of people who do not have the time, or perhaps may not be willing, to become trustees themselves or could only do so at the risk of increasing the number of members of the board until it becomes unworkable. Power to delegate to a committee of the board will usually be set out in an express provision in the charity's constitution.

8.113 Committees of the board often encountered include:

- the audit (or finance) committee, with overall responsibility for overseeing a charity's finances and financial scrutiny and accountability;

---

[15] See **6.2** and **7.3** for more in relation to this.
[16] Trustee Act 2000, s 23(1).

- a remuneration committee, responsible for reviewing the terms on which a charity's senior employees are engaged (in much the same way as the non-executive directors sitting on a commercial company's remuneration committee); and

- a strategy committee, to engage with the charity's strengths, weaknesses and the opportunities for, and threats to, it.

8.114 The basis on which the trustees' powers are delegated to committees of the board of this kind will usually be set out in Terms of Reference. These should obviously be set by the board itself, and should also be reviewed from time to time in order to ensure that they remain appropriate. The Terms made will vary from charity to charity but examples of the sort of provisions that might be made are set out below.

Audit Committee

Terms of Reference

The board (the **'Board'**) of trustees (the **'Trustees'**) of the [Charity] (the **'Charity'**) has established a committee of the Board to be known as the Audit Committee (the **'Committee'**). These are its terms of reference.

Membership

The Committee will be appointed by the Board and will comprise no more than and no fewer than members, of whom one will be the Treasurer of the Charity and a majority (including the Treasurer) will be Trustees.

The Board will appoint one of the members of the Committee as its chairman (the **'Chairman'**).

The Committee will elect a Secretary to the Committee.

Attendance

The Committee may ask the Chief Executive and the Finance Director and any other senior executive to attend meetings of the Committee either regularly or by invitation. Invitees have no right to attend Committee meetings.

The Committee will ask a representative of the external auditors and the head of internal audit to attend all meetings. The Committee will have at least one annual meeting, or part of one meeting, with each of the external auditor and the head of internal audit without the senior executives being present.

Voting

Only those members of the Committee who are Trustees will be entitled to vote and count in the quorum at meetings of the Committee. The quorum at any meeting of the Committee will be Trustee-members. The Chairman will have a casting vote on an equality of votes. ➡

The Committee will be competent to exercise all or any of the authority, powers and discretions vested in or exercisable by the Committee.

Meetings

The Committee shall meet quarterly on such dates as shall be determined by the Committee from time to time and at such other time as the Secretary shall specify at the request of any member of the Committee.

Meetings can be requested by the external or internal auditors if they consider that one is necessary.

Unless otherwise agreed, notice of each meeting confirming the venue, date and time together with an agenda shall be sent to each member of the Committee and any other person invited or required to attend no fewer than 7 working days prior to the date of the meeting.

Minutes

The Secretary will minute the proceedings and resolutions of the Committee and ascertain, at the beginning of each meeting, the existence of any conflicts of interest and minute them accordingly.

Minutes of each Committee meeting will be sent to all members of the Committee and the Board within 7 working days of the meeting.

Authority

The Committee is authorised by the Board to investigate any activity within its terms of reference. It is authorised to seek any information it requires from any employee and all employees are directed to cooperate with any request made by the Committee.

The Committee is authorised by the Board to obtain outside legal or other independent professional advice and to secure the attendance of any person at any Committee meeting with relevant experience and expertise if it considers this necessary.

Duties

The duties of the Committee shall be:

- to consider the appointment of the external auditor, the audit fee, and any questions of resignation or dismissal;

- to discuss with the external auditor before the audit commences the nature and scope of the audit;

- to review the annual financial statements before submission to the board of trustees, focussing particularly on:
  - any changes in accounting policies and practices
  - areas involving a significant degree of judgement

➡

      – significant adjustments resulting from the audit
      – the going concern assumption
      – compliance with accounting standards
      – compliance with legal requirements
      – the clarity of disclosures
      – the consistency of accounting policies from year to year

- to discuss problems and reservations arising from the audit and any matters the external auditor may wish to discuss (in the absence of the management where necessary);

- to act as the body to whom the head of internal audit reports on the internal audit function and to discuss any issue that the head of internal audit may wish to raise (in the absence of the management where necessary);

- to review the internal audit function, consider the major findings of internal audit investigations and the management's response, and ensure co-ordination between the internal and external auditors;

- to keep under review the effectiveness of internal control systems, and in particular review the external auditor's management letter and the management's response;

- to consider other topics, as defined by the Board from time to time; and

- to review, on a regular basis, its own performance, constitution and terms of reference to ensure it is operating at maximum effectiveness.

In discharging its duties, the aims of the Audit Committee are to:

- facilitate good communication between the Charity and its external auditor;

- increase the credibility and objectivity of financial reporting;

- strengthen the independence of the audit function; and

- improve the quality of the accounting and auditing functions.

Remuneration Committee

Terms of Reference

The board (the **'Board'**) of trustees (the **'Trustees'**) of the [Charity] (the **'Charity'**) has established a committee of the Board to be known as the Remuneration Committee (the **'Committee'**). These are its terms of reference.

Membership

The Committee will be appointed by the Board and will comprise no more than and no fewer than members, of whom a majority will be Trustees. ➡

Those members of the Committee who are Trustees will elect a Trustee-member to be the chairman (the **'Chairman'**) of the Committee.

The Committee will elect a Secretary to the Committee.

Attendance

The Committee may ask the Chief Executive and the Finance Director and any other senior executive to attend meetings of the Committee either regularly or by invitation. Invitees have no right to attend Committee meetings.

The Committee may also ask any other person whose attendance they consider necessary or desirable to attend any meeting either regularly or by invitation. Invitees have no right to attend Committee meetings.

Voting

Only those members of the Committee who are Trustees will be entitled to vote and count in the quorum at meetings of the Committee. The quorum at any meeting of the Committee will be Trustee-members. The Chairman will have a casting vote on any equality of votes.

The Committee will be competent to exercise all or any of the authorities, powers and discretions vested in or exercisable by the Committee.

Meetings

The Committee shall meet quarterly on such dates as shall be determined by the Committee from time to time and at such other time as the Secretary shall specify at the request of any member of the Committee.

Unless otherwise agreed, notice of each meeting confirming the venue, date and time together with an agenda shall be sent to each member of the Committee and any other person invited or required to attend no fewer than 7 working days prior to the date of the meeting.

Minutes

The Secretary will minute the proceedings and resolutions of the Committee and ascertain, at the beginning of each meeting, the existence of any conflicts of interest and minute them accordingly.

Minutes of each Committee meeting will be sent to all members of the Committee and the Board within 7 working days of the meeting.

Authority

The Committee is authorised by the Board to investigate any activity within its terms of reference. It is authorised to seek any information it requires from any employee and all employees are directed to co-operate with any request made by the Committee.

➡

The Committee is authorised by the Board to obtain outside legal or other independent professional advice if it considers this necessary.

Duties

The duties of the Committee shall be:

- to consider, determine and keep under review a framework or policy for the remuneration, benefits and incentives of the Chief Executive and the Finance Director and such other senior executives as the Board shall from time to time direct;

- in determining that framework, to seek evidence of the remuneration, benefits and incentives paid to senior executives in comparable employment within the commercial and voluntary sectors;

- to consider the outcome of every appraisal of the performance of the Chief Executive and the Finance Director and such other senior executives as the Board shall from time to time direct;

- to make recommendations to the Board as to the remuneration, benefit and incentives that should be paid to the Chief Executive and the Finance Director and such other senior executives as the Board shall from time to time direct with a view to ensuring that they are encouraged to enhance their performance and are, in a fair and responsible manner, rewarded for their individual contributions to the success of the Charity and its progress towards fulfilling its objectives;

- to make recommendations to the Board as to the remuneration, benefits and incentives of newly appointed senior executives;

- to determine the policy for and scope of pension arrangements, service agreements for the senior executives, termination payments and compensation commitments;

- to consider other topics, as defined by the Board from time to time; and

- to review, on a regular basis, its own performance, constitution and terms of reference to ensure it is operating at maximum effectiveness.

Strategy Committee

Terms of Reference

The board (the **'Board'**) of trustees (the **'Trustees'**) of the [Charity] (the **'Charity'**) has established a committee of the Board to be known as the Strategy Committee (the **'Committee'**). These are its terms of reference. ➡

Membership

The Committee will be appointed by the Board and will comprise no more than and no fewer than members, of whom a majority will be Trustees.

Those members of the Committee who are Trustees will elect a Trustee-member to be the chairman (the **'Chairman'**) of the Committee.

The Committee will elect a Secretary to the Committee.

Attendance

The Committee may ask the Chief Executive and the Finance Director and any other senior executive to attend meetings of the Committee either regularly or by invitation. Invitees have no right to attend Committee meetings.

The Committee may also ask any other person whose attendance they consider necessary or desirable to attend any meeting either regularly or by invitation. Invitees have no right to attend Committee meetings.

Voting

Only those members of the Committee who are Trustees will be entitled to vote and count in the quorum at meetings of the Committee. The quorum at any meeting of the Committee will be Trustee-members. The Chairman will have a casting vote on an equality of votes.

The Committee will be competent to exercise all or any of the authorities, powers and discretions vested in or exercisable by the Committee.

Meetings

The Committee shall meet quarterly on such dates as shall be determined by the Committee from time to time and at such other time as the Secretary shall specify at the request of any member of the Committee.

Unless otherwise agreed, notice of each meeting confirming the venue, date and time together with an agenda shall be sent to each member of the Committee and any other person invited or required to attend no fewer than 7 working days prior to the date of the meeting.

Minutes

The Secretary will minute the proceedings and resolutions of the Committee and ascertain, at the beginning of each meeting, the existence of any conflicts of interest and minute them accordingly.

Minutes of each Committee meeting will be sent to all members of the Committee and the Board within 7 working days of the meeting.   ➡

Authority

The Committee is authorised by the Board to investigate any activity within its terms of reference. It is authorised to seek any information it requires from any employee and all employees are directed to co-operate with any request made by the Committee.

The Committee is authorised by the Board to obtain outside legal or other independent professional advice if it considers this necessary.

Duties

The duties of the Committee shall be:

- to identify, seek evidence of and monitor the Charity's strengths and weaknesses and the threats and opportunities to and for it in the future;

- to evaluate the skills and expertise of the Trustees with a view to identifying potential gaps in their skills and expertise and the other requirements that the Charity will need in the future;

- to make recommendations to the Board as to how any gap in the skills and expertise of the Trustees can be remedied by succession planning;

- to make recommendations to the Board as to the changes that may be required to the Charity's business plan (or any other aspects of the Charity's activities) in order to deal with the strengths and weaknesses and threats and opportunities that the Committee identifies;

- to make recommendations to the Board as regards plans for succession for the Chief Executive and the Finance Director and any other senior executive the Board considers relevant;

- to identify any risks that should be added to or deleted from the risk management policy adopted by the Board from time to time;

- to consider other topics, as defined by the Board from time to time; and

- to review, on a regular basis, its own performance, constitution and terms of reference to ensure it is operating at maximum effectiveness.

EXECUTION OF DOCUMENTS

8.115 The way in which a charity executes documents often depends upon the existence and exercise of powers of delegation.

Charitable companies

8.116 The Companies Acts sets out a specific regime for the execution of documents by companies, including charitable companies. Essentially, this regime is as follows:

- A 'simple' contract (that is, any contract which is not required to be executed as a deed) can be made by a charitable company in writing using its common seal (if it has one, although there is no requirement that it should have) or on behalf of the charitable company by a person acting under its express or implied authority. In practice, any charity trustee will have implied authority to make simple contracts of this kind on behalf of a charitable company. A charitable company's constitution may make express provisions to this effect or the board itself may exercise an express power in the constitution to authorise one of their number to sign.

- Any document which needs to be signed as a deed can be validly executed by the charitable company by fixing its common seal (again, if it has one) or by being signed by two trustees or a trustee and the company secretary (if there is one) or, subject to the coming into force of the Companies Act 2006, by a single trustee in the presence of a witness who attests the trustee's signature and signs and adds his or her own name, address and occupation.[17]

- In order for any document validly executed by a company to take effect as a deed, it will also need to be 'delivered' as a deed.

- Any charitable company can appoint an attorney to execute deeds and other documents on its behalf.[18]

Unincorporated charities

8.117 There is no single statutory regime that governs the execution of documents by unincorporated charities. The starting point is that an unincorporated charity can only enter into deeds and other documents by its trustees. So every contract between the charity and a third party will actually be made between the third party and the trustees of the charity at the time the contract is entered into.

8.118 This means that, in order to validly execute a document, all of the trustees of a charity must execute it (either by signing a simple contract or by executing a deed in the presence of a witness who attests his or her signature) unless the trustees can use an appropriate power to delegate responsibility for signing to one or more of the trustees or to any other person. The relevant powers of delegation are as follows:

- The charity's constitution may confer an express power of delegation or an express power in relation to the signing of documents that will enable the trustees to properly authorise one or more of the trustees or any other person to sign a particular document or deed on their behalf.

- In addition, but subject to the provisions of the charity's constitution, the general authority to delegate conferred by s 11 of the Trustee Act 2000 will be sufficiently wide to authorise the signature of any document which sets out the terms of an agreement that the trustees have already decided to enter into.

- The Charities Act 1993, s 82 gives charity trustees an express power (subject to the provisions of the charity's constitution) to confer on any two or more of the trustees a general authority, or a limited authority if the trustees consider it more

---

[17]   Companies Act 2006, s 44.
[18]   Companies Act 2006, s 47.

appropriate, to execute documents and deeds in the names and on behalf of the trustees. Provided the documents give effect to transactions to which the trustees are a party, signature under a 'section 82' power of this kind will have the same effect as if executed by all of the trustees. Provided the document states that it is executed under a section 82 power, then it is conclusively presumed to have been properly executed by all of the trustees in favour of a person who acts in good faith and acquires (for money or money's worth) any interest in, or charge on, property as a consequence.

8.119 The section 82 power is particularly useful and many charities will wish to pass a general authority for any two or more of the trustees to sign documents and deeds on their behalf. Once given, the authority continues notwithstanding any changes to the charity trustees as if it refers to the charity trustees at the relevant time. The trustees also have the ability to restrict the basis on which documents can be signed. This could include, for example, only signing any document that has been properly approved by resolution of the charity trustees as a body.

8.120 Because a third party acting in good faith has given money or money's worth can only rely upon a section 82 power where a document 'purports to be executed in pursuance of', such a power should be expressly referred to in any document which is intended to be signed on the charity's behalf.

8.121 A section 82 power itself can be given in writing or by resolution of a meeting of the charity trustees. Section 82 expressly provides that any power given this way is sufficient to authorise two or more trustees to sign any deed or other written instruments. This is an exception to the usual rule that any delegated authority to sign a deed must be given by deed.

EMPLOYEES

8.122 Many charities have employees whose role is to help advance their purposes in accordance with the strategy and decisions of the board of trustees. In larger and more complex charities, the role played by the charity's chief executive, finance director and chief operating officer are very often significant.

8.123 While they may have wide-ranging powers and authority, a charity's employees do not have the power or authority to take the strategic decisions that are reserved to the charity trustees alone. In other words, they have no power or authority to take decisions at the highest level that affect the way in which the charity is managed and controlled. In larger charities, the employees will have significant day-to-day powers and discretions, but the exercise of those powers and discretions will be aimed at giving effect to the strategic decisions of the trustees.

8.124 There are no hard and fast legal rules about what constitutes a 'strategic' decision. Ultimately, one can only look at the test of charity trusteeship set by the Charities Act 1993. The decisions taken by the charity trustees are those that relate to the management and control of the charity in question.

8.125 Having said this, the trustees of larger charities will often wish to ensure that senior employees have Terms of Reference that set out clearly the scope of their roles and responsibilities. These will usually be set by the board as part of the exercise of a power to employ individuals to advance the charity's purposes (and must be consistent with the employees' contracts of employment). Terms of this kind will vary from charity to charity but may look something like this:

Chief Executive

Terms of Reference

The board (the **'Board'**) of trustees (the **'Trustees'**) of the [Charity] (the **'Charity'**) has adopted the following terms of reference in respect of the Charity's Chief Executive.

Role

The Chief Executive's role is to act as the chief executive of the Charity and, in particular:

- to take primary responsibility for the implementation of the business plan and the budget;

- to provide clear and effective leadership of the Charity's employees;

- to represent the chief public face of the Charity to its beneficiaries and other stakeholders, the media and the public at large;

- to engage actively with other charities and social enterprises, particularly those with objectives or activities similar to the Charity, with a view to ensuring that the Charity's own vision is fulfilled;

- to assist the Board to identify the strengths and weaknesses and the threats and opportunities for the Charity.

The Chief Executive's responsibility for these matters is delegated to him by the Board but there are a number of matters that must be presented to the Board:

- specific risk management policies, including insurance and borrowing limits;

- avoidance of wrongful or fraudulent trading;

- acquisition and disposal of assets or liabilities over 5% of net assets/income;

- investment and capital projects over a similar level;

- substantial commitments including pension funding, contracts of more than one year's duration and giving security over the Charity's assets; and

- contracts not in the ordinary course of business.

Delegation

In fulfilling his or her role, the Chief Executive is assisted by the Finance Director.➡

In particular, the day-to-day implementation of the business plan and budget is delegated by the Chief Executive to the Finance Director.

The Finance Director (and such other senior executives as the Chief Executive may decide from time to time) report to the Chief Executive at monthly management meetings and, between those meetings, on an ad hoc basis as and when the Chief Executive considers necessary.

Reporting

The Chief Executive reports on every aspect of his or her role and, in particular, the implementation of the business plan and budget, to the Board at every meeting. A report is made in writing. The Chief Executive also attends the meeting to discuss the report, other relevant issues and answer questions.

The Chief Executive also reports between Board meetings on an ad hoc basis to the Chairman of the Board.

Appraisal

The Chief Executive's performance is appraised annually by the Chairman and another Trustee selected by the Board.

The Chairman and the other Trustee selected by the Board consult the Finance Director in relation to the performance of the Chief Executive before the appraisal takes place.

Conflicts of interest

The Chief Executive must disclose any personal interest he or she may have in any agreement or proposed agreement with the Charity or in any other matter in which the Charity has an interest.

Any interests which are disclosed are recorded in a register of interests maintained by the Charity.

Finance Director

Terms of Reference

The board (the **'Board'**) of trustees (the **'Trustees'**) of the [Charity] (the **'Charity'**) has adopted the following terms of reference in respect of the Charity's Finance Director.

Role

The Finance Director's role is to act as the chief financial officer of the Charity and, in particular: ➡

- to take day-to-day responsibility for the financial aspects of the implementation of the business plan and the budget under the direction of the Chief Executive;

- to provide clear and effective leadership of the Charity's employees;

- to take responsibility for all aspects of the Charity's finances;

- to work with the Chief Executive to manage the Charity's assets and liabilities;

- to assist the Board to identify the strengths and weaknesses and the threats and opportunities for the Charity.

The Finance Director's responsibility for these matters is delegated to him or her by the Board but there are a number of matters that must be presented to the Board:

- specific risk management policies, including insurance and borrowing limits;

- avoidance of wrongful or fraudulent trading;

- acquisition and disposal of assets or liabilities over 5% of net assets/income;

- investment and capital projects over a similar level;

- substantial commitments including pension funding, contracts of more than one year's duration and giving security over the Charity's assets; and

- contracts not in the ordinary course of business.

Delegation

In fulfilling his or her role, the Finance Director works in conjunction with the Chief Executive.

The Finance Director is responsible for ensuring that the Charity has sufficient well-qualified employees to assist him or her to fulfil his role as effectively as possible.

Reporting

The Finance Director reports on every aspect of his role and, in particular, the financial aspects of the implementation of the business plan and budget, to the Board at every meeting. A report is made in writing. The Finance Director also attends the meeting to discuss the report and other relevant issues and to answer questions.

The Finance Director also reports between Board meetings on an ad hoc basis to the Chief Executive.

➡

Appraisal

The Finance Director's performance is appraised annually by the Chief Executive.

Conflicts of interest

The Finance Director must disclose any personal interest he or she may have in any agreement or proposed agreement with the Charity or in any other matter in which the Charity has an interest.

Any interests which are disclosed are recorded in a register of interests maintained by the Charity.

8.126 If a charity does have employees, their relationship with its trustees will be very important, particularly at the level of the chief executive and the chairman. Trustees may be less visible in the operation of the charity than the senior employees and, notwithstanding that the trustees have ultimate responsibility for the charity; this may mean that a relationship is more difficult to establish.

8.127 Effective management will depend in part on a clear understanding of the scope of the role of the senior employees (as set out in the relevant Terms of Reference) but also in part on an effective appraisal process for senior employees (who will themselves appraise more junior staff). This task can in reality only fall to the trustees.

CONFLICTS OF INTEREST

8.128 Every charity trustee has a duty to avoid any conflict between his or her duties to their charity and their own personal interests. Charity trustees also have a duty to avoid any conflict between their duties to their charity and the duties they may owe some other entity notwithstanding that they have no personal interest in it. It is perhaps more accurately described as a 'conflict of duty' but is generally referred to as a 'conflict of interest'.

8.129 The fundamental issue is that a conflict of interest may compromise a trustee's ability to act solely in the best interests of his or her charity. The Charity Commission[19] takes the following position:

'We recognise that it is inevitable that conflicts of interest occur. The issue is not the integrity of the trustee concerned, but the management of any potential to profit for a person's position as trustee, or for a trustee to be influenced by conflicting loyalty. Even the appearance of a conflict of interest can damage the charity's reputation, so conflicts need to be managed carefully.

The need to declare and manage conflicts of interest does not just apply to charity trustees. The Committee on Standards in the Public Life (the Wicks Committee) set up by the Government with the aim of ensuring the highest standards of propriety in public life, acknowledge the need to declare and manage conflicts of interest, in its 'Seven Principles of Public Life', which it believes should apply to everyone who holds a public office. These

---

[19] The Charity Commission's 'Guide to conflicts of interest for charity trustees'.

principles state that holders of public office should declare any private interest relating to their public duties and should take steps to resolve any conflicts in a way which protects the public interest.'

8.130 The most obvious, and most frequently encountered, example of a conflict of interest arises where a charity trustee wishes to receive any sort of benefit from the charity. The Commission's guidance makes it clear that 'benefit' includes 'any property, goods or services which have a monetary value, as well as money'. There is more about trustee benefits at **6.35**. The fundamental issue is well summarised by the Charity Commission in their Guide to conflicts of interest:

'The rule that a trustee cannot receive any benefit from his or her charity without explicit authority is based on the principle that trustees should not be in a position where their personal interests and their duty to the charity conflict, unless the possibility of personal benefit from which the conflict of interest arises is transparent. Transparency is achieved by requiring explicit authorisation of the benefit, and by ensuring that any particular conflict of interest is properly and openly managed.

It is the potential, rather than the actual, benefit from which the conflict of interest arises which requires authority. In order to avoid the breach of trust and to ensure transparency, authority is required where there is a possibility of benefit. This will avoid accusations of impropriety, which could in turn have a damaging effect on the charity's reputation.'

8.131 This point is well made. The fact that a trustee may not actually receive any benefit from his or her charity or that the charity has received valuable goods, services in return is irrelevant. It is the potential for the trustee to benefit that is significant.

8.132 The Commission's Guide states that:

'Where we find, or are alerted to, an unauthorised benefit, the action we take will depend on the extent of the benefit and cumulative interest and the impact which it has on the charity. We will also take into account other factors such as the reason why the trustees did not obtain authority. We are likely to be more supportive if the trustees can show that the failure to obtain authority was an oversight. However, we will generally not take a sympathetic line where we have previously advised the trustees that the benefit needs to be authorised or where a solicitor is acting for the trustees.

Where the arrangements are in the interests of a charity we will give advice on the management of conflicts of interest and the authorisation of future benefits to trustees. However, we will open a formal inquiry, with the possibility that we might use our statutory powers, in cases where trustees appear to have placed their personal or other interests ahead of those of the charity in order to derive significant benefit at the charity's expense, and where they have deliberately ignored the requirements of the law or of previous advice'.

8.133 Although, as we have indicated, most cases of conflict of interest arise in the context of benefits received by trustees, other forms of conflict can arise. This could be, for example, where there is a conflict of duties, such as where a trustee is appointed by a stakeholder member to whom duties as a trustee or employee are owed.

Managing conflicts of interest

8.134 There are three key aspects of managing trustees' conflicts of interest. These are:

- ensuring that any trustee benefits are properly authorised;

- ensuring that conflicts of interest and potential conflicts of interest are properly identified and disclosed; and

- ensuring that any trustee who has a conflict of interest does not participate in any decision by the board of trustees that relates to it.

Charitable companies

8.135 Trustees of charitable companies are subject to a specific statutory regime in relation to conflicts of interest imposed by the Companies Acts. Section 317 of the Companies Act 1985 imposes an obligation on every trustee of a charitable company to declare the nature of his or her interest in any contract or proposed contract with the charity at the first board meeting at which it is discussed or, if the trustee is not at that meeting, the next meeting he or she attends. Once it comes into force, the Companies Act 2006 will introduce a more comprehensive regime for disclosure. Section 175 of the 2006 Act states that:

> 'A director of a company must avoid a situation in which he has, or can have, a direct or indirect interest that conflicts, or possibly may conflict, with the interests of the company.

8.136 Section 175(4) will provide that this duty is not infringed if either the situation in question cannot reasonably be regarded as likely to give rise to a conflict of interest or if the matter has been authorised by the directors. Section 175(3) provides that the duty does not apply to a conflict of interest arising in relation to a 'transaction or arrangement' with the company itself. Both of these provisions are modified by s 181 in relation to charitable companies. This section requires any conflict to be specifically authorised by the charitable company's constitution and provides that this may be done 'only in relation to the descriptions of transactions or arrangement specified in' the constitution. In addition, the charitable company's trustees can only authorise the conflict if there is a provision enabling them to do so in its constitution.

8.137 The Companies Act 2006 will also impose an express duty on trustees to declare the nature and extent of any interest, whether direct or indirect, which he or she may have in a proposed transaction or arrangement with the company. The declaration has to be made before the company enters into the transaction or arrangement in question. However, it need not be declared if it cannot reasonably be regarded as likely to give rise to a conflict of interest or if the other trustees are already aware of it. In addition, the trustee does not need to declare any interest where he or she is not actually aware of the transaction or arrangement in question.

8.138 The declaration can be made in any way but s 177(2) of the Companies Act specifically provides that it may be made either by giving notice to a meeting of the trustees or by giving notice in accordance with an additional statutory duty placed upon all trustees to declare any interest in any existing transaction or arrangements.

8.139 The duty in relation to existing transactions or arrangements will be imposed by s 182 of the 2006 Act and is in very similar form to the duty imposed by s 177. It provides that:

> 'Where a director of a company is in any way, directly or indirectly, interested in a transaction or arrangement that has been entered into by the company, he must declare the nature and extent of the interest of the other directors in accordance with this section'.

8.140 The declaration must be made as soon as is reasonably practicable. A similar set of exemptions applies to the duty imposed by s 182 of the Companies Act 2006 as applies to the duty imposed by s 177.

8.141 There will therefore be three ways (subject to the coming into force of the Companies Act 2006) in which a trustee can declare an interest in the proposed or existing transaction or arrangement with his or her charitable company:

- by making a declaration at a meeting of the trustees;

- by sending a written notice to all of the other trustees (provided that it is properly sent in accordance with the provisions of the Companies Act 2006, s 184 it is treated as if the declaration had been made at the next meeting of the trustees after the notice is given); or

- by giving a 'general notice' to the trustees of the charitable company that the trustee in question has an interest (as a member, officer or employee or in any other way) in a particular body corporate or firm or connected person and is to be regarded as interested in any transaction or arrangement that may, after the day of the notice, be made with the body corporate, firm or connected person in question. The general notice is not required to be made in writing. However, it is not effective unless it is given at a meeting of the trustees or the trustee in question takes reasonable steps to ensure that it is brought up and read at the next meeting of the trustees after it is given.

8.142 Any failure to declare any conflict relating to any proposed transaction or arrangement will be a breach of trust. The consequences of failing to declare any conflict relating to an existing transaction or arrangement are more significant because the Companies Act 2006, s 183 makes a failure to comply with the requirements of s 182 a criminal offence (it will also obviously be a breach of trust). Section 317(7) of the Companies Act 1985 already makes any trustee who fails to comply with the provisions of s 317 liable to a fine.

8.143 Additional safeguards are imposed by the Companies Acts and s 66 Charities Act 1993 in relation to the potential conflicts of interest of the directors of all companies. Essentially, a company's members must approve certain transactions and arrangements. If not, the transaction or arrangement in question is generally either void or voidable. The provisions in question include:

- directors' long-term service contracts;

- substantial property transactions with directors); and

- payments to directors for loss of office.

8.144 Many of these provisions are unlikely to be relevant to the trustees of a charitable companies (for example, it is very unlikely that any charitable company's constitution will authorise it to pay to trustees under service contracts), but the consent of the Charity Commission is in any event required for any of these transactions or arrangements even if they are approved by the charitable company's members.

Unincorporated charities

8.145 Although there are statutory rules which govern the position in relation to conflicts of interest for the trustees of charities set up as companies, the constitutions of many unincorporated charities may contain express provisions dealing with conflicts. Typically, these may include:

- provisions authorising any trustee benefits;

- provisions obliging trustees to disclose any conflict of interest or potential conflict of interest to the other trustees; and

- provisions which oblige a trustee who has a conflict of interest or a potential conflict not to take part in any decision in relation to the transaction in question.

8.146 Where there are express provisions of this kind in a charity's constitution, they must obviously be adhered to. But the trustees of a charity which does not include express provisions of this kind will still need to take the same steps in relation to conflicts of interest and potential conflicts. They may take the view, therefore, that it will be sensible to alter their charity's constitution to specifically include provisions of this kind. Specific express provisions will be required in order to authorise trustee benefits in any event. There is more about altering constitutional provisions at **15.3**.

Conflict of interests policy

8.147 Regardless of the way in which a charity is set up, its trustees should consider putting in place a policy in relation to conflicts of interest. This should explain in clear and simple terms:

- The purpose of the policy in seeking to identify and manage conflicts of interest and potential conflicts.

- The conflicts of interest (and conflicts of duty) with which the policy is concerned, particularly in relation to benefits to trustees.

- A summary of any provisions which authorise trustees to benefit from the charity.

- The use of a register of interests (if the charity has one).

- An explanation of the way in which trustees should disclose their interest in relation to particular transactions (whether by way of written notice to the charity or a declaration at a trustees' meeting).

- The restrictions on a trustee's ability to vote on (and possibly also to participate in a discussion about) a transaction in which he or she has an interest.

8.148 The charity's trustees may also operate a register of interests in which a record of all other relevant interests, posts, employments and other matters is kept. This is not a legal requirement, but is a sensible part of a wider policy on managing conflicts of interest.

RETIREMENT

8.149 In general, a charity trustee can only retire if there is an express or an implied power to do so. Many charity constitutions will include express powers. But even if there is no express power, a trustee appointed for a fixed term of office will generally have an implied power (and a corresponding obligation) to retire when that term comes to an end.

8.150 In the case of an unincorporated charity, a trustee who wishes to retire may be able to rely upon the statutory power conferred by the Trustee Act 1925, s 39. This will allow the trustees to retire either on the appointment of a new trustee in his or her place or, if there is to be no such new appointment, if at least two trustees or a trust corporation will continue to hold office as trustees of the charity. If there is no trust corporation acting or fewer than two trustees will be left after his or her retirement, the trustee will not be able to rely upon s 39.

REMOVAL

8.151 A trustee of an unincorporated charity may be removed from office as a consequence of the exercise of powers conferred by the Trustee Act 1925, s 36. This will only be relevant where one or more new trustees are to be appointed in place of the retiring trustee. There is more about s 36 at **8.64**.

8.152 A charity trustee will be removed from office where he or she is disqualified from acting as a charity trustee. The circumstances in which a charity trustee is disqualified from acting are set out in the Charities Act 1993, s 72 (and summarised above at **8.29**). Many charities' constitutions will expressly include the circumstances specified by the Charities Act 1993, s 72 as grounds for the removal or automatic retirement of trustees. However, the provisions are overriding, so that they will apply to a charity trustee even if they are not included in the charity's constitution.

8.153 Where a charity trustee is disqualified from acting as a director of a company under the Company Directors Disqualification Act 1986, he or she will also be disqualified from acting as a trustee of any charity, whether set up as a company or not (unless the Charity Commission is willing and able to exercise its discretion to allow them to act). There is more about this at **8.32**.

8.154 A charity's constitution may also include other express circumstances in which a charity trustee is removed from office. Some of the more often encountered examples are:

- Where a trustee is convicted of an offence which does not involve dishonesty or deception (and will not, therefore lead to disqualification under the Charities Act 1993, s 72), the charity's constitution may give its trustees a discretion to remove the trustee who has been convicted of the offence if they reasonably conclude that it will damage the interests of the charity.

- Where a trustee fails to attend a specified number of meetings (usually two or three) the other trustees may be given a discretion to remove the absentee from office. This is usually subject to certain safeguards; the resolution may need to be unanimous and the trustees may need reasonable grounds in order to exercise their discretion. A power of this kind usually only relates to absence without the consent of the trustees, to cater for a trustee who is, for example, absent over the long term due to illness or work overseas.

- The trustees of a charity may occasionally have a power to remove one of their number if they conclude that anything he or she has done is contrary to the best interests of the charity. Again, this will often be subject to certain safeguards; typically the power must be exercised unanimously (with the exception of the trustee who is being removed) and on reasonable grounds.

8.155 In some cases, a charity's constitution may include an express power for its members (or other third parties) to remove a trustee. Typically, 'stakeholder members' of charities may have an express power to appoint and remove one or more individuals as trustees of the charity. A stakeholder member exercising a power of this kind will need to ensure that any restrictions on the power are properly observed. The duty owed by a member to a charity is unclear (except in relation to a CIO or where there is an express duty incorporated into the constitution). In our view, the likelihood is that the court will conclude that any member should act in good faith in the interests of the charity. A stakeholder member that wishes to remove its appointee as a trustee should therefore only do so if it considers that this is in the best interests of the charity. There is more about members' duties at **5.22** and stakeholder members at **5.84**.

8.156 A trustee of a charitable company can be removed by ordinary resolution of the majority of its members. There is a specific procedure for removing a trustee using this power which is set out in the Companies Acts.[20] Broadly, the members have to give the company special notice of the proposed resolution to remove the trustee. The trustee is able to attend and speak at the meeting at which the resolution is proposed. He or she can also require the charity to circulate their written representations in relation to the proposed resolution to the members.

Removal by the court

8.157 The High Court has an inherent jurisdiction to remove any charity trustee and appoint a new trustee in his or her place. An application to remove a trustee can be made by the charity itself, or by any of the charity trustees or by any person interested in the charity (or by any two or more local residents if the charity is a 'local charity'). The application will constitute 'charity proceedings' under the Charities Act 1993, s 33. This means that the consent of the Charity Commission is required before the application can be brought.

8.158 Broadly, the High Court has the power to remove a charity trustee where he or she has committed a wilful breach of trust. Where there is no wilful breach of trust, the courts are likely to be more reluctant to remove a trustee.

Removal by the Charity Commission

8.159 The Charity Commission has jurisdiction to remove any charity trustee on an application by the charity or where the High Court has made an order directing a Scheme under the Charities Act 1993, s 16(4).

---

[20] Companies Act 1985, s 303; Companies Act 2006, ss 168, 169.

8.160 The Charity Commission also has the power to remove a charity trustee where:

- Within the last 5 years, the trustee:
  - having previously been adjudged bankrupt or had his estate sequestrated, has been discharged; or
  - having previously made a composition or arrangement with, or granted a trust deed for, his creditors, has been discharged in respect of it.

- Where the trustee is a corporation in liquidation.

- Where the trustee is incapable of acting by reason of mental disorder within the meaning of the Mental Health Act 1983.

- Where the trustee has not acted and will not declare his willingness or unwillingness to act.

- Where the trustee is outside England and Wales or cannot be found or does not act and his absence or failure to act impedes the proper administration of the charity.[21]

8.161 Where the Charity Commission has opened an Inquiry into a charity, it also has all of the remedial powers conferred upon it by the Charities Act 1993, s 18, which include a power to remove any charity trustee. The Commission's jurisdiction depends upon it being satisfied that there has been any misconduct or mismanagement in the administration of the charity and that it is necessary or desirable to remove the trustee in order to protect the property of the charity.

8.162 Where the Commission exercises its powers under the Charities 1993, s 18 after the opening of the Inquiry to remove a charity trustee, the Commission will also (subject to the coming into force of the Charities Act 2006) have the power to terminate his or her membership of the charity.[22] This provision is intended to allow the Commission to prevent a trustee who has been removed on the grounds of misconduct or mismanagement to continue to exercise his or her powers as a member of the charity in question.

DISCHARGE

8.163 A retiring charity trustee (or a trustee who is being removed) will wish to ensure that he or she is properly discharged from his office as trustee (and, therefore, his duties and liabilities in relation to the charity) once he or she has retired.

Charitable companies

8.164 The position in relation to charitable companies is straightforward. A retiring trustee will give notice of his retirement in accordance with the charity's constitution. The retirement must be notified to Companies House on form 288b, which must be signed by one of the charity's trustees or its secretary (if it has one). The charitable company should amend its register of trustees accordingly.

---

[21]   Charities Act 1993, s 18(4).
[22]   Charities Act 1993, s 18A; expected to come into force in early 2008.

Unincorporated charities

8.165 An unincorporated charity has no legal personality separate from its trustees, so that they are personally liable in respect of liabilities incurred in relation to the charity and will in general hold its assets in their own names (or via a nominee). In order to obtain a discharge from their duties and liabilities, the trustees will need to comply with the requirements of the charity's constitution in respect of retirement, but will also need to ensure that:

- there is a power for the trustee to retire;

- title to the charity's assets is vested in the continuing trustees; and

- the retiring trustee is indemnified in respect of the liabilities he or she has incurred in relation to the charity.

Power to retire

8.166 The powers of retirement available to trustees are explained at **8.149**. Where a new trustee is to be appointed in the place of a retiring trustee of an unincorporated charity, it will be important to ensure that there are at least two continuing trustees of the charity (or a trust corporation acting as trustee) in order to ensure that the retiring trustee is properly discharged. This restriction is imposed by the Trustee Act 1925, s 37 (although it is subject to anything to the contrary in the charity's constitution).

Vesting of assets

8.167 Where a trustee of an unincorporated charity retires using the statutory power conferred by the Trustee Act 1925, s 39 and he or she does so by deed, the Trustee Act 1925, s 40 provides that, unless the deed contains provisions to the contrary, it will vest all of the charity's assets in the continuing trustees. Section 40 does not apply to every asset (for example, mortgages of land, transfers of shares or securities or transfers of registered land). Assets of this kind will need to be dealt with individually.

8.168 Section 40 of the Trustee Act 1925 does not apply where a trustee retires under an express or an implied power. In practice, therefore, a trustee should retire using a deed which recites that he or she relies upon the power conferred by s 39 (and any other power, express or implied, available to them). This will bring into effect the provisions of the Trustee Act 1925, s 40, provided the retirement is by deed.

8.169 Where no deed is used, the same effect can be achieved by discharging the retiring trustee by resolution of a meeting of the charity trustees, members or other persons who have power to give the discharge.[23] In general, the power to give a discharge will be vested in the continuing trustees, but the position may vary from charity to charity.

Indemnity

8.170 As a general principle, every charity trustee is entitled to an indemnity against the charity's assets in respect of liabilities that he or she has properly incurred in relation to it. The right to an indemnity continues after the trustees' retirement. A charity's

---

[23] Charities Act 1993, s 83.

constitution may contain an express power for the continuing trustees to give an express indemnify to a retiring trustee on this basis. If there is no express power, it should be possible to imply a power (on the basis that the legal right to an indemnity exists in any event), but this will be subject to the same restrictions as any express power. In other words, the liabilities that can be indemnified against must be 'properly' incurred. This excludes any indemnity in respect of liabilities incurred as a consequence of any breach of trust. See **6.22** for more in relation to this.

8.171 Although a charity trustee's right to an indemnity in respect of properly incurred liabilities arises automatically, many retiring trustees will prefer to see an express indemnity (appropriately qualified in relation to liabilities incurred in breach of trust) set out in a deed of retirement which is signed by both the retiring trustee and the continuing trustees.

Notification

8.172 There is no obligation to notify the Charity Commission of the retirement of a charity trustee. The fact that he or she has retired will be picked up in the charity's annual return for the period during which the trustee has retired.

9

CHARITY ASSETS

9.1   This chapter is intended to summarise the legal basis on which charities hold assets. As we will explain, there are a number of legal concepts in this area that are unique to charities. This is of more than simply academic interest. The basis on which a charity holds a particular asset will determine the powers and duties its trustees have in relation to it. It may mean that the asset in question can only be applied for a particular charitable purpose within a wider range of purposes for which the charity has been established. Or it may mean that the charity has no power to sell the asset or, if it does, that there will be restrictions on the way in which it can apply the proceeds of sale.

9.2   The basis on which assets are held will also have an impact on the way in which the trustees of a charity formulate their reserves policy. This is explained in detail. We also go on to explain some of the specific considerations that apply to charities holding land, including the restrictions on its disposal imposed by the Charities Act 1993.

GOVERNANCE

9.3   Understanding the way in which a charity holds it assets is an important governance issue for its trustees. Failure to observe particular legal restrictions may mean that the trustees act in breach of trust, with the potential for personal liability as a consequence (see **6.18** for more on this). As importantly, the trustees must understand the way in which a particular asset can be used as part of their strategic planning for the charity generally. For example, trustees who wish to raise finance to develop one aspect of their charity's activities by using the proceeds of sale of a particular asset will be frustrated by a restriction on their ability to sell that asset or, if it is capable of being sold, on their ability to apply the proceeds of sale. Trustees must also be able to formulate a reserves policy for their charity, something that will be difficult to do unless the basis on which assets are held is clear and understood.

UNINCORPORATED CHARITIES

9.4   In looking at the way in which charities hold their assets, there is a fundamental distinction to be drawn between incorporated and unincorporated charities. Broadly, the assets of an unincorporated charity are almost invariably held on trust. The assets of a charitable trust are, as the name suggests, always held on trust. And while the assets of a charitable unincorporated association can be held in a number of different ways, assets held by a charitable unincorporated association will generally be held on trust for its charitable purposes. This is consistent with the fact that the individual members of a charitable unincorporated association have no personal entitlement to its assets.[1]

---

[1]   *Re Morrison* (1967) 111 SJ 758; *Re Finger's Will Trusts* [1972] Ch 286.

INCORPORATED CHARITIES

9.5   The assets of a charitable company are almost invariably held as corporate, rather than trust, assets. In other words, the assets are beneficially owned by the company itself rather than being held on trust by it. The constitution of the company will oblige it to apply its assets for its charitable purposes. In that sense, the company's 'beneficial' ownership of the assets is qualitatively different to the beneficial ownership of a commercial company's assets. But while the company's trustees can be liable for a 'breach of trust' if they mis-apply its assets, the assets themselves are not held on a trust of the kind found in the context of unincorporated charities.

9.6   The leading case in this area confirms that, while a company may hold its assets as a 'trustee' for charitable purposes where its constitution places a binding obligation on it to apply its assets for exclusively charitable purposes, a company is not a 'trustee' in 'the strict sense' of its corporate assets. Rather, the company is in a position 'analogous to that of a trustee in relation to its corporate assets'.[2] This decision was at least partly based upon the inconsistency that the court thought would arise if a company could incur liabilities without holding any of its assets beneficially and therefore available to meet those liabilities.

9.7   The position is likely to be similar in relation to other charitable corporations. The approach the court will take to CIOs remains to be seen, but the likelihood is that, given their limited liability status, this will be the same as the approach to charitable companies.

TRUST ASSETS

9.8   The fact that incorporated charities do not hold their corporate assets on trust does not mean that they cannot hold particular assets on trust. Many incorporated charities hold trust assets of this kind, particularly where they have been given an asset for a particular purpose or on terms that restrict the charity's ability to dispose of the asset or apply its proceeds. There is more about restrictions of this kind at **9.27**.

9.9   This is an important governance issue for the trustees of incorporated charities. At the most basic level, the powers the charity has to deal with trust assets will depend upon the terms of the trust itself rather than the constitution of the charitable company. So while a power to charge corporate assets in a charitable company's constitution may be clear, it will not apply to any trust assets held by the charity. If the trustees do something with a trust asset that they do not have power to do, they may be personally liable for a breach of trust as a consequence. In addition, assets held on trust will not generally be available to the charitable company's creditors in the event of its liquidation except where the company has contracted in its capacity as trustee in respect of the asset in question and/or granted security over it.

9.10   It is very important, therefore, that the trustees of an incorporated charity identify any trust assets held by the charity and distinguish them from its corporate assets. The first point of call will usually be the charity's accounts, which should give some guidance on the basis on which assets are held (see **9.59** for more in relation to this). Having said that, the charity's accounts are not definitive. They will generally

---

[2]   *Liverpool and District Hospital for Diseases of the Heart v Att-Gen* [1981] Ch 193.

depend upon whether the underlying legal position has been correctly interpreted. This can, in turn, depend upon whether the terms of, for example, a gift of a particular asset to the charity has been correctly interpreted.

9.11 All of this means that charity assets are trust assets where:

- the charity is unincorporated; or

- the charity is incorporated but holds the assets in question on trust.

9.12 Why is it important to recognise trust assets? We have explained the significance of trust assets held by incorporated charities at **9.8**. But there is a wider significance, which is that the terms of the trust may impose certain restrictions on the way in which the trust assets can be applied. There are two types of restriction that may apply:

- Restrictions that mean that the assets can only be applied for particular charitable purposes within a charity's wider charitable purposes (usually referred to as a 'special trust').

- Restrictions that control how trust assets can be used or applied for particular charitable purposes, rather than restrictions on the purposes themselves (usually referred to as 'endowment').

SPECIAL TRUSTS

9.13 The restrictions may mean that the assets can only be applied for particular charitable purposes within the wider charitable purposes of the charity that holds them on trust. For example, a school might hold a portfolio of investments to pay for music scholarships for pupils. This is a charitable educational purpose, but one that is narrower than the general educational purposes of the school. Therefore, the school cannot use the trust assets to pay for any other aspect of its operations.

9.14 Restrictions of this kind will usually be imposed by the person who has given the trust assets to the charity in the first place, although the charity itself may have exercised a power under its constitution to impose the restrictions itself.

9.15 Assets held on this basis are usually held on what is referred to as a 'special trust'. There is a definition of 'special trust' in the 1993 Act:

> "'Special trust" means property which is held and administered by or on behalf of the charity, and is so held and administered on separate trusts relating only to that property...'[3]

9.16 This definition applies for the purposes of the 1993 Act but is used by the Charity Commission generally. See, for example, the Commission's Glossary of terms used in their Operational Guidance which confirms that:

> 'It follows that the objects of a special trust must be narrower than those of the main charity'.

---

[3]   Charities Act 1993, s 97(1).

This is consistent with the definition of 'special trust' in the 1993 Act, which goes on to say that while property held on a special trust is 'held and administered on separate trusts relating only to that property', a special trust 'shall not, by itself, constitute a charity' for the purpose of reporting under the Act.

9.17   Assets held on a special trust should be identified in a charity's accounts as a 'restricted fund'. There is more about this at **9.59**.

9.18   Assets held on a special trust can also be income or endowment. This is explained in more detail at **9.19**.

INCOME AND ENDOWMENT

9.19   The other kind of restrictions that may be imposed on trust assets relate to how they can be used or applied for particular charitable purposes rather than restrictions on those purposes. Charity lawyers often refer to the 'expenditure' of charity assets rather than their use or application. This reflects the terminology used by the Charities Act 1993 Act, but the term really means no more than how the assets can be used or applied.

9.20   Restrictions of the kind mentioned in **9.19** will make the trust assets 'endowment'. But in order to understand fully what constitutes a charity's endowment, it is important to understand how a charity holds other assets that its trustees are free to apply for its purposes without restriction. Assets of this kind are usually referred to as 'income'. The Charity Commission explains the position in another way by stating that income is all of the financial resources 'that become available to a charity and that the trustees are required to apply in furtherance of its charitable purposes within a reasonable time of receipt'. This is quite correct (and there is more about trustees' duties to apply income at **9.64**), but the point is essentially this; a charity's trustees are free to apply its income for the charity's purposes (subject only to any restriction on the purposes for which the income can be applied where the relevant assets are held on a special trust) and are obliged to do so within a reasonable time of its receipt.

9.21   As is often the case in relation to charity law, the terminology used in this context can be confusing although, unusually, perhaps more so for the lawyer than the layman. This is because trusts law (as it applies to private trusts) distinguishes between the 'income' and the 'capital' of assets and has developed rules to distinguish between the two things and the way in which a trust's beneficiaries are entitled to them. In the context of trusts law, 'capital' means the principal of an asset, while 'income' is whatever return it produces that is not an increase in the value of the principal itself.

9.22   In a charitable context, 'income' can include assets that a trusts lawyer would categorise as capital as well as those he or she would categorise as income. So a portfolio of investments held by a charity without any restriction on its application will be 'income' notwithstanding that the portfolio is made up of capital assets and can produce both capital gains and income. This is also true of the corporate assets of an incorporated charity, although its trustees owe a different duty in respect of the application or expenditure of those assets from the duty owed by the trustees of an unincorporated charity (there is more about this at **9.64**).

9.23   As we have explained, if a charity's trust assets are not 'income' then they are 'endowment'. There is no statutory definition of 'endowment' which, as we have said, refers essentially to those assets of a charity that are under a legal restriction that obliges them to be retained by the charity for its benefit and which the trustees are not, therefore, free to apply. Endowment assets take two forms; 'expendable endowment' and 'permanent endowment'. These are dealt with in more detail below.

9.24   Endowment held by a charity is broadly equivalent to the capital of private trusts. In fact, endowment is often referred to as 'capital' in the Charity Commission's published guidance.

EXPENDABLE ENDOWMENT

9.25   The Charity Commission's definition of 'expendable endowment' is as follows:

> 'An expendable endowment fund is a fund that must be invested to produce income. Depending on the conditions attached to the endowment, the trustees will have a legal power to convert all or part of it into an income fund which can then be spent.'

In other words, an expendable endowment asset can be applied by the trustees of a charity, but the general duty to apply it for their charity's purposes within a reasonable period of receipt does not apply. The Commission confirm this:

> 'An expendable endowment differs from an income fund in that there is no actual requirement to spend the principal for the purposes of the charity unless or until the trustees decide to.'

The reference here to 'principal' is to 'capital' or 'endowment'. They go on to say:

> 'However, income generated from expendable endowment ... should be spent for the purposes of the charity within a reasonable time of receipt.'[4]

The reference to 'income' here must be to 'income' in the sense it is used in relation to private trusts.

9.26   Why is it important to identify expendable endowment? Essentially, because the trustees should understand their power to apply it at their discretion rather than subject to the duty in respect of income to apply it within a reasonable time of receipt, which will in turn affect their judgement about the level of their charity's reserves and probably also their strategic financial planning for its operations.

PERMANENT ENDOWMENT

9.27   Unlike expendable endowment, 'permanent endowment' is defined by the Charities Act 1993. The definition is:

---

4   Charity Commission's Glossary for its Operational Guidance.

'"permanent endowment' means, in relation to any charity, property held subject to a restriction on its being expended for the purposes of the charity.'[5]

This is the definition that applies for the purposes of the 1993 Act. The Commission's Operational Guidance expands upon this:

'Permanent endowment is property of the charity (including land, buildings, cash or investments) which the trustees may not spend as if it were income. It must be held permanently, sometimes to be used in furthering the charity's purposes, sometimes to produce an income for the charity.[6]

9.28 The concept of holding assets permanently on trust is unique to charity law. In the context of private trusts there is a body of law devoted to preventing what is usually referred to as the 'alienation' of assets permanently (these are the rules against perpetuities and excessive accumulations). And yet this concept is accepted in relation to charities, presumably because society has always accepted that donors to charity should be free to set whatever restrictions they choose on assets that they give away and that there will always be a requirement for charity.

9.29 In practice, charity permanent endowment is often land and is often held to be used 'in furthering the charity's purposes', usually because a donor has given it to the charity or the charity has acquired it (often in the dim and distant past) to be used for the purposes of the charity. So, for example, an almshouse charity is likely to hold its almshouses as permanent endowment assets for use by its beneficiaries. Land used in this way is often referred to by the Charity Commission as 'specie land' (their definition is 'land required to be used for a particular charitable purpose').[7]

9.30 The other form of permanent endowment often encountered (and used 'to produce an income for the charity') is an investment portfolio, made up of cash and investment assets.

Identifying permanent endowment

9.31 How does one identify permanent endowment in the first place? This is often difficult, particularly where an asset (often land) has been held by a charity for a very long period of time, with no or limited written evidence of the position. And in assessing the status of charity assets, one has to apply a presumption set out in the Charities Act 1993:

'A charity shall be deemed for the purposes of this Act to have a permanent endowment unless all property held for the purposes of the charity may be expended for those purposes without distinction between capital and income.'[8]

9.32 Effectively, therefore, a charity's asset is presumed to be permanent endowment unless there is some evidence that the trustees have the power to apply or spend it as income. This definition applies only for the purposes of the 1993 Act and not to the construction a court might place on the documents relating to a particular asset, but any application to the Commission for an Order or Scheme under the 1993 Act 9 as to

---

[5]   Charities Act 1993, s 96(3).
[6]   Charity Commission's Glossary for its Operational Guidance.
[7]   Or 'functional land'.
[8]   Charities Act 1993, s 96(3).

which, see **4.19** and **4.26**) will obviously bring the presumption into play. For practical purposes, therefore, it is generally advisable to assume that the presumption applies.

9.33   There is no corresponding definition in relation to expendable endowment (see **9.25**). In fact, the Commission's guidance confirms that in relation to donated assets:

> 'If there is really no evidence, either direct or circumstantial, as to a donor's intention, then a gift should be treated as income.'[9]

9.34   More often than not, whether an asset is permanent endowment will depend upon the way in which the documents recording its gift or acquisition are construed. A reference to the gift of an asset 'in perpetuity' is likely to be very clear evidence that the gift is permanent endowment. Other cases may be more difficult to interpret and may also lead to disagreement with the Charity Commission.

9.35   A charity may hold a permanent endowment asset subject to an obligation to retain it permanently and with no power to sell or otherwise dispose of it. Alternatively, a charity may hold permanent endowment but with a power to sell it and reinvest the proceeds in other permanent endowment assets. This will often be true, for example, of a permanent endowment investment portfolio, within which investments are regularly sold and the proceeds reinvested. It would also be true of land held for, eg recreational purposes that is sold in order to buy replacement land. The Charity Commission's guidance recognises this:

> 'The terms of the endowment may permit assets within the fund to be sold and reinvested, or may provide that some or all of the assets are retained indefinitely (for example, a particular building)'.[10]

9.36   What is the significance of a charity holding permanent endowment? The Charity Commission sum the position up as follows:

> 'Normally, trustees cannot spend any part of the charity's permanent endowment. Not only would it be contrary to the trusts of the charity, but if they did, the capital would de depleted and therefore would generate less income, thus reducing the charity's capacity to carry out its work. Eventually the charity might simply cease to exist because of lack of funds, whereas the intention was that the help or facilities provided by the charity would last forever and thereby serve successive generations of the community.'[11]

Buildings

9.37   As we have indicated, some permanent endowment assets may be held with a power to dispose of them and apply the proceeds in purchasing other permanent endowment assets. It is worth mentioning the Charity Commission's approach to buildings in this context. Many charities hold permanent endowment land which, for one reason or another, they wish to sell. This might be because the land can no longer be used effectively for the purpose for which it is given or that its investment value (as, say development land) can, if unlocked, make a real difference to a charity's operational capabilities.

---

[9]   OG 43 B4.
[10]   Charity Commission's Glossary for its Operational Guidance.
[11]   CC 38.

9.38   In this context, it is worth remembering that the Charity Commission takes the view that buildings are not generally permanent endowment assets. This means that if a charity sells a piece of permanent endowment land with a view to using the proceeds to build facilities on other land it owns, the Charity Commission will treat this as the expenditure of the permanent endowment. This is on the basis that buildings are 'wasting assets', with a value that will decline over time, presumably in contrast to an investment portfolio or land. Because of their limited lifespan, buildings are assumed not to be able to hold their value permanently.

9.39   This approach can lead to some strange practical consequences. A charity may need a new building to operate effectively but cannot use the proceeds of sale of a piece of permanent endowment land which is held as an investment to pay for it to be built (at least not without an order for 'recoupment', as described below).

Recoupment

9.40   Where permanent endowment assets are held without a power to sell them and reinvest the proceeds in replacement property, the Charity Commission's consent will be required (usually by way of Order (see **4.16** for more on this)) to the disposal. Where a charity has a power of sale, no Order will generally be required where the proceeds of sale are to be used to purchase replacement property.

9.41   Where the charity's trustees have a power to dispose of a permanent endowment asset but no power to spend the proceeds of sale on some operational activity rather than replacing the asset, the Commission's consent will also be required but will generally only be available on the basis of what is usually referred to as 'recoupment'.

9.42   The trustees of a charity that holds permanent endowment have a duty to retain it permanently. For this reason, the Charity Commission will generally only authorise the expenditure of permanent endowment on the basis that whatever is spent must be reimbursed by the charity out of its future income. In other words, the permanent endowment that is spent is treated as a loan made to the charity for its general purposes that must be repaid over a particular period. This is 'recoupment' (sometimes referred to as 'replacement').

9.43   For this reason, where the Charity Commission agrees to the expenditure of a charity's permanent endowment, it will generally only do so by making an Order that provides for recoupment. This is likely to be on the following basis:

> 'Replacement is on the basis of a simple pound-for-pound repayment by the investment of annual instalments for an agreed number of years out of the income of the charity. As an example, £10,000 borrowed from capital would require annual instalments of £500 if paid back over 20 years or annual instalments of £1,000 if paid back over 10 years. The income from the invested annual instalments does not have to be reinvested and can be used for the charity's purposes.'[12]

9.44   The Charity Commission does not generally require the payment of any interest in respect of the recouped funds. The recouped funds are effectively loaned to the charity on an interest free basis.

---

[12]   CC 38.

Security

9.45 Notwithstanding the restrictions on the disposal of permanent endowment, the consent of the Charity Commission is not required to the grant of security over it, except as required by the Charities Act 1993, s 38. This is dealt with in more detail in **Chapter 12**. There is obviously a degree of contradiction here. While permanent endowment land cannot be sold to generate income for a charity without the Commission's consent, it can be charged as security for a loan which may be spent by the charity in the same way as income without the Commission's consent, notwithstanding that a failure by the charity to meet its obligations to the lender may result in the forced sale of the land by the lender under its security to meet the charity's liabilities.

CONVERTING PERMANENT ENDOWMENT INTO INCOME

9.46 The Commission's power to make Orders for the disposal of permanent endowment requiring recoupment is based upon the provisions of the 1993 Act that authorise it to issue directions binding on a charity's trustees which may include directions 'requiring expenditure charged to capital to be recouped out of income within a specified time'.[13]

9.47 The Charity Commission regards itself as bound to make Orders that include directions for recoupment, but may in exceptional circumstances consider whether to do so without recoupment. This is generally where a charity has specie or functional property comprised in its permanent endowment which it can no longer afford to maintain or improve to meet the charity's purposes. The Commission may be willing to authorise the expenditure of permanent endowment to pay for its maintenance or improvement but this is only likely to be on the basis that the trustees make the case for the making of an Order without recoupment by showing that:

- retaining the property is essential in order to allow the charity to advance its purposes;

- there are no other funds available (including funds borrowed from a commercial lender) to pay for the maintenance and improvement of the property and the charity's income is insufficient to meet an Order for recoupment; and

- the buildings are long lasting and the charity will be able to make provision for repairs out of its future income.

STATUTORY POWERS TO CONVERT PERMANENT ENDOWMENT INTO INCOME

9.48 Subject to the coming into force of the relevant provisions of the Charities Act 2006 (which is expected in early 2008), the Charities Act 1993 contains statutory provisions which may authorise an unincorporated charity to spend its permanent endowment assets, except for any specie or functional land ('land held on trusts which stipulate that it is to be used for the purposes, or any particular purposes, of the

---

[13] Charities Act 1993, s 26(4).

charity').[14] The provisions introduced by the 2006 Act will significantly widen a charity's power to convert permanent endowment into income. The existing provisions of the Charities Act 1993 (ss 74 and 75) are limited to very small charities. In summary, the new provisions are as follows:

- Where the trustees of an unincorporated charity with gross income in its last financial year of more than £1,000 and permanent endowment (excluding specie or functional land) given by one or more individuals or institutions with a value in excess of £10,000 conclude that the trust on which the endowment is held could be carried out more effectively if the capital of the fund could be spent as well as the fund's income, rather than just the income, they can resolve that the capital of the endowment (or a part of it) should be spent.

- The trustees must send a copy of the resolution to the Charity Commission. The Commission can then do a number of things. It can direct the trustees to give public notice of the resolution and take into account any representations made by anyone interested in the charity who responds to the notice. The Commission can also direct the trustees to provide it with additional information in relation to the resolution.

- The Commission must then consider the resolution, taking into account any evidence which is available in relation to the wishes of the person who originally gave the endowment to the charity and any changes in the circumstances of the charity since the gift was made (these include 'its financial position, the needs of its beneficiaries, and the social, economic and legal environment in which it operates').

- The Commission has three months from the date on which it receives the resolution (or the date on which public notice is given, if this is directed by the Commission) to consider whether to agree to the resolution. If it notifies the trustees that it does agree to the resolution within that period or they hear nothing from the Commission, the trustees are entitled to go ahead and spend the endowment in accordance with the resolution.

- The Commission cannot agree to the resolution if they conclude that its implementation will not 'accord with the spirit' of the original gift of the endowment or that the trustees have not complied with their obligations in respect of the statutory power to spend the endowment.

9.49   The Charities Act 2006 will introduce into the Charities Act 1993 (expected to come into force in early 2008) a similar statutory power in respect of any unincorporated charity with gross income in its last financial year of £1,000 or less or permanent endowment given by one or more individuals or institutions with a value of £10,000 or less. The power enables the trustees to resolve to spend all or part of the endowment (excluding specie or functional land) without the Charity Commission's consent provided that they conclude that the trust on which the endowment is held could be carried out more effectively if the capital of the fund could be spent as well as the fund's income, rather than just the income. There is no obligation to notify the Commission that the resolution has been passed.[15]

---

14   Charities Act 1993, s 75A.
15   Charities Act 1993, s 75A.

9.50 The Charities Act 2006 will also introduce into the Charities Act 1993 (expected to come into force in early 2008) a statutory power to spend endowment held on certain special trusts (see **9.13** for more on this). The power applies where a special trust is treated by the Commission as a 'distinct charity' for the purposes of the 1993 Act. In other words, where a charity or its trustees hold permanent endowment for the charity's purposes but as part of a separately registered charity. Essentially, the trustees have a power to spend permanent endowment (other than specie or functional land) held on a special trust on the same basis as any other charity with endowment.[16] This can include endowment held on special trust by an incorporated charity. The procedure to be adopted in relation to the expenditure of the endowment will depend upon the level of the charity's income and the value of the endowment (as to which, see **9.48**).

CONVERTING INCOME INTO ENDOWMENT

9.51 Some unincorporated charities will have a power in their constitution to convert income into endowment. As is the case in the context of private trusts, this is usually referred to as a power of 'accumulation'. By exercising the power, the charity's trustees can accumulate income and change it into endowment.

9.52 Powers of accumulation are not common and the Charity Commission take the view that they cannot be exercised 'in default'. In other words, the power must be expressly exercised by the trustees with the deliberate intention of changing income into endowment. Income cannot be changed into endowment by a simple failure to apply it over the long term. This sort of 'thoughtless accumulation' is likely to do no more than put the trustees in breach of their duty to apply the income within a reasonable time of its receipt (see **9.64** in relation to this). The Commission have this to say on the subject:

> 'If trustees are allowed power to accumulate income, that power must be consciously exercised in a proper way with the good of the charity's beneficiaries in mind. A failure to consider the matter and simply to allow the income to accumulate without good reason amounts to a breach of trust.'[17]

9.53 The trustees of a charity which has no constitutional power to accumulate income may occasionally seek the Charity Commission's authority for accumulation. This might be because, for example, the charity has received an exceptionally large amount of income which the trustees cannot hope to spend in line with their duty to apply it within a reasonable time of receipt. The Charity Commission give the example of 'an exceptionally large dividend or other distribution from a company, which is technically 'income' but in common sense appears to be a return of part of the capital investment'. Where the charity's trustees have a duty to maintain a balance between capital income and trusts, a distribution of this kind may upset that balance if it is treated as income. Authority for accumulation will be given by way of a Scheme or Order.

9.54 There are three situations where, at first glance, income may appear to be converted into endowment. It is important to distinguish these situations from accumulation because the legal analysis is that the assets remain as income. The three situations are:

---

[16] Charities Act, s 74B.
[17] Charity Commission report 1992, paragraph 98.

- designation;

- reserves; and

- total return approach to investment.

Designation

9.55   The trustees of a charity will often earmark a part of its income for a particular purpose or project. Earmarking income in this way is usually referred to as 'designation' and the income which is earmarked as 'designated funds'. The key point to appreciate is that the designation does not in any way restrict or commit the charity to spend the income for the purpose for which it has been designated. The trustees are free to use designated funds for some other purpose if the charity's circumstances change. This is expressly confirmed by the Charity Commission:

> 'The act of designating particular funds neither:
>
> - allows those funds to be used for a purpose for which they could not previously be used; nor
> - by itself provides the justification of their use for the designated purpose.'[18]

9.56   Designated funds must be expressly identified in a charity's accounts.

Reserves

9.57   Many charities reserve part of their income from one financial year with a view to spending it in future financial years. The legal position in relation to reserves is explained at **9.64**. The important point to appreciate is that, unless accumulated using an express power of accumulation, reserving income does not change it into endowment.

Total return approach to investment

9.58   Charities with permanent endowment made up of investment assets will often ask the Charity Commission to authorise its investment on a 'total return' basis using an Order. This is explained in more detail at **10.103**. An Order of this kind will generally have the effect of treating the investment return as endowment unless and until the charity's trustees allocate it to a 'trust for application' (essentially, treating it as income). However, the underlying legal analysis is that the income received continues to be income and is not converted into capital.

RESTRICTED AND UNRESTRICTED FUNDS

9.59   It is obviously essential that assets held on trust are accounted for in such a way that a charity's accounts gives an overall view of its financial position. For accounting purposes, a distinction is drawn between the restricted and unrestricted funds of a charity. Looking at a charity's accounts is often the best starting point for an assessment of how it holds its property and it is obviously important that the terminology used in the accounts is intelligible.

---

[18]   CC 19.

9.60 A charity's unrestricted funds are all of the assets capable of being applied by the trustees without restriction. In other words, a charity's income will be its unrestricted funds. Some unrestricted funds are described as 'designated funds' for accounting purposes. As we have explained, this means no more than that they have been earmarked by trustees as available for a particular charitable purpose, but are not subject to a legally binding restriction.

9.61 The Charity Commission defines restricted funds as follows:

> Restricted funds are funds subject to specific trusts which may be declared by the donor(s), or with their authority (eg, in a public appeal), but still within the objects of the charity. Restricted funds may be restricted income funds, which are expendable at the discretion of the trustees in furtherance of some particular aspect(s) of the objects of the charity, or they may be capital funds, where the assets are required to be invested, or retained for actual use, rather than expended.

9.62 This definition is drawn from the Charities SORP 2005. The reference to 'specific trusts' must be to 'special trusts'. The reference to restricted income funds is clear. The reference to restricted capital funds is a reference to endowment.

9.63 It follows that 'unrestricted funds' are 'expendable at the discretion of the trustees in furtherance of the charity's objects'. Again, this definition is drawn from the Charities SORP 2005. See **Chapter 14** for more in relation to the SORP 2005.

RESERVES

9.64 The trustees of an unincorporated charity have duties to ensure that:

- the income of the charity is applied as income unless it is endowment; and

- the income is applied for the charity's purposes within a reasonable time of receipt (subject to any provision in the charity's constitution which authorises the accumulation of all or part of the income as capital).

9.65 The duty to apply the income of a charity within a reasonable time of receipt is based upon the case of *A-G v Alford* (1855) 4 De G M & G 843. This is an old case, but the Charity Commission point to more recent case law in the context of private trusts which by analogy, suggest that a failure to distribute income within a reasonable time of receipt is likely to constitute a breach of trust by the trustee.

Charitable companies

9.66 The duty to apply income within a reasonable time of receipt applies to trust assets held by charitable companies. It does not, however, apply to the corporate assets of a charitable company. As the Commission recognises, company law does not impose any duty on the directors of a charitable company to apply its corporate property within a reasonable time of its receipt. But in the Commission's view, this does not 'sanction its indefinite aggregation' and 'it is legitimate to expect that a charitable company's income resources should be used to further its objects'.[19]

---

[19] OG 43 B2.

9.67   The Commission bases this 'legitimate expectation' on a case relating to a trading company whose members, the court held, had a legitimate expectation that they would receive dividends out of its profit.[20] Whatever the correctness of this analogy, the trustees of a charitable company will obviously do well to plan on the basis that this is the approach the Commission will take notwithstanding that they have a greater degree of flexibility in relation to the application of income than the trustees of an unincorporated charity.

Power to hold reserves

9.68   Notwithstanding the duty imposed on the trustees of an unincorporated charity to apply its income within a reasonable time of receipt, there are likely to be many cases where, for good practical reasons, it is not possible or appropriate for all of the charity's income to be distributed promptly. The Charity Commission recognises this:

> 'It is recognised that the charity may need to retain some reserve of income in order to ensure the continued furtherance of its objects. This is reflected by the inclusion of the word "reasonable" in the phrase "within a reasonable period of receipt". But it is clearly not "reasonable" to retain income when there is no connection between doing so and ensuring the proper administration of the trust.'[21]

9.69   The key point is ensuring that the reserve of income is made in order to ensure the 'proper administration' of the charity in question.

9.70   Some charity constitutions may give their trustees an express power to hold income in reserve, although provisions of this kind are relatively unusual. More often, trustees will need to rely upon an implied power to make a reserve. Clearly, it is likely to be impossible to imply a power where there are any other express provisions in a charity's constitution which are inconsistent with this approach.

9.71   Ensuring that they have a sufficiently wide expressly implied power to hold reserves is an important consideration for a charity's trustees because, without it, holding reserves will amount to a breach of trust. The Commission says this:

> 'Before trustees can use income funds in a way which does not comply with this duty, they need to have a legal power which overrides this general duty. Holding income funds in reserve rather than expanding them is one use that does not comply with the duty, since the trustees are delaying the application beyond what the law would normally accept as a reasonable time. Trustees therefore need a legal power to hold income funds in reserve.'[22]

9.72   As with all powers, it is not enough for the trustees simply to exercise their power to hold reserves of income. The matter will only be exercisable by them without giving rise to a breach of trust if they consider that what they are doing is necessary and in the best interests of the charity. In the words of the Commission, 'if it is done without justification, the holding of income in reserve may amount to a breach of trust'.

---

[20]   *Re A company No 370 of 987* [1988] 1 WLR 1068.
[21]   OG 43 B2.
[22]   CC 19.

Defining reserves

9.73 Before a charity's trustees can take any decision in relation to the exercise of an express or implied power to earn income, it is important that they understand which part of the charity's income will constitute 'reserves'. The Charity Commission's approach is as follows:

> 'The term 'reserves' has a variety of technical and ordinary meanings, depending on the context in which it is used. As in SORP 2000, here we use the term 'reserves' (unless otherwise indicated) to describe that part of a charity's income funds that is freely available for its general purposes. 'Reserves' are therefore the resources the charity has or can make available to spend for any or all of the charity's purposes once it has met its commitments and covered its other planned expenditure.
>
> More specifically SORP 2000 defines reserves as income which becomes available to the charity and is to be spent at the trustees' discretion in furtherance of any of the charity's objects (sometimes referred to as 'general purpose' income); but which is not yet spent, committed or designated (i.e. is 'free'). This definition of reserves therefore excludes:
>
> - permanent endowment;
> - expendable endowment;
> - restricted funds;
> - designated funds; and
> - income funds which could only be realised by disposing of fixed assets held for charity use.'[23]

9.74 Accumulated income will feature in this list, as either permanent or expendable endowment.

Expendable endowment and designated funds

9.75 The Commission say this in relation to expendable endowment (see **9.25**) and designated funds (see **9.55**):

> 'There is an argument for saying that expendable endowment and designated income funds ought to be counted as reserves. The argument is that in each case the trustees are free to regard the funds, if they so choose, as available for general purpose expenditure. There are no legal restrictions preventing trustees treating those two types of funds as free, general purpose funds. But there are practical reasons, explained below, why the funds should not normally be regarded as free (though there are exceptions).'[24]

9.76 As regards expendable endowment, the practical reason is that many charities with an expendable endowment depend upon the income it produces to fund their operations. Spending the endowment is likely to reduce the income available to the charity and may jeopardise its operations as a result. That may leave the charity to seek income from other sources or cut back on the scope of its operations. In that sense, the expendable endowment is not treated by the Charity Commission as funds 'freely available' for the charity's general purposes.

9.77 Having said this, it is important to bear in mind that income generated by expendable endowment is income subject to the trustees' general duty to spend it within

---

[23] CC 19.
[24] CC 19.

a reasonable time of receipt. Reinvesting the income as part of the expendable endowment will not have the effect of converting the income into endowment (unless the trustees have a power of accumulation).

9.78 The practical reason for excluding designated funds from the definition of 'reserves' is presumably that a charity's trustees need the flexibility to build up funds for particular purposes or projects and on the basis that the assets held in a designated fund are at an appropriate level for the project or purpose that the trustees have in mind. On this basis, the Charity Commission accepts that designated funds can be excluded from charity's reserves. However, they state that:

> 'A charity will not be justified in creating, or transferring resources to, a designated fund where the main purpose of doing that is to allow the charity to show a reduced level of reserves.'[25]

Restricted funds

9.79 The Commission say this about restricted funds in the context of reserves:

> '... restricted funds can never be regarded as general purpose funds. Restricted income funds do not fall within the scope of reserves as the term is used in this guidance. Nevertheless, the legal principles on the retention of income apply to restricted income funds, as do the principles of justifying and explaining any retention. For the purpose of applying the principles in this guidance it is suggested that trustees treat each restricted income fund as if it were a separate charity. Thus, each material restricted income fund could have its own "reserve", which should be justified and (if practicable) explained in its own right.'[26]

Tax

9.80 There are also tax reasons why the trustees of a charity must take care to ensure that they comply with their duty to apply the charity's income within a reasonable time of receipt. The exemptions from direct tax available to charities depend upon their income and capital gains being applied for charitable purposes only. Income that is retained by a charity without either a legal power of accumulation or proper justification will not be 'applied' for charitable purposes, with the result that exemption from tax may be lost. There is more information about this at **11.45**.

Donations

9.81 The Charity Commission acknowledges that 'people who give or leave money to charities do not usually specify whether their donation or legacy should be treated as income or as permanent or expendable endowment'. The key issue is the available evidence of a donor's intention, whether formal, informal or circumstantial. As we have mentioned, the Commission's view is that 'if there is really no evidence, either direct or circumstantial, as to the donor's intention then the gift should be applied as income consistently with the terms of the charity's governing document in a way the trustees think will benefit the charity'.[27] The key point for the charity will obviously be to try, where possible, to ensure that there is evidence of the donor's intention. Generally, the charity will wish to have the flexibility to treat a gift as expendable endowment, though the position will vary from case to case.

---

[25] CC 19.
[26] CC 19.
[27] OG 43 84.

Justifying reserves

9.82 As we have indicated, the Charity Commission acknowledge and accept that charity trustees are often justified in creating reserves of income in order to ensure that their charities are financially viable and better able to withstand financial setbacks or problems. At the same time, the Commission acknowledges the public interest in knowing that charities are actually applying their assets for their charitable purposes. As the Commission say, 'underlying much public discussion of charity reserves is the belief that holding a significant amount of reserves is tantamount to hoarding'.[28]

9.83 The Commission's approach to reserves strikes a balance between the strategic and operational requirements of charities and the public interest in seeing that they apply their assets. The key point is that the Commission has no objection to a charity making reserves if its trustees can justify why they are doing it. Their guidance in this area is helpful:

> 'The fact that the charity holds, or does not hold, reserves is not in itself a reason either to criticise or to commend a charity. In our view, a charity should be judged on whether or not its level of reserves, whatever it is, is justified and clearly explained. Justifying reserves...does not mean excusing or being defensive about reserves. It means being able to demonstrate, by reference to a charity's current position and future prospects, why holding a particular level of reserves is right for the charity at that time.'[29]

9.84 Charity trustees are required by the SORP 2005 to make a statement in their annual report about the level of reserves their charity holds and why. However, in most cases, trustees will need to justify the reserve they are holding by developing a reserves policy based upon, in the Commission's words, 'a realistic assessment of their reserve needs'.

Reserves policy

9.85 The key points in relation to reserves policy are as follows:

- The policy should be agreed upon by the trustees and set out in writing, notwithstanding that it may be drafted by senior employees of the charity or a sub-committee of the trustees.

- The policy should, as a minimum, cover the following points:
    - Why the charity needs reserves (or does not need them as the case may be).
    - What level or range of reserves the trustees think the charity needs.
    - What steps the charity is going to take to establish or maintain reserves at the agreed level or range.
    - What arrangements the trustees are going to make for monitoring and reviewing the policy.

- The amount of time invested in preparing and reviewing the policy should be in proportion to the scale and complexity of the charity's affairs.

- Even if the charity is not in a position to build up reserves to the level required or perhaps at all, its trustee should consider what level of reserves would be appropriate.

---

[28]   CC 19.
[29]   CC 19.

- An established charity with a low level of reserves will need to have a policy which makes it clear whether there are no financial problems or, as the case may be, that there are financial problems which the trustees are seeking to resolve.

- A decision to hold no reserves does not mean that a reserves policy is not required. The trustees would still need to justify why they have decided not to hold any reserves at all.

- The trustees should put together a reserves policy taking into account their understanding of its operations and finances and, in particular, its forecast levels of income and expenditure over future years, the trustees' analysis of any future needs, opportunities, contingencies or risks and the likelihood of those risks becoming a reality.

9.86   The Charity Commission guidance in this area is helpful.[30] It discusses the risk to charities of retaining funds that could be used with immediate effect to alleviate acute need. The guidance also highlights the fact that the giving public are 'not generally concerned with legal and accounting technicalities'. Bearing in mind the implications for raising funds from the general public and the likelihood that other funders may regard reserves as either too high (eliminating the need for additional funds) or too low (implying financial problems), it is obviously essential from the point of view of good governance that trustees invest an appropriate amount of time and effort in their reserves policy and communicate it effectively to all of those with an interest in its operations and activity.

9.87   The Charity Commission publish a number of helpful examples of what they regard as good and bad examples of reserves policies.[31]

LAND

9.88   Many charities own freehold or leasehold land, some using it for their charitable purposes ('specie' or 'functional' land), while others may hold it as an investment that produces income to support their operations.

Acquiring land

9.89   Incorporated charities will generally have an express power to acquire and hold both functional and investment land under their constitution. Unincorporated charities may have a similar express power but, failing that, can rely upon a statutory power to purchase functional or investment land under s 8 of the Trustee Act 2000. This power will also apply to the acquisition of land on trust by an incorporated charity but is subject to any provisions to the contrary in a charity's constitution. Except where a charity has no power to acquire land (or the trustees propose to spend permanent endowment to acquire land and buildings), the consent of the Charity Commission is not required to the acquisition of land by a charity.

---

[30]   CC 19.
[31]   These are all available at http://www.charity-commission.gov.uk/supportingcharities/ogs/g043e003.asp.

9.90 Charity trustees acquiring land should familiarise themselves with the Charity Commission's guidance in this area.[32] Much of this is common sense, but trustees should bear in mind that the Commission will expect them to have considered the following issues:

- The trustees will need to have taken reasonable steps to ensure that the land is suitable for its intended use and is not subject to any legal or planning restrictions which might conflict with that use.

- The trustees must also have taken reasonable steps to ensure that the charity can afford the purchase and, where it is being bought with the aid of a mortgage, the charity can cope with projected rises in interest rates.

- While there is no legal requirement to do so, the Commission 'strongly recommends' that the trustees obtain a surveyor's report which deals with valuation, the maximum price the trustees ought to have to pay, a description of any repairs or alterations the trustees will need to make and their cost and a 'positive recommendation (with reasons) that is in the interest of the charity to purchase the land'.

9.91 Specific considerations apply where a charity's trustees wish to acquire land using a mortgage. These are dealt with in more detail in the context of borrowing by charities in **Chapter 12**.

Disposing of land

9.92 An incorporated charity will usually also have express powers under its constitution to sell, lease or mortgage its land. The trustees of an unincorporated charity have all of the powers of an 'absolute owner' of land under s 8 of the Trustee Act 2000 (which can be restricted by the charity's constitution) and s 6 of the Trusts of Land and Appointment of Trustees Act 1996 (which cannot). These powers will generally be sufficiently wide to authorise a sale, lease or mortgage of land. Mortgages of land are dealt with in the context of borrowing by charities in **Chapter 12**. This chapter deals with the sale and lease of land.

9.93 Some express powers of disposal may be subject to particular restrictions. Where a disposal is stated to be subject to the consent of the Charity Commission, the Charities Act 1993, s 36 frees the charity and its trustees from this restriction. When the exercise of a power of disposal is subject to the consent of the court, an Order of the Commission may be required (see **4.16** for more on this), depending upon the power that is being exercised and the way in which the restriction is worded.

9.94 Notwithstanding that a charity may have the powers it needs, the sale or lease of land by a charity is subject to certain other restrictions:

- If the land is specie or functional land (see **9.29** for more on this) that is to be used for the charity's purposes and it does not have an express power to sell it, the charity can rely on the statutory power of sale provided that the trustees intend to buy replacement property with the proceeds. However, if the land is to be sold without replacing it, a Scheme (see **4.29** for more on this) will be required in order

---

[32] CC 33.

to authorise the sale (on the basis that the sale will alter the purposes of the charity). The Scheme will specify how the proceeds of sale must be spent (cy-près).

- If the land is held as an investment or part of the charity's permanent endowment, an Order of the Commission will be required if the proceeds of sale are to be spent by the charity rather than being reinvested in replacement investments. No Order will be required to authorise a sale if the proceeds are used to buy replacement investments provided that the charity has a power of sale.

- The charity's trustees must conclude that the sale or lease is in the charity's best interests. Where functional land is being replaced, the new land must be at least as suitable for the charity's operational needs. Where investment land is sold, the trustees will need to be satisfied that investing the proceeds in other land or asset classes is likely to produce a better return for the charity. Where a lease is being granted, the trustees will generally need to take advice on its terms.

- The terms of the sale must be the best reasonably obtainable. This may mean that the trustees must take advice on the best way of marketing the land and the price that should be obtained (this is certainly the Charity Commission's view).

- In certain circumstances, the consent of the Charity Commission to a sale or lease may be required. This depends upon the provisions of the Charities Act 1993, s 36. This is dealt with in more detail below.

Charities Act 1993, s 36

9.95   The Charities Act 1993, s 36 provides that land in England or Wales held 'by or in trust for' a charity (other than an exempt charity) cannot be 'sold, leased or otherwise disposed of' without a court order or an Order of the Charity Commission. The words 'in trust for' ensure that land held by a third party for a charity (such as a nominee or custodian trustee) is subject to the restrictions. The words 'sold, leased or otherwise disposed of' have a wide meaning but do not include the grant of a mortgage or other security over the land.

9.96   There are two exceptions to this general principle. The first applies to the grant of any lease by a charity for seven years or less where the charity receives no premium in return. No court order or Order of the Commission is required provided that:

- The trustees obtain and consider the advice of any person that they reasonably believe has the ability and experience to advise them competently on the grant of the lease.

- The trustees are satisfied (taking into account the advice they have received) that the terms on which the lease is being granted are the best that can reasonably be obtained in the circumstances.

- The land is not being leased to a 'connected person'.

9.97   The 'connected person' requirement is intended to prevent charity trustees from disposing of land at an undervalue to people who are able to pass on the benefit of the undervalue to them or retain them for their own benefit. They are:

(i)   A charity trustee or a 'trustee for the charity' (ie a nominee or custodian).

(ii) Anyone who has given any land (not just the land in question) to the charity (at any time).

(iii) A child, parent, grandchild, grandparent or sibling of the trustee.

(iv) An officer, agent or employee of the charity.

(v) A spouse or civil partner of the trustee or anyone within (i) to (iv).

(vi) Any 'institution' controlled by the trustee or anyone within (i) to (v) above (whether acting alone or together). 'Control' means that the relevant person can secure that the affairs of the 'institution' are conducted in accordance with his wishes.

(vii) Any 'body corporate' in which the trustee or anyone within (i) to (vi) has a 'substantial interest' (whether alone or taken together). A substantial interest is more than 20% of the share capital or voting rights in the relevant 'body corporate'.

9.98 The second exception relates to any other sale or lease of a charity's land. A court order or an Order of the Commission is not required provided that the trustees:

- obtain and consider a written report on the proposed disposal from a qualified surveyor instructed by the trustees and acting exclusively for the charity (there are special requirements both for the surveyor's qualifications and for the contents of the surveyor's report, which are explained below);

- advertise the property in accordance with the surveyor's advice (but if the surveyor advises that advertising or marketing the property would not be in the best interests of the charity, then the property need not be advertised);

- having considered the surveyor's report, they must satisfy themselves that the terms of the disposal they intend to make are the best that can reasonably be obtained; or

- are not selling or leasing the land to a 'connected person' (as defined at **9.97**).

9.99 The surveyor must be a Fellow or Professional Associate of the Royal Institution of Chartered Surveyors (RICS). He or she will be entitled to use the letters FRICS, ARICS, FSVA or ASVA after their name. The content of the report prepared by the surveyor is specified by the Charities (Qualified Surveyors Reports) Regulations (SI 1992/2980) and includes advice on how best to sell the land and its likely value but the Charity Commission quite rightly encourage charity trustees to engage with their surveyor's advice pro-actively with a view to obtaining the best deal for their charity. The Commission's guidance is that:

'We would advise trustees to urge their surveyor to report to them on any other matters which the surveyor feels are relevant in the circumstances, or on which the trustees wish to receive advice. The surveyor could, for example, always be asked to assess the offers actually made for the land and give a positive recommendation if they believe that one offer represents the best obtainable in the circumstances. In some cases the surveyor may need, for instance, to give specific advice about the effect of a sale on the value of adjoining land retained by the trustees. It may also be that trustees will need to receive more than one report, at different stages of the transaction.'[33]

9.100 In most circumstances the trustees are under a duty to accept the best price for the charity's land without regard to their own personal preferences. This includes a duty to consider a higher offer at any time before exchange of contracts unless the trustees reasonably consider that the prospective purchaser's ability to complete the purchase is doubtful. There is some helpful guidance about this from the Commission:[34]

'Trustees cannot sell at less than the best price simply in order to avoid selling to a purchaser whom they find objectionable: the interests of a charity must come before the trustees' personal preferences. However, trustees may reject an offer where they have reasonable grounds for believing that the purchaser will use the land in a way which will either:

- affect other land which they are retaining; or
- be directly contrary to the purposes of the charity.

Where they accept a lower price, they must be clear that this is to the overall advantage of the charity. The surveyor or other adviser must be instructed to assess the value of any non-monetary elements in an offer.'

Functional land

9.101 The Charities Act 1993, s 36 imposes additional restrictions where a charity wishes to dispose of any functional or specie land (see **9.29** for more on this) which its constitution requires should be used for its purposes (eg land used for recreational purposes). Unless waived by the Charity Commission, the trustees are required to give public notice of their intention to sell the land with a view to allowing anyone affected by the disposal to make representations to the charity's trustees. The notice must give at least one month's notice of the end date for the submission of representations to the charity. The Commission's guidance says this about the notice:

'The form and extent of the notice will depend on the size and type of the charity. In the case of a local charity it will usually be acceptable for the trustees to put up a notice on the property itself and to insert a second notice in a local newspaper. Larger charities, or charities with specialised activities, will have to consider advertising in newspapers of wider circulation or in specialised publications connected with the charity's activities. In publishing the notices, it is recommended that trustees aim to reach as many beneficiaries, and other people who may have an interest in the charity, as is possible at reasonable cost.'[35]

There is helpful guidance available on the content of the notice and its publication and the trustees' approach to any to representations received.[36]

9.102 The provisions of Charities Act 1993, s 36 do not apply (and no consent is required from the Charity Commission) in certain circumstances:

- Where a disposal is authorised by a statutory provision or a Scheme made by the Charity Commission.[37]

---

[33]   CC 28.
[34]   CC 28.
[35]   CC 28.
[36]   OG 54 B3.
[37]   Charities Act 1993, s 36(9)(a).

- Where a charity sells or leases land to another charity at less than its full value and is authorised to do so by its constitution (because it has a power to transfer the land and the transfer is the best way of advancing its charitable purposes and is not expressly prohibited by anything in its constitution).[38]

- Where a charity grants a lease to a beneficiary at less than full value (described as 'less than the best rent reasonably obtainable') and the lease is authorised by the charity's constitution.[39]

9.103 In order to give those purchasing land from charities a degree of protection, the Charities Act 1993, s 37 obliges trustees to include certain statements and certificates in the contract they make with the purchaser and the transfer of the land itself. Charities Act 1993, s 37(1) requires a contract for sale and transfer to state that the land is held by or in trust for a charity and that either restrictions apply on its disposition or that it is exempt. The trustees must also certify in the transfer that either the Charity Commission's consent or a court order has been obtained or that the charity trustees have the power under the charity's constitution to make the disposition.

9.104 If the trustees give this certificate but have not actually complied with the restrictions in the Charities Act 1993, s 36, the disposal is still valid in favour of the purchaser if he or she acted in good faith for money or money's worth. However, the Court has held that where the statement required by s 37 is included in a contract for sale but the requirements of s 36 have not actually been complied with, the contract itself is unenforceable.[40] As a consequence, a purchaser may seek evidence that s 36 has been complied with before exchange of contracts for the sale of land by a charity.

9.105 The Charity Commission takes the view that the certificate required by the Charities Act 1993, s 37 must be given by a charity's trustees rather than the charity itself. This is consistent with the legislation, although it is possible for trustees to delegate responsibility for signing the certificate using whatever powers of delegation they have available to them. Where an incorporated charity sells land, therefore, the parties to the transfer will be the charity, its trustees (or their delegates authorised to give a certificate on their behalf) and the purchaser. Where the sale is by an unincorporated charity, the parties will be the trustees or their delegates (who will make the transfer and sign the certificate) and the purchaser.

NOMINEES AND CUSTODIANS

9.106 Many charities use nominees and custodians to hold their assets. A 'nominee' will hold legal title to the charity's assets on its behalf, almost invariably on trust. The charity will remain beneficially entitled to the assets, but it is the nominee's name which will appear on the legal title. In the context of shares and other securities, it is the nominee's name which will appear in the relevant share register. Where the nominee holds registered land on behalf of the charity, the nominee will appear as the registered proprietor of the land at HM Land Registry.

9.107 A 'custodian' may also hold legal title to an asset on behalf of a charity, but the expression is more often used to describe a person who has physical custody of

---

[38] Charities Act 1993, s 36(9)(b).
[39] Charities Act 1993, s 36(9)(c).
[40] *Bayoumi v Women's Total Abstinence Educational Union Limited and Another* [2003] 1 All ER 864.

particular documents or other evidence of the charity's title to its assets. This could include, for example, share certificates. However, neither 'nominee' nor 'custodian' has any very precise legal definition and in practice they are often used interchangeably.

9.108 The main advantage of using a nominee or custodian is to avoid the administrative difficulties posed by vesting assets in a body of trustees whose identity will change from time to time. This is generally only an issue in relation to unincorporated charities. Because they lack legal personality, their assets must be held in the names of their trustees from time to time. When a trustee retires and a new trustee is appointed in his or her place, arrangements must be made for the title of the charity's assets to be vested in the new trustee alongside the continuing trustees. This issue can be dealt with to an extent by ensuring that trustees retire and are appointed by way of deed, but unincorporated charities still face the administrative task of changing records of legal title. Although this is really no more than an administrative burden, a failure to deal with title to a charity's assets can lead to significant problems in practice. Where, for example, a charity's trustees wish to dispose of an asset, they may find it very difficult to do so if title to it is still with individuals who have long since retired as trustees and may subsequently have disappeared or died. There is more about how a charity's assets should be dealt with in the context of the appointment and retirement of trustees at **8.64**.

9.109 This kind of administrative problem is much less of an issue in relation to incorporated charities, which are capable of holding assets in their own name regardless of changes in the identity of their trustees. Having said that, nominees and custodians may still be used by an incorporated charity, often to facilitate the rapid sale and purchase of investments where a charity has engaged an investment manager to invest its assets. There is more about this in **Chapter 10**.

9.110 Both incorporated and unincorporated charities may wish to use a custodian in any event to hold important title documents with a view to safeguarding them against loss and the delay and expense that may ensue as a consequence.

POWERS TO APPOINT NOMINEES AND CUSTODIANS

9.111 An unincorporated charity may have an express power to engage a nominee or custodian in its constitution. If not, the charity's trustees can rely upon the statutory powers to appoint nominees and custodians in the Trustee Act 2000.[41] The power can be used to appoint a person as both nominee and custodian in relation to all or any of the assets of the charity. It is in addition to, but can also be excluded by, any express power contained in the charity's constitution.

9.112 The statutory power conferred by the Trustee Act 2000 also applies to assets held on trust by an incorporated charity. It is not available to an incorporated charity in respect of its corporate assets, although many incorporated charity's constitutions will contain an express power to appoint a nominee or custodian.

9.113 The statutory power does not apply in some specific circumstances. These are:

- It cannot be used by common investment funds or common deposit funds.

---

[41]   Trustees Act 2000, ss 16 and 17.

- It does not apply to any land held in the name of the Official Custodian for Charities.

- It cannot be used where the charity already has a custodian trustee under the terms of its constitution.

9.114 The statutory powers in the Trustee Act 2000 were designed to balance flexibility for charities in relation to using nominees and custodians (for the good practical reasons we have mentioned earlier) against a concern that a charity's assets held by a nominee or custodian will not be secure. In the words of the Charity Commission's guidance:

'A balance has to be struck between economy and convenience of trust administration on the one hand, and security for the trust property on the other.'[42]

9.115 One of the main safeguards in the Trustee Act 2000 is a provision that a charity's trustees can only appoint as a nominee or a custodian:

- a person who carries on a business which includes acting as nominee or custodian;

- a corporate body controlled by the trustees of the charity; or

- a solicitors' nominee company (under s 9 of the Administration of Justice Act 1985).

9.116 Providing services as a nominee or custodian will in certain circumstances constitute 'investment business' for the purpose of the Financial Services and Markets Act 2000. Authorisation by the Financial Services Authority to carry on business as a nominee or custodian will obviously ensure that the first of the requirements mentioned in **9.115** is satisfied.

9.117 There are a number of other safeguards built into the Trustee Act 2000. If the nominee or custodian is to be appointed on terms of business which allow it to appoint a substitute to carry out its work on its behalf, or which limit its liability to the charity, or which allow a nominee or custodian to act in circumstances capable of giving rise to conflicts of interest, the charity's trustees must conclude that it is 'reasonably necessary to do so'. This obviously imports an objective standard into this test. Having said that, the terms of business of many professional nominees or custodians will include provisions of this kind. It may be that the trustees of the charity conclude that it is reasonably necessary to include terms of this kind if only because there are no other nominees or custodians who will not also insist on terms of this kind as part of their appointment.

9.118 There are other safeguards:

- A sole trustee cannot appoint itself as a nominee or custodian and a body of trustees can only appoint one of their number to act as a nominee or custodian if it is a trust corporation.

---

[42] CC 42.

- The trustees must ensure that they discharge the statutory duty of care applied by the Trustee Act 2000 when selecting the nominee or custodian and in agreeing the terms on which it should act. There is more about the statutory duty of care in **Chapter 6**.

- The appointment of the nominee or custodian must be in, or be evidenced by, writing. Professional nominees or custodians (and in particular, those authorised by the Financial Services Authority) will not generally agree to act without a written agreement in any event.

- The charity's trustees are under an obligation to review the arrangements under which the nominee or custodian acts and whether it is appropriate to give directions to it or to determine its appointment. The statutory duty of care under the Trustee Act 2000 also applies to this duty to review the position (see **6.2** for more on this).

9.119 While none of these safeguards will apply to the exercise of a power to appoint a nominee or custodian in the constitution of an incorporated charity (except where the express power itself contains provisions of this kind), it is likely that the court would, if called upon to do so, apply similar principles to the exercise of the trustees' duties in respect of the appointment. For practical purposes therefore, the trustees of an incorporated charity should assume that safeguards of the kind we have summarised above should apply to the exercise of their express powers of appointment.

9.120 The other significant provision contained in the Trustee Act 2000 is that the trustees of a charity (other than an exempt charity) exercising the statutory power must act in accordance with any guidance given by the Charity Commission in relation to the selection of nominees or custodians using the statutory power. The Commission has this to say in relation to the guidance:

> 'The guidance only applies directly to the exercise of the powers in the act to appoint nominees/custodians. It does not apply directly to the exercise of any other power to appoint a nominee/custodian, but we recommend that charity trustees exercising such a power should nonetheless bear this guidance in mind.'[43]

9.121 The Commission's guidance also makes the point that a nominee or custodian which is routinely used by a charity's investment manager to hold investments on its behalf will still be 'selected' by the charity's trustees notwithstanding that the investment manager may (as agent) have in practice selected it to act.

9.122 The Commission's guidance in CC 42 covers four areas:

- The relationship between the nominee and the charity.
  As we have stated earlier in this chapter, a nominee will usually hold assets on trust for a charity. This means that only legal title to the assets is with the nominee while beneficial ownership remains with the charity. This is important, because the existence of the trust prevents creditors of the nominee claiming any asset to meets it liabilities. Where, on the other hand, a nominee is only contractually obliged to a charity, the assets it holds will be at risk to creditors' claims in the event that it becomes insolvent. The Commission's guidance is that 'charity trustees must normally avoid selecting a nominee who insists on a purely

---

[43]   CC 42.

contractual relationship'. It goes on to say that it is '...important for trustees to ensure that the proposed arrangements with the selected nominee do, in fact, make it clear that the shares or other property which the nominee is to hold on behalf of the charitable trust do, in fact, belong to the trust'.

- The qualification and location of the nominee or custodian.
  The Commission's guidance acknowledges that a nominee or custodian engaged in the business of providing a nominee or custodian services may, but need not necessarily, be authorised by the Financial Services Authority. The Commission also acknowledges that trustees may exercise their statutory power to appoint a nominee or custodian who is not under their control or subject to the sort of regulations imposed by the Financial Services and Markets Act 2000 (or, in fact, any regulation at all). The Commission acknowledges that an appointment of this kind may be necessary where investments are made outside the UK but state that '... charity trustees need to consider the legal risks associated with the transfer of the trust property to the jurisdiction where the nominee/custodian is located. These risks should be factored into any decision as to whether the relevant location is or is not a suitable one for the investment of the charity's assets, and into the process of reviewing investments'. The Commission's guidance goes on to make the point that the trustees must understand what sort of legal constraints an overseas nominee or custodian is under and how its obligations to the charity can be enforced.

- The independence of the nominee or custodian from each other and from any person to whom the charity's trustees have delegated the function of managing the charity's investments.
  While the statutory power to the Trustee Act 2000 allows a charity to appoint the same person as both nominee and custodian, the Commission's guidance recognises that the person appointed as a discretionary investment manager may also act as a nominee or custodian (or both). The guidance reminds trustees that a nominee or custodian should only be appointed on terms which allow it to act in circumstances that are capable of giving rise to conflicts of interest if it 'reasonably necessary to do so'. Their guidance states: 'Charity trustees need to recognise the possible risks associated with the lack of independence in the persons responsible for the process of administering the charity's investments on its behalf'.

- Reporting by the nominee or custodian to the charity.
  As part of the duty on charity trustees to review the performance of a nominee or custodian appointed by them, the Charity Commission's guidance is that 'it is important for charity trustees to ensure that any nominee/custodian whom they propose to select is prepared to agree to satisfactory reporting arrangements'. The Commission also recommends ensuring that any agreement with a nominee or custodian obliges them to report to the charity on an agreed basis.

9.123 The Charity Commission's guidance makes a number of other useful points in relation to these four areas and the appointment of custodians generally. Trustees looking to appoint a nominee or custodian (whether or not as part of appointing a discretionary investment manager) should bear in mind that it is binding upon them and refer to it.

10

INVESTMENT

10.1 This chapter deals with the powers and duties of charity trustees in relation to the investment of their assets. This will not be relevant to every charity, particularly those whose financial resources are such that they have no surplus income. However, it will be relevant to charities with endowment assets or those with sufficient surplus income to enable them to build up reserves. There is more about endowment and reserves in **Chapter 9**.

10.2 What do we mean by investment? The legal meaning of 'investment' is simply this; an investment is any asset which produces income.[1] This is 'income' in the sense used in the context of trusts law generally and therefore excludes assets which produce only capital gains. It should be distinguished from 'income' for the purposes of charity law, which can include both income in the traditional sense and capital gains. There is more about this in **Chapter 9**.

10.3 Investment is no more than one of a number of ways in which a charity can seek to exploit its assets with a view to generating financial resources to support its activities. However, there are a number of methods of generating resources that should be clearly distinguished from investment, not least because the powers and duties which apply to them are different. The most significant examples are:

- Trading, usually by selling goods, services or other assets for money. There is more about how to identify a trade and the most important of aspects of trading by charities in **Chapter 13**.

- Raising funds by way of grant and donation.

- Buying assets which are so speculative that the purchaser is in reality doing little more than betting on a rise or fall in their value. The usual examples are commodities, works of art and premium bonds.

10.4 The distinction between trading and investment is particularly important and is often narrow. The best example of this is the acquisition of land. Land purchased by a charity with the intention of letting it at a rent will be an 'investment'. Land purchased by a charity with a view to selling it on for development at a higher price will constitute a 'trade'. The fact that land acquired by charity is subsequently sold for development does not necessarily mean that it was not bought and held as an investment rather than as a trading asset. The key issue is what the charity intended at the time it bought the land.

---

[1]   See *Johnston v Heath* [1970] 1 WLR 1567.

10.5 The Charity Commission's analysis of what constitutes an 'investment' departs from the strict legal definition we have mentioned. The Commission's guidance on the investment of charitable funds says this:

> 'In order that an asset can be regarded as an "investment", funds must at some stage have been provided by an investor to an "investee". This expression is used in this guidance to describe someone who agrees to provide some form of benefit in return for the use of funds provided by the "investor".'[2]

10.6 The guidance goes on to say that '… if there is no 'investee' in the sense indicated above, there is no 'investment'. This is not an unhelpful way of analysing the position. It certainly rules out treating the purchase of 'speculative' assets such as commodities as 'investments'. In the Commission's words:

> 'There is no 'investee' where trustees simply purchase an asset in a speculative hope that they will eventually be able to obtain a higher price from a purchaser than they have paid for the asset, or whether the trustees are, in substance, merely gambling with the charity's funds'.[3]

10.7 The usual classes of asset in which charities invest are:

- quoted shares and securities (including loan stock issued by companies and local authorities and sovereign debt);

- units in authorised unit trusts and other listed collective investment schemes;

- investment land; and

- cash deposits with banks, building societies and other financial institutions.

10.8 Modern investment practice has meant that more charities are now investing in other asset classes (so called 'alternative investments'), including hedge and private equity funds. There is more about this at **10.50** and **10.55**.

SOCIAL INVESTMENT

10.9 The investment of a charity's assets in order to produce a financial return must be distinguished from 'social' investment. Social investment (sometimes referred to as 'programme-related' investment) is any investment of a charity's assets which is intended to advance its charitable purposes rather than produce an investment return.

10.10 Superficially, a social investment may resemble a financial investment in the sense that it will generally involve making funds available on an ostensibly 'commercial' basis, often involving the purchase of shares or the making of a loan. However, social investment will be intended to provide the 'investee' (to use the Commission's terminology) with funds to develop activities that will advance the charity's charitable purposes. While the investment may produce a financial return (in the sense that the shares may pay a dividend or the loan may pay interest) this is not the purpose of making the investment.

---

2   CC 14 (Investment of Charitable Funds: Detailed guidance).
3   CC 14.

10.11 Social investment which combines some of the rigour and discipline of financial investment with charitable (or 'social') objectives is becoming increasingly important. It is important to appreciate that social and financial investment are two fundamentally different things. None of the considerations we mention in this chapter relating to financial investment apply to social investment. The Charity Commission has published some helpful guidance in relation to social investment.[4]

INVESTMENT POWERS

10.12 As is so often the case, the investment powers which are available to a particular charity will depend upon whether it is an incorporated or an unincorporated charity.

UNINCORPORATED CHARITIES

10.13 An unincorporated charity may have an express power of investment in its constitution. However, its trustees can also rely upon the statutory power of investment conferred by the Trustee Act 2000, s 3. This authorises them to invest the charity's assets in any kind of investment in which they could invest if they were the absolute owner of the assets. This power (usually referred to as the 'general power of investment') gives charity trustees the widest possible discretion to invest. It is subject to two conditions:

- it is subject to any restriction or exclusion in the charity's constitution; and

- it does not authorise charity trustees to invest in land.

There is more about each of these conditions below.

Restriction or exclusion

10.14 Whether a charity's constitution does 'restrict or exclude' the general power of investment will obviously depend upon what is in the constitution. The Charity Commission's guidance in this area is helpful. It states that:

> 'A provision in the governing document of a charity will only be a "restriction or exclusion" . . . if it is intended to prevent the trustees from making a particular form of investment which will be within the scope of the general power, or if it is intended to apply a procedural restriction to the making of an investment (for example, a requirement of consent from the person who set the charity up).'[5]

10.15 The guidance goes on to give a number of examples of provisions often encountered in charity constitutions which the Commission do and do not regard as representing restrictions or exclusions. Some of the more important examples are:

- A positive direction in a charity's constitution to invest only in a particular way will be a restriction (although, as the Commission rightly points out, a provision of this kind may not be enforceable by the court on the basis that it may conflict with the general duty of the charity trustees in relation to investment).

---

[4]   'Charities and Social Investment'.
[5]   CC 14.

- A provision which is part of the definition of a power of investment that is intended to be wider than a statutory power of investment that may have been in force in the past should not be treated as a restriction or exclusion. This sort of provision will usually spell out the charity's power to invest in a range of specified investment assets, often prefaced by the words '... and in particular to invest in ...' or something similar.

- Declaratory statements that are intended to do no more than explain or confirm the scope of a particular power of investment are not usually regarded by the Charity Commission as restrictions or exclusions. They often do no more than reflect how the law was understood at a particular time. The Commission gives the example of investment powers which specifically state that they do not authorise the use of derivative instruments on the basis that powers of this kind were drafted at a time when derivatives were not (as they are now) an accepted part of investment practice for charities.

- Any investment provision contained in a charity's constitution made before 3 August 1961 is deemed not to be a restriction or exclusion, provided the charity is not constituted by an Act of Parliament or delegated legislation.

- The general power of investment is not available to common investment funds or common deposit funds. There is more about funds of this kind at **10.75**.

10.16 These examples are, of course the Commission's interpretation of the legal position and the way in which they think the court would construe particular types of investment power. Generally speaking, only the court can definitely answer a question of this kind, but the Commission's guidance is obviously helpful and is likely to be considered by the court should it ever have to make a judgment about provisions of this kind.

Land

10.17 Although investment in land is not authorised by the general power of investment, the trustees of an unincorporated charity can exercise another statutory power (conferred by the Trustee Act 2000, s 8) to acquire freehold or leasehold land in the UK as an investment. This power is available on exactly the same basis as the general power of investment. Clearly, land outside the UK is excluded. Charities that wish to invest in overseas property will generally need to use a collective investment scheme whose underlying assets include property overseas (see **10.69–10.74** for more on this).

Corporate assets

10.18 The general power of investment is not available to the trustees of an incorporated charity in respect of its corporate assets (see **10.19** for more detail in relation to this). However, the general power does apply in relation to trust assets held by an incorporated charity (see **9.8–9.12** for more on this). This means that any restriction or exclusion on investment set out in the incorporated charity's constitution will not operate to restrict or exclude the scope of the general power in relation to trust assets. There is more about the corporate and trust assets of incorporated charities in **Chapter 9**.

INCORPORATED CHARITIES

10.19 As we have explained, incorporated charities cannot take advantage of the general power of investment conferred by the Trustee Act 2000, s 3 in relation to their corporate assets. An incorporated charity must rely upon an express power of investment in its constitution. Many such charities will have an express power, often in very similar terms to the general power of investment.

10.20 In the unlikely event that an unincorporated charity does not have an express power of investment or its power is not sufficiently wide to authorise an investment it proposes to make, it will generally be possible to exercise a power of amendment in the charity's constitution to include a new express power or alter an existing express power. In the context of charitable companies, the Charity Commission has confirmed that it is 'prepared routinely to give the consent' which is required to changes of this kind. There is more guidance on amending charity constitutions in **Chapter 15**.

TRUSTEE'S DUTIES

10.21 There are several significant aspects to the duty owed by charity trustees when making investments. These are:

- The trustees must ensure that they have an appropriate power of investment and are acting within its scope.

- The Trustee Act 2000 imposes statutory duties in respect of the exercise of any power of investment by charity trustees.

- There is also a statutory duty of care owed by trustees imposed by the Trustee Act 2000.

- The trustees must ensure that the tax implications of any investment they make are understood and taken into account in exercising their discretion.

Powers of investment

10.22 The scope of the express and statutory powers of investment available to trustees are explained earlier in this chapter. See **Chapter 7** for more in relation to the exercise of powers.

Statutory duties

10.23 In exercising any power of investment (whether an express or statutory power), a charity's trustees must have regard to the 'standard investment criteria' specified by the Trustee Act 2000.[6] There are two criteria:

- The suitability to the charity of 'investments in the same kind as any particular investment proposed to be made, and of that particular investment as an investment of that kind'. This is usually referred to as 'suitability'.

---

[6]   Trustee Act 2000, s 4(3).

- The need for diversification of the charity's investments 'in so far as is appropriate to the circumstances' of the charity. This is usually referred to as 'diversification'.

10.24 The trustees must also review the charity's investments from time to time with a view to deciding whether, having regard to the standard investment criteria, the investments should be retained or changed.

10.25 Before they exercise any power of investment (again, whether an express or statutory power), a charity's trustees must obtain and consider 'proper advice' about the way in which the power should be exercised, having regard to the investment criteria we have mentioned. There is an important exception to this which is mentioned at **10.32**.

10.26 The trustees have a similar duty to obtain and consider proper advice when they review whether investments should be retained or changed.

Incorporated charities

10.27 The trustees of an incorporated charity are not subject to these statutory duties when they exercise their power of investment in respect of the charity's corporate assets. However, it is clear that an incorporated charity is in the position 'analogous to that of a trustee in relation to its corporate assets'.[7] On this basis, the likelihood is that a court would regard the trustees of an incorporated charity as owing duties comparable to the statutory duties imposed upon the trustees of an unincorporated charity. This is certainly the approach taken by the Charity Commission. For practical purposes, therefore, it is advisable to assume that the trustees of an incorporated charity owe duties in relation to investments which are substantially similar to the duties owed by the trustees of an unincorporated charity.

Suitability and diversification

10.28 Suitability relates to both the allocation of a charity's funds between different classes of assets (usually referred to in the investment world as 'asset allocation') and the merits of individual investments within each asset class.

10.29 Diversification means ensuring that the assets invested in are sufficiently diverse to reduce the risk to the charity of significant fluctuations in the value of a particular asset class or an individual investment within each asset class. As the Commission point out:

> 'The extent to which diversification is practicable will depend upon the amount of resources which are available for investment and, in some cases, on the nature of the investment assets which are currently held.'[8]

10.30 Suitability and diversification are aimed at managing the risk to the charity of investments which fail or under perform. In the context of investment, risk is usually categorised as 'counterparty risk' and 'investment risk'. Counterparty risk is the possibility that an entity with which the charity does business in relation to investment (such as an investment manager) defaults on its obligations. Investment risk relates to the risk inherent in any investment of failure or under performance.

---

[7]   *Liverpool and District Hospital for Diseases of the Heart v Att-Gen* [1981] Ch 193.
[8]   CC 14.

10.31 Some charity constitutions will expressly provide that trustees are not under a duty to consider the suitability or (more often) the diversification of the charity's investments. The Commission's stance in relation to clauses of this kind is that they 'have no legal effect'. While it is certainly true that a court is unlikely to treat provisions of this kind as ousting these duties altogether, our view is that their existence is certainly one of the factors trustees can legitimately take into account in exercising their investment powers and, is likely to be one of the 'circumstances' in the context of the diversification that may be relevant to the charity.

Advice

10.32 The 'proper advice' a charity's trustees are obliged to obtain before exercising any investment power is the advice of 'a person who is reasonably believed by the trustee to be qualified to give it by his ability in and practical experience of financial and other matters relating to the proposed investment'. This need not necessarily be a person authorised to give investment advice by the Financial Services Authority pursuant to the Financial Services and Markets Act 2000, although some charity constitutions make it a requirement that the adviser is appropriately authorised (and it may not be possible for anyone other than an FSA authorised person to give certain advice in any event).

10.33 There is no objection in principle to an adviser not being authorised by the FSA (unless his or her advice relates to an area that is regulated by the FSA), and it is also possible for a trustee who is appropriately qualified to advise his co-trustees. While this may be a more cost-effective option for the charity than consulting an independent adviser, trustees looking to rely on the advice of one of their co-trustees are obviously under a particular duty to consider the advice they receive objectively. And, as the Commission points out, the trustee who does give advice may be liable to the charity if the advice he or she has given proves to be negligent.

10.34 There is an important exception to the duty to seek advice where the trustees reasonably conclude that, in all the circumstances, it is unnecessary or inappropriate to do so. The key word here is 'reasonably'. It would be reasonable to expect trustees not to seek advice where the value of the funds they are seeking to invest is so small that the cost of the advice would be disproportionate. Equally, it is likely to be unreasonable for trustees to conclude that they will not take advice because they have some limited experience of making investments in their personal capacity and do not wish to incur any fees. The general duty on trustees to consider taking advice in relation to matters which they are not qualified to consider themselves is clear (see **7.45** for more on this). The fact that the advice may need to be paid for is not, of itself, a sufficient justification not to take it.

Statutory duty of care

10.35 In exercising any power of investment (and the specific duties in relation to investment imposed by the Trustee Act 2000) the trustees of an unincorporated charity are subject to the statutory duty of care imposed by the 2000 Act. The trustees of incorporated charities are likely to be subject to a similar duty. There is more about the statutory duty of care at **6.2**.

Tax implications

10.36 The wide range of exemptions and reliefs from tax available to charities can be restricted where they incur 'non-charitable expenditure'. One form of non-charitable expenditure is investment in assets outside the asset classes specified in the Income and Corporation Taxes Act 1988. This will include, for example, investments in private equity and hedge funds. Investments of this kind are only at risk of being treated as non-charitable expenditure if made for tax avoidance purposes. This will not often be the case, but it is obviously essential that a charity's trustees appreciate the significance of investing in asset classes of this kind. There is more detail about this in **Chapter 11**.

10.37 More generally, trustees should ensure that the tax implications of a particular investment are understood. Because of the 'patchwork' of exemptions and reliefs from tax available to charities, not every investment that may be made by a charity will give rise to an investment return which is free of tax. This does not necessarily mean that a charity cannot invest in assets of this kind, but the fact that they may produce a taxable return whereas other investments will not is an important fact to be taken into account by the trustees in exercising their investment powers in accordance with their duty of care.

ETHICAL INVESTMENT

10.38 Increasing numbers of charities are engaging in 'ethical investment'. The Commission's guidance on investment contains a helpful description:

> '"Ethical investment" is a wide phrase which is used to cover many different approaches to investment strategies. An ethical investment policy may involve looking for companies which demonstrate best practice in areas like environmental protection, employment and human rights, or for companies whose businesses contribute directly to a cleaner environment or healthier society. Or it may involve negative screening, to avoid investments in a particular business or sector. Many ethical investors' investment funds adopt a combination of positive and negative criteria.'[9]

10.39 Charity trustees who wish to adopt an ethical investment policy are bound by the principles set out in the leading case, *Harries (Bishop of Oxford) v Church Commissioners for England*.[10] The starting point is that the trustees of every charity are under a duty to act in the best interests of the charity and that those interests will generally best be advanced by maximising (in a way which is consistent with the trustees' duty in relation to investment) the financial return for its investments regardless of other considerations, whether ethical or otherwise.

10.40 As the Commission points out in its guidance:

> 'An ethical investment policy may be entirely consistent with this principle of seeking the best return. For example, there is an increasingly held view that companies which act in a socially responsible way are more likely to flourish and to deliver the best long term balance between risk and return. The trustees are free to adopt any ethical investment policy which they reasonably believe will provide the best balance or risk and reward for their charity.'[11]

10.41 Notwithstanding this, the *Bishop of Oxford* case recognised the circumstances in which the trustees of a charity can allow ethical considerations to carry more weight than 'financial' considerations:

---

[9]   CC 14.
[10] [1992] 1 WLR 1241.
[11] CC 14.

- Where there is a clear conflict between the operations of a particular investment and the operations of the charity, the charity is able to rule it out as an investment. This will, for example, allow a charity that relieves those suffering from cancer to exclude investments in the tobacco industry.

- Investments which might cause a charity problems in practice (perhaps because they alienate beneficiaries, members, volunteers etc) can be excluded provided that the trustees consider that the risk to the charity posed by, say, alienating its supporters is greater than the risk of financial under-performance.

- More generally, trustees of a charity are free to make an ethical investment if they conclude that it will leave them in no worse financial position than any other investment. This condition is likely to become easier to satisfy as more and more professional investment managers offer 'ethical' funds and other forms of collective investment schemes that appear to offer returns comparable to 'unethical' funds.

10.42 The Charity Commission recommends that, as a point of good practice, charities should disclose any ethical policy they might have in relation to investment in their annual report, although there is no legal requirement to do so. They also offer some helpful practical guidance to trustees in relation to formulating an ethical investment policy:

- Consider the aims and objectives of the charity.
- Keep in mind the fundamental principle of maximising return. If an ethical policy is adopted, it should be set out in writing and should be clear both on positive aims and any exclusions.
- If companies or sectors are excluded, the reasons for exclusions should be clearly thought through. The more restrictive the policy (in terms of exclusions) the greater may be the risk to returns.
- Trustees need to evaluate the effect which any proposed policy may have on potential investment returns, and this will usually require expert advice.
- If a proposed policy increases the risk of lower returns, this must be balanced against the risk of alienating support and damage to reputation. This cannot be an exact calculation. It is just one of many areas where trustees have to identify and manage risk.
- Trustees are unlikely to be criticised for adopting a particular policy if they have considered the correct issues, taking appropriate advice and reached a rational result.'[12]

10.43 It may be, of course, that the express power of investment given to a particular charity specifically excludes investment in particular assets or particular classes of assets. So, for example, those establishing a charity to assist people who are injured by landmines may decide to state in the charity's constitution that it is not permitted to invest in shares or securities in companies engaged in the arms trade. Provisions of this kind will be binding on the charity's trustees.

---

[12]   CC 14.

SPECIFIC INVESTMENTS

10.44 As we suggested earlier in this chapter, there are a number of different investments (including 'alternative investments') that now form part of the modern investment portfolio for many charities alongside more 'traditional' asset classes. These are considered in more detail below.

Derivatives

10.45 'Derivatives' is the way in which a wide range of different financial instruments are described. What they have in common is that, while they are not 'investments' in their own right, they generally relate to an investment and will give rise to a financial return (or loss) which is dependant upon the way in which the relevant investment performs.

10.46 The other factor common to the derivatives is that they are intended to protect against (or 'hedge') the financial risk which may attach to particular investments. A good example of this is an interest rate 'swap'. This is essentially an agreement which allows a party that has financial exposure to a floating rate of interest (eg under a floating rate loan) to 'swap' that rate for a fixed rate of interest. The counterparty to the swap will generally be a bank or other financial institution. The counterparty receives a premium for taking on the risk that floating rates of interest will rise above the fixed rate specified in the swap. The other party has the comfort of knowing that its financial exposure to a rise in interest rates has been capped. Other forms of derivative include currency rate swaps, options, and futures.

10.47 Notwithstanding that derivatives are not 'investments', the Charity Commission's stated policy is that their use is acceptable (and is authorised by the general power of investment) when it is 'ancillary' to the investment process. There are three conditions that the Commission will expect to see satisfied if the use of derivatives is to be 'ancillary' to the investment process. These are as follows:

- The derivative in question must be ancillary to a particular investment transaction (or an intended transaction). So, for example, a charity which proposes to sell a significant proportion of its equity based portfolio of investments in the short to medium term to fund a particular project may purchase a put option from a bank or another financial institution which has the effect of fixing the value of the investments which are to be sold in the interim.

- The derivative must have been entered into either to manage risk or to manage transaction costs in relation to the investment process (or both).

- The derivative must be 'economically appropriate' to the investment in question. The Commission's guidance on this point is helpful:

  'This means that trustees (when entering into and reviewing [the derivative]), should be satisfied that its value is such that the transaction can fairly be regarded as related to the object of managing risk, or of managing transaction costs in the investment process. The economic appropriateness of the transaction will be determined by the relationship between the size of the payments to be made or received under it and the fluctuations in the value of the investment transaction(s) to which it relates. The amount of the capital on which the derivative transaction is based should not significantly exceed the capital of the investment transaction. But a precise correlation between the value of the derivative transaction(s) and the value of the related investment transaction(s) is not required. Such a correlation would often, in practice, be unrealistically expensive to achieve.'[13]

10.48 Most derivatives are complex financial instruments used by sophisticated investors which generate significant income for the banks and financial institutions which provide them. It will generally be particularly important for charity trustees to seek advice in relation to a derivative transaction they are proposing to enter into in order to understand its financial implications and the risks attached to it.

10.49 The tax treatment of derivatives is more complex than the tax treatment of investments. Trustees should ensure that they understand the tax implications of the derivative transaction they are proposing to enter into. Professional advice will generally be required under the general duty to consider taking appropriate advice.

Hedge funds

10.50 Hedge funds have become an increasingly 'mainstream' investment asset in recent years, prompted, no doubt, by the apparently significant investment returns they are reported to produce. Investors generally are looking to include hedge fund investments as part of their portfolios and many charities are no exception to this.

10.51 A hedge fund is essentially a collective investment scheme that uses investors' funds to buy a wide range of assets, particularly assets that are not closely correlated to movements in more traditional asset classes, such as listed shares and securities.

10.52 Hedge funds are often highly 'leveraged'. In other words, their managers borrow significantly in order to buy assets. This can obviously increase the gains that a fund may make on assets that perform well. Equally, it can exaggerate the losses that a fund may experience if assets do not perform as expected. Hedge funds are also generally unregulated, often operating out of offshore jurisdictions with no (or very 'light touch') regulatory regimes. This means that obtaining reliable and verifiable information about the way in which hedge funds perform is often difficult.

10.53 Having said all this, hedge funds have, as we have explained, become more of a mainstream investment in recent years and the approach many charities take is to invest in a 'fund of funds'. In other words, a charity may invest in a collective investment scheme which itself invests in a wide range of hedge funds adopting different investment strategies, with a view to mitigating risk. Given the duties owed by charity trustees in relation to investment, this is obviously likely to be a sensible approach. However, any investment in any hedge fund (whether directly or via a collective investment scheme) is likely to carry a higher degree of risk than investing in the more 'traditional' asset classes. Charity trustees are unlikely to be able to assess the risks in investing in hedge funds or retaining their investments without taking professional advice.

10.54 Any investment in a hedge fund is not 'charitable expenditure' where it is made to avoid tax. This issue will need to be addressed by a charity's trustees before they make any investment in a hedge fund. They will also need to ensure that they understand the tax implications of the investment and any financial return it produces. Again, they are unlikely to be able to do this without taking professional advice.

---

[13] CC 14.

Private equity

10.55 'Private equity' means buying shares in a private company, as opposed to shares which are traded on a stock exchange. Investment by charities in private equity was unusual in the past (except perhaps where a charity held shares transferred by a donor), but the emergence of collective investment schemes specialising in private equity investment has meant that private equity investment, like investment in hedge funds, is becoming more mainstream for investors generally, including charities.

10.56 The most significant issue for charity trustees looking to invest in private equity is that their ability to exit from the investment is likely to be limited because there will be no market on which shares that are bought can be traded and sold. This risk may be mitigated to a certain extent by investing in private equity via units or shares in a collective investment scheme specialising in the area.

10.57 A direct investment in private equity by a charity is likely to be difficult without taking professional advice, which may well make the investment disproportionately expensive. It will be particularly important to understand the control (if any) the charity will acquire over the private company it is investing in. This will obviously determine the charity's ability to exercise control over the way in which the company's business is operated. Charity trustees should also bear in mind that the governance and other regulatory requirements in relation to private companies will be lighter than those which apply to the shares of a public company listed on the stock exchange.

10.58 Like hedge funds, private equity investments are not 'charitable expenditure' for tax purposes where they are made in order to avoid tax. A charity's trustees will need to take professional advice on this issue before investing.

Underwriting

10.59 Charities may occasionally be invited to underwrite a new issues of shares by a listed company. Essentially, the underwriter is asked to buy newly issued shares at an agreed price in the event that they are not subscribed for by anyone else. Generally speaking, the obligation to subscribe will arise where the expected subscription price is not being met, so that the price paid by the underwriter is higher than the price for the shares in the market. The underwriter will, however, receive a fee for agreeing to underwrite the subscription.

10.60 Charity trustees would need to consider an invitation of this kind very carefully, not least because of the risk of the charity being obliged to buy a significant number of shares at a price which is higher than they can be purchased in the market. The Charity Commission's view is that the trustees' duties in respect of investment will not have been discharged if the purpose of the underwriting is simply speculative, balancing the fee payable by the share issuer 'against the loss resulting from possibly having to sell the subscribed shares at a discount.'

10.61 Underwriting fees which are received are likely to be taxable. A charity's trustees should take professional advice on this point before agreeing to underwrite shares.

Stock lending

10.62 'Stock lending' is a technique used by many pension trustees and other 'institutional' investors to maximise the return from their investment portfolios.

10.63 A 'stock loan' describes the economic effect of the transaction, rather than the actual legal position. The reality is that stock lending involves the transfer of shares or other securities by one party (a 'lender') to another party (a 'borrower') on the basis of an undertaking from the borrower to re-deliver exactly the same number and type of securities after a specified period. The borrower pays the lender a fee in respect of the 'loan'.

10.64 Borrowers are typically banks and other large investment houses which need particular stock to satisfy other obligations they may owe to third parties. For example, a bank may sell shares in a particular company short and not be able to comply with its delivery obligations unless it can 'borrow' shares from another source. The borrower will also agree to pay to the lender amounts equal to any dividends or other distributions paid on the borrowed shares during the loan. From the lender's perspective, therefore, a stock loan maximises the investment return from the shares it holds.

10.65 Stock loans are usually secured by the borrower, who will deliver collateral to the lender as security for its re-delivery obligations. Because the availability of collateral, the risk to the lender of a failure by the borrower to comply with its obligations should be limited to the possibility of default in respect of the collateral itself. Acceptable collateral is usually limited to cash and other near cash obligations such as sovereign debt. Having said that, there are clearly risks associated with stock lending that charity trustees should understand and consider before they agree to lend shares within their charity's investment portfolio. In particular, trustees will need to consider the terms on which they engage an agent to arrange stock loans (an agent will almost always be required on the basis that most charities that wish to engage in stock lending would have great difficulty in identifying potential borrowers or making appropriate arrangements with them).

10.66 Fees payable to the charity in respect of the stock loan are liable to tax. This may not be an issue if the trustees can conclude that the fees are an additional financial return which would not otherwise have been received in respect of the relevant shares and that the risk of the stock loan as against the net fees receivable is acceptable.

10.67 Stock loans are treated by HM Revenue & Customs as non-charitable expenditure where they are made in order to avoid tax. The trustees of a charity who are considering engaging in stock lending should ensure that they understand the position and are likely to need to take professional advice in order to do so.

Insurance policies

10.68 While the Charity Commission believe that purchasing life insurance policies is within the general power of investment, HM Revenue & Customs will treat the premiums payable by the charity as non-charitable expenditure. On this basis, charity trustees should not generally consider purchasing life insurance policies as an investment. Gains on policies are, in any event, liable to tax. See **11.27** for more in relation to this.

Land

10.69 An incorporated charity will generally have an express power to acquire investment land under its constitution. Unincorporated charities (or incorporated charities which hold trust assets) may have a similar express power but, failing that, can rely upon the statutory power to purchase investment land conferred by the Trustee Act 2000, s 8. This statutory power is subject to any provisions to the contrary in a charity's constitution.

10.70 The Charity Commission's guidance on acquiring investment land[14] mentions a number of considerations which charity trustees should take into account when considering buying land as an investment:

- Land may require more active management than other investment assets. This would include, for example, ensuring the investment property is kept in repair and fully let to tenants.

- In comparison to cash, listed investments etc, land is illiquid.

- Managing investment land requires different skills and experience from managing listed investments.

- The cost of investing in a sufficiently diversified portfolio of investment land (particularly commercial property) may not be practicable for an individual charity acting alone.

- The ownership of investment land may impose financial obligations on the charity.

10.71 The Charity Commission goes on to say that:

'We would recommend that this type of investment is normally only suitable for a charity which either:

- has traditionally held land as an investment; or
- has a sufficiently wide and varied portfolio of investments into which land could reasonably be introduced.'[15]

10.72 While these comments are helpful, most of these issues may be answered (to a greater or lesser extent) by investing in collective investment schemes which specialise in property. This will usually enable a charity to invest in land (albeit indirectly) with the same liquidity as an investment in any other listed investment and with responsibility for the day-to-day management of the underlying property vested in professional managers.

10.73 Where, on the other hand, a charity proposes a direct investment in land, the Commission's guidance should be carefully considered. So too should their recommendation that trustees proposing to buy land for investment purposes should obtain a report from a qualified surveyor (although there is no legal obligation to do so).

10.74 The statutory power conferred by s 8 of the Trustee Act 2000 applies only to land in England and Wales. In the absence of an express power in a charity's constitution, it would be a breach of trust for its trustees to acquire land overseas. While the investment return from overseas land will generally be exempt from UK tax, overseas tax may be withheld, with no entitlement for credit under a double tax treaty (even if there is one in place between the UK and the relevant jurisdiction).

---

[14]   CC 33.
[15]   CC 33.

Common investment and deposit funds

10.75 Common deposit funds are arrangements under which charities can deposit cash with a view to generating interest on the deposit they have made. Common deposit funds are themselves charities and are set up by way of a Scheme made by the Commission under the Charities Act 1993.[16]

10.76 The Charity Commission has a similar power to make common investment schemes.[17] Common investment schemes enable participating charities to pool their assets for investment purposes, with a view to gaining access to a wider range of investments. Common investment schemes are themselves charities and are very similar in the way they are structured to any other collective investment scheme. Investing charities acquire an interest in the common investment scheme (usually 'units' or 'shares') rather than in the underlying assets of the scheme itself.

DELEGATION OF INVESTMENT MANAGEMENT

10.77 Many charities employ a professional management adviser to manage their assets. In some cases, investment managers of this kind may act on an 'execution only' and 'advisory' basis. In other words, they may advise a charity's trustees on their investment strategy and deal with the purchase and sale of investments at their direction. More often, charities will engage a 'discretionary' investment manager and authorise it to exercise its own discretion to buy and sell assets on behalf of the charity within an investment policy laid down by the trustees.

10.78 In legal terms, engaging a discretionary investment manager is a delegation of the trustee's power to invest their charity's assets. Delegation by trustees is considered in more detail in **Chapter 8**, but it is helpful to remember that the starting point is that every charity trustee should exercise his or her powers personally unless they are expressly authorised by someone else to exercise them. This means that every charity trustee is obliged to make decisions about investment personally unless they are able to delegate responsibility for investment decisions to someone else.

10.79 The powers of delegation available to trustees in relation to investment management depend upon whether the charity in question is incorporated or unincorporated.

Incorporated charities

10.80 Most incorporated charities will have a power in their constitution expressly authorising their trustees to delegate investment management to a third party. Powers of this kind will usually impose certain restrictions on the exercise of the power, including provisions in relation to the competence and experience of the investment management. If an incorporated charity does not have an appropriate power of delegation, it will need to exercise a power of amendment or addition under its constitution to add one. This is usually a straightforward matter for a charitable company.[18] See **15.24–15.33** for more detail in relation to this.

---

[16] Charities Act 1993, s 25.
[17] Charities Act 1993, s 24.
[18] Charities Act 1993, s 64.

Unincorporated charities

10.81 The trustees of an unincorporated charity may also have an express power of delegation under its constitution. Failing that, s 11 of the Trustee Act 2000 gives trustees the power to delegate functions relating to the investment of charity assets. The power is conferred by the 2000 Act in addition to any powers of delegation expressly set out in the charity's constitution (or which are otherwise available to the charity's trustees under some other legal provision). See **8.101–8.111** for detail in relation to this.

10.82 The statutory power conferred by the Trustee Act 2000 can be restricted or excluded by provisions in the charity's constitution. The statutory power applies to trust assets held by an incorporated charity (but not to its corporate assets).

10.83 The statutory power is wide enough to authorise the trustees to appoint one of their number as a discretionary investment manager (although the prohibition under the Financial Services and Markets Act 2000 on anyone other than an authorised person providing investment management advice may preclude this).

Investment management agreements

10.84 Charity trustees must ensure that any agreement they enter into with any investment manager is appropriate. The trustees of an unincorporated charity who wish to rely upon the power of delegation conferred upon them by the Trustee Act 2000 must comply with a number of statutory restrictions on their discretion to agree terms with an investment manager.[19] Essentially, the trustees have a discretion to determine the basis on which any delegate should be appointed but cannot, unless it is reasonably necessary, agree to terms which:

- permit the investment manager to appoint a substitute to act in its place;

- include any exemption clause restricting the investment manager's liability to the charity; or

- permit the investment manager to act in circumstances which give rise to potential conflicts of interest.

10.85 While these restrictions do not strictly apply to the trustees of an incorporated charity entering into an investment management agreement in relation to its corporate assets, the Charity Commission takes the view that 'these restrictions apply whether or not the statutory power of delegation is being relied upon'. In other words, any charity trustee looking to enter into an investment management agreement must observe the Trustee Act 2000 restrictions we have mentioned. There does not appear to be any direct authority to substantiate the Commission's view. However, it is likely that the court would, if called upon, take into account statutory restrictions imposed on the trustees of an unincorporated charity in assessing the comparable position of the trustees of an incorporated charity. For practical purposes, therefore, all charity trustees should assume that these restrictions apply to them.

10.86 In practice, restrictions of this kind form part of the terms and conditions of business of many professional investment managers. In that sense, they are by no means unusual. On this basis, charity trustees may well conclude that it is 'reasonably

---

[19]   Trustee Act 2000, s 14.

necessary' to agree to terms of this kind on the basis that most (if not all) other professional investment managers will only agree to act on the same basis. The Commission's guidance makes the point that trustees will normally need to consider the basis on which a number of different investment managers will act before deciding on an appointment and that:

> '... a willingness or otherwise to modify these terms, perhaps by means of a "side letter" may be an important consideration for some charities. Insistence on one or more of the special terms ... is one of the factors which trustees should take into account when selecting an investment manager. It would not be "reasonably necessary" to prefer an institution which insists on one or more of these terms to one which does not, unless there is some good reason for the trustees to do so.'[20]

10.87 The investment management agreement must be in writing or 'be evidenced in writing'. In practice, no professional investment manager authorised by the Financial Services Authority will agree to act unless it has been appointed in writing.

Duty of care

10.88 In appointing a discretionary investment manager, a charity's trustees are under the general duty to exercise due care and skill we have mentioned at **10.35**. This includes the determination of whether the sort of terms we have mentioned at **10.84** are 'reasonably necessary' within the investment management agreement. Trustees looking to appoint an investment manager will generally need to consider more than one potential provider of investment management services and look in some detail at comparative service levels and costs in order to comply with their general duty.

Investment manager's duty of care

10.89 Once appointed, an investment manager will owe exactly the same duties in relation to the investments it makes on the charity's behalf as the trustees themselves. This will mean, therefore, that the investment manager must pay due regard to the 'standard investment criteria' of suitability and diversification. An investment manager will not, though, be under the same obligation as the charity's trustees to consider taking advice in relation to a particular investment. This is on the basis that the manager is a person from whom the charity's trustees could properly have taken advice from if they were exercising the power of investment themselves.[21]

10.90 An investment manager does not owe the same duty of care and skill as the charity's trustees. The duty of care owed to the charity will be regulated by the investment management agreement. Trustees should be aware of the Commission's view that:

> '... a lowering of the duty of care which would normally be applied by the law of contract would be a special term, and the trustees would have to be satisfied that it was "reasonably necessary" to agree to it'.[22]

---

[20] CC 14.
[21] Trustee Act 2000, s 13(2).
[22] CC 14.

Investment policy

10.91 The Trustee Act 2000[23] obliges the trustees of any unincorporated charity to prepare an investment policy before they exercise any power (whether conferred by the 2000 Act or not) to delegate responsibility for investment to an investment manager. The investment policy is intended to guide the investment manager in relation to the exercise of the functions delegated to it in the best interests of the charity. The policy itself has to be in writing and the charity's trustees are personally responsible for preparing it without delegating it to the investment manager in question. The Charity Commission recommends that a charity's trustees should prepare their policy in consultation with any investment manager that they propose to appoint. As the Commission points out, '... the manager is obliged to comply with the policy statement and may, therefore, be in difficulty if he finds impracticable a policy statement which the trustees have prepared without ... consultation'. The investment management agreement itself must also include a provision requiring the manager to comply with the policy statement.

10.92 The duty of care we have mentioned earlier in this chapter at **10.35** applies to the trustees in relation to preparing and reviewing the investment policy.

10.93 Because the requirement to prepare an investment policy and ensure that an investment manager is obliged to comply with it is imposed by the Trustee Act 2000, it does not strictly apply to the trustees of an incorporated charity in relation to its corporate assets. However, this is another area where the Commission takes the view that an investment policy is required irrespective of the power of delegation that is being relied upon. The constitutions of many incorporated charities will, in any event, require the preparation of an investment policy. For practical purposes, therefore, all charity trustees should assume that an investment policy is required.

10.94 The Charity Commission 'strongly recommends' that the trustees of every charity with investments should formulate an investment policy and keep it under review notwithstanding that they do not propose to delegate investment management to a professional manager.

10.95 The Trustee Act 2000 does not specify the content or form of an investment policy. Because the investment manager will need to agree to comply with it, its terms need to be reasonably specific if they are to be capable of being complied with. Subject to that, the content of the policy is likely to be determined by the circumstances of individual charities and their particular investment objectives. The Charity Commission suggests general areas which might be dealt with in an investment policy. These are:

• The charity's aim in investing its funds, including the charity's position on risk. The trustees' assessment of risk will mean striking a balance between the level of investment return required and the risk associated with it which, as the Commission points out, will be influenced by the operational needs of the charity in question. The position will need to be clearly stated to the investment manager.

• The asset allocation strategy. Some charities may have particular requirements in relation to asset allocation where, for example, they are adopting a particular ethical investment policy or have a particular requirement for liquidity. Many charities will agree a range of percentage values of the managed fund as a whole for allocation between particular asset classes.

---

23   Trustee Act 2000, s 15.

- The investment managers' benchmarks and targets. Benchmarking an investment managers' performance is clearly essential. Identifying the right benchmark is clearly a key consideration. Many investment managers will suggest benchmarks against which they should be assessed. It may be difficult for charity trustees with limited experience in relation to investment management to assess whether or not the benchmarks suggested are appropriate. It may conclude that advice from an independent third party is required.

- The charity's stance on ethical investment. Any ethical investment policy must clearly be spelt out, including any requirements in relation to positive and negative screening.

- The balance between capital and income. This will not be relevant to every charity, but those with endowment, (in particular, permanent endowment) will be particularly concerned to ensure that the right balance is struck between income and capital gains. There is more about endowment in **Chapter 9**. The investment position will be altered where a charity with permanent endowment has adopted the so called 'total return' approach to investment. There is more about this at **10.103**.

- Scope of the investment. Any restrictions on the trustee's powers of investment should be clearly identified with a view to ensuring that the investment manager does not inadvertently breach them. The policy may also usefully set out the classes of investment that may be regarded as non-charitable expenditure for tax purposes.

- The Trustee Act 2000 obliges charity trustees to keep their investment policy under review. An investment policy should normally state the basis on which it will be reviewed and the intervals on which this is expected to happen.

10.96 An example of an investment policy for a newly established grant making charity (without endowment assets and intending to operate overseas) is as follows:

Investment policy

Background

[The Charity] is a registered charity (registered number [ ]) and a company limited by guarantee (registered number [ ]) with the following charitable objects:
    [charitable objects]

Investment powers

The Charity has a wide power to invest or deposit funds in any manner (subject to an obligation to invest only after taking such advice as the trustees consider is reasonably necessary).

The Charity (and [ ] in its capacity as discretionary investment manager) should ensure that, in managing the investments, they have regard to:

- the *suitability* to the Charity of investments of the same kind as any proposed investment;

➡

- the *suitability* of the proposed investment as an investment of that kind; and

- the need for *diversification* of the investments of the Charity so far as is appropriate to its circumstances.

There are no factors which limit the need for diversification of the Charity's investments.

The investment powers of the Charity authorise an investment in hedge funds, subject to the requirements of suitability and diversification.

Investment restrictions

As a registered charity, investment by the Charity in any assets other than 'qualifying investments' within section 506 and Schedule 20 Income and Corporation Taxes Act 1988 may constitute non-charitable expenditure in certain circumstances and lead to the restriction of the tax exemptions available to the Charity in respect of its investment income and gains.

Any foreign withholding taxes should be taken into account in making investments.

Investment aims

The Charity's aim over the first 5 years of its lifespan is to invest its initial assets with a view to increasing their value. The return should be considered on a total return basis and the income generated will be re-invested. After the expiry of the first 5 year period, the Charity expects to start to use its investment return to support [ ] in respect of its activities within the Charity's objects.

The Charity's total lifespan is expected to be between [ ] and [ ] years.

Special preferences and constraints

Currency

The majority of the liabilities of the Charity will be in the currencies of the [ ] countries in which it operates, although no significant liabilities are expected to arise during the first 5 years of the Charity's lifespan. The impact of this on the currency exposure of the investments must be taken into account.

Investments in fixed interest securities should be restricted to Sterling, Euro and the US dollar denominations, in government debt or corporate bonds at or above a Standard & Poor's 'A' credit rating.

Yield

There are no restrictions on the yield of the investment portfolio.   ➡

Risk profile

The investment portfolio should carry a medium to low risk profile.

- The majority of equity investments will be in the major world companies with collective investment vehicles used to cover specialised areas such as smaller company investment.

- All investments should be readily marketable in normal stock market conditions.

- For the equity section of the portfolio no single holding should exceed 5% of the total valuation of the portfolio. Nor should any single holding produce more than 5% of the total income of the portfolio. Should either of these limits be exceeded that holding should be reduced, subject to market considerations. Larger holdings in fixed interest stocks and in collectives are permitted provided that they do not compromise the overall requirement to spread the risk of the portfolio.

Liquidity

During the first 5 years of the Charity's lifespan, liquidity will only be required to pay investment management fees and other administrative costs and expenses.

Socially Responsible Investment constraints

As the Foundation wishes to invest in a way that helps to promote its objects, investment should not normally be made in companies known to be operating in the following sectors.

Asset Allocation

Initial asset allocation / strategic range	Index	Range for Portfolio
Fixed Interest and cash	50%	[40%–60]%
International Equities	50%	[40%–60]%

Benchmark

The portfolio should be benchmarked against an index weighted 50% on the Salomon Government Bonds World Index and 50% against the FTSE World Index. These figures will be provided by [ ] as part of its half yearly reporting.

Reviews and reporting

Valuations and performance figures are expected every half year with details of the income received and other information as required by the auditors at the Charity's year end. Additional reports on performance and strategy may be➡

> requested by the Charity from time to time. This investment policy and the
> delegation of the Charity's discretionary investment management will be reviewed
> by the Charity annually.

Review

10.97 Charity trustees are under a duty to review their investment management arrangements.[24] The Charity Commission's guidance confirms that 'review' in this context does not necessarily mean seeking alternative bids for the investment management work from other investment managers.

10.98 Clearly, identifying an appropriate benchmark at the outset and ensuring performance is regularly measured against those benchmarks will be the fundamental point in relation to any review. Where necessary, a charity's trustee may need to think about obtaining professional advice from a third party if they conclude that they are not themselves in a position to make an assessment.

10.99 The Charity Commission highlights the issue of 'transaction costs' in relation to reviews. The aim of the trustees should be to seek clarity in relation to the fee structure that applies and the actual cost being met by the charity in relation to the investment management agreement. Generally speaking, the fee payable to the investment manager (which will often be a percentage to the value of the funds under management payable on an annual basis) will be clear. What are often less clear are the fees that may be payable in respect of the investments which make up the portfolio itself, particularly where funds are being invested in collective investment schemes. Those operating collective investment schemes are generally entitled to charge management fees which it may be much more difficult for the charity's trustees to assess.

NOMINEES AND CUSTODIANS

10.100 As part of most investment management agreements, the investment manager will agree to hold their charity client's investments in the name of a nominee company established by the investment manager. Beneficial ownership of the investments remains with the charity, but using a nominee company will usually make buying and selling investments within the charity's portfolio much more straightforward.

10.101 The trustees of an unincorporated charity have a statutory power under the Trustee Act 2000 to appoint a nominee or custodian of any of the charity's assets.[25] This is in addition to any powers to appoint a nominee or custodian in the charity's own constitution.

10.102 The trustees of an incorporated charity cannot rely upon the Trustee Act 2000 in respect of its corporate assets, but will generally have an express power to put assets into the name of a nominee or custodian in the charity's constitution. There is more about this in **Chapter 9.**

---

[24]   Trustee Act 2000, s 22.
[25]   Trustee Act 2000, ss 16, 17.

TOTAL RETURN APPROACH TO INVESTMENT

10.103 Specific investment considerations apply to the trustees of any charity with permanent endowment. Permanent endowment is the term applied to any charity asset which is held on trust to retain it for the purposes of the charity. Permanent endowment will often be land used for a charity's particular purposes. However, permanent endowment may also be investment assets held with a view to generating income capable of supporting the charity's operations. See **9.27–9.36** for more detail in relation to permanent endowment.

10.104 In this sense, permanent endowment is very similar to the capital assets of a private trust which are held to generate an income for certain beneficiaries, while the endowment assets themselves are held for other beneficiaries. In the context of a charity, trustees are required to hold the balance between its present and future needs. The charity's present requirements will be met out of the income generated by the endowment assets. But the endowment assets themselves must be retained in order to maintain a capital base which can generate income to meet the charity's requirements in the future.

10.105 An issue highlighted by the bull market in many investments in recent years (giving rise to significant capital gains) has been the discrepancy between the way in which charities with permanent endowment can apply the investment return from the endowment itself and what might be considered, in investment terms alone, the best possible approach for the benefit of the charity. The Charity Commission put it this way:

> 'Trustees are selecting investments which they judge should produce returns that, when the rules are applied to them, will break down into a mix of income needed by the charity to carry out its charitable purposes for the benefit of the current beneficiaries and of capital growth for the benefit of future beneficiaries. This reflects their duty to maintain a fair balance between capital and income interests.
>
> In theory, this approach does not seem problematic. However, the need to comply with the rules has led trustees to select investment portfolios because they will "fit" the rules for the treatment of investment returns, rather than because the portfolio's mix of investments will give the charity the best total level of economic return. A charity's scope for investment and the total level of returns it is able to realise can be negatively affected as a result.'[26]

10.106 In other words, charity trustees may feel (and in fact are) obliged to allow the legal constraints on the way in which they can apply income and capital gains generated by their invested endowment to take precedence over the investment approach that might otherwise be taken to produce the best overall return for the charity. The 'total return approach to investment' is the Charity Commission's response to this issue. It is a policy which is intended to enable the trustees of any charity with permanent endowment to invest their charity's assets in a way that will produce the best overall financial return for the charity, regardless of whether this is made up of income or capital gains or both.

10.107 The Charity Commission's guidance explains how the total return approach to investment works:

---

[26]   Consultation Document July 2000; OG 83 CI.

'Under the standard rules the form in which investment returns arise is important. By contrast, under the total return approach the form in which investment returns are received is irrelevant. Instead, investments are managed so as to optimise the investment return generated by them regardless of whether this is obtained by way of dividends, interest or capital gains. With this approach it is the level of the investment return rather than the composition of the return that is important.'[27]

10.108 In essence, the total return approach is as follows:

- On an application by a charity's trustees, the Charity Commission may agree to give them the power to allocate all or part of the 'investment return' on the charity's endowment assets to a 'trust for application (income)'.

- The 'investment return' includes income such as interest and dividends but will also include any form of capital gain which would otherwise ordinarily form part of the capital or endowment of the charity (and is referred to in the context of total return as the 'trust for application (capital)'). Any capital losses have to be deducted from the 'investment return'.

- By allocating all or part of the investment return to the trust for application (income), the charity's trustees are able to spend it for the charity's purposes in the same way as the charity's other income. Any part of the investment return that is not allocated in this way must be allocated to the trust for application (capital). In other words, it must be added to the existing endowment.

- The trustees will continue to have the capacity to spend any part of the investment return received previously by the charity which has been added to the trust for application. The Commission refer to this as the 'unapplied total return'. The authority given to a charity's trustees will allow them to decide which part of this unapplied total return should be held on the trust for application (income) and spent by the charity accordingly.

10.109 The Charity Commission will usually make an Order under the Charities Act 1993, s 26 authorising the trustees of a charity to adopt a total return approach on the basis that it is 'expedient in the interest of the charity that the trustees should have the power to do so'. A Scheme will generally only be required if the charity's constitution contains a specific prohibition on the use of the total return approach, perhaps by specifying that the charity's capital gains derived from its endowment cannot be spent by it. Provisions of this kind will be unusual in practice, so that most total return powers will be conferred by way of an Order.

10.110 The Charity Commission regard the power to allocate all or part of the investment return in the way we have explained as no more than an 'administrative power'. On that basis, the Commission's guidance[28] confirms that they have no objection to the use of a power of amendment conferred by a charity's constitution to adopt provisions authorising the total return approach provided they include the sort of safeguards usually contained in the Commission's own Orders.

10.111 The key point in relation to the total return approach to investment is that it is intended to give the charity trustees the freedom to allocate investment return as they

---

[27]   OG 83 AI.
[28]   OG 83 B1.

think fit, with the consequence that they can determine their investment policy solely on the basis of investment considerations. It is essential that the trustees exercise the power they are given in the best interests of the charity. This is reflected in the directions the Commission will include in any Order regulating the way in which the power it gives trustees should be exercised. Of these, the most important is the direction that 'the trustees should only use the power … in such a way as not to prejudice the ability of the charity to meet the present and future needs which are designated by its trusts'. It is this provision which obliges a charity's trustees to take into account the position of both the charity's present and future beneficiaries.

10.112 There are other directions which are relevant. Before exercising the power, a charity's trustees must obtain and consider proper advice about the way in which the power ought to be exercised. The proper advice is the advice of a person whom the trustees reasonably believe to be qualified to give it by 'his or her ability and practical experience of investment or actuarial matters'. There is a limited exception where the trustees 'reasonably conclude' that 'in all the circumstances it is unnecessary or inappropriate to do so'. Clearly, the use of the word 'reasonably' imports an objective standard into these criteria.

10.113 There are other directions, including an obligation on the trustees to keep a careful record of which part of a charity's assets represents its 'unapplied total return' and a requirement to state in the charity's annual report for each financial year the consideration and policies which are relevant to the exercise of the total return power by the trustees.

10.114 Before giving trustees authority to adopt the total return approach to investment, the Charity Commission will usually wish to be satisfied in relation to three points:

- That the charity in question does actually hold endowment. Clearly, if there is no endowment, the charity will not need a total return Order.

- The trustees for the charity must also be able to distinguish between the endowment assets of the charity and assets which represent the 'unapplied total return' it has received previously. The Commission states that 'we will not expect trustees to carry out an elaborate tracing exercise in this respect, as this will often not be practical – particularly in the case of that part of the unapplied investment return which takes the form of investment gains, rather than the form of retained investment income'. The guidance goes on to say, 'In many cases trustees will have to make a reasonable estimate as to which part of their overall resources represent the unapplied return from the investment of the gifts they have received'.[29]

- The Commission must be able to conclude that having the power to apply the total return approach would be in the charity's best interests. Trustees should write to the Commission setting out why they consider that a power of this kind would be beneficial to their charity. The Commission's guidance states that 'in the absence of any other information we should normally accept the trustees' conclusions'. However, if there is an indication that authorising a total return approach might be opposed by a significant donor to the charity or its supporters generally, they may ask the trustees to give public notice of the application before authorising the use of the power.

---

[29] OG 83 B1.

10.115 The Commission's guidance states that the power to adopt a total return approach does not authorise the expenditure of the charity's 'investment fund', which is defined by the Commission to mean a charity's permanent endowment together with any part of the unapplied total return which cannot be allocated to the trust for application (income). Expenditure of the investment fund using a total return Order would require an additional Order. Essentially, this will only allow the expenditure of the investment fund on the basis of 'recoupment'. There is more about recoupment in **Chapter 9**. On this basis, the Commission's view is that:

> 'It is therefore clear that the concept of permanent endowment (i.e. assets held on trust for investment (capital)) is not affected by the power we propose to give trustees. We recognise a donor's rights to create a charity that will have future as well as present beneficiaries.'[30]

10.116 In one sense this is true. The policy requires a charity's trustees to take account of both its present and future needs. However, the reality is that the policy allows charity trustees to treat capital gains (which would otherwise be considered to be part of permanent endowment) as income. One view is that the Charity Commission has no legal authority to authorise this sort of expenditure by way of Order implementing the total return policy. While this may be correct as a strict legal interpretation of the position, our view is that charity trustees do not have a great deal to fear in adopting an approach which is so clearly delineated by the Charity Commission. It may, though, mean that trustees will prefer to seek an express Order than to exercise their own powers to add similar provisions.

10.117 The Charity Commission's guidance also indicates that, in their view, 'trustees will not normally need to retain funds for any length of time in the trust for application (income)'. This is on the basis that any part of the charity's unapplied total return can be applied to the trust for application (income) at any time provided that the trustees conclude that the interests of the present and future beneficiaries are not prejudiced as a consequence. As the Commission points out, a charity's trustees do not therefore need to build up reserves in the trust for application (income) in anticipation of any year when investment returns are lower than expected. If reserves are made, the Charity Commission will expect this to be in accordance with the charity's reserves policy. There is more about reserves at **9.64–9.87**.

---

[30]   OG 83 A2.

11

TAXATION

11.1 There is a popular misconception that charities are eligible for a blanket exemption from tax in respect of all and any of their activities. In reality, the blanket is more of a patchwork, with scope for liabilities for tax to arise where particular activities or transactions are not properly considered or structured by a charity's trustees beforehand.

11.2 Why is this a governance issue? The Charity Commission's view (expressed in their 1988 Report) is that charity trustees may be

'... personally liable to account for taxation liabilities which are unnecessarily incurred directly or indirectly as a result of the inefficient administration of the charity.'

11.3 From the point of view of good governance, therefore, the duty owed by a charity's trustees in relation to tax liabilities is clear. Given the scope of activities within which liability to tax can arise (whether in relation to investment, trading or fundraising), this duty is fairly onerous.

11.4 The way in which charities are taxed is the subject of a book in itself. In this chapter, we do no more than summarise the framework for the taxation of charities with the view to highlighting some of the more significant issues that may arise in practice. In order to do this, we explain:

- what constitutes a 'charity' for tax purposes;

- how the income and capital gains of incorporated and unincorporated charities are charged to tax, subject to any exemptions;

- the exemptions from tax on the income and capital gains of charities that are available;

- the restrictions on these exemptions that are aimed at countering tax avoidance; and

- the tax treatment of donations of cash and other assets by individuals and commercial entities.

'CHARITY' FOR TAX PURPOSES

11.5 As we have mentioned in **Chapter 1** a 'charity' is defined differently for the purposes of charity law and tax, although the definitions are very similar. For income tax purposes, a 'charity' is 'any body or persons or trust established for charitable purposes only'.[1] There is no statutory definition for the purposes of capital gains tax, although the meaning is essentially the same.

11.6   The leading case for tax purposes is *Camille and Henry Dreyfus Foundation Inc v IRC*.[2] Essentially, in order to be 'established for charitable purposes only' an institution must be '... so constituted or regulated as to be subject to the jurisdiction of the courts which can alone define and regulate those purposes'. In simple terms, therefore, whether an entity is a charity for tax purposes depends upon the way in which it is constituted. In the case of a charitable trust, the courts will look at the governing law of the charity and where the trustees are resident. Where the charity is a company, they will look at the place in which it is incorporated and where its directors are resident. They will also look in any event at where the charity is administered and where its assets are located.

11.7   In practice, HM Revenue & Customs will look to the Charity Commission for a determination of whether a particular entity has been registered as a charity or not. Although the tests for the purposes of charity and tax law are slightly different (because they depend upon different lines of case law), the practical position is fundamentally the same. A charitable company must be incorporated in England and Wales. A charitable trust must be governed by English law and must also have at least one trustee who is resident here.

EU LAW

11.8   The restriction of exemptions from UK tax to entities that are 'charities' for UK tax purposes (and which therefore have the kind of connection with the UK we have mentioned) may be a breach of certain of the fundamental freedoms under the EC Treaty. The European Commission has made a complaint to the UK under article 226 of the Treaty that the exemptions available to charities for UK tax purposes are in breach of several of the articles in the Treaty, including the freedom of movement of capital and the freedom of establishment. The complaint reflects previous European Court of Justice decisions in relation to other jurisdictions (Belgium and Germany). Depending upon the response made by the UK to the EC's complaint, it is possible that the scope of exemptions from UK tax will be extended to charities established under the laws of other EU jurisdictions.

LIABILITY TO TAX

11.9   The way in which a charity is constituted will determine the tax to which it will be liable in the event that there is no exemption available.

11.10   Charitable trusts are potentially liable to pay income tax on their taxable income and capital gains tax on their capital gains. The liability to income tax is the basic rate (presently 22%) or, where the income in question is less than £2,150, the lower rate (presently 10%). Charitable trusts are not subject to the 'rate applicable to trusts' paid by private trusts,[3] which would bring the rate of income tax up to 40%. However, a

---

[1]   Income and Corporation Taxes Act 1988, s 506(1).
[2]   [1954] 2 All ER 466.
[3]   Income and Corporation Taxes Act 1988, s 686A(4)(c).

charitable trust does pay capital gains tax at the 'rate applicable to trusts' on its capital gains. The rate is therefore presently 40%, subject to an annual exemption.

11.11 Charitable companies, and any other charity which is a 'corporation' for tax purposes, pay corporation tax in respect of both their income and capital profits. The rate of tax that applies will depend upon the level of taxable profit. Profits of less than £300,000 are charged to tax at 19%. Profits in excess of £1,500,000 are charged at 30%. Where profits fall between these two figures a 'marginal' rate of tax applies.

11.12 For tax purposes, a 'corporation' will include charitable companies limited by guarantee and by shares, CIOs, industrial and provident societies, friendly societies, corporations and also charitable unincorporated associations.

11.13 Where a charitable company is 'close', it is likely to be a 'close investment-holding company'. This means that the company is not entitled to pay corporation tax at the lower rate of 19%.[4] A company is 'close' if it is under the control of five or fewer participators or any number of participators who are also its directors. A 'participator' is any person who exercises voting rights in relation to a company. This will include not only the members of charitable companies, but also the members of any charitable unincorporated association. In many cases, a charitable company's trustees will also be its members, so that the company will be close irrespective of the number of trustees.

11.14 A charitable close company will generally be an 'investment-holding' company. This is because its charitable purposes will prevent it from qualifying for any of the exceptions in the tax legislation from the definition of 'investment-holding'. These include, for example, existing wholly or mainly for the purpose of carrying on a trade. While a charitable company may well carry on a trade, it will not exist wholly and mainly for this purpose.

EXEMPTIONS FROM TAX ON INCOME

11.15 Section 505(1)(c) of the Income and Corporation Taxes Act 1988 gives charities a number of significant exemptions from tax on particular types of income. This reflects the scheme of the income tax legislation generally, which categorises and taxes different types of income according to their 'source'.

11.16 There are two general requirements that must be satisfied in order for each of the specific exemptions to apply. The first is that the income in question is actually the income of a 'charity' for tax purposes. The second is that the income must be 'applied to charitable purposes only'. We look at the way in which income is applied to charitable purposes only in more detail at **11.45**.

Trading income

11.17 There are a series of specific exemptions that apply to a charity's trading income. These are explained in more detail in **Chapter 13**. In general, the exemptions summarised below relate to a charity's investment income. There is more about investment generally in **Chapter 10**.

---

4   Income and Corporation Taxes Act 1988, s 13(1).

Deduction of tax

11.18 Many of the sources of income mentioned below (e g bank interest) will have tax deducted from them at source. The availability of an exemption from tax will enable the charity to reclaim the tax deducted. There is more about tax reclaims at **11.145**.

Income from land

11.19 There is an exemption from tax on rent and other profit and gains received in respect of land (whether inside or outside the UK). This includes a beneficial interest in land vested in the charity, where the legal title is held by a nominee on its behalf.[5]

11.20 There is a specific anti-avoidance provision which charges to income tax gains arising from the disposal of land by charity.[6] Although this is an 'anti-avoidance' provision, it is wide enough to catch any land that is obtained, held or developed with the intention of realising a gain on its disposal. In practice, a charge is often triggered where charity trustees selling land with the potential for development do so on the basis that they are entitled to a share in any profits that are realised if the land is actually subsequently developed.

11.21 It is also possible that, in certain circumstances, HM Revenue & Customs may argue that a disposal of land is part of a trade of property development being carried out by the charity. Because property development cannot be a primary purpose trade of a charity, any trading profits are unlikely to qualify for exemption for tax. There is more about this in **Chapter 13**.

11.22 The key issue for charity trustees in relation to any proposal to disposal of land is to seek professional tax advice on the position at an early stage.

Interest and annual payments

11.23 Section 505(1)(b)(ii) of the Income and Corporation Taxes Act 1988 exempts all payments of interest to a charity from tax. These include, for example, interest payable on bonds and loan notes issued by companies, local authorities, governments etc. It does not matter whether or not the interest has a UK 'source'. In other words, the exemption applies whether the interest is paid by an entity that is resident inside or outside the UK.

11.24 The same provision also exempts from tax 'annual payments', again irrespective of whether they have UK or an overseas source. Annual payments are explained in more detail in **13.68**. For the purposes of this exemption, they include royalties and gift aid donations payable to the charity.

Dividends

11.25 There is an exemption from tax for dividends received in respect of shares held by a charity.[7] This exemption also extends to all other forms of 'distribution' by a company in which a charity owns shares, irrespective of whether the company is resident in the UK or overseas. The exemption also applies to distributions from unit trusts, OEICs and other forms of collective investment schemes.

---

[5] Income and Corporation Taxes Act 1988), s 505(a).
[6] Income and Corporation Taxes Act 1988, s 776.
[7] Income and Corporation Taxes Act 1988, s 505(b)(iii) and (iv).

11.26 Although dividends and other distributions are exempt from tax, they will have been paid out of the company's taxed profits. Charities are not able to reclaim the tax paid by a UK resident company, which will be tax at a rate of 19% to 30%. In the case of an overseas company, the tax paid by it on its profits it will be at whatever rate applies in the overseas jurisdiction (but see the comments at **11.39** for more on this).

Insurance policies

11.27 Where a charity invests in an insurance policy, a tax charge can arise when the policy matures or in certain other circumstances specified by the tax legislation. The rules governing the way in which policies are taxed are complicated, depending in part upon the type of policy in question and the terms on which it is issued.

11.28 The key point is that any gain in the value of the policy (which will reflect any increase in the value of the insurer's underlying investments) will be liable to tax in the hands of the charity. A tax credit is available to a charitable trust in certain circumstances, but an incorporated charity (including an unincorporated association) does not qualify for an exemption.

11.29 There are in any event two other significant issues that need to be taken into account by a charity that is looking to invest in insurance policies. First, HM Revenue & Customs do not regard them as 'qualifying investments' for the purpose of the rules on charitable expenditure (there is more about this at **11.56**). Second, any return on the policy will be net of the tax paid by the insurer, which may mean that the net benefit to the charity is lower than the net benefit that can be received from other forms of investment.

Stock lending

11.30 The tax treatment of stock loans and stock lending fees is complex and may give rise to tax liabilities for charities. Trustees should seek professional advice before entering into stock loans.

Swaps

11.31 Where a charity enters into swap arrangements as part of its investment strategy, (and HM Revenue & Customs will assess whether the charity has complied with the Charity Commission's guidance in relation to the appropriate use of swaps in this context),[8] an incorporated charity or unincorporated association can claim an exemption in respect of any profits arising from the swap. However, where the swap transaction is entered into by a charitable trust, an exemption is only likely to be available under the small trades exemption. There is more about this in **13.38**.

11.32 If HM Revenue & Customs conclude that a swap transaction is entered into as part of a trade rather than as an investment, any profits received by the charity will qualify for exemption on the same basis as any other trading income. There is more about this in **13.25**.

---

8   HM Revenue & Customs' Tax Bulletin 66.

Futures and options

11.33 Where a charitable trust (but not a charitable company) enters into futures and options as part of its investment strategy, and the futures and options and questions are structured in such a way that they produce a return which is both guaranteed and is substantially the same as interest, it will pay income tax on the payments unless they fall within the exemption for small trades. There is more about this in **13.38**. An incorporated charity or an unincorporated association will generally be able to claim an exemption from tax.[9]

Underwriting fees

11.34 Underwriting fees are not generally exempt from tax. Trustees will need to take professional advice on the tax treatment of such fees.

EXEMPTION FROM TAX ON CAPITAL GAINS

11.35 Section 256(1) of the Taxation of Chargeable Gains Act 1992 exempts from tax capital gains that accrue to a charity and are 'applicable and applied for charitable purposes'. In essence, therefore, there are two general requirements that must be satisfied in order for this exemption to apply. These are essentially the same as the requirements that apply to the exemptions from tax on income. The first is that the capital gains are actually capital gains of a 'charity' for tax purposes. As we have indicated, there is no statutory definition of 'charity' for capital gains tax purposes. In practice, a charity that satisfies the definition for the purposes of income tax will also be a charity for the purposes of capital gains tax.

11.36 The second requirement of the capital gains tax exemption requires that the capital gains must be 'applied for charitable purposes'. This has essentially the same meaning as the phrase 'applied to charitable purposes only' for income tax purposes.[10]

11.37 The capital gains in question must also be 'applicable for' charitable purposes. It is difficult to see what this adds to the other two requirements given that, between them, they ensure that the exemption is only available where the charity is actually a charity (and therefore established for charitable purposes) and that the capital gain must only be applied for those charitable purposes.

11.38 Unlike the different exemptions that apply in relation to tax on different types of income, there is only a single exemption in respect of tax on capital gains. This will apply in almost every situation providing the requirements we have mentioned above are satisfied. However, it is worth mentioning that capital gains can in certain circumstances be deemed to arise. Given the practical difficulty of showing that deemed gains have been applied for charitable purposes, it is possible that HM Revenue & Customs may not allow exemption in certain circumstances. The most notable example of this is where a close company which is resident for tax purposes outside the UK realises gains. The anti-avoidance provisions in the capital gains tax legislation will deem the gains to have

---

9   Income and Corporation Taxes Act 1988, s 505(1)(c)(ii).
10   *IRC v Helen Slater Charitable Trust Limited* (1981) 55 TC 230.

been realised by certain participators in the company. Where this includes a charity, an exemption from capital gains tax is unlikely to be available.[11] There is more about close companies at **11.13**.

OVERSEAS INVESTMENTS

11.39 As we have explained, the exemptions from income and capital gains available to charities will generally apply irrespective of whether the investment that generates the income or gains is inside or outside the UK. In terms of UK tax, this obviously gives a charity's trustees the flexibility to consider including overseas investments as part of their overall investment strategy.

11.40 Having said this, it is obviously important that the charity's trustees take into account any foreign taxes that may be payable in respect of particular investments. While, for example, rental income from land in an overseas jurisdiction may be free of UK tax, there is unlikely to be an exemption within that jurisdiction for rental income payable to a UK charity. Any overseas tax that is payable will obviously reduce the net returns of the charity on its investment. This is a very important consideration for trustees when they are determining their investment strategy.

11.41 In practice, relief from overseas tax will generally only be available under a 'double tax treaty' between the UK and the overseas jurisdiction in question. The UK has a very wide range of double tax treaties. While most will not refer to charities expressly, it may be possible to claim double treaty relief from overseas tax in certain circumstances. There are a number of potential issues for charities in relation to double tax treaties, not least that relief is usually only available to entities which are 'liable to tax'. While there is a good argument that charities are liable to UK tax, subject only to the wide range of exemptions and reliefs that are available, the position is not absolutely certain.

11.42 In practice, any charity looking to invest overseas will need to take advice on any foreign taxes which are payable and then look in some detail at the availability of double taxation relief.

GIFTS AND DONATIONS

11.43 While gifts and donations to a charity will form part of its income for the purposes of charity law, they are not 'income' for tax purposes. This means that, with two exceptions, there is no specific exemption from tax in respect of funds donated to a charity.

11.44 The exceptions we have mentioned are donations by individuals that qualify for gift aid relief and donations made between charities. Both of these kinds of donation are deemed by the tax legislation to be taxable income of the charity that receives them. However, both also qualify for a specific exemption from tax (they are, in fact, treated in the same way as 'annual payments'; there is more about this at **11.23**).

---

[11]   Taxation of Chargeable Gains Act 1992, s 13; Budget notice 5/01.

APPLICATION FOR CHARITABLE PURPOSES ONLY

11.45 As we have mentioned, the exemptions from tax on both income and capital gains are subject to a requirement that the income and gains in question are applied for (or 'to') charitable purposes only. This requirement relates only to a charity's income and capital gains and not, for example, to the way in which it may spend any other financial resources. There are specific rules relating to 'charitable expenditure' which are intended to deal with this wider issue. These are explained in more detail at **11.56**.

11.46 Income and gains will be applied by a charity for charitable purposes only where the way in which they are applied is authorised by the charity's constitution. Clearly, this will include grants for the charity's purposes and operational activities that advance those purposes. But it will also include expenditure on the costs of maintaining and administering the charity so that it can continue to advance its charitable purposes.

11.47 Equally clearly, income and gains will not have been applied for charitable purposes only where they are applied in breach of the charity's constitution. This would include, for example, making a payment to a trustee in circumstances where the trustee is not entitled to be paid and has done nothing in return for the charity or where the charity makes payments for purposes that are not charitable (eg funding a political party or campaign).

11.48 In principle, applying income and gains for a purpose that is charitable but is not one of the charitable purposes specified in the charity's constitution will not breach the requirement.[12] HM Revenue & Customs appear to accept that this may be the case, while reserving their position:

> 'If expenditure is clearly of a charitable nature, but it is not authorised by the terms of the governing document to the charity, it will not necessarily be refused for tax refunds.'[13]

11.49 Clearly, the application of funds for a charitable purpose which is outside the charity's own purposes will be a breach of the restrictions imposed by charity law and is also likely to be a breach of trust by the charity's trustees.

11.50 Where the Charity Commission make an Order under Charities Act 1993, s 26 which deems a charity's trustees to have power to do something they do not otherwise have a power to do, there is a good argument that any income and gains applied pursuant to the Order will have been applied for charitable purposes only. The position is different where a charity's trustees seek Advice, because this merely protects trustees from personal liability rather than deeming them to have a power that they do not otherwise have. There is more about Advice and Orders at **4.16** and **4.19** respectively.

11.51 In certain circumstances, a charity may take the decision not to spend income that it receives. Its trustees may decide, for example, to make a reserve of income that can be spent to fund future projects. Or they may have a formal power to add the income to the charity's capital assets. This is usually referred to as 'accumulation'. There is more about reserves and accumulation at **9.64** and **9.51** respectively.

11.52 HM Revenue & Customs' view is that:

---

[12] *Ofrex (George Drexler) Foundation (Trustees) v IRC* [1965] 3 All ER 529.
[13] HM Revenue & Customs' Guidance Note Annex II.2.

'Where a charity accumulates income, or builds up reserves, we need to decide if this is within the meaning of the phrase "applied for charitable purposes only".'[14]

11.53 Clearly, the concern is that the income that is held in reserve or added to capital cannot have actually been 'applied'. But the Courts have concluded previously that income that is accumulated or reserved can be treated as 'applied for charitable purposes' where this is properly done.[15] Provided, therefore, that income is properly accumulated in accordance with a power conferred upon a charity's trustees or added to its reserves in accordance with the duties imposed upon the trustees in relation to reserves generally, the income will have been applied for charitable purposes only.

11.54 HM Revenue & Customs mention two other circumstances in which they will argue that accumulated and reserved income has not been applied for charitable purposes only:

'IR Charities will not challenge accumulations of income except in the rare cases in which it is:

- Not invested at all but kept in cash or in a current account; or
- Where it becomes apparent that accumulated income is being invested in some project in which there is a potential conflict of interest between the interest of the charitable trust and the interest of the trustee or provider of the trust funds.'[16]

11.55 In certain circumstances, a charity's trustees may enter into a transaction that is in breach of the charity's constitution and also qualifies as a breach of trust by the trustees. This might be because, for example, the charity enters into a transaction with one of the trustees that is not authorised by its constitution. The courts have concluded previously that where a breach of trust of this kind does not result in any disadvantage to the charity, any income or capital gains paid by the charity to the trustee will still have been applied for charitable purposes only, notwithstanding that a breach of trust may have occurred. The position will be different where the breach of trust has clearly resulted in the trustee benefiting at the expense of the charity.

CHARITABLE EXPENDITURE

11.56 As we have explained, the charitable expenditure rules supplement the requirement for the expenditure of income and capital gains for charitable purposes only. The rules are essentially straightforward:

- The tax legislation distinguishes between 'charitable expenditure' and 'non-charitable expenditure'. Charitable expenditure is expenditure that is 'exclusively for charitable purposes'. All other expenditure (and certain things that, although not strictly 'expenditure', are deemed to be expenditure by a charity) is non-charitable.

- 'Expenditure which is exclusively for charitable purposes' is not defined by the tax legislation but, in our view, it has the same meaning as 'applied for charitable purposes only'.

---

14 HM Revenue & Customs' Guidance Note Annex II.3.
15 *Nightingale v Price* [1996] STC (SCD) 116.
16 HM Revenue & Customs' Guidance Note Annex II.3.

- Certain things are deemed by the tax legislation to be non-charitable expenditure. These are:
  - any investment made by the charity that is not a 'qualifying investment'
  - any loan made by the charity that is not an investment and also fails to meet the criteria for a 'qualifying loan'
  - any payment to an overseas body where the charity has failed to take reasonable steps to ensure that the payment will be applied for charitable purposes
  - certain payments made to a 'substantial donor' to the charity.

  Each of these four categories of non-charitable expenditure is explained in more detail below.

- Where a charity incurs any non-charitable expenditure, the charity's ability to claim exemption from tax on its income and capital gains is restricted. The exemption the charity could otherwise claim is restricted by an amount equal to its non-charitable expenditure. This is on a 'pound for pound' basis.

- If the charity's non-charitable expenditure exceeds both its income and capital gains and any non-taxable income (including donations), the excess can be carried back to previous 'chargeable periods' and set against the income and gains and non-taxable income of previous years. It cannot be carried back for more than 6 years before the end of the chargeable period in which the non-charitable expenditure was actually incurred.

- The 'chargeable period' in respect of which a charity's relevant income and gains and non-charitable expenditure is assessed will depend upon the way in which it is constituted. The chargeable period for a charitable trust is the tax year ending 5 April. For a charity that is incorporated or a charitable unincorporated association, the chargeable period is the period in respect of which it makes up its accounts (often the period of 12 months to 31 December or 31 March in each year).

11.57 Essentially, therefore, whether or not the charitable expenditure rules give rise to a liability to tax for a charity will depend whether it has incurred any expenditure which is not exclusively for charitable purposes and, in particular, whether it has made any non-qualifying investments or loans, made payments to an overseas body without taking reasonable steps to ensure that the funds paid over can only be applied for charitable purposes or entered into any transactions with any of its substantial donors. Each of these four items of non-charitable expenditure is examined in more detail below.

11.58 Because a charity must self-assess itself in respect of its liability to tax, it is obviously essential that its trustees understand how the charitable expenditure rules work and their implications and take professional advice where required.

Non-qualifying investments

11.59 A non-qualifying investment is any investment made by a charity which does not feature on a list of 'qualifying' investments set out in the Income and Corporation Taxes Act 1988, Schedule 20, Part 1. There is more about what constitutes an 'investment' in **Chapter 10**.

11.60 The investments mentioned in Schedule 20 are as follows:

- Any investment falling within Trustee Investment Act 1961, Schedule 1, Parts I, II or III (with the exception of Part III, paragraph 13).
  The 1961 Act specifies a number of 'safe' investments considered suitable for trustees in 1961. They include National Savings Certificates and UK Government bonds.

- Any investment in a common investment fund or common deposit fund.
  There is more about funds of this kind in **Chapter 10**.

- Any interest in land (except an interest in land which is held as security for a debt).

- Shares or securities issued by a company that are listed on a 'recognised stock exchange'.
  HM Revenue & Customs maintain a list of recognised stock exchanges for tax purposes. This includes shares listed on the Alternative Investment Market (or 'AIM').

- Units and authorised unit trusts and shares in an OEIC (open ended investment company).[17]

- Any deposit with a bank where the bank pays interest at a commercial rate (except where the deposit is made as part of an arrangement (usually the giving of 'back to back' security) under which a loan is made by the bank to some other person on the strength of the deposit by the charity).

- Uncertificated eligible debt security units.[18]

- Certificates of deposit.

- Any loan or other investment which HM Revenue & Customs are satisfied is made for the benefit of the charity and not for the avoidance of tax (whether by the charity or by any other person). For this purpose, a loan includes a loan which is secured by a mortgage or a charge over any land.

11.61 Clearly, this final category will be very important where a charity wishes to invest in any asset that does not appear in any of the other categories we have mentioned. The best examples are a direct investment in private equity (because buying unlisted shares in a company is not one of the specified categories of qualifying investment) or an interest in a hedge fund.

11.62 The first requirement for an asset to be a qualifying investment under this category is that it is made for 'the benefit of the charity'. There is no statutory definition of this test nor of what 'benefit' means, but HM Revenue & Customs will assess the position at the time the investment or loan in question is made. HM Revenue & Customs also state in their guidance that:

---

[17] Financial Services and Markets Act 2000, Part XVII.
[18] Income Tax (Trading and Other Income) Act 2005, s 552(2).

'An investment or loan will normally be "for the benefit of the charity" where it is made on sound commercial terms. Whether or not an investment or loan is commercially sound should be considered by reference to the circumstances prevailing at the time it was made.'[19]

11.63 In our view, the test of what is for the 'benefit' of a charity includes both an objective and a subjective element, in much the same way as the statutory duty of care imposed upon charity trustees in relation to the exercise of certain powers by the Trustee Act 2000, s 1. In this sense, trustees considering whether to buy a particular asset or to make a particular loan is for the benefit of their charity should ensure that there is some objective justification for their decision. HM Revenue & Customs' guidance is that:

'There is no one test of commercial soundness, and each case must be viewed on its own facts. Where a loan or investment:

- carries a commercial rate of interest; and
- is adequately secured; and
- is made under a formal written agreement which includes reasonable repayment terms

we will normally expect that the investment or loan is for the benefit of the charity.'[20]

11.64 It will obviously be essential from the point of view of the charity's trustees that they ensure that a full written record of their reasons for making a particular loan or investment is kept, together with any supporting advice or other evidence. Again, HM Revenue & Customs' guidance is helpful:

'All investment decisions should be properly monitored, including the factors on which the decisions were based. Depending upon the size of the proposed investment, the decision may be based on the following:

- Business plans
- Cash flow forecasts
- Projections of future profits.'[21]

11.65 In practice, the question of whether or not a particular investment or loan can qualify on this basis is thrown into sharp relief where a charity is considering investing in its trading subsidiary. There is more information about the considerations that should be taken into account by a charity's trustees in relation to any investment in a trading subsidiary in **13.80**.

For the avoidance of tax

11.66 Again, there is no statutory definition of what constitutes tax avoidance, although a long line of decisions by the courts indicate that they are often reluctant to conclude that the avoidance of tax is a motive for a particular transaction, particularly where there is some commercial purpose involved.

11.67 The fact that a charity is making an investment or a loan that it considers will be a qualifying investment and will not, therefore, be liable to tax is not, in itself, tax avoidance. In our view, the same is true of any investment in a charity's trading subsidiary. While, on one analysis, this avoids tax on trading income that would have

---

[19]   HM Revenue & Customs' Guidance Note Annex III.4.
[20]   HM Revenue & Customs' Guidance Note Annex III.4.
[21]   HM Revenue & Customs' Guidance Note Annex IV.62.

been payable had the charity carried out the trade itself, the arrangement is so clearly approved of by both HM Revenue & Customs and the Charity Commission that it is difficult to foresee the circumstances in which HM Revenue & Customs would argue that using a subsidiary is for the avoidance of tax.

Qualifying loans

11.68 Loans that are made as investments may be 'qualifying investments' under the rules explained above. Loans which are not made 'by way of investment' will only qualify as charitable expenditure if they fall within one of four specific categories:

- A loan made by one charity to another charity for charitable purposes only.

- A loan to a beneficiary of the charity that is made in the course of carrying out the purposes of the charity.

- Money placed on a current account with a bank (except where this is part of an arrangement under which a loan is made by the bank to some other person).

- Any other loan made for the benefit of the charity and not for the avoidance of tax (whether by the charity or some other person).

11.69 The provisions which require that the loan must be for the benefit of the charity and not for the avoidance of tax apply in exactly the same way as they do to qualifying investments.

Claims

11.70 Investments and loans fall into the categories mentioned in **11.60**(i) and **11.68**(d) above will only constitute qualifying investments and qualifying loans if HM Revenue & Customs are satisfied 'on a claim made to them in that behalf' that the investment or loan in question is made for the benefit of the charity and not for the avoidance of tax.

11.71 However, there is no formal mechanism for a claim to be made in advance of the making of any investment or loan and, in practice, HM Revenue & Customs will usually refuse to comment on the position in advance. In practice, therefore, a claim can only really be made by a charity by assessing itself to tax on the basis that the investments and loan its makes are qualifying and ensuring that sufficient information is made available to HM Revenue & Customs in relation to the terms of the investment or loan to enable them to query the position if they consider it necessary either by way of a tax return or by making a formal claim. HM Revenue & Customs' guidance in relation to this is set out in Annex III.9.

Payments to overseas bodies

11.72 Section 506(3) of the Income and Corporation Taxes Act 1988 states that:

> 'A payment made (or to be made) to a body situated outside the United Kingdom shall not be charitable expenditure . . . unless the charity concerned has taken such steps as may be reasonable in the circumstances to ensure that the payment will be applied for charitable purposes.'

11.73 The aim is obviously to seek to ensure that funds paid to the bodies that may qualify as charities under the law of their own jurisdiction will apply them for purposes that are charitable under English law. As HM Revenue & Customs state in their guidance:

> '"Applies for charitable purposes" means applied for purposes which are regarded as charitable under UK law. It is not sufficient for the charity to establish that the overseas entity is a charity under its domestic law.'[22]

11.74 This makes sense, because registration as a charity in an overseas jurisdiction is no guarantee that it must apply its funds for purposes that are charitable under English law (for example, charity law in an overseas jurisdiction may allow charities to apply funds for 'political' purposes, which would not be acceptable under English law). Charities established in overseas jurisdictions may also be subject to a much lighter regulatory regime than the regime to which UK charities are subject. HM Revenue & Custom's guidance states that:

> 'The steps taken are to "ensure" that the payment will be applied for charitable purposes. If the recipient body overseas is not bound by its own domestic law to apply all of its income for charitable purposes, then the UK charity should consider seeking a legally binding agreement to ensure that the payment will be applied charitably. It the overseas body declines to enter into such an agreement, the trustees may have difficulty ensuring that the payment is applied for charitable purposes. If an agreement is entered into the UK charity will need to have a means of establishing whether the agreement has been complied with.'[23]

11.75 HM Revenue & Customs' general guidance is also helpful:

> 'The legislation makes it clear that payments to bodies situated outside the UK are not [charitable expenditure], unless the trustees take steps to ensure that the payments will be applied for charitable purposes.
>
> The first requirement is that the charity must take "such steps as are reasonable in the circumstances". The charity trustees must be able to describe the steps they have taken, demonstrate that the steps taken were reasonable and produce evidence that the steps were, in fact, taken.
>
> When considering whether the steps taken by the charity were "reasonable in the circumstances", [HM Revenue & Customs] will have regard to:
>
> - The charity's knowledge of the overseas body.
> - Previous relations with and past history of that body.
>
> Trustees are expected to make adequate enquiries to find out such information as is reasonably available about the overseas body and what evidence will be provided by that body to show that payment(s) will or have been applied for charitable purposes.
>
> The nature of the steps will depend upon the scale of operations and size of the sums involved.
>
> In the case of small one-off payments an exchange of correspondence between the charity and the overseas body will normally be sufficient. Where possible, the correspondence should be on headed paper and:

---

[22]   HM Revenue & Customs' Guidance Note Annex II.4.7.
[23]   HM Revenue & Customs' Guidance Note Annex II.4.6.

- give details of the payment and the purpose for which it is given; and
- give confirmation that the sum has or will be applied for the purposes given.

More thorough work by the trustees will be required where the sums involved are large or where a transfer forms part of an ongoing commitment. This might include independent verification of the overseas body's status and activities; and reporting and verification of the manner of application of resources provided. The steps required can be reviewed in the light of evidence of proper use of funds and resources from earlier involvement with a particular project.'[24]

11.76 If HM Revenue & Customs look at a payment to an overseas body in any detail, they will generally ask the charity's trustees to provide information about:

- To whom the payment was given
- For what charitable purpose it was given
- What guarantees have been given that the payment will be applied for the purpose for which it was given
- What steps the trustees took to ensure the payment will be applied for charitable purposes
- What follow-up action the trustees took to confirm the payments were applied properly

If [HM Revenue & Customs] is not provided with sufficient evidence it is unlikely that the expenditure is accepted as qualifying and this may give rise to a liability to tax.'[25]

11.77 Finally, HM Revenue & Customs' guidance confirms that:

'There is no requirement for a charity to make an application to [HM Revenue & Customs] for advance clearance in respect of overseas donations.'[26]

11.78 This is true, although the reality is that there is no mechanism for a charity to apply for clearance in any event.

Substantial donors

11.79 Section 54 of the Finance Act 2006 introduced provisions aimed at individuals donating cash or other assets to charities with a view to obtaining relief from tax while also retaining the economic benefit of the cash or assets that have been given away. This might be, for example, by way of a gift aid donation of cash that is then loaned back to the donor on an interest-free basis. Broadly, the provisions work as follows:

- They are aimed at transactions between charities and 'substantial donors'. A 'substantial donor' to a charity in respect of any 'chargeable period' is anyone who has given £25,000 or more to the charity in any period of 12 months that falls wholly or partly within the chargeable period or has given £100,000 or more over a period of 6 years falling wholly or partly within the chargeable period.

- The donations must have qualified for relief from tax in order for the donor to be a 'substantial donor'. This will include gift aid relief, gifts of shares and other securities and gifts of land.

---

[24] HM Revenue & Customs' Guidance Note Annex II.4
[25] HM Revenue & Customs' Guidance Note Annex II.4.
[26] HM Revenue & Customs' Guidance Note Annex II.4.11.

- The 'chargeable period' for a charity is, in the case of a charitable trust, the period of 12 months to 5 April in each year and, in the case of an incorporated charity or unincorporated association, its accounting period (often the 12-month period to 31 December or 31 March in each year).

- Individuals who would have been substantial donors on the basis of either of the criteria mentioned above in the previous five chargeable periods of the charity will be deemed to be substantial donors.

- The rules treat any payment made by a charity to a 'substantial donor' in the course of or for the purposes of a number of specified transactions as 'non-charitable expenditure'.

- The transactions in question are:
    - the sale or letting of property by a substantial donor to the charity or vice versa;
    - the provision of services by a substantial donor to a charity or vice versa;
    - an exchange of property between a charity and a substantial donor;
    - the provision of financial assistance by a substantial donor to a charity or vice versa; and
    - investment by a charity in the business of a substantial donor.

- In addition, HM Revenue & Customs has a power to determine the cost to the charity of any payments it makes to a substantial donor where these are 'less beneficial to the charity than terms which might be expected in a transactions at arm's length'. The amount HM Revenue & Customs decides has been overpaid by the charity will also be deemed to be non-charitable expenditure. In other words, a market value can be put on the transaction in calculating the amount of non-charitable expenditure.

- Any payment of remuneration by a charity to a substantial donor is deemed to be non-charitable expenditure unless it is remuneration for his or her services as a trustee which has been approved by the Charity Commission, the courts or any other body with responsibility for regulating charities (such as the principal regulator of an exempt charity). Clearly, this will treat payments to a substantial donor for services other than acting as a trustee (e g professional services) provided to a charity as non-charitable expenditure even where they are authorised by a charity's constitution.

11.80 There are a number of exceptions from the substantial donor provisions. Broadly, these are:

- Transactions with a charity's trading subsidiary (which cannot be treated as a substantial donor in relation to the charity).

- Any investment in shares in listed companies.

- 'Arm's-length' business relationships between the charity and a substantial donor which do not form part of an arrangement for the avoidance of tax.

- Charitable service provision on terms that are no more favourable to the substantial donor than to anyone else.

- Any transaction at an undervalue that qualifies for exemption from capital gains tax.

- The provision of 'financial assistance' to a charity by a substantial donor, again on arm's-length terms where the assistance is not part of an arrangement for the avoidance of tax.

- Any transaction at an undervalue under which relief for gifts of shares or securities and/or land can be claimed.

11.81 Clearly, it is essential that a charity is able to identify who its 'substantial donors' are and whether or not they have entered into any transactions with the charity that may give rise to a restriction of tax or relief under the 'charitable expenditure' rules, not least because of the requirement that the charity should self-assess itself to tax. This is made more complicated by the provisions in the Finance Act 2006 that deem two or more 'connected' charities to be a single charity for the purposes of the substantial donor rules. 'Connected' means connected in a matter 'relating to the structure, administration or control of a charity'.[27] This is a very wide definition.

11.82 Other provisions deem certain donors to be 'connected' for the purposes of the rules, so that their donation must be looked at together in assessing whether either or both of them are substantial donors. Again, there is a wide definition of 'connected'.

11.83 The rules relating to substantial donors may potentially give rise to significant tax liabilities for charities deemed to have incurred non-charitable expenditure as a consequence. The key areas of difficulty are:

- The rules are solely a concern for the charity. Even if the donor proves to be a substantial donor and has subsequently entered into a transaction with the charity, the tax relief he or she may have claimed on their original gift to the charity is not at risk. The risk in relation to the rules lies, therefore, solely with the charity.

- There is no link between the amount of the original gift and the amount of the non-charitable expenditure the charity may incur under the rules. Clearly, a donor will need to have made a significant gift in the first place in order to qualify as a substantial donor, but even sums of this size may be small in comparison to the amount of non-charitable expenditure that may be incurred in relation to a later transaction.

- A donor may not become a 'substantial' donor for the purposes of the rules when he first makes a gift to the charity. It may only be the cumulative total of gifts made by the donor that bring the rules into play. Clearly, the onus is on the charity to maintain sufficiently detailed records of donations to it over a sufficiently long period of time (potentially up to 11 years) to ensure that it can identify who its substantial donors are.

11.84 The obvious example is the acquisition by a charity of shares in a private unlisted company in which a substantial donor also owns shares. The provisions will also catch the payment of any unauthorised remuneration by a charity to a substantial donor.

---

[27]   Income and Corporation Taxes Act 1988, s 506C(5).

DONATIONS BY INDIVIDUALS

11.85 As we have explained earlier in this Chapter, most donations by individuals will not form part of a charity's taxable income. One of the exceptions is donations that qualify for gift aid relief, which are made liable to tax in the charity's hands by one provision in the tax legislation and exempted by another.

11.86 Essentially, there are four tax incentives available to individuals who wish to make donations to charity. These are:

- 'gift aid' relief from income and capital gains tax for gifts for donations of cash;

- income tax relief for gifts of shares and securities;

- income tax relief for gifts of land to charity; and

- income tax relief for payroll giving.

Each of these incentives is explained in more detail below.

11.87 In addition to these tax incentives, there are two other exemptions from tax gifts to charity which are, in tax terms at least, generally neutral.

- Gifts to charity do not give rise to a liability to capital gains tax.

- Gifts to charity are wholly exempt from inheritance tax.

GIFT AID

11.88 Gift aid relief is reasonably straightforward. It works as follows:

- Where an individual makes a donation of, say, £1,000 to a charity, he or she is treated for tax purposes as having made a donation of £1,282 from which basic rate income tax (at 22%) has been deducted.

- If the donor signs a gift aid declaration the charity can reclaim the basic rate tax (£282) from HM Revenue & Customs. The total value of the donation to the charity is therefore £1,282. The total cost to the donor is £1,000.

- In addition, higher rate taxpayers can claim additional tax relief on donations on their tax returns. The relief is the difference between the basic and higher rates of income tax (ie 18%, at present rates) on the full amount of the gift (ie £1,282). The tax repayment due to the donor (£231) further reduces the total cost of the gift to the donor to £769. And, if the donor has insufficient income to fully utilise this relief, the donor can claim it against his or her capital gains. The relief can also be carried back for one tax year.

- Relief may be at a different rate where the donor has dividend income because the rate of tax that applies to dividends paid to individuals differs from the rate that applies to other income.

- Higher rate taxpayers can donate their tax repayments to the charity (or any other charity) using their tax return. In the above example, the donor could opt to donate the £231 tax repayment to the charity. There is a list of potential charitable beneficiaries to choose from, and taxpayers can opt to donate all or part of the refund. Charities must be registered with HM Revenue & Customs in order to be included in the list.

- The donor must pay an amount of income tax or capital gains tax equal to the basic rate tax that the charity reclaims on the gift.

- Gift aid donations must be payments of cash. The waiver of a loan previously made to a charity by one of its supporters will not qualify for gift aid relief.

- The donor cannot receive any material benefit in return for the donations. There are, though, rules that allow donors benefits with a monetary value that falls within certain specified limits. These would include, for example, free or reduced entry to heritage property or free or reduced subscriptions for a charity's publications. The limits are as follows:

Donations	Maximum benefit allowed
£0 – £100	25% of the value of the donation
£101 – £1,000	£25
£1,000 +	2.5% of the value of the donation up to a maximum of £250

- There are complicated rules that apply to 'annualise' the benefits received by donors. HM Revenue & Customs take the view that the value of the benefit is judged by the value to the donor. Where these restrictions are likely to be breached, there may be scope for tax planning by using 'split payments'. This is explained in more detail in **13.62**.

11.89 In order to ensure that the gift aid regime is not abused, every donor is required to make a gift aid 'declaration' in respect of his or her donations. The charity will need a declaration in place before it can reclaim basic rate tax on the donations it receives.

11.90 Gift aid declarations are reasonably flexible. They can be given at any time, whether before or after a donation is made. They can also relate to a single donation or donations made at any time by the donor to the charity. In principle, they can also be made orally provided that the charity makes a written record of the oral declaration.

11.91 Written gift aid declarations must contain the following details:

- the donor's name and address;

- the name of the recipient charity;

- a description of the donation;

- a declaration that the donation is to be treated as a gift aid donation; and

- a note explaining that the donor must pay income and/or capital gains tax equal to the tax recoverable by the charity on the donations.

11.92 There is no requirement that the declaration should be signed, but this is useful proof of the position.

11.93 A charity will need to be able to produce its gift aid records to HM Revenue & Customs in order to support its claims for tax to be repaid. There is a useful model form of declaration on HM Revenue & Customs' website (www.hmrc.gov.uk/charities).

11.94 Gift aid donations can be made under a deed of covenant that obliges a donor to make payments to a charity, but there is no requirement for a covenant in order to claim tax relief (as there was in the past).

Gifts of shares and securities

11.95 Income tax relief is available in respect of gifts and sales at an undervalue of certain qualifying investments to UK charities. The following are qualifying investments:

- listed shares and securities (including AIM listed shares);

- units in an authorised unit trust;

- shares in an OEIC; and

- interests in offshore funds.

11.96 Relief is given on the market value of the investment that is given away. Where the investment is sold to a charity at less than its market value, relief is given on the gift element, ie on the difference between the market value and the sale price. The relief also takes into account the incidental costs incurred by the donor in making the gift and in respect of certain (but not all) sales.

11.97 The relief is given by deducting the amount of the gift from the donor's total income before deducting personal allowances and reliefs. So a donor should consider limiting the donation to his or her total taxable income or (to maximise the tax advantage) total taxable income subject to higher rate income tax.

11.98 The relief can only be set against a donor's income and not against chargeable gains, but any gain arising on the gift or sale of the investment to the charity is exempt from capital gains tax.

Gifts of land

11.99 Gifts of freehold or leasehold land also qualify for income tax relief, essentially on the market value of the land. Relief can only be claimed if the donor receives a certificate from the charity identifying the land, specifying the date of the gift and containing a statement that the charity has acquired it.

11.100 Joint owners of land must all agree to give it to a charity if the relief is to apply; they cannot simply give away their shares in it. But they can agree between them how to share the relief, irrespective of the shares in which they actually own the land.

Payroll giving

11.101 Under the payroll-giving scheme, employees can authorise their employer to deduct donations to charity from their wages before income tax is deducted under the PAYE scheme. This means that income tax relief is given at the highest rate at which the employee pays tax.

11.102 The relief given under the scheme is essentially the same as gift aid relief, except that the employee does not need to fill in a gift aid declaration, the charity is paid gross and relief is only available against PAYE income. The employer must also have agreed to operate the scheme.

STRUCTURING DONATIONS

11.103 Where a donor has the capacity to give cash or investments or land to a charity, the position will need to be looked at carefully in order to work out the optimum position for both donor and charity. The donor will need to consider carefully whether it is better to sell investments or land and give away the cash proceeds or to give away the assets themselves bearing in mind that:

- Gifts of cash qualify for gift aid, with 22% of the tax saving passing to the charity and up to 18% to the donor.

- A sale of investments or land to generate cash for a gift aid donation may give rise to capital gains (or losses).

- For some donors, optimum relief can be achieved by selling investments to charity at a value that does not give rise to a gain or a loss.

11.104 The fundamental point is that both charity and donor need to look carefully at the real cost to the donor of the gift (whether cash, shares or land) and the real benefit to the charity (again, whether cash, shares or land but taking into account the tax that can be reclaimed in respect of gift aid donations).

CAPITAL GAINS TAX RELIEF

11.105 A gift can give rise to a capital gain that is liable to tax. This is because any 'disposal' of an asset is treated as if it had been made for market value. However, the Taxation of Chargeable Gains Act 1992, s 257 provides that the disposal of an asset at arm's length to a charity is treated as a disposal which gives rise to 'neither a gain nor a loss'.

11.106 However, where the asset in question is disposed of by the donor to a charity in return for some 'consideration', tax is calculated on the basis of the consideration that is received by the donor rather than the market value of the assets. 'Consideration' is not defined by the Taxation of Chargeable Gains Act 1992 but is a fundamental part of the English law of contract. Put simply, 'consideration' is the price that one party pays to another in exchange for an undertaking to do something.

11.107 We mention the concept of 'consideration' because of the possibility that a charity may be asked to give a donor an indemnity in respect of liabilities that are attached to a particular asset. For example, a donor who wishes to give away land to a charity may (quite reasonably) ask the charity to indemnify him or her in respect of any environmental or other claims that attach to the land and may come out of the woodwork subsequently. Whether indemnities of this kind constitute consideration will need to be looked at carefully by both the charity and the donor in the context of the transaction as a whole, although our view is that seeking protection from liabilities that are an inherent part of an asset will not generally be 'consideration' in the sense intended by the legislation.

11.108 As we have indicated earlier in this Chapter, both the charity and the donor should give careful thought to whether it would be better for the donor to sell an asset (giving rise to a capital gains tax liability) and give the proceeds to a charity (giving rise to relief from income and/or capital gains tax) or to give the asset itself to the charity (where the asset in question is listed shares or land, the donor can claim income tax relief as well as capital gains tax exemption on the gift). The optimum position for both donor and charity will vary from case to case.

INHERITANCE TAX

11.109 Gifts to a charity by an individual are wholly exempt from inheritance tax under the Inheritance Tax Act 1984, s 23, although they may also qualify for relief as 'normal expenditure out of income'.

11.110 Inheritance tax planning for individuals is a complex area. Existing charities can form part of tax planning arrangements, but only on the basis that the donor is willing to give up (both for him or herself and his or her estate) any claims to the assets which are given away.

DONATIONS BY COMPANIES

11.111 Gift aid donations by companies qualify for relief from corporation tax. They are, however, subject to similar restrictions to those that apply to gift aid donations by individuals. The most significant difference is that the benefit of gift aid for relief in respect of a donation by a company accrues wholly to the company itself. A donation by an individual will pass the benefit of basic rate tax relief to the charity, with higher rate tax relief available to the donor.

11.112 This is because relief for gift aid donations by a company is given by treating the donation as a 'charge on income'. This can be deducted from the company's taxable profits in calculating its liability to corporation tax. In other respects, the rules that govern gift aid donations by companies are very similar to those which govern gift aid donations by individuals. Donations must be of cash (rather than, say, by way of a loan). And, while there is no minimum amount that qualifies for relief, there are restrictions on the benefits that the company can receive in return for the donations.

11.113 A non-resident company can claim gift aid relief provided that it is liable to pay corporation tax on its profits. Like individual donations, relief can also be claimed in respect of payments made under a deed of covenant that obliges the company to pay a charity a particular sum, although there is no requirement for a covenant.

11.114 There is no requirement that a claim needs to be made by the company to HM Revenue & Customs and no gift aid declaration is required. In practice, HM Revenue & Customs may ask to see some evidence that the donation has actually been paid to a charity.

11.115 It is possible that HM Revenue & Customs may argue in certain circumstances that a payment by a company which is owned wholly or partly by a charity may be a 'distribution' rather than a gift aid donation. A 'distribution'[28] includes both dividends and 'any other distribution of assets of the company (whether in cash or otherwise) in respect of shares in the company'.

11.116 This is an argument that HM Revenue & Customs has raised previously, on the basis that a subsidiary company making payments to a parent charity has made a 'distribution' which is clearly 'out of the assets of the company' and is ostensibly 'in respect of shares in the company'. In practice, HM Revenue & Customs appears to accept that a payment by a wholly owned trading subsidiary to its parent charity should not be treated as a distribution, provided it is clearly a gift rather than a distribution in respect of shares. Where, on the other hand, a trading subsidiary held by a charity and one or more other shareholders makes gifts to its shareholders in proportion to their shareholdings, HM Revenue & Customs is likely to take the view that the payments are distributions in respect of shares in the subsidiary. That is not to say that every payment by a partly owned trading subsidiary to a shareholder charity will be a distribution. The position will depend upon whether the payment is genuinely a gift or is, in reality, a distribution in respect of the charity's shareholdings.

OTHER TAX-FREE GIFTS BY BUSINESS

11.117 Certain payments by businesses count as 'business expenses' and are therefore deductible in calculating their tax liabilities. In outline, these are donations for technical education conducted at approved institutes and for approved scientific research and small gifts to charity under HM Revenue & Customs' Extra Statutory Concession B7. In each case, the education, research or projects must be related to the trade of the business making the payment.

11.118 Certain gifts in kind to schools and universities of trading stock and other articles used as plant and machinery in the course of carrying out a trade by a donor are also tax deductible, as are articles manufactured or sold in the course of the donor's trade or machinery or plant used in the donor's trade.

STAMP DUTY LAND TAX

11.119 Stamp duty land tax (or 'SDLT') applies to the purchase or lease of land in the UK (as well as to certain transactions which relate to land). SDLT is, in general, paid by the person acquiring land or an interest in land. Rates vary from 1 to 4 % of the price paid in relation to the sale or lease of the land.

---

[28] Income and Corporation Taxes Act 1988, s 209(2)(a).

11.120 Charities qualify for an exemption from SDLT where they buy or lease land provided that they intend to hold the land for one of two 'qualifying charitable purposes'. These are:

- For use in furtherance of the charitable purposes of the purchaser or of another charity.
- As an investment from which the profits are applied to the charitable purposes of the purchaser.'[29]

11.121 There is no definition of 'use and furtherance of the charitable purposes' of a charity for SDLT but in our view this is likely to be interpreted by HM Revenue & Customs in a similar way to 'applied for charitable purposes only' in the context of income, capital gains and corporation tax (see **11.45** for more in relation to this).

11.122 It is easy to assume that any purchase of an interest in land by a charity is exempt from SDLT. But the conditions we have mentioned will need to be satisfied if SDLT relief is to be available. By way of example, these conditions will exclude SDLT relief where a charity purchases land as part of a trading transaction (in other words, if it proposes to buy land with a view to selling it on to the third party at a profit).

11.123 It is also important to appreciate that there are certain 'disqualifying events' which may make SDLT payable. These include the land in question ceasing to be used by the charity that has bought it for 'qualifying charitable purposes'.

11.124 The availability of SDLT relief is also subject to there being no tax avoidance motive in relation to the purchase.

11.125 The charity's trustees should also bear in mind that a non-charitable subsidiary of the charity will not qualify for relief from SDLT.

RATING RELIEF

11.126 Mandatory relief from 80% of non-domestic rates is available to a ratepayer that is a charity and in occupation of premises used wholly or mainly for charitable purposes. Where the mandatory relief applies, the local authority also has a discretion to relieve the 20% balance of the rates due.

11.127 In order to claim the mandatory relief, the charity must be in exclusive occupation of the premises but, provided that part of the premises is used 'wholly or mainly' for 'charitable purposes', relief will be available in respect of it. 'Mainly' is usually regarded as meaning 'more than half', although there is no established precedent for this in the context of rating. However, there is clearly some scope for use of the charity's premises by, say, its trading subsidiary without an adverse effect on the availability of rating relief.

---

[29]   Finance Act 2003, Schedule 8, paragraph 1.

CLIMATE CHANGE LEVY

11.128 Supplies of electricity and other non-renewable energy sources are exempt from the climate change levy when they are made to a charity for its 'non-business' activities.

11.129 There is no definition of what constitutes a 'business' for the purposes of the levy, but HM Revenue & Customs have adopted an interpretation that is similar to the interpretation they use for the purposes of VAT. This is reflected in their guidance, which states that a VAT certificate is required if the exemption is to be claimed.

VAT

11.130 VAT is a particularly difficult area for charities. A detailed discussion of the impact of VAT on charities is a book in itself. But from a governance point of view, it is important that a charity's trustees appreciate the VAT significance of particular operations or activities they may wish to see their charity undertake.

11.131 The particular difficulty for charities is that, while they qualify for a wide range of exemptions from direct tax, the way in which VAT works means that, in many cases, charities are put in a much worse financial position than many commercial entities.

11.132 There are a number of reasons for this, but most relate to the way in which VAT works, which is intrinsically different to the way in which income, capital gains or corporation tax apply.

11.133 Fundamentally, VAT is intended to be a tax on spending by consumers. This determines the way in which it is structured which, broadly, is as follows:

- VAT is payable by any 'taxable person' who supplies goods or services in the course of a 'business'. The supply has to be made in the UK.

- A taxable person is anyone who makes supplies of goods or services with a value in excess of a specified threshold (presently £61,000) over certain specified periods of time.

- Supplies are 'taxable', 'zero-rated' or 'exempt'. Taxable supplies are subject to VAT at a standard rate of 17.5% or a reduced rate of 5% on their value, depending on what is being supplied. Zero-rated and exempt supplies do not give rise to a liability on the supplier to pay VAT.

- In general, a supplier will add the amount of the VAT it is due to account for to HM Revenue & Customs in respect of a taxable supply (usually referred to as 'output VAT') to the invoice it gives its customer. It can then use the amount in respect of VAT paid by the customer when it pays the invoice to meet its liability to pay output VAT to HM Revenue & Customs.

- Where the customer is itself a taxable person and uses the goods or services supplied to it to make its own taxable or zero-rated supplies for VAT purposes, the VAT legislation allows it to credit the VAT it has paid (usually referred to as 'input VAT') against the output VAT it is due to pay to HM Revenue & Customs.

- The net effect of this where an entity is buying in VATable goods or services in order to make taxable or zero-rated supplies is that there is no net cost to it. The cost of VAT is aimed at the consumer, who will not be using goods or services supplied to him or to her to make their own taxable or zero-rated supplies.

- Where, however, an entity uses VATable goods or services to make exempt supplies, or supplies outside the scope of VAT altogether, its ability to recover its input VAT will be limited.

11.134 The difficulties faced by charities in relation to VAT are generally because of two aspects of the way in which the VAT legislation works. These are what constitute a 'business' for VAT purposes and the treatment of exempt supplies.

'Business' supplies

11.135 The concept of 'business' for VAT is far wider than that of 'trade', particularly because there is no requirement that a profit should be intended. It can include, therefore, the provision of services by a charity to its beneficiaries (e g the provisions of residential care to the elderly and infirm by a charity set up to relieve the elderly in need).

11.136 However, where a charity is not carrying out a VAT 'business', supplies made by it are outside the scope of VAT altogether. There is no VAT due on the supply, so that no VAT cost is passed on to the charity's customers, but the charity will not be able to credit the input VAT it has incurred in buying the goods and services it has bought in to make it supplies.

'Exempt supplies'

11.137 There is a similar problem in relation to 'exempt' supplies. There are a number of such supplies made by charities:

- the provision of education or research by educational establishments and professional training by charities;

- providing care, treatment or instruction to promote the welfare of elderly, sick, distressed or disabled persons;

- goods and services closely linked to the protection of children and young persons; and

- goods and services supplied by a charity in connection with certain fundraising events (see **13.45** for more in relation to this).

11.138 The difficulty for charities is that, while no output VAT is due on these supplies (because they are 'exempt'), they do not enable the charity to claim a credit for all of the input VAT it has paid on supplies made to it which it has used to make its exempt supplies. There are some rules that may allow a proportion of the input VAT to be credited, but these are complex.

Zero-rated supplies

11.139 Charities can, on the other hand, make a number of zero-rated supplies:

- supplies of talking books for the blind and handicapped;

- supplies of equipment for the relief of the chronically sick and disabled;

- the sale of donated goods; and

- the export of goods.

11.140 The advantage of zero-rating is that no output VAT is due on the supply, which is deemed to be a taxable supply in calculating entitlement to credit for input VAT.

Buildings

11.141 Charities often face particular VAT issues in relation to the construction or alteration of buildings. The rules in relation to land and buildings are generally fairly complicated, but particularly so for charities.

11.142 In summary, there are very few areas of a charity's operations that are unlikely to have some VAT implications. A charity's trustees must ensure that they identify activities that are potentially problematic and take appropriate steps, usually by taking specialist VAT advice.

TAX COMPLIANCE

11.143 Charities are subject to the self-assessment regime in respect of their tax liabilities. This means that they are not obliged to submit a tax return to HM Revenue & Customs unless required to do so by the Revenue or because they have a liability to tax that must be returned to the Revenue (in which case, they should write to HM Revenue & Customs and ask for a self-assessment tax return to be issued).

11.144 HM Revenue & Custom's guidance in relation to tax returns is:

> 'The great majority of charities will not be required to complete a Self-Assessment return on a regular basis. Formal returns and notices to file will be issued to a sample of charities each year, selected through a risk assessment system or on a random basis. The type of return required will be specified in the notice issued to the charities concerned. This will depend on whether the charity is a trust or a company for tax purposes.
>
> Those charities receiving returns will be required to self assess. A copy of the charity's accounts will need to be submitted in support of the return made.'[30]

11.145 Charities can also claim back any income tax deducted from certain other types of income they receive:

- net bank or building society interest;

---

[30] HM Revenue & Customs' Guidance Notes, chapter 6.

- gift aid donations;

- net interest from Government stocks; and

- royalties and other types of annual payment.

11.146 The tax must be reclaimed using form R68 unless the charity must file a self-assessment tax return, in which case the claim is made in the return itself.

11.147 A charitable trust must make any claim within 5 years of 31 January in the year following the end of the tax year to which the claim relates. A charitable company or unincorporated association must make any claim within 6 years from the end of the accounting period to which the claim relates.

11.148 The key governance point for trustees is that the self assessment tax regime puts the onus on them to decide that all of a charity's income and gains have been applied 'for charitable purposes only', constitute charitable expenditure and otherwise qualify for exemption from tax. This is obviously a significant burden, and one that the trustees must understand, even if only in outline.

12

BORROWING

12.1 This chapter deals with borrowing by charities. It will not be relevant to every charity, but as the range and complexity of services provided by charities increases, the ability to borrow on commercial terms is becoming more important.

12.2 The ability of a charity to borrow will depend primarily upon whether it has a power to borrow and, if relevant, to charge its assets as security for the borrowing. This will depend primarily upon the way in which the charity has been set up. We consider the position in relation to both incorporated and unincorporated charities below.

12.3 We have assumed that, in most cases, lenders will want security for their loans. Where a charity wishes to grant a mortgage over its land as security for a loan, it must also generally comply with the provisions of the Charities Act 1993, s 38. Section 38 applies only to mortgages over land and not to any other assets. This position is explained in more detail below.

INCORPORATED CHARITIES

Charitable companies

12.4 The position in relation to charitable companies looking to borrow funds is reasonably straightforward. Many charitable companies will have an express power in their constitution to borrow, often alongside a power to charge their assets as security for the loan. The charity's trustees will need to assess the scope of the power to ensure that any restrictions which apply to it are observed. An express power will generally cover the grant by a charity of both fixed and floating charges over its assets.

12.5 Where a charitable company does not have an express power to borrow and charge its assets, it will generally be possible for a 75% majority of its members to pass a special resolution to alter its constitution in order to add the power that is required. A straightforward power to borrow and charge assets will not generally constitute an alteration which requires the prior written consent of the Charity Commission under the Charities Act 1993, s 64. There is more about constitutional changes at **15.24**.

12.6 The provisions of the Companies Acts which state that the capacity of a company is not limited by its memorandum and give its directors power to bind the company do not apply to a charitable company except in favour of a person who:

- gives full consideration (in money or money's worth) in relation to the act in question and does not know that the act is not permitted by the company's memorandum or is beyond the directors' powers; or

- who does not know that the company is a charity.[1]

12.7 Clearly, therefore, anyone who does not meet these criteria (and many lenders who deal with charities are likely to ask for confirmation of its powers so that they will have actual or constructive notice that the charity lacks a power or that is subject to restrictions) cannot rely upon the protection conferred by the Companies Acts. There is more about this at **7.12**.

12.8 It will generally be possible to imply a power into a charitable company's constitution using the 'sweep-up' provision often included. This usually states that the company has power to do 'such other lawful things as are necessary to assume its objects'. The powers that can be applied using a provision of this kind will be limited to carrying out the charity's charitable purposes. A power can also be implied in the context of a trading charity to borrow a reasonable amount for the purpose of its trade. In practice, most lenders will want to see an express power authorising a charity to borrow and charge its assets and will not be interested in the risk inherent in implying a power when the position can only ever be conclusively determined by the courts. The lender's concern is obviously that any borrowing outside a charity's powers will be *ultra vires* and unenforceable against it.

CIOs

12.9 CIOs are likely to be in a very similar position to charitable companies. Their constitution may include an express power to borrow and charge its assets. If there is no express power, a 75% majority of the members of a CIO have the power to pass a resolution to add an express power. This will not generally constitute an alteration requiring the Charity Commission's consent under the Charities Act 1993, Schedule 5B. There is more about altering the constitutions of CIOs at **15.34**.

12.10 CIOs will be subject to an *ultra vires* rule that is modelled on the rule that applies in relation to companies under the Companies Acts.[2] As with charitable companies, a lender is unlikely to be able to rely upon these provisions because they are likely to ask for confirmation of the CIO's powers so that they will have actual or constructive notice that it lacks a power or that it is subject to restrictions.

12.11 The Charities Act 1993 (Schedule 5B) gives a CIO the power to do anything that is 'calculated to further its purposes', together with a statutory power to do anything that is 'conducive or incidental' to those purposes. Lenders are likely to adopt a similar approach to powers implied under these provisions as they do in relation to charitable companies. In practice, therefore, an express power is likely to be required by a lender.

12.12 Where a CIO holds trust assets, it will be in the same position as a charitable company. The powers in the CIO's own constitution will apply only to its corporate assets. Its power to deal with the assets held on trust will depend upon the terms of the trust itself and the statutory powers that apply to unincorporated charities.

Other incorporated charities

12.13 Other incorporated charities may have express powers to borrow in their constitutions depending upon the way in which they are set up. Failing that, charities

---

[1]   Companies Act 1985, s 35; Charities Act 1993, s 65; Companies Act 2006, s 42.
[2]   Charities Act 1993, Schedule 5B; expected to come into force in early 2008.

constituted by Royal Charter may be able to obtain a Supplemental Charter conferring an express power to borrow and charge assets, while charities governed by Act of Parliament may require a further Act of Parliament in order to make a constitutional change which will add an express power.

UNINCORPORATED CHARITIES

12.14 The position in relation to charitable trusts and charitable unincorporated associations is a little more complicated than the position in relation to incorporated charities.

Charitable trusts

12.15 Because a trust has no legal personality separate from its trustees, a loan can only be made to its trustees, who will be personally liable to repay the debt due, usually on a joint and several basis.

12.16 While the trustees' liability to the lender is personal, trustees will not generally need to have recourse to their own assets in order to meet their liabilities because of their right to indemnify themselves out of the trust assets, either under an express provision in the charitable trust or under the Trustee Act 2000, s 31 (see **6.22** for more in relation to this). The statutory right of indemnity is limited to liabilities that are 'properly incurred' by the trustees in acting on behalf of the charity and any express power will generally be subject to a similar restriction. To the extent that liabilities are incurred as a consequence of a breach of trust (eg in breach of an express restriction imposed by the trust), the indemnity will not be available. And even if the indemnity is available, there may not be sufficient trust assets to meet a liability in full.

12.17 In most cases, therefore, the charity's trustees will want to agree with the lender that its recourse against them in respect of its loan is limited to the amount of the charity's assets from time to time. Provided this is agreed to by the lender, it will have no right to claim against the trustee's personal assets in the event of default on the loan. In order to ensure that this provision is effective, it is important that there is an express limitation on the trustee's liability to the assets of the charity from time to time. Doing no more than providing for the trustees to contract with the lender in their capacity as trustees will not limit their liability. An express statement is required. In practice, most lenders will understand the trustees' reluctant to incur liability in respect of their personal assets and will, in any event, assess the credit-worthiness of the charity on the basis of its assets alone and not the personal assets of the trustees.

12.18 Because the lender's recourse to the charity's assets depends on the trustees' right of indemnity, it may wish to seek security for its loan. Where trustees grant fixed security over a trust asset, the creditor will have recourse to the asset irrespective of the availability of the trustees' indemnity, which will then generally only be an issue where the liability it secures is in excess of the value of the charged asset and the creditor wishes to enforce its rights against the charity's other assets.

12.19 Lenders will often seek both fixed and floating charges as security for their loans. A fixed charge secures the lender's rights over particular assets. A floating charge is used to improve the lender's position, by securing all, or substantially all, of the charity's assets which are not subject to fixed charges. This will usually include cash held at the bank, debts owed by third parties and other intangible assets such as goodwill. A floating charge is, however, only capable of being given by an incorporated charity. The trustees of a charitable trust are not generally considered to be capable of granting a floating charge alongside the fixed charges they grant over particular assets. Most lenders' standard form documentation will provide for both fixed and floating charges. They will obviously need to be amended where the loan is being taken by the trustees of a charitable trust.

12.20 Because a charity's trustees may change from time to time, a lender will wish to ensure that the loan binds the successors of the trustees who take out the original loan. This is usually done by ensuring that, on a change of trustees, the retiring trustees are only relieved of their personal liability in respect of the loan to the extent that the new trustees agree to be bound by it. This will often be regulated by a 'deed of adherence' in an agreed form scheduled to the loan documentation.

12.21 In many cases, the trustees of a charitable trust will have an express power to borrow and charge the charity's assets. Any restrictions on the express power must obviously be observed. If a charitable trust has no express power to borrow and charge, it may be possible for one to be added by the trustees using a power to add to the trust's provisions. Adding a provision of this kind using this power would not usually require the consent of the Charity Commission. There is more about constitutional changes at **15.5**.

12.22 If there is no express power and one cannot be added, the trustees may be able to rely upon a statutory power. The statutory power to borrow conferred on the trustees of private trusts by the Trustee Act 1925, s 16 does not apply to charities. However, a trading charitable trust will have a power similar to that of a trading charitable company to borrow what it requires for the purposes of its trade,[3] provided that the expenditure cannot reasonably be financed without borrowing. A power to borrow can also be implied under the Trusts of Land and Appointment of Trustees Act 1996 and the Trustee Act 2000, s 8 (on the basis that the trustees are given all of the powers of an 'absolute owner') but only for any purpose connected with the repair, maintenance, improvement of buildings or the purchase of land. The power will also allow the land to be charged.

12.23 Some lenders take the view that the statutory powers are not sufficiently wide to authorise borrowing and the grant of charges because they do not refer to these powers expressly. Some also take the view that, while the statutory powers authorise borrowing, they do not extend to unsecured loans. The Charity Commission's view is that:

> '...an "absolute owner" undoubtedly has power to borrow money on the security of their property' and 'the power to borrow for any purpose relating to the repair, maintenance, improvement etc of buildings and land which the charity trustees own also applies to unsecured loans.'[4]

12.24 However, the Charity Commission does acknowledge that its view is not accepted 'by all the corporate lenders which charity trustees may approach for finance'. The Commission states that: 'This difference arises from differing interpretations of the

---

3   See *Mansell v Viscount Cobham* (1905) 1 Ch 568.
4   OG 22 B1.

law rather than questioning the financial viability of lending to a charity.'[5] In practice, therefore, many lenders are reluctant to rely on statutory or implied powers to borrow and charge assets.

12.25 Trustees without an appropriate express power may obtain an express authority from the Charity Commission, generally by way of an Order. The Charity Commission is aware of lenders' reluctance to rely on a statutory or implied power to borrow and is usually willing to make a 'comfort' Order if it considers that it is for the benefit of the charity. The Commission's guidance states that:

> 'Lenders tend to be concerned that, even though the trustees have complied with the requirement to obtain proper advice, and certify this on the deed of charge, their security will be invalid if the trustees did not have the necessary power to enter into the mortgage in the first place...the lender may attempt to influence the trustees to apply for an Order to safeguard its position.'[6]

12.26 The Commission's guidance goes on to say that: 'Where the circumstances of the case indicate that the matter is genuinely urgent, we should be prepared to make an Order for the avoidance of doubt where agreement cannot quickly be reached' and:

> 'We should also make an Order where the borrowing is demonstrably in the interests of the charity and the lender ultimately insists on an explicit Order being given. Provided therefore that:
>
> - the borrowing is clearly shown to be expedient in the interests of the charity; and
> - proper financial advice has been taken (which we should ask the trustees to provide us with);
>
> we will have to continue to make Orders in such cases to safeguard the interests of the charity (as opposed to those of the lender).'[7]

There is more about applying for Orders generally at **4.19**.

12.27 If there is no power to borrow, a loan is not necessarily invalid or unenforceable. *De Vigier v IRC*[8] suggests that a loan made to trustees may be recoverable from the trust assets (rather than from the trustees personally) on the basis that the doctrine of *ultra vires* was developed in the context of the limited capacity of corporations and that the fact that taking a loan might constitute a breach of trust does not of itself mean that a loan cannot be valid and enforceable. Lenders are obviously unlikely to want to rely on this.

Unincorporated associations

12.28 Like a charitable trust, a charitable unincorporated association has no legal personality separate from its trustees or members. The validity of the acts undertaken by the trustees and members of the association depends upon the provisions of its constitution.

---

[5]   OG 22 B1.
[6]   OG 22 B1.
[7]   OG 22 B1.
[8]   [1964] 1 WLR 1073.

12.29 An association's constitution will usually provide for the direction and supervision of its affairs to be vested in a governing body of trustees with specified functions and powers. Provided that the trustees act within the powers conferred on them, they will bind (as agents) the association's members (as principals) and will also usually be entitled to an express or implied indemnity against the association's assets in respect of the liabilities they take on.

12.30 An unauthorised liability will not bind an association's members. Those who incurred it will incur personal liability and will not usually be entitled to indemnify themselves from the association's assets.

12.31 A lender will need to check that an association's constitution confers an express power to borrow and grant security. An association's assets will usually be held by one or more of its members as nominees or custodians. The identity of those holding the assets over which security is granted should be verified and their capacity to act under the constitution checked.

12.32 Like the trustees of a charitable trust, it is considered that the trustees of a charitable unincorporated association cannot grant a floating charge. Lenders' standard form documentation may need to be amended to reflect this.

CHARITIES ACT 1993, S 38

12.33 As we have mentioned earlier in this chapter, any charity (with the exception of an exempt charity) must comply with the provisions of Charities Act 1993, s 38 if it is granting a mortgage over its land. It does not apply to security granted over any asset other than land. Section 38 requires the charity's trustees to obtain the prior consent of the Charity Commission to the grant of the mortgage unless the trustees have obtained and considered 'proper advice' in writing in relation to the mortgage.

12.34 The advice that is required differs depending upon the purpose of the mortgage. Where it is to secure the repayment of a loan or a grant, the things that need to be advised on are:

- Whether the loan or grant is necessary in order for the charity trustees to be able to pursue the particular course of action in connection with which they are seeking the loan or grant.

- Whether the terms of the loan or grant are reasonable having regard to the status of the charity as the prospective recipient of the loan or grant.

- The ability of the charity to repay the loan or grant on the terms on which they are made.

12.35 In the case of a mortgage which is given as security in respect of any other obligation, the advice must relate to whether it is reasonable for the charity trustees to undertake to discharge the obligation, having regard to the charity's charitable purposes.

12.36 The advice has to come from someone the trustees believe is qualified to give it and who has no financial interest in relation to the loan, grant or other obligation in relation to which the advice is given. This could include an employee of the charity (eg a finance director). In practice, charity trustees are sometimes keen for one of the charity's employees to give the advice they need, partly because the employee may be best placed to give it but often also because they will avoid the cost of taking professional advice from a third party.

12.37 Clearly, a charity's trustees will need to consider very carefully whether it is appropriate for an employee to give the advice. In particular, they should consider the implications if the advice given proves to be negligent. An employee's ability to meet any claims the charity may have for negligent advice may be very limited in comparison to that of a professional adviser, who will generally carry professional indemnity insurance in respect of the advice they give. The employee will also need to consider his or her own position carefully. They may only be willing to advise on the basis that the advice is given without personal liability, which will obviously be a very relevant consideration for the trustees in considering whether or not the advice they give can be relied upon.

12.38 In practice, whether it is appropriate for an employee to give advice is likely to depend upon the value of the liability that the mortgage secures and the complexity of the transaction in question. While an employee may be able to advise on the grant of a mortgage to secure an overdraft, he or she is much less likely to be able to advise on the terms of a loan incorporating interest rate options.

12.39 Having said this, advice in relation to a mortgage to secure obligations other than loans or grants may be difficult to procure from a third party, on the basis that they may not consider themselves able to have due regard to the 'charity's purposes' in giving the advice. Again, the position is likely to vary depending upon the obligation in question.

12.40 In practice, most lenders' standard form charge documents (including those for a secured overdraft facility) will make any mortgage an 'all monies' charge which will secure any future borrowings by the charity. This obviously makes good commercial sense for the lender, but the charity's trustees will need to ensure that they take new advice whenever they wish to borrow additional amounts under the 'all monies' mortgage.

12.41 The prior consent of the Commission will be required where land is mortgaged to secure a guarantee or indemnity or the payment of deferred consideration. It is not possible for the charity's trustees to rely on advice in relation to these transactions.

CHARITIES ACT 1993, S 39

12.42 Section 39 of the Charities Act 1993 (as amended by the Land Registration Rules 2003, r 180[9]) requires a mortgage granted by any charity (including an exempt charity) to include a statement that the land is held by or in trust for the charity and that the restrictions of s 38 apply. The statement is that the land is held by or in trust for a charity whether the charity is an exempt charity and whether the mortgage has been generally or specially authorised by the Charity Commission or that the mortgage is subject to the restrictions of s 38. The form of the statement is specified by the Land Registry. The *Land Registry Practice Guide* spells out the full requirements for the statement.

---

[9]   SI 2003/1417.

12.43 The trustees are also required to certify in the mortgage that it has either been sanctioned by an appropriate order of the Commission or that the charity has power to grant the mortgage and that the trustees have taken advice on it.

12.44 Where the certificate is given (even falsely), the s 38 procedure is deemed to have been complied with in favour of anyone who acquires the land (whether or not under the mortgage) in good faith for money or money's worth unless the purchaser knows that the certificate was false and that the transaction was not in the interests of the charity. If no certificate is given, the mortgage will still be valid in favour of a purchaser for good faith in money or money's worth on the same basis. A certificate and statement should always therefore be included in a mortgage.

12.45 It is important that a charity's trustees ensure that provisions of s 39 are complied with in full. The protection it offers to third parties applies only from completion of a transaction[10] and the relevant statement and certificate should be included in any contract entered into by the charity in anticipation of the mortgage. If not, the contract may be void or voidable.

12.46 The certificate must be given by the charity's trustees. This is the case even in relation to an incorporated charity. The Land Registry's guidance indicates that the trustees must be a party to the mortgage in order to give the certificate in addition to the charity itself. The Charity Commission's guidance states that:

> 'The trustees are required to give the certificate of the mortgage deed, but in the case of a charitable company, the mortgage will be executed by the company itself not by the directors, who are the trustees. Although the matter is not free from doubt, it should be approached on the basis that the persons executing the mortgage on behalf of the charity, company or not, can give the certificate as agent for the trustees.'[11]

In practice, therefore, the certificate can usually be dealt with by ensuring that the trustees delegate responsibility for giving it to two or more of the trustees (or, in certain circumstances, non-trustees) either under an express power of delegation or using a statutory power. There is more about the powers of delegation that can be used at **8.87**.

PERMANENT ENDOWMENT

12.47 As we have explained in an earlier chapter (see **9.27**), there are restrictions on any charity's power to dispose of its permanent endowment assets, which will often include land. These restrictions will generally mean that land can only be sold or leased by a charity with the prior consent of the Charity Commission. However, the Commission's consent is not required to the grant of security over permanent endowment land, except where this is required by the Charities Act 1993, s 38 or in the event that a charity has no power to grant the mortgage. This is the case, notwithstanding that the grant of a mortgage may ultimate lead to the disposal of the permanent endowment land by the lender under the terms of the mortgage in the event that the charity defaults on its loan.

---

[10] *Bayoumi v Women's Total Abstinence Educational Union Ltd* [2004] 3 All ER 110.
[11] OG 22 C1.

INTEREST RATE SWAPS

12.48 Charities with significant borrowings may sometimes wish to enter into interest rate swaps in order to manage their debt as effectively as possible. An interest rate swap is essentially a contract between two parties under which one party agrees to pay interest at a 'floating' rate (in other words, a rate that fluctuates depending upon the fluctuations in a particular base rate) in exchange for payments of interest at a fixed rate. The payments are not, in reality 'interest' at all but cash which is intended to compensate the charity in respect of its exposure to a particular fixed or floating rate of interest.

12.49 So, for example, a charity that has borrowed a significant sum from a bank on the basis that it will pay interest at a floating rate (often a percentage that moves in line with the 'London Interbank Offer Rate' or 'LIBOR') may conclude that its interests would best be served by fixing the rate of interest it pays on the borrowing, so that it can manage its debt obligations (particularly as regards cash flow) more effectively. This could be achieved by entering into an interest rate swap with a bank or other financial institution under which the charity agrees to pay the bank a notional amount of fixed rate interest on the principal of its borrowings in return for a payment from the bank or financial institution equal to the floating rate of interest actually due on the borrowings.

12.50 In some cases, banks and other financial institutions may only agree to lend to a charity on the basis that its floating rate obligations are effectively fixed by entering into a swap. This may be before a loan is agreed upon or in connection with an existing loan.

12.51 Whether a charity can enter into an interest rate swap in relation to its borrowings depends upon two issues:

- whether the charity has a power to enter into the swap; and

- whether the power can properly be exercised by the charity's trustees.

12.52 In *Hazell v Hammersmith and Fulham Borough Council* [12] the court considered a number of interest rate swaps entered into by local authorities. While the powers of local authorities to borrow are different from the powers available to most charities, this case established certain principles which apply by analogy to charities in relation to swaps. Lenders will always be concerned to ensure that a charity's powers to enter into a swap do not infringe the principles set out in *Hazell*. The Charity Commission also bases its guidance in relation to swaps on the principles established by the case.

12.53 A charity's constitution will not generally contain an express power authorising it to enter into a swap transaction. The Charity Commission does not regard a power of this kind as consistent with charitable status, on the basis that 'it is not appropriate that trustees should be given the power to speculate'. Generally speaking, therefore, a charity's power to enter into a swap must be incidental to the exercise of a charity's power to borrow by its trustees. The Commission's guidance states that:

> 'In the case of an existing borrowing, it may be more difficult to argue that the swap was incidental to the exercise of a borrowing power, although it may be easier to see the justification where a swap is in connection with a proposed new borrowing. The issue in each case must be carefully examined to decide whether the swap is:

---

[12]   [1991] 2 WLR 372.

- really an integral part of managing the charity's debt; or
- a speculative venture.'[13]

12.54 This guidance reflects the court's decision in *Hazell*. Essentially, the court concluded that a swap entered into by a local authority as an essential part of its approach to debt management would be within its powers, while a swap which did no more than gamble on the possibility of a rise or fall in interest rates would be too speculative to fall within its powers. On the facts of the case, the courts concluded that the local authority in question was doing no more than speculating on the possibility that interest rates would rise or, as the case may be, fall with a view to generating additional income. This is not consistent with the authority's duties in relation to the exercise of its powers. Again, the Commission's guidance is helpful:

'For example, a swap in relation to an existing borrowing might be justifiable where a charity enters into a borrowing in a period where borrowing rates are relatively stable, but subsequently borrowing rates become unstable with wide fluctuations. In such a case, a charity may seek to stabilise its borrowing rate by taking out a swap. Clearly, this would fall in the category of managing the charity's debt and not a speculative venture.'[14]

12.55 If a charity has no express power to enter into a swap transaction and the power cannot be implied as incidental to its borrowing power, the Charity Commission's consent to the swap will be required by way of an Order. However, the likelihood is that, in circumstances where entering into a swap is not incidental to the exercise of a borrowing power, the Commission will not make an Order.

12.56 On an application for an Order, the Charity Commission will look at the charity's reasons for wishing to enter into the swap. Again, the Commission's guidance is helpful:

'In all cases it will be necessary for the staff to explore in some detail why the swap is proposed and why the trustees consider it advantageous.'[15]

12.57 Even if a charity has a power to enter into a swap, its trustees must also be satisfied that they can properly exercise the power to enter into the swap which is proposed. The trustees will need to be very clear about the purpose of entering into the swap. The issue is, again, whether the swap is intended to involve speculation or eliminate speculation. The Charity Commission's guidance recognises that: 'This type of transaction can be very complex and the issue of the speculation or its elimination can be very finely balanced.'[16]

12.58 In practice, the Charity Commission takes the view that swap transactions which are entered into solely on the basis of forecasting future interest trends will not be consistent with the proper exercise of their powers by a charity's trustees. The Commission appears to draw a distinction between new and existing borrowings:

'Generally, where staff are dealing with an existing loan, and a swap transaction is proposed, the transaction will normally be one involving speculation on future interest rate movements, and therefore in conflict with the duties of trustees. On the other hand, a charity may be proposing to take up a new borrowing and the trustees may see a swap as a means of

---

[13] OG 22 B9.
[14] OG 22 B9.
[15] OG 22 B9.
[16] OG 22 B9.

enabling the charity to obtain a loan on terms which are in the charity's best interests. This may well be an appropriate exercise of the trustees' discretion.'[17]

12.59 In some respects, this distinction between existing and new loans seems arbitrary. A charity's trustees may well conclude that their charity's financial circumstances (or economic circumstances generally) have changed since a loan was originally made and that the changes in question justify them seeking, for example, to fix a floating rate of interest. In practice, the position will vary from charity to charity. However, the trustees are likely to be in a stronger position where they can show that they have taken appropriate financial advice on the terms of the swap as part of their debt management arrangements. The Charity Commission considers that taking advice is, in any event, essential for any charity which proposes to enter into a swap.

12.60 The charity's trustees should also consider the following points, which the Charity Commission's guidance indicates they will look at:

'What fee will be paid for the swap?

Why is it proposed?

What are the advantages to the charity?

What risks are there and do the advantages outweigh any risks?'[18]

12.61 Where possible, it may be better for a charity's trustees to seek to incorporate an interest rate option into the terms of a loan. An interest rate option will have the same economic effect as a swap in allowing the charity to convert the fixed or floating rate payable on the loan. By ensuring that the option is the term of the loan itself, the trustees are more likely to be able to conclude that swapping a fixed or floating rate of interest is incidental to the exercise of their borrowing power. Whether an interest rate option can be included will depend, of course, upon the commercial terms that can be agreed with the lender.

12.62 The charity's trustees should also be aware that lenders will often look for an opinion from the charity's legal advisers in relation to its capacity to enter into a swap. A legal opinion will help to minimise the risk to the lender in respect of its loan but will obviously mean that the charity's legal advisers must be able to conclude that the swap is within the charity's powers.

ENFORCING SECURITY

12.63 As we explain at **15.120**, charitable companies are subject to the winding-up regime imposed by the Insolvency Act 1986 (as amended by the Enterprise Act 2002). The courts also have jurisdiction to make an administration order under Part II of the 1986 Act in relation to a body incorporated by Royal Charter as well as companies incorporated under the Companies Acts.[19]

---

[17] OG 22 B9.
[18] OG 22 B9.
[19] See *The Salvage Association,* (2003) *The Times,* 21 May.

12.64 Unincorporated charities (ie trusts and unincorporated associations) cannot become 'insolvent' within the regime imposed by the Insolvency Act 1986 (as amended by the Enterprise Act 2002). This is because they have no separate legal personality and cannot incur liabilities in their own right. However, an unincorporated charity may reach the financial state where it is 'insolvent' in the sense that the value of the charity's assets that are available to its trustees to settle their liabilities is insufficient. Ultimately, creditors' claims against the trustees may mean that they are made personally bankrupt.

12.65 There are some issues that are likely to be particularly important where a charity has become insolvent. In summary, these are as follows:

LIQUIDATION/ADMINISTRATION

12.66 As mentioned earlier in this Chapter, assets held by a company as trustee do not form part of its corporate property and are not available for distribution to its creditors in a liquidation or administration. It may therefore be a breach of trust for a charitable company to discharge its liabilities out of the trust property unless they are liabilities properly incurred in the administration of the trust in question (when the Trustee Act 2000, s 31 will apply to provide a statutory indemnity). This may be a concern to an administrator or liquidator who is responsible for committing a charity to a breach of this kind because he or she may be in breach of their own fiduciary duty to the charity as a consequence.

12.67 Another aspect of concern will be whether an administrator or liquidator has the power to realise security by selling a particular asset. This may be because the powers conferred by the order appointing him or her relate only to corporate property and the powers contained in the trust of the asset in question do not authorise a sale. In those circumstances, the administrator or liquidator may need to obtain an order or Scheme from the Charity Commission authorising a sale before he or she can proceed.

12.68 The liquidator or administrator may also need to comply with the Charities Act 1993, s 36, which makes a sale of any land owned by a charity subject to the consent of the Charity Commission unless he or she obtains a surveyor's report on the sale and acts in accordance with the advice it contains. There is more about s 36 at **9.95**.

RECEIVERSHIP

12.69 Where a receiver is appointed under a validly granted mortgage, his or her powers to deal with the charged assets derive from the mortgage itself. The Charity Commission has no published view on the position of a receiver in relation to trust property held by a charitable company, but the approach taken appears to be that he or she is free to exercise the power of sale under the mortgage and to discharge the debt due to the mortgagee without giving rise to any breach of duty to the charity. The receiver's duty is owed to both the mortgagee and the charity and is to take reasonable care to obtain a fair value for the asset.

12.70 This appears to be the approach that would be taken by the Charity Commission to permanent endowment property, which will almost always be held on trust. If a receiver is exercising a power of sale over land, he or she will need to consider whether the Charities Act 1993, s 36 applies. On a strict construction of the Act, a report is required but this runs contrary to the scheme of the legislation, which is intended to ensure that the trustees (rather than a receiver) consider whether the sale is in the best interests of their charity. There is more about s 36 at **9.95**.

CHECKLIST

12.71 In agreeing to borrow, the charity's trustees should ensure that they have dealt with the following points:

- Do the charity's trustees have an express power under the charity's constitution to borrow and charge the charity's assets as security for the loan?

- If there is no express power, can the charity amend its constitution to add an express power or, if the charity is unincorporated, can an order giving authority to borrow be applied for from the Charity Commission?

- If there is no express power, can a power be implied and will this be acceptable to the lender?

- In the case of an unincorporated charity (or an incorporated charity which wishes to borrow in its capacity as trustee of the trust assets), are the statutory powers to borrow sufficiently wide and will this be acceptable to the lender?

- Where the lender requires security over the charity's land, can the trustees comply with the provisions of the Charities 1993, s 38?

- Do the trustees of an unincorporated charity wish to limit their liability in respect of the loan to the assets of the charity from time to time?

- If the charity's trustees need to take advice in order to comply with the Charities Act 1993, s 38, from whom should they take advice? Should this be from an employee of the charity or a professional adviser?

- If the charity is unincorporated, is the lender looking for a floating charge over its assets?

- If the charity is borrowing additional funds under an 'all monies' charge, have the trustees taken further advice?

- Has the prior consent of the Charity Commission been obtained where the land is charged to secure a guarantee or indemnity or the payment of deferred consideration?

- Have the charity's trustees complied with the provisions of the Charities Act 1993, s 39 in relation to the required statement and certificate?

- Have the trustees properly delegated their power to give the certificate?

- Where the charity proposes to enter into a swap in relation to a loan, does it have an express power to do so, or can one be implied as incidental to its borrowing power?

- If a charity has a power to enter into a swap, is the swap entered into as part of the charity's debt management strategy or is it 'speculative'?

- Have the charity's trustees taken professional advice in relation to the terms of any swap that is proposed?

- Would an interest rate option be a better way of achieving the charity's financial objective than entering into a free-standing swap transaction?

13

TRADING

13.1 Trading is (like investment and fundraising) one of the ways in which many charities exploit their assets in order to generate funds to advance their charitable purposes. In this Chapter, we look at:

- what constitutes a 'trade';

- the governance implications of trading;

- the kinds of trade that a charity can properly carry out; and

- how (and why) charities use trading subsidiaries.

13.2 It is important to remember that whether a charity can trade has governance implications in respect of both charity and tax law, which is why this chapter draws on the guidance issued by both the Charity Commission and HM Revenue & Customs. The governance implications are explained in more detail at **13.18**.

WHAT IS A 'TRADE'?

13.3 There is no single clear statutory definition of what constitutes a 'trade' which applies for the purposes of both tax and charity law. There is a partial statutory definition for the purposes of tax ('"trade" includes every trade, manufacture, adventure or concern in the nature of trade'[1]) but this does not do much more than confirm that it can encompass a wide range of different activities. Fortunately, the courts have developed some tests that they will apply to any income generating activity in order to determine whether it constitutes a trade or not. These are:

- where a charity buys in goods or services in order to sell them on to a third party, it is likely to be trading;

- an activity carried out by a charity on a one-off basis is less likely to be trading;

- activities carried out by a charity with the intention of making a profit are more likely to be trading; and

- if the charity has developed a mechanism for selling its good or services, this is likely to point to it carrying out a trade. This could include, for example, sales via shops or a website.

---

[1]   Income and Corporation Taxes Act 1988, s 832(1).

13.4   These tests are usually referred to as the 'badges' of trade. They help to identify whether a particular activity is a trade or not, but they are not hard and fast rules. So, for example, the courts have concluded that a one-off activity can constitute a trade and also that a trade may be carried out where there is no intention to make a profit. In other words, while the badges point to the existence of a trade, none of them is, of itself, conclusive.

13.5   HM Revenue & Custom's guidance states that:

> 'Usually, trading involves the provision of goods or services to customers on a commercial basis'

but goes on to say:

> 'Whether an activity is, or is not, a trade depends on the facts of each case. When it is not clear it will be necessary for HMRC Charities to look at all the circumstances surrounding the charity'.[2]

13.6   It may help to consider some of the activities presently carried out by charities that do constitute trading. These include, for example, being paid by a government department to provide services to disabled people, selling educational materials on-line, charging admission to a zoo or historical buildings, selling theatre tickets, educating children in return for school fees and licensing a charity's name and logo to a commercial entity which hopes to increase its sales of a particular product by associating itself with the charity in question.

INVESTMENT AND FUNDRAISING

13.7   Because trading is a varied and wide-ranging concept, there are some nebulous areas where the dividing line between trading and other ways in which a charity may wish to exploit their assets can become blurred. These are investment and fundraising. It is important to understand how they differ from trading because the powers charities have to carry them out, and their tax and charity law implications, are different from those that apply in relation to trading. This obviously raises significant governance issues for a charity's trustees.

13.8   At a basic level, investment and trading are very similar in that they both involve the buying and selling of assets with a view to generating financial resources. But if one looks a little more closely at a charity's intentions, it is possible to draw a distinction between them. The best example of this is the acquisition of land. Land purchased by a charity with the intention of letting it for rent will be an 'investment'. While the charity intends to make a profit in the form of rental income from the land (one of the badges of trade we have mentioned), it does not intend to do so by way of re-sale, there is no mechanism for re-selling and the acquisition will be a one-off transaction. Where, on the other hand, land is purchased by a charity with a view to selling it on for development at a higher price, it will carry out a 'trade' (the trade of property development). Here, the charity intends to make a profit but also intends to re-sell the land.

---

[2]   HM Revenue & Customs' Guidance Note Annex IV.2.

13.9   The distinction between investment and trading is not always clear cut. So the fact that land acquired by a charity is subsequently sold for development does not necessarily mean that it was not bought and held as an investment rather than as a trading asset. As we have said, the key issue is what the charity intended at the time it bought the land in question.

13.10   The distinction between 'trading' and 'fundraising' is even more nebulous, not least because 'fundraising' has no legal meaning in this context and, in the everyday sense, encompasses a very wide range of activities. Trading is certainly one way of raising funds for a charity, but this does not mean that all forms of fund-raising are trading. Again, the true position will vary from case to case and will depend upon the way in which the badges of trade apply. So, for example, a charity may decide to hold an event to raise funds for a particular project. It might decide to hold a concert for which tickets are sold to the charity's supporters. While the charity intends to make a profit from the event, it will be a 'one-off' with no established mechanism for the sale of tickets. On this basis, it is likely to constitute a fundraising event rather than trading. If, however, the event is a success and the charity decides to hold a series of concerts, it is much more likely to be trading as a result. The fact that the event is put on repeatedly, presumably with a more formal mechanism for selling tickets, will, when combined with the profit motive, mean that the events are a trade by the charity.

13.11   Other cases will be more clear cut. A charity may invite the public to make a donation in response to a particular event or to fund a particular project. Invitations of this kind (where the public are promised nothing in return) can never constitute trading notwithstanding that, in the most basic sense, the charity intends to profit from them. Where, on the other hand, a charity provides goods or services in exchange for payment, it will almost invariably be trading. This would include, for example, a charity that charges employers to provide training in first aid to their employees.

13.12   One of the greyer areas is the sponsorship of charities and charitable events by commercial entities. Whether payments made by a commercial entity to a charity in order to be associated with the charity or a particular event put on by the charity constitute trading or fundraising income will generally depend on the way in which the association is presented to the public. There is more about this at **13.142**.

13.13   It is important to bear in mind that the fact that a particular activity raises funds for a charity's charitable purposes (rather than for shareholders, as is the aim for commercial entities) does not mean that the activity cannot be a trade. The courts have considered this question on a number of occasions and have always concluded that what a charity does with the profits it may generate from a trade does not alter the fact that it is a trade.

SALE OF DONATED GOODS

13.14   Before we move on to consider the governance implications of trading, we should mention the specific treatment of the sale by a charity of goods which have been given to a charity specifically for the purpose of raising funds. The classic example of this is goods given to a charity and re-sold by the charity in a shop, but the principle applies in the same way to donated goods which are re-sold to the public in other ways. Both HM Revenue & Customs and the Charity Commission accept that selling donated goods in this way is no more than the realisation by the charity of the value of a gift to it. As HM Revenue & Customs state: 'for this reason the sale of donated goods is generally not regarded as a trade for tax purposes'.[3]

13.15 The Charity Commission also confirm that this is not the exercise of a trade,[4] although both HM Revenue & Customs and the Commission make the point that if donated goods are substantially altered or improved before sale (e g where raw materials are turned into finished goods or the donated goods are subject to 'significant refurbishment or to any process which brings them into a different condition for sale purposes than that in which they have donated') their sale will be trading.

13.16 The Charity Commission's guidance suggests that the sale of any donated asset (including goods, land, buildings and investments) which has been given to a charity specifically for the purpose of raising funds will not constitute a trade. HM Revenue & Customs' guidance is specifically restricted to donated 'goods'. In our view, there is no reason in principle to distinguish between goods and any other sort of donated asset but it is worthwhile bearing in mind that HM Revenue & Customs' guidance is more restricted than this.

13.17 Some charity shops may sell a mixture of donated goods and stock which has been bought in specifically for re-sale. Clearly, the sale of the bought in stock will constitute a trade, whereas the sale of donated goods will not. The distinction between the two is usually dealt with by arranging for the charity to sell the bought in stock as agent for a subsidiary trading company. By acting as the subsidiary's agent, the charity can avoid trading in breach of the restrictions imposed upon it by charity and tax law, whilst also maintaining a claim for mandatory rating relief in respect of the shop premises. There is more guidance in relation to this in the Charity Commission's publication *Charities and trading*.[5]

GOVERNANCE ISSUES

13.18 There are three significant governance issues for charity trustees raised by trading. These are:

- the tax implications of the trade;

- the charity law implications of the trade; and

- the implications of the trade in respect of liability and risk.

Tax implications

13.19 Exemptions and reliefs from tax available to charities only apply to certain types of trading income. This is explained in much more detail at **13.25**. From the point of view of good governance, the key point for charity trustees is that allowing their charity to engage in a trade which gives rise to taxable profits is likely to constitute a breach of

---

[3]   HM Revenue & Customs' Guidance Note Annex IV.21.
[4]   CC 35 ('Charities and trading').
[5]   CC 35.

trust by them which may mean that they are personally liable to compensate the charity for any tax it has to pay but which could have been avoided had the trade been structured appropriately.

13.20 The possibility that a charity may trade at a loss also has potentially significant tax implications. This is because of the rules which restrict the availability of the exemptions and reliefs from tax available generally to a charity where it incurs 'non-charitable expenditure'. As we explain in more detail at **13.25**, certain trading activities carried out by charities generate income which is not exempt from tax (we call this 'non-exempt trading'). HM Revenue & Customs take the view that losses incurred in any non-exempt trading activity cannot be charitable expenditure. This may lead to a restriction on the charity's ability to claim exemptions and reliefs from tax in respect of its other, non-trading, income. HM Revenue & Customs do, however, ignore trading losses which arise as a result of the allocation of a proportion of the charity's fixed costs (ie its overheads) to the trade provided that the charity has realised profits from the trade after deducting its direct trading costs and would have incurred the fixed costs in any event.

Charity law implications

13.21 Generally speaking, the restrictions on a charity's ability to trade with the benefit of exemptions and reliefs from tax mirror the restrictions on its ability to trade under charity law. Where the profits of a trade are exempt from tax, the Charity Commission accept that the trade in question can properly be carried out without infringing charity law. Where there are no exemptions or reliefs, the trade is likely to be carried out in breach of the restrictions imposed by charity law. Again, the consequence for the charity's trustees is likely to be the potential for personal liability for losses that the charity would not have suffered had it not engaged in the trade. This is likely to encompass tax liabilities but also any trading losses.

13.22 The charity law restrictions on trading derive from the constitutional arrangements that must be adopted in order to qualify as a charity. Every charity will have one or more charitable purposes for which it is established. And every charity will have a range of powers which can only be exercised in order to give effect to those charitable purposes. Broadly (and there is more in detail about this at **13.55**), the exercise of a charity by its powers to carry out trades that directly advance its charitable purposes are acceptable. Those trades that do not directly exercise a charity's charitable purposes are (broadly speaking) not acceptable, on the basis that its powers cannot be exercised in a way that does not directly advance its charitable purposes.

Liability and risk

13.23 While charity trustees have to contend with the framework of charity and tax law within which they must operate, they also need to take into account the wide range of trading issues that may give rise to liabilities and increase the risk of carrying out the trade to the charity. A discussion of the liabilities and risk associated with trading is the subject of a book in itself and is outside the scope of this chapter. But there are obviously issues relating to employees, consumer contracts, intellectual property, unfair contract terms etc that must be taken into account as well as the possibility of trading at a loss.

13.24 The risk associated with liabilities of this kind is particular important for charities which carry out both trading and other activities. While a charity which does no more than carry out a particular trade may be willing to accept the risk associated with it (and look at ways in which those risks can be mitigated), a charity with significant investment assets which is looking at engaging in a trade for the first time will obviously want to think long and hard about whether (and how) it can ring fence those assets from liabilities associated with the trade.

TAXATION OF TRADING

13.25 There are six exemptions from tax available to a charity in respect of its trading income. Trading income which falls outside the exemptions will be liable to tax (as we have mentioned, we call this 'non-exempt trading'). Some of the exemptions are more significant than others. They are as follows:

- primary purpose trades;

- beneficiary trades;

- small trades;

- fundraising events;

- lotteries; and

- agricultural shows.

13.26 The tax for which a charity may be liable will depend upon how it is constituted. Broadly, charitable companies and other incorporated charities will be liable to corporation tax, while unincorporated charities will usually be liable to income tax. We refer to both as 'tax' in this chapter. There is more about this in **11.9**.

Primary purpose trading

13.27 The Income and Corporation Taxes Act 1988, s 505(1)(e)(i) exempts from tax the income from any trade which is 'exercised in the course of the actual carrying out of a primary purpose' of a charity. For obvious reasons, trades of this kind are referred to as 'primary purpose' trades. The primary purpose in question will be one (or more) of the charitable purposes specified in a charity's constitution.

13.28 The key to this exemption is that the trade in question is 'exercised in the course of the actual carrying out' of the primary purpose. It may help to consider some examples. HM Revenue & Customs' guidance gives these examples of primary purpose trades:

- The provision of educational services by a school or college in return for course fees.
- The holding of an exhibition by an art gallery or museum in return for admission fees.
- The sale of tickets for a theatrical production staged by a theatre.
- The provision of health-care services by a hospital in return for payment.
- The provision of serviced residential accommodation by a residential care home in return for payment.
- The sale of certain educational goods by an art gallery or museum.'[6]

---

6   HM Revenue & Customs' Guidance Note Annex IV.12.

13.29 What each of these examples have in common is that the income is received by the charity in return for goods or services which are an intrinsic part of the way in which the charity in question advances its charitable purposes. So, for example, while a school which charges fees for providing education to its pupils will be carrying out a primary purpose trade, letting its facilities to third parties out of term time for use as conference facilities has nothing to do with its charitable educational purposes and will not be an exempt trade (notwithstanding that the funds generated will be used to support those purposes).

13.30 HM Revenue & Customs also accepts that:

'The exemption from tax can also extend to other trading, which is not overtly primary purpose in nature but which is ancillary to the carrying out of a primary purpose so that they can be said to be exercised in the course of the actual carrying out of a primary purpose. It is therefore part of the primary purpose trade'[7]

13.31 The Charity Commission's guidance is in line with this and suggests that 'an ancillary trade is one that does not directly further a primary purpose but is exercised in the course of the actual carrying out of a primary purpose of the charity'.[8] HM Revenue & Customs' examples are helpful:

- The sale of relevant goods or services, for the benefit of students by a school or college (text books, for example).
- The provision of a crèche for the children of students by a college or school in return for payment.
- The sale of food and drink in a cafeteria to visitors to exhibits by an art gallery or museum.
- The sale of food and drink in a restaurant or bar to members of the audience by a theatre.
- The sale of confectionary, toiletries and flowers to patients and their visitors by a hospital.'[9]

13.32 HM Revenue & Customs also accepts that certain 'mixed' trades (in other words, a trade which has both primary purpose and non-primary purpose elements) may be treated as a primary purpose trade for tax purposes. Again, the Revenue's examples are helpful:

- A shop in an art gallery or museum which sells a range of goods, some of which are related to a primary purpose of the activity i.e. education and the preservation of property for the public benefit (e.g. direct reproductions of exhibits and catalogues) and some which are not (e.g. promotional pens, mugs, tea towels, stamps etc).
- The letting of accommodation for students in term-time (primary purpose), and for tourists out of term (non primary purpose) by a school or college.
- The sale of food and drink in a theatre restaurant or bar both to members of the audience (beneficiaries of the charity) and the general public (non-beneficiaries).'[10]

13.33 HM Revenue & Customs' practice is to accept that all of the profits of a trade will be exempt for tax if the part of the trade which is not primary purpose is not 'large in absolute terms' and that its turnover is less than 10% of the turnover of the trade as a whole. For this purpose turnover derived from the non-primary purpose trade of £50,000 or less will be considered 'not large'. The Revenue's guidance is as follows:

---

7   HM Revenue & Customs' Guidance Note Annex IV.13.
8   CC 35.
9   HM Revenue & Customs' Guidance Note Annex IV.13.
10   HM Revenue & Customs' Guidance Note Annex IV.14.

'... a mixed trade with a non-primary turnover of less than £50,000 and representing less than 10% of the total trade turnover would satisfy this test. Where the profits of trade cannot be exempted because part of the trade is not related to a primary purpose and it represents 10% or more of the whole trade or, the non-primary purpose turnover is greater than £50,000 per annum the whole of the profits may be liable to tax, including that part of them which is related to a primary purpose'.[11]

13.34 While this has been HM Revenue & Custom's longstanding practice in relation to 'mixed' trades, it was given a statutory basis by the Finance Act 2006, s 56. This provision[12] enables HM Revenue & Customs to treat a charity as carrying out two separate trades. Previously, there was an argument that the Revenue was legally obliged to treat any charity as carrying out only a single trade. This would have meant that the non-primary purpose trade would 'taint' the primary purpose trade with the effect that none of the charity's trading income would be exempt from tax.

Beneficiary trades

13.35 The Income and Corporation Taxes Act 1988, s 505(1)(e)(ii) exempts from tax the income a charity derives from any trade which consists of work 'mainly carried out by beneficiaries of the charity'.

13.36 This exemption is directed at the kind of trading that is perhaps less common now than it was previously eg the sale of goods which have been manufactured by people with disabilities who are also beneficiaries of the charity selling the goods. Trades of this kind may often be primary purpose trades as well as beneficiary trades because they will advance the charity's charitable purposes. This will include, for example, a charity established to relieve the need for disabled people by providing them with paid employment in a workshop producing goods for sale. HM Revenue & Customs' guidance is helpful:

'Some of the work of a trade may be carried out by employees, contractors or volunteer workers who will not rank as beneficiaries of the charity. In these circumstances exemption under s 505(1)(e)(ii) will still be available provided it can be shown that a greater part of the work in connection with the trade is carried out by beneficiaries of the charity.

A charity may wish to pay salaries to beneficiaries who work in a trade carried on by the charity. This will mean that the beneficiaries will become employees of the charity. Provided that they can still properly be regarded as beneficiaries of the charity, the exemption of the trading profits will not be affected. PAYE must be operated on the earnings of beneficiaries who are employed by a charity in the same way as for other employees'.[13]

13.37 There is no definition of 'mainly' for this exemption, although in other contexts it means more than 50%. Where the work in connection with a trade is carried out partly (but not mainly) by a charity's beneficiaries, Finance Act 2006, s 56 allows HM Revenue & Customs to treat the work carried on by the beneficiaries and the work carried on by non-beneficiaries as separate trades. This ensures that the non-beneficiary trade does not 'taint' the beneficiary trade, leading to a loss of tax relief for the trade as a whole.

---

[11] HM Revenue & Customs' Guidance Note Annex IV.15.
[12] With effect in respect of chargeable periods beginning on or after 22 March 2006.
[13] HM Revenue & Customs' Guidance Note Annex IV.17/18.

Small trades

13.38 There is a specific exemption from tax on profits of certain 'small trades' carried out by charities. The exemption is available where a charity's gross trading income (in other words, the income it receives before deducting any of its trading expenses) is equal to or less than the greater of £5,000 and whichever is the lesser of £50,000 and 25% of all of the charity's 'incoming resources' during a tax year.

13.39 In this context, 'incoming resources' is much wider than the 'gross income' of the trade. It includes, for example, all of the income the charity may receive from its investment assets and all of the donations it may receive over the same period.

13.40 This means that a charity which has incoming resources of more than £200,000 during a tax year can only rely on the 'small trades' exemption if its trading income is £50,000 or less. If the trading income is higher than this limit, the exemption is not available in respect of any of the trading income received.[14]

13.41 The exception to this is where the charity can show that, at the beginning of the tax year, it had a reasonable expectation that its gross income from its trade during the year would not exceed the limit. HM Revenue & Customs' guidance states that:

> 'If the total turnover of taxable fund-raising activities does exceed the limits, profits may still be exempt if the charity can show that, at the start of the relevant accounting period, it was reasonable for it to expect that the turnover would not exceed the limit. This might be because:
>
> - The charity expected the turnover to be lower than it turned out to be; or
> - The charity expected that its gross income would be higher than it turned out to be.
>
> The Inland Revenue will consider any evidence the charity may have to satisfy the reasonable expectation test.'[15]

It may be the case that the charity has carried out the activity for a number of years and might be able to show that the turnover increased unexpectedly compared with earlier years. Alternatively, the charity might have started carrying out the fund-raising activity in the year in question and might be able to show that the turnover was higher than it forecasted when it decided to start the activity.

13.42 The key to meeting the 'reasonable expectation' test is obviously being able to produce clear and convincing evidence of what the charity expected might happen at the start of the tax year. HM Revenue & Customs suggest producing minutes of meetings, copies of cash flow forecasts, business plans and the previous year's accounts as evidence. Clear minutes are likely to be essential.

13.43 The Charity Commission accepts that, where a charity can trade within the limits of the 'small trades' exemption, there is no intrinsic objection under charity law. Their guidance says:

> 'Our view is that any charity may trade within the limits of this exemption, provided that the governing document does not generally prohibit non-primary purpose trading. The familiar

---

[14] Finance Act 2000, s 46.
[15] HM Revenue & Customs' Guidance Note Annex IV.22.

provision which, in the context of confirming a power to raise funds, prohibits 'substantial' trading should not be treated as prohibiting trading which falls within this exemption'.[16]

13.44 This confirmation is helpful, because many charities' constitutions will include an express prohibition on 'substantial' trading activities. In our view, the Commission is likely to take the same approach to any prohibition on 'permanent' trading activities.

Fundraising events

13.45 As we have mentioned earlier in this chapter, the line between fundraising and trading is often difficult to draw, particularly in relation to fundraising events such as, concerts, dinners, shows, participation in sporting events, auctions and festivals. By concession, HM Revenue & Customs accepts that:

> 'Certain events arranged by voluntary organisations or charities for the purpose of raising funds for charity may fall within the definition of 'trade' in section 832, ICTA 1988, with the result that any profits will be liable to income tax or corporation tax. Tax will not be charged on such profits provided:
>
> •   the event is of a kind which falls within the exemption from VAT under Group 12 of Schedule 9 of the VATA 1994; and
> •   the profits are transferred to charities or otherwise applied for charitable purposes.'[17]

13.46 The requirements of this concession (Extra-Statutory Concession 4 or 'ESC4') are:

•   The event must be organised and promoted exclusively to raise money for the charity and people attending or participating in the event must be aware that raising funds is its primary purpose.

•   An event is only an event if it does not include the provision of accommodation for more than two nights. This means that most 'challenge events' (which will generally involve travelling and staying overseas for a number of nights in order to complete a particular journey or task) will fall outside ESC4.

•   There must be no more than 15 events of the same type in any one location within any one financial year. So, for example, a raffle held in the same place on more than 15 occasions during a financial year will fall outside ESC4.

13.47 Where the exemption is available, it also covers all the income from supplies of goods and services made by the charity in connection with a particular event including, for example, the sale of brochures and sponsorship payments which are directly connected with the event.

13.48 Although there is a requirement that the profits from the event are 'transferred to charities' ESC4 is not available to a charity's trading subsidiary. The restriction that the profits should be 'otherwise applied for charitable purposes' is common to all of the exemptions from tax on trading by charities. There is more about this at **13.52**.

---

16   OG 63 B2.
17   Extra Statutory Concession 4.

Lotteries

13.49 Lotteries are defined by the Lotteries and Amusements Act 1976. A charity's trustees should understand the legal implications of raising money by way of a lottery (and also those fundraising events which, while not intended to be lotteries, may fall within the statutory definition), not least because promoting an unlawful lottery is a criminal offence. The 1976 Act will be repealed in the Gambling Act 2005 once it has come fully into force (which is expected to happen in autumn 2007).

13.50 The exemption from tax on the profits of a lottery applies to particular kinds of 'small' and 'societies' lotteries. Clearly, a charity's trustees will need to understand how to promote lotteries of this kind rather than any other kind of lottery in order to ensure that the exemption from tax is available (although it is worth remembering that not every lottery will constitute a trade by a charity). Trustees will need to ensure that they understand the changes that will be made to the regulation of lotteries by the 2005 Act.

Agricultural shows

13.51 There is specific exemption for the profits of shows of agricultural societies. In many cases, a charitable agricultural show's profits may in any event be derived from a primary purpose trade.[18]

Application of profits

13.52 Each of these exemptions (with the exception of ESC4) applies only to the extent that the trading profits in question are applied 'solely to the purposes of the charity'. In other words, the profits must be properly applied to advance the charity's purposes in accordance with charity law if the exemptions are to be available.

13.53 ESC4 works in a slightly different way. There, the profits derived from a fundraising event must be applied for the 'charitable purposes'. In principle, therefore, a charity could apply profits for a charitable purpose which is not one of its own charitable purposes and still claim the benefit of ESC4.

13.54 It is also worth remembering that each of the exemptions from tax on trading profits requires *all* of the profits to be applied for charitable purposes. Even if a part of the profits were applied for non-charitable purposes, the exemptions will be lost in their entirety.

CHARITY LAW

13.55 As we have said earlier in this Chapter, the charity law restrictions on trading derive from the constitutional arrangements that must be adopted in order to qualify as a charity, with the consequence that a power to trade can only be used to advance directly the charity's charitable purposes.

13.56 The Charity Commission's guidance gives a different reason:

'Charity law does not permit charities to carry out non-primary purpose trading themselves on a substantial basis in order to raise additional funds. This is because of the general

---

[18]   Income and Corporation Taxes Act 1988, s 510.

expectation that contributions made to a charity will be used for its purposes or invested prudently, rather than being risked in trading activities simply to raise money.'[19]

13.57 While there is undoubtedly some truth in this statement, it is debatable whether this is actually the legal basis for the charity law restriction on charities carrying out non-primary purpose trading.

13.58 Notwithstanding this, the Charity Commission do accept that trading which can be carried out by a charity without giving rise to a liability to tax on its profits can also properly be carried out by the charity as a matter of charity law. This is, though, subject to a requirement that a charity which wishes to carry out a particular trade has the powers it needs in order to do so.

13.59 Where a charity trades without a power to do so, its trustees will be acting in breach of trust and the charity itself will be acting *ultra vires*. There is more about the consequences of this in **Chapter 7**. There are no statutory powers that can be relied upon by charities in order to trade, so the position will be determined by the provisions of a charity's constitution. Many charities will have an express power to trade, although any restrictions on that power should be carefully observed. See **13.43** for the Charity Commission's views in relation to a prohibition on 'substantial' trading activities.

13.60 If a charity does not have an appropriate power to trade, it may be possible to amend its constitution in order to add one. There is more about amendments to charity constitutions in **Chapter 15**.

TAX PLANNING

13.61 Where a charity wishes to carry out a trade which does not fall within one of the exemptions we have summarised earlier in this chapter, there may be other ways of structuring the trade so that there is no liability to tax on profits. The most common forms of tax planning are:

- split payments;
- annual payments; and
- trading subsidiaries.

Each of these possibilities is examined in more detail below.

SPLIT PAYMENTS

13.62 This is a tax planning approach that may be useful where a charity wishes to raise funds from its supporters where (from the supporters' perspective) a significant part of the funds given are donations whereas (from the point of view of tax law), the fact that it is making available goods or services in return for the funds it receives from the supporter means that it is in receipt of trading income.

---

[19] CC 35.

13.63 This is not unusual in the context of charity fundraising, where supporters may make payments which are primarily intended to be donations but are also receiving some tangible benefits from the charity in return. The best example is probably a fundraising event which has a specified ticket price. The price payable for each ticket will be trading income, notwithstanding that the price paid by a supporter may be much greater than the financial value of the benefit they receive in return (e g the cost to the charity of allowing the supporters to bring a certain number of guests to a dinner).

13.64 A possible solution to this problem is to split the payments received by the charity between payments for goods and services and payments which constitute donations. In this way, the donations can be clearly earmarked as donations with the consequence that they are likely to be eligible for gift aid relief and will not constitute trading income for the charity. The payments received by the charity for the supply of goods or services in question will be trading income.

13.65 The fundamental requirement in relation to this approach is that the payment is split in a way which is reasonable. Any charge made for the supply of goods or services must reflect the value of those goods and services so that it can reasonably be said that the 'donation' is clearly a donation.

13.66 HM Revenue & Customs acknowledge that this approach is workable in the context of fundraising events:

> '…it may be possible to organise [a fundraising event] so as to minimise the amount of tax payable. For instance, the charity might set a basic minimum charge (which will be taxable as trading income) and invite those attending the event to supplement this with a voluntary donation. The additional contributions will not be taxable if all of the following conditions are met:
>
> - It is clearly stated in all publicity material, including tickets, that anyone paying only the minimum charge will be admitted without further payment.
> - The additional payment does not secure any particular benefit (for example, admission to a better seat in the auditorium) beyond the limits specified in Gift Aid legislation.
> - The extent of further contributions is ultimately left to ticket holders to decide (even if the organiser indicates a desired level of donation).
> - For film or theatre performances, concerts, sporting fixtures and similar events the minimum charge is not less than the usual price for the particular seats at a normal commercial event of the same type.
> - For dances, dinners and similar functions the sum of the basic minimum charges is not less than the total costs incurred in arranging the event.'[20]

13.67 These are all reasonable requirements aimed at ensuring that the trading income represents the 'market value' of the benefits provided and that the additional donation that is paid by a supporter is truly a donation, with no obligations attached to it. In that sense, the acid test is whether a supporter could decide to pay the specified minimum charge and still attend the event without making any sort of donation whatsoever. There is obviously a judgement to be made by the charity about the value of the tax saved as against the possibility that its supporters will not put their hands deep enough into their pockets.

---

[20] HM Revenue & Customs' Guidance Note Annex IV.43.

ANNUAL PAYMENTS

13.68 Increasingly, charities may be able to exploit the value in their 'brand' (in other words, their name and/or logo), by licensing its use to commercial entities which hope to sell more of their goods and services by associating themselves with the charity.

13.69 This would normally be achieved by arranging for a charity to license its name and or logo to a commercial entity for use in relation to a particular product or service. There are other issues that a charity should be aware of in relation to this (not least the rules in relation to commercial participators imposed by the Charities Act 1992). These are summarised below at **13.142**.

13.70 Provided royalties payable to the charity under the licence are 'annual payments' for tax purposes, they will qualify for income tax relief in the hands of the charity. In some cases, the royalties must be paid after deducting tax but this can be reclaimed by the charity. The key advantage is however, that the royalties are not treated as non-exempt trading income and are not liable, therefore, to tax. Unless royalties are 'annual payments' in the hands of a charity, they will almost inevitably be trading income because there are very few circumstances in which exploiting the goodwill associated with a charity's name and logo would fall within its charitable purposes so that it constitutes primary purpose trading income.

13.71 In order to ensure that royalties are 'annual payments' for tax purposes, the charity must ensure that it does no more than license its name and or logo to the commercial entity, that it incurs no other expenses in relation to the licence and that the licence itself is capable for lasting for more than one year. Commercial entities may often require a licence of this kind to be made in conjunction with a licence to use, say, the charity's database of supporters, which would mean that payments received by the charity would not constitute annual payments. Where this is a risk, a charity should consider making the licence arrangement via a wholly-owned trading subsidiary.

TRADING SUBSIDIARIES

13.72 One of the most common approaches taken by charities to minimising tax liabilities in relation to non-exempt trading is to use a trading subsidiary. In principle, this is a straightforward structure to put in place. Broadly, it works in the following way:

- Where a charity wishes to carry out a trade which does not fall within any of the available exemptions from tax for its profits, the trustees may decide to establish a non-charitable trading company, which will usually be wholly owned by the charity.

- The purpose of the subsidiary company is to carry on the non-exempt trade which the charity cannot carry out itself (hence the usual reference to a 'trading subsidiary').

- The trading subsidiary operates in much the same way as any other commercial company. To the extent that it makes profits from the trade it carries, it will have a liability to corporation tax.

- However, this tax liability can be reduced (or eliminated altogether) by the trading subsidiary making a 'gift aid' donation to its parent charity.

- The donation is free of tax in the hands of the charity and is deductible (as a 'charge on income') by the trading subsidiary in calculating its liability to corporation tax.

- The net effect should be (in principle, at least) that the trading subsidiary has traded profitably with the full benefit of those profits passing (tax free) to its parent charity.

13.73 Strictly, a company is only a 'subsidiary' where it is owned by another company. We use the term 'trading subsidiary' in the wider sense in which it is used by the Charity Commission, to include any trading company wholly owned by any incorporated or unincorporated charity.

13.74 Both the Charity Commission and HM Revenue & Customs expressly approve of trading subsidiary arrangements, notwithstanding that, in some respects at least, they appear to represent a rather artificial solution to the problems posed for charities by non-exempt trading. The Charity Commission's guidance states:

> 'Where a charity wishes to benefit substantially from permanent trading for the purpose of fund-raising, trustees should creating a subsidiary trading company. This avoids the risk of committing a breach of trust, and the profits of the trade may be passed by the charity in a tax-efficient way under the gift aid scheme.'[21]

13.75 Although establishing a trading subsidiary will generally be driven by tax considerations, there may be circumstances in which a charity concludes that it would prefer to carry out a trade via a trading subsidiary in order to ensure that any liabilities and risks associated with the trade in question are ring-fenced from the charity's other assets and activities. Where the trade in question is a primary purpose trade that the charity could have carried out itself under both tax and charity law, its ability to invest in the subsidiary will be subject to different considerations from an investment in a subsidiary which has been established to carry out a non-exempt trade. Essentially, the relationship between a charity and a trading subsidiary established for this purpose need not be on arm's length terms, as the relationship with any other trading subsidiary must be.

13.76 Although the relationship between a charity and its trading subsidiary is easily summarised, there are a number of other issues which make the position more complex for a charity's trustees. These relate to both the setting up and initial investment in a trading subsidiary and its subsequent operations.

13.77 Fundamental to many of these issues is the principle that a trading subsidiary will, notwithstanding that it may be wholly owned by a charity and have been established by it for a particular purpose, still be (and will be treated by HM Revenue & Customs and the Charity Commission) as a separate commercial entity which the charity must deal with in the same way as it would deal with any other separate commercial entity (in other words, on arm's length terms).

---

[21] CC 35.

Set-up

13.78 There are a number of issues that will need to be addressed by a charity's trustees in relation to the setting-up of a trading subsidiary. These are explained below.

Corporate structure

13.79 Generally, a trading subsidiary will be a company limited by shares. A company limited by guarantee can be used while retaining the benefits of limited liability, but this would exclude the possibility of the charity investing in the company by subscribing for shares in it.

Investment

13.80 In line with the principle that the charity should deal with the trading as a subsidiary in the same way as it would deal with any other commercial entity, any investment the charity proposes to make in the subsidiary must be on arm's length terms. In other words, it must be treated by the trustees in the same way as they would treat any other proposed investment of the charity's assets. The Commission's guidance is that:

> 'Three questions which the trustees (with advice from their own professional advisors as necessary) will need to address are:
>
> - Whether the charity's investment powers permit the making of an investment in the subsidiary trading company.
> - Whether an investment of this sort in a trading venture is too speculative for a charity (i.e. is the proposed company likely to be successful and have appropriate business plans and financial forecasts been prepared?)
> - Whether investment in a subsidiary trading company is in line with the charity's current investment policy.'[22]

13.81 HM Revenue & Customs' guidance reflects the guidance issued by the Commission:

> 'When deciding whether to make an investment, charities should bear in mind the requirements of charity law in relation to:
>
> - Objectivity in the selection of investments;
> - The need to avoid undue risk or speculation; and
> - The need for a proper spread of investments.'[23]

13.82 There is more about the considerations that are applied to the exercise of power of investment by a charity's trustees in **Chapter 10**. These include an obligation to observe the 'standard investment criteria'. The key point is that a charity's trustees are expected to approach an investment in its trading subsidiary in the same way as they would approach an investment in, say, shares in Marks & Spencer. In practice, it is often difficult to justify investing the charity's funds in what is essentially a start-up company as against investing them in listed shares in an established trading company.

13.83 In this context, 'investment' does not mean the charity's initial subscription for shares in the trading subsidiary. As the Commission's guidance states:

---

[22] CC 35.
[23] HM Revenue & Customs' Guidance Note Annex IV.62.

'The authorised share capital in such companies is usually small, perhaps £100, of which only 2 shares may be issued. The charity can freely make nominal subscription of share capital in the trading subsidiary.'[24]

13.84 However, where the charity needs to make a more substantial investment in the trading subsidiary in order to fund its trading activities, all of the considerations that apply to investment generally will apply. Again, the Commissions' guidance states that:

'Such an investment must be:

- Within the investment powers of the charity; and
- A commercially sound proposition.'[25]

13.85 In practice, the Commission will expect the charity's trustees to take the sort of steps that they should take in relation to any proposed investment in order to ensure that the trading subsidiary is a 'commercially sound proposition'. These will include:

- assessing the financial viability of the trading subsidiary by reviewing its business plan, cash flow forecast, profit projections, risk analysis and any other relevant information;

- considering the length of time during which funds may be tied up in investment in the trading subsidiary and the fact that the investment is likely to be illiquid; and

- the form the investment in the trading subsidiary should take.

13.86 Again, HM Revenue & Customs' guidance reflects the Commission's guidance:

'Depending on the size of a proposed investment, the decision may be based on the following:

- Business plans.
- Cashflow forecast.
- Projections of future profits.'[26]

13.87 Investment by the charity can take one of two forms. The charity could subscribe for shares in the trading subsidiary. Alternatively, the charity could make loans to the trading subsidiary which may or may not be secured. The key consideration is that shareholders subscribing for shares in a trading subsidiary will rank behind lenders. Lenders will rank with other ordinary creditors, unless they take security for their loan. The Commission's guidance is:

'Charities should not ordinarily subscribe anything more than nominal sums for the issue of share capital by the subsidiary trading company (in order to satisfy the formal requirements of company law). The subscription of shares in a subsidiary trading company by the charity normally exposes the charity's investment to greater risk (because the repayment of share capital, in the event of the liquidation of the subsidiary trading company, has a lower priority than the repayment of loans).'[27]

---

[24] CC 35.
[25] CC 35.
[26] HM Revenue & Customs' Guidance Note Annex IV.62.
[27] CC 35.

13.88 In general, therefore, charity trustees should look to lend money to a trading subsidiary in order to provide the funds required for its activities. Again the Commission state that:

> 'Normally, investment in a subsidiary trading company should take the form of secured loans by the charity on market terms.'

and

> 'Charities should not normally make unsecured or interest free loans to a subsidiary trading company. Such loans are not compatible with the proper discharge of the duties and responsibility of charity trustees. If a subsidiary trading company fails the trustees may find themselves personally liable for any losses to the charity's funds if they have acted in breach of trust.'[28]

13.89 The starting point, therefore, should be that all loans must:

- charge a proper rate of interest;

- be secured; and

- include repayment terms.

13.90 Clearly, an interest free loan by a charity to its trading subsidiary will not satisfy the general principle that funding should be made available on an arm's length basis. A proper rate of interest should be charged by the charity, although the rate that is set will need to take into account the risk of default by the trading subsidiary (which is a factor that any commercial lender would take into account) and the rate that the charity might otherwise obtain by depositing the funds with a bank or other financial institution. Interest payments should actually be made by the trading subsidiary of the charity (and not simply added to the principal outstanding on the loan).

13.91 Taking security may have no real value in the context of a start-up company which may have few fixed or other assets that have any realisable value in the event of default on the loan. But it is obviously advisable for a charity's trustees to seek fixed and floating charges where this is possible.

13.92 The loan must set out the basis on which the principal will be repaid. There is no requirement that the loan should be repayable on demand by the charity but, equally, no commercial lender would agree to lend funds without specifying the term of the loan.

13.93 The Charity Commission does acknowledge that there may be circumstances in which investing in a trading subsidiary by way of loan may have the effect of making it insolvent. The Commission's guidance states:

> 'For example, the taxable profits of the trading subsidiary in a particular financial period may exceed its accounting profits. If, in order to maximise its tax relief, the subsidiary pays over the whole of the taxable profit to the charity, it may have to be financed by the charity to bridge a gap between the taxable and the accounting profits. A loan for this purpose could have the effect of making a subsidiary trading company insolvent, and the professional advisers of the charity may advise it to subscribe for equity capital in the company instead.'[29]

---

[28]   CC 35.
[29]   CC 35.

13.94 The Charity Commission recommends that 'proper consideration' should be given by a charity's trustees to the possibility of financing its subsidiary trading company by way of commercial loan. As the Commission quite rightly points out, involving a commercial lender is more likely to ensure that the viability of the subsidiary's trading activities is objectively assessed by someone with no direct involvement in the trade.

13.95 The Commission also makes the point that arranging for a trading subsidiary to borrow from a commercial lender will protect the charity's assets from exposure to the financial risks of the trade the subsidiary is carrying out. The Commission's view is that:

'The additional cost of commercial lending, as compared with lending by the charity, may be regarded as a reasonable price to be paid for the acceptance by the commercial lender, rather than the charity, of the risk of loss.'[30]

13.96 While this would be a good outcome for most charities, most commercial lenders are shrewd enough to look for security from the parent charity where they take the view that the trading subsidiary's activities and assets present them with any sort of risk of default on the loan. This is obviously particularly likely to be an issue where a trading subsidiary routinely pays all or most of its trading profits up to its parent charity, with little opportunity to accrue value within the subsidiary itself.

13.97 The Charity Commission's guidance in relation to security granted by a charity in respect of the liabilities of its trading subsidiary is:

'Whether such security takes the form of an indirect loan arrangement, a guarantee, or a charge over charity property, it essentially has the effect of re-exposing the charity's assets to the financial risks to the business. This negates the effect of involving the commercial lender at all and we would not normally regard the giving of such security as being in the best interests of the charity.'[31]

13.98 Where a charity is not able to guarantee its trading subsidiary's liabilities directly, a commercial lender may agree to lend on the basis of a 'letter of comfort' from the charity which indicates that it will consider meeting any liabilities to the lender which the trading subsidiary cannot meet itself. A letter of comfort must be carefully worded in order to ensure that it is not legally binding on the charity. Even if it is not, our view is that comfort of this kind blurs the distinction between a charity and its trading subsidiary. It is only likely to be appropriate for a letter of comfort of this kind to be given where the charity's trustees are confident that trading subsidiary will be profitable and that the letter is, therefore, genuinely given only as 'comfort'.

Tax

13.99 Any investment in a trading subsidiary (whether by subscribing for shares or loans) will only qualify as 'charitable expenditure' for tax purposes if it is made for charitable purposes only, is for the benefit of charity and is not for the avoidance of tax. If the investment does not qualify as charitable expenditure, the charity may lose all or part of its exemptions and reliefs from tax on its other sources of income and gains. There is more information about this at **11.56**.

---

[30] CC 35.
[31] CC 35.

13.100 HM Revenue & Customs' guidance makes it clear that:

> 'An investment or loan will normally be 'for the benefit of the charity' where it is made on sound commercial terms...There is no one test of commercial soundness and each case must be viewed on its own facts. Where a loan or investment:
>
> - carries a commercial rate of interest;
> - is adequately secure; and
> - is made under a formal written agreement which includes reasonable repayment terms we will normally accept that the investment or loan is for the benefit of the charity.'[32]

13.101 In assessing whether or not investments in a trading subsidiary do qualify as charitable expenditure, HM Revenue & Customs' approach is to ask whether the charity's trustees have followed the Charity Commission's guidance.

Governance

13.102 Irrespective of the charity and tax implications of setting up a trading subsidiary, a charity's trustees should give careful consideration to governance arrangements, particularly as regards the board of directors of the trading subsidiary. The Commission's guidance states that:

> 'An individual who is both a trustee of the charity and a director of a subsidiary trading company will have two different sets of responsibilities to fulfil even though the company was established as a means of raising funds for the charity. It can be difficult to balance these responsibilities.'[33]

13.103 The potential for conflicts of interest is clearly an issue given the fundamental requirement that arrangements between the charity and its trading subsidiary should be on an arm's length basis. Where all of the trustees of the charity are all also directors of the trading subsidiary, the scope for a conflict of interest which will leave the trading subsidiary without directors capable of making a decision is reasonably high. On this basis, the Commission's guidance is:

> 'We recommend that there should be at least one person who is a trustee of the charity and not a director of the trading company, and at least one person who is a director of the trading company and not a trustee of the charity. The people without dual interests can be expected to give suitable advice to their colleagues as to the proper course of action in a conflict of interest situation and this should reduce the risk of any transaction between the charity and the company being challenged or questioned.'[34]

13.104 A director of the trading subsidiary who is not also a trustee of the charity will often be the charity's chief executive or chief financial officer.

13.105 The scope for conflicts of interest to put individual directors of the trading subsidiary in a very difficult position is a real one. In the worst case, where the trading subsidiary is bordering on insolvency and is unlikely to avoid becoming insolvent without continued financial support from its parent charity, the subsidiary's directors may be concerned about their liabilities for any claims in respect of wrongful trading which may be brought by the subsidiary's liquidator. In this sense, the directors may have an interest in the charity continuing to provide financial support in circumstances

---

[32] HM Revenue & Customs' Guidance Note Annex III.4.
[33] CC 35.
[34] CC 35.

where, as trustees, they would find it difficult to do so. The solution to this problem in practice is to ensure that the directors of the subsidiary are fully advised in relation to insolvency issues in general and wrongful trading in particular, but the potential for conflict is clear. There is more about wrongful trading at **6.14**.

13.106 Charity trustees who also act as directors of a trading subsidiary should bear in mind that they cannot be paid for doing so unless the charity's constitution authorises them to benefit. There is more about trustee benefits of this kind at **6.35**.

Costs

13.107 Trustees should take into account the likelihood that setting up and running a separate trading subsidiary will increase the administrative and professional costs of the charity. The trustees will need to be sure that the costs in question do not exceed the tax saved by setting the subsidiary up.

Rating relief

13.108 While a charity qualifies for 80% mandatory (and 20% discretionary) relief from non-domestic rates, the same is not true of a trading subsidiary. In order to qualify for relief, a property must be occupied by a charity and be occupied wholly or mainly for its charitable purposes. As the Commission's guidance states:

> '"Charitable purposes" normally exclude fund-raising but include the sale of donated goods. Premises used partly by a charity for its purposes and partly by non-charitable subsidiary trading company will qualify for relief only in respect of the part actually occupied by the charity.'[35]

13.109 It may be possible for the trading subsidiary to occupy a charity's premises under licence or for the charity to act as agent for the subsidiary, so that the charity continues to be in occupation wholly or mainly for its charitable purposes.

Operational issues

13.110 In addition to the issues that charity trustees need to take into account on setting up a trading subsidiary, there are number of operational issues that are likely to arise in practice.

Additional investment

13.111 The charity's trustees will need to treat any additional investment in the trading subsidiary in exactly the same way as their initial investment. All of the same considerations in relation to looking for funding from commercial lenders and whether the charity should make funds available by loan or by subscribing for additional shares will apply.

13.112 In many cases, the trustees will wish to see the trading subsidiary making gift aid donations of all of its taxable profit up to the charity in order to avoid any liability to corporation tax (see **13.123**). This will mean that there is no real scope for the trading subsidiary to build up any value. This will, in turn, make it more difficult for the trading

---

[35] CC 35.

subsidiary to obtain funding from a commercial lender and for the trustees to conclude that the trading subsidiary is an appropriate investment for the charity.

13.113 Problems often arise in practice where the trading subsidiary is loss making. Where losses are accruing on a regular basis and without a particular justification in trading terms, the trustees are likely to be faced with a difficult decision. On the one hand, they may wish to see the charity continuing to support the trading subsidiary and its directors and employees. On the other hand, they are faced with the prospect of investing further funds for the charity in a trading company which is unlikely to produce an investment return. The Commission states:

> 'If the trustees sink further funds in supporting an ailing subsidiary at a time when it was reasonably clear that the failure of the company was likely or inevitable, then this could constitute a breach of trust on the part of the trustees putting them at personal risk to make good any losses to the charity. Trustees facing these circumstances should take advice from their professional advisers as to the course of action which they should follow.'[36]

Third party investment

13.114 An alternative to further investment by the charity or commercial loans may be to issue shares to a commercial entity which is willing to invest funds. This would usually be because the trading subsidiary's activities have some synergy with the commercial entity's own trading activities or because the commercial entity concludes that shares in the trading subsidiary are a good investment.

13.115 There is no objection in principle to a charity co-owning a trading subsidiary with a commercial entity where this is justified on the basis of the commercial entity's financial investment in the subsidiary, or the particular skills and expertise it has in relation to the subsidiary's operational activities.

13.116 However, a charity should only consider entering into a co-ownership arrangement of this kind on the basis of a carefully considered and properly drafted shareholders' agreement which deals with all of the issues that arise in these circumstances. These include, for example:

- whether shareholders will have rights to appoint and remove directors to and from the board of the subsidiary;

- whether shareholders have any rights of veto over material transactions with which the subsidiary may become involved (such as taking on a lease, employing senior executives or incurring material liabilities);

- the financial investment and management skills that each shareholder will bring to the subsidiary; and

- the basis on which shares can be transferred by a shareholder to a third party, perhaps with 'drag along' or 'tag along' rights in the event that a third party makes an offer to buy out one shareholder's shares.

13.117 An association with a commercial entity in this way can obviously have potentially serious implications for a charity's reputation. The shareholders' agreement

---

[36]   CC 35.

should regulate the use of the charity's name and/or logo, but the charity should also think hard about the commercial entity with which it is entering into an agreement and the scope for its activities to adversely affect the charity.

13.118 Co-owning a trading subsidiary with a non-charity will affect when the subsidiary can pay profits to the charity by way of gift aid. There is more about this at **13.129**.

13.119 Where a trading subsidiary is co-owned by a charity and a non-charity, it is possible that HM Revenue & Customs will argue that gift aid payments to the charity are distributions of its profits rather than donations (with the consequence that they must be paid out of the subsidiary's taxed income). There is more about this at **13.131**.

Employee investment

13.120 Many commercial companies use employee incentives in order to help improve their profitability. The incentives in question will generally be shares issued to employees at a discount or options enabling employees to purchase shares at a discount, usually using one of the tax efficient arrangements for issuing employee incentives, such as the Employee Management Incentives scheme.

13.121 There is no reason in principle why a charity's trading subsidiary cannot issue share incentives to its employees where they are tied to appropriate targets. However, there is obviously some scope for a conflict of interest to arise for employees of the subsidiary who are also employees of the charity because they may start to do more to increase the subsidiary's profitability at the expense of the charity's own operations.

13.122 The scope for conflicts of interest to arise will obviously vary from case to case, but a charity's trustees should consider any proposal to issue employee incentives very carefully.

Profit retention

13.123 As we have mentioned, a charity's trustees may wish to see the charity's trading subsidiary making gift aid donations of all of its taxable profits to the charity, with a view to eliminating any liability to corporation tax. But trustees will need to ensure they take into account the working capital requirements of the trading subsidiary. These may mean that, in order to develop its trading activities, the subsidiary requires working capital which, if it cannot be obtained from the charity or a commercial lender, can only be obtained by leaving some profits within the subsidiary (giving rise, therefore, to a liability to tax).

13.124 The Commission suggests that:

'Some charities may prefer to accept the tax consequences as a measure of profit retention by the subsidiary trading company. This can enable the subsidiary trading company to function in a normal commercial way, and reduce or eliminate the need for the charity to invest (at risk) its own money in the subsidiary trading company.'[37]

13.125 This is helpful because, indirectly at least, it confirms the Commission's view that a charity's trustees can in certain circumstances properly decide not to seek a gift

---

[37]   CC 35.

aid payment of all of a subsidiary's profits. The Commission has stated previously that charity trustees have a duty to consider the tax effectiveness of arrangements with its subsidiary and that they may be personally liable for tax liabilities unnecessarily incurred as a result of the inefficient administration of the charity. Clearly, this does not extend to a considered decision to leave profits with a subsidiary to help develop its business.

13.126 HM Revenue & Customs' guidance makes a similar point:

> 'Most commercial companies keep part of their profits to provide them with funds for day-to-day expenses, working capital and normal development of their business. However, companies which intend to donate all of their profits to charity every year may not be able to retain the funds they need to carry on in business. Charities may therefore want to ensure when a company is set up that it is provided with enough capital to enable it to shed its profits every year. The passing of profits up to the parent charity may result in a serious drain on the company's cash. If so, care should be taken to avoid a pattern of frequent injections of funds by the charity in order to keep the company in business. Such a practice might put at risk both the charity's tax exemptions and the company's deductions for its Gift Aid payments. In some cases where there is a serious cash drain in the company, it would be necessary for the company to change its practice so that it keeps part of its profits. In these circumstances some tax will become payable by the company.'[38]

13.127 Again, it is helpful to have HM Revenue & Customs' acknowledgement that there are circumstances in which taxable profits can properly be left within a trading subsidiary.

13.128 Clearly, there is a difficult balance to be struck by a charity's trustees between a desire to minimise liability to tax and the advantage of leaving funds within a trading subsidiary in order to enable it to develop its own business without resorting to further investment by the charity and the complications that this may entail. The fact that there is a balance to be struck is a strong argument for avoiding the use of a deed of covenant between the subsidiary and the charity which obliges the subsidiary to pay up all or part of its taxable profits to the charity. There is more about deeds of covenant at **13.132**.

Gift aid

13.129 Providing a trading subsidiary is wholly owned by a charity, it has 9 months from the end of its accounting period to make donations to its parent charity. This means that it will have the time to establish its taxable and accounting profits after the end of the accounting period and can then make an appropriate donation. The same is true of a trading company which is owned by more than one charity.

13.130 However, a trading company which is owned in part by anyone other than a charity does not qualify for this treatment. It can only claim gift aid relief in respect of payments made within the company's accounting period, with no ability to carry the relief back to an accounting period ending in the pervious 9 months.

13.131 As we have mentioned earlier in this Chapter, payments by a subsidiary to a charity which co-owns the subsidiary with a non-charity may be treated by HM Revenue & Customs as 'distributions' for tax purposes. This will mean that HMRC will treat the payments to the charity as made out of the subsidiary's taxed income, with a

---

[38]   HM Revenue & Customs' Guidance Note Annex IV.63.

corporation tax liability for the subsidiary and no repayable credit for the charity for the tax withheld on the distribution. There is more about this at **11.115**.

Deeds of covenant

13.132 There is no requirement that a gift aid donation is made under a deed of covenant, although some charities may want to see a binding legal obligation imposed upon their trading subsidiary to give to the charity an amount equal to its taxable profits (or perhaps a particular proportion of those taxable profits). The argument against this, which we have mentioned earlier in this Chapter, is that it will be better to maintain the capacity to retain profits with the subsidiary and rely upon the charity's control of the subsidiary to influence the payments that are made.

13.133 A deed of covenant imposes a legal obligation to make payments to the charity and will need to be drafted carefully. Problems can arise where there is any discrepancy between the trading subsidiary's accounting and taxable profits. Where, for example, items of expenditure are allowed for accounting purposes but not allowed as deductions against tax, the trading subsidiary may have insufficient cash with which to meet its total corporation tax liability. This can be avoided by careful drafting of the deed of covenant.

Cost sharing

13.134 In line with the principle that arrangements between the charity and its trading subsidiary should be at arm's length, there should be an appropriate cost sharing arrangement in relation to any shared facilities. This might be because, for example, the trading subsidiary occupies part of the charity's premises, uses its IT or other facilities, or some of the charity's employees spend part of their time working for the subsidiary. The costs shared, therefore, should include both direct and indirect costs.

13.135 More generally, a charity's trustees should ensure that an appropriate distinction is drawn between the charity and its subsidiary in relation to all operational activities. This will mean ensuring that:

- The trustees of the charity and the directors of the trading subsidiary hold separate meetings and that separate minutes of each meeting are produced. There is no objection to holding both meetings on the same day (because the day on which a trustees' meeting is held may often be a good opportunity for the directors of the subsidiary to meet), but the two entities have a separate legal existence and it is important that this is recognised and properly recorded.

- The trading subsidiary will require its own letter headed paper, invoices etc, all of which must comply with the requirements of the companies legislation by confirming its registered name, office and company number, its place of incorporation and either all of its directors or none of them.

- The charity and its subsidiary should use separate bank accounts and their funds should not be mixed.

13.136 All of these operational issues can be dealt with alongside cost sharing in a formal agreement between the charity and the subsidiary. This might also deal with, for example, the basis on which the subsidiary is able to use the charity's name and/or logo. This agreement should be reviewed by both the charity and the subsidiary on a regular basis.

13.137 The Charity Commission recommends that a trading subsidiary which uses part of its parent charity's premises should enter into a 'formal lease or licence of the property'. The Commission also recommends that the trading subsidiary should pay a market rent or fee for the use of the property. This is obviously in line with the principle that arrangements between the charity and its trading subsidiary should be at arm's length. The charity's trustees should bear in mind that a lease of any part of its premises to the trading subsidiary will require the Commission's consent under the Charities Act 1993, s 36 (see **9.95** for more information in relation to this). In practice, the charity will often grant a licence to its trading subsidiary. Provided the licence is actually a licence (and the distinction between leases and licences is not always absolutely clear), the Commission's consent will not be required. The charity will need to take advice to ensure that it grants a licence rather than a lease if this is what is intended.

Charity Commission guidance

13.138 It is worth bearing in mind the Charity Commission's guidance in relation to the use of trading subsidiaries generally.

'Based on our experience of cases, where substantial amounts of charities' money have been lost as a result of ill-considered investments in subsidiary trading companies, we would expect trustees to consider the following points:

- The financial structure of the charity and the subsidiary trading company ought to be kept separate.
- Separate identities of the charity and the subsidiary trading company should be made clear in all publicity material and in deals with suppliers.
- The names of the charity and the subsidiary trading company should be distinguished from each other to prevent confusion between the activities of the two organisations.
- The establishment of a trading subsidiary, where the directors of that company are the same people as the trustees of the charity, cannot be used as a means of paying the charity's trustees 'by the back door'.
- The charity must not settle the debts of the subsidiary trading company.
- The charity should not feel any moral obligation to fund the subsidiary trading company.
- Any financial support the charity can give to the subsidiary trading company including non-cash commitments (e.g. staff, office space and equipment) should be carefully assessed.
- The charity buying stock and donating to its subsidiary trading company should be avoided.
- Plan for the subsidiary trading company to be financially viable as soon as possible. Normally this will be within its first five years of operation.
- The need to obtain the Commission's authority to any proposal for a lease of property by a charity to a subsidiary trading company.
- To ensure that investments in a subsidiary trading company are qualifying investments for tax purposes.'[39]

Transfer pricing

13.139 The 'transfer pricing' rules allow HM Revenue & Customs to treat transactions between certain connected parties as made on an arm's length basis for tax purposes.

---

[39]   CC 35.

The aim is to ensure that tax is not avoided by manipulating the profitability of contracts and other transactions. In principle, arrangements between a charity and trading subsidiary will be caught by the rules, although HM Revenue & Customs' own guidance in this area suggests that the position is unlikely to be looked at critically where the charity follows the guidance issued by the Charity Commission in relation to investment in trading subsidiaries.

13.140 In general, where a charity and its subsidiary are dealing with each other on an arm's length basis, the scope for the application on the transfer pricing rules is likely to be fairly restricted. However, the rules are complicated and the charity's trustees should seek advice if they are in any doubt about the position.

VAT

13.141 A detailed discussion of the VAT implications of trading by charities and their trading subsidiaries is outside the scope of this chapter. VAT is a complex tax which in many ways operates very differently to the direct charges to income and corporation tax we have discussed earlier in this chapter. Because of the sort of activities that many charities undertake, it can penalise them financially to a far greater extent than commercial entities. If in any doubt about the VAT implications of a particular trading activity (and it will generally be best to assume that there will be VAT implications unless and until it is confirmed otherwise), a charity's trustee should seek professional advice.

BUSINESS SPONSORSHIP

13.142 Many charities receive donations from commercial entities. Sometimes, this relationship may be more complex than that of donor and donee. So, eg, the charity may agree to acknowledge the commercial entity's support to the general public. This is usually referred to as 'sponsorship'. Other arrangements may involve a commercial entity paying a charity for a licence of its name and/or logo to help promote sales of particular goods or services because of the value of the charity's 'brand' among the general public. This is usually referred to as 'cause-related marketing'.

13.143 Payments received by a charity from a commercial entity under a sponsorship or cause related marketing arrangement can in certain circumstances constitute a trade (the trade of advertising). This will vary from case to case and the way in which the 'badges' of trade apply to a particular arrangement between the charity and commercial entity. HM Revenue & Customs' guidance is helpful:

> 'Just because a sponsor derives good publicity or public relations benefits from payments to charity, does not automatically mean that payments by the sponsor are trading income in the hands of the charity.
>
> If the charity does not provide goods or services in return for payment, payments will normally have the character of charitable donations rather than trading income in the charity's hands. The fact that the business sponsor takes steps to publicise or exploit the affinity with the charity will not change the treatments of the payments in the hands of the charity, unless the charity also publicises the affinity itself.'[40]

---

[40] HM Revenue & Customs' Guidance Note Annex IV.28.

13.144 The key question is whether or not the charity is providing anything to the sponsor in return for the payment it is making. If nothing is received in return, then the payment will generally be a donation. This is likely to be reflected in the way in which the commercial entity accounts for the payment. A donation is likely to be paid out of its charity budget and be treated as a 'charge on income' in calculating its corporation tax liability. A payment in return for goods of services received from the charity will, on the other hand, probably be paid out of the commercial entity's advertising budget and will be deducted as a trading expense in calculating its liability to tax.

13.145 HM Revenue & Customs' guidance goes on to say:

'If the charity provides some goods or services in return for the sponsorship payments they may be treated as trading income. Most commonly, a charity will play a part in publicising the business sponsor's affinity with the charity by including references to the sponsor in publications, posters, etc. and the events organised by the charity. Provided that such references amount to no more than acknowledgements of the sponsor's contributions they will not cause the payments to be regarded as trading income. However, references to a sponsor which amount to advertisements will cause the payments to be treated as trading income.'[41]

13.146 HM Revenue & Customs goes on to give some helpful examples of references to a sponsor it will regard as advertisements:
　　　　'Large and prominent displays of the sponsor's logo
　　　　Large and prominent displays of the sponsor's corporate colours
　　　　A description of the sponsor's products or services.'[42]

13.147 However, it goes on to say:

'...If a project organised by a charity is sponsored by a well-known company, and acknowledgment of the support of this company in the form of its name and logo is inserted in the corner of a project report, this would not be considered to be advertising. However, if the name and logo was substantially and widely displayed throughout the report, this might be considered to be advertising in return for the sponsorship payment.'[43]

13.148 HM Revenue & Customs will also look at other services that a charity might provide to a sponsor alongside advertising in deciding whether or not sponsorship payments are donations or trading income. These may include a right for the sponsor to use the charity's mailing list of supporters, the use of its logo or an endorsement of the sponsor's goods or services.

13.149 HM Revenue & Customs takes a similar approach to cause-related marketing arrangements:

'Where a charity allows its logo to be used, in return for payment, by a business as an endorsement for one or more of the business' products or services, and the charity likewise promotes the endorsement in its own literature, the payments are likely to be trading income of the charity.'[44]

13.150 On this basis, arrangements under which, for example, a charity licences its name and/or logo to appear on a commercial entity's product containing a statement

---

[41]　HM Revenue & Customs' Guidance Note Annex IV.29.
[42]　HM Revenue & Customs' Guidance Note Annex IV.29.
[43]　HM Revenue & Customs' Guidance Note Annex IV.29.
[44]　HM Revenue & Customs' Guidance Note Annex IV.31.

that a percentage of the sale price will be donated to the charity will constitute a trade. So too will any arrangement under which a charity is paid to licence its name and/or logo as part of the endorsement of a commercial entity's goods or services. This would include, for example, the wide range of 'affinity' credit cards marketed by banks and other financial institutions under the name of particular charities.

13.151 Providing advertising services to commercial entities is not a primary purpose trading activity for a charity. However, there are some circumstances in which trading income of this kind will not be taxable:

- The income may fall within the small trades exemption (see **13.38**).

- Where the sponsorship is intended to fund or subsidise another trading activity of a charity, HM Revenue & Customs will treat the sponsorship payments as part of the income of that trade. Where the trade in question is primary purpose, the sponsorship payments will be treated as part of the income of that primary purpose trade. This would include, for example, sponsorship payments made to a charitable theatre in relation to a particular production.

- Where payments are made under a cause-related marketing arrangement solely for the use of the charity's name and/or logo under licence, the payments may be 'annual payments'. There is more about this at **13.68** above. Annual payments are exempt from tax if received by a charity, but the charity must not provide the commercial entity with anything other than a licence of its name and/or logo (eg, a licence to use its database of supporters or agreeing to endorse the commercial entity's goods or services).

- In circumstances where payments by a sponsor involve a degree of altruism, it may be possible to 'split' the payment between a payment for services provided by the charity and a payment that is a donation. There is more about this at **13.62** above.

13.152 Where none of these options is available, a charity will need to ensure that trading activities associated with business sponsorship or cause-related marketing are carried out via a trading subsidiary. This will generally involve the charity licensing the subsidiary to exploit its name and/or logo. There is more about trading subsidiaries at **13.72** above.

13.153 Entering into sponsorship and cause-related marketing agreements with commercial entities obviously involves issues other than just tax. In particular, a charity's trustees will want to assess how the commercial entity will use its association with the charity and the risk that there is any damage to the commercial entity's name or reputation may pose to the charity as a consequence. The Charity Commission's guidance in relation to cause-related marketing arrangements (which applies in the same way the business sponsorship) is:

> 'The charity's name is a valuable asset. It is the means by which it is identified in the central register of charities and to the public. Before allowing the use of a charity name on a commercial basis, the charity trustees must first consider the needs of the charity and whether funds can be raised by other methods ...If a charity's name is used commercially it must be shown that the arrangement is:
> Expedient
> In the interests of the charity
> On terms which are advantageous to the charity.

Any such arrangements must be precisely defined by the charity trustees and every detail kept under review.'[45]

Commercial participators

13.154 In addition to these considerations, a charity's trustees will need to take into account the restrictions imposed by the Charities Act 1992, Part II on 'commercial participators'. A commercial participator is anyone who encourages the sale of their goods or services on the basis that some of the proceeds will be given to charity. The actual legal definition is:

'In relation to any charitable institution any person who:

(a)   carries on for gain a business other than a fundraising business; but
(b)   in the course of that business, engages in any promotional venture in the course of which it is represented that charitable contributions are to be given to or applied for the benefit of the institution.'[46]

13.155 Most cause-related marketing agreements with commercial entities will make them 'commercial participators'. The Charities Act 1992 provides that any agreement between a commercial participator and a charity is unlawful if it does not meet certain minimum requirements. These include the period for which the agreement is to remain in effect and how each of the charity and the commercial participator are to benefit under the agreement.

13.156 The Charities Act 1992 also imposes an obligation on the commercial participator to ensure that it makes a clear statement of the proportion of the purchase price for goods and services that will be given to the charity or the sums that will be given to it as a consequence of their sale or supply. A failure to comply with this requirement is a criminal offence.

13.157 A charity's trading subsidiary is not subject to the restrictions imposed by the Charities Act 1992 in relation to commercial participators. The Home Office has recommended in the past that, as a matter of good practice, trading subsidiaries should comply with the restrictions. This is, though, no more than suggested good practice.

13.158 While the sanctions for breach of the Charities Act 1992 are aimed at the commercial participator, many charities find in practice that they are expected to ensure compliance with the 1992 Act. In practice, a charity will often need to brief a potential commercial participator in relation to the restrictions and ensure that they are understood and accepted before a commercial participator agreement is prepared and agreed.

---

[45]   CC 35.
[46]   Charities Act 1992, s 58(1).

14

REPORTING AND ACCOUNTING

14.1   The importance of proper financial and other forms of reporting by charities to good governance cannot be overstated. If donors, beneficiaries and other stakeholders are to have confidence in charities then they must be subject to a regime that ensures that there is transparency in terms of how a charity's funds have been spent. The key to this is the accounting and reporting framework.

THE ACCOUNTING AND REPORTING FRAMEWORK

14.2   The accounting and reporting framework applying to charities in England and Wales is largely contained within the Charities Act 1993, the Charities Act 2006, the Statement of Recommended Practice: Accounting and Reporting by Charities issued in March 2005 ('the SORP') and the Charities (Accounts and Reports) Regulations 2005 ('the Regulations').

14.3   In addition to these requirements, charitable companies must also comply with the requirements of the Companies Acts. Some charities may also be required to comply with specific legislation relating to their particular type of organisation (eg registered social landlords).

14.4   The framework is designed to meet the need for consistent and transparent public accountability for the resources held by charities without adding unnecessarily to the burden on trustees. Accordingly, the requirements to be met by smaller charities are less onerous than those for larger charities.

THE SORP

14.5   The SORP explains how charities should prepare their accounts and apply accounting standards. It applies to all charities in the UK unless a separate SORP exists for a particular class of charities. For example, there are additional SORPs applicable to registered social landlords and further and higher education institutions.

14.6   Although the SORP is a statement of recommended practice only, it has been developed under an Accounting Standards Board (ASB) code of practice and any non-compliance with its recommendation must be disclosed in a charity's accounts. This may lead to a qualified audit opinion. Many of its provisions are also underpinned, in England and Wales, by the Regulations.

BASIC REQUIREMENTS FOR ALL CHARITIES

14.7 The minimum requirements for keeping accounting records applying to all charities are set out in Charities Act 1993, Part VI as amended by the Charities Act 2006.

14.8 All charities must:

- Prepare and maintain accounting records. These records (cash books, invoices, receipts etc) must be retained for at least 6 years (at least 3 years in the case of charitable companies).

- Prepare accounts.

- Make their accounts available to the public on request. This is a vital underpinning to the principle of public accountability, and must be complied with in all cases. It is open to trustees to make a reasonable charge to cover the costs of complying with the request (eg photocopying and postage). As a matter of good practice the Charity Commission recommends that a copy of the trustees' annual report should, wherever possible, be sent with the accounts.

ADDITIONAL REQUIREMENTS

14.9 In addition to the basic requirements applicable to all charities, there are additional accounting and reporting requirements that may have to be met which depend largely on the levels of income and expenditure of the charity. Broadly speaking, the larger the charity the more onerous the requirements although the precise details depend on the type of charity. However it should be noted that the charity's constitution may also contain specific rules on accounts, reports and auditing which may be more onerous than the requirements of the general accounting and reporting framework. If this is the case then the trustees must follow the requirements set out in the constitution, or else amend the constitution in order to relax them. There is more about alterations to charity constitutions at **15.3**.

14.10 The levels of income and expenditure of a charity and whether it is a charitable company will impact on four key areas:

- the accounting basis on which the charity's accounts are prepared;

- whether the charity is required to have its accounts scrutinised by independent examination or audited by a registered auditor;

- whether the charity is required to prepare a trustees' annual report; and

- the type of information that the charity is required to send to the Charity Commission by way of annual return, information update form or summary information return.

These four aspects of accounting and reporting are discussed in more detail below.

BASIS OF PREPARATION OF ACCOUNTS

14.11 There are two bases on which charity accounts may be prepared: the receipts and payments basis and the accruals basis.

Receipts basis

14.12 Charities that are not set-up as companies and which have a gross income of £100,000 or less during the financial year may prepare their accounts on the receipts and payments basis.[1] This simply entails the preparation of an account summarising all money received and paid out by the charity in the year in question together with a statement giving details of its assets and liabilities at the end of the year.

Accruals basis

14.13 Charities that are not set-up as companies and with gross income over £100,000 during the financial year and all charitable companies must prepare their accounts on the accruals basis. This entails the preparation of a balance sheet showing the charity's financial position at the end of the year in question, a statement of financial activities during the year (and sometimes an income and expenditure account) and explanatory notes. Accounts of this kind are normally required, in accountancy terms, to show a 'true and fair view' and must apply the methods and principles of the SORP unless a more specialist SORP applies.[2]

REQUIREMENT FOR AN AUDIT OR INDEPENDENT EXAMINATION

14.14 All charities (regardless of how they are set-up) with a gross income over £250,000 in the relevant financial year are required to have their accounts audited.[3] In addition, charitable companies are required to have their accounts audited in the circumstances set out in **14.48** below. If an audit is required then this means that the accounts must be scrutinised by a registered auditor who must apply auditing standards and should apply the guidance contained in Audit Practice Note 11: The Audit of Charities produced by the Auditing Practices Board. A registered auditor must be registered with a recognised supervisory body in accordance with the Companies Act 1989. In the case of some charities, eg those connected with the NHS or local authorities, alternative auditing arrangements may be possible.[4]

14.15 Independent examination is a less onerous form of scrutiny than an audit. Examiners report whether specific matters which are identified in the Regulations have come to their attention. The Commission has issued guidance to trustees on the selection of examiners and directions for examiners on carrying out an examination (Independent Examination of Charity Accounts: Directions & Guidance Notes – CC 63).

---

[1] Charities Act 1993, s 42(3).
[2] The Regulations, reg 3.
[3] Charities Act 1993, s 43(1) and Companies Act 1985, s 226 and s 227, but see also **14.51–14.53** in relation to prospective changes to be introduced under the Charities Act 2006.
[4] Charities Act 1993, s 43A and s 43B in relation to auditing arrangements where charities are connected with the NHS.

14.16 An audit exemption report or accountant's report is a less onerous form of scrutiny than an audit for charitable companies where the charity is below the audit threshold (see **14.48**). An accountant's report can only be made by qualified persons in an approved format, set out in the 'Accounts and Auditing Reference Dates' guidance available from Companies House.

TRUSTEES' ANNUAL REPORT

14.17 This is a concise but comprehensive review of a charity's activities, prepared by the trustees for each accounting year. The basic requirements of the report are set out in the Regulations and more detailed guidance is given in the SORP. A charity which is under the audit threshold may prepare a simplified annual report, the contents of which are set out in Appendix 5 to the SORP.

RETURNS

14.18 All charities with a gross income or total expenditure for the year of over £10,000 are required to complete an annual return and submit it to the Commission.[5] The annual return is used by the Commission to monitor the activities of charities and to ensure that the register of charities is kept up to date. The annual return is made up of three parts and charities are required to complete the relevant parts based on their income in the previous financial year.

14.19 Smaller charities are only required to complete an annual information update form.

14.20 Charities with an income of over £1million are required to complete an annual Summary Information Return (SIR) highlighting key qualitative and quantitative information about the charity's work, with a focus on how it sets objectives and measures its outcomes and its impact.[6]

14.21 The information to be provided in a SIR is covered under the following eight question headings:[7]

- The charity's aims.

- Who benefits.

- The charity's strategy.

- Objectives and achievements.

- Income and expenditure.

---

[5]   Charities Act 1993, s 48(1).

[6]   What do charities need to submit to the Charity Commission each year? www.charitycommission.gov.uk/investigations/ccmonsub.asp.

[7]   Guidance Notes for the Summary Information Return, www.charitycommission.gov.uk/investigations/sir2005notes.asp.

- The charity's financial health.

- The next year.

- The charity's governance.

APPLICATION OF FRAMEWORK PRINCIPLES TO CATEGORIES OF CHARITY

14.22 Broadly speaking, the principles referred to above are applied to charities falling into a number of basic categories as follows:

- Charities that are not set-up as companies
    - Where neither the gross income nor total expenditure of the charity exceeds £10,000 in the charity's relevant financial year
    - Where the gross income or total expenditure of the charity exceeds £10,000 (but the gross income does not exceed £100,000) in the relevant financial year
    - Where the gross income of the charity exceeds £100,000 (but the gross income does not exceed £250,000) in the relevant financial year
    - Where the gross income exceeds £500,000 in the relevant financial year
    - Where the gross income exceeds £1,000,000 in the relevant financial year.

- Charitable companies.

- Excepted charities.

- Exempt charities.

The accounting and reporting requirements for charities falling into each of these categories is discussed in further detail below.

Charities not set up as companies

Neither gross income nor total expenditure exceeds £10,000 in the charity's relevant financial year

14.23 The requirements for charities that fall into this band are as follows:

Basis of preparation

14.24 Accounts may be prepared on either the receipts and payments or the accruals basis – if the latter, they must be prepared in accordance with the methods and principles of the SORP and the Regulations (see **14.12–14.13**).

External scrutiny

14.25 There is no requirement to have the accounts independently examined or audited, unless the charity's constitution requires it, but the Charity Commission has the power to require an audit in exceptional circumstances. The only other exceptions to this are for charities which:

- have an income of less than £10,000 but whose total expenditure exceeds £250,000 in the same year;[8] or

- have an income of less than £10,000 in the year for which accounts are being prepared but which in either of the two previous financial years have had a gross income or total expenditure exceeding £250,000.[9]

In these circumstances, an audit by a registered auditor must be carried out.[10]

Trustees' annual report

14.26 An annual report must be prepared but it may be simplified (see **14.17**).

Information to be sent to the Commission

14.27 Charities with an income of up to £10,000 in their financial year receive an annual information update form, which includes information forming part of the charity's entry on the register of charities, including trustee details. Although not legally obliged to complete an annual return, small charities are asked to complete the annual information update as a good way of meeting their obligation to update their register details. Charities with income of less than £10,000 are not required to send a copy of their annual report and accounts to the Commission unless it asks for them.

Gross income or total expenditure exceeds £10,000 (but gross income does not exceed £100,000) in the relevant financial year

14.28 Within this band, the requirements are as follows:

Basis of preparation

14.29 Accounts may be prepared on either the receipts and payments or the accruals basis – if the latter, they must be prepared in accordance with the methods and principles of the SORP and the Regulations (see **14.12–14.13**).

External scrutiny

14.30 Accounts must be subject to outside scrutiny but trustees may choose either independent examination or audit by a registered auditor, unless the charity's constitution requires one or the other (also, the Commission has the power to require an audit in exceptional circumstances).[11] The exception mentioned in **14.25** also applies and an audit, by a registered auditor, is required where total expenditure in the year exceeds £250,000 or the income/expenditure thresholds have been exceeded in either of the two previous financial years.[12]

Trustees' annual report

14.31 An annual report must be prepared but it may be simplified (see **14.17**).

---

[8] Charities Act 1993, s 43(4).
[9] Charities Act 1993, s 43(1).
[10] But see also **14.51–14.53** in relation to prospective changes to be introduced under the Charities Act 2006.
[11] Charities Act 1993, s 43(2).
[12] But see also **14.51–14.53** in relation to prospective changes to be introduced under the Charities Act 2006.

Information to be sent to the Commission

14.32 Charities with an income of between £10,000 and £100,000 are legally required to complete an annual return requesting essential information required to update the charity's details.[13] Those charities in this category but with a previous income in excess of £100,000 will be invited to submit their details online. The charity's annual report and accounts must normally be sent to the Commission within 10 months of the end of the charity's financial year.[14]

Gross income exceeds £100,000 (but does not exceed £250,000) in the relevant financial year

14.33 For charities falling within this band:

Basis of preparation

14.34 Accounts must be prepared on the accruals basis in accordance with the methods and principles of the SORP and the Regulations (see **14.13**).

External scrutiny

14.35 Accounts must be subject to outside scrutiny but trustees may choose either independent examination or audit by a registered auditor, unless the charity's governing document stipulates one or the other – if an independent examination is chosen then the Commission recommends that the examiner is a qualified accountant (also, the Commission has the power to require an audit in exceptional circumstances). The exception mentioned in **14.25** also applies and an audit, by a registered auditor, is required where total expenditure in the year exceeds £250,000 or the income/expenditure thresholds have been exceeded in either of the two previous financial years.[15]

Trustees' annual report

14.36 An annual report must be prepared but it may be simplified (see **14.17**).

Information to be sent to the Commission

14.37 Charities with an income between £100,000 and £250,000 will receive an annual return which they are legally required to complete. This form will ask the trustees for essential information required to update the charity's details. The annual report and accounts must normally be sent to the Commission within 10 months of the end of the charity's financial year (see **14.32**).

Gross income over £250,000 in the relevant financial year

14.38 For charities falling within this band:

---

[13] Charities Act 1993, s 48(1).
[14] Charities Act 1993, s 48(2).
[15] But see also **14.51–14.53** in relation to prospective changes to be introduced under the Charities Act 2006.

Basis of preparation

14.39 Accounts must be prepared on the accruals basis and in accordance with the methods and principles of the SORP and the Regulations (see **14.13**).

External scrutiny

14.40 Accounts must be audited by a registered auditor.[16]

Trustees' annual report

14.41 A full annual report must be prepared.[17]

Information to be sent to the Commission

14.42 Charities with an income exceeding £250,000 but less than or equal to £1,000,000 must complete an annual return comprised of both essential information and a series of regulatory questions which are used to monitor charities' activities. The annual report and accounts must normally be sent to the Commission within 10 months of the end of the charity's financial year.

Gross income over £1,000,000 in the relevant financial year

14.43 Charities with an income exceeding £1,000,000 must meet all the requirements set out in the previous band relating to charities with income over £250,000. In addition, charities in this band are legally required to complete the summary information return (SIR) that forms the third part of the annual return (see **14.20** and **14.21**). The Commission normally asks larger charities to complete these forms online.

Charitable companies

14.44 The SORP applies to charitable companies as well as unincorporated charities.

14.45 A charitable company must prepare a directors' report and accounts under the Companies Acts and must file these with Companies House.[18] The accounts must be prepared on an accruals basis.

14.46 The requirements for the trustees' annual report are the same as those for other charities and therefore the charity must comply with the Regulations. In practice charitable companies normally produce a directors' report and that report is expanded to contain all the information required by the Regulations and recommended by the SORP to be included in the trustees' annual report.

14.47 If the charitable company's income or expenditure is over £10,000, the trustees must also send a trustees' annual report (or a suitably modified directors' report), the accounts and its annual return to the Commission. The Commission's requirements for an annual return are the same as those for non-company charities.[19]

---

[16]   Charities Act 1993, s 43(2).
[17]   Charities Act 1993, s 45(1).
[18]   Companies Act 1985, s 226, s 227 and s 234.
[19]   SORP, paragraphs 420–422.

14.48 Charitable companies are required to have their accounts audited by a registered auditor if either of the following conditions apply:

- gross income exceeds £250,000; or

- gross assets exceed £1.4m.[20]

However, if the gross assets are below £1.4m and gross income is the range £90,001–£250,000, an accountant's report (audit exemption report) may normally be prepared instead of a full audit report. If gross assets are less than £1.4m and gross income is £90,000 or less, no external scrutiny is normally required.

Excepted charities

14.49 If the trustees have chosen to register, they will have to fulfil the same accounting and reporting requirements as any other registered charity. If they do not register they must still produce annual accounts in the same way as a registered charity of the same type (company or non-company). They must provide copies of their accounts to members of the public on request, but should not send them to the Commission unless they ask for them. There is more about excepted charities in **4.58–4.59**.

Exempt charities

14.50 Exempt charities have to keep proper accounting records and prepare accounts. Where they are required to prepare accounts giving a true and fair view, they should follow the SORP in the preparation of those accounts, unless a more specialised SORP applies. They must provide copies of their accounts to members of the public on request. There is more about exempt charities in **4.55–4.57**.

CHARITIES ACT 2006

14.51 The Charities Act 2006 will shortly simplify the rules as to when a professional audit is required and will apply similar thresholds to both charities which are companies and those which are not.

A non-company charity's accounts must be audited if it has:

- gross annual income over £500,000 or

- an aggregate value of assets over £2.8m and gross annual income over £100,000.

Below this threshold, for non-company charities, an independent examiner can be used instead of an auditor. An independent examination is not required if the charity's income is below £10,000. If the income is above £250,000 then the independent examiner must have an appropriate accountancy qualification.[21]

---

[20] Companies Act 1985, s 249A, but see also **14.51–14.53** in relation to prospective changes to be introduced under the Charities Act 2006.
[21] Charities Act 2006, s 28.

14.52 For charities which are companies, accounts must be audited if the charity has:

- gross annual income over £500,000; or

- a balance sheet total (aggregate assets) over £2.8m.[22]

14.53 Charitable companies with an income between £90,000 and £500,000 and assets of £2.8m or less are not required to have their accounts audited if they provide an accountant's report. For a charitable company with income of £90,000 or less then neither a professional audit nor an accountant's report is required unless its assets are over £2.8m.[23]

FURTHER HELP WITH PREPARING ACCOUNTS

14.54 Various publications relating to the accounting framework have been produced by the Commission and are available on its website (www.charitycommission.gov.uk).

14.55 In particular, the Commission's website pages 'Help with preparing Charity Accounts and Reports' provide additional guidance, example accounts and reports and links to other useful websites providing information on accounting and external scrutiny issues.

SOCIAL REPORTING – THE TRUSTEES' ANNUAL REPORT

14.56 Outsiders who are interested in assessing the performance of a particular charity cannot really do so simply by looking at the charity's financial figures alone. The success of a charity will largely depend upon how successful it has been in fulfilling its charitable objects and this is not something that can always be communicated through a profit and loss account or balance sheet (although these may be indirect indicators of success). For this reason, the trustees' annual report is a vital means of communicating to interested parties just what it is that a particular charity has been doing over the course of a financial year. From this, third parties should be better able to make an assessment as to the effectiveness of a particular charity.

14.57 The SORP and the Regulations set out what a trustees' annual report should contain. Among other things, the report should contain:[24]

- A summary of the objects of the charity.

- A brief summary of the main activities and achievements of the charity during the year in relation to the charity's objects.

- The methods adopted for the recruitment and appointment of new trustees, including details of any constitutional provisions relating to appointments. Where any other person or external body is entitled to appoint one or more of the charity trustees this should be explained together with the name of that person.

---

[22]   Charities Act 2006, s 32(1).
[23]   Charities Act 2006, s 32(1).
[24]   The Regulations, reg 11 and SORP, paragraphs 41–59.

- A description of the policies (if any) which have been adopted by the charity trustees:
  - for the purpose of determining the level of reserves which it is appropriate for the charity to maintain in order to meet effectively the needs designated by its trusts;
  - details of the amount and purpose of any material commitments and planned expenditure not provided for in the balance sheet which have been deducted from the assets in the unrestricted fund of the charity in calculating the amount of reserves, and where no such policies have been adopted, a statement to this effect; and
  - where any fund is materially in deficit at the beginning of the financial year in question, and particulars of the steps taken by the charity trustees to eliminate the deficit.

14.58 If the charity is subject to a statutory audit then the annual report prepared must include:

- Instead of a brief summary of achievements and activities, a review of all activities, including:
  - details of the aims and objectives which the charity trustees have set for the charity in the year, and details of the strategies adopted, and of significant activities undertaken, in order to achieve those aims and objectives;
  - details of the achievements of the charity during the year, measured by reference to the aims and objectives which have been set;
  - details of the principal funding sources of the charity;
  - the details of significant activities provided should focus on those activities that the charity trustees consider to be significant in the circumstances of the charity as a whole and, as a minimum, explain the objectives, activities and projects or services identified within the analysis note accompanying charitable activities in the Statement of Financial Activities; and
  - how expenditure in the year under review has supported the key objectives of the charity.

- Where the charity is part of a wider network then the relationship involved should be explained where this impacts on the operating policies adopted by the charity.

- The relationship between the charity and related parties, including its subsidiaries and with any other charities and organisations with which it co-operates in the pursuit of its charitable objectives.

- Where social or programme-related investment activities are material in the context of charitable activities undertaken, the policies adopted in making such investments should be explained.

- A statement as to whether the charity trustees have given consideration to:
  - the major risks to which the charity is exposed; and
  - systems or procedures designed to manage those risks (see **14.59**).

- A description of the policies and procedures (if any) which have been adopted by the charity trustees for the induction and training of charity trustees, and where no such policies have been adopted, a statement to this effect.

- A description of the policies (if any) which have been adopted by the charity trustees for the selection of individuals and institutions who are to receive grants, or other forms of financial support, out of the assets of the charity.

- Where fundraising activities are undertaken, details of performance achieved against fundraising objectives set, commenting on any material expenditure for future income generation and explaining the effect on the current period's fundraising return and anticipated income generation in future periods.

- Comment on those factors within and outside the charity's control which are relevant to the achievement of its objectives.

- A description of the aims and objectives which the charity trustees have set for the charity in the future, and of the activities contemplated in furtherance of those aims and objectives.

It should be noted, however, that these are only guidelines and the SORP expressly states that charity trustees should consider providing such additional information as is needed to give donors, beneficiaries and the general public a greater insight into the charity's activities and achievements.[25]

RISK REPORTING

14.59 As stated above, the SORP requires trustees to make a statement in their annual report confirming that 'the major risks to which the charity is exposed, as identified by the trustees, have been reviewed and systems have been established to mitigate those risks'.[26]

14.60 The SORP focuses on major risks. Major risks are those which, if they occur, would have a severe impact on operational performance, objectives or reputation of the charity and which have a high likelihood of occurring.

14.61 The Regulations place a legal requirement on charities whose gross income is over £250,000 for the trustees' annual report to 'contain a statement as to whether the charity trustees have given consideration to the major risks to which the charity is exposed and systems designed to mitigate those risks'. All charities in England and Wales with gross income exceeding £250,000 are therefore required to make a risk management statement.[27]

14.62 Trustees of smaller charities with gross income not over £250,000 (who should still be concerned about the risks their charity faces) are encouraged to make a statement as a matter of best practice.

Identifying risk

14.63 The first step for any charity is therefore to identity the risks to which it is exposed. The risks faced by charities may fall into different categories including:

---

[25] SORP, paragraph 10.
[26] SORP, paragraph 45.
[27] The Regulations, reg 11(3), but see also 14.51–14.53 in relation to the prospective changes to be introduced under the Charities Act 2006 which will increase the gross income threshold from £250,000 to £500,000.

- Governance risks (eg inappropriate organisational structure, difficulties recruiting trustees with relevant skills, conflict of interests).

- Operational risks (eg service quality and development, contract pricing, employment issues; health and safety issues; fraud and misappropriation).

- Financial risks (eg accuracy and timeliness of financial information, adequacy of reserves and cash flow, diversity of income sources, investment management).

- External risks (eg public perception and adverse publicity, demographic changes, government policy).

- Compliance with law and regulation (eg breach of trust law, employment law, and regulative requirements of particular activities such as fund-raising or the running of care facilities).

The process of risk identification should be charity specific as it needs to reflect the activities, structure and environment in which a particular charity operates.

Evaluating risk

14.64 Having identified the risks faced by a particular charity, it is then necessary to put those risks into perspective in terms of the potential severity of impact and likelihood of their occurrence. One method is to consider each identified risk and decide for each the likelihood of it occurring and the severity of the impact of its occurrence on the charity.

14.65 Some charities operate a scoring system to assess which risks need further work. For example, the severity of impact could be scored on a scale of 1 (least serious) to 5 (most serious) and similarly the likelihood of occurrence could be scored from 1 (remote) to 5 (almost certain). The impact score is usually multiplied by the score for likelihood and the product of the scores used to rank those risks that the trustees regard as most serious.

Drawing up an action plan

14.66 Once each risk has been evaluated, the trustees should draw up a plan for any action that needs to be taken. This action plan and the implementation of appropriate systems or procedures allows the trustees to make a positive statement as to risk mitigation.

14.67 For each of the major risks identified, trustees will need to consider any additional action that needs to be taken to mitigate the risk, either by lessening the likelihood of the event occurring, or lessening its impact if it does.

14.68 There are essentially four basic strategies that can be applied to an identified risk:

- transferring the financial consequences to third parties or sharing it (eg insurance, outsourcing);

- avoiding the activity giving rise to the risk completely (eg a potential grant or contract not taken up);

- management or mitigation of risk; or

- acceptance of the risk (eg it is assessed as an inherent risk that cannot be avoided if the activity is to continue).

14.69 Risk mitigation is aimed at reducing the 'gross level' of risk identified to a 'net level' of risk that remains after appropriate action has been taken. This identification of 'gross risk', the control procedures put in place to mitigate the risk, and the identification of the residual or 'net risk' is often scheduled in a risk register. Trustees should form a view as to the acceptability of the residual or 'net risk' that remains after mitigation. It is possible that the process may also identify areas where the current control processes are disproportionately costly or onerous compared to the risk they seek to address.

Periodic monitoring and assessment

14.70 The risk management process needs to be dynamic so as to ensure that new risks are addressed as they arise and whether any previously identified risks have changed. The process therefore requires regular monitoring and assessment.

14.71 One method of codifying such an approach is through the use of a risk register. The register seeks to pull together the key aspects of the risk management process. It schedules identified risks and their assessment, the controls in place and the residual risks, and can identify responsibilities, monitoring procedures and follow up action required.

15

RESTRUCTURING

15.1 A charity, like any other entity, will change and develop over time. This may be, for example, because its sources of funding change or its trustees decide to advance its charitable purposes in a new way or perhaps because its trustees decide that its charitable purposes would best be served by transferring the charity's assets to another charity.

15.2 This chapter highlights a number of different ways in which a charity may re-structure itself:

- constitutional changes;

- mergers and transfers;

- incorporation; or

- dissolution.

CONSTITUTIONAL CHANGES

15.3 Some restructurings may not require any more than a change to the constitutional provisions that govern a charity's charitable purposes, its powers or its governance arrangements. This might be because its governance arrangements are outdated or inadequate or no longer reflect how the charity operates in practice. Or a charity's purposes may no longer be appropriate, perhaps because its beneficiaries are no longer in need, or their needs have changed.

15.4 The way in which a charity can alter its constitution depends primarily on the way in which it is constituted. Specific legal provisions apply to charitable companies and CIOs. These rules are explained in more detail below. The position in relation to unincorporated charities is a little more complicated and we explain this first.

Unincorporated charities

15.5 The constitution of an unincorporated charity may give its trustees an express power to alter the terms of the constitution itself. If there is an express power, it will need to be exercised carefully in accordance with any restrictions imposed upon it. Where the charity is a trust, its trustees are likely to be able to exercise the power. Where the charity is an unincorporated association, the power is more likely to be vested in the members.

15.6 It is unlikely that even the most widely expressed power of amendment will authorise the charity's trustees to alter its charitable purposes or to insert provisions that would enable the trustees to dispose of the charity's assets for anything other than those purposes. Good examples of this sort of change are the addition of a provision enabling trustees to benefit personally from the charity's assets or a change to a provision dealing with the charity's assets in the event of its dissolution. Even if a power of amendment were to be exercised this widely, it could not be validly used to make changes of this kind because they will be inconsistent with the principle that a charity's assets can only ever be applied for its charitable purposes. The Charity Commission's guidance reflect this:

> '... trusts law prevents the use of powers of constitutional amendment in ... ways which conflict with the provisions of charity law.'[1]

15.7 It is, though, open to anyone setting up an unincorporated charity to give its trustees a wide power to amend or add to the provisions of the constitution insofar as its administrative or governance arrangements are concerned. Powers of this kind can be used to deal with alterations to, for example, provisions governing trustees' meetings, the powers exercisable by a charity's trustees and arrangements for assets to be held in nominee names (although the position will obviously vary from charity to charity).

15.8 If trustees wish to alter a charity's purposes or change the way in which its assets can be disposed of or if there is no express power of amendment (or there is a power, but it is not wide enough to authorise the change that a charity's trustees wish to make), there are three courses of action that may be open to them:

- to exercise the statutory power to modify powers or procedures;

- to exercise the statutory power to replace the purposes of a 'small' unincorporated charity; or

- to apply to the Charity Commission for an Order or Scheme.

Statutory power to modify powers or procedures

15.9 Section 74D of the Charities Act 1993 gives the trustees of an unincorporated charity a statutory power to resolve to modify the provisions of the charity's constitution insofar as they relate to any of the powers exercisable by the trustees in the administration of the charity or regulate the procedures to be followed in connection with its administration. Where the charity has a body of members which is distinct from the charity's trustees (which, in principle at least, would include a group of trustees who also act as the members of a charitable unincorporated association under its constitution), they must also resolve to approve the trustees' resolution at a general meeting (by a majority of not less than two-thirds of the members entitled to attend and vote at the meeting who actually vote on the resolution unless the decision is taken at a meeting without a vote and none of the members present expresses any dissent in relation to the resolution).

15.10 Provided these requirements are met, the charity's constitution is deemed to be modified from the date specified in the trustees' resolution or (if later) the date in which the members pass their resolution approving it.

---

[1]   OG 47 A1.

15.11 This is obviously a very useful power for charity trustees. In cases where there is some doubt about the scope of their administrative powers in relation to a particular aspect of the charity's operations, it obviously offers a simple and straightforward way of putting the position beyond doubt. Clearly, it does not give a charity's trustees the authority to make any changes to the charity's purposes, because this would not be a change to the administration of the charity. This will require an application to the Charity Commission unless the statutory power to replace purposes is exercisable.

Statutory power to replace purposes

15.12 This power (under the Charities Act 1993, s 74C) will be introduced by the Charities Act 2006[2] and will enable the trustees of a 'small' unincorporated charity to resolve that its charitable purposes can be modified by replacing them with any other charitable purposes. The trustees can only pass the resolution if they are satisfied that it is expedient in the charity's interests for the purposes to be replaced and that 'so far as is reasonably practical' the new purposes consist of or include purposes that are similar in character to those that are to be replaced.

15.13 A 'small charity' for this purpose will have gross income (ie income from all sources, before allowing for expenditure) in its last financial year of no more than £10,000 and must not hold any 'designated land'. Designated land is any land held on the basis that it must be used for the purposes of the charity (what the Charity Commission usually refer to as 'specie' or 'functional' land).

15.14 The resolution must be passed by a majority of not less than two-thirds of the charity trustees who actually vote on the resolution (rather than two-thirds of all of the charity trustees). The trustees are obliged to send a copy of the resolution to the Charity Commission together with a statement of their reasons for passing it. The Commission may decide to direct the trustees to give public notice of the resolution and then take into account any representations received in response to the notice. The Commission can also direct the trustees to provide them with further information and explanation in relation to their reasons for passing the resolution.

15.15 The Commission has 60 days from the date on which it receives a copy of the trustees' resolution to notify them in writing that it objects to the resolution, either on 'procedural grounds' or on the merits of the proposals contained in the resolution. On 'procedural grounds' means that the trustees have not complied with one of the specific provisions under the Charities Act 1993, s 74C for the passing of the resolution. If the Commission does decide to direct the charity trustees to give public notice of the resolution, the 60 day period is suspended from the date on which the direction is given until 42 days after the date on which public notice is given by the trustees. The same is true where the Commission directs the charity trustees to provide additional information; the 60 day period is suspended from the date on which the direction is given until the information is provided to the Commission.

15.16 If the Commission does notify the trustees that it objects to the resolution, whether on procedural grounds or on the merits of the proposals in the resolution, then the resolution is deemed never to have been passed by the trustees.

---

[2]   Charities Act 2006, s 40; expected to come into force in early 2008.

Charity Commission Orders and Schemes

15.17 Where a charity's trustees cannot rely upon any of the express or statutory powers we have mentioned, their only other option in relation to a proposed constitutional change will be to apply to the Charity Commission for an Order or Scheme. Which of these is relevant will depend upon the changes that are required by trustees. The Commission's guidance is that:

> 'Where a change to the administrative powers is needed and the trustees are not able to make the changes themselves ... we will always aim to give them a power to make the changes by making an Order, unless the changes which the charity needs go beyond the scope of our power to make Orders.'[3]

15.18 There is more information about the differences between Orders and Schemes at **4.19** and **4.26**. But it is important to appreciate that the Commission will not make an Order or a Scheme if the trustees already have a power to amend their charity's constitution. Essentially, this will be one of the express or statutory powers we have mentioned above.

15.19 The Commission's guidance in relation to Orders is helpful:

> 'An Order will normally be sufficient in the following specific cases if the trustees make a case for us to:
>
> - Confer on the trustees a power of amendment, subject to certain limitations.
> - Provide additional powers if not currently available in the governing document.
> - Give the trustees power to add or amend specific administrative provisions in the charity's governing document.'[4]

15.20 The Charity Commission will normally make a Scheme rather than an Order where a charity's trustees either wish to change its charitable purposes or their proposed changes to the charity's constitution go beyond the scope of the Commission's power to make Orders. Again, the Commission's guidance is helpful:

> 'Typically, a Scheme will be appropriate where:
>
> - The governing document needs completely replacing.
> - The purposes of the charity need changing.
> - Other changes are required which the governing document or an Act of Parliament expressly prohibit.
> - Charities wish to merge and the effect would be to change their purposes or allow something which the constitutional arrangements or an Act of Parliament expressly prohibits.
>
> These are all areas where we cannot make Orders. In addition we would not make an Order where the changes are sensitive or controversial.'[5]

15.21 Although the Charity Commission can make a Scheme to alter a charity's charitable purposes, there are limits on this. A Scheme can only be made where the purposes of the charity have 'failed' in some way, which will allow its assets to be applied 'cy-près' for similar charitable purposes. The rules on cy-près applications are set out in

---

[3]   CC 36 (Amending Charities' Governing Documents: Orders and Schemes).
[4]   CC 36.
[5]   CC 36.

the Charities Act 1993, ss 13 and 14. A detailed explanation of the scope of the cy-près rules is beyond the scope of this book, but the examples given by the Charity Commission in their guidance are a helpful summary of the position:

> 'Our powers to change the purposes of a charity are limited to the circumstances defined at section 13 of the 1993 Act. Broadly, these are when there has been a 'failure' of some sort in the purposes, for example, where they:
>
> - Can no longer be carried out in the way laid down in the governing document (for example, if the people to benefit from the charity are defined by reference to a class of person which has ceased to be suitable, or if the charity provides a service which is no longer required).
> - May have been adequately provided for in other ways (perhaps if provision is now adequately made out of public funds).
> - May have stopped being a useful way of using the property of the charity (such as where the income of the charity is to be applied by the payment of very small gifts).'[6]

15.22 Where a charity's trustees require changes to its constitution, the Charity Commission's policy is to consider whether the trustees could introduce the change themselves if the Commission were to give them an appropriate power of amendment (either by way of Order or Scheme). Also, when the Commission makes an Order or Scheme, it will usually include a power for the Charity's trustees to amend certain of the provisions of the charity's constitution in the future without requiring a further Order or Scheme. A power of amendment of this kind will obviously not extend to changes to the charity's purposes or any other constitutional provisions which affect the way in which the charity's assets can be applied for its charitable purposes.

15.23 The procedure for obtaining an Order or a Scheme is set out in more detail at **4.25** and **4.34**.

Charitable companies

15.24 As we have indicated in **Chapter 2**, the members of a charitable company (whether limited by shares or guarantee) have a statutory power to alter its constitution. A 'special resolution' of a 75% majority of the members voting in a general meeting is required, unless all of the members are willing to sign a written resolution.

15.25 The ability to alter the provisions of a charitable company's memorandum is subject to certain restrictions. There is a specific power to alter the company's objects by special resolution.[7] Any other part of the memorandum can only be altered by special resolution if it could lawfully have been contained in the company's articles.[8] These provisions are the company's name, where its registered office is situated, the limitation on members' liability and (in the case of a company limited by guarantee) the members' guarantee of the company's debts.[9] Every other provision of the company's memorandum (such as the company's powers or a dissolution provision) can therefore be altered by special resolution unless the memorandum either expressly prohibits the alteration or provides for a different procedure for amending its provisions. The Companies Act 2006 will simplify the position by providing that the memorandum will contain no more than a statement by the company's subscribers and that all of the

---

[6]   CC 36.
[7]   Companies Act 1985, s 4.
[8]   Companies Act 1985, s 17.
[9]   Companies Act 1985, s 2.

provisions of the company's articles can be amended by special resolution except where they contain provisions entrenching them.[10] The 2006 Act will also deem all of the existing provisions of a company's memorandum other than the subscribers' statement to form part of the articles, so that they too can be altered by special resolution.[11]

The power of a charitable company's members to alter its constitution is subject to the Charities Act 1993, s 64. Section 64 will be amended by the Charities Act 2006[12] to provide that any 'regulated alteration' by a charitable company requires the prior written consent of the Charity Commission and is ineffective if that consent has not been obtained. 'Regulated alterations' are:

- any alteration to the charitable company's charitable objects (as set out in its memorandum of association);

- any alteration of any provision in its constitution 'directing the application of property of the company on its dissolution'; and

- any alteration of any provision of its constitution 'where the alteration will provide authorisation for any benefit to be obtained by directors or members of the company or persons connected with them'.

The existing provisions of the Charities Act 1993, s 64 impose similar restrictions on proposed alterations, but these will be tightened up by the Charities Act 2006.

15.26 For the purposes of the rules on regulated alterations, 'directors' means 'trustees'. 'Benefit' and 'connected' have the meanings they are given in the context of the statutory power to pay trustees for providing services to a charity. There is more information about this at **6.35**. It is worth mentioning, however, that 'benefit' does not include any remuneration for the provision of goods and services which a trustee is authorised to receive by the Charities Act 1993, s 73A.[13]

15.27 The approach the Commission takes to an application to make regulated alterations will depend primarily upon the changes that are proposed. As far as proposed changes to the charity's purposes are concerned (by an amendment to its 'objects clause') the Commission's policy is to:

> '... ensure that good reasons exist in the interests of the charity for making the changes. When considering what changes can be agreed, our concern is to ensure that no changes are made which would alter the purposes of the company in a way which is so radical that it would not reasonably have been contemplated by those who have supported the company.'[14]

'Support' is not defined, but is aimed primarily at financial support in the form of gifts and donations.

15.28 The Commission will expect a charity's trustees to make their case in writing in support of the proposed changes to the charity's purposes, explaining in particular why

---

[10] Companies Act 2006, ss 21, 22.
[11] Companies Act 2006, s 28.
[12] Charities Act 2006, s 31; expected to come into force in early 2008.
[13] Charities Act 2006, s 36; expected to come into force in early 2008.
[14] OG 47 A1.

they are expected to be for the benefit of the charity. The Commission identifies three 'typical' applications in relation to the objects clause of a charitable company:

- Where the proposed alteration will make a 'material' change to the charity's purposes, the Commission will need to be satisfied that there are good reasons in the interests of the charity for making the changes and that no changes are made which would alter the purposes of the charity in a way which is, as we have mentioned, 'so radical that it would not reasonably have been contemplated by those who have supported it'.

  The Commission do not adopt as rigorous an approach in relation to changes to the purposes of a charitable company as they do in relation to application for a cy-près Scheme in respect of an unincorporated charity under the Charity Act 1993 (see **15.21** above). There is, therefore, no requirement for 'failure' although this is likely to, in the Commission's words, 'add weight to any application'. Ultimately, the key point for the Commission is:

  > 'In practice we need to be satisfied that there are good reasons for making the changes and that those reasons could be seen to benefit the charity.'[15]

  The Commission's guidance in relation to changes which might not have been contemplated by those who have supported the charity in the past is also helpful:

  > 'The fact that it remains reasonably practicable for the company to continue to operate within its existing objects does not prevent us from agreeing to changes to the objects. Someone who contributes to a charitable company must be taken to be aware of the broad statutory power of the members to change the constitution. We should not use the consent power to inhibit, say, the adoption by a company of wider objects in the same general area of charity, if that appears to be socially more beneficial, simply because it remains reasonably practical for the company to continue to operate within the existing objects.'[16]

  In considering whether changes are reasonably likely to have been contemplated by a charity's supporters, they will look particularly hard at changes that 'prejudice' the original charitable purposes or add a completely unrelated purpose.

- Where a proposed change to the objects clause does not materially affect the charity's charitable purposes (eg where the intention is to clarify the meaning of the words used, perhaps to update them) the Commission will normally consent 'without difficulty'.[17]

- Where the change to the objects clause does not actually affect the charity's charitable purposes, the Commission will consent unless the reasons for the changes are 'manifestly unreasonable'.

15.29 The other two categories of 'regulated alteration' relate to the application of the Charity's assets on its dissolution and any change which would authorise trustees or members to benefit from the charity's assets. Again, the Commission's guidance is helpful:

---

[15]   OG 47 B2.
[16]   OG 47 B2.
[17]   OG 47 B2.

'In the case of other changes where our consent is required, they are likely to fall into two main categories; extension of provisions which can benefit the directors personally, and the extension of powers relating to the administration of the company's property.'[18]

15.30 Insofar as consent to provisions which enable a charity's trustees to benefit personally from its assets are concerned, the Charity Commission will adopt the approach they take in relation to trustees' benefits generally (see **6.35** for more in relation to this).

15.31 Where changes to a charity's administrative provisions are concerned, the Commission's guidance is:

'We should adopt a relaxed approach to the question of giving consent to the extension of powers relating to the administration of the company's property. ... While neither we, nor charitable companies, can ignore the present law, we should therefore be prepared to give consent to the extension of powers relating to the administration of the company's property as a matter of routine.'[19]

15.32 There are obviously a wide range of changes to a charity's constitution that do not require the Charity Commission's consent. These include, for example, changes that do not affect the way in which a charity's assets are used (eg procedures for holding meetings, voting, appointing trustees or altering the charity's internal rules) and also alterations to allow the delegation of investment management or appointment of a nominee.

15.33 A charitable company is required by the Companies Acts to deliver a copy of any resolution altering its constitution to the Registrar of Companies. The Registrar will not accept resolutions making changes to the constitution which are not accompanied by the Charity Commission's consent. This is the Commission's 'prior written' consent to the changes in question. The Commission's preference is for a resolution to be submitted to it in draft for approval (usually by way of an endorsement) before it is passed. In practice, it is often much easier to arrange for a resolution to be passed which is conditional on the Commission's consent. The Commission does not appear to approve of this approach, although in our view it satisfies the requirements of the Charities Act 1993, s 64 provided that the resolution is clearly conditional on consent and cannot take effect without it.

Charitable incorporated organisations

15.34 The provisions in the Charities Act 1993 which will govern CIOs include provisions governing constitutional changes. These are modelled closely on the provisions of the Companies Acts as they apply to charitable companies. So, for example, a resolution to make changes must be passed by a resolution of a 75% majority of the members of the CIO voting at a general meeting or all of the members in a written resolution.

15.35 Any changes which the members do resolve to make will be subject to the prior written consent of the Charity Commission where they constitute 'regulated alterations'. These are identical to the 'regulated alterations' which will, subject to the

---

[18]   OG 47 A1.
[19]   OG 47 A1.

coming into force of the relevant provisions of the Charities Act 2006 (expected in early 2008), apply to charitable companies (see **15.25** for more on this).

15.36 There are additional provisions in relation to CIOs which will be imposed by Charities Act 1993, Schedule 5B. A CIO which amends its constitution must send a copy of the constitution (as amended) to the Charity Commission within 16 days of the date of the members' resolution making the changes. The Commission will register the changes unless it decides that the CIO has no power to make them or the amendment would change the name of the CIO or because the Commission's consent to any 'regulated alteration' has not been obtained. If the Commission refuses to register the changes, they have no legal effect.

Other incorporated charities

15.37 Other incorporated charities may have express powers to amend their constitutions depending upon the way in which they are set up. Failing that, charities constituted by Royal Charter may be able to obtain a Supplemental Charter, while charities governed by Act of Parliament may require a further Act of Parliament in order to make any changes.

15.38 The requirement for the prior written consent of the Charity Commission to constitutional alterations under the Charities Act 1993, s 64 does not apply to any 'body corporate' (ie any incorporated body other than a Companies Act company) which has a power to alter the provisions of its constitution. However, s 64 does provide that no exercise of the power that has the effect of the body corporate ceasing to be a charity has any effect upon the assets held before the change.

Notification

15.39 Section 3 of the Charities Act 1993[20] obliges the trustee of any charity (however it is constituted) to notify the Charity Commission if there is any change to any provision of its constitution and to send the Commission copies of any new constitutional provisions that have been adopted. In practice, the Commission will require a copy of any new constitution certified by one of the charity's trustees or officers.

MERGERS AND TRANSFERS

15.40 Essentially, any arrangement under which:

- one charity transfers its assets to another and then ceases to exist; or

- two or more charities transfer their assets to another charity and then both cease to exist

may be variously described as a 'merger' or 'transfer', or occasionally as an 'amalgamation'. None of these terms has any precise legal meaning, although all three are referred to in different contexts by the Charities Act 1993 (and there is a definition of what constitutes a 'relevant charity merger' for certain purposes).

---

[20] See also Charities Act 1993, s 3B(3); expected to come into force in early 2008.

15.41 What each of these arrangements has in common is that the trustees of a charity have concluded that its charitable purposes will be better advanced by pooling its assets and other resources with the assets and other resources of another charity. This may be because, for example, two charities are able to raise more funds if they become a single entity or because a single entity's requirements will deliver financial savings based upon economies of scale. Whatever the motivation, the key point is that the charity will generally cease to exist in its present form after transferring its assets. We refer in this chapter to all such arrangements as 'mergers'.

15.42 There are two key aspects of any merger. These are:

- Whether the charity making the transfer (we refer to it below as the 'transferor') has a power to do so and whether the recipient charity (we refer to it below as the 'transferee') has corresponding power to accept the transfer (which may involve accepting both assets and liabilities).

- The range of commercial, financial, tax and other issues which may be raised by the transfer, depending upon the complexity of the assets and any liabilities which are transferred.

We consider each of these aspects in more detail below.

Powers to transfer

15.43 The powers exercisable by a charity's trustees in order to facilitate a merger will depend primarily upon the way in which the charity is constituted. Incorporated and unincorporated charities are considered in more detail below.

Incorporated charities

Charitable companies

15.44 In general, charitable companies may be able to rely upon one of three different provisions in order to arrange a transfer of their assets as part of a merger. These are:

- Many charitable companies will have an express power to make grants and donations which can be used to transfer all of their assets to another charity which has charitable purposes identical to, or narrower than, the purposes of the transferor. In this context, 'narrower' means that the transferee's charitable purposes are a sub-set of the transferor's purposes.

- Some charitable companies may have an express power to merge with other charities. Powers will vary from charity to charity but it is likely that this power can only be used to transfer assets to a transferee charity with purposes identical to, or narrower than, those of the transferor.

- A charitable company will almost inevitably have a 'dissolution' clause that provides for the way in which its assets must be dealt with in the event that it is dissolved. A 75% majority of the members of a charitable company have the right under the Companies Acts to pass a special resolution at any time that will have the effect of dissolving it. The dissolution clause will generally spell out how the charity's assets must then be applied for its charitable purposes. Clauses will vary, with some providing for assets to pass to another charity with identical purposes, perhaps to a charity with similar purposes or perhaps just for similar charitable purposes.

The discretion to apply the charity's assets in these circumstances will often lie with the charity's trustees, but some dissolution clauses vest this power in a charity's members. Clearly, the terms of the clause must be observed.

15.45 In the (somewhat unlikely) event that a charitable company does not have a power of this kind, one can be added by the members by passing a special resolution. A clause of this kind will be caught by the Charities Act 1993, s 64 and will therefore require the prior written consent of the Charity Commission. See **15.25** for more in relation to this.

15.46 The powers contained in a charitable company's constitution will generally relate only to its corporate assets. Where a charitable company holds trust assets, its trustees will need to ensure that the terms of the trust (rather than the charitable company's constitution) contain an appropriate power.

15.47 Where a charitable company holds trust assets, it will usually only be possible for it to transfer them to another charity on the basis that they will continue to be held on the same trust by the transferee. This is because the trust assets were held separately from the charitable company's corporate assets and, as a consequence, 'ring fenced' from its liabilities. Were the trust assets simply to be transferred to the transferee to be held by it as part of its own unrestricted assets, they will be exposed to its liabilities. For this reason, the transferee charity must usually agree to hold the trust assets as trustee. This will almost invariably be true of permanent endowment, although certain other trust assets may be held on trusts that give the transferor a power to transfer them free of any restrictions. The position will vary from asset to asset.

Charitable incorporated organisations

15.48 There are three specific statutory provisions which are likely to facilitate CIO mergers:

- The Charities Act 1993, s 69K[21] will give any two or more CIOs the power to apply to the Charity Commission to be 'amalgamated', with the effect that a new CIO is incorporated and registered as their successor.

  A 75% majority of the members of each CIO must vote for the amalgamation at a meeting (or all of the members can pass a written resolution). An application is then made to the Commission, which can refuse the application on certain specified grounds, including where it is not satisfied that the new CIO would be able properly to pursue its charitable purposes, would not actually be a charity at the time it is registered, does not comply with any of the statutory requirements in relation to CIO constitutions or that the constitution of the new CIO does not properly provide for its charitable purposes, the application of its property on dissolution or the benefits its trustees or members are entitled to receive.

---

[21] Expected to come into force in early 2008.

- The Charities Act 1993, s 69M[22] will give any CIO a power to resolve that all of its property, rights and liabilities should be transferred to another CIO. The resolution must be passed by a 75% majority of the members at a meeting (or by all of them in a written resolution).

  Once a resolution has been passed, an application must be made to the Charity Commission, which has a discretion to refuse the application on certain specified grounds. These are broadly similar to those that apply in relation to an amalgamation.

- The Charities Act 1993, s 69M provides for regulations to be made to govern the winding up of CIOs, their insolvency and their dissolution. It is likely that the regulations will contain specific provisions that determine what should happen to its surplus assets (including trust assets) on dissolution. The regulations are also likely to enable a CIO's members to resolve whether it should be dissolved, with the consequence that its assets are transferred to another charity.

Other incorporated charities

15.49 The ability of other types of incorporated types of charity to merge will primarily depend upon whether they have appropriate express powers in their constitution or an express power that they can use to add the powers that they need. Failing that, the Charity Commission may be able to make an Order or Scheme to give a charity the powers it needs. The Commission does not, though, have jurisdiction to make Schemes in relation to charities established by Royal Charter or by an Act of Parliament.

Unincorporated charities

15.50 Many charitable trusts and charitable unincorporated associations will have express powers in their constitutions in a very similar form to those found in the constitutions of charitable companies:

- powers to make grants and donations to other charities;

- express powers to merge with other charities; and

- an express dissolution clause which enables a charity to be dissolved and its surplus assets transferred to another charity.

15.51 The terms of powers of this kind will obviously vary from charity to charity. A dissolution clause in the constitution of a charitable trust is likely to vest the power of dissolution in its trustees. A dissolution clause in the constitution of an unincorporated association is more likely to vest the power of dissolution in its members than its trustees, although this too will vary from case to case.

Statutory power to transfer assets

15.52 There is also a statutory power that may apply to allow certain unincorporated charities to transfer their assets. This power is conferred by the Charities Act 1993, s 74. The Charities Act 2006 has made a number of changes to the provisions of s 74: subject

---

[22] Expected to come into force in early 2008.

to those changes coming into force,[23] s 74 will apply to any charity which had gross income (in other words, income from all sources) in its last financial year of £10,000 or less, and which does not hold any 'designated land'. Designated land is land held on trust by the charity to be used for its purposes (what the Charity Commission usually refers to as 'specie' or 'functional' land). The existing provisions of s 74 apply in a similar way but only where the gross income of the charity in its last financial year did not exceed £5,000.

15.53 Where the statutory power applies, the charity's trustees can only transfer all of the charity's assets, but can do so to one or more other charities. Because all of the charity's assets must be transferred, it will be dissolved as a consequence.

15.54 The trustees must also be satisfied that it is expedient in the interests of the charity for the assets to be transferred and that the transferee's charitable purposes are substantially similar to some or all of those of the transferor.

15.55 The resolution has to be voted for by a majority of two-thirds or more of the trustees who vote on it (rather than two-thirds or more of the total number of trustees). The trustees must then send a copy of the resolution to the Charity Commission, together with a statement of their reasons for passing it. The Commission may then decide to direct the trustees to give public notice of the resolution and take into account any representations received in response to the notice. The Commission can also direct their trustees to provide them with further information about the circumstances in which they have decided to exercise the statutory power.

15.56 The Commission has 60 days from the date on which it receives a copy of the trustees' resolution to notify them in writing that it objects to the resolution, either on 'procedural grounds' or on the merits of the proposals contained in the resolution. On 'procedural grounds' means that the trustees have not complied with one of the specific provisions under the Charities Act 1993, s 74 for the passing of the resolution. If the Commission does decide to direct the charity trustees to give public notice of the resolution, the 60-day period is suspended from the date on which the direction is given until 42 days after the date on which public notice is given by the trustees. The same is true where the Commission directs that the charity trustees provide additional information; the 60-day period is suspended from the date on which the direction is given until the information is provided to the Commission.

15.57 If the Commission does notify the trustees that it objects to the resolution, whether on procedural grounds or on the merits of the proposals in the resolution, then the resolution is deemed never to have been passed by the trustees.

15.58 If, on the other hand, the resolution takes effect, the charity trustees are then obliged to arrange for the transfer of all of the charity's assets in accordance with the resolution. Any of the charity's assets that are held subject to any restrictions on their expenditure (e g restricted funds held for particular charitable purposes), can only be transferred subject to the same restrictions.

15.59 In addition, the Charities Act 2006 will introduce[24] specific provisions in relation to the transfer of permanent endowment assets under the Charities Act 1993, s 74B . Broadly, these provisions will oblige the charity's trustees to be satisfied that the

---

23   Charities Act 2006, s 40: expected to come into force in early 2008.
24   Charities Act 2006, s 40: expected to come into force in early 2008.

transferee charity has charitable purposes which are 'substantially similar' to *all* of the purposes of the transferor (rather than *some or all*, as is the case for the charity's non-endowment assets). The trustees are also obliged to take account of any guidance given by the Charity Commission in relation to the transfer of permanent endowment. It remains to be seen what form that guidance will take and the approach the Commission will adopt in relation to the transfer of permanent endowment assets in these circumstances.

15.60 Where the statutory power is exercised, there is an obligation on the trustees of the transferee charity to ensure that, so far as is reasonably practical, the assets are applied for such of its charitable purposes as are substantially similar to those of the transferor charity. However, there is an exception to this; the requirement does not apply if the transferor's trustees consider that complying with it would not result in a 'suitable and effective method' of applying the assets.

Other statutory powers

15.61 We should also mention in this context the statutory powers conferred upon the trustees of unincorporated charities to spend the capital of endowment assets (including those held on a special trust) under the Charities Act 1993, ss 75, 75A and 75B. These provisions have been introduced into the Charities Act 1993 by the Charities Act 2006[25] and will replace the existing provisions of the Charities Act 1993, s 75 (which apply only to any charity with gross income in its last financial year of £1,000 or less and are therefore of limited assistance in practice). The provisions introduced by the Charities Act 2006 are explained in more detail at **9.48**, but they may be used in certain circumstances to facilitate a merger by allowing a charity's trustees to transfer endowment assets free of the restrictions imposed upon them.

Charity Commission Orders and Schemes

15.62 In the absence of an express power or the availability of one of the statutory powers we have mentioned, its trustees will need to apply to the Charity Commission for an Order or a Scheme to give them an appropriate power. There is more about this at **4.19**, **4.26** and **15.17**. Typically, an Order will be sufficient to authorise the trustees of a charity to transfer its assets to another charity, although when they wish to facilitate a merger which has the effect of changing the transferor charity's purposes, a Scheme is likely to be required.

Power to receive

15.63 The position of the transferee charity should not be forgotten. Its trustees will obviously wish to ensure that it is able to accept a transfer of assets. This will often be in exchange for an indemnity from the transferee to the transferor or its trustees in respect of the transferor charity's liabilities (there is more about this below at **15.70**).

15.64 In many cases, the charity's constitution will contain an express power to accept gifts and donations, although express powers to give indemnities in respect of associated liabilities are less likely to be included. Our view is that the trustees of any charity have a discretion to consider whether to accept any gift, whether outright or on particular terms. Provided the trustees comply with their duty of care and take into account all

---

[25]   Charities Act 2006, s 43; expected to come into force in early 2008.

relevant circumstances in considering whether accepting the transfer is in their charity's best interests, we think it is unlikely that trustees would be criticised by the court for giving an indemnity in respect of liabilities which is a condition of a transfer of assets even where they have no express power to do so.

15.65 Clearly, where it is possible to rely upon an express power, this will be the best approach. Charitable companies and CIOs may be able to rely upon their members passing an appropriate resolution to add a power to their constitution. The trustees of an unincorporated charity may be able to exercise an appropriate power of amendment or seek an Order from the Charity Commission.

15.66 Other incorporated charities will need to check whether their constitutions contain an appropriate power to transfer their assets. If not, charities constituted by Royal Charter may be able to obtain a Supplemental Charter. A charity governed by an Act of Parliament may require a further Act of Parliament in order to make any changes to its constitution.

Merger issues

15.67 It is obviously essential that the trustees of any charity involved in a merger exercise their powers to transfer or receive assets and liabilities in its best interests. This will involve an assessment of all of the relevant circumstances and some clear thinking about the pros and cons of the merger that is proposed. There is some helpful guidance on the Charity Commission's approach to this in its publication CC 34 (Collaborative Working and Mergers).

15.68 There are also a number of specific issues that are likely to arise in relation to any merger. These are explained in a little more detail below.

Trust assets

15.69 As we have explained earlier in this chapter, assets held on trust for particular charitable purposes (on a special trust) or subject to restrictions on the way in which they can be spent (endowment) can generally only be transferred to another charity on the basis that it will act as trustee in place of the transferor. This ensures that the existing legal restrictions in relation to the assets are maintained after the transfer. So, for example, a charity that holds land as a permanent endowment asset cannot transfer it to another charity to be held as one of its unrestricted assets. This would expose it to the risk of the transferee's insolvency along with all of its other unrestricted assets.

Liabilities

15.70 Generally, the trustees of a charity will only be willing to transfer its assets to another charity on the basis that a transferee takes responsibility for all and any associated liabilities. This will ensure that the transferor's assets and undertaking will be transferred as a 'going concern'. It will obviously also give the trustees of the transferor comfort that the liabilities will be met. This is obviously of particular importance to the trustees of an unincorporated charity, who are potentially personally responsible for the liabilities of their charity.

15.71 Liabilities can only vest in the transferee with the consent of the person who benefits from them, either by way of assignment or novation. Where an assignment or novation cannot be arranged, or at least not within the time available to complete a merger, the usual approach is for the transferee to agree to discharge the transferor's liabilities in full and to give an indemnity against any liabilities that do arise.

15.72 From the point of view of the trustees of the transferor, an indemnity is usually preferable to a covenant or warranty to meet the liabilities. An indemnity will generally cover liabilities in full, with no obligation on the person seeking to enforce it to mitigate any losses that they have suffered. The duty to mitigate would apply in relation to a warranty or covenant, in much the same way as a breach of any other contractual liability.

15.73 This is a reasonable enough position for the trustees of the transferor charity but there will need to be some limitations on the scope of the indemnity. The trustees of the transferee could not, for example, agree to an indemnity against any liabilities that have not properly been incurred by the trustees of the transferor or against any liabilities arising as a result of a breach of trust. Agreeing an indemnity that contains provisions of this kind would expose the transferee's assets to claims that are likely to mean that its own trustees are in breach of trust.

Gifts

15.74 A major objection to mergers of charities in the past was the legal principle that a gift to a charity that has ceased to exist will generally fail, notwithstanding that the charity in question may have previously transferred all of its assets and undertakings to another charity with the same charitable purposes. This was obviously more of an issue for those charities which rely to a significant extent for their funding on legacy income, given the likelihood that most failed gifts will result from wills or trusts made by individuals in the past which have not been updated to reflect any change in relation to the charity.

15.75 The possibility that a charity may lose a significant amount of legacy funding (and other gifts) where a merger takes place is obviously a major disincentive for mergers in the charity sector. Fortunately, the Charities Act 2006 will introduce a new s 75C into the Charities Act 1993.[26] This contains a mechanism that allows merging charities to register their merger with the Charity Commission.

15.76 The merger in question must be a 'relevant charity merger', which is defined by the Charities Act 1993, s 75C. Essentially, a relevant charity merger involves:

• one or more charities transfer their respective assets to one or more other charities and then cease to exist; or

• two or more charities transfer their assets to a new charity and then both cease to exist.

15.77 Clearly, a merger that involves a transferor charity remaining in place after the merger has taken place (even if only as a shell), will prevent it from qualifying as a relevant charity merger because it will not have ceased to exist. That would not be an unusual position in relation to certain mergers where, for example, a charity cannot transfer all of its assets immediately because of restrictions on them. There is no

---

[26]   Charities Act 2006, s 44; expected to come into force in the second half of 2007.

definition of what 'ceasing to exist' means, but in our view the courts are likely to interpret this to mean that the charity in question has been dissolved (as to which see **15.102** below).

15.78 The position is different where a transferor charity has permanent endowment assets. The requirement that the transferor must cease to exist does not then apply.

15.79 There is no obligation to notify the Commission (except where a 'vesting declaration' is in place; see **15.83** for more on this) but, if a declaration is given, this must be after the last asset transfer has taken place as part of the merger. The notice must be given by the transferee's charity trustees and specify which transfers took place and when and confirm that 'appropriate arrangements have been made with respect to the discharge of any liabilities of the transferor charity'. The arrangements required are not specified, but are likely to include indemnity arrangements of the kind mentioned at **15.70**.

15.80 Provided the Commission is notified that a merger has taken place, gifts to a charity which take effect after the date of registration will become payable to the charity to which the charity which would otherwise have been entitled to the gift has transferred its assets. This does not include gifts that are intended to be held as part of a charity's permanent endowment. Notwithstanding this, the provision for mergers is obviously helpful to a charity's trustees in considering the advantages and disadvantages of a proposed merger.

15.81 There are corresponding provisions in relation to gifts to CIOs where the statutory powers in relation to their amalgamation and the transfer of their assets and undertaking apply. Very broadly, any gift which is expressed as a gift to a transferor CIO will take effect as a gift to the new CIO once it has been registered by the Charity Commission.[27]

Transfer agreements

15.82 It will usually be sensible for the terms of any transfer to be set out in a written agreement, not least because the trustees of the transferor will wish to establish the terms of their indemnity in respect of liabilities. The agreement may be capable of transferring title to some assets but others (for example, shares) will still need to be subject to a separate transfer. Others (for example, computer equipment) may be able to be transferred by way of delivery.

15.83 The Charities Act 2006 will introduce a new s 75E into the Charities Act 1993.[28] Section 75E will contain a provision for the trustees of the transferor to make a 'vesting declaration' in connection with their merger which confirms that the transferor's assets are vested in the transferee from a date specified in the declaration. The merger in question must be a 'relevant charity merger' (see the definition of this at **15.76**). The declaration then operates to vest legal title to certain of the transferor's assets in the transferee 'without the need for any further documentation'. There are some important exceptions to this:

- shares and other securities;

---

[27] Charities Act 2006, s 34; expected to come into force in early 2008.
[28] Charities Act 2006, s 44; expected to come into force in the second half of 2007.

- permanent endowment;

- leases which can only be assigned with the landlord's consent (where that consent has not been obtained); and

- land charged as security by the charity.

15.84 Each of these assets will need to be dealt with on an individual basis in order to ensure that they are properly transferred. The transferor and transferree will also need to deal expressly with the transfer of contractual rights and obligations, which cannot be vested in the transferee by using a vesting declaration. There is more about contracts at **15.90**.

15.85 A vesting declaration must be made by the charity trustees of the transferor and must confirm that all of the transferor's property will vest in the transferee on a specified date. The declaration must be made as a deed. It must also be notified to the Charity Commission by the transferee.

15.86 A vesting declaration may be useful in certain circumstances, eg where the transferor's assets include only cash, computer equipment and other tangible assets. However:

- it cannot be used to transfer shares, lease and other assets commonly held by charities; and

- it does not deal with the liabilities of the transferor charity (or its charity trustees, where it is unincorporated) but will have the effect of transferring some or all of the assets that are required in order to meet its liabilities or the liabilities of the trustees.

15.87 In our view, a vesting declaration will be most useful as part of a wider agreement in relation to a merger which deals more comprehensively with liabilities. If so, it is important to ensure that the agreement is executed as a deed, because this is one of the requirements in relation to a valid declaration.

Employees

15.88 In general, the transfer of a charity's assets and undertakings to another charity will result in the automatic transfer of employees' contracts of employment from the transferor to the transferee under the Transfer of Undertakings (Protection of Employment) Regulations 2006. Where the terms and conditions of employee's contracts do not change, employment issues may be reasonably straightforward, although there are duties to inform and consult with employees prior to the transfer.

VAT

15.89 While the transfer of a charity's assets and undertakings to another charity will generally have no adverse direct tax or SDLT implications, it can give rise to a liability to VAT. In practice, this is usually avoided by ensuring that the transfer qualifies as a 'transfer of a going concern' (TOGC) for the purposes of the VAT legislation. However, the requirements for TOGC treatment are fairly technical and will need to be complied with in detail. A written agreement between the transferor and the transferee is usually essential in order to regulate this.

Contracts

15.90 The transfer agreement will usually regulate the position in relation to the transferor's contracts, including grant funding agreements. Generally, the best approach will be to oblige both transferor and transferee to seek the consent of the counter party to each contract to the assignment or novation of the transferor's obligations to the transferee. Pending this, the transferee will usually agree to carry out the transferor's obligations under the contract and to indemnify the transferor in respect of them.

15.91 It will obviously be essential to ensure that the transfer will not trigger any early termination clauses or any other relevant provision in any contracts to which the transferor is party. This should obviously form an important part of the due diligence that the transferee is likely to carry out in relation to the transferor.

Due diligence

15.92 Before agreeing to the transfer, the trustees of the charities concerned will normally want to carry out a certain amount of financial and legal due diligence in relation to the merger and, in particular, the transferor's and transferee's assets and liabilities. It is obviously essential that the transferee's trustees understand the scope of any liabilities that they are taking on, particularly in the light of the indemnity that the transferor's trustees are likely to seek from them.

15.93 The transferor's trustees are more likely to focus on the financial viability of the transferee both pre and post merger. The scope of the due diligence involved will generally depend upon the value of the assets being transferred and the complexity of the transferor's operation, but the transferee may be particularly concerned to assess potential liabilities in relation to employees, pensions, tax, VAT, litigation and any environmental claims. Some of these liabilities and potential liabilities may not be immediately obvious to the transferee's trustees. They may need to take professional advice in order to understand the position in full.

15.94 The Charity Commission's guidance indicates the sort of general areas that should be looked at as part of a due diligence exercise:

> 'The main elements of due diligence tend to include commercial, financial and legal matters. Other issues such as fundraising strategy, evaluation of future income sources, property, pensions and the provision and maintenance of information technology systems will often also need to be covered.'[29]

There is more guidance about the specific commercial, financial and legal issues the Charity Commission expect to be assessed in their publication CC 34 (Collaborative Working and Mergers).

15.95 There is no objection to the trustees of charities considering a merger paying professional costs to assist them in relation to due diligence. The Commission's guidance is:

> 'Whilst trustee bodies of all charities considering mergers should conduct a due diligence exercise, it can be undertaken with or without external professional advice. If trustees have adequate experience, the due diligence exercise can be wholly performed by them. The

---

[29]   CC 34.

advantage of external advice is that professionals with special expertise can act independently and objectively. They can also be used to ask the awkward questions and request documentary evidence to support the answers.'[30]

15.96 Clearly, extensive due diligence will add to the cost of any merger. The Commission suggests that the nature of the due diligence carried out should be proportionate to the size and nature of the proposed merger, the amount of income and expenditure involved and the nature of existing and planned activities. The Commission accepts that more rigorous due diligence may be required where one or more of the following elements is involved in the merger:

- complex service delivery arrangements;

- high profile of sensitive work undertaken;

- links with affiliated charities;

- operations in a number of geographical locations;

- one or more trading subsidiaries;

- extensive property holdings and assets; or

- restricted funds or permanent endowment.

The key point is clearly that the due diligence that is carried out is in proportion to the size and complexity of the merger which is proposed and the risks involved in it. Where the amounts at stake are small, the cost of due diligence should be kept in proportion.

15.97 There are a number of other issues over and above the strict legal, commercial and financial position in relation to a merger that the trustees of a transferor and transferee must consider very carefully. The Charity Commission's guidance in this area is helpful. They mention the following issues:

- '• Whether the merger will be in the best interests of the charity's beneficiaries.
- How to maintain confidentiality.
- Proper assessment of employment issues, such as any TUPE requirements, pension liabilities (in particular, final salary schemes) and compliance with employment law.
- Sensitive handling of staffing issues, such as managing any staff reductions, (including in some cases the chief executive and other senior staff) and addressing staff morale in the period of change.
- An assessment of the risks attached to the proposed merger, including any operational and reputational risks.'[31]

Other forms of merger

15.98 One other form of merger that is sometime encountered (although it is not really a 'merger' at all) is where one charity obtains control of another. This is usually on the basis that:

---

[30]   CC 34.
[31]   CC 34.

- Both charities' charitable purposes are the same, or the purposes of one charity are narrower than the purposes of the other.

- One charity becomes a member of the other, giving it rights to control, for example, the appointment of its trustees, changes to its constitution and any resolution in relation to its dissolution.

- One charity's trustees may also act as the trustees of the other charity, with a view to running both charities in parallel.

15.99 This sort of arrangement is not a true 'merger' because both charities remain in existence (nor is it a 'relevant charity merger'; see **15.76** for more on this). While the Charity Commission may direct that two charities with the same charity trustees should be treated as a single charity for registration, accounting or any other purposes of the Charities Act 1993, the two charities continue to be separate legal entities.[32]

15.100 An arrangement of this kind is often simpler to arrange than a true merger, if only because it will not involve any transfer of assets or liabilities. Generally speaking, its feasibility will depend upon the powers one charity has to appoint the other as its member and/or to appoint the other's trustees as its own trustees. Clearly, this will depend upon the provisions of the relevant charities' constitutions.

15.101 It is important to appreciate that individuals acting as trustees of both charities owe separate and distinguishable duties to each of them. While their charitable purposes may be identical or overlap, it is possible that a conflict between the two entities may arise, with the end result that the trustees have a conflict between their duties to each of their respective charities. In practice, this is perhaps unlikely, but the trustees should bear it in mind in considering whether the arrangement is more appropriate than, say, a true merger of the two charities.

15.102 Where a charity ceases to exist as a result of merger, its trustees have a duty to notify the Charity Commission, so that the Commission can update the register of charities.[33] The Commission usually asks for some evidence of the dissolution of a charity. There is more on this at **15.139**.

INCORPORATION

15.103 'Incorporation' is the term generally used to describe a decision by the trustees of an unincorporated charity to transfer its assets and undertaking to a newly established incorporated charity with a view to avoiding many of the problems posed by unincorporated status. The aim, therefore, is generally to avoid potential personal liability for the trustees in relation to the liabilities of the charity, whilst also allowing the charity to own assets and enter into agreements in its own name. There is more about this issue at **2.55**.

15.104 Generally, the new incorporated charity will have been established with charitable purposes that are identical to the charitable purposes of the old unincorporated charity. The new charity's governance arrangements may well reflect the

---

[32] Charities Act 1993, s 96(6).
[33] Charities Act 1993, s 3.

governance arrangements of the old charity, although many trustees take the opportunity to update governance arrangements where possible.

15.105 Clearly, an arrangement of this kind is not in any strict legal sense an 'incorporation' of the old charity. It will cease to exist following the transfer of its assets and liabilities to the new charity. However, arrangements of this kind are often referred to as 'incorporation'. They should be distinguished from the trustees of an unincorporated charity opting to become an incorporated body under the Charities Act 1993, Part VII (ss 50–62) or a decision by them to appoint a corporate trustee in their place. Neither of these arrangements (which are explained in more detail at **6.26**) makes any fundamental change to the unincorporated status of the existing charity.

15.106 The incorporation of an unincorporated charity raises almost all of the same issues in relation to transfer of its assets and liabilities as a merger (as to which, see **15.67**). The significant difference is that the new charity is generally under the sole control of the trustees of the old charity. They will need to ensure that they take into account the duties they owe to each of the charities with a view to ensuring that there is no conflict between the two. Generally, the scope for conflict will be limited where the charities have identical charitable purposes.

15.107 As with any charity merger, the key issues in relation to an incorporation are usually:

- The terms of the transfer and an indemnity for liabilities.

- The status of trust assets and arrangements for the transfer of permanent endowment.
  As we have explained earlier in this chapter, this will generally be on the basis that the new charity becomes a trustee of the permanent endowment assets of the old charity. This will usually involve the Charity Commission making a new fully regulating Scheme governing the permanent endowment assets under the old charity's registered number. The new charity will act as trustee of the endowment assets under the Scheme and will obviously wish to ensure that the scope of its powers in relation to borrowing, disposal etc of the permanent endowment are sufficiently wide and flexible. They will also wish to ensure that the Commission make a uniting direction pursuant to the Charities Act 1993, s 96(5) which will enable the two charities to prepare a single set of accounts and be treated for other purposes of the 1993 Act as the same charity.

- The transfer should generally qualify as a TOGC for VAT purposes but this will need to be checked carefully (see **15.89** for more in relation to this). The position in relation to land owned by the charity will need to be checked particularly carefully, where provisions that allow land to be 'opted' to VAT need to be taken into account.

- The transfer of assets and undertakings by the charity to the new charity will generally constitute a 'relevant charity merger' for the purposes of the register of mergers maintained by the Charity Commission. The provisions in respect of pre-merger vesting declarations will also apply. These should obviously be taken advantage of. There is more about this at **15.76** and **15.83**.

- All of the other issues in relation to contracts, employees, pensions, etc that we have mentioned above at **15.67** will need to be addressed.

15.108 The trustees of an unincorporated charity will obviously need to ensure that they have the powers required to transfer the charity's assets and undertakings to the new charity. These may be express or statutory powers (as we have explained earlier in this Chapter) or, failing that, an Order or Scheme of the Charity Commission may be required.

15.109 There have been a number of incorporations of charities in more recent years, driven primarily by trustees' concerns about personal liability. The Charity Commission now offers a separate set of documents that can be used to apply for the registration of any new charity set up as part of an incorporation. The relevant forms (APP2 and DEC2) are available online, together with guidance on the application process (www.charitycommission.gsi.gov.uk).

15.110 In addition, there are some specific provisions in relation to CIOs that will be implemented by the Charities Act 2006[34] that are clearly designed to encourage 'incorporation' as a CIO. Section 69O of the Charities Act 1993 will give the trustees of any unincorporated charity a power to transfer all of its assets to a CIO (provided that it does not hold any 'designated land').

15.111 This is obviously potentially a very useful statutory power, particularly where an unincorporated charity does not have express powers that will facilitate an incorporation. Section 69G of the Charities Act 1993 will also contain provisions for charitable companies and industrial and provident societies to convert into CIOs provided they follow a regime set out in the 1993 Act.[35] This will obviously not constitute an 'incorporation', but may be useful in certain circumstances.

DISSOLUTION

15.112 We have explained the basis on which different types of charity may be dissolved earlier in this chapter. Where there is an express power for a charity's dissolution and this is exercised in accordance with its terms, this will generally result in the charity's dissolution, although it is worth remembering that certain types of charity (eg charitable companies) can only finally be dissolved by using a formal statutory process. This is explained in more detail at **15.116** and **15.120** below.

15.113 It is also worth remembering that certain other types of charity (eg charitable trusts) can be dissolved by doing no more than distributing all of their assets using a power to make gifts and donations. A charitable trust cannot exist without any assets, so that a distribution of all of a charity's assets will ensure that it is dissolved. This is what happens where the trustees of an unincorporated charity decide to 'incorporate' by transferring all of its assets and undertakings to a new charitable company.

15.114 Where the trustees of a charitable trust decide to distribute all of its assets with a view to ensuring that it is dissolved, they will need to take careful steps to ensure that its debts and liabilities are met in full. As we have explained at **6.22**, the trustees of a charitable trust are potentially personally liable in respect of all of the liabilities they

---

[34] Charities Act 2006, s 34; expected to come into force in early 2008.
[35] Charities Act 2006, s 34; expected to come into force in early 2008.

incur in respect of the charity. While they have an indemnity against the charity's assets in respect of their properly incurred liabilities, this indemnity will generally cease once the assets have been distributed.

15.115 The rules of a charitable unincorporated association will generally contain a provision providing for dissolution by a resolution of its members. If there is no express power to this effect, a dissolution could be achieved by agreement between all of the members of the association. Failing that, the court may order a winding up of the association under its general equitable distribution.

15.116 A charitable company, whether limited by guarantee or shares can be wound up under the Insolvency Act 1986. A winding-up petition can be presented by the company itself, or by its members or (on an insolvency) by its creditors. The Charity Commission also has a power to petition for a winding-up where it has instituted an Inquiry in relation to the company.

15.117 The constitution of a charitable company will almost invariably contain a dissolution clause that will govern how any surplus assets on a dissolution should be dealt with. Generally, they must be applied for charitable purposes that are the same as or are similar to, the charitable purposes of the company itself.

15.118 As we have indicated earlier in this chapter, the trustees of any charity that ceases to exist have a duty to notify the Charity Commission so that it can update the register of charities.[36] This is explained in more detail at **15.139**.

INSOLVENCY

15.119 Charities are as much at risk of insolvency as their counterparts in the commercial world. Incorporated and unincorporated charities become insolvent in different ways. This is explained in more detail below.

Charitable companies

15.120 As we have indicated earlier in this chapter, charitable companies are subject to the winding-up regime imposed by the Insolvency Act 1986 (as amended by the Enterprise Act 2002). This will apply where a charitable company is insolvent. There are two tests of insolvency:

• Whether the charitable company is unable to pay its debts as they fall due. This is usually referred to as the 'going concern' test of insolvency. It looks at whether the charity has sufficient resources available to meet all of its immediate liabilities and is likely to be able to do so over the short term.

• Whether the value of the charity's assets is less than the amount of its liabilities (taking into account its possible and prospective liabilities).
This is usually referred to as the 'balance sheet' test which looks at whether the charity has sufficient assets (both fixed and current) to meet all of its actual and anticipated liabilities in the long term.

---

[36] Charities Act 1993, s 3.

15.121 While the regime imposed by the Insolvency Act 1986 will apply to a charitable company's corporate assets, any trust assets that are held by the company will not be subject to it and can only be dealt with in the same way as the assets of an unincorporated charity.

15.122 The court has jurisdiction to make an administration order under Part II of the 1986 Act in relation to a body incorporated by Royal charter as well as companies incorporated under the Companies Acts (see *The Salvage Association* (2003) *The Times*, 21 May).

Unincorporated charities

15.123 Unincorporated charities (ie trusts and unincorporated associations) cannot become 'insolvent' within the regime imposed by the Insolvency Act 1986. This is because they have no separate legal personality and cannot incur liabilities in their own right. However, an unincorporated charity may reach the financial state where it is 'insolvent' in the sense that the value of the charity's assets that are available to its trustees to settle their liabilities is insufficient. Ultimately, creditors' claims against the trustees may mean that they are made personally bankrupt.

15.124 As we have explained at **6.22**, the trustees of an unincorporated charity have a right to indemnify themselves from the charity's assets against liabilities properly incurred on its behalf. In an insolvency situation, the concern is obviously that there are insufficient assets to meet the liabilities that the trustees owe personally to third parties.

15.125 Although unincorporated charities are not the subject of the regime imposed by the Insolvency Act 1986, the Charity Commission recommends that:

> '... as a matter of good practice, a similar approach is adopted for unincorporated charities.'[37]

15.126 The Charity Commission also recommends that the going concern and balance sheet tests of insolvency which apply to charitable companies may also be useful is assessing whether an unincorporated charity is 'insolvent'.

Governance implications

15.127 The possibility that a charity may become insolvent is a significant governance issue because managing the risk of insolvency is one of the many obligations of charity trustees. As the Commission's guidance states:

> 'It is essential for a trustee body to have a good knowledge and understanding of the charity and its finances. Although it can be difficult to prevent the overnight collapse, even if it is anticipated, it ought to be possible to prevent or delay the onset of creeping insolvency.
>
> The action necessary can be summed up as being "effective management and control". The responsibility for creating this environment rests with the trustees, but will involve all staff members whether paid or volunteers.'[38]

---

[37] CC 12 (Managing Financial Difficulties and Insolvency in Charities).
[38] CC 12.

15.128 The Charity Commission go on to make a number of recommendations about the way in which trustees should exercise effective management control over their charity's finances. The key points are:

- A charity's trustees should have a mix of skills and experience which will enable them to understand and monitor its finances and trustees generally must be able to find the time to devote to running the charity.

- Proper financial reporting is essential. If trustees are to monitor the charity's financial position, they need to receive regular budgets, cash flow forecasts and other financial reports on a regular basis, together with projects of income and expenditure.

- Actual income and expenditure should be monitored regularly against projected income and expenditure.

- The trustees should spend some time analysing the sources of the charity's income and the way in which that income is spent, with a view to identifying where the risks of insolvency lie (for example, over reliance on an single source of income).

- Trustees should take professional advice on significant capital expenditure or other material liabilities they propose to incur.

- Systems of internal financial control should be comprehensive and robust.

- The charity's investment portfolio should be sufficiently diversified (in order to manage risk) and invested in accordance with an appropriate investment policy. There is more about this in **Chapter 10**.

15.129 There are other aspects of the way in which the charity is structured and owns its assets that the trustees must understand if they are to exercise effective management control over its finances. The most significant aspects are:

- Trustees must understand which assets (if any) are held by the charity on a 'special trust' for particular charitable purposes or held as endowment assets subject to restrictions on the way in which they can be spent. Restrictions of this kind mean that the charity's trustees may not be able to apply trust assets in order to meet the charity's liabilities without giving rise to a breach of trust, unless the liabilities in question were properly incurred in the administration of the relevant trust. The Commission's position on this is clear:

   'An understanding of the nature of the separate funds of a charity is crucial to the understanding of the financial position. Such considerations must be taken into account when analysing the insolvency of a charity.'[39]

- The restrictions on a charity's ability to dispose of any 'functional' or 'specie' land which is obliged to be used for its purposes will also be relevant in assessing the charity's financial position because this will make them more than usually illiquid.

- The Charity Commission recommends the use of a reserves policy (identifying the level of free reserves a charity needs in order to ensure that its operations will

---

[39] CC 12.

continue in accordance with its overall strategy) as a way of providing financial stability. There is more about reserves at **9.64**.

- Trustees should understand that the way in which the value of assets and liabilities is recognised in the charity's accounts can vary depending upon the charity's solvency or insolvency. For example, assets that may have a particular market value on a solvent basis, may have a much lower basis in the context of insolvency (when they need to be disposed of by way of a 'fire sale'). Insolvency may also give rise to additional liabilities including redundancy and professional costs.

15.130 Where insolvency appears to be approaching, but insolvency proceedings have not yet started, the Charity Commission recommends that the trustees take professional advice with a view to taking action to stabilise the charity's financial position. This could include:

- Ceasing some operational activities or transferring them to other charities.

- Looking at the possibility of merging with another charity.

- Re-financing, perhaps by borrowing from a bank or commercial entity on the basis of security over the charity's fixed assets. The Commission accepts that a charity may also be able to 'borrow' from permanent endowment assets in order to fund deficits. This would require an Order or a Scheme from the Commission.

- The Insolvency Act 1986 provides for any company (including a charitable company) to enter into a compulsory voluntary arrangement with its creditors under which they agree to accept a part repayment of the liabilities due to them or payment on a delayed basis. There is no corresponding arrangement for the individual trustees of an unincorporated charity, although it is open to them to come to a 'private' arrangement with their creditors in certain circumstances.

15.131 While the limited liability of a charitable company will usually protect its trustees and members from personal liability, its trustees may be liable in the context of insolvency in respect of wrongful or fraudulent trading. Personal liability on this basis is explained in more detail at **6.14**.

15.132 We have already mentioned potential personal liability to trustees where they allow trust assets to be used to discharge liabilities owed to the charitable company's creditors except where the liabilities in question have been properly incurred for the administration of the trust in question. This will generally constitute a breach of trust.

The Charity Commission

15.133 The Charity Commission's role in relation to charities that are, or may be, insolvent is relatively restricted. As the Commission's own guidance states:

> 'We are precluded by law from becoming involved in the internal administration of a charity, including restructuring and refinancing. Questions of financial viability must remain a matter for the charity trustees and their professional advisers.'[40]

---

[40]   CC 12.

15.134 Having said this, the Commission will be interested in a charity's insolvency from the point of view of good regulation. Again, their guidance states:

> 'When solvency is an issue we may have a regulatory interest. In these cases we may need to ensure that proper control of the charity exists and that the trustees are aware of their responsibilities and duties in such difficult circumstances.'[41]

15.135 Where there is doubt about why a charity has become insolvent, the Charity Commission may well look at the position in detail, perhaps asking for detailed information from the trustees which will enable the Commission to determine whether robust internal financial controls are in place, the trustees have received and monitored financial information on a regular basis, professional advice has been taken where necessary and that the trustees have approached the insolvency with a clear plan to address it.

Interim manager

15.136 Where the Commission suspects that a charity has been subject to mismanagement or maladministration by the trustees, they have the power to open an Inquiry (under the Charities Act 1993, s 8). There is more about this at **4.35**. Once an Inquiry has been opened, the Commission has the power to appoint an 'interim manager' under the Charities Act 1993, s 18. The 'interim manager' will be introduced by the Charities Act 2006 and is presently referred to by the Charities Act 1993 as a 'receiver and manager'.

15.137 An appointment can be made in respect of any charity, whether or not it is incorporated. An interim manager acts as the trustee of a charity while his appointment continues. His role is essentially to try to identify and rectify whatever mismanagement or misconduct has taken place. He will also usually need to make an assessment of whether the charity should continue or be wound-up. He has the power to petition the court for the winding-up of a charitable company in certain circumstances.

15.138 The Commission's guidance states that:

> 'Such appointments can be made where we are satisfied that the trustees have not acted properly, or where we perceive there to be a risk to charitable property. In some cases the appointment may be made in co-operation with the trustees.'[42]

Notification

15.139 The trustees of any charity which is dissolved as a consequence of its insolvency have a duty to notify the Charity Commission, so that it can update the register of charities. Where the charity is a company, the Commission will usually expect the company's liquidator to inform them when the liquidation has been completed and the company has been formally dissolved under the Companies Acts.

15.140 Where the charity is unincorporated, the Charity Commission will usually require some supporting evidence in relation to the dissolution. This is likely to include

---

[41]   CC 12.
[42]   CC 12.

a copy of the relevant resolution to wind-up the charity, a final set of accounts and a statement of the final distribution of the charity's assets (if this is not clear from the accounts themselves).

Appendix 1

CHARITIES ACT 1993

Note—Amendments made by the Charities Act 2006 are prospective unless otherwise indicated.

PART I
THE [CHARITY COMMISSION][1] AND THE OFFICIAL CUSTODIAN FOR CHARITIES

1 ...[2]

Amendment—Charities Act 2006, ss 6(6), 75(2), Sch 9.

[1A The Charity Commission

(1) There shall be a body corporate to be known as the Charity Commission for England and Wales (in this Act referred to as 'the Commission').

(2) In Welsh the Commission shall be known as 'Comisiwn Elusennau Cymru a Lloegr'.

(3) The functions of the Commission shall be performed on behalf of the Crown.

(4) In the exercise of its functions the Commission shall not be subject to the direction or control of any Minister of the Crown or other government department.

(5) But subsection (4) above does not affect—

    (a)   any provision made by or under any enactment;
    (b)   any administrative controls exercised over the Commission's expenditure by the Treasury.

(6) The provisions of Schedule 1A to this Act shall have effect with respect to the Commission.][3]

Amendment—Charities Act 2006, s 6(1).

[1B The Commission's objectives

(1) The Commission has the objectives set out in subsection (2).

(2) The objectives are—

    1.   The public confidence objective.
    2.   The public benefit objective.
    3.   The compliance objective.
    4.   The charitable resources objective.
    5.   The accountability objective.

(3) Those objectives are defined as follows—

---

[1]   Amendment: Words substituted: Charities Act 2006, s 75(1), Sch 8, paras 96, 97.
[2]   Amendment: Section repealed: Charities Act 2006, ss 6(6), 75(2), Sch 9.
[3]   Amendment: Section inserted: Charities Act 2006, s 6(1).

1. The public confidence objective is to increase public trust and confidence in charities.
2. The public benefit objective is to promote awareness and understanding of the operation of the public benefit requirement.
3. The compliance objective is to promote compliance by charity trustees with their legal obligations in exercising control and management of the administration of their charities.
4. The charitable resources objective is to promote the effective use of charitable resources.
5. The accountability objective is to enhance the accountability of charities to donors, beneficiaries and the general public.

(4) In this section 'the public benefit requirement' means the requirement in section 2(1)(b) of the Charities Act 2006 that a purpose falling within section 2(2) of that Act must be for the public benefit if it is to be a charitable purpose.]⁴

Amendment—Charities Act 2006, s 7.

[1C The Commission's general functions

(1) The Commission has the general functions set out in subsection (2).

(2) The general functions are—

1. Determining whether institutions are or are not charities.
2. Encouraging and facilitating the better administration of charities.
3. Identifying and investigating apparent misconduct or mismanagement in the administration of charities and taking remedial or protective action in connection with misconduct or mismanagement therein.
4. Determining whether public collections certificates should be issued, and remain in force, in respect of public charitable collections.
5. Obtaining, evaluating and disseminating information in connection with the performance of any of the Commission's functions or meeting any of its objectives.
6. Giving information or advice, or making proposals, to any Minister of the Crown on matters relating to any of the Commission's functions or meeting any of its objectives.

(3) The Commission's fifth general function includes (among other things) the maintenance of an accurate and up-to-date register of charities under section 3 below.

(4) The Commission's sixth general function includes (among other things) complying, so far as is reasonably practicable, with any request made by a Minister of the Crown for information or advice on any matter relating to any of its functions.

(5) In this section 'public charitable collection' and 'public collections certificate' have the same meanings as in Chapter 1 of Part 3 of the Charities Act 2006.]⁵

Amendment—Charities Act 2006, s 7.

[1D The Commission's general duties

(1) The Commission has the general duties set out in subsection (2).

(2) The general duties are—

---

4 Amendment: Section inserted: Charities Act 2006, s 7.
5 Amendment: Section inserted: Charities Act 2006, s 7.

1. So far as is reasonably practicable the Commission must, in performing its functions, act in a way—
   (a) which is compatible with its objectives, and
   (b) which it considers most appropriate for the purpose of meeting those objectives.
2. So far as is reasonably practicable the Commission must, in performing its functions, act in a way which is compatible with the encouragement of—
   (a) all forms of charitable giving, and
   (b) voluntary participation in charity work.
3. In performing its functions the Commission must have regard to the need to use its resources in the most efficient, effective and economic way.
4. In performing its functions the Commission must, so far as relevant, have regard to the principles of best regulatory practice (including the principles under which regulatory activities should be proportionate, accountable, consistent, transparent and targeted only at cases in which action is needed).
5. In performing its functions the Commission must, in appropriate cases, have regard to the desirability of facilitating innovation by or on behalf of charities.
6. In managing its affairs the Commission must have regard to such generally accepted principles of good corporate governance as it is reasonable to regard as applicable to it.][6]

Amendment—Charities Act 2006, s 7.

[1E The Commission's incidental powers

(1) The Commission has power to do anything which is calculated to facilitate, or is conducive or incidental to, the performance of any of its functions or general duties.

(2) However, nothing in this Act authorises the Commission—

(a) to exercise functions corresponding to those of a charity trustee in relation to a charity, or
(b) otherwise to be directly involved in the administration of a charity.

(3) Subsection (2) does not affect the operation of section 19A or 19B below (power of Commission to give directions as to action to be taken or as to application of charity property).][7]

Amendment—Charities Act 2006, s 7.

2 The official custodian for charities

(1) There shall continue to be an officer known as the official custodian for charities (in this Act referred to as 'the official custodian') whose function it shall be to act as trustee for charities in the cases provided for by this Act; and the official custodian shall be by that name a corporation sole having perpetual succession and using an official seal which shall be officially and judicially noticed.

[(2) Such individual as the Commission may from time to time designate shall be the official custodian.][8]

---

[6] Amendment: Section inserted: Charities Act 2006, s 7.
[7] Amendment: Section inserted: Charities Act 2006, s 7.
[8] Amendment: Subsection substituted: Charities Act 2006, s 75(1), Sch 8, paras 96, 98(1), (2), for transitional provisions see s 75(3), Sch 10, para 19.

(3) The official custodian shall perform his duties in accordance with such general or special directions as may be given him by the [Commission][9], and his expenses (except those re-imbursed to him or recovered by him as trustee for any charity) shall be defrayed by the [Commission][10].

(4) Anything which is required to or may be done by, to or before the official custodian may be done by, to or before any [member of the staff of the Commission][11] generally or specially authorised [by it][12] to act for him during a vacancy in his office or otherwise.

(5) The official custodian shall not be liable as trustee for any charity in respect of any loss or of the mis-application of any property unless it is occasioned by or through the wilful neglect or default of the custodian or of any person acting for him; but the Consolidated Fund shall be liable to make good to a charity any sums for which the custodian may be liable by reason of any such neglect or default.

(6) The official custodian shall keep such books of account and such records in relation thereto as may be directed by the Treasury and shall prepare accounts in such form, in such manner and at such times as may be so directed.

(7) The accounts so prepared shall be examined and certified by the Comptroller and Auditor General...[13].

[(8) The Comptroller and Auditor General shall send to the Commission a copy of the accounts as certified by him together with his report on them.

(9) The Commission shall publish and lay before Parliament a copy of the documents sent to it under subsection (8) above.][14]

Amendments—Charities Act 2006, s 75, Sch 8, paras 96, 98, Sch 9.

[PART 1A
THE CHARITY TRIBUNAL

[2A The Charity Tribunal

(1) There shall be a tribunal to be known as the Charity Tribunal (in this Act referred to as 'the Tribunal').

(2) In Welsh the Tribunal shall be known as 'Tribiwnlys Elusennau'.

(3) The provisions of Schedule 1B to this Act shall have effect with respect to the constitution of the Tribunal and other matters relating to it.

(4) The Tribunal shall have jurisdiction to hear and determine—

    (a)   such appeals and applications as may be made to the Tribunal in accordance with Schedule 1C to this Act, or any other enactment, in respect of decisions, orders or directions of the Commission, and

    (b)   such matters as may be referred to the Tribunal in accordance with Schedule 1D to this Act by the Commission or the Attorney General.

---

[9]   Amendment: Word substituted: Charities Act 2006, s 75(1), Sch 8, paras 96, 98(1), (3).
[10]   Amendment: Word substituted: Charities Act 2006, s 75(1), Sch 8, paras 96, 98(1), (3).
[11]   Amendment: Words substituted: Charities Act 2006, s 75(1), Sch 8, paras 96, 98(1), (4)(a).
[12]   Amendment: Words substituted: Charities Act 2006, s 75(1), Sch 8, paras 96, 98(1), (4)(b).
[13]   Amendment: Words omitted: Charities Act 2006, s 75, Sch 8, paras 96, 98(1), (5), Sch 9.
[14]   Amendment: Subsections inserted: Charities Act 2006, s 75(1), Sch 8, paras 96, 98(1), (6).

(5) Such appeals, applications and matters shall be heard and determined by the Tribunal in accordance with those Schedules, or any such enactment, taken with section 2B below and rules made under that section.][15]

Amendment—Charities Act 2006, s 8(1).

2B Practice and procedure

(1) The Lord Chancellor may make rules—

(a) regulating the exercise of rights to appeal or to apply to the Tribunal and matters relating to the making of references to it;

(b) about the practice and procedure to be followed in relation to proceedings before the Tribunal.

(2) Rules under subsection (1)(a) above may, in particular, make provision—

(a) specifying steps which must be taken before appeals, applications or references are made to the Tribunal (and the period within which any such steps must be taken);

(b) specifying the period following the Commission's final decision, direction or order within which such appeals or applications may be made;

(c) requiring the Commission to inform persons of their right to appeal or apply to the Tribunal following a final decision, direction or order of the Commission;

(d) specifying the manner in which appeals, applications or references to the Tribunal are to be made.

(3) Rules under subsection (1)(b) above may, in particular, make provision—

(a) for the President or a legal member of the Tribunal (see paragraph 1(2)(b) of Schedule 1B to this Act) to determine preliminary, interlocutory or ancillary matters;

(b) for matters to be determined without an oral hearing in specified circumstances;

(c) for the Tribunal to deal with urgent cases expeditiously;

(d) about the disclosure of documents;

(e) about evidence;

(f) about the admission of members of the public to proceedings;

(g) about the representation of parties to proceedings;

(h) about the withdrawal of appeals, applications or references;

(i) about the recording and promulgation of decisions;

(j) about the award of costs.

(4) Rules under subsection (1)(a) or (b) above may confer a discretion on—

(a) the Tribunal,

(b) a member of the Tribunal, or

(c) any other person.

(5) The Tribunal may award costs only in accordance with subsections (6) and (7) below.

---

[15] Amendment: Section inserted: Charities Act 2006, s 8(1).

(6) If the Tribunal considers that any party to proceedings before it has acted vexatiously, frivolously or unreasonably, the Tribunal may order that party to pay to any other party to the proceedings the whole or part of the costs incurred by that other party in connection with the proceedings.

(7) If the Tribunal considers that a decision, direction or order of the Commission which is the subject of proceedings before it was unreasonable, the Tribunal may order the Commission to pay to any other party to the proceedings the whole or part of the costs incurred by that other party in connection with the proceedings.

(8) Rules of the Lord Chancellor under this section—

    (a)   shall be made by statutory instrument, and
    (b)   shall be subject to annulment in pursuance of a resolution of either House of Parliament.

(9) Section 86(3) below applies in relation to rules of the Lord Chancellor under this section as it applies in relation to regulations and orders of the Minister under this Act.][16]

Amendment—Charities Act 2006, s 8(1).

2C Appeal from Tribunal

(1) A party to proceedings before the Tribunal may appeal to the High Court against a decision of the Tribunal.

(2) Subject to subsection (3) below, an appeal may be brought under this section against a decision of the Tribunal only on a point of law.

(3) In the case of an appeal under this section against a decision of the Tribunal which determines a question referred to it by the Commission or the Attorney General, the High Court—

    (a)   shall consider afresh the question referred to the Tribunal, and
    (b)   may take into account evidence which was not available to the Tribunal.

(4) An appeal under this section may be brought only with the permission of—

    (a)   the Tribunal, or
    (b)   if the Tribunal refuses permission, the High Court.

(5) For the purposes of subsection (1) above—

    (a)   the Commission and the Attorney General are to be treated as parties to all proceedings before the Tribunal, and
    (b)   rules under section 2B(1) above may include provision as to who else is to be treated as being (or not being) a party to proceedings before the Tribunal.][17]

Amendment—Charities Act 2006, s 8(1).

2D Intervention by Attorney General

(1) This section applies to any proceedings—

    (a)   before the Tribunal, or
    (b)   on an appeal from the Tribunal,

---

[16]   Amendment: Section inserted: Charities Act 2006, s 8(1).
[17]   Amendment: Section inserted: Charities Act 2006, s 8(1).

to which the Attorney General is not a party.

(2) The Tribunal or, in the case of an appeal from the Tribunal, the court may at any stage of the proceedings direct that all the necessary papers in the proceedings be sent to the Attorney General.

(3) A direction under subsection (2) may be made by the Tribunal or court—

(a) of its own motion, or
(b) on the application of any party to the proceedings.

(4) The Attorney General may—

(a) intervene in the proceedings in such manner as he thinks necessary or expedient, and
(b) argue before the Tribunal or court any question in relation to the proceedings which the Tribunal or court considers it necessary to have fully argued.

(5) Subsection (4) applies whether or not the Tribunal or court has given a direction under subsection (2).][18]

Amendment—Charities Act 2006, s 8(1).

PART II
REGISTRATION AND NAMES OF CHARITIES
Registration of charities

[3 Register of charities

(1) There shall continue to be a register of charities, which shall be kept by the Commission.

(2) The register shall be kept by the Commission in such manner as it thinks fit.

(3) The register shall contain—

(a) the name of every charity registered in accordance with section 3A below (registration), and
(b) such other particulars of, and such other information relating to, every such charity as the Commission thinks fit.

(4) The Commission shall remove from the register—

(a) any institution which it no longer considers is a charity, and
(b) any charity which has ceased to exist or does not operate.

(5) If the removal of an institution under subsection (4)(a) above is due to any change in its trusts, the removal shall take effect from the date of that change.

(6) A charity which is for the time being registered under section 3A(6) below (voluntary registration) shall be removed from the register if it so requests.

(7) The register (including the entries cancelled when institutions are removed from the register) shall be open to public inspection at all reasonable times.

(8) Where any information contained in the register is not in documentary form, subsection (7) above shall be construed as requiring the information to be available for public inspection in legible form at all reasonable times.

---

[18] Amendment: Section inserted: Charities Act 2006, s 8(1).

(9) If the Commission so determines, subsection (7) shall not apply to any particular information contained in the register that is specified in the determination.

(10) Copies (or particulars) of the trusts of any registered charity as supplied to the Commission under section 3B below (applications for registration etc) shall, so long as the charity remains on the register—

  (a)   be kept by the Commission, and
  (b)   be open to public inspection at all reasonable times.][19]

Amendments—Teaching and Higher Education Act 1998, s 44(1), Sch 3, para 9; School Standards and Framework Act 1998, s 140(1), Sch 30, para 48; Charities Act 2006, s 9.

[3A Registration of charities

(1) Every charity must be registered in the register of charities unless subsection (2) below applies to it.

(2) The following are not required to be registered—

  (a)   any exempt charity (see Schedule 2 to this Act);
  (b)   any charity which for the time being—
         (i)   is permanently or temporarily excepted by order of the Commission, and
         (ii)   complies with any conditions of the exception,
         and whose gross income does not exceed £100,000;
  (c)   any charity which for the time being—
         (i)   is, or is of a description, permanently or temporarily excepted by regulations made by the Secretary of State, and
         (ii)   complies with any conditions of the exception,
         and whose gross income does not exceed £100,000; and
  (d)   any charity whose gross income does not exceed £5,000.

(3) For the purposes of subsection (2)(b) above—

  (a)   any order made or having effect as if made under section 3(5)(b) of this Act (as originally enacted) and in force immediately before the appointed day has effect as from that day as if made under subsection (2)(b) (and may be varied or revoked accordingly); and
  (b)   no order may be made under subsection (2)(b) so as to except on or after the appointed day any charity that was not excepted immediately before that day.

(4) For the purposes of subsection (2)(c) above—

  (a)   any regulations made or having effect as if made under section 3(5)(b) of this Act (as originally enacted) and in force immediately before the appointed day have effect as from that day as if made under subsection (2)(c) (and may be varied or revoked accordingly);
  (b)   such regulations shall be made under subsection (2)(c) as are necessary to secure that all of the formerly specified institutions are excepted under that provision (subject to compliance with any conditions of the exception and the financial limit mentioned in that provision); but
  (c)   otherwise no regulations may be made under subsection (2)(c) so as to except on or after the appointed day any description of charities that was not excepted immediately before that day.

---

[19]   Amendment: Section substituted: Charities Act 2006, s 9.

(5) In subsection (4)(b) above 'formerly specified institutions' means—

- (a) any institution falling within section 3(5B)(a) or (b) of this Act as in force immediately before the appointed day (certain educational institutions); or
- (b) any institution ceasing to be an exempt charity by virtue of section 11 of the Charities Act 2006 or any order made under that section.

(6) A charity within—

- (a) subsection (2)(b) or (c) above, or
- (b) subsection (2)(d) above,

must, if it so requests, be registered in the register of charities.

(7) The Minister may by order amend—

- (a) subsection (2)(b) and (c) above, or
- (b) subsection (2)(d) above,

by substituting a different sum for the sum for the time being specified there.

(8) The Minister may only make an order under subsection (7) above—

- (a) so far as it amends subsection (2)(b) and (c), if he considers it expedient to so with a view to reducing the scope of the exception provided by those provisions;
- (b) so far as it amends subsection (2)(d), if he considers it expedient to do so in consequence of changes in the value of money or with a view to extending the scope of the exception provided by that provision,

and no order may be made by him under subsection (7)(a) unless a copy of a report under section 73 of the Charities Act 2006 (report on operation of that Act) has been laid before Parliament in accordance with that section.

(9) In this section 'the appointed day' means the day on which subsections (1) to (5) above come into force by virtue of an order under section 79 of the Charities Act 2006 relating to section 9 of that Act (registration of charities).

(10) In this section any reference to a charity's 'gross income' shall be construed, in relation to a particular time—

- (a) as a reference to the charity's gross income in its financial year immediately preceding that time, or
- (b) if the Commission so determines, as a reference to the amount which the Commission estimates to be the likely amount of the charity's gross income in such financial year of the charity as is specified in the determination.

(11) The following provisions of this section—

- (a) subsection (2)(b) and (c),
- (b) subsections (3) to (5), and
- (c) subsections (6)(a), (7)(a), (8)(a) and (9),

shall cease to have effect on such day as the Minister may by order appoint for the purposes of this subsection.][20]

Amendment—Charities Act 2006, s 9.

---

[20]   Amendment: Section substituted for section 3: Charities Act 2006, s 9.

3B Duties of trustees in connection with registration

(1) Where a charity required to be registered by virtue of section 3A(1) above is not registered, it is the duty of the charity trustees—

    (a)   to apply to the Commission for the charity to be registered, and

    (b)   to supply the Commission with the required documents and information.

(2) The 'required documents and information' are—

    (a)   copies of the charity's trusts or (if they are not set out in any extant document) particulars of them,

    (b)   such other documents or information as may be prescribed by regulations made by the Minister, and

    (c)   such other documents or information as the Commission may require for the purposes of the application.

(3) Where an institution is for the time being registered, it is the duty of the charity trustees (or the last charity trustees)—

    (a)   to notify the Commission if the institution ceases to exist, or if there is any change in its trusts or in the particulars of it entered in the register, and

    (b)   (so far as appropriate), to supply the Commission with particulars of any such change and copies of any new trusts or alterations of the trusts.

(4) Nothing in subsection (3) above requires a person—

    (a)   to supply the Commission with copies of schemes for the administration of a charity made otherwise than by the court,

    (b)   to notify the Commission of any change made with respect to a registered charity by such a scheme, or

    (c)   if he refers the Commission to a document or copy already in the possession of the Commission, to supply a further copy of the document.

(5) Where a copy of a document relating to a registered charity—

    (a)   is not required to be supplied to the Commission as the result of subsection (4) above, but

    (b)   is in the possession of the Commission,

a copy of the document shall be open to inspection under section 3(10) above as if supplied to the Commission under this section.][21]

Amendment—Charities Act 2006, s 9.

4 Effect of, and claims and objections to, registration

(1) An institution shall for all purposes other than rectification of the register be conclusively presumed to be or to have been a charity at any time when it is or was on the register of charities.

(2) Any person who is or may be affected by the registration of an institution as a charity may, on the ground that it is not a charity, object to its being entered by [the Commission][22] in the register, or apply [to the Commission][23] for it to be removed from

---

[21]   Amendment: Section substituted for section 3: Charities Act 2006, s 9.
[22]   Amendment: Words substituted: Charities Act 2006, s 75(1), Sch 8, paras 96, 99(1), (2)(a).
[23]   Amendment: Words substituted: Charities Act 2006, s 75(1), Sch 8, paras 96, 99(1), (2)(b).

the register; and provision may be made by regulations made by the Secretary of State as to the manner in which any such objection or application is to be made, prosecuted or dealt with.

(3) ...[24]

(4) If there is an appeal to the [Tribunal][25] against any decision of [the Commission][26] to enter an institution in the register, or not to remove an institution from the register, then until [the Commission is][27] satisfied whether the decision of [the Commission][28] is or is not to stand, the entry in the register shall be maintained, but shall be in suspense and marked to indicate that it is in suspense; and for the purposes of subsection (1) above an institution shall be deemed not to be on the register during any period when the entry relating to it is in suspense under this subsection.

(5) Any question affecting the registration or removal from the register of an institution may, notwithstanding that it has been determined by a decision on appeal under [Schedule 1C to this Act][29], be considered afresh by [the Commission][30] and shall not be concluded by that decision, if it appears to [the Commission][31] that there has been a change of circumstances or that the decision is inconsistent with a later judicial decision...[32].

Amendments—Charities Act 2006, s 75, Sch 8, paras 96, 99, Sch 9.

5 Status of registered charity (other than small charity) to appear on official publications etc

(1) This section applies to a registered charity if its gross income in its last financial year exceeded [£10,000][33].

(2) Where this section applies to a registered charity, the fact that it is a registered charity shall be stated ...[34] in legible characters—

    (a)   in all notices, advertisements and other documents issued by or on behalf of the charity and soliciting money or other property for the benefit of the charity;

    (b)   in all bills of exchange, promissory notes, endorsements, cheques and orders for money or goods purporting to be signed on behalf of the charity; and

    (c)   in all bills rendered by it and in all its invoices, receipts and letters of credit.

---

[24]   Amendment: Subsection omitted: Charities Act 2006, s 75, Sch 8, paras 96, 99(1), (3), Sch 9, for transitional provisions see s 75(3), Sch 10, para 18.

[25]   Amendment: Word substituted: Charities Act 2006, s 75(1), Sch 8, paras 96, 99(1), (4)(a), for transitional provisions see s 75(3), Sch 10, para 18.

[26]   Amendment: Words substituted: Charities Act 2006, s 75(1), Sch 8, paras 96, 99(1), (4)(b).

[27]   Amendment: Words substituted: Charities Act 2006, s 75(1), Sch 8, paras 96, 99(1), (4)(c).

[28]   Amendment: Words substituted: Charities Act 2006, s 75(1), Sch 8, paras 96, 99(1), (4)(b).

[29]   Amendment: Words substituted: Charities Act 2006, s 75(1), Sch 8, paras 96, 99(1), (5)(a), for transitional provisions see s 75(3), Sch 10, para 18.

[30]   Amendment: Words substituted: Charities Act 2006, s 75(1), Sch 8, paras 96, 99(1), (5)(b).

[31]   Amendment: Words substituted: Charities Act 2006, s 75(1), Sch 8, paras 96, 99(1), (5)(b).

[32]   Amendment: Words omitted: Charities Act 2006, s 75, Sch 8, paras 96, 99(1), (5)(c), Sch 9, for transitional provisions see s 75(3), Sch 10, para 18.

[33]   Amendment: Figure substituted: The Charities Act 1993 (Substitution of Sums) Order 1995, SI 1995/2696, art 2(2).

[34]   Amendment: Words omitted: Welsh Language Act 1993, ss 32(2), 35, Sch 2

[(2A) The statement required by subsection (2) above shall be in English, except that, in the case of a document which is otherwise wholly in Welsh, the statement may be in Welsh if it consists of or includes the words 'elusen cofrestredig' (the Welsh equivalent of 'registered charity').][35]

(3) Subsection (2)(a) above has effect whether the solicitation is express or implied, and whether the money or other property is to be given for any consideration or not.

(4) If, in the case of a registered charity to which this section applies, any person issues or authorises the issue of any document falling within paragraph (a) or (c) of subsection (2) above [which does not contain the statement][36] required by that subsection, he shall be guilty of an offence and liable on summary conviction to a fine not exceeding level 3 on the standard scale.

(5) If, in the case of any such registered charity, any person signs any document falling within paragraph (b) of subsection (2) above [which does not contain the statement][37] required by that subsection, he shall be guilty of an offence and liable on summary conviction to a fine not exceeding level 3 on the standard scale.

(6) The Secretary of State may by order amend subsection (1) above by substituting a different sum for the sum for the time being specified there.

Amendments—The Charities Act 1993 (Substitution of Sums) Order 1995, SI 1995 No 2696, art 2(2); Welsh Language Act 1993, s 32.

Charity names

6 Power of [Commission][38] to require charity's name to be changed

(1) Where this subsection applies to a charity, the [Commission][39] may give a direction requiring the name of the charity to be changed, within such period as is specified in the direction, to such other name as the charity trustees may determine with the approval of the [Commission][40].

(2) Subsection (1) above applies to a charity if—

    (a)   it is a registered charity and its name ('the registered name')—
        (i)   is the same as, or
        (ii)   is in the opinion of the [Commission][41] too like,
        the name, at the time when the registered name was entered in the register in respect of the charity, of any other charity (whether registered or not);
    (b)   the name of the charity is in the opinion of the [Commission][42] likely to mislead the public as to the true nature—
        (i)   of the purposes of the charity as set out in its trusts, or
        (ii)   of the activities which the charity carries on under its trusts in pursuit of those purposes;
    (c)   the name of the charity includes any word or expression for the time being specified in regulations made by the Secretary of State and the inclusion in its

---

[35] Amendment: Subsection inserted: Welsh Language Act 1993, s 32(3).
[36] Amendment: Words substituted: Welsh Language Act 1993, s 32(4).
[37] Amendment: Words substituted: Welsh Language Act 1993, s 32(5).
[38] Amendment: Word substituted: Charities Act 2006, s 75(1), Sch 8, paras 96, 100(1), (2).
[39] Amendment: Word substituted: Charities Act 2006, s 75(1), Sch 8, paras 96, 100(1), (2).
[40] Amendment: Word substituted: Charities Act 2006, s 75(1), Sch 8, paras 96, 100(1), (2).
[41] Amendment: Word substituted: Charities Act 2006, s 75(1), Sch 8, paras 96, 100(1), (2).
[42] Amendment: Word substituted: Charities Act 2006, s 75(1), Sch 8, paras 96, 100(1), (2).

name of that word or expression is in the opinion of the [Commission][43] likely to mislead the public in any respect as to the status of the charity;

(d) the name of the charity is in the opinion of the [Commission][44] likely to give the impression that the charity is connected in some way with Her Majesty's Government or any local authority, or with any other body of persons or any individual, when it is not so connected; or

(e) the name of the charity is in the opinion of the [Commission][45] offensive;

and in this subsection any reference to the name of a charity is, in relation to a registered charity, a reference to the name by which it is registered.

(3) Any direction given by virtue of subsection (2)(a) above must be given within twelve months of the time when the registered name was entered in the register in respect of the charity.

(4) Any direction given under this section with respect to a charity shall be given to the charity trustees; and on receiving any such direction the charity trustees shall give effect to it notwithstanding anything in the trusts of the charity.

(5) Where the name of any charity is changed under this section, then (without prejudice to [section 3B(3)][46] it shall be the duty of the charity trustees forthwith to notify the [Commission][47] of the charity's new name and of the date on which the change occurred.

(6) A change of name by a charity under this section does not affect any rights or obligations of the charity; and any legal proceedings that might have been continued or commenced by or against it in its former name may be continued or commenced by or against it in its new name.

(7) Section 26(3) of the Companies Act 1985 (minor variations in names to be disregarded) shall apply for the purposes of this section as if the reference to section 26(1)(c) of that Act were a reference to subsection (2)(a) above.

(8) Any reference in this section to the charity trustees of a charity shall, in relation to a charity which is a company, be read as a reference to the directors of the company.

(9) ...[48]

Amendments—Charities Act 2006, ss 12, 75, Sch 5, para 1, Sch 8, paras 96, 100, Sch 9.

7 Effect of direction under s. 6 where charity is a company

(1) Where any direction is given under section 6 above with respect to a charity which is a company, the direction shall be taken to require the name of the charity to be changed by resolution of the directors of the company.

(2) Section 380 of the Companies Act 1985 (registration etc of resolutions and agreements) shall apply to any resolution passed by the directors in compliance with any such direction.

(3) Where the name of such a charity is changed in compliance with any such direction, the registrar of companies—

---

43 Amendment: Word substituted: Charities Act 2006, s 75(1), Sch 8, paras 96, 100(1), (2).
44 Amendment: Word substituted: Charities Act 2006, s 75(1), Sch 8, paras 96, 100(1), (2).
45 Amendment: Word substituted: Charities Act 2006, s 75(1), Sch 8, paras 96, 100(1), (2).
46 Amendment: Words substituted: Charities Act 2006, s 75(1), Sch 8, paras 96, 100(1), (3).
47 Amendment: Word substituted: Charities Act 2006, s 75(1), Sch 8, paras 96, 100(1), (2).
48 Amendment: Subsection omitted: Charities Act 2006, ss 12, 75(2), Sch 5, para 1, Sch 9.

(a)   shall, subject to section 26 of the Companies Act 1985 (prohibition on registration of certain names), enter the new name on the register of companies in place of the former name, and

(b)   shall issue a certificate of incorporation altered to meet the circumstances of the case;

and the change of name has effect from the date on which the altered certificate is issued.

PART III
[INFORMATION POWERS][49]

8 General power to institute inquiries

(1) [The Commission][50] may from time to time institute inquiries with regard to charities or a particular charity or class of charities, either generally or for particular purposes, but no such inquiry shall extend to any exempt charity [except where this has been requested by its principal regulator.][51]

(2) [The Commission][52] may either conduct such an inquiry [itself][53] or appoint a person to conduct it and make a report [to the Commission][54].

(3) For the purposes of any such inquiry [the Commission, or a person appointed by the Commission][55] to conduct it, may direct any person (subject to the provisions of this section)—

(a)   to furnish accounts and statements in writing with respect to any matter in question at the inquiry, being a matter on which he has or can reasonably obtain information, or to return answers in writing to any questions or inquiries addressed to him on any such matter, and to verify any such accounts, statements or answers by statutory declaration;

(b)   to furnish copies of documents in his custody or under his control which relate to any matter in question at the inquiry, and to verify any such copies by statutory declaration;

(c)   to attend at a specified time and place and give evidence or produce any such documents.

(4) For the purposes of any such inquiry evidence may be taken on oath, and the person conducting the inquiry may for that purpose administer oaths, or may instead of administering an oath require the person examined to make and subscribe a declaration of the truth of the matters about which he is examined.

(5) [The Commission][56] may pay to any person the necessary expenses of his attendance to give evidence or produce documents for the purpose of an inquiry under this section, and a person shall not be required in obedience to a direction under paragraph (c) of subsection (3) above to go more than ten miles from his place of residence unless those expenses are paid or tendered to him.

---

[49]   Amendment: Words substituted: Charities Act 2006, s 75(1), Sch 8, paras 96, 101.

[50]   Amendment: Words substituted: Charities Act 2006, s 75(1), Sch 8, paras 96, 102(1), (2).

[51]   Amendment: Words inserted: Charities Act 2006, s 12, Sch 5, para 2.

[52]   Amendment: Words substituted: Charities Act 2006, s 75(1), Sch 8, paras 96, 102(1), (3)(a).

[53]   Amendment: Word substituted: Charities Act 2006, s 75(1), Sch 8, paras 96, 102(1), (3)(b).

[54]   Amendment: Words substituted: Charities Act 2006, s 75(1), Sch 8, paras 96, 102(1), (3)(c).

[55]   Amendment: Words substituted: Charities Act 2006, s 75(1), Sch 8, paras 96, 102(1), (4).

[56]   Amendment: Words substituted: Charities Act 2006, s 75(1), Sch 8, paras 96, 102(1), (5).

(6) Where an inquiry has been held under this section, [the Commission][57] may either—

(a) cause the report of the person conducting the inquiry, or such other statement of the results of the inquiry as [the Commission thinks][58] fit, to be printed and published, or

(b) publish any such report or statement in some other way which is calculated in [the Commission's opinion][59] to bring it to the attention of persons who may wish to make representations [to the Commission][60] about the action to be taken.

(7) The council of a county or district, the Common Council of the City of London and the council of a London borough may contribute to the expenses of [the Commission][61] in connection with inquiries under this section into local charities in the council's area.

Amendments—Charities Act 2006, ss 12, 75(1), Sch 5, para 2, Sch 8, paras 96, 102.

9 Power to call for documents and search records

(1) [The Commission][62] may by order—

(a) require any person to [furnish the Commission][63] with any information in his possession which relates to any charity and is relevant to the discharge of [the Commission's functions][64] or of the functions of the official custodian;

(b) require any person who has in his custody or under his control any document which relates to any charity and is relevant to the discharge of [the Commission's functions][65] or of the functions of the official custodian—

    (i) to [furnish the Commission][66] with a copy of or extract from the document, or

    (ii) (unless the document forms part of the records or other documents of a court or of a public or local authority) to transmit the document itself to [the Commission for its][67] inspection.

(2) Any [member of the staff of the Commission, if so authorised by it][68], shall be entitled without payment to inspect and take copies of or extracts from the records or other documents of any court, or of any public registry or office of records, for any purpose connected with the discharge of the functions of [the Commission][69] or of the official custodian.

(3) [The Commission][70] shall be entitled without payment to keep any copy or extract furnished [to it][71] under subsection (1) above; and where a document transmitted [to the

---

[57] Amendment: Words substituted: Charities Act 2006, s 75(1), Sch 8, paras 96, 102(1), (6)(a).
[58] Amendment: Words substituted: Charities Act 2006, s 75(1), Sch 8, paras 96, 102(1), (6)(b).
[59] Amendment: Words substituted: Charities Act 2006, s 75(1), Sch 8, paras 96, 102(1), (6)(c).
[60] Amendment: Words substituted: Charities Act 2006, s 75(1), Sch 8, paras 96, 102(1), (6)(d).
[61] Amendment: Words substituted: Charities Act 2006, s 75(1), Sch 8, paras 96, 102(1), (7).
[62] Amendment: Words substituted: Charities Act 2006, s 75(1), Sch 8, paras 96, 103(1), (2)(a).
[63] Amendment: Words substituted: Charities Act 2006, s 75(1), Sch 8, paras 96, 103(1), (2)(b).
[64] Amendment: Words substituted: Charities Act 2006, s 75(1), Sch 8, paras 96, 103(1), (2)(c).
[65] Amendment: Words substituted: Charities Act 2006, s 75(1), Sch 8, paras 96, 103(1), (2)(c).
[66] Amendment: Words substituted: Charities Act 2006, s 75(1), Sch 8, paras 96, 103(1), (2)(b).
[67] Amendment: Words substituted: Charities Act 2006, s 75(1), Sch 8, paras 96, 103(1), (2)(d).
[68] Amendment: Words substituted: Charities Act 2006, s 75(1), Sch 8, paras 96, 103(1), (3)(a).
[69] Amendment: Words substituted: Charities Act 2006, s 75(1), Sch 8, paras 96, 103(1), (3)(b).
[70] Amendment: Words substituted: Charities Act 2006, s 75(1), Sch 8, paras 96, 103(1), (4)(a).
[71] Amendment: Words substituted: Charities Act 2006, s 75(1), Sch 8, paras 96, 103(1), (4)(b).

Commission][72] under that subsection for [it to inspect][73] relates only to one or more charities and is not held by any person entitled as trustee or otherwise to the custody of it, [the Commission][74] may keep it or may deliver it to the charity trustees or to any other person who may be so entitled.

(4) ...[75]

(5) The rights conferred by subsection (2) above shall, in relation to information recorded otherwise than in legible form, include the right to require the information to be made available in legible form for inspection or for a copy or extract to be made of or from it.

[(6) In subsection (2) the reference to a member of the staff of the Commission includes the official custodian even if he is not a member of the staff of the Commission.][76]

Amendments—Charities Act 2006, ss 12, 75, Sch 5, para 3, Sch 8, paras 96, 103, Sch 9.

[10 Disclosure of information to Commission

(1) Any relevant public authority may disclose information to the Commission if the disclosure is made for the purpose of enabling or assisting the Commission to discharge any of its functions.

(2) But Revenue and Customs information may be disclosed under subsection (1) only if it relates to an institution, undertaking or body falling within one (or more) of the following paragraphs—

    (a)   a charity;
    (b)   an institution which is established for charitable, benevolent or philanthropic purposes;
    (c)   an institution by or in respect of which a claim for exemption has at any time been made under section 505(1) of the Income and Corporation Taxes Act 1988;
    (d)   a subsidiary undertaking of a charity;
    (e)   a body entered in the Scottish Charity Register which is managed or controlled wholly or mainly in or from England or Wales.

(3) In subsection (2)(d) above 'subsidiary undertaking of a charity' means an undertaking (as defined by section 259(1) of the Companies Act 1985) in relation to which—

    (a)   a charity is (or is to be treated as) a parent undertaking in accordance with the provisions of section 258 of, and Schedule 10A to, the Companies Act 1985, or
    (b)   two or more charities would, if they were a single charity, be (or be treated as) a parent undertaking in accordance with those provisions.

(4) For the purposes of the references to a parent undertaking—

    (a)   in subsection (3) above, and
    (b)   in section 258 of, and Schedule 10A to, the Companies Act 1985 as they apply for the purposes of that subsection,

---

[72]   Amendment: Words substituted: Charities Act 2006, s 75(1), Sch 8, paras 96, 103(1), (4)(c).
[73]   Amendment: Words substituted: Charities Act 2006, s 75(1), Sch 8, paras 96, 103(1), (4)(d).
[74]   Amendment: Words substituted: Charities Act 2006, s 75(1), Sch 8, paras 96, 103(1), (4)(e).
[75]   Amendment: Subsection omitted: Charities Act 2006, ss 12, 75(2), Sch 5, para 3, Sch 9.
[76]   Amendment: Subsection inserted: Charities Act 2006, s 75(1), Sch 8, paras 96, 103(1), (5).

'undertaking' includes a charity which is not an undertaking as defined by section 259(1) of that Act.][77]

Amendment—Charities Act 2006, s 75, Sch 8, paras 96, 104.

[10A Disclosure of information by Commission

(1) Subject to subsections (2) and (3) below, the Commission may disclose to any relevant public authority any information received by the Commission in connection with any of the Commission's functions—

(a) if the disclosure is made for the purpose of enabling or assisting the relevant public authority to discharge any of its functions, or

(b) if the information so disclosed is otherwise relevant to the discharge of any of the functions of the relevant public authority.

(2) In the case of information disclosed to the Commission under section 10(1) above, the Commission's power to disclose the information under subsection (1) above is exercisable subject to any express restriction subject to which the information was disclosed to the Commission.

(3) Subsection (2) above does not apply in relation to Revenue and Customs information disclosed to the Commission under section 10(1) above; but any such information may not be further disclosed (whether under subsection (1) above or otherwise) except with the consent of the Commissioners for Her Majesty's Revenue and Customs.

(4) Any responsible person who discloses information in contravention of subsection (3) above is guilty of an offence and liable—

(a) on summary conviction, to imprisonment for a term not exceeding 12 months or to a fine not exceeding the statutory maximum, or both;

(b) on conviction on indictment, to imprisonment for a term not exceeding two years or to a fine, or both.

(5) It is a defence for a responsible person charged with an offence under subsection (4) above of disclosing information to prove that he reasonably believed—

(a) that the disclosure was lawful, or

(b) that the information had already and lawfully been made available to the public.

(6) In the application of this section to Scotland or Northern Ireland, the reference to 12 months in subsection (4) is to be read as a reference to 6 months.

(7) In this section 'responsible person' means a person who is or was—

(a) a member of the Commission,

(b) a member of the staff of the Commission,

(c) a person acting on behalf of the Commission or a member of the staff of the Commission, or

(d) a member of a committee established by the Commission.][78]

Amendment—Charities Act 2006, s 75, Sch 8, paras 96, 104.

---

[77] Amendment: Section substituted: Charities Act 2006, s 75(1), Sch 8, paras 96, 104.

[78] Amendment: Section substituted for s 10: Charities Act 2006, s 75(1), Sch 8, paras 96, 104, for transitional provisions see s 75(3), Sch 10, para 20.

[10B Disclosure to and by principal regulators of exempt charities

(1) Sections 10 and 10A above apply with the modifications in subsections (2) to (4) below in relation to the disclosure of information to or by the principal regulator of an exempt charity.

(2) References in those sections to the Commission or to any of its functions are to be read as references to the principal regulator of an exempt charity or to any of the functions of that body or person as principal regulator in relation to the charity.

(3) Section 10 above has effect as if for subsections (2) and (3) there were substituted—

'(2) But Revenue and Customs information may be disclosed under subsection (1) only if it relates to—

   (a)   the exempt charity in relation to which the principal regulator has functions as such, or
   (b)   a subsidiary undertaking of the exempt charity.

(3) In subsection (2)(b) above "subsidiary undertaking of the exempt charity" means an undertaking (as defined by section 259(1) of the Companies Act 1985) in relation to which—

   (a)   the exempt charity is (or is to be treated as) a parent undertaking in accordance with the provisions of section 258 of, and Schedule 10A to, the Companies Act 1985, or
   (b)   the exempt charity and one or more other charities would, if they were a single charity, be (or be treated as) a parent undertaking in accordance with those provisions.'

(4) Section 10A above has effect as if for the definition of 'responsible person' in subsection (7) there were substituted a definition specified by regulations under section 13(4)(b) of the Charities Act 2006 (regulations prescribing principal regulators).

(5) Regulations under section 13(4)(b) of that Act may also make such amendments or other modifications of any enactment as the Secretary of State considers appropriate for securing that any disclosure provisions that would otherwise apply in relation to the principal regulator of an exempt charity do not apply in relation to that body or person in its or his capacity as principal regulator.

(6) In subsection (5) above 'disclosure provisions' means provisions having effect for authorising, or otherwise in connection with, the disclosure of information by or to the principal regulator concerned.][79]

Amendment—Charities Act 2006, s 75, Sch 8, paras 96, 104.

[10C Disclosure of information: supplementary

(1) In sections 10 and 10A above 'relevant public authority' means—

   (a)   any government department (including a Northern Ireland department),
   (b)   any local authority,
   (c)   any constable, and
   (d)   any other body or person discharging functions of a public nature (including a body or person discharging regulatory functions in relation to any description of activities).

---

[79]   Amendment: Section substituted for s 10: Charities Act 2006, s 75(1), Sch 8, paras 96, 104.

(2) In section 10A above 'relevant public authority' also includes any body or person within subsection (1)(d) above in a country or territory outside the United Kingdom.

(3) In sections 10 to 10B above and this section—

'enactment' has the same meaning as in the Charities Act 2006;
'Revenue and Customs information' means information held as mentioned in section 18(1) of the Commissioners for Revenue and Customs Act 2005.

(4) Nothing in sections 10 and 10A above (or in those sections as applied by section 10B(1) to (4) above) authorises the making of a disclosure which—

(a)   contravenes the Data Protection Act 1998, or
(b)   is prohibited by Part 1 of the Regulation of Investigatory Powers Act 2000.][80]

Amendment—Charities Act 2006, s 75, Sch 8, paras 96, 104.

11 Supply of false or misleading information to [Commission][81], etc

(1) Any person who knowingly or recklessly provides the [Commission][82] with information which is false or misleading in a material particular shall be guilty of an offence if the information—

(a)   is provided in purported compliance with a requirement imposed by or under this Act; or
(b)   is provided otherwise than as mentioned in paragraph (a) above but in circumstances in which the person providing the information intends, or could reasonably be expected to know, that it would be used by the [Commission][83] for the purpose of discharging [its functions][84] under this Act.

(2) Any person who wilfully alters, suppresses, conceals or destroys any document which he is or is liable to be required, by or under this Act, to produce to the [Commission][85] shall be guilty of an offence.

(3) Any person guilty of an offence under this section shall be liable—

(a)   on summary conviction, to a fine not exceeding the statutory maximum;
(b)   on conviction on indictment, to imprisonment for a term not exceeding two years or to a fine, or both.

(4) In this section references to the [Commission][86] include references to any person conducting an inquiry under section 8 above.

12 ...[87]

Amendments—Data Protection Act, s 74(2), Sch 16; Charities Act 2006, s 75(1), Sch 8, paras 96, 105.

---

[80]   Amendment: Section substituted for s 10: Charities Act 2006, s 75(1), Sch 8, paras 96, 104.
[81]   Amendment: Word substituted: Charities Act 2006, s 75(1), Sch 8, paras 96, 105(1), (2).
[82]   Amendment: Word substituted: Charities Act 2006, s 75(1), Sch 8, paras 96, 105(1), (2).
[83]   Amendment: Word substituted: Charities Act 2006, s 75(1), Sch 8, paras 96, 105(1), (2).
[84]   Amendment: Word substituted: Charities Act 2006, s 75(1), Sch 8, paras 96, 105(1), (3).
[85]   Amendment: Word substituted: Charities Act 2006, s 75(1), Sch 8, paras 96, 105(1), (2).
[86]   Amendment: Word substituted: Charities Act 2006, s 75(1), Sch 8, paras 96, 105(1), (2).
[87]   Amendment: Section repealed: Data Protection Act s 74(2), Sch 16.

PART IV
APPLICATION OF PROPERTY CY-PRÈS AND ASSISTANCE AND
SUPERVISION OF CHARITIES BY COURT [AND COMMISSION][88]

Extended powers of court and variation of charters

13 Occasions for applying property cy-près

(1) Subject to subsection (2) below, the circumstances in which the original purposes of a charitable gift can be altered to allow the property given or part of it to be applied cy-près shall be as follows—

   (a)   where the original purposes, in whole or in part—
      (i)   have been as far as may be fulfilled; or
      (ii)   cannot be carried out, or not according to the directions given and to the spirit of the gift; or
   (b)   where the original purposes provide a use for part only of the property available by virtue of the gift; or
   (c)   where the property available by virtue of the gift and other property applicable for similar purposes can be more effectively used in conjunction, and to that end can suitably, regard being had to [the appropriate considerations][89], be made applicable to common purposes; or
   (d)   where the original purposes were laid down by reference to an area which then was but has since ceased to be a unit for some other purpose, or by reference to a class of persons or to an area which has for any reason since ceased to be suitable, regard being had to [the appropriate considerations][90], or to be practical in administering the gift; or
   (e)   where the original purposes, in whole or in part, have, since they were laid down,—
      (i)   been adequately provided for by other means; or
      (ii)   ceased, as being useless or harmful to the community or for other reasons, to be in law charitable; or
      (iii)   ceased in any other way to provide a suitable and effective method of using the property available by virtue of the gift, regard being had to [the appropriate considerations][91].

[(1A) In subsection (1) above 'the appropriate considerations' means—

   (a)   (on the one hand) the spirit of the gift concerned, and
   (b)   (on the other) the social and economic circumstances prevailing at the time of the proposed alteration of the original purposes.][92]

(2) Subsection (1) above shall not affect the conditions which must be satisfied in order that property given for charitable purposes may be applied cy-près except in so far as those conditions require a failure of the original purposes.

(3) References in the foregoing subsections to the original purposes of a gift shall be construed, where the application of the property given has been altered or regulated by a scheme or otherwise, as referring to the purposes for which the property is for the time being applicable.

---

[88]   Amendment: Word substituted: Charities Act 2006, s 75(1), Sch 8, paras 96, 106.
[89]   Amendment: Words substituted: Charities Act 2006, s 15(1), (2).
[90]   Amendment: Words substituted: Charities Act 2006, s 15(1), (2).
[91]   Amendment: Words substituted: Charities Act 2006, s15(1), (2).
[92]   Amendment: Subsection inserted: Charities Act 2006, s 15(1), (3).

(4) Without prejudice to the power to make schemes in circumstances falling within subsection (1) above, the court may by scheme made under the court's jurisdiction with respect to charities, in any case where the purposes for which the property is held are laid down by reference to any such area as is mentioned in the first column in Schedule 3 to this Act, provide for enlarging the area to any such area as is mentioned in the second column in the same entry in that Schedule.

(5) It is hereby declared that a trust for charitable purposes places a trustee under a duty, where the case permits and requires the property or some part of it to be applied cy-près, to secure its effective use for charity by taking steps to enable it to be so applied.

Amendments—Charities Act 2006, s 15.

14 Application cy-près of gifts of donors unknown or disclaiming

(1) Property given for specific charitable purposes which fail shall be applicable cy-près as if given for charitable purposes generally, where it belongs—

    (a)   to a donor who after—
        (i)   the prescribed advertisements and inquiries have been published and made, and
        (ii)   the prescribed period beginning with the publication of those advertisements has expired,
        cannot be identified or cannot be found; or

    (b)   to a donor who has executed a disclaimer in the prescribed form of his right to have the property returned.

(2) Where the prescribed advertisements and inquiries have been published and made by or on behalf of trustees with respect to any such property, the trustees shall not be liable to any person in respect of the property if no claim by him to be interested in it is received by them before the expiry of the period mentioned in subsection (1)(a)(ii) above.

(3) For the purposes of this section property shall be conclusively presumed (without any advertisement or inquiry) to belong to donors who cannot be identified, in so far as it consists—

    (a)   of the proceeds of cash collections made by means of collecting boxes or by other means not adapted for distinguishing one gift from another; or

    (b)   of the proceeds of any lottery, competition, entertainment, sale or similar money-raising activity, after allowing for property given to provide prizes or articles for sale or otherwise to enable the activity to be undertaken.

(4) The court [or the Commission][93] may by order direct that property not falling within subsection (3) above shall for the purposes of this section be treated (without any advertisement or inquiry) as belonging to donors who cannot be identified where it appears to the court [or the Commission][94] either—

    (a)   that it would be unreasonable, having regard to the amounts likely to be returned to the donors, to incur expense with a view to returning the property; or

    (b)   that it would be unreasonable, having regard to the nature, circumstances and amounts of the gifts, and to the lapse of time since the gifts were made, for the donors to expect the property to be returned.

---

[93]   Amendment: Words inserted: Charities Act 2006, s 16(1), (2).
[94]   Amendment: Words inserted: Charities Act 2006, s 16(1), (2).

(5) Where property is applied cy-près by virtue of this section, the donor shall be deemed to have parted with all his interest at the time when the gift was made; but where property is so applied as belonging to donors who cannot be identified or cannot be found, and is not so applied by virtue of subsection (3) or (4) above—

(a)   the scheme shall specify the total amount of that property; and

(b)   the donor of any part of that amount shall be entitled, if he makes a claim not later than six months after the date on which the scheme is made, to recover from the charity for which the property is applied a sum equal to that part, less any expenses properly incurred by the charity trustees after that date in connection with claims relating to his gift; and

(c)   the scheme may include directions as to the provision to be made for meeting any such claim.

(6) Where—

(a)   any sum is, in accordance with any such directions, set aside for meeting any such claims, but

(b)   the aggregate amount of any such claims actually made exceeds the relevant amount,

then, if [the Commission so directs][95], each of the donors in question shall be entitled only to such proportion of the relevant amount as the amount of his claim bears to the aggregate amount referred to in paragraph (b) above; and for this purpose 'the relevant amount' means the amount of the sum so set aside after deduction of any expenses properly incurred by the charity trustees in connection with claims relating to the donors' gifts.

(7) For the purposes of this section, charitable purposes shall be deemed to 'fail' where any difficulty in applying property to those purposes makes that property or the part not applicable cy-près available to be returned to the donors.

(8) In this section 'prescribed' means prescribed by regulations made by [the Commission][96]; and such regulations may, as respects the advertisements which are to be published for the purposes of subsection (1)(a) above, make provision as to the form and content of such advertisements as well as the manner in which they are to be published.

(9) Any regulations made by [the Commission][97] under this section shall be published by [the Commission][98] in such manner as [it thinks fit][99].

(10) In this section, except in so far as the context otherwise requires, references to a donor include persons claiming through or under the original donor, and references to property given include the property for the time being representing the property originally given or property derived from it.

(11) This section shall apply to property given for charitable purposes, notwithstanding that it was so given before the commencement of this Act.

Amendments—Charities Act 2006, ss 16, 75(1), Sch 8, paras 96, 107.

---

[95]   Amendment: Words substituted: Charities Act 2006, s 75(1), Sch 8, paras 96, 107(1), (2).
[96]   Amendment: Words substituted: Charities Act 2006, s 75(1), Sch 8, paras 96, 107(1), (3).
[97]   Amendment: Words substituted: Charities Act 2006, s 75(1), Sch 8, paras 96, 107(1), (4)(a).
[98]   Amendment: Words substituted: Charities Act 2006, s 75(1), Sch 8, paras 96, 107(1), (4)(a).
[99]   Amendment: Words substituted: Charities Act 2006, s 75(1), Sch 8, paras 96, 107(1), (4)(b).

14A Application cy-près of gifts made in response to certain solicitations

(1) This section applies to property given—

    (a)   for specific charitable purposes, and

    (b)   in response to a solicitation within subsection (2) below.

(2) A solicitation is within this subsection if—

    (a)   it is made for specific charitable purposes, and

    (b)   it is accompanied by a statement to the effect that property given in response to it will, in the event of those purposes failing, be applicable cy-près as if given for charitable purposes generally, unless the donor makes a relevant declaration at the time of making the gift.

(3) A 'relevant declaration' is a declaration in writing by the donor to the effect that, in the event of the specific charitable purposes failing, he wishes the trustees holding the property to give him the opportunity to request the return of the property in question (or a sum equal to its value at the time of the making of the gift).

(4) Subsections (5) and (6) below apply if—

    (a)   a person has given property as mentioned in subsection (1) above,

    (b)   the specific charitable purposes fail, and

    (c)   the donor has made a relevant declaration.

(5) The trustees holding the property must take the prescribed steps for the purpose of—

    (a)   informing the donor of the failure of the purposes,

    (b)   enquiring whether he wishes to request the return of the property (or a sum equal to its value), and

    (c)   if within the prescribed period he makes such a request, returning the property (or such a sum) to him.

(6) If those trustees have taken all appropriate prescribed steps but—

    (a)   they have failed to find the donor, or

    (b)   the donor does not within the prescribed period request the return of the property (or a sum equal to its value),

section 14(1) above shall apply to the property as if it belonged to a donor within paragraph (b) of that subsection (application of property where donor has disclaimed right to return of property).

(7) If—

    (a)   a person has given property as mentioned in subsection (1) above,

    (b)   the specific charitable purposes fail, and

    (c)   the donor has not made a relevant declaration,

section 14(1) above shall similarly apply to the property as if it belonged to a donor within paragraph (b) of that subsection.

(8) For the purposes of this section—

    (a)   'solicitation' means a solicitation made in any manner and however communicated to the persons to whom it is addressed,

    (b)   it is irrelevant whether any consideration is or is to be given in return for the property in question, and

(c)   where any appeal consists of both solicitations that are accompanied by statements within subsection (2)(b) and solicitations that are not so accompanied, a person giving property as a result of the appeal is to be taken to have responded to the former solicitations and not the latter, unless he proves otherwise.

(9) In this section 'prescribed' means prescribed by regulations made by the Commission, and any such regulations shall be published by the Commission in such manner as it thinks fit.

(10) Subsections (7) and (10) of section 14 shall apply for the purposes of this section as they apply for the purposes of section 14.][100]

Amendment—Charities Act 2006, s 17.

[14B Cy-près schemes

(1) The power of the court or the Commission to make schemes for the application of property cy-près shall be exercised in accordance with this section.

(2) Where any property given for charitable purposes is applicable cy-près, the court or the Commission may make a scheme providing for the property to be applied—

(a)   for such charitable purposes, and
(b)   (if the scheme provides for the property to be transferred to another charity) by or on trust for such other charity,

as it considers appropriate, having regard to the matters set out in subsection (3).

(3) The matters are—

(a)   the spirit of the original gift,
(b)   the desirability of securing that the property is applied for charitable purposes which are close to the original purposes, and
(c)   the need for the relevant charity to have purposes which are suitable and effective in the light of current social and economic circumstances.

The 'relevant charity' means the charity by or on behalf of which the property is to be applied under the scheme.

(4) If a scheme provides for the property to be transferred to another charity, the scheme may impose on the charity trustees of that charity a duty to secure that the property is applied for purposes which are, so far as is reasonably practicable, similar in character to the original purposes.

(5) In this section references to property given include the property for the time being representing the property originally given or property derived from it.

(6) In this section references to the transfer of property to a charity are references to its transfer—

(a)   to the charity, or
(b)   to the charity trustees, or
(c)   to any trustee for the charity, or
(d)   to a person nominated by the charity trustees to hold it in trust for the charity,

---

[100]   Amendment: Section inserted: Charities Act 2006, s 17.

as the scheme may provide.][101]

Amendment—Charities Act 2006, s 18.

15 Charities governed by charter, or by or under statute

(1) Where a Royal charter establishing or regulating a body corporate is amendable by the grant and acceptance of a further charter, a scheme relating to the body corporate or to the administration of property held by the body (including a scheme for the cy-près application of any such property) may be made by the court under the court's jurisdiction with respect to charities notwithstanding that the scheme cannot take effect without the alteration of the charter, but shall be so framed that the scheme, or such part of it as cannot take effect without the alteration of the charter, does not purport to come into operation unless or until Her Majesty thinks fit to amend the charter in such manner as will permit the scheme or that part of it to have effect.

(2) Where under the court's jurisdiction with respect to charities or the corresponding jurisdiction of a court in Northern Ireland, or under powers conferred by this Act or by any Northern Ireland legislation relating to charities, a scheme is made with respect to a body corporate, and it appears to Her Majesty expedient, having regard to the scheme, to amend any Royal charter relating to that body, Her Majesty may, on the application of that body, amend the charter accordingly by Order in Council in any way in which the charter could be amended by the grant and acceptance of a further charter; and any such Order in Council may be revoked or varied in like manner as the charter it amends.

(3) The jurisdiction of the court with respect to charities shall not be excluded or restricted in the case of a charity of any description mentioned in Schedule 4 to this Act by the operation of the enactments or instruments there mentioned in relation to that description, and a scheme established for any such charity may modify or supersede in relation to it the provision made by any such enactment or instrument as if made by a scheme of the court, and may also make any such provision as is authorised by that Schedule.

[Powers of Commission][102] to make schemes and act for protection of charities etc

16 Concurrent jurisdiction with High Court for certain purposes

(1) Subject to the provisions of this Act, [the Commission][103] may by order exercise the same jurisdiction and powers as are exercisable by the High Court in charity proceedings for the following purposes—

(a) establishing a scheme for the administration of a charity;
(b) appointing, discharging or removing a charity trustee or trustee for a charity, or removing an officer or employee;
(c) vesting or transferring property, or requiring or entitling any person to call for or make any transfer of property or any payment.

(2) Where the court directs a scheme for the administration of a charity to be established, the court may by order refer the matter to [the Commission for it][104] to prepare or settle a scheme in accordance with such directions (if any) as the court sees fit

---

[101] Amendment: Section inserted: Charities Act 2006, s 18, for transitional provisions see s 75(3), Sch 10, para 3.
[102] Amendment: Words substituted: Charities Act 2006, s 75(1), Sch 8, paras 96, 108.
[103] Amendment: Words substituted: Charities Act 2006, s 75(1), Sch 8, paras 96, 109(1), (2).
[104] Amendment: Words substituted: Charities Act 2006, s 75(1), Sch 8, paras 96, 109(1), (3)(a).

to give, and any such order may provide for the scheme to be put into effect by order of [the Commission][105] as if prepared under subsection (1) above and without any further order of the court.

(3) [The Commission][106] shall not have jurisdiction under this section to try or determine the title at law or in equity to any property as between a charity or trustee for a charity and a person holding or claiming the property or an interest in it adversely to the charity, or to try or determine any question as to the existence or extent of any charge or trust.

(4) Subject to the following subsections, [the Commission shall not exercise its][107] jurisdiction under this section as respects any charity, except—

    (a)   on the application of the charity; or
    (b)   on an order of the court under subsection (2) above; or
    (c)   ...[108] on the application of the Attorney General.

(5) In the case of a charity ...[109] whose [gross income does not][110] exceed £500 a year, [the Commission may exercise its][111] jurisdiction under this section on the application—

    (a)   of any one or more of the charity trustees; or
    (b)   of any person interested in the charity; or
    (c)   of any two or more inhabitants of the area of the charity if it is a local charity.

(6) Where in the case of a charity, other than an exempt charity, [the Commission is][112] satisfied that the charity trustees ought in the interests of the charity to apply for a scheme, but have unreasonably refused or neglected to do so and [the Commission has][113] given the charity trustees an opportunity to make representations to them, [the Commission][114] may proceed as if an application for a scheme had been made by the charity but [the Commission][115] shall not have power in a case where [it acts][116] by virtue of this subsection to alter the purposes of a charity, unless forty years have elapsed from the date of its foundation.

(7) Where—

    (a)   a charity cannot apply to [the Commission][117] for a scheme by reason of any vacancy among the charity trustees or the absence or incapacity of any of them, but
    (b)   such an application is made by such number of the charity trustees as [the Commission considers][118] appropriate in the circumstances of the case,

[the Commission][119] may nevertheless proceed as if the application were an application made by the charity.

---

[105]   Amendment: Words substituted: Charities Act 2006, s 75(1), Sch 8, paras 96, 109(1), (3)(b).
[106]   Amendment: Words substituted: Charities Act 2006, s 75(1), Sch 8, paras 96, 109(1), (4).
[107]   Amendment: Words substituted: Charities Act 2006, s 75(1), Sch 8, paras 96, 109(1), (5).
[108]   Amendment: Words omitted: Charities Act 2006, ss 12, 75(2), Sch 5, para 4(1), (2), Sch 9.
[109]   Amendment: Words omitted: Charities Act 2006, ss 12, 75(2), Sch 5, para 4(1), (3), Sch 9.
[110]   Amendment: Words substituted: Charities Act 2006, s 75(1), Sch 8, paras 96, 109(1), (6)(a).
[111]   Amendment: Words substituted: Charities Act 2006, s 75(1), Sch 8, paras 96, 109(1), (6)(b).
[112]   Amendment: Words substituted: Charities Act 2006, s 75(1), Sch 8, paras 96, 109(1), (7)(a).
[113]   Amendment: Words substituted: Charities Act 2006, s 75(1), Sch 8, paras 96, 109(1), (7)(b).
[114]   Amendment: Words substituted: Charities Act 2006, s 75(1), Sch 8, paras 96, 109(1), (7)(c).
[115]   Amendment: Words substituted: Charities Act 2006, s 75(1), Sch 8, paras 96, 109(1), (7)(c).
[116]   Amendment: Words substituted: Charities Act 2006, s 75(1), Sch 8, paras 96, 109(1), (7)(d).
[117]   Amendment: Words substituted: Charities Act 2006, s 75(1), Sch 8, paras 96, 109(1), (8)(a).
[118]   Amendment: Words substituted: Charities Act 2006, s 75(1), Sch 8, paras 96, 109(1), (8)(b).
[119]   Amendment: Words substituted: Charities Act 2006, s 75(1), Sch 8, paras 96, 109(1), (8)(a).

(8) [The Commission][120] may on the application of any charity trustee or trustee for a charity exercise [its jurisdiction][121] under this section for the purpose of discharging him from his trusteeship.

(9) Before exercising any jurisdiction under this section otherwise than on an order of the court, [the Commission shall give notice of its][122] intention to do so to each of the charity trustees, except any that cannot be found or has no known address in the United Kingdom or who is party or privy to an application for the exercise of the jurisdiction; and any such notice may be given by post, and, if given by post, may be addressed to the recipient's last known address in the United Kingdom.

(10) [The Commission shall not exercise its][123] jurisdiction under this section in any case (not referred to them by order of the court) which, by reason of its contentious character, or of any special question of law or of fact which it may involve, or for other reasons, [the Commission][124] may consider more fit to be adjudicated on by the court.

(11)–(14) ...[125]

(15) If the Secretary of State thinks it expedient to do so—

(a)   in consequence of changes in the value of money, or
(b)   with a view to increasing the number of charities in respect of which [the Commission may exercise its][126] jurisdiction under this section in accordance with subsection (5) above,

he may by order amend that subsection by substituting a different sum for the sum for the time being specified there.

Amendments—Charities Act 2006, ss 12, 75, Sch 5, para 4, Sch 8, paras 96, 109, Sch 9.

17 Further powers to make schemes or alter application of charitable property

(1) Where it appears to [the Commission][127] that a scheme should be established for the administration of a charity, but also that it is necessary or desirable for the scheme to alter the provision made by an Act of Parliament establishing or regulating the charity or to make any other provision which goes or might go beyond the powers exercisable [by the Commission][128] apart from this section, or that it is for any reason proper for the scheme to be subject to parliamentary review, then (subject to subsection (6) below) [the Commission][129] may settle a scheme accordingly with a view to its being given effect under this section.

(2) A scheme settled by [the Commission][130] under this section may be given effect by order of the Secretary of State, and a draft of the order shall be laid before Parliament.

(3) Without prejudice to the operation of section 6 of the Statutory Instruments Act 1946 in other cases, in the case of a scheme which goes beyond the powers

---

[120]   Amendment: Words substituted: Charities Act 2006, s 75(1), Sch 8, paras 96, 109(1), (9)(a).
[121]   Amendment: Words substituted: Charities Act 2006, s 75(1), Sch 8, paras 96, 109(1), (9)(b).
[122]   Amendment: Words substituted: Charities Act 2006, s 75(1), Sch 8, paras 96, 109(1), (10).
[123]   Amendment: Words substituted: Charities Act 2006, s 75(1), Sch 8, paras 96, 109(1), (11)(a).
[124]   Amendment: Words substituted: Charities Act 2006, s 75(1), Sch 8, paras 96, 109(1), (11)(b).
[125]   Amendment: Subsections omitted: Charities Act 2006, s 75, Sch 8, paras 96, 109(1), (12), Sch 9, for transitional provisions see s 75(3), Sch 10, para 18.
[126]   Amendment: Words substituted: Charities Act 2006, s 75(1), Sch 8, paras 96, 109(1), (13).
[127]   Amendment: Words substituted: Charities Act 2006, s 75(1), Sch 8, paras 96, 110(1), (2)(a).
[128]   Amendment: Words substituted: Charities Act 2006, s 75(1), Sch 8, paras 96, 110(1), (2)(b).
[129]   Amendment: Words substituted: Charities Act 2006, s 75(1), Sch 8, paras 96, 110(1), (2)(a).
[130]   Amendment: Words substituted: Charities Act 2006, s 75(1), Sch 8, paras 96, 110(1), (3).

exercisable apart from this section in altering a statutory provision contained in or having effect under any public general Act of Parliament, the order shall not be made unless the draft has been approved by resolution of each House of Parliament.

(4) Subject to subsection (5) below, any provision of a scheme brought into effect under this section may be modified or superseded by the court or [the Commission][131] as if it were a scheme brought into effect by order of [the Commission][132] under section 16 above.

(5) Where subsection (3) above applies to a scheme, the order giving effect to it may direct that the scheme shall not be modified or superseded by a scheme brought into effect otherwise than under this section, and may also direct that that subsection shall apply to any scheme modifying or superseding the scheme to which the order gives effect.

(6) The [Commission][133] shall not proceed under this section without the like application and the like notice to the charity trustees, as would be required [if the Commission was][134] proceeding (without an order of the court) under section 16 above; but on any application for a scheme, or in a case where [it acts][135] by virtue of subsection (6) or (7) of that section, the [Commission][136] may proceed under this section or that section as appears [to it][137] appropriate.

(7) Notwithstanding anything in the trusts of a charity, no expenditure incurred in preparing or promoting a Bill in Parliament shall without the consent of the court or [the Commission][138] be defrayed out of any moneys applicable for the purposes of a charity ...[139].

(8) Where [the Commission is][140] satisfied—

(a)   that the whole of the income of a charity cannot in existing circumstances be effectively applied for the purposes of the charity; and

(b)   that, if those circumstances continue, a scheme might be made for applying the surplus cy-près; and

(c)   that it is for any reason not yet desirable to make such a scheme;

then [the Commission][141] may by order authorise the charity trustees at their discretion (but subject to any conditions imposed by the order) to apply any accrued or accruing income for any purposes for which it might be made applicable by such a scheme, and any application authorised by the order shall be deemed to be within the purposes of the charity.

(9) An order under subsection (8) above shall not extend to more than £300 out of income accrued before the date of the order, nor to income accruing more than three years after that date, nor to more than £100 out of the income accruing in any of those three years.

---

[131]   Amendment: Words substituted: Charities Act 2006, s 75(1), Sch 8, paras 96, 110(1), (4).
[132]   Amendment: Words substituted: Charities Act 2006, s 75(1), Sch 8, paras 96, 110(1), (4).
[133]   Amendment: Word substituted: Charities Act 2006, s 75(1), Sch 8, paras 96, 110(1), (5)(a).
[134]   Amendment: Words substituted: Charities Act 2006, s 75(1), Sch 8, paras 96, 110(1), (5)(b).
[135]   Amendment: Words substituted: Charities Act 2006, s 75(1), Sch 8, paras 96, 110(1), (5)(c).
[136]   Amendment: Word substituted: Charities Act 2006, s 75(1), Sch 8, paras 96, 110(1), (5)(a).
[137]   Amendment: Words substituted: Charities Act 2006, s 75(1), Sch 8, paras 96, 110(1), (5)(d).
[138]   Amendment: Words substituted: Charities Act 2006, s 75(1), Sch 8, paras 96, 110(1), (6).
[139]   Amendment: Words omitted: Charities Act 2006, ss 12, 75(2), Sch 5, para 5, Sch 9.
[140]   Amendment: Words substituted: Charities Act 2006, s 75(1), Sch 8, paras 96, 110(1), (7)(a).
[141]   Amendment: Words substituted: Charities Act 2006, s 75(1), Sch 8, paras 96, 110(1), (7)(b).

Amendments—Charities Act 2006, ss 12, 75, Sch 5, para 5, Sch 8, paras 96, 110, Sch 9.

18 Power to act for protection of charities

(1) Where, at any time [after it has][142] instituted an inquiry under section 8 above with respect to any charity, [the Commission is][143] satisfied—

(a) that there is or has been any misconduct or mismanagement in the administration of the charity; or

(b) that it is necessary or desirable to act for the purpose of protecting the property of the charity or securing a proper application for the purposes of the charity of that property or of property coming to the charity,

[the Commission may of its][144] own motion do one or more of the following things—

(i) by order suspend any trustee, charity trustee, officer, agent or employee of the charity from the exercise of his office or employment pending consideration being given to his removal (whether under this section or otherwise);

(ii) by order appoint such number of additional charity trustees [as it considers][145] necessary for the proper administration of the charity;

(iii) by order vest any property held by or in trust for the charity in the official custodian, or require the persons in whom any such property is vested to transfer it to him, or appoint any person to transfer any such property to him;

(iv) order any person who holds any property on behalf of the charity, or of any trustee for it, not to part with the property without the approval of [the Commission][146];

(v) order any debtor of the charity not to make any payment in or towards the discharge of his liability to the charity without the approval of [the Commission][147];

(vi) by order restrict (notwithstanding anything in the trusts of the charity) the transactions which may be entered into, or the nature or amount of the payments which may be made, in the administration of the charity without the approval of [the Commission][148];

(vii) by order appoint (in accordance with section 19 below) [an interim manager, who shall act as receiver][149] and manager in respect of the property and affairs of the charity.

(2) Where, at any time after [it has][150] instituted an inquiry under section 8 above with respect to any charity, [the Commission is][151] satisfied—

(a) that there is or has been any misconduct or mismanagement in the administration of the charity; and

(b) that it is necessary or desirable to act for the purpose of protecting the property of the charity or securing a proper application for the purposes of the charity of that property or of property coming to the charity,

---

142 Amendment: Words substituted: Charities Act 2006, s 75(1), Sch 8, paras 96, 111(1), (2)(a).
143 Amendment: Words substituted: Charities Act 2006, s 75(1), Sch 8, paras 96, 111(1), (2)(b).
144 Amendment: Words substituted: Charities Act 2006, s 75(1), Sch 8, paras 96, 111(1), (2)(c).
145 Amendment: Words substituted: Charities Act 2006, s 75(1), Sch 8, paras 96, 111(1), (2)(d).
146 Amendment: Words substituted: Charities Act 2006, s 75(1), Sch 8, paras 96, 111(1), (2)(e).
147 Amendment: Words substituted: Charities Act 2006, s 75(1), Sch 8, paras 96, 111(1), (2)(e).
148 Amendment: Words substituted: Charities Act 2006, s 75(1), Sch 8, paras 96, 111(1), (2)(e).
149 Amendment: Words substituted: Charities Act 2006, s 75(1), Sch 8, paras 96, 111(1), (2)(f).
150 Amendment: Words substituted: Charities Act 2006, s 75(1), Sch 8, paras 96, 111(1), (3)(a).
151 Amendment: Words substituted: Charities Act 2006, s 75(1), Sch 8, paras 96, 111(1), (3)(b).

[the Commission may of its]^{152} own motion do either or both of the following things—

(i)   by order remove any trustee, charity trustee, officer, agent or employee of the charity who has been responsible for or privy to the misconduct or mismanagement or has by his conduct contributed to it or facilitated it;

(ii)   by order establish a scheme for the administration of the charity.

(3) The references in subsection (1) or (2) above to misconduct or mismanagement shall (notwithstanding anything in the trusts of the charity) extend to the employment for the remuneration or reward of persons acting in the affairs of the charity, or for other administrative purposes, of sums which are excessive in relation to the property which is or is likely to be applied or applicable for the purposes of the charity.

(4) [The Commission]^{153} may also remove a charity trustee by order made of [its own motion]^{154}—

(a)   where, within the last five years, the trustee—
(i)   having previously been adjudged bankrupt or had his estate sequestrated, has been discharged, or
(ii)   having previously made a composition or arrangement with, or granted a trust deed for, his creditors, has been discharged in respect of it;
(b)   where the trustee is a corporation in liquidation;
(c)   where the trustee is incapable of acting by reason of mental disorder within the meaning of the Mental Health Act 1983;
(d)   where the trustee has not acted, and will not declare his willingness or unwillingness to act;
(e)   where the trustee is outside England and Wales or cannot be found or does not act, and his absence or failure to act impedes the proper administration of the charity.

(5) [The Commission may by order made of its]^{155} own motion appoint a person to be a charity trustee—

(a)   in place of a charity trustee [removed by the Commission]^{156} under this section or otherwise;
(b)   where there are no charity trustees, or where by reason of vacancies in their number or the absence or incapacity of any of their number the charity cannot apply for the appointment;
(c)   where there is a single charity trustee, not being a corporation aggregate, and [the Commission is of]^{157} opinion that it is necessary to increase the number for the proper administration of the charity;
(d)   where [the Commission is of]^{158} opinion that it is necessary for the proper administration of the charity to have an additional charity trustee because one of the existing charity trustees who ought nevertheless to remain a charity trustee either cannot be found or does not act or is outside England and Wales.

---

^{152} Amendment: Words substituted: Charities Act 2006, s 75(1), Sch 8, paras 96, 111(1), (3)(c).
^{153} Amendment: Words substituted: Charities Act 2006, s 75(1), Sch 8, paras 96, 111(1), (4)(a).
^{154} Amendment: Words substituted: Charities Act 2006, s 75(1), Sch 8, paras 96, 111(1), (4)(b).
^{155} Amendment: Words substituted: Charities Act 2006, s 75(1), Sch 8, paras 96, 111(1), (5)(a).
^{156} Amendment: Words substituted: Charities Act 2006, s 75(1), Sch 8, paras 96, 111(1), (5)(b).
^{157} Amendment: Words substituted: Charities Act 2006, s 75(1), Sch 8, paras 96, 111(1), (5)(c).
^{158} Amendment: Words substituted: Charities Act 2006, s 75(1), Sch 8, paras 96, 111(1), (5)(c).

(6) The powers of [the Commission][159] under this section to remove or appoint charity trustees of [its own motion][160] shall include power to make any such order with respect to the vesting in or transfer to the charity trustees of any property as [the Commission][161] could make on the removal or appointment of a charity trustee [by it][162] under section 16 above.

(7) Any order under this section for the removal or appointment of a charity trustee or trustee for a charity, or for the vesting or transfer of any property, shall be of the like effect as an order made under section 16 above.

(8)–(10) ...[163]

(11) The power of [the Commission][164] to make an order under subsection (1)(i) above shall not be exercisable so as to suspend any person from the exercise of his office or employment for a period of more than twelve months; but (without prejudice to the generality of section 89(1) below), any such order made in the case of any person may make provision as respects the period of his suspension for matters arising out of it, and in particular for enabling any person to execute any instrument in his name or otherwise act for him and, in the case of a charity trustee, for adjusting any rules governing the proceedings of the charity trustees to take account of the reduction in the number capable of acting.

(12) Before exercising any jurisdiction under this section otherwise than by virtue of subsection (1) above, [the Commission][165] shall give notice of [its intention][166] to do so to each of the charity trustees, except any that cannot be found or has no known address in the United Kingdom; and any such notice may be given by post and, if given by post, may be addressed to the recipient's last known address in the United Kingdom.

(13) [The Commission][167] shall, at such intervals as [it thinks fit][168], review any order made [by it][169] under paragraph (i), or any of paragraphs (iii) to (vii), of subsection (1) above; and, if on any such review it appears [to the Commission][170] that it would be appropriate to discharge the order in whole or in part, [the Commission shall][171] so discharge it (whether subject to any savings or other transitional provisions or not).

(14) If any person contravenes an order under subsection (1)(iv), (v) or (vi) above, he shall be guilty of an offence and liable on summary conviction to a fine not exceeding level 5 on the standard scale.

(15) Subsection (14) above shall not be taken to preclude the bringing of proceedings for breach of trust against any charity trustee or trustee for a charity in respect of a contravention of an order under subsection (1)(iv) or (vi) above (whether proceedings in respect of the contravention are brought against him under subsection (14) above or not).

---

[159] Amendment: Words substituted: Charities Act 2006, s 75(1), Sch 8, paras 96, 111(1), (6)(a).
[160] Amendment: Words substituted: Charities Act 2006, s 75(1), Sch 8, paras 96, 111(1), (6)(b).
[161] Amendment: Words substituted: Charities Act 2006, s 75(1), Sch 8, paras 96, 111(1), (6)(a).
[162] Amendment: Words substituted: Charities Act 2006, s 75(1), Sch 8, paras 96, 111(1), (6)(c).
[163] Amendment: Subsections omitted: Charities Act 2006, s 75, Sch 8, paras 96, 111(1), (7), Sch 9, for transitional provisions see s 75(3), Sch 10, para 18.
[164] Amendment: Words substituted: Charities Act 2006, s 75(1), Sch 8, paras 96, 111(1), (8).
[165] Amendment: Words substituted: Charities Act 2006, s 75(1), Sch 8, paras 96, 111(1), (9)(a).
[166] Amendment: Words substituted: Charities Act 2006, s 75(1), Sch 8, paras 96, 111(1), (9)(b).
[167] Amendment: Words substituted: Charities Act 2006, s 75(1), Sch 8, paras 96, 111(1) 10(a).
[168] Amendment: Words substituted: Charities Act 2006, s 75(1), Sch 8, paras 96, 111(1) 10(b).
[169] Amendment: Words substituted: Charities Act 2006, s 75(1), Sch 8, paras 96, 111(1) 10(c).
[170] Amendment: Words substituted: Charities Act 2006, s 75(1), Sch 8, paras 96, 111(1) 10(d).
[171] Amendment: Words substituted: Charities Act 2006, s 75(1), Sch 8, paras 96, 111(1) 10(e).

[(16) In this section—

(a)   subsections (1) to (3) apply in relation to an exempt charity, and

(b)   subsections (4) to (6) apply in relation to such a charity at any time after the Commission have instituted an inquiry under section 8 with respect to it,

and the other provisions of this section apply accordingly.][172]

Amendments—Charities Act 2006, ss 12, 75, Sch 5, para 6, Sch 8, para 96, 111, Sch 9.

[18A Power to suspend or remove trustees etc from membership of charity

(1) This section applies where the Commission makes—

(a)   an order under section 18(1) above suspending from his office or employment any trustee, charity trustee, officer, agent or employee of a charity, or

(b)   an order under section 18(2) above removing from his office or employment any officer, agent or employee of a charity,

and the trustee, charity trustee, officer, agent or employee (as the case may be) is a member of the charity.

(2) If the order suspends the person in question from his office or employment, the Commission may also make an order suspending his membership of the charity for the period for which he is suspended from his office or employment.

(3) If the order removes the person in question from his office or employment, the Commission may also make an order—

(a)   terminating his membership of the charity, and

(b)   prohibiting him from resuming his membership of the charity without the Commission's consent.

(4) If an application for the Commission's consent under subsection (3)(b) above is made five years or more after the order was made, the Commission must grant the application unless satisfied that, by reason of any special circumstances, it should be refused.][173]

Amendment—Charities Act 2006, s 19.

19 Supplementary provisions relating to [interim manager][174] appointed for a charity

[(1) The Commission may under section 18(1)(vii) above appoint to be interim manager in respect of a charity such person (other than a member of its staff) as it thinks fit.][175]

(2) Without prejudice to the generality of section 89(1) below, any order made by [the Commission][176] under section 18(1)(vii) above may make provision with respect to the functions to be discharged by the [interim manager][177] appointed by the order; and those functions shall be discharged by him under the supervision of [the Commission][178].

(3) In connection with the discharge of those functions any such order may provide—

---

[172]   Amendment: Subsection substituted: Charities Act 2006, s 12, Sch 5, para 6.
[173]   Amendment: Section inserted: Charities Act 2006, s 19, for transitional provisions see s 75(3), Sch 10, para 4.
[174]   Amendment: Words substituted: Charities Act 2006, s 75(1), Sch 8, paras 96, 112(1), (7).
[175]   Amendment: Subsection substituted: Charities Act 2006, s 75(1), Sch 8, paras 96, 112(1), (2).
[176]   Amendment: Words substituted: Charities Act 2006, s 75(1), Sch 8, paras 96, 112(1), (3)(a).
[177]   Amendment: Words substituted: Charities Act 2006, s 75(1), Sch 8, paras 96, 112(1), (3)(b).
[178]   Amendment: Words substituted: Charities Act 2006, s 75(1), Sch 8, paras 96, 112(1), (3)(a).

(a)　for the [interim manager][179] appointed by the order to have such powers and duties of the charity trustees of the charity concerned (whether arising under this Act or otherwise) as are specified in the order;

(b)　for any powers or duties exercisable or falling to be performed by the [interim manager][180] by virtue of paragraph (a) above to be exercisable or performed by him to the exclusion of those trustees.

(4) Where a person has been appointed [interim manager][181] by any such order—

(a)　section 29 below shall apply to him and to his functions as a person so appointed as it applies to a charity trustee of the charity concerned and to his duties as such; and

(b)　[the Commission][182] may apply to the High Court for directions in relation to any particular matter arising in connection with the discharge of those functions.

(5) The High Court may on an application under subsection (4)(b) above—

(a)　give such directions, or

(b)　make such orders declaring the rights of any persons (whether before the court or not),

as it thinks just; and the costs of any such application shall be paid by the charity concerned.

(6) Regulations made by the Secretary of State may make provision with respect to—

(a)　the appointment and removal of persons appointed in accordance with this section;

(b)　the remuneration of such persons out of the income of the charities concerned;

(c)　the making of reports to [the Commission][183] by such persons.

(7) Regulations under subsection (6) above may, in particular, authorise [the Commission][184]—

(a)　to require security for the due discharge of his functions to be given by a person so appointed;

(b)　to determine the amount of such a person's remuneration;

(c)　to disallow any amount of remuneration in such circumstances as are prescribed by the regulations.

Amendments—Charities Act 2006, s 75(1), Sch 8, paras 96, 112.

[19A Power to give specific directions for protection of charity

(1) This section applies where, at any time after the Commission has instituted an inquiry under section 8 above with respect to any charity, it is satisfied as mentioned in section 18(1)(a) or (b) above.

(2) The Commission may by order direct—

---

[179]　Amendment: Words substituted: Charities Act 2006, s 75(1), Sch 8, paras 96, 112(1), (4).

[180]　Amendment: Words substituted: Charities Act 2006, s 75(1), Sch 8, paras 96, 112(1), (4).

[181]　Amendment: Words substituted: Charities Act 2006, s 75(1), Sch 8, paras 96, 112(1), (5)(a).

[182]　Amendment: Words substituted: Charities Act 2006, s 75(1), Sch 8, paras 96, 112(1), (5)(b).

[183]　Amendment: Words substituted: Charities Act 2006, s 75(1), Sch 8, paras 96, 112(1), (6).

[184]　Amendment: Words substituted: Charities Act 2006, s 75(1), Sch 8, paras 96, 112(1), (6).

    (a)   the charity trustees,

    (b)   any trustee for the charity,

    (c)   any officer or employee of the charity, or

    (d)   (if a body corporate) the charity itself,

to take any action specified in the order which the Commission considers to be expedient in the interests of the charity.

(3) An order under this section—

    (a)   may require action to be taken whether or not it would otherwise be within the powers exercisable by the person or persons concerned, or by the charity, in relation to the administration of the charity or to its property, but

    (b)   may not require any action to be taken which is prohibited by any Act of Parliament or expressly prohibited by the trusts of the charity or is inconsistent with its purposes.

(4) Anything done by a person or body under the authority of an order under this section shall be deemed to be properly done in the exercise of the powers mentioned in subsection (3)(a) above.

(5) Subsection (4) does not affect any contractual or other rights arising in connection with anything which has been done under the authority of such an order.][185]

Amendment—Charities Act 2006, s 20.

[19B Power to direct application of charity property

(1) This section applies where the Commission is satisfied—

    (a)   that a person or persons in possession or control of any property held by or on trust for a charity is or are unwilling to apply it properly for the purposes of the charity, and

    (b)   that it is necessary or desirable to make an order under this section for the purpose of securing a proper application of that property for the purposes of the charity.

(2) The Commission may by order direct the person or persons concerned to apply the property in such manner as is specified in the order.

(3) An order under this section—

    (a)   may require action to be taken whether or not it would otherwise be within the powers exercisable by the person or persons concerned in relation to the property, but

    (b)   may not require any action to be taken which is prohibited by any Act of Parliament or expressly prohibited by the trusts of the charity.

(4) Anything done by a person under the authority of an order under this section shall be deemed to be properly done in the exercise of the powers mentioned in subsection (3)(a) above.

(5) Subsection (4) does not affect any contractual or other rights arising in connection with anything which has been done under the authority of such an order.][186]

Amendment—Charities Act 2006, s 21.

---

[185]   Amendment: Section inserted: Charities Act 2006, s 20, for transitional provisions see s 75(3), Sch 10, para 5.

[186]   Amendment: Section inserted: Charities Act 2006, s 21.

[19C Copy of order under section 18, 18A, 19A or 19B, and Commission's reasons, to be sent to charity

(1) Where the Commission makes an order under section 18, 18A, 19A or 19B, it must send the documents mentioned in subsection (2) below—

(a) to the charity concerned (if a body corporate), or

(b) (if not) to each of the charity trustees.

(2) The documents are—

(a) a copy of the order, and

(b) a statement of the Commission's reasons for making it.

(3) The documents must be sent to the charity or charity trustees as soon as practicable after the making of the order.

(4) The Commission need not, however, comply with subsection (3) above in relation to the documents, or (as the case may be) the statement of its reasons, if it considers that to do so—

(a) would prejudice any inquiry or investigation, or

(b) would not be in the interests of the charity;

but, once the Commission considers that this is no longer the case, it must send the documents, or (as the case may be) the statement, to the charity or charity trustees as soon as practicable.

(5) Nothing in this section requires any document to be sent to a person who cannot be found or who has no known address in the United Kingdom.

(6) Any documents required to be sent to a person under this section may be sent to, or otherwise served on, that person in the same way as an order made by the Commission under this Act could be served on him in accordance with section 91 below.][187]

Amendment—Charities Act 2006, s 75(1), Sch 8, paras 96, 113.

[20 Publicity relating to schemes

(1) The Commission may not—

(a) make any order under this Act to establish a scheme for the administration of a charity, or

(b) submit such a scheme to the court or the Minister for an order giving it effect,

unless, before doing so, the Commission has complied with the publicity requirements in subsection (2) below.

This is subject to any disapplication of those requirements under subsection (4) below.

(2) The publicity requirements are—

(a) that the Commission must give public notice of its proposals, inviting representations to be made to it within a period specified in the notice; and

(b) that, in the case of a scheme relating to a local charity (other than an ecclesiastical charity) in a parish or in a community in Wales, the Commission must communicate a draft of the scheme to the parish or community council (or, where a parish has no council, to the chairman of the parish meeting).

---

[187] Amendment: Section inserted: Charities Act 2006, s 75(1), Sch 8, paras 96, 113.

(3) The time when any such notice is given or any such communication takes place is to be decided by the Commission.

(4) The Commission may determine that either or both of the publicity requirements is or are not to apply in relation to a particular scheme if it is satisfied that—

  (a)   by reason of the nature of the scheme, or
  (b)   for any other reason,

compliance with the requirement or requirements is unnecessary.

(5) Where the Commission gives public notice of any proposals under this section, the Commission—

  (a)   must take into account any representations made to it within the period specified in the notice, and
  (b)   may (without further notice) proceed with the proposals either without modifications or with such modifications as it thinks desirable.

(6) Where the Commission makes an order under this Act to establish a scheme for the administration of a charity, a copy of the order must be available, for at least a month after the order is published, for public inspection at all reasonable times—

  (a)   at the Commission's office, and
  (b)   if the charity is a local charity, at some convenient place in the area of the charity.

Paragraph (b) does not apply if the Commission is satisfied that for any reason it is unnecessary for a copy of the scheme to be available locally.

(7) Any public notice of any proposals which is to be given under this section—

  (a)   is to contain such particulars of the proposals, or such directions for obtaining information about them, as the Commission thinks sufficient and appropriate, and
  (b)   is to be given in such manner as the Commission thinks sufficient and appropriate.][188]

Amendment—Charities Act 2006, s 22.

20A Publicity for orders relating to trustees or other individuals

(1) The Commission may not make any order under this Act to appoint, discharge or remove a charity trustee or trustee for a charity, other than—

  (a)   an order relating to the official custodian, or
  (b)   an order under section 18(1)(ii) above,

unless, before doing so, the Commission has complied with the publicity requirement in subsection (2) below.

This is subject to any disapplication of that requirement under subsection (4) below.

(2) The publicity requirement is that the Commission must give public notice of its proposals, inviting representations to be made to it within a period specified in the notice.

(3) The time when any such notice is given is to be decided by the Commission.

---

[188]   Amendment: Section substituted: Charities Act 2006, s 22.

(4) The Commission may determine that the publicity requirement is not to apply in relation to a particular order if it is satisfied that for any reason compliance with the requirement is unnecessary.

(5) Before the Commission makes an order under this Act to remove without his consent—

(a)   a charity trustee or trustee for a charity, or
(b)   an officer, agent or employee of a charity,

the Commission must give him not less than one month's notice of its proposals, inviting representations to be made to it within a period specified in the notice.

This does not apply if the person cannot be found or has no known address in the United Kingdom.

(6) Where the Commission gives notice of any proposals under this section, the Commission—

(a)   must take into account any representations made to it within the period specified in the notice, and
(b)   may (without further notice) proceed with the proposals either without modifications or with such modifications as it thinks desirable.

(7) Any notice of any proposals which is to be given under this section—

(a)   is to contain such particulars of the proposals, or such directions for obtaining information about them, as the Commission thinks sufficient and appropriate, and
(b)   (in the case of a public notice) is to be given in such manner as the Commission thinks sufficient and appropriate.

(8) Any notice to be given under subsection (5)—

(a)   may be given by post, and
(b)   if given by post, may be addressed to the recipient's last known address in the United Kingdom.][189]

Amendment—Charities Act 2006, s 22.

Property vested in official custodian

21 Entrusting charity property to official custodian, and termination of trust

(1) The court may by order—

(a)   vest in the official custodian any land held by or in trust for a charity;
(b)   authorise or require the persons in whom any such land is vested to transfer it to him; or
(c)   appoint any person to transfer any such land to him;

but this subsection does not apply to any interest in land by way of mortgage or other security.

(2) Where property is vested in the official custodian in trust for a charity, the court may make an order discharging him from the trusteeship as respects all or any of that property.

---

[189]   Amendment: Section substituted: Charities Act 2006, s 22.

(3) Where the official custodian is discharged from his trusteeship of any property, or the trusts on which he holds any property come to an end, the court may make such vesting orders and give such directions as may seem to the court to be necessary or expedient in consequence.

(4) No person shall be liable for any loss occasioned by his acting in conformity with an order under this section or by his giving effect to anything done in pursuance of such an order, or be excused from so doing by reason of the order having been in any respect improperly obtained.

22 Supplementary provisions as to property vested in official custodian

(1) Subject to the provisions of this Act, where property is vested in the official custodian in trust for a charity, he shall not exercise any powers of management, but he shall as trustee of any property have all the same powers, duties and liabilities, and be entitled to the same rights and immunities, and be subject to the control and orders of the court, as a corporation appointed custodian trustee under section 4 of the Public Trustee Act 1906 except that he shall have no power to charge fees.

(2) Subject to subsection (3) below, where any land is vested in the official custodian in trust for a charity, the charity trustees shall have power in his name and on his behalf to execute and do all assurances and things which they could properly execute or do in their own name and on their own behalf if the land were vested in them.

(3) If any land is so vested in the official custodian by virtue of an order under section 18 above, the power conferred on the charity trustees by subsection (2) above shall not be exercisable by them in relation to any transaction affecting the land, unless the transaction is authorised by order of the court or of [the Commission][190].

(4) Where any land is vested in the official custodian in trust for a charity, the charity trustees shall have the like power to make obligations entered into by them binding on the land as if it were vested in them; and any covenant, agreement or condition which is enforceable by or against the custodian by reason of the land being vested in him shall be enforceable by or against the charity trustees as if the land were vested in them.

(5) In relation to a corporate charity, subsections (2), (3) and (4) above shall apply with the substitution of references to the charity for references to the charity trustees.

(6) Subsections (2), (3) and (4) above shall not authorise any charity trustees or charity to impose any personal liability on the official custodian.

(7) Where the official custodian is entitled as trustee for a charity to the custody of securities or documents of title relating to the trust property, he may permit them to be in the possession or under the control of the charity trustees without thereby incurring any liability.

Amendment—Charities Act 2006, s 75(1), Sch 8, paras 96, 114.

23 Divestment in the case of land subject to Reverter of Sites Act 1987

(1) Where—

    (a)   any land is vested in the official custodian in trust for a charity, and

---

[190]   Amendment: Words substituted: Charities Act 2006, s 75(1), Sch 8, paras 96, 114.

(b)   it appears to [the Commission]¹⁹¹ that section 1 of the Reverter of Sites Act 1987 (right of reverter replaced by [trust]¹⁹²) will, or is likely to, operate in relation to the land at a particular time or in particular circumstances,

the jurisdiction which, under section 16 above, is exercisable by [the Commission]¹⁹³ for the purpose of discharging a trustee for a charity may, at any time before section 1 of that Act ('the 1987 Act') operates in relation to the land, be exercised [by the Commission of its own]¹⁹⁴ motion for the purpose of—

(i)   making an order discharging the official custodian from his trusteeship of the land, and

(ii)   making such vesting orders and giving such directions as [appear to the Commission]¹⁹⁵ to be necessary or expedient in consequence.

(2) Where—

(a)   section 1 of the 1987 Act has operated in relation to any land which, immediately before the time when that section so operated, was vested in the official custodian in trust for a charity, and

(b)   the land remains vested in him but on the trust arising under that section,

the court or [the Commission (of its own motion)]¹⁹⁶ may—

(i)   make an order discharging the official custodian from his trusteeship of the land, and

(ii)   (subject to the following provisions of this section) make such vesting orders and give such directions as appear to it …¹⁹⁷ to be necessary or expedient in consequence.

(3) Where any order discharging the official custodian from his trusteeship of any land—

(a)   is made by the court under section 21(2) above, or by [the Commission]¹⁹⁸ under section 16 above, on the grounds that section 1 of the 1987 Act will, or is likely to, operate in relation to the land, or

(b)   is made by the court or [the Commission]¹⁹⁹ under subsection (2) above,

the persons in whom the land is to be vested on the discharge of the official custodian shall be the relevant charity trustees (as defined in subsection (4) below), unless the court or (as the case may be) [the Commission is]²⁰⁰ satisfied that it would be appropriate for it to be vested in some other persons.

(4) In subsection (3) above 'the relevant charity trustees' means—

(a)   in relation to an order made as mentioned in paragraph (a) of that subsection, the charity trustees of the charity in trust for which the land is vested in the official custodian immediately before the time when the order takes effect, or

---

¹⁹¹   Amendment: Words substituted: Charities Act 2006, s 75(1), Sch 8, paras 96, 115(1), (2)(a).
¹⁹²   Amendment: Words substituted: Trusts of Land and Appointment of Trustees Act 1996, s 25(1), Sch 3, para 26, for savings see 25(4), (5).
¹⁹³   Amendment: Words substituted: Charities Act 2006, s 75(1), Sch 8, paras 96, 115(1), (2)(a).
¹⁹⁴   Amendment: Words substituted: Charities Act 2006, s 75(1), Sch 8, paras 96, 115(1), (2)(b).
¹⁹⁵   Amendment: Words substituted: Charities Act 2006, s 75(1), Sch 8, paras 96, 115(1), (2)(c).
¹⁹⁶   Amendment: Words substituted: Charities Act 2006, s 75(1), Sch 8, paras 96, 115(1), (3)(a).
¹⁹⁷   Amendment: Words omitted: Charities Act 2006, s 75, Sch 8, paras 96, 115(1), (3)(b), Sch 9.
¹⁹⁸   Amendment: Words substituted: Charities Act 2006, s 75(1), Sch 8, paras 96, 115(1), (4)(a).
¹⁹⁹   Amendment: Words substituted: Charities Act 2006, s 75(1), Sch 8, paras 96, 115(1), (4)(a).
²⁰⁰   Amendment: Words substituted: Charities Act 2006, s 75(1), Sch 8, paras 96, 115(1), (4)(b).

(b) in relation to an order made under subsection (2) above, the charity trustees of the charity in trust for which the land was vested in the official custodian immediately before the time when section 1 of the 1987 Act operated in relation to the land.

(5) Where—

(a) section 1 of the 1987 Act has operated in relation to any such land as is mentioned in subsection (2)(a) above, and

(b) the land remains vested in the official custodian as mentioned in subsection (2)(b) above,

then (subject to subsection (6) below), all the powers, duties and liabilities that would, apart from this section, be those of the official custodian as [trustee][201] of the land shall instead be those of the charity trustees of the charity concerned; and those trustees shall have power in his name and on his behalf to execute and do all assurances and things which they could properly execute or do in their own name and on their own behalf if the land were vested in them.

(6) Subsection (5) above shall not be taken to require or authorise those trustees to sell the land at a time when it remains vested in the official custodian.

(7) Where—

(a) the official custodian has been discharged from his trusteeship of any land by an order under subsection (2) above, and

(b) the land has, in accordance with subsection (3) above, been vested in the charity trustees concerned or (as the case may be) in any persons other than those trustees,

the land shall be held by those trustees, or (as the case may be) by those persons, as [trustees][202] on the terms of the trust arising under section 1 of the 1987 Act.

(8) The official custodian shall not be liable to any person in respect of any loss or misapplication of any land vested in him in accordance with that section unless it is occasioned by or through any wilful neglect or default of his or of any person acting for him; but the Consolidated Fund shall be liable to make good to any person any sums for which the official custodian may be liable by reason of any such neglect or default.

(9) In this section any reference to section 1 of the 1987 Act operating in relation to any land is a reference to a [trust][203] arising in relation to the land under that section.

Amendments—Trusts of Land and Appointment of Trustees Act 1996, s 25(1), Sch 3, para 26; Charities Act 2006, s 75, Sch 8, paras 96, 115, Sch 9.

---

[201] Amendment: Words substituted: Trusts of Land and Appointment of Trustees Act 1996, s 25(1), Sch 3, para 26, for savings see 25(4), (5).

[202] Amendment: Words substituted: Trusts of Land and Appointment of Trustees Act 1996, s 25(1), Sch 3, para 26, for savings see 25(4), (5).

[203] Amendment: Words substituted: Trusts of Land and Appointment of Trustees Act 1996, s 25(1), Sch 3, para 26, for savings see 25(4), (5).

Establishment of common investment or deposit funds

24 Schemes to establish common investment funds

(1) The court or [the Commission][204] may by order make and bring into effect schemes (in this section referred to as 'common investment schemes') for the establishment of common investment funds under trusts which provide—

(a) for property transferred to the fund by or on behalf of a charity participating in the scheme to be invested under the control of trustees appointed to manage the fund; and

(b) for the participating charities to be entitled (subject to the provisions of the scheme) to the capital and income of the fund in shares determined by reference to the amount or value of the property transferred to it by or on behalf of each of them and to the value of the fund at the time of the transfers.

(2) The court or [the Commission][205] may make a common investment scheme on the application of any two or more charities.

(3) A common investment scheme may be made in terms admitting any charity to participate, or the scheme may restrict the right to participate in any manner.

[(3A) A common investment scheme may provide for appropriate bodies to be admitted to participate in the scheme (in addition to the participating charities) to such extent as the trustees appointed to manage the fund may determine.

(3B) In this section 'appropriate body' means—

(a) a Scottish recognised body, or

(b) a Northern Ireland charity,

and, in the application of the relevant provisions in relation to a scheme which contains provisions authorised by subsection (3A) above, 'charity' includes an appropriate body.

'The relevant provisions' are subsections (1) and (4) to (6) and (in relation only to a charity within paragraph (b)) subsection (7).][206]

(4) A common investment scheme may make provision for, and for all matters connected with, the establishment, investment, management and winding up of the common investment fund, and may in particular include provision—

(a) for remunerating persons appointed trustees to hold or manage the fund or any part of it, with or without provision authorising a person to receive the remuneration notwithstanding that he is also a charity trustee of or trustee for a participating charity;

(b) for restricting the size of the fund, and for regulating as to time, amount or otherwise the right to transfer property to or withdraw it from the fund, and for enabling sums to be advanced out of the fund by way of loan to a participating charity pending the withdrawal of property from the fund by the charity;

(c) for enabling income to be withheld from distribution with a view to avoiding fluctuations in the amounts distributed, and generally for regulating distributions of income;

---

[204] Amendment: Words substituted: Charities Act 2006, s 75(1), Sch 8, paras 96, 116.
[205] Amendment: Words substituted: Charities Act 2006, s 75(1), Sch 8, paras 96, 116.
[206] Amendment: Subsections inserted: Charities Act 2006, s 23(1).

(d)   for enabling money to be borrowed temporarily for the purpose of meeting payments to be made out of the funds;

(e)   for enabling questions arising under the scheme as to the right of a charity to participate, or as to the rights of participating charities, or as to any other matter, to be conclusively determined by the decision of the trustees managing the fund or in any other manner;

(f)   for regulating the accounts and information to be supplied to participating charities.

(5) A common investment scheme, in addition to the provision for property to be transferred to the fund on the basis that the charity shall be entitled to a share in the capital and income of the fund, may include provision for enabling sums to be deposited by or on behalf of a charity on the basis that (subject to the provisions of the scheme) the charity shall be entitled to repayment of the sums deposited and to interest thereon at a rate determined by or under the scheme; and where a scheme makes any such provision it shall also provide for excluding from the amount of capital and income to be shared between charities participating otherwise than by way of deposit such amounts (not exceeding the amounts properly attributable to the making of deposits) as are from time to time reasonably required in respect of the liabilities of the fund for the repayment of deposits and for the interest on deposits, including amounts required by way of reserve.

(6) Except in so far as a common investment scheme provides to the contrary, the rights under it of a participating charity shall not be capable of being assigned or charged, nor shall any trustee or other person concerned in the management of the common investment fund be required or entitled to take account of any trust or other equity affecting a participating charity or its property or rights.

(7) The powers of investment of every charity shall include power to participate in common investment schemes unless the power is excluded by a provision specifically referring to common investment schemes in the trusts of the charity.

(8) A common investment fund shall be deemed for all purposes to be a charity...[207].

(9) Subsection (8) above shall apply not only to common investment funds established under the powers of this section, but also to any similar fund established for the exclusive benefit of charities by or under any enactment relating to any particular charities or class of charity.

Amendments—Charities Act 2006, ss 11(10), 23(1), 75, Sch 8, paras 96, 116, Sch 9.

25 Schemes to establish common deposit funds

(1) The court or [the Commission][208] may by order make and bring into effect schemes (in this section referred to as 'common deposit schemes') for the establishment of common deposit funds under trusts which provide—

(a)   for sums to be deposited by or on behalf of a charity participating in the scheme and invested under the control of trustees appointed to manage the fund; and

(b)   for any such charity to be entitled (subject to the provisions of the scheme) to repayment of any sums so deposited and to interest thereon at a rate determined under the scheme.

---

[207]   Amendment: Words omitted: Charities Act 2006, ss 11(10), 75(2), Sch 9.
[208]   Amendment: Words substituted: Charities Act 2006, s 75(1), Sch 8, paras 96, 117.

(2) Subject to subsection (3) below, the following provisions of section 24 above, namely—

    (a)   [subsections (2), (3) and (4)][209], and

    (b)   subsections (6) to (9),

shall have effect in relation to common deposit schemes and common deposit funds as they have effect in relation to common investment schemes and common investment funds.

(3) In its application in accordance with subsection (2) above, subsection (4) of that section shall have effect with the substitution for paragraphs (b) and (c) of the following paragraphs—

    '(b)   for regulating as to time, amount or otherwise the right to repayment of sums deposited in the fund;

    (c)   for authorising a part of the income for any year to be credited to a reserve account maintained for the purpose of counteracting any losses accruing to the fund, and generally for regulating the manner in which the rate of interest on deposits is to be determined from time to time;'

[(4) A common deposit scheme may provide for appropriate bodies to be admitted to participate in the scheme (in addition to the participating charities) to such extent as the trustees appointed to manage the fund may determine.

(5) In this section 'appropriate body' means—

    (a)   a Scottish recognised body, or

    (b)   a Northern Ireland charity,

and, in the application of the relevant provisions in relation to a scheme which contains provisions authorised by subsection (4) above, 'charity' includes an appropriate body.

(6) 'The relevant provisions' are—

    (a)   subsection (1) above, and

    (b)   subsections (4) and (6) of section 24 above, as they apply in accordance with subsections (2) and (3) above, and

    (c)   (in relation only to a charity within subsection (5)(b) above) subsection (7) of that section, as it so applies.][210]

Amendments—Charities Act 2006, ss 23(2), (3), 75(1), Sch 8, paras 96, 117.

[25A Meaning of 'Scottish recognised body' and 'Northern Ireland charity' in sections 24 and 25

(1) In sections 24 and 25 above 'Scottish recognised body' means a body—

    (a)   established under the law of Scotland, or

    (b)   managed or controlled wholly or mainly in or from Scotland,

to which the Commissioners for Her Majesty's Revenue and Customs have given intimation, which has not subsequently been withdrawn, that relief is due under section 505 of the Income and Corporation Taxes Act 1988 in respect of income of the body which is applicable and applied to charitable purposes only.

---

[209]   Amendment: Words substituted: Charities Act 2006, s 23(2).

[210]   Amendment: Subsections added: Charities Act 2006, s 23(3).

(2) In those sections 'Northern Ireland charity' means an institution—

(a)   which is a charity under the law of Northern Ireland, and

(b)   to which the Commissioners for Her Majesty's Revenue and Customs have given intimation, which has not subsequently been withdrawn, that relief is due under section 505 of the Income and Corporation Taxes Act 1988 in respect of income of the institution which is applicable and applied to charitable purposes only.][211]

Amendment—Charities Act 2006, s 23(4).

[Additional powers of Commission][212]

26 Power to authorise dealings with charity property etc

(1) Subject to the provisions of this section, where it appears to [the Commission][213] that any action proposed or contemplated in the administration of a charity is expedient in the interests of the charity, [the Commission may][214] by order sanction that action, whether or not it would otherwise be within the powers exercisable by the charity trustees in the administration of the charity; and anything done under the authority of such an order shall be deemed to be properly done in the exercise of those powers.(2) An order under this section may be made so as to authorise a particular transaction, compromise or the like, or a particular application of property, or so as to give a more general authority, and (without prejudice to the generality of subsection (1) above) may authorise a charity to use common premises, or employ a common staff, or otherwise combine for any purpose of administration, with any other charity.

(3) An order under this section may give directions as to the manner in which any expenditure is to be borne and as to other matters connected with or arising out of the action thereby authorised; and where anything is done in pursuance of an authority given by any such order, any directions given in connection therewith shall be binding on the charity trustees for the time being as if contained in the trusts of the charity; but any such directions may on the application of the charity be modified or superseded by a further order.

(4) Without prejudice to the generality of subsection (3) above, the directions which may be given by an order under this section shall in particular include directions for meeting any expenditure out of a specified fund, for charging any expenditure to capital or to income, for requiring expenditure charged to capital to be recouped out of income within a specified period, for restricting the costs to be incurred at the expense of the charity, or for the investment of moneys arising from any transaction.

(5) An order under this section may authorise any act notwithstanding that it is prohibited by any of the disabling Acts mentioned in subsection (6) below or that the trusts of the charity provide for the act to be done by or under the authority of the court; but no such order shall authorise the doing of any act expressly prohibited by Act of Parliament other than the disabling Acts or by the trusts of the charity or shall extend or alter the purposes of the charity.

---

[211]   Amendment: Section inserted: Charities Act 2006, s 23(4).
[212]   Amendment: Words substituted: Charities Act 2006, s 75(1), Sch 8, paras 96, 118.
[213]   Amendment: Words substituted: Charities Act 2006, s 75(1), Sch 8, paras 96, 119(a).
[214]   Amendment: Words substituted: Charities Act 2006, s 75(1), Sch 8, paras 96, 119(b).

(6) The Acts referred to in subsection (5) above as the disabling Acts are ͭͪe Ecclesiastical Leases Act 1571, the Ecclesiastical Leases Act 1572, the Ecclesiastical Leases Act 1575 and the Ecclesiastical Leases Act 1836.

(7) An order under this section shall not confer any authority in relation to a building which has been consecrated and of which the use or disposal is regulated, and can be further regulated, by a scheme having effect under the Union of Benefices Measures 1923 to 1952, the Reorganisation Areas Measures 1944 and 1954, the Pastoral Measure 1968 or the Pastoral Measure 1983, the reference to a building being taken to include part of a building and any land which under such a scheme is to be used or disposed of with a building to which the scheme applies.

Amendments—Charities Act 2006, s 75(1), Sch 8, paras 96, 119.

27 Power to authorise ex gratia payments etc

(1) Subject to subsection (3) below, [the Commission][215] may by order exercise the same power as is exercisable by the Attorney General to authorise the charity trustees of a charity—

(a) to make any application of property of the charity, or

(b) to waive to any extent, on behalf of the charity, its entitlement to receive any property,

in a case where the charity trustees—

(i) (apart from this section) have no power to do so, but

(ii) in all the circumstances regard themselves as being under a moral obligation to do so.

(2) The power conferred on [the Commission][216] by subsection (1) above shall be exercisable [by the Commission][217] under the supervision of, and in accordance with such directions as may be given by, the Attorney General; and any such directions may in particular require [the Commission][218], in such circumstances as are specified in the directions—

(a) to refrain from exercising that power; or

(b) to consult the Attorney General before exercising it.

(3) Where—

(a) an application is made to [the Commission for it][219] to exercise that power in a case where [it is not][220] precluded from doing so by any such directions, but

(b) [the Commission considers][221] that it would nevertheless be desirable for the application to be entertained by the Attorney General rather than [by the Commission][222],

[the Commission shall][223] refer the application to the Attorney General.

---

[215] Amendment: Words substituted: Charities Act 2006, s 75(1), Sch 8, paras 96, 120(1), (2).

[216] Amendment: Words substituted: Charities Act 2006, s 75(1), Sch 8, paras 96, 120(1), (3)(a).

[217] Amendment: Words substituted: Charities Act 2006, s 75(1), Sch 8, paras 96, 120(1), (3)(b).

[218] Amendment: Words substituted: Charities Act 2006, s 75(1), Sch 8, paras 96, 120(1), (3)(a).

[219] Amendment: Words substituted: Charities Act 2006, s 75(1), Sch 8, paras 96, 120(1), (4)(a).

[220] Amendment: Words substituted: Charities Act 2006, s 75(1), Sch 8, paras 96, 120(1), (4)(b).

[221] Amendment: Words substituted: Charities Act 2006, s 75(1), Sch 8, paras 96, 120(1), (4)(c).

[222] Amendment: Words substituted: Charities Act 2006, s 75(1), Sch 8, paras 96, 120(1), (4)(d).

[223] Amendment: Words substituted: Charities Act 2006, s 75(1), Sch 8, paras 96, 120(1), (4)(e).

(4) It is hereby declared that where, in the case of any application made [to the Commission][224] as mentioned in subsection (3)(a) above, [the Commission determines][225] the application by refusing to authorise charity trustees to take any action falling within subsection (1)(a) or (b) above, that refusal shall not preclude the Attorney General, on an application subsequently made to him by the trustees, from authorising the trustees to take that action.

Amendments—Charities Act 2006, s 75(1), Sch 8, paras 96, 120.

28 Power to give directions about dormant bank accounts of charities

(1) Where [the Commission][226]—

    (a)   [is informed][227] by a relevant institution—
        (i)   that it holds one or more accounts in the name of or on behalf of a particular charity ('the relevant charity'), and
        (ii)   that the account, or (if it so holds two or more accounts) each of the accounts, is dormant, and
    (b)   [is unable][228], after making reasonable inquiries, to locate that charity or any of its trustees,

[it may give][229] a direction under subsection (2) below.

(2) A direction under this subsection is a direction which—

    (a)   requires the institution concerned to transfer the amount, or (as the case may be) the aggregate amount, standing to the credit of the relevant charity in the account or accounts in question to such other charity as is specified in the direction in accordance with subsection (3) below; or
    (b)   requires the institution concerned to transfer to each of two or more other charities so specified in the direction such part of that amount or aggregate amount as is there specified in relation to that charity.

(3) The [Commission][230] may specify in a direction under subsection (2) above such other charity or charities as [it considers][231] appropriate, having regard, in a case where the purposes of the relevant charity are known [to the Commission][232], to those purposes and to the purposes of the other charity or charities; but the [Commission][233] shall not so specify any charity unless [it has received][234] from the charity trustees written confirmation that those trustees are willing to accept the amount proposed to be transferred to the charity.

(4) Any amount received by a charity by virtue of this section shall be received by the charity on terms that—

    (a)   it shall be held and applied by the charity for the purposes of the charity, but

---

[224] Amendment: Words substituted: Charities Act 2006, s 75(1), Sch 8, paras 96, 120(1), (5)(a).
[225] Amendment: Words substituted: Charities Act 2006, s 75(1), Sch 8, paras 96, 120(1), (5)(b).
[226] Amendment: Words substituted: Charities Act 2006, s 75(1), Sch 8, paras 96, 121(1), (2)(a).
[227] Amendment: Words substituted: Charities Act 2006, s 75(1), Sch 8, paras 96, 121(1), (2)(b).
[228] Amendment: Words substituted: Charities Act 2006, s 75(1), Sch 8, paras 96, 121(1), (2)(c).
[229] Amendment: Words substituted: Charities Act 2006, s 75(1), Sch 8, paras 96, 121(1), (2)(d).
[230] Amendment: Word substituted: Charities Act 2006, s 75(1), Sch 8, paras 96, 121(1), (3)(a).
[231] Amendment: Words substituted: Charities Act 2006, s 75(1), Sch 8, paras 96, 121(1), (3)(b).
[232] Amendment: Words substituted: Charities Act 2006, s 75(1), Sch 8, paras 96, 121(1), (3)(c).
[233] Amendment: Word substituted: Charities Act 2006, s 75(1), Sch 8, paras 96, 121(1), (3)(a).
[234] Amendment: Words substituted: Charities Act 2006, s 75(1), Sch 8, paras 96, 121(1), (3)(d).

(b)   it shall, as property of the charity, nevertheless be subject to any restrictions on expenditure to which it was subject as property of the relevant charity.

(5) Where—

(a)   [the Commission has been]²³⁵ informed as mentioned in subsection (1)(a) above by any relevant institution, and

(b)   before any transfer is made by the institution in pursuance of a direction under subsection (2) above, the institution has, by reason of any circumstances, cause to believe that the account, or (as the case may be) any of the accounts, held by it in the name of or on behalf of the relevant charity is no longer dormant,

the institution shall forthwith notify those circumstances in writing to [the Commission]²³⁶; and, if it appears to [the Commission]²³⁷ that the account or accounts in question is or are no longer dormant, [it shall revoke]²³⁸ any direction under subsection (2) above which has previously been given [by it]²³⁹ to the institution with respect to the relevant charity.

(6) The receipt of any charity trustees or trustee for a charity in respect of any amount received from a relevant institution by virtue of this section shall be a complete discharge of the institution in respect of that amount.

(7) No obligation as to secrecy or other restriction on disclosure (however imposed) shall preclude a relevant institution from disclosing any information to [the Commission]²⁴⁰ for the purpose of enabling [the Commission to discharge its functions]²⁴¹ under this section.

(8) For the purposes of this section—

(a)   an account is dormant if no transaction, other than—

    (i)   a transaction consisting in a payment into the account, or

    (ii)   a transaction which the institution holding the account has itself caused to be effected,

has been effected in relation to the account within the period of five years immediately preceding the date when [the Commission is informed]²⁴² as mentioned in paragraph (a) of subsection (1) above;

(b)   a 'relevant institution' means—

    (i)   the Bank of England;

    [(ii)   a person who has permission under Part 4 of the Financial Services and Markets Act 2000 to accept deposits;

    (iii)   an EEA firm of the kind mentioned in paragraph 5(b) of Schedule 3 to that Act which has permission under paragraph 15 of that Schedule (as a result of qualifying for authorisation under paragraph 12(1) of that Schedule) to accept deposits; or

    (iv)   such other person who may lawfully accept deposits in the United Kingdom as may be prescribed by the Secretary of State;]²⁴³ and

²³⁵   Amendment: Words substituted: Charities Act 2006, s 75(1), Sch 8, paras 96, 121(1), (4)(a).
²³⁶   Amendment: Words substituted: Charities Act 2006, s 75(1), Sch 8, paras 96, 121(1), (4)(b).
²³⁷   Amendment: Words substituted: Charities Act 2006, s 75(1), Sch 8, paras 96, 121(1), (4)(b).
²³⁸   Amendment: Words substituted: Charities Act 2006, s 75(1), Sch 8, paras 96, 121(1), (4)(c).
²³⁹   Amendment: Words substituted: Charities Act 2006, s 75(1), Sch 8, paras 96, 121(1), (4)(d).
²⁴⁰   Amendment: Words substituted: Charities Act 2006, s 75(1), Sch 8, paras 96, 121(1), (5)(a).
²⁴¹   Amendment: Words substituted: Charities Act 2006, s 75(1), Sch 8, paras 96, 121(1), (5)(b).
²⁴²   Amendment: Words substituted: Charities Act 2006, s 75(1), Sch 8, paras 96, 121(1), (6).
²⁴³   Amendment: Paragraphs substituted: The Financial Services and Markets Act 2000 (Consequential Amendments and Repeals) Order 2001, SI 2001/3649, art 339(1), (2).

(c)   references to the transfer of any amount to a charity are references to its transfer—
    (i)   to the charity trustees, or
    (ii)   to any trustee for the charity,
    as the charity trustees may determine (and any reference to any amount received by a charity shall be construed accordingly).

[(8A) Sub-paragraphs (ii) to (iv) of the definition of 'relevant institution' in subsection (8)(b) must be read with—

(a)   section 22 of the Financial Services and Markets Act 2000;
(b)   any relevant order under that section; and
(c)   Schedule 2 to that Act.][244]

(9) For the purpose of determining the matters in respect of which any of the powers conferred by section 8 or 9 above may be exercised it shall be assumed that [the Commission has][245] no functions under this section in relation to accounts to which this subsection applies (with the result that, for example, a relevant institution shall not, in connection with the functions of [the Commission][246] under this section, be required under section 8(3)(a) above to furnish any statements, or answer any questions or inquiries, with respect to any such accounts held by the institution).

This subsection applies to accounts which are dormant accounts by virtue of subsection (8)(a) above but would not be such accounts if sub-paragraph (i) of that provision were omitted.

(10) ...[247]

Amendments—The Financial Services and Markets Act 2000 (Consequential Amendments and Repeals) Order 2001, SI 2001/3649, art 339; Charities Act 2006, ss 12, 75, Sch 5, para 7, Sch 8, paras 96, 121, Sch 9.

[29 Power to give advice and guidance

(1) The Commission may, on the written application of any charity trustee or trustee for a charity, give that person its opinion or advice in relation to any matter—

(a)   relating to the performance of any duties of his, as such a trustee, in relation to the charity concerned, or
(b)   otherwise relating to the proper administration of the charity.

(2) A charity trustee or trustee for a charity who acts in accordance with any opinion or advice given by the Commission under subsection (1) above (whether to him or to another trustee) is to be taken, as regards his responsibility for so acting, to have acted in accordance with his trust.

(3) But subsection (2) above does not apply to a person if, when so acting, either—

(a)   he knows or has reasonable cause to suspect that the opinion or advice was given in ignorance of material facts, or
(b)   a decision of the court or the Tribunal has been obtained on the matter or proceedings are pending to obtain one.

---

[244]   Amendment: Subsection inserted: The Financial Services and Markets Act 2000 (Consequential Amendments and Repeals) Order 2001, SI 2001/3649, art 339(1), (3).
[245]   Amendment: Words substituted: Charities Act 2006, s 75(1), Sch 8, paras 96, 121(1), (7)(a).
[246]   Amendment: Words substituted: Charities Act 2006, s 75(1), Sch 8, paras 96, 121(1), (7)(b).
[247]   Amendment: Subsection omitted: Charities Act 2006, ss 12, 75(2), Sch 5, para 7, Sch 9.

(4) The Commission may, in connection with its second general function mentioned in section 1C(2) above, give such advice or guidance with respect to the administration of charities as it considers appropriate.

(5) Any advice or guidance so given may relate to—

(a)   charities generally,
(b)   any class of charities, or
(c)   any particular charity,

and may take such form, and be given in such manner, as the Commission considers appropriate.][248]

Amendment—Charities Act 2006, s 24.

[29A Power to determine membership of charity

(1) The Commission may—

(a)   on the application of a charity, or
(b)   at any time after the institution of an inquiry under section 8 above with respect to a charity,

determine who are the members of the charity.

(2) The Commission's power under subsection (1) may also be exercised by a person appointed by the Commission for the purpose.

(3) In a case within subsection (1)(b) the Commission may, if it thinks fit, so appoint the person appointed to conduct the inquiry.][249]

Amendment—Charities Act 2006, s 25.

30 Powers for preservation of charity documents

(1) [The Commission][250] may provide books in which any deed, will or other document relating to a charity may be enrolled.

(2) The [Commission][251] may accept for safe keeping any document of or relating to a charity, and the charity trustees or other persons having the custody of documents of or relating to a charity (including a charity which has ceased to exist) may with the consent of the [Commission][252] deposit them with the [Commission][253] for safe keeping, except in the case of documents required by some other enactment to be kept elsewhere.

(3) Where a document is enrolled by [the Commission][254] or is for the time being deposited [with the Commission][255] under this section, evidence of its contents may be given by means of a copy certified by any [member of the staff of the Commission generally or specially authorised by the Commission][256] to act for this purpose; and a document purporting to be such a copy shall be received in evidence without proof of

---

[248]   Amendment: Section substituted: Charities Act 2006, s 24.
[249]   Amendment: Section inserted: Charities Act 2006, s 25.
[250]   Amendment: Words substituted: Charities Act 2006, s 75(1), Sch 8, paras 96, 122(1), (2).
[251]   Amendment: Word substituted: Charities Act 2006, s 75(1), Sch 8, paras 96, 122(1), (3).
[252]   Amendment: Word substituted: Charities Act 2006, s 75(1), Sch 8, paras 96, 122(1), (3).
[253]   Amendment: Word substituted: Charities Act 2006, s 75(1), Sch 8, paras 96, 122(1), (3).
[254]   Amendment: Words substituted: Charities Act 2006, s 75(1), Sch 8, paras 96, 122(1), (4)(a).
[255]   Amendment: Words substituted: Charities Act 2006, s 75(1), Sch 8, paras 96, 122(1), (4)(b).
[256]   Amendment: Words substituted: Charities Act 2006, s 75(1), Sch 8, paras 96, 122(1), (4)(c).

the official position, authority or handwriting of the person certifying it or of the original document being enrolled or deposited as aforesaid.

(4) Regulations made by the Secretary of State may make provision for such documents deposited with [the Commission][257] under this section as may be prescribed by the regulations to be destroyed or otherwise disposed of after such period or in such circumstances as may be so prescribed.

(5) Subsections (3) and (4) above shall apply to any document transmitted to [the Commission][258] under section 9 above and kept [by the Commission][259] under subsection (3) of that section, as if the document had been deposited [with the Commission][260] for safe keeping under this section.

Amendments—Charities Act 2006, s 75(1), Sch 8, paras 96, 122.

31 Power to order taxation of solicitor's bill

(1) [The Commission][261] may order that a solicitor's bill of costs for business done for a charity, or for charity trustees or trustees for a charity, shall be taxed, together with the costs of the taxation, by a taxing officer in such division of the High Court as may be specified in the order, or by the taxing officer of any other court having jurisdiction to order the taxation of the bill.

(2) On any order under this section for the taxation of a solicitor's bill the taxation shall proceed, and the taxing officer shall have the same powers and duties, and the costs of the taxation shall be borne, as if the order had been made, on the application of the person chargeable with the bill, by the court in which the costs are taxed.

(3) No order under this section for the taxation of a solicitor's bill shall be made after payment of the bill unless [the Commission is][262] of opinion that it contains exorbitant charges; and no such order shall in any case be made where the solicitor's costs are not subject to taxation on an order of the High Court by reason either of an agreement as to his remuneration or the lapse of time since payment of the bill.

Amendments—Charities Act 2006, s 75(1), Sch 8, paras 96, 123.

[31A Power to enter premises

(1) A justice of the peace may issue a warrant under this section if satisfied, on information given on oath by a member of the Commission's staff, that there are reasonable grounds for believing that each of the conditions in subsection (2) below is satisfied.

(2) The conditions are—

    (a)   that an inquiry has been instituted under section 8 above;

    (b)   that there is on the premises to be specified in the warrant any document or information relevant to that inquiry which the Commission could require to be produced or furnished under section 9(1) above; and

    (c)   that, if the Commission were to make an order requiring the document or information to be so produced or furnished—

---

[257] Amendment: Words substituted: Charities Act 2006, s 75(1), Sch 8, paras 96, 122(1), (5).

[258] Amendment: Words substituted: Charities Act 2006, s 75(1), Sch 8, paras 96, 122(1), (6)(a).

[259] Amendment: Words substituted: Charities Act 2006, s 75(1), Sch 8, paras 96, 122(1), (6)(b).

[260] Amendment: Words substituted: Charities Act 2006, s 75(1), Sch 8, paras 96, 122(1), (6)(c).

[261] Amendment: Words substituted: Charities Act 2006, s 75(1), Sch 8, paras 96, 123(1), (2).

[262] Amendment: Words substituted: Charities Act 2006, s 75(1), Sch 8, paras 96, 123(1), (3).

(i)   the order would not be complied with, or

(ii)   the document or information would be removed, tampered with, concealed or destroyed.

(3) A warrant under this section is a warrant authorising the member of the Commission's staff who is named in it—

(a)   to enter and search the premises specified in it;

(b)   to take such other persons with him as the Commission considers are needed to assist him in doing anything that he is authorised to do under the warrant;

(c)   to take possession of any documents which appear to fall within subsection (2)(b) above, or to take any other steps which appear to be necessary for preserving, or preventing interference with, any such documents;

(d)   to take possession of any computer disk or other electronic storage device which appears to contain information falling within subsection (2)(b), or information contained in a document so falling, or to take any other steps which appear to be necessary for preserving, or preventing interference with, any such information;

(e)   to take copies of, or extracts from, any documents or information falling within paragraph (c) or (d);

(f)   to require any person on the premises to provide an explanation of any such document or information or to state where any such documents or information may be found;

(g)   to require any such person to give him such assistance as he may reasonably require for the taking of copies or extracts as mentioned in paragraph (e) above.

(4) Entry and search under such a warrant must be at a reasonable hour and within one month of the date of its issue.

(5) The member of the Commission's staff who is authorised under such a warrant ('the authorised person') must, if required to do so, produce—

(a)   the warrant, and

(b)   documentary evidence that he is a member of the Commission's staff,

for inspection by the occupier of the premises or anyone acting on his behalf.

(6) The authorised person must make a written record of—

(a)   the date and time of his entry on the premises;

(b)   the number of persons (if any) who accompanied him onto the premises, and the names of any such persons;

(c)   the period for which he (and any such persons) remained on the premises;

(d)   what he (and any such persons) did while on the premises; and

(e)   any document or device of which he took possession while there.

(7) If required to do so, the authorised person must give a copy of the record to the occupier of the premises or someone acting on his behalf.

(8) Unless it is not reasonably practicable to do so, the authorised person must comply with the following requirements before leaving the premises, namely—

(a)   the requirements of subsection (6), and

(b)   any requirement made under subsection (7) before he leaves the premises.

(9) Where possession of any document or device is taken under this section—

(a) the document may be retained for so long as the Commission considers that it is necessary to retain it (rather than a copy of it) for the purposes of the relevant inquiry under section 8 above, or

(b) the device may be retained for so long as the Commission considers that it is necessary to retain it for the purposes of that inquiry,

as the case may be.

(10) Once it appears to the Commission that the retention of any document or device has ceased to be so necessary, it shall arrange for the document or device to be returned as soon as is reasonably practicable—

(a) to the person from whose possession it was taken, or

(b) to any of the charity trustees of the charity to which it belonged or related.

(11) A person who intentionally obstructs the exercise of any rights conferred by a warrant under this section is guilty of an offence and liable on summary conviction—

(a) to imprisonment for a term not exceeding 51 weeks, or

(b) to a fine not exceeding level 5 on the standard scale,

or to both.][263]

Amendment—Charities Act 2006, s 26(1).

Legal proceedings relating to charities

32 Proceedings by [Commission][264]

(1) Subject to subsection (2) below, [the Commission][265] may exercise the same powers with respect to—

(a) the taking of legal proceedings with reference to charities or the property or affairs of charities, or

(b) the compromise of claims with a view to avoiding or ending such proceedings,

as are exercisable by the Attorney General acting ex officio.

(2) Subsection (1) above does not apply to the power of the Attorney General under section 63(1) below to present a petition for the winding up of a charity.

(3) The practice and procedure to be followed in relation to any proceedings taken by [the Commission][266] under subsection (1) above shall be the same in all respects (and in particular as regards costs) as if they were proceedings taken by the Attorney General acting ex officio.

(4) No rule of law or practice shall be taken to require the Attorney General to be a party to any such proceedings.

(5) The powers exercisable by [the Commission][267] by virtue of this section shall be exercisable [by the Commission of its own][268] motion, but shall be exercisable only with the agreement of the Attorney General on each occasion.

---

[263] Amendment: Section inserted: Charities Act 2006, s 26(1), for transitional provisions see s 75(3), Sch 10, para 6.

[264] Amendment: Word substituted: Charities Act 2006, s 75(1), Sch 8, paras 96, 124(1), (4).

[265] Amendment: Words substituted: Charities Act 2006, s 75(1), Sch 8, paras 96, 124(1), (2).

[266] Amendment: Words substituted: Charities Act 2006, s 75(1), Sch 8, paras 96, 124(1), (2).

[267] Amendment: Words substituted: Charities Act 2006, s 75(1), Sch 8, paras 96, 124(1), (3)(a).

[268] Amendment: Words substituted: Charities Act 2006, s 75(1), Sch 8, paras 96, 124(1), (3)(b).

Amendments—Charities Act 2006, s 75(1), Sch 8, paras 96, 124.

33 Proceedings by other persons

(1) Charity proceedings may be taken with reference to a charity either by the charity, or by any of the charity trustees, or by any person interested in the charity, or by any two or more inhabitants of the area of the charity if it is a local charity, but not by any other person.

(2) Subject to the following provisions of this section, no charity proceedings relating to a charity …[269] shall be entertained or proceeded with in any court unless the taking of the proceedings is authorised by order of [the Commission][270].

(3) [The Commission][271] shall not, without special reasons, authorise the taking of charity proceedings where in [its opinion][272] the case can be dealt with [by the Commission][273] under the powers of this Act other than those conferred by section 32 above.

(4) This section shall not require any order for the taking of proceedings in a pending cause or matter or for the bringing of any appeal.

(5) Where the foregoing provisions of this section require the taking of charity proceedings to be authorised by an order of [the Commission][274], the proceedings may nevertheless be entertained or proceeded with if, after the order had been applied for and refused, leave to take the proceedings was obtained from one of the judges of the High Court attached to the Chancery Division.

(6) Nothing in the foregoing subsections shall apply to the taking of proceedings by the Attorney General, with or without a relator, or to the taking of proceedings by [the Commission][275] in accordance with section 32 above.

(7) Where it appears to [the Commission][276], on an application for an order under this section or otherwise, that it is desirable for legal proceedings to be taken with reference to any charity …[277] or its property or affairs, and for the proceedings to be taken by the Attorney General, [the Commission][278] shall so inform the Attorney General, and send him such statements and particulars as [the Commission thinks][279] necessary to explain the matter.

(8) In this section 'charity proceedings' means proceedings in any court in England or Wales brought under the court's jurisdiction with respect to charities, or brought under the court's jurisdiction with respect to trusts in relation to the administration of a trust for charitable purposes.

Amendments—Charities Act 2006, ss 12, 75, Sch 5, para 8, Sch 8, paras 96, 125, Sch 9.

---

[269] Amendment: Words omitted: Charities Act 2006, ss 12, 75(2), Sch 5, para 8(1), (2), Sch 9.
[270] Amendment: Words substituted: Charities Act 2006, s 75(1), Sch 8, paras 96, 125(1), (2).
[271] Amendment: Words substituted: Charities Act 2006, s 75(1), Sch 8, paras 96, 125(1), (3)(a).
[272] Amendment: Words substituted: Charities Act 2006, s 75(1), Sch 8, paras 96, 125(1), (3)(b).
[273] Amendment: Words substituted: Charities Act 2006, s 75(1), Sch 8, paras 96, 125(1), (3)(c).
[274] Amendment: Words substituted: Charities Act 2006, s 75(1), Sch 8, paras 96, 125(1), (4).
[275] Amendment: Words substituted: Charities Act 2006, s 75(1), Sch 8, paras 96, 125(1), (4).
[276] Amendment: Words substituted: Charities Act 2006, s 75(1), Sch 8, paras 96, 125(1), (5)(a).
[277] Amendment: Words omitted: Charities Act 2006, ss 12, 75(2), Sch 5, para 8(1), (3), Sch 9.
[278] Amendment: Words substituted: Charities Act 2006, s 75(1), Sch 8, paras 96, 125(1), (5)(a).
[279] Amendment: Words substituted: Charities Act 2006, s 75(1), Sch 8, paras 96, 125(1), (5)(b).

34 Report of s 8 inquiry to be evidence in certain proceedings

(1) A copy of the report of the person conducting an inquiry under section 8 above shall, if certified by [the Commission]²⁸⁰ to be a true copy, be admissible in any proceedings to which this section applies—

(a)   as evidence of any fact stated in the report; and

(b)   as evidence of the opinion of that person as to any matter referred to in it.

(2) This section applies to—

(a)   any legal proceedings instituted by [the Commission]²⁸¹ under this Part of this Act; and

(b)   any legal proceedings instituted by the Attorney General in respect of a charity.

(3) A document purporting to be a certificate issued for the purposes of subsection (1) above shall be received in evidence and be deemed to be such a certificate, unless the contrary is proved.

Amendments—Charities Act 2006, s 75(1), Sch 8, paras 96, 126.

Meaning of 'trust corporation'

35 Application of provisions to trust corporations appointed under s 16 or 18

(1) In the definition of 'trust corporation' contained in the following provisions—

(a)   section 117(xxx) of the Settled Land Act 1925,

(b)   section 68(18) of the Trustee Act 1925,

(c)   section 205(xxviii) of the Law of Property Act 1925,

(d)   section 55(xxvi) of the Administration of Estates Act 1925, and

(e)   section 128 of the [Supreme Court Act 1981]²⁸²,

the reference to a corporation appointed by the court in any particular case to be a trustee includes a reference to a corporation appointed by [the Commission]²⁸³ under this Act to be a trustee.

(2) This section shall be deemed always to have had effect; but the reference to section 128 of the [Supreme Court Act 1981]²⁸⁴ shall, in relation to any time before 1 January 1982, be construed as a reference to section 175(1) of the Supreme Court of Judicature (Consolidation) Act 1925.

Amendments—Constitutional Reform Act, s 59(5), Sch 11, para 1(2); Charities Act 2006, s 75(1), Sch 8, paras 96, 127.

---

280   Amendment: Words substituted: Charities Act 2006, s 75(1), Sch 8, paras 96, 126.
281   Amendment: Words substituted: Charities Act 2006, s 75(1), Sch 8, paras 96, 126.
282   Prospective amendment: Words substituted: Constitutional Reform Act 2005, s 59(5), Sch 11, para 1(2), as from a date to be appointed. New text= 'Senior Courts Act 1981'.
283   Amendment: Words substituted: Charities Act 2006, s 75(1), Sch 8, paras 96, 127.
284   Prospective amendment: Words substituted: Constitutional Reform Act 2005, s 59(5), Sch 11, para 1(2), as from a date to be appointed. New text= 'Senior Courts Act 1981'.

PART V
CHARITY LAND

36 Restrictions on dispositions

(1) Subject to the following provisions of this section and section 40 below, no land held by or in trust for a charity shall be [conveyed, transferred][285], leased or otherwise disposed of without an order of the court or of [the Commission][286].

(2) Subsection (1) above shall not apply to a disposition of such land if—

(a) the disposition is made to a person who is not—
   (i) a connected person (as defined in Schedule 5 to this Act), or
   (ii) a trustee for, or nominee of, a connected person; and
(b) the requirements of subsection (3) or (5) below have been complied with in relation to it.

(3) Except where the proposed disposition is the granting of such a lease as is mentioned in subsection (5) below, [the requirements mentioned in subsection (2)(b) above are that][287] the charity trustees must, before entering into an agreement for the sale, or (as the case may be) for a lease or other disposition, of the land—

(a) obtain and consider a written report on the proposed disposition from a qualified surveyor instructed by the trustees and acting exclusively for the charity;
(b) advertise the proposed disposition for such period and in such manner as the surveyor has advised in his report (unless he has there advised that it would not be in the best interests of the charity to advertise the proposed disposition); and
(c) decide that they are satisfied, having considered the surveyor's report, that the terms on which the disposition is proposed to be made are the best that can reasonably be obtained for the charity.

(4) For the purposes of subsection (3) above a person is a qualified surveyor if—

(a) he is a fellow or professional associate of the Royal Institution of Chartered Surveyors or of the Incorporated Society of Valuers and Auctioneers or satisfies such other requirement or requirements as may be prescribed by regulations made by the Secretary of State; and
(b) he is reasonably believed by the charity trustees to have ability in, and experience of, the valuation of land of the particular kind, and in the particular area, in question;

and any report prepared for the purposes of that subsection shall contain such information, and deal with such matters, as may be prescribed by regulations so made.

(5) Where the proposed disposition is the granting of a lease for a term ending not more than seven years after it is granted (other than one granted wholly or partly in consideration of a fine), [the requirements mentioned in subsection (2)(b) above are that][288] the charity trustees must, before entering into an agreement for the lease—

---

[285] Amendment: Words substituted: Charities Act 2006, s 75(1), Sch 8, paras 96, 128(1), (2)(a).
[286] Amendment: Words substituted: Charities Act 2006, s 75(1), Sch 8, paras 96, 128(1), (2)(b).
[287] Amendment: Words inserted: Charities Act 2006, s 75(1), Sch 8, paras 96, 128(1), (3).
[288] Amendment: Words inserted: Charities Act 2006, s 75(1), Sch 8, paras 96, 128(1), (4).

(a) obtain and consider the advice on the proposed disposition of a person who is reasonably believed by the trustees to have the requisite ability and practical experience to provide them with competent advice on the proposed disposition; and

(b) decide that they are satisfied, having considered that person's advice, that the terms on which the disposition is proposed to be made are the best that can reasonably be obtained for the charity.

(6) Where—

(a) any land is held by or in trust for a charity, and

(b) the trusts on which it is so held stipulate that it is to be used for the purposes, or any particular purposes, of the charity,

then (subject to subsections (7) and (8) below and without prejudice to the operation of the preceding provisions of this section) the land shall not be [conveyed, transferred][289], leased or otherwise disposed of unless the charity trustees have [before the relevant time][290]—

(i) given public notice of the proposed disposition, inviting representations to be made to them within a time specified in the notice, being not less than one month from the date of the notice; and

(ii) taken into consideration any representations made to them within that time about the proposed disposition.

[(6A) In subsection (6) above 'the relevant time' means—

(a) where the charity trustees enter into an agreement for the sale, or (as the case may be) for the lease or other disposition, the time when they enter into that agreement, and

(b) in any other case, the time of the disposition.][291]

(7) Subsection (6) above shall not apply to any such disposition of land as is there mentioned if—

(a) the disposition is to be effected with a view to acquiring by way of replacement other property which is to be held on the trusts referred to in paragraph (b) of that subsection; or

(b) the disposition is the granting of a lease for a term ending not more than two years after it is granted (other than one granted wholly or partly in consideration of a fine).

(8) [The Commission][292] may direct—

(a) that subsection (6) above shall not apply to dispositions of land held by or in trust for a charity or class of charities (whether generally or only in the case of a specified class of dispositions or land, or otherwise as may be provided in the direction), or

(b) that that subsection shall not apply to a particular disposition of land held by or in trust for a charity,

---

[289] Amendment: Words substituted: Charities Act 2006, s 75(1), Sch 8, paras 96, 128(1), (5)(a).
[290] Amendment: Words substituted: Charities Act 2006, s 75(1), Sch 8, paras 96, 128(1), (5)(b).
[291] Amendment: Subsection inserted: Charities Act 2006, s 75(1), Sch 8, paras 96, 128(1), (6).
[292] Amendment: Words substituted: Charities Act 2006, s 75(1), Sch 8, paras 96, 128(1), (7)(a).

if, on an application made to them in writing by or on behalf of the charity or charities in question, [the Commission is satisfied][293] that it would be in the interests of the charity or charities [for the Commission][294] to give the direction.

(9) The restrictions on disposition imposed by this section apply notwithstanding anything in the trusts of a charity; but nothing in this section applies—

(a)   to any disposition for which general or special authority is expressly given (without the authority being made subject to the sanction of an order of the court) by any statutory provision contained in or having effect under an Act of Parliament or by any scheme legally established; or

(b)   to any disposition of land held by or in trust for a charity which—

   (i)   is made to another charity otherwise than for the best price that can reasonably be obtained, and

   (ii)   is authorised to be so made by the trusts of the first-mentioned charity; or

(c)   to the granting, by or on behalf of a charity and in accordance with its trusts, of a lease to any beneficiary under those trusts where the lease—

   (i)   is granted otherwise than for the best rent that can reasonably be obtained; and

   (ii)   is intended to enable the demised premises to be occupied for the purposes, or any particular purposes, of the charity.

(10) Nothing in this section applies—

(a)   to any disposition of land held by or in trust for an exempt charity;

(b)   to any disposition of land by way of mortgage or other security; or

(c)   to any disposition of an advowson.

(11) In this section 'land' means land in England or Wales.

Amendments—Charities Act 2006, s 75(1), Sch 8, paras 96, 128.

37 Supplementary provisions relating to dispositions

(1) Any of the following instruments, namely—

(a)   any contract for the sale, or for a lease or other disposition, of land which is held by or in trust for a charity, and

(b)   any conveyance, transfer, lease or other instrument effecting a disposition of such land,

shall state—

(i)   that the land is held by or in trust for a charity,

(ii)   whether the charity is an exempt charity and whether the disposition is one falling within paragraph (a), (b) or (c) of subsection (9) of section 36 above, and

(iii) if it is not an exempt charity and the disposition is not one falling within any of those paragraphs, that the land is land to which the restrictions on disposition imposed by that section apply.

---

[293]   Amendment: Words substituted: Charities Act 2006, s 75(1), Sch 8, paras 96, 128(1), (7)(b).
[294]   Amendment: Words substituted: Charities Act 2006, s 75(1), Sch 8, paras 96, 128(1), (7)(c).

(2) Where any land held by or in trust for a charity is [conveyed, transferred][295], leased or otherwise disposed of by a disposition to which subsection (1) or (2) of section 36 above applies, the charity trustees shall certify in the instrument by which the disposition is effected—

  (a)   (where subsection (1) of that section applies) that the disposition has been sanctioned by an order of the court or of [the Commission][296] (as the case may be), or

  (b)   (where subsection (2) of that section applies) that the charity trustees have power under the trusts of the charity to effect the disposition, and that they have complied with the provisions of that section so far as applicable to it.

(3) Where subsection (2) above has been complied with in relation to any disposition of land, then in favour of a person who (whether under the disposition or afterwards) acquires an interest in the land for money or money's worth, it shall be conclusively presumed that the facts were as stated in the certificate.

(4) Where—

  (a)   any land held by or in trust for a charity is [conveyed, transferred][297], leased or otherwise disposed of by a disposition to which subsection (1) or (2) of section 36 above applies, but

  (b)   subsection (2) above has not been complied with in relation to the disposition,

then in favour of a person who (whether under the disposition or afterwards) in good faith acquires an interest in the land for money or money's worth, the disposition shall be valid whether or not—

  (i)   the disposition has been sanctioned by an order of the court or of [the Commission][298], or

  (ii)   the charity trustees have power under the trusts of the charity to effect the disposition and have complied with the provisions of that section so far as applicable to it.

(5) Any of the following instruments, namely—

  (a)   any contract for the sale, or for a lease or other disposition, of land which will, as a result of the disposition, be held by or in trust for a charity, and

  (b)   any conveyance, transfer, lease or other instrument effecting a disposition of such land,

shall state—

  (i)   that the land will, as a result of the disposition, be held by or in trust for a charity,

  (ii)   whether the charity is an exempt charity, and

  (iii) if it is not an exempt charity, that the restrictions on disposition imposed by section 36 above will apply to the land (subject to subsection (9) of that section).

(6) ...[299]

---

[295]   Amendment: Words substituted: Charities Act 2006, s 75(1), Sch 8, paras 96, 129(a).
[296]   Amendment: Words substituted: Charities Act 2006, s 75(1), Sch 8, paras 96, 129(b).
[297]   Amendment: Words substituted: Charities Act 2006, s 75(1), Sch 8, paras 96, 129(a).
[298]   Amendment: Words substituted: Charities Act 2006, s 75(1), Sch 8, paras 96, 129(b).
[299]   Amendment: Subsection repealed: Trusts of Land and Appointment of Trustees Act 1996, s 25(2), Sch 4, for savings see s 25(4), (5).

and expressions used in this subsection which are also used in that Act have the same meaning as in that Act.

[(7) Where the disposition to be effected by any such instrument as is mentioned in subsection (1)(b) or (5)(b) above will be—

(a)   a registrable disposition, or

(b)   a disposition which triggers the requirement of registration,

the statement which, by virtue of subsection (1) or (5) above, is to be contained in the instrument shall be in such form as may be prescribed by land registration rules.

(8) Where the registrar approves an application for registration of—

(a)   a disposition of registered land, or

(b)   a person's title under a disposition of unregistered land,

and the instrument effecting the disposition contains a statement complying with subsections (5) and (7) above, he shall enter in the register a restriction reflecting the limitation under section 36 above on subsequent disposal.][300]

(9) Where—

(a)   any such restriction is entered in the register in respect of any land, and

(b)   the charity by or in trust for which the land is held becomes an exempt charity,

the charity trustees shall apply to the registrar for [the removal of the entry][301]; and on receiving any application duly made under this subsection the registrar shall [remove the entry][302].

(10) Where—

(a)   any registered land is held by or in trust for an exempt charity and the charity ceases to be an exempt charity, or

(b)   any registered land becomes, as a result of a declaration of trust by the registered proprietor, land held in trust for a charity (other than an exempt charity),

the charity trustees shall apply to the registrar for such a restriction as is mentioned in subsection (8) above to be entered in the register in respect of the land; and on receiving any application duly made under this subsection the registrar shall enter such a restriction in the register in respect of the land.

(11) In this section—

(a)   references to a disposition of land do not include references to—

(i)   a disposition of land by way of mortgage or other security,

(ii)   any disposition of an advowson, or

(iii) any release of a rentcharge falling within section 40(1) below; and

(b)   'land' means land in England or Wales;

and subsections (7) to (10) above shall be construed as one with the [Land Registration Act 2002][303].

Amendments—Trusts of Land and Appointment of Trustees Act 1996, s 25(2), Sch 4; Land Registration Act 2002, s 133, Sch 11, para 29; Charities Act 2006, s 75(1), Sch 8, paras 96, 129.

---

[300]   Amendment: Subsections substituted: Land Registration Act 2002, s 133, Sch 11, para 29(1), (2).

[301]   Amendment: Words substituted: Land Registration Act 2002, s 133, Sch 11, para 29(1), (3)(a).

[302]   Amendment: Words substituted: Land Registration Act 2002, s 133, Sch 11, para 29(1), (3)(b).

[303]   Amendment: Words substituted: Land Registration Act 2002, s 133, Sch 11, para 29(1), (4).

38 Restrictions on mortgaging

(1) Subject to subsection (2) below, no mortgage of land held by or in trust for a charity shall be granted without an order of the court or of [the Commission][304].

[(2) Subsection (1) above shall not apply to a mortgage of any such land if the charity trustees have, before executing the mortgage, obtained and considered proper advice, given to them in writing, on the relevant matters or matter mentioned in subsection (3) or (3A) below (as the case may be).

(3) In the case of a mortgage to secure the repayment of a proposed loan or grant, the relevant matters are—

    (a)   whether the loan or grant is necessary in order for the charity trustees to be able to pursue the particular course of action in connection with which they are seeking the loan or grant;

    (b)   whether the terms of the loan or grant are reasonable having regard to the status of the charity as the prospective recipient of the loan or grant; and

    (c)   the ability of the charity to repay on those terms the sum proposed to be paid by way of loan or grant.

(3A) In the case of a mortgage to secure the discharge of any other proposed obligation, the relevant matter is whether it is reasonable for the charity trustees to undertake to discharge the obligation, having regard to the charity's purposes.

(3B) Subsection (3) or (as the case may be) subsection (3A) above applies in relation to such a mortgage as is mentioned in that subsection whether the mortgage—

    (a)   would only have effect to secure the repayment of the proposed loan or grant or the discharge of the proposed obligation, or

    (b)   would also have effect to secure the repayment of sums paid by way of loan or grant, or the discharge of other obligations undertaken, after the date of its execution.

(3C) Subsection (3D) below applies where—

    (a)   the charity trustees of a charity have executed a mortgage of land held by or in trust for a charity in accordance with subsection (2) above, and

    (b)   the mortgage has effect to secure the repayment of sums paid by way of loan or grant, or the discharge of other obligations undertaken, after the date of its execution.

(3D) In such a case, the charity trustees must not after that date enter into any transaction involving—

    (a)   the payment of any such sums, or

    (b)   the undertaking of any such obligations,

unless they have, before entering into the transaction, obtained and considered proper advice, given to them in writing, on the matters or matter mentioned in subsection (3)(a) to (c) or (3A) above (as the case may be).][305]

(4) For the purposes of [this section][306] proper advice is the advice of a person—

---

[304]   Amendment: Words substituted: Charities Act 2006, s 75(1), Sch 8, paras 96, 130.

[305]   Amendment: Subsections substituted: Charities Act 2006, s 27(1), (2).

[306]   Amendment: Words substituted: Charities Act 2006, s 27(1), (3)(a).

(a) who is reasonably believed by the charity trustees to be qualified by his ability in and practical experience of financial matters; and

(b) who has no financial interest in [relation to the loan, grant or other transaction in connection with which his advice is given][307];

and such advice may constitute proper advice for those purposes notwithstanding that the person giving it does so in the course of his employment as an officer or employee of the charity or of the charity trustees.

(5) This section applies notwithstanding anything in the trusts of a charity; but nothing in this section applies to any mortgage for which general or special authority is given as mentioned in section 36(9)(a) above.

(6) In this section—

'land' means land in England or Wales;
'mortgage' includes a charge.

(7) Nothing in this section applies to an exempt charity.

Amendments—Charities Act 2006, ss 27, 57(1), Sch 8, paras 96, 130.

39 Supplementary provisions relating to mortgaging

(1) Any mortgage of land held by or in trust for a charity shall state—

(a) that the land is held by or in trust for a charity,

(b) whether the charity is an exempt charity and whether the mortgage is one falling within subsection (5) of section 38 above, and

(c) if it is not an exempt charity and the mortgage is not one falling within that subsection, that the mortgage is one to which the restrictions imposed by that section apply;

and where the mortgage will be a registered disposition any such statement shall be in such form as may be prescribed [by land registration rules][308].

[(1A) Where any such mortgage will be one to which section 4(1)(g) of the Land Registration Act 2002 applies—

(a) the statement required by subsection (1) above shall be in such form as may be prescribed by land registration rules; and

(b) if the charity is not an exempt charity, the mortgage shall also contain a statement, in such form as may be prescribed by land registration rules, that the restrictions on disposition imposed by section 36 above apply to the land (subject to subsection (9) of that section).

(1B) Where—

(a) the registrar approves an application for registration of a person's title to land in connection with such a mortgage as is mentioned in subsection (1A) above,

(b) the mortgage contains statements complying with subsections (1) and (1A) above, and

(c) the charity is not an exempt charity,

the registrar shall enter in the register a restriction reflecting the limitation under section 36 above on subsequent disposal.

---

[307] Amendment: Words substituted: Charities Act 2006, s 27(1), (3)(b).
[308] Amendment: Words substituted: Land Registration Act 2002, s 133, Sch 11, para 29(1), (5).

(1C) Section 37(9) above shall apply in relation to any restriction entered under subsection (1B) as it applies in relation to any restriction entered under section 37(8).][309]

(2) Where subsection (1) or (2) of section 38 above applies to any mortgage of land held by or in trust for a charity, the charity trustees shall certify in the mortgage—

(a)   (where subsection (1) of that section applies) that the mortgage has been sanctioned by an order of the court or of [the Commission][310] (as the case may be), or

(b)   (where subsection (2) of that section applies) that the charity trustees have power under the trusts of the charity to grant the mortgage, and that they have obtained and considered such advice as is mentioned in that subsection.

(3) Where subsection (2) above has been complied with in relation to any mortgage, then in favour of a person who (whether under the mortgage or afterwards) acquires an interest in the land in question for money or money's worth, it shall be conclusively presumed that the facts were as stated in the certificate.

(4) Where—

(a)   subsection (1) or (2) of section 38 above applies to any mortgage of land held by or in trust for a charity, but

(b)   subsection (2) above has not been complied with in relation to the mortgage,

then in favour of a person who (whether under the mortgage or afterwards) in good faith acquires an interest in the land for money or money's worth, the mortgage shall be valid whether or not—

(i)   the mortgage has been sanctioned by an order of the court or of [the Commission][311], or

(ii)   the charity trustees have power under the trusts of the charity to grant the mortgage and have obtained and considered such advice as is mentioned in subsection (2) of that section.

[(4A) Where subsection (3D) of section 38 above applies to any mortgage of land held by or in trust for a charity, the charity trustees shall certify in relation to any transaction falling within that subsection that they have obtained and considered such advice as is mentioned in that subsection.

(4B) Where subsection (4A) above has been complied with in relation to any transaction, then, in favour of a person who (whether under the mortgage or afterwards) has acquired or acquires an interest in the land for money or money's worth, it shall be conclusively presumed that the facts were as stated in the certificate.][312]

(5) ...[313]

(6) In this section—

'mortgage' includes a charge, and 'mortgagee' shall be construed accordingly;
'land' means land in England or Wales;

---

[309]   Amendment: Subsections substituted: Land Registration Act 2002, s 133, Sch 11, para 29(1), (6).

[310]   Amendment: Words substituted: Charities Act 2006, s 75(1), Sch 8, paras 96, 131(1), (2).

[311]   Amendment: Words substituted: Charities Act 2006, s 75(1), Sch 8, paras 96, 131(1), (2).

[312]   Amendment: Subsections inserted: Charities Act 2006, s 75(1), Sch 8, paras 96, 131(1), (3).

[313]   Amendment: Subsection repealed: Trusts of Land and Appointment of Trustees Act 1996, s 25(2), Sch 4, for savings see s 25(4), (5).

[and subsections (1) to (1B) above shall be construed as one with the Land Registration Act 2002.][314]

Amendments—Trusts of Land and Appointment of Trustees Act 1996, s 25(2), Sch 4; Land Registration Act 1997, s 4(21), Sch 1, para 6(2); Land Registration Act 2002, s 133, Sch 11, para 29; Charities Act 2006, s 75(1), Sch 8, paras 96, 131.

40 Release of charity rentcharges

(1) Section 36(1) above shall not apply to the release by a charity of a rentcharge which it is entitled to receive if the release is given in consideration of the payment of an amount which is not less than ten times the annual amount of the rentcharge.

(2) Where a charity which is entitled to receive a rentcharge releases it in consideration of the payment of an amount not exceeding £500, any costs incurred by the charity in connection with proving its title to the rentcharge shall be recoverable by the charity from the person or persons in whose favour the rentcharge is being released.

(3) Neither section 36(1) nor subsection (2) above applies where a rentcharge which a charity is entitled to receive is redeemed under sections 8 to 10 of the Rentcharges Act 1977.

(4) The Secretary of State may by order amend subsection (2) above by substituting a different sum for the sum for the time being specified there.

PART VI
CHARITY ACCOUNTS, REPORTS AND RETURNS

41 Duty to keep accounting records

(1) The charity trustees of a charity shall ensure that accounting records are kept in respect of the charity which are sufficient to show and explain all the charity's transactions, and which are such as to—

    (a) disclose at any time, with reasonable accuracy, the financial position of the charity at that time, and

    (b) enable the trustees to ensure that, where any statements of accounts are prepared by them under section 42(1) below, those statements of accounts comply with the requirements of regulations under that provision.

(2) The accounting records shall in particular contain—

    (a) entries showing from day to day all sums of money received and expended by the charity, and the matters in respect of which the receipt and expenditure takes place; and

    (b) a record of the assets and liabilities of the charity.

(3) The charity trustees of a charity shall preserve any accounting records made for the purposes of this section in respect of the charity for at least six years from the end of the financial year of the charity in which they are made.

(4) Where a charity ceases to exist within the period of six years mentioned in subsection (3) above as it applies to any accounting records, the obligation to preserve those records in accordance with that subsection shall continue to be discharged by the

---

[314] Amendment: Words substituted: Land Registration Act 2002, s 133, Sch 11, para 29(1), (7).

last charity trustees of the charity, unless [the Commission consents]³¹⁵ in writing to the records being destroyed or otherwise disposed of.

(5) Nothing in this section applies to a charity which is a company.

Amendment—Charities Act 2006, s 75(1), Sch 8, paras 96, 132.

42 Annual statements of accounts

(1) The charity trustees of a charity shall (subject to subsection (3) below) prepare in respect of each financial year of the charity a statement of accounts complying with such requirements as to its form and contents as may be prescribed by regulations made by the Secretary of State.

(2) Without prejudice to the generality of subsection (1) above, regulations under that subsection may make provision—

    (a)   for any such statement to be prepared in accordance with such methods and principles as are specified or referred to in the regulations;

    (b)   as to any information to be provided by way of notes to the accounts;

and regulations under that subsection may also make provision for determining the financial years of a charity for the purposes of this Act and any regulations made under it.

[(2A) Such regulations may, however, not impose on the charity trustees of a charity that is a charitable trust created by any person ('the settlor') any requirement to disclose, in any statement of accounts prepared by them under subsection (1)—

    (a)   the identities of recipients of grants made out of the funds of the charity, or

    (b)   the amounts of any individual grants so made,

if the disclosure would fall to be made at a time when the settlor or any spouse or civil partner of his was still alive.]³¹⁶

(3) Where a charity's gross income in any financial year does not exceed [£100,000]³¹⁷, the charity trustees may, in respect of that year, elect to prepare the following, namely—

    (a)   a receipts and payments account, and

    (b)   a statement of assets and liabilities,

instead of a statement of accounts under subsection (1) above.

(4) The charity trustees of a charity shall preserve—

    (a)   any statement of accounts prepared by them under subsection (1) above, or

    (b)   any account and statement prepared by them under subsection (3) above,

for at least six years from the end of the financial year to which any such statement relates or (as the case may be) to which any such account and statement relate.

(5) Subsection (4) of section 41 above shall apply in relation to the preservation of any such statement or account and statement as it applies in relation to the preservation of any accounting records (the references to subsection (3) of that section being read as references to subsection (4) above).

---

³¹⁵ Amendment: Words substituted: Charities Act 2006, s 75(1), Sch 8, paras 96, 132.
³¹⁶ Amendment: Subsection inserted: Charities Act 2006, s 75(1), Sch 8, paras 96, 133(1), (2).
³¹⁷ Amendment: Figure substituted: The Charities Act 1993 (Substitution of Sums) Order 1995, SI 1995/2696, art 2(3).

(6) The Secretary of State may by order amend subsection (3) above by substituting a different sum for the sum for the time being specified there.

(7) Nothing in this section applies to a charity which is a company.

[(8) Provisions about the preparation of accounts in respect of groups consisting of certain charities and their subsidiary undertakings, and about other matters relating to such groups, are contained in Schedule 5A to this Act (see section 49A below).][318]

Amendments—The Charities Act 1993 (Substitution of Sums) Order 1995, SI 1995/2696, art 2(3); Charities Act 2006, s 75(1), Sch 8, paras 96, 133.

43 Annual audit or examination of charity accounts

[(1) Subsection (2) below applies to a financial year of a charity if—

- (a) the charity's gross income in that year exceeds £500,000; or
- (b) the charity's gross income in that year exceeds the accounts threshold and at the end of the year the aggregate value of its assets (before deduction of liabilities) exceeds £2.8 million.

'The accounts threshold' means £100,000 or such other sum as is for the time being specified in section 42(3) above.][319].

(2) If this subsection applies to a financial year of a charity, the accounts of the charity for that year shall be audited by a person who—

- [(a) would be eligible for appointment as auditor of the charity under Part 2 of the Companies Act 1989 if the charity were a company, or][320]
- (b) is a member of a body for the time being specified in regulations under section 44 below and is under the rules of that body eligible for appointment as auditor of the charity.

(3) If subsection (2) above does not apply to a financial year of a charity [but its gross income in that year exceeds £10,000,][321] the accounts of the charity for that year shall, at the election of the charity trustees, either—

- (a) be examined by an independent examiner, that is to say an independent person who is reasonably believed by the trustees to have the requisite ability and practical experience to carry out a competent examination of the accounts, or
- (b) be audited by such a person as is mentioned in subsection (2) above.

[This is subject to the requirements of subsection (3A) below where the gross income exceeds £250,000, and to any order under subsection (4) below.][322]

[(3A) If subsection (3) above applies to the accounts of a charity for a year and the charity's gross income in that year exceeds £250,000, a person qualifies as an independent examiner for the purposes of paragraph (a) of that subsection if (and only if) he is an independent person who is—

---

[318] Amendment: Subsection added: Charities Act 2006, s 75(1), Sch 8, paras 96, 133(1), (3).

[319] Amendment: Subsection substituted: Charities Act 2006, s 28(1), (2), for transitional provisions see s 75(3), Sch 10, para 7.

[320] Amendment: Paragraph substituted: Charities Act 2006, s 28(1), (3), for transitional provisions see s 75(3), Sch 10, para 7.

[321] Amendment: Words substituted: Charities Act 2006, s 28(1), (4)(a), for transitional provisions see s 75(3), Sch 10, para 7.

[322] Amendment: Words inserted: Charities Act 2006, s 28(1), (4)(b), for transitional provisions see s 75(3), Sch 10, para 7.

(a)   a member of a body for the time being specified in section 249D(3) of the Companies Act 1985 (reporting accountants);

(b)   a member of the Chartered Institute of Public Finance and Accountancy; or

(c)   a Fellow of the Association of Charity Independent Examiners.][323]

(4) Where it appears to [the Commission][324]—

(a)   that subsection (2), or (as the case may be) subsection (3) above, has not been complied with in relation to a financial year of a charity within ten months from the end of that year, or

(b)   that, although subsection (2) above does not apply to a financial year of a charity, it would nevertheless be desirable for the accounts of the charity for that year to be audited by such a person as is mentioned in that subsection,

[the Commission][325] may by order require the accounts of the charity for that year to be audited by such a person as is mentioned in that subsection.

(5) If [the Commission makes][326] an order under subsection (4) above with respect to a charity, then unless—

(a)   the order is made by virtue of paragraph (b) of that subsection, and

(b)   the charity trustees themselves appoint an auditor in accordance with the order,

the auditor shall be a person appointed by [the Commission][327].

(6) The expenses of any audit carried out by an auditor appointed by [the Commission][328] under subsection (5) above, including the auditor's remuneration, shall be recoverable by [the Commission][329]—

(a)   from the charity trustees of the charity concerned, who shall be personally liable, jointly and severally, for those expenses; or

(b)   to the extent that it appears to [the Commission][330] not to be practical to seek recovery of those expenses in accordance with paragraph (a) above, from the funds of the charity.

(7) [The Commission][331] may—

(a)   give guidance to charity trustees in connection with the selection of a person for appointment as an independent examiner;

(b)   give such directions as [it thinks][332] appropriate with respect to the carrying out of an examination in pursuance of subsection (3)(a) above;

and any such guidance or directions may either be of general application or apply to a particular charity only.

[(8) The Minister may by order—

---

[323]   Amendment: Subsection inserted: Charities Act 2006, s 28(1), (5), for transitional provisions see s 75(3), Sch 10, para 7.

[324]   Amendment: Words substituted: Charities Act 2006, s 75(1), Sch 8, paras 96, 134(1), (2).

[325]   Amendment: Words substituted: Charities Act 2006, s 75(1), Sch 8, paras 96, 134(1), (2).

[326]   Amendment: Words substituted: Charities Act 2006, s 75(1), Sch 8, paras 96, 134(1), (3)(a).

[327]   Amendment: Words substituted: Charities Act 2006, s 75(1), Sch 8, paras 96, 134(1), (3)(b).

[328]   Amendment: Words substituted: Charities Act 2006, s 75(1), Sch 8, paras 96, 134(1), (4).

[329]   Amendment: Words substituted: Charities Act 2006, s 75(1), Sch 8, paras 96, 134(1), (4).

[330]   Amendment: Words substituted: Charities Act 2006, s 75(1), Sch 8, paras 96, 134(1), (4).

[331]   Amendment: Words substituted: Charities Act 2006, s 75(1), Sch 8, paras 96, 134(1), (5)(a).

[332]   Amendment: Words substituted: Charities Act 2006, s 75(1), Sch 8, paras 96, 134(1), (5)(b).

(a) amend subsection (1)(a) or (b), (3) or (3A) above by substituting a different sum for any sum for the time being specified there;

(b) amend subsection (3A) by adding or removing a description of person to or from the list in that subsection or by varying any entry for the time being included in that list.][333]

(9) Nothing in this section applies to a charity which is a company.

[(10 Nothing in this section applies in relation to a financial year of a charity where, at any time in the year, a charity is an English National Health Service charity or Welsh National Health Service charity (as defined in sections 43A and 43B respectively).][334]

Amendments—Deregulation and Contracting Out Act 1994, s 28; The Charities Act 1993 (Substitution of Sums) Order 1995, SI 1995/2696, art 2(4); The Regulatory Reform (National Health Service Charitable and Non-Charitable Trust Accounts and Audit) Order 2005, SI 2005/1074, art 3(1), (2); Charities Act 2006, ss 28, 75(1), Sch 8, paras 96, 134.

[43A Annual audit or examination of English National Health Service charity accounts

(1) This section applies in relation to a financial year of a charity where, at any time in the year, the charity is an English National Health Service charity.

(2) In any case where [paragraph (a) or (b) of section 43(1) is satisfied in relation to][335] a financial year of an English National Health Service charity, the accounts of the charity for that financial year shall be audited by a person appointed by the Audit Commission.

(3) In any other case, the accounts of the charity for that financial year shall, at the election of the Audit Commission, be—

(a) audited by a person appointed by the Audit Commission; or
(b) examined by a person so appointed.

(4) Section 3 of the Audit Commission Act 1998 (c 18) applies in relation to any appointment under subsection (2) or (3)(a).

(5) [The Commission][336] may give such directions as [it thinks][337] appropriate with respect to the carrying out of an examination in pursuance of subsection (3)(b); and any such directions may either be of general application or apply to a particular charity only.

(6) The Comptroller and Auditor General may at any time examine and inspect—

(a) the accounts of the charity for the financial year;
(b) any records relating to those accounts; and
(c) any report of a person appointed under subsection (2) or (3) to audit or examine those accounts.

(7) In this section—

'Audit Commission' means the Audit Commission for Local Authorities and the National Health Service in England and Wales; and

---

[333] Amendment: Subsection substituted: Charities Act 2006, s 28(1), (6), for transitional provisions see s 75(3), Sch 10, para 7.

[334] Amendment: Subsection inserted: The Regulatory Reform (National Health Service Charitable and Non-Charitable Trust Accounts and Audit) Order 2005, SI 2005/1074, art 3(1), (2).

[335] Amendment: Words substituted: Charities Act 2006, s 75(1), Sch 8, paras 96, 135(1), (2).

[336] Amendment: Words substituted: Charities Act 2006, s 75(1), Sch 8, paras 96, 135(1), (3)(a).

[337] Amendment: Words substituted: Charities Act 2006, s 75(1), Sch 8, paras 96, 135(1), (3)(b).

'English National Health Service charity' means a charitable trust, the trustees of which are—

(a)   a Strategic Health Authority;

(b)   a Primary Care Trust;

(c)   a National Health Service trust all or most of whose hospitals, establishments and facilities are situated in England;

(d)   trustees appointed in pursuance of section 11 of the National Health Service and Community Care Act 1990 (c 19), or special trustees appointed in pursuance of section 29(1) of the National Health Service Reorganisation Act 1973 (c 32) and section 95(1) of the National Health Service Act 1977 (c 49), for a National Health Service trust falling within paragraph (c); or

(e)   trustees for a Primary Care Trust appointed in pursuance of section 96B of the National Health Service Act 1977.][338]

Amendments—The Regulatory Reform (National Health Service Charitable and Non-Charitable Trust Accounts and Audit) Order 2005, SI 2005/1074, art 3(1), (3); Charities Act 2006, s 75(1), Sch 8, paras 96, 135.

[43B Annual audit or examination of Welsh National Health Service charity accounts

(1) This section applies in relation to a financial year of a charity where, at any time in the year, the charity is a Welsh National Health Service charity.

(2) In any case where [paragraph (a) or (b) of section 43(1) is satisfied in relation to][339] a financial year of a Welsh National Health Service charity, the accounts of the charity for that financial year shall be audited by the Auditor General for Wales.

(3) In any other case, the accounts of the charity for that financial year shall, at the election of the Auditor General for Wales, be audited or examined by the Auditor General for Wales.

(4) In this section—

'Welsh National Health Service charity' means a charitable trust, the trustees of which are—

(a)   a Local Health Board;

(b)   a National Health Service trust all or most of whose hospitals, establishments and facilities are situated in Wales; or

(c)   trustees appointed in pursuance of section 11 of the National Health Service and Community Care Act 1990 (c 19), or special trustees appointed in pursuance of section 29(1) of the National Health Service Reorganisation Act 1973 (c 32) and section 95(1) of the National Health Service Act 1977 (c 49), for a National Health Service trust falling within paragraph (b).][340]

[(5) References in this Act to an auditor or an examiner have effect in relation to this section as references to the Auditor General for Wales acting under this section as an auditor or examiner.][341]

Amendments—The Regulatory Reform (National Health Service Charitable and Non-Charitable Trust Accounts and Audit) Order 2005, SI 2005/1074, art 3(1), (3); Charities Act 2006, s 75(1), Sch 8, paras 96, 136.

---

[338]   Amendment: Section inserted: The Regulatory Reform (National Health Service Charitable and Non-Charitable Trust Accounts and Audit) Order 2005, SI 2005/1074, art 3(1),(3).

[339]   Amendment: Words substituted: Charities Act 2006, s 75(1), Sch 8, paras 96, 136(1), (2).

[340]   Amendment: Section inserted: The Regulatory Reform (National Health Service Charitable and Non-Charitable Trust Accounts and Audit) Order 2005, SI 2005/1074, art 3(1), (3).

[341]   Amendment: Subsection added: Charities Act 2006, s 75(1), Sch 8, paras 96, 136(1), (3).

44 Supplementary provisions relating to audits etc

(1) The Secretary of State may by regulations make provision—

(a)   specifying one or more bodies for the purposes of section 43(2)(b) above;

(b)   with respect to the duties of an auditor carrying out an audit under section 43[, 43A or 43B][342] above, including provision with respect to the making by him of a report on—

    (i)   the statement of accounts prepared for the financial year in question under section 42(1) above, or

    (ii)   the account and statement so prepared under section 42(3) above,

    as the case may be;

[(c)   with respect to the making of a report—

    (i)   by an independent examiner in respect of an examination carried out by him under section 43 above; or

    (ii)   by an examiner in respect of an examination carried out by him under section 43A or 43B above;][343]

(d)   conferring on such an auditor or on an independent examiner [or examiner][344] a right of access with respect to books, documents and other records (however kept) which relate to the charity concerned;

(e)   entitling such an auditor or an independent examiner [or examiner][345] to require, in the case of a charity, information and explanations from past or present charity trustees or trustees for the charity, or from past or present officers or employees of the charity;

(f)   enabling [the Commission][346], in circumstances specified in the regulations, to dispense with the requirements of section 43(2) or (3) above in the case of a particular charity or in the case of any particular financial year of a charity.

(2) If any person fails to afford an auditor or an independent examiner [or examiner][347] any facility to which he is entitled by virtue of subsection (1)(d) or (e) above, [the Commission][348] may by order give—

(a)   to that person, or

(b)   to the charity trustees for the time being of the charity concerned,

such directions as [the Commission thinks][349] appropriate for securing that the default is made good.

(3) ...[350]

Amendments—Charities Act 2006, s 75, Sch 8, paras 96, 137, Sch 9.

[44A Duty of auditors etc to report matters to Commission

(1) This section applies to—

(a)   a person acting as an auditor or independent examiner appointed by or in relation to a charity under section 43 above,

---

[342]   Amendment: Words inserted: Charities Act 2006, s 75(1), Sch 8, paras 96, 137(1), (2)(a).

[343]   Amendment: Paragraph substituted: Charities Act 2006, s 75(1), Sch 8, paras 96, 137(1), (2)(b).

[344]   Amendment: Words inserted: Charities Act 2006, s 75(1), Sch 8, paras 96, 137(1), (2)(c).

[345]   Amendment: Words inserted: Charities Act 2006, s 75(1), Sch 8, paras 96, 137(1), (2)(c).

[346]   Amendment: Words substituted: Charities Act 2006, s 75(1), Sch 8, paras 96, 137(1), (2)(d).

[347]   Amendment: Words inserted: Charities Act 2006, s 75(1), Sch 8, paras 96, 137(1), (3)(a).

[348]   Amendment: Words substituted: Charities Act 2006, s 75(1), Sch 8, paras 96, 137(1), (3)(b).

[349]   Amendment: Words substituted: Charities Act 2006, s 75(1), Sch 8, paras 96, 137(1), (3)(c).

[350]   Amendment: Subsection omitted: Charities Act 2006, s 75, Sch 8, paras 96, 137(1), (4), Sch 9.

(b)   a person acting as an auditor or examiner appointed under section 43A(2) or (3) above, and

(c)   the Auditor General for Wales acting under section 43B(2) or (3) above.

(2) If, in the course of acting in the capacity mentioned in subsection (1) above, a person to whom this section applies becomes aware of a matter—

(a)   which relates to the activities or affairs of the charity or of any connected institution or body, and

(b)   which he has reasonable cause to believe is likely to be of material significance for the purposes of the exercise by the Commission of its functions under section 8 or 18 above,

he must immediately make a written report on the matter to the Commission.

(3) If, in the course of acting in the capacity mentioned in subsection (1) above, a person to whom this section applies becomes aware of any matter—

(a)   which does not appear to him to be one that he is required to report under subsection (2) above, but

(b)   which he has reasonable cause to believe is likely to be relevant for the purposes of the exercise by the Commission of any of its functions,

he may make a report on the matter to the Commission.

(4) Where the duty or power under subsection (2) or (3) above has arisen in relation to a person acting in the capacity mentioned in subsection (1), the duty or power is not affected by his subsequently ceasing to act in that capacity.

(5) Where a person makes a report as required or authorised by subsection (2) or (3), no duty to which he is subject is to be regarded as contravened merely because of any information or opinion contained in the report.

(6) In this section 'connected institution or body', in relation to a charity, means—

(a)   an institution which is controlled by, or

(b)   a body corporate in which a substantial interest is held by,

the charity or any one or more of the charity trustees acting in his or their capacity as such.

(7) Paragraphs 3 and 4 of Schedule 5 to this Act apply for the purposes of subsection (6) above as they apply for the purposes of provisions of that Schedule.][351]

Amendment—Charities Act 2006, s 29(1).

45 Annual reports

(1) The charity trustees of a charity shall prepare in respect of each financial year of the charity an annual report containing—

(a)   such a report by the trustees on the activities of the charity during that year, and

(b)   such other information relating to the charity or to its trustees or officers,

as may be prescribed by regulations made by the Secretary of State.

---

[351]   Amendment: Section inserted: Charities Act 2006, s 29(1), for transitional provisions see s 75(3), Sch 10, para 8.

(2) Without prejudice to the generality of subsection (1) above, regulations under that subsection may make provision—

(a)　for any such report as is mentioned in paragraph (a) of that subsection to be prepared in accordance with such principles as are specified or referred to in the regulations;

(b)　enabling [the Commission]³⁵² to dispense with any requirement prescribed by virtue of subsection (1)(b) above in the case of a particular charity or a particular class of charities, or in the case of a particular financial year of a charity or of any class of charities.

(3) [Where [a charity's gross income in any financial year]³⁵³ exceeds £10,000, [a copy of]³⁵⁴ the annual report required to be prepared under this section in respect of that year]³⁵⁵ shall be transmitted to [the Commission]³⁵⁶ by the charity trustees—

(a)　within ten months from the end of that year, or

(b)　within such longer period as [the Commission]³⁵⁷ may for any special reason allow in the case of that report.

[(3A) Where [a charity's gross income in any financial year does not exceed]³⁵⁸ £10,000, [a copy of]³⁵⁹ the annual report required to be prepared under this section in respect of that year shall, if [the Commission so requests, be transmitted to it]³⁶⁰ by the charity trustees—

(a)　in the case of a request made before the end of seven months from the end of the financial year to which the report relates, within ten months from the end of that year, and

(b)　in the case of a request not so made, within three months from the date of the request,

or, in either case, within such longer period as [the Commission]³⁶¹ may for any special reason allow in the case of that report.]³⁶²

[(3B) But in the case of a charity which is constituted as a CIO—

(a)　the requirement imposed by subsection (3) applies whatever the charity's gross income is, and

(b)　subsection (3A) does not apply.]³⁶³

(4) Subject to subsection (5) below, [any [copy of an annual report transmitted to the Commission]³⁶⁴ under this section]³⁶⁵ shall have attached to it [a copy of]³⁶⁶ the

---

³⁵² Amendment: Words substituted: Charities Act 2006, s 75(1), Sch 8, paras 96, 138(1), (2).
³⁵³ Amendment: Words substituted: Charities Act 2006, s 75(1), Sch 8, paras 96, 138(1), (3)(a).
³⁵⁴ Amendment: Words inserted: Charities Act 2006, s 75(1), Sch 8, paras 96, 138(1), (3)(b).
³⁵⁵ Amendment: Words substituted: Deregulation and Contracting Out Act 1994, s 29(1).
³⁵⁶ Amendment: Words substituted: Charities Act 2006, s 75(1), Sch 8, paras 96, 138(1), (3)(c).
³⁵⁷ Amendment: Words substituted: Charities Act 2006, s 75(1), Sch 8, paras 96, 138(1), (3)(c).
³⁵⁸ Amendment: Words substituted: Charities Act 2006, s 75(1), Sch 8, paras 96, 138(1), (4)(a).
³⁵⁹ Amendment: Words inserted: Charities Act 2006, s 75(1), Sch 8, paras 96, 138(1), (4)(b).
³⁶⁰ Amendment: Words substituted: Charities Act 2006, s 75(1), Sch 8, paras 96, 138(1), (4)(c).
³⁶¹ Amendment: Words substituted: Charities Act 2006, s 75(1), Sch 8, paras 96, 138(1), (4)(d).
³⁶² Amendment: Subsection inserted: Deregulation and Contracting Out Act 1994, s 29(2).
³⁶³ Amendment: Subsection inserted: Charities Act 2006, s 34, Sch 7, Pt 2, paras 3, 4.
³⁶⁴ Amendment: Words substituted: Charities Act 2006, s 75(1), Sch 8, paras 96, 138(1), (5)(a).
³⁶⁵ Amendment: Words substituted: Deregulation and Contracting Out Act 1994, s 29(3).
³⁶⁶ Amendment: Words inserted: Charities Act 2006, s 75(1), Sch 8, paras 96, 138(1), (5)(b).

statement of accounts prepared for the financial year in question under section 42(1) above or (as the case may be) [a copy of][367] the account and statement so prepared under section 42(3) above, together with—

(a) where the accounts of the charity for that year have been audited under section 43[, 43A or 43B][368] above, a copy of the report made by the auditor on that statement of accounts or (as the case may be) on that account and statement;

(b) where the accounts of the charity for that year have been examined under section 43[, 43A or 43B][369] above, a copy of the report made by the [person carrying out the examination][370].

(5) Subsection (4) above does not apply to a charity which is a company, and any [copy of an][371] annual report transmitted by the charity trustees of such a charity under [this section][372] shall instead have attached to it a copy of the charity's annual accounts prepared for the financial year in question under Part VII of the Companies Act 1985, together with a copy of [any auditors report or report made for the purposes of section 249A(2) of that Act][373] on those accounts.

(6) Any [copy of an][374] annual report transmitted to [the Commission][375] under [this section][376], together with the documents attached to it, shall be kept by [the Commission][377] for such period as [it thinks fit][378].

[(7) The charity trustees of a charity shall preserve, for at least six years from the end of the financial year to which it relates, any annual report prepared by them under subsection (1) above [of which they have not been required to transmit a copy to the Commission.][379]

(8) Subsection (4) of section 41 above shall apply in relation to the preservation of any such annual report as it applies in relation to the preservation of any accounting records (the references [to subsection (3)][380] of that section being read as references to subsection (7) above).

(9) The Secretary of State may by order amend subsection (3) or (3A) above by substituting a different sum for the sum for the time being specified there.][381]

Amendments—Deregulation and Contracting Out Act 1994, s 29; The Companies Act 1985 (Audit Exemption) Regulations 1994, SI 1994/1935, reg 4, Sch 1, para 6; The Regulatory Reform (National Health Service Charitable and Non-Charitable Trust Accounts and Audit) Order 2005, SI 2005/1074, art 3(1), (4)(a); Charities Act 2006, ss 34, 75(1), Sch 7, Pt 2, paras 3, 4, Sch 8, paras 96, 138.

---

[367] Amendment: Words inserted: Charities Act 2006, s 75(1), Sch 8, paras 96, 138(1), (5)(b).
[368] Amendment: Words inserted: The Regulatory Reform (National Health Service Charitable and Non-Charitable Trust Accounts and Audit) Order 2005, SI 2005/1074, art 3(1), (4)(a).
[369] Amendment: Words inserted: The Regulatory Reform (National Health Service Charitable and Non-Charitable Trust Accounts and Audit) Order 2005, SI 2005/1074, art 3(1), (4)(a).
[370] Amendment: Words inserted: The Regulatory Reform (National Health Service Charitable and Non-Charitable Trust Accounts and Audit) Order 2005, SI 2005/1074, art 3(1), (4)(b).
[371] Amendment: Words inserted: Charities Act 2006, s 75(1), Sch 8, paras 96, 138(1), (6).
[372] Amendment: Words substituted: Deregulation and Contracting Out Act 1994, s 29(4).
[373] Amendment: Words substituted: The Companies Act 1985 (Audit Exemption) Regulations 1994, SI 1994/1935, reg 4, Sch 1, para 6.
[374] Amendment: Words inserted: Charities Act 2006, s 75(1), Sch 8, paras 96, 138(1), (7)(a).
[375] Amendment: Words substituted: Charities Act 2006, s 75(1), Sch 8, paras 96, 138(1), (7)(b).
[376] Amendment: Words substituted: Deregulation and Contracting Out Act 1994, s 29(5).
[377] Amendment: Words substituted: Charities Act 2006, s 75(1), Sch 8, paras 96, 138(1), (7)(b).
[378] Amendment: Words substituted: Charities Act 2006, s 75(1), Sch 8, paras 96, 138(1), (7)(c).
[379] Amendment: Words substituted: Charities Act 2006, s 75(1), Sch 8, paras 96, 138(1), (8).
[380] Amendment: Words substituted: Charities Act 2006, s 75(1), Sch 8, paras 96, 138(1), (9).
[381] Amendment: Subsection inserted: Deregulation and Contracting Out Act 1994, s 29(6).

46 Special provision as respects accounts and annual reports of exempt and other excepted charities

(1) Nothing in [sections 41 to 44 or section 45][382] above applies to any exempt charity; but the charity trustees of an exempt charity shall keep proper books of account with respect to the affairs of the charity, and if not required by or under the authority of any other Act to prepare periodical statements of account shall prepare consecutive statements of account consisting on each occasion of an income and expenditure account relating to a period of not more than fifteen months and a balance sheet relating to the end of that period.

(2) The books of accounts and statements of account relating to an exempt charity shall be preserved for a period of six years at least unless the charity ceases to exist and [the Commission consents][383] in writing to their being destroyed or otherwise disposed of.

[(2A) Section 44A(2) to (7) above shall apply in relation to a person appointed to audit, or report on, the accounts of an exempt charity which is not a company as they apply in relation to a person such as is mentioned in section 44A(1).

(2B) But section 44A(2) to (7) so apply with the following modifications—

    (a)   any reference to a person acting in the capacity mentioned in section 44A(1) is to be read as a reference to his acting as a person appointed as mentioned in subsection (2A) above; and

    (b)   any reference to the Commission or to any of its functions is to be read as a reference to the charity's principal regulator or to any of that person's functions in relation to the charity as such.][384]

[(3) Except in accordance with subsections (3A) and (3B) below, nothing in section 43, 44, 44A or 45 applies to any charity which—

    (a)   falls within section 3A(2)(d) above (whether or not it also falls within section 3A(2)(b) or (c)), and

    (b)   is not registered.

(3A) Section 44A above applies in accordance with subsections (2A) and (2B) above to a charity mentioned in subsection (3) above which is also an exempt charity.

(3B) Sections 44 and 44A above apply to a charity mentioned in subsection (3) above which is also an English National Health Service charity or a Welsh National Health Service charity (as defined in sections 43A and 43B above).][385]

(4) Except in accordance with subsection (7) below, nothing in section 45 above applies to any charity [which—

    (a)   falls within section 3A(2)(b) or (c) above but does not fall within section 3A(2)(d), and

    (b)   is not registered.][386]

---

[382]   Amendment: Words substituted: Charities Act 2006, s 29(2)(a).
[383]   Amendment: Words substituted: Charities Act 2006, s 75(1), Sch 8, paras 96, 139(1), (2).
[384]   Amendment: Subsections inserted: Charities Act 2006, s 29(2)(b).
[385]   Amendment: Subsections substituted: Charities Act 2006, s 75(1), Sch 8, paras 96, 139(1), (3).
[386]   Amendment: Words substituted: Charities Act 2006, s 75(1), Sch 8, paras 96, 139(1), (4).

(5) If requested to do so by [the Commission][387], the charity trustees of any such charity as is mentioned in subsection (4) above shall prepare an annual report in respect of such financial year of the charity as is specified in [the Commission's request][388].

(6) Any report prepared under subsection (5) above shall contain—

(a)   such a report by the charity trustees on the activities of the charity during the year in question, and

(b)   such other information relating to the charity or to its trustees or officers,

as may be prescribed by regulations made under section 45(1) above in relation to annual reports prepared under that provision.

[(7) The following provisions of section 45 above shall apply in relation to any report required to be prepared under subsection (5) above as if it were an annual report required to be prepared under subsection (1) of that section—

(a)   subsection (3), with the omission of the words preceding 'a copy of the annual report', and

(b)   subsections (4) to (6).][389]

(8) ...[390]

Amendments—Deregulation and Contracting Out Act 1994, s 29; The Regulatory Reform (National Health Service Charitable and Non-Charitable Trust Accounts and Audit) Order 2005, SI 2005/1074, art 3(1), (5), Charities Act 2006, ss 29(2), 75, Sch 8, paras 96, 139, Sch 9.

47 Public inspection of annual reports etc

(1) [Any document kept by the Commission][391] in pursuance of section 45(6) above shall be open to public inspection at all reasonable times—

(a)   during the period for which it is so kept; or

(b)   if [the Commission so determines][392], during such lesser period as [it may][393] specify.

(2) Where any person—

(a)   requests the charity trustees of a charity in writing to provide him with a copy of the charity's most recent accounts [or (if subsection (4) below applies) of its most recent annual report][394], and

(b)   pays them such reasonable fee (if any) as they may require in respect of the costs of complying with the request,

those trustees shall comply with the request within the period of two months beginning with the date on which it is made.

(3) In subsection (2) above the reference to a charity's most recent accounts is—

(a)   ...[395]

---

[387]   Amendment: Words substituted: Charities Act 2006, s 75(1), Sch 8, paras 96, 139(1), (5)(a).

[388]   Amendment: Words substituted: Charities Act 2006, s 75(1), Sch 8, paras 96, 139(1), (5)(b).

[389]   Amendment: Subsection substituted: Charities Act 2006, s 75(1), Sch 8, paras 96, 139(1), (6).

[390]   Amendment: Subsection omitted: Charities Act 2006, s 75, Sch 8, paras 96, 139(1), (7), Sch 9.

[391]   Amendment: Words substituted: Charities Act 2006, s 75(1), Sch 8, paras 96, 140(1), (2)(a).

[392]   Amendment: Words substituted: Charities Act 2006, s 75(1), Sch 8, paras 96, 140(1), (2)(b).

[393]   Amendment: Words substituted: Charities Act 2006, s 75(1), Sch 8, paras 96, 140(1), (2)(c).

[394]   Amendment: Words inserted: Charities Act 2006, s 75(1), Sch 8, paras 96, 140(1), (3).

[395]   Amendment: Paragraph omitted: Deregulation and Contracting Out Act 1994, ss 39, 81(1), Sch 11, para 12(a), Sch 17.

(b)   in the case of [a charity other than one falling within paragraph (c) or (d)
       below][396], a reference to the statement of accounts or account and statement
       prepared in pursuance of section 42(1) or (3) above in respect of the last
       financial year of the charity in respect of which a statement of accounts or
       account and statement has or have been so prepared;

[(c)   in the case of a charity which is a company, a reference to the most recent
       annual accounts of the company prepared under Part VII of the Companies
       Act 1985 in relation to which any of the following conditions is satisfied—
       (i)   they have been audited
       (ii)   a report required for the purposes of section 249A(2) of that Act has
               been made in respect of them; or
       (iii)   they relate to a year in respect of which the company is exempt from
               audit by virtue of section 249A(1) of that Act; and][397]

(d)   in the case of an exempt charity, a reference to the accounts of the charity
       most recently audited in pursuance of any statutory or other requirement or, if
       its accounts are not required to be audited, the accounts most recently
       prepared in respect of the charity.

[(4) This subsection applies if an annual report has been prepared in respect of any
financial year of a charity in pursuance of section 45(1) or 46(5) above.

(5) In subsection (2) above the reference to a charity's most recent annual report is a
reference to the annual report prepared in pursuance of section 45(1) or 46(5) in respect
of the last financial year of the charity in respect of which an annual report has been so
prepared.][398]

Amendments—Deregulation and Contracting Out Act 1994, ss 39, 81(1), Sch 11, para 12(a), Sch 17; The
Companies Act 1985 (Audit Exemption) Regulations 1994, SI 1994/1935, reg 4, Sch 1, para 7; Charities Act 2006,
s 75(1), Sch 8, paras 96, 140.

48 Annual returns by registered charities

(1) [Subject to subsection (1A) below,][399] every registered charity shall prepare in
respect of each of its financial years an annual return in such form, and containing such
information, as may be prescribed by regulations made by [the Commission][400].

[(1A) Subsection (1) above shall not apply in relation to any financial year of a charity
in which [the charity's gross income does not exceed][401] £10,000 [(but this subsection
does not apply if the charity is constituted as a CIO)][402].][403]

(2) Any such return shall be transmitted to [the Commission][404] by the date by which
the charity trustees are, by virtue of section 45(3) above, required to transmit [to the
Commission][405] the annual report required to be prepared in respect of the financial
year in question.

---

[396]   Amendment: Words substituted: Deregulation and Contracting Out Act 1994, s 39, Sch 11, para 12(b).
[397]   Amendment: Paragraph substituted: The Companies Act 1985 (Audit Exemption) Regulations 1994,
        SI 1994/1935, reg 4, Sch 1, para 7.
[398]   Amendment: Subsections added: Charities Act 2006, s 75(1), Sch 8, paras 96, 140(1), (4).
[399]   Amendment: Words inserted: Deregulation and Contracting Out Act 1994, s 30(1), (2).
[400]   Amendment: Words substituted: Charities Act 2006, s 75(1), Sch 8, paras 96, 141(1), (2).
[401]   Amendment: Words substituted: Charities Act 2006, s 75(1), Sch 8, paras 96, 141(1), (3).
[402]   Amendment: Words added: Charities Act 2006, s 34, Sch 7, Pt 2, paras 3, 5.
[403]   Amendment: Subsection inserted: Deregulation and Contracting Out Act 1994, s 30(1), (3).
[404]   Amendment: Words substituted: Charities Act 2006, s 75(1), Sch 8, paras 96, 141(1), (4)(a).
[405]   Amendment: Words substituted: Charities Act 2006, s 75(1), Sch 8, paras 96, 141(1), (4)(b).

(3) [The Commission]⁴⁰⁶ may dispense with the requirements of subsection (1) above in the case of a particular charity or a particular class of charities, or in the case of a particular financial year of a charity or of any class of charities.

[(4) The Secretary of State may by order amend subsection (1A) above by substituting a different sum for the sum for the time being specified there.]⁴⁰⁷

Amendments—Deregulation and Contracting Out Act 1994, s 30; Charities Act 2006, ss 34, 75(1), Sch 7, Pt 2, paras 3, 5, Sch 8, paras 96, 141.

[49 Offences

(1) If any requirement imposed—

   (a)   by section 45(3) or (3A) above (taken with section 45(3B), (4) and (5), as applicable), or
   (b)   by section 47(2) or 48(2) above,

is not complied with, each person who immediately before the date for compliance specified in the section in question was a charity trustee of the charity shall be guilty of an offence and liable on summary conviction to the penalty mentioned in subsection (2).

(2) The penalty is—

   (a)   a fine not exceeding level 4 on the standard scale, and
   (b)   for continued contravention, a daily default fine not exceeding 10% of level 4 on the standard scale for so long as the person in question remains a charity trustee of the charity.

(3) It is a defence for a person charged with an offence under subsection (1) to prove that he took all reasonable steps for securing that the requirement in question would be complied with in time.]⁴⁰⁸

Amendments—Deregulation and Contracting Out Act 1994, s 29(8); Charities Act 2006, s 75(1), Sch 8, paras 96, 142.

[49A Group accounts

The provisions of Schedule 5A to this Act shall have effect with respect to—

   (a)   the preparation and auditing of accounts in respect of groups consisting of parent charities and their subsidiary undertakings (within the meaning of that Schedule), and
   (b)   other matters relating to such groups.]⁴⁰⁹

Amendment—Charities Act 2006, s 30(1).

PART VII
INCORPORATION OF CHARITY TRUSTEES

50 Incorporation of trustees of a charity

(1) Where—

---

⁴⁰⁶   Amendment: Words substituted: Charities Act 2006, s 75(1), Sch 8, paras 96, 141(1), (5).
⁴⁰⁷   Amendment: Subsection inserted: Deregulation and Contracting Out Act 1994, s 30(1), (4).
⁴⁰⁸   Amendment: Section substituted: Charities Act 2006, s 75(1), Sch 8, paras 96, 142.
⁴⁰⁹   Amendment: Section inserted: Charities Act 2006, s 30(1).

(a)   the trustees of a charity, in accordance with section 52 below, apply to [the Commission][410] for a certificate of incorporation of the trustees as a body corporate, and

(b)   [the Commission considers][411] that the incorporation of the trustees would be in the interests of the charity,

[the Commission][412] may grant such a certificate, subject to such conditions or directions as [the Commission thinks fit][413] to insert in it.

(2) [The Commission][414] shall not, however, grant such a certificate in a case where the charity appears [to the Commission][415] to be required to be registered [in accordance with section 3A][416] above but is not so registered.

(3) On the grant of such a certificate—

(a)   the trustees of the charity shall become a body corporate by such name as is specified in the certificate; and

(b)   (without prejudice to the operation of section 54 below) any relevant rights or liabilities of those trustees shall become rights or liabilities of that body.

(4) After their incorporation the trustees—

(a)   may sue and be sued in their corporate name; and

(b)   shall have the same powers, and be subject to the same restrictions and limitations, as respects the holding, acquisition and disposal of property for or in connection with the purposes of the charity as they had or were subject to while unincorporated;

and any relevant legal proceedings that might have been continued or commenced by or against the trustees may be continued or commenced by or against them in their corporate name.

(5) A body incorporated under this section need not have a common seal.

(6) In this section—

'relevant rights or liabilities' means rights or liabilities in connection with any property vesting in the body in question under section 51 below; and
'relevant legal proceedings' means legal proceedings in connection with any such property.

Amendments—Charities Act 2006, s 75(1), Sch 8, paras 96, 143.

51 Estate to vest in body corporate

The certificate of incorporation shall vest in the body corporate all real and personal estate, of whatever nature or tenure, belonging to or held by any person or persons in trust for the charity, and thereupon any person or persons in whose name or names any stocks, funds or securities are standing in trust for the charity, shall transfer them into the name of the body corporate, except that the foregoing provisions shall not apply to property vested in the official custodian.

---

[410]   Amendment: Words substituted: Charities Act 2006, s 75(1), Sch 8, paras 96, 143(1), (2)(a).
[411]   Amendment: Words substituted: Charities Act 2006, s 75(1), Sch 8, paras 96, 143(1), (2)(b).
[412]   Amendment: Words substituted: Charities Act 2006, s 75(1), Sch 8, paras 96, 143(1), (2)(a).
[413]   Amendment: Words substituted: Charities Act 2006, s 75(1), Sch 8, paras 96, 143(1), (2)(c).
[414]   Amendment: Words substituted: Charities Act 2006, s 75(1), Sch 8, paras 96, 143(1), (3)(a).
[415]   Amendment: Words substituted: Charities Act 2006, s 75(1), Sch 8, paras 96, 143(1), (3)(b).
[416]   Amendment: Words substituted: Charities Act 2006, s 75(1), Sch 8, paras 96, 143(1), (3)(c).

52 Applications for incorporation

(1) Every application to [the Commission][417] for a certificate of incorporation under this Part of this Act shall—

    (a)   be in writing and signed by the trustees of the charity concerned; and

    (b)   be accompanied by such documents or information as [the Commission][418] may require for the purpose of the application.

(2) [The Commission][419] may require—

    (a)   any statement contained in any such application, or

    (b)   any document or information supplied under subsection (1)(b) above,

to be verified in such manner as [it may specify][420].

Amendments—Charities Act 2006, s 75(1), Sch 8, paras 96, 144.

53 Nomination of trustees, and filling up vacancies

(1) Before a certificate of incorporation is granted under this Part of this Act, trustees of the charity must have been effectually appointed to the satisfaction of [the Commission][421].

(2) Where a certificate of incorporation is granted vacancies in the number of the trustees of the charity shall from time to time be filled up so far as required by the constitution or settlement of the charity, or by any conditions or directions in the certificate, by such legal means as would have been available for the appointment of new trustees of the charity if no certificate of incorporation had been granted, or otherwise as required by such conditions or directions.

Amendment—Charities Act 2006, s 75(1), Sch 8, paras 96, 145.

54 Liability of trustees and others, notwithstanding incorporation

After a certificate of incorporation has been granted under this Part of this Act all trustees of the charity, notwithstanding their incorporation, shall be chargeable for such property as shall come into their hands, and shall be answerable and accountable for their own acts, receipts, neglects, and defaults, and for the due administration of the charity and its property, in the same manner and to the same extent as if no such incorporation had been effected.

55 Certificate to be evidence of compliance with requirements for incorporation

A certificate of incorporation granted under this Part of this Act shall be conclusive evidence that all the preliminary requirements for incorporation under this Part of this Act have been complied with, and the date of incorporation mentioned in the certificate shall be deemed to be the date at which incorporation has taken place.

[417]   Amendment: Words substituted: Charities Act 2006, s 75(1), Sch 8, paras 96, 144(1), (2).
[418]   Amendment: Words substituted: Charities Act 2006, s 75(1), Sch 8, paras 96, 144(1), (2).
[419]   Amendment: Words substituted: Charities Act 2006, s 75(1), Sch 8, paras 96, 144(1), (3)(a).
[420]   Amendment: Words substituted: Charities Act 2006, s 75(1), Sch 8, paras 96, 144(1), (3)(b).
[421]   Amendment: Words substituted: Charities Act 2006, s 75(1), Sch 8, paras 96, 145.

56 Power of [Commission]⁴²² to amend certificate of incorporation

(1) [The Commission]⁴²³ may amend a certificate of incorporation either on the application of the incorporated body to which it relates or [of the Commission's own motion]⁴²⁴.

(2) Before making any such amendment [of its own motion, the Commission]⁴²⁵ shall by notice in writing—

(a)   inform the trustees of the relevant charity of [its proposals]⁴²⁶, and

(b)   invite those trustees to make representations [to it]⁴²⁷ within a time specified in the notice, being not less than one month from the date of the notice.

(3) [The Commission]⁴²⁸ shall take into consideration any representations made by those trustees within the time so specified, and may then (without further notice) proceed with [its proposals]⁴²⁹ either without modification or with such modifications as appear [to it]⁴³⁰ to be desirable.

(4) [The Commission]⁴³¹ may amend a certificate of incorporation either—

(a)   by making an order specifying the amendment; or

(b)   by issuing a new certificate of incorporation taking account of the amendment.

Amendments—Charities Act 2006, s 75(1), Sch 8, paras 96, 146.

57 Records of applications and certificates

(1) [The Commission]⁴³² shall keep a record of all applications for, and certificates of, incorporation under this Part of this Act and shall preserve all documents sent [to it]⁴³³ under this Part of this Act.

(2) Any person may inspect such documents, under the direction of [the Commission]⁴³⁴, and any person may require a copy or extract of any such document to be certified by a certificate signed by [a member of the staff of the Commission]⁴³⁵.

Amendments—Charities Act 2006, s 75(1), Sch 8, paras 96, 147.

58 Enforcement of orders and directions

All conditions and directions inserted in any certificate of incorporation shall be binding upon and performed or observed by the trustees as trusts of the charity, and section 88 below shall apply to any trustee who fails to perform or observe any such

---

422   Amendment: Word substituted: Charities Act 2006, s 75(1), Sch 8, paras 96, 146(1), (6).
423   Amendment: Words substituted: Charities Act 2006, s 75(1), Sch 8, paras 96, 146(1), (2)(a).
424   Amendment: Words substituted: Charities Act 2006, s 75(1), Sch 8, paras 96, 146(1), (2)(b).
425   Amendment: Words substituted: Charities Act 2006, s 75(1), Sch 8, paras 96, 146(1), (3)(a).
426   Amendment: Words substituted: Charities Act 2006, s 75(1), Sch 8, paras 96, 146(1), (3)(b).
427   Amendment: Words substituted: Charities Act 2006, s 75(1), Sch 8, paras 96, 146(1), (3)(c).
428   Amendment: Words substituted: Charities Act 2006, s 75(1), Sch 8, paras 96, 146(1), (4)(a).
429   Amendment: Words substituted: Charities Act 2006, s 75(1), Sch 8, paras 96, 146(1), (4)(b).
430   Amendment: Words substituted: Charities Act 2006, s 75(1), Sch 8, paras 96, 146(1), (4)(c).
431   Amendment: Words substituted: Charities Act 2006, s 75(1), Sch 8, paras 96, 146(1), (5).
432   Amendment: Words substituted: Charities Act 2006, s 75(1), Sch 8, paras 96, 147(1), (2)(a).
433   Amendment: Words substituted: Charities Act 2006, s 75(1), Sch 8, paras 96, 147(1), (2)(b).
434   Amendment: Words substituted: Charities Act 2006, s 75(1), Sch 8, paras 96, 147(1), (3)(a).
435   Amendment: Words substituted: Charities Act 2006, s 75(1), Sch 8, paras 96, 147(1), (3)(b).

condition or direction as it applies to a person guilty of disobedience to any such order of [the Commission][436] as is mentioned in that section.

Amendment—Charities Act 2006, s 75(1), Sch 8, paras 96, 148.

59 Gifts to charity before incorporation to have same effect afterwards

After the incorporation of the trustees of any charity under this Part of this Act every donation, gift and disposition of property, real or personal, lawfully made before the incorporation but not having actually taken effect, or thereafter lawfully made, by deed, will or otherwise to or in favour of the charity, or the trustees of the charity, or otherwise for the purposes of the charity, shall take effect as if made to or in favour of the incorporated body or otherwise for the like purposes.

60 Execution of documents by incorporated body

(1) This section has effect as respects the execution of documents by an incorporated body.

(2) If an incorporated body has a common seal, a document may be executed by the body by the affixing of its common seal.

(3) Whether or not it has a common seal, a document may be executed by an incorporated body either—

(a)   by being signed by a majority of the trustees of the relevant charity and expressed (in whatever form of words) to be executed by the body; or

(b)   by being executed in pursuance of an authority given under subsection (4) below.

(4) For the purposes of subsection (3)(b) above the trustees of the relevant charity in the case of an incorporated body may, subject to the trusts of the charity, confer on any two or more of their number—

(a)   a general authority, or

(b)   an authority limited in such manner as the trustees think fit,

to execute in the name and on behalf of the body documents for giving effect to transactions to which the body is a party.

(5) An authority under subsection (4) above—

(a)   shall suffice for any document if it is given in writing or by resolution of a meeting of the trustees of the relevant charity, notwithstanding the want of any formality that would be required in giving an authority apart from that subsection;

(b)   may be given so as to make the powers conferred exercisable by any of the trustees, or may be restricted to named persons or in any other way;

(c)   subject to any such restriction, and until it is revoked, shall, notwithstanding any change in the trustees of the relevant charity, have effect as a continuing authority given by the trustees from time to time of the charity and exercisable by such trustees.

(6) In any authority under subsection (4) above to execute a document in the name and on behalf of an incorporated body there shall, unless the contrary intention appears, be

---

[436]   Amendment: Words substituted: Charities Act 2006, s 75(1), Sch 8, paras 96, 148.

implied authority also to execute it for the body in the name and on behalf of the official custodian or of any other person, in any case in which the trustees could do so.

(7) A document duly executed by an incorporated body which makes it clear on its face that it is intended by the person or persons making it to be a deed has effect, upon delivery, as a deed; and it shall be presumed, unless a contrary intention is proved, to be delivered upon its being so executed.

(8) In favour of a purchaser a document shall be deemed to have been duly executed by such a body if it purports to be signed—

    (a)   by a majority of the trustees of the relevant charity, or

    (b)   by such of the trustees of the relevant charity as are authorised by the trustees of that charity to execute it in the name and on behalf of the body,

and, where the document makes it clear on its face that it is intended by the person or persons making it to be a deed, it shall be deemed to have been delivered upon its being executed.

For this purpose 'purchaser' means a purchaser in good faith for valuable consideration and includes a lessee, mortgagee or other person who for valuable consideration acquires an interest in property.

61 Power of [Commission][437] to dissolve incorporated body

(1) Where [the Commission is][438] satisfied—

    (a)   that an incorporated body has no assets or does not operate, or

    (b)   that the relevant charity in the case of an incorporated body has ceased to exist, or

    (c)   that the institution previously constituting, or [treated by the Commission][439] as constituting, any such charity has ceased to be, or (as the case may be) was not at the time of the body's incorporation, a charity, or

    (d)   that the purposes of the relevant charity in the case of an incorporated body have been achieved so far as is possible or are in practice incapable of being achieved,

[the Commission may of its own motion][440] make an order dissolving the body as from such date as is specified in the order.

(2) Where [the Commission is][441] satisfied, on the application of the trustees of the relevant charity in the case of an incorporated body, that it would be in the interests of the charity for that body to be dissolved, [the Commission][442] may make an order dissolving the body as from such date as is specified in the order.

(3) Subject to subsection (4) below, an order made under this section with respect to an incorporated body shall have the effect of vesting in the trustees of the relevant charity, in trust for that charity, all property for the time being vested—

    (a)   in the body, or

    (b)   in any other person (apart from the official custodian),

[437]   Amendment: Word substituted: Charities Act 2006, s 75(1), Sch 8, paras 96, 149(1), (6).
[438]   Amendment: Words substituted: Charities Act 2006, s 75(1), Sch 8, paras 96, 149(1), (2)(a).
[439]   Amendment: Words substituted: Charities Act 2006, s 75(1), Sch 8, paras 96, 149(1), (2)(b).
[440]   Amendment: Words substituted: Charities Act 2006, s 75(1), Sch 8, paras 96, 149(1), (2)(c).
[441]   Amendment: Words substituted: Charities Act 2006, s 75(1), Sch 8, paras 96, 149(1), (3)(a).
[442]   Amendment: Words substituted: Charities Act 2006, s 75(1), Sch 8, paras 96, 149(1), (3)(b).

in trust for that charity.

(4) If [the Commission so directs][443] in the order—

(a) all or any specified part of that property shall, instead of vesting in the trustees of the relevant charity, vest—

   (i) in a specified person as trustee for, or nominee of, that charity, or

   (ii) in such persons (other than the trustees of the relevant charity) as may be specified;

(b) any specified investments, or any specified class or description of investments, held by any person in trust for the relevant charity shall be transferred—

   (i) to the trustees of that charity, or

   (ii) to any such person or persons as is or are mentioned in paragraph (a)(i) or (ii) above;

and for this purpose 'specified' means specified by [the Commission][444] in the order.

(5) Where an order to which this subsection applies is made with respect to an incorporated body—

(a) any rights or liabilities of the body shall become rights or liabilities of the trustees of the relevant charity; and

(b) any legal proceedings that might have been continued or commenced by or against the body may be continued or commenced by or against those trustees.

(6) Subsection (5) above applies to any order under this section by virtue of which—

(a) any property vested as mentioned in subsection (3) above is vested—

   (i) in the trustees of the relevant charity, or

   (ii) in any person as trustee for, or nominee of, that charity; or

(b) any investments held by any person in trust for the relevant charity are required to be transferred—

   (i) to the trustees of that charity, or

   (ii) to any person as trustee for, or nominee of, that charity.

(7) ...[445]

Amendments—Charities Act 2006, s 75, Sch 8, paras 96, 149, Sch 9.

62 Interpretation of Part VII

In this Part of this Act—

'incorporated body' means a body incorporated under section 50 above;

'the relevant charity', in relation to an incorporated body, means the charity the trustees of which have been incorporated as that body;

'the trustees', in relation to a charity, means the charity trustees.

---

[443] Amendment: Words substituted: Charities Act 2006, s 75(1), Sch 8, paras 96, 149(1), (4)(a).
[444] Amendment: Words substituted: Charities Act 2006, s 75(1), Sch 8, paras 96, 149(1), (4)(b).
[445] Amendment: Subsection omitted: Charities Act 2006, s 75, Sch 8, paras 96, 149(1), (5), Sch 9.

PART VIII
CHARITABLE COMPANIES

63 Winding up

(1) Where a charity may be wound up by the High Court under the Insolvency Act 1986, a petition for it to be wound up under that Act by any court in England or Wales having jurisdiction may be presented by the Attorney General, as well as by any person authorised by that Act.

(2) Where a charity may be so wound up by the High Court, such a petition may also be presented by [the Commission][446] if, at any time after [it has instituted][447] an inquiry under section 8 above with respect to the charity, [it is satisfied][448] as mentioned in section 18(1)(a) or (b) above.

(3) Where a charitable company is dissolved, [the Commission][449] may make an application under section 651 of the Companies Act 1985 (power of court to declare dissolution of company void) for an order to be made under that section with respect to the company; and for this purpose subsection (1) of that section shall have effect in relation to a charitable company as if the reference to the liquidator of the company included a reference to [the Commission][450].

(4) Where a charitable company's name has been struck off the register of companies under section 652 of the Companies Act 1985 (power of registrar to strike defunct company off register), [the Commission][451] may make an application under section 653(2) of that Act (objection to striking off by person aggrieved) for an order restoring the company's name to that register; and for this purpose section 653(2) shall have effect in relation to a charitable company as if the reference to any such person aggrieved as is there mentioned included a reference to [the Commission][452].

(5) The powers exercisable by [the Commission][453] by virtue of this section shall be exercisable [by the Commission of its own motion][454], but shall be exercisable only with the agreement of the Attorney General on each occasion.

(6) In this section 'charitable company' means a company which is a charity.

Amendments—Charities Act 2006, s 75(1), Sch 8, paras 96, 150.

64 Alteration of objects clause

(1) Where a charity is a company or other body corporate having power to alter the instruments establishing or regulating it as a body corporate, no exercise of that power which has the effect of the body ceasing to be a charity shall be valid so as to affect the application of—

(a)   any property acquired under any disposition or agreement previously made otherwise than for full consideration in money or money's worth, or any property representing property so acquired,

---

[446]   Amendment: Words substituted: Charities Act 2006, s 75(1), Sch 8, paras 96, 150(1), (2)(a).
[447]   Amendment: Words substituted: Charities Act 2006, s 75(1), Sch 8, paras 96, 150(1), (2)(b).
[448]   Amendment: Words substituted: Charities Act 2006, s 75(1), Sch 8, paras 96, 150(1), (2)(c).
[449]   Amendment: Words substituted: Charities Act 2006, s 75(1), Sch 8, paras 96, 150(1), (3).
[450]   Amendment: Words substituted: Charities Act 2006, s 75(1), Sch 8, paras 96, 150(1), (3).
[451]   Amendment: Words substituted: Charities Act 2006, s 75(1), Sch 8, paras 96, 150(1), (4).
[452]   Amendment: Words substituted: Charities Act 2006, s 75(1), Sch 8, paras 96, 150(1), (4).
[453]   Amendment: Words substituted: Charities Act 2006, s 75(1), Sch 8, paras 96, 150(1), (5)(a).
[454]   Amendment: Words substituted: Charities Act 2006, s 75(1), Sch 8, paras 96, 150(1), (5)(b).

(b)   any property representing income which has accrued before the alteration is made, or

(c)   the income from any such property as aforesaid.

[(2) Where a charity is a company, any regulated alteration by the company—

(a)   requires the prior written consent of the Commission, and

(b)   is ineffective if such consent has not been obtained.

(2A) The following are 'regulated alterations'—

(a)   any alteration of the objects clause in the company's memorandum of association,

(b)   any alteration of any provision of its memorandum or articles of association directing the application of property of the company on its dissolution, and

(c)   any alteration of any provision of its memorandum or articles of association where the alteration would provide authorization for any benefit to be obtained by directors or members of the company or persons connected with them.

(2B) For the purposes of subsection (2A) above—

(a)   'benefit' means a direct or indirect benefit of any nature, except that it does not include any remuneration (within the meaning of section 73A below) whose receipt may be authorised under that section; and

(b)   the same rules apply for determining whether a person is connected with a director or member of the company as apply, in accordance with section 73B(5) and (6) below, for determining whether a person is connected with a charity trustee for the purposes of section 73A.][455]

(3) Where a company has made [a regulated alteration][456] in accordance with subsection (2) above and—

(a)   in connection with the alteration is required by virtue of—

(i)   section 6(1) of the Companies Act 1985 (delivery of documents following alteration of objects), or

(ii)   that provision as applied by section 17(3) of that Act (alteration of condition in memorandum which could have been contained in articles),

to deliver to the registrar of companies a printed copy of its memorandum, as altered, or

(b)   is required by virtue of section 380(1) of that Act (registration etc of resolutions and agreements) to forward to the registrar a printed or other copy of the special resolution effecting the alteration,

the copy so delivered or forwarded by the company shall be accompanied by a copy of [the Commission's consent][457].

(4) Section 6(3) of that Act (offences) shall apply to any default by a company in complying with subsection (3) above as it applies to any such default as is mentioned in that provision.

Amendments—Charities Act 2006, ss 31, 75(1), Sch 8, paras 96, 151.

---

[455]   Amendment: Subsection substituted: Charities Act 2006, s 31(1), (2).
[456]   Amendment: Words substituted: Charities Act 2006, s 31(1), (3).
[457]   Amendment: Words substituted: Charities Act 2006, s 75(1), Sch 8, paras 96, 151.

65 Invalidity of certain transactions

(1) Sections 35 and 35A of the Companies Act 1985 (capacity of company not limited by its memorandum; power of directors to bind company) do not apply to the acts of a company which is a charity except in favour of a person who—

(a)   gives full consideration in money or money's worth in relation to the act in question, and

(b)   does not know that the act is not permitted by the company's memorandum or, as the case may be, is beyond the powers of the directors,

or who does not know at the time the act is done that the company is a charity.

(2) However, where such a company purports to transfer or grant an interest in property, the fact that the act was not permitted by the company's memorandum or, as the case may be, that the directors in connection with the act exceeded any limitation on their powers under the company's constitution, does not affect the title of a person who subsequently acquires the property or any interest in it for full consideration without actual notice of any such circumstances affecting the validity of the company's act.

(3) In any proceedings arising out of subsection (1) above the burden of proving—

(a)   that a person knew that an act was not permitted by the company's memorandum or was beyond the powers of the directors, or

(b)   that a person knew that the company was a charity,

lies on the person making that allegation.

(4) Where a company is a charity, the ratification of an act under section 35(3) of the Companies Act 1985, or the ratification of a transaction to which section 322A of that Act applies (invalidity of certain transactions to which directors or their associates are parties), is ineffective without the prior written consent of [the Commission][458].

Amendments—Charities Act 2006, s 75(1), Sch 8, paras 96, 152.

66 Requirement of consent of [Commission][459] to certain acts

(1) Where a company is a charity—

(a)   any approval given by the company for the purposes of any of the provisions of the Companies Act 1985 specified in subsection (2) below, and

(b)   any affirmation by it for the purposes of section 322(2)(c) of that Act (affirmation of voidable arrangements under which assets are acquired by or from a director or person connected with him),

is ineffective without the prior written consent of the [Commission][460].

(2) The provisions of the Companies Act 1985 referred to in subsection (1)(a) above are—

(a)   section 312 (payment to director in respect of loss of office or retirement);

(b)   section 313(1) (payment to director in respect of loss of office or retirement made in connection with transfer of undertaking or property of company);

(c)   section 319(3) (incorporation in director's service contract of term whereby his employment will or may continue for a period of more than five years);

---

[458]   Amendment: Words substituted: Charities Act 2006, s 75(1), Sch 8, paras 96, 152.
[459]   Amendment: Word substituted: Charities Act 2006, s 75(1), Sch 8, paras 96, 153.
[460]   Amendment: Word substituted: Charities Act 2006, s 75(1), Sch 8, paras 96, 153.

(d)   section 320(1) (arrangement whereby assets are acquired by or from director or person connected with him);

(e)   section 337(3)(a) (provision of funds to meet certain expenses incurred by director).

Amendments—Charities Act 2006, s 75(1), Sch 8, paras 96, 153.

67 Name to appear on correspondence etc

Section 30(7) of the Companies Act 1985 (exemption from requirements relating to publication of name etc) shall not, in its application to any company which is a charity, have the effect of exempting the company from the requirements of section 349(1) of that Act (company's name to appear in its correspondence etc).

68 Status to appear on correspondence etc

(1) Where a company is a charity and its name does not include the word 'charity' or the word 'charitable'[then, subject to subsection (1A)][461], the fact that the company is a charity shall be stated ...[462] in legible characters—

(a)   in all business letters of the company,

(b)   in all its notices and other official publications,

(c)   in all bills of exchange, promissory notes, endorsements, cheques and orders for money or goods purporting to be signed on behalf of the company,

(d)   in all conveyances purporting to be executed by the company, and

(e)   in all bills rendered by it and in all its invoices, receipts, and letters of credit.

[(1A) Where a company's name includes the word 'elusen' or the word 'elusennol' (the Welsh equivalents of the words 'charity' and 'charitable'), subsection (1) above shall not apply in relation to any document which is wholly in Welsh.

(1B) The statement required by subsection (1) above shall be in English, except that, in the case of a document which is otherwise wholly in Welsh, the statement may be in Welsh if it consists of or includes the word 'elusen' or the word 'elusennol'.][463]

(2) In subsection (1)(d) above 'conveyance' means any instrument creating, transferring, varying or extinguishing an interest in land.

(3) Subsections (2) to (4) of section 349 of the Companies Act 1985 (offences in connection with failure to include required particulars in business letters etc) shall apply in relation to a contravention of subsection (1) above, taking the reference in subsection (3)(b) of that section to a bill of parcels as a reference to any such bill as is mentioned in subsection (1)(e) above.

Amendments—Welsh Language Act 1992, s 33.

[68A Duty of charity's auditors etc to report matters to Commission

(1) Section 44A(2) to (7) above shall apply in relation to a person acting as—

(a)   an auditor of a charitable company appointed under Chapter 5 of Part 11 of the Companies Act 1985 (auditors), or

(b)   a reporting accountant appointed by a charitable company for the purposes of section 249C of that Act (report required instead of audit),

---

[461]   Amendment: Words inserted: Welsh Language Act 1993, s 33(1), (2).

[462]   Amendment: Words omitted: Welsh Language Act 1993, s 33(1), (2), Sch 2.

[463]   Amendment: Subsections inserted: Welsh Language Act 1993, s 33(1), (3).

as they apply in relation to a person such as is mentioned in section 44A(1).

(2) For this purpose any reference in section 44A to a person acting in the capacity mentioned in section 44A(1) is to be read as a reference to his acting in the capacity mentioned in subsection (1) of this section.

(3) In this section 'charitable company' means a charity which is a company.][464]

Amendment—Charities Act 2006, s 33

69 Investigation of accounts

(1) In the case of a charity which is a company [the Commission][465] may by order require that the condition and accounts of the charity for such period as [the Commission thinks fit][466] shall be investigated and audited by an auditor appointed [by the Commission][467], being a person eligible for appointment as a company auditor under section 25 of the Companies Act 1989.

(2) An auditor acting under subsection (1) above—

(a)   shall have a right of access to all books, accounts and documents relating to the charity which are in the possession or control of the charity trustees or to which the charity trustees have access;

(b)   shall be entitled to require from any charity trustee, past or present, and from any past or present officer or employee of the charity such information and explanation as he thinks necessary for the performance of his duties;

(c)   shall at the conclusion or during the progress of the audit make such reports to [the Commission][468] about the audit or about the accounts or affairs of the charity as he thinks the case requires, and shall send a copy of any such report to the charity trustees.

(3) The expenses of any audit under subsection (1) above, including the remuneration of the auditor, shall be paid by [the Commission][469].

(4) If any person fails to afford an auditor any facility to which he is entitled under subsection (2) above [the Commission][470] may by order give to that person or to the charity trustees for the time being such directions as [the Commission thinks][471] appropriate for securing that the default is made good.

Amendments—Charities Act 2006, s 75(1), Sch 8, paras 96, 154.

---

[464]   Amendment: Section inserted: Charities Act 2006, s 33, for transitional provisions see s 75(3), Sch 10, para 10.

[465]   Amendment: Words substituted: Charities Act 2006, s 75(1), Sch 8, paras 96, 154(1), (2)(a).

[466]   Amendment: Words substituted: Charities Act 2006, s 75(1), Sch 8, paras 96, 154(1), (2)(b).

[467]   Amendment: Words substituted: Charities Act 2006, s 75(1), Sch 8, paras 96, 154(1), (2)(c).

[468]   Amendment: Words substituted: Charities Act 2006, s 75(1), Sch 8, paras 96, 154(1), (3).

[469]   Amendment: Words substituted: Charities Act 2006, s 75(1), Sch 8, paras 96, 154(1), (3).

[470]   Amendment: Words substituted: Charities Act 2006, s 75(1), Sch 8, paras 96, 154(1), (4)(a).

[471]   Amendment: Words substituted: Charities Act 2006, s 75(1), Sch 8, paras 96, 154(1), (4)(b).

[PART 8A
CHARITABLE INCORPORATED ORGANISATIONS

Nature and constitution

69A Charitable incorporated organisations

(1) In this Act, a charitable incorporated organisation is referred to as a 'CIO'.

(2) A CIO shall be a body corporate.

(3) A CIO shall have a constitution.

(4) A CIO shall have a principal office, which shall be in England or in Wales.

(5) A CIO shall have one or more members.

(6) The members may be either—

(a) not liable to contribute to the assets of the CIO if it is wound up, or
(b) liable to do so up to a maximum amount each.

Amendment—Charities Act 2006, s 34, Sch 7, Pt 1, para 1.

69B Constitution

(1) A CIO's constitution shall state—

(a) its name,
(b) its purposes,
(c) whether its principal office is in England or in Wales, and
(d) whether or not its members are liable to contribute to its assets if it is wound up, and (if they are) up to what amount.

(2) A CIO's constitution shall make provision—

(a) about who is eligible for membership, and how a person becomes a member,
(b) about the appointment of one or more persons who are to be charity trustees of the CIO, and about any conditions of eligibility for appointment, and
(c) containing directions about the application of property of the CIO on its dissolution.

(3) A CIO's constitution shall also provide for such other matters, and comply with such requirements, as are specified in regulations made by the Minister.

(4) A CIO's constitution—

(a) shall be in English if its principal office is in England,
(b) may be in English or in Welsh if its principal office is in Wales.

(5) A CIO's constitution shall be in the form specified in regulations made by the Commission, or as near to that form as the circumstances admit.

(6) Subject to anything in a CIO's constitution: a charity trustee of the CIO may, but need not, be a member of it; a member of the CIO may, but need not, be one of its charity trustees; and those who are members of the CIO and those who are its charity trustees may, but need not, be identical.

Amendment—Charities Act 2006, s 34, Sch 7, Pt 1, para 1.

69C Name and status

(1) The name of a CIO shall appear in legible characters—

(a)   in all business letters of the CIO,

(b)   in all its notices and other official publications,

(c)   in all bills of exchange, promissory notes, endorsements, cheques and orders for money or goods purporting to be signed on behalf of the CIO,

(d)   in all conveyances purporting to be executed by the CIO, and

(e)   in all bills rendered by it and in all its invoices, receipts, and letters of credit.

(2) In subsection (1)(d), 'conveyance' means any instrument creating, transferring, varying or extinguishing an interest in land.

(3) Subsection (5) applies if the name of a CIO does not include—

(a)   'charitable incorporated organisation', or

(b)   'CIO', with or without full stops after each letter, or

(c)   a Welsh equivalent mentioned in subsection (4) (but this option applies only if the CIO's constitution is in Welsh),

and it is irrelevant, in any such case, whether or not capital letters are used.

(4) The Welsh equivalents referred to in subsection (3)(c) are—

(a)   'sefydliad elusennol corfforedig', or

(b)   'SEC', with or without full stops after each letter.

(5) If this subsection applies, the fact that a CIO is a CIO shall be stated in legible characters in all the documents mentioned in subsection (1).

(6) The statement required by subsection (5) shall be in English, except that in the case of a document which is otherwise wholly in Welsh, the statement may be in Welsh.

Amendment—Charities Act 2006, s 34, Sch 7, Pt 1, para 1.

69D Offences connected with name and status

(1) A charity trustee of a CIO or a person on the CIO's behalf who issues or authorises the issue of any document referred to in paragraph (a), (b), (d) or (e) of section 69C(1) above which fails to comply with the requirements of section 69C(1), (5) or (6) is liable on summary conviction to a fine not exceeding level 3 on the standard scale.

(2) A charity trustee of a CIO or a person on the CIO's behalf who signs or authorises to be signed on behalf of the CIO any document referred to in paragraph (c) of section 69C(1) above which fails to comply with the requirements of section 69C(1), (5) or (6)—

(a)   is liable on summary conviction to a fine not exceeding level 3 on the standard scale, and

(b)   is personally liable to the holder of the bill of exchange (etc) for the amount of it, unless it is duly paid by the CIO.

(3) A person who holds any body out as being a CIO when it is not (however he does this) is guilty of an offence and is liable on summary conviction to a fine not exceeding level 3 on the standard scale.

(4) It is a defence for a person charged with an offence under subsection (3) to prove that he believed on reasonable grounds that the body was a CIO.

Amendment—Charities Act 2006, s 34, Sch 7, Pt 1, para 1.

Registration

69E Application for registration

(1) Any one or more persons ('the applicants') may apply to the Commission for a CIO to be constituted and for its registration as a charity.

(2) The applicants shall supply the Commission with—

   (a)   a copy of the proposed constitution of the CIO,
   (b)   such other documents or information as may be prescribed by regulations made by the Minister, and
   (c)   such other documents or information as the Commission may require for the purposes of the application.

(3) The Commission shall refuse such an application if—

   (a)   it is not satisfied that the CIO would be a charity at the time it would be registered, or
   (b)   the CIO's proposed constitution does not comply with one or more of the requirements of section 69B above and any regulations made under that section.

(4) The Commission may refuse such an application if—

   (a)   the proposed name of the CIO is the same as, or is in the opinion of the Commission too like, the name of any other charity (whether registered or not), or
   (b)   the Commission is of the opinion referred to in any of paragraphs (b) to (e) of section 6(2) above (power of Commission to require change in charity's name) in relation to the proposed name of the CIO (reading paragraph (b) as referring to the proposed purposes of the CIO and to the activities which it is proposed it should carry on).

Amendment—Charities Act 2006, s 34, Sch 7, Pt 1, para 1.

69F Effect of registration

(1) If the Commission grants an application under section 69E above it shall register the CIO to which the application relates as a charity in the register of charities.

(2) Upon the registration of the CIO in the register of charities, it becomes by virtue of the registration a body corporate—

   (a)   whose constitution is that proposed in the application,
   (b)   whose name is that specified in the constitution, and
   (c)   whose first member is, or first members are, the applicants referred to in section 69E above.

(3) All property for the time being vested in the applicants (or, if more than one, any of them) on trust for the charitable purposes of the CIO (when incorporated) shall by virtue of this subsection become vested in the CIO upon its registration.

(4) The entry relating to the charity's registration in the register of charities shall include—

   (a)   the date of the charity's registration, and

(b) a note saying that it is constituted as a CIO.

(5) A copy of the entry in the register shall be sent to the charity at the principal office of the CIO.

Amendment—Charities Act 2006, s 34, Sch 7, Pt 1, para 1.

Conversion, amalgamation and transfer

69G Conversion of charitable company or registered industrial and provident society

(1) The following may apply to the Commission to be converted into a CIO, and for the CIO's registration as a charity, in accordance with this section—

(a) a charitable company,
(b) a charity which is a registered society within the meaning of the Industrial and Provident Societies Act 1965.

(2) But such an application may not be made by—

(a) a company or registered society having a share capital if any of the shares are not fully paid up, or
(b) an exempt charity.

(3) Such an application is referred to in this section and sections 69H and 69I below as an 'application for conversion'.

(4) The Commission shall notify the following of any application for conversion—

(a) the appropriate registrar, and
(b) such other persons (if any) as the Commission thinks appropriate in the particular case.

(5) The company or registered society shall supply the Commission with—

(a) a copy of a resolution of the company or registered society that it be converted into a CIO,
(b) a copy of the proposed constitution of the CIO,
(c) a copy of a resolution of the company or registered society adopting the proposed constitution of the CIO,
(d) such other documents or information as may be prescribed by regulations made by the Minister, and
(e) such other documents or information as the Commission may require for the purposes of the application.

(6) The resolution referred to in subsection (5)(a) shall be—

(a) a special resolution of the company or registered society, or
(b) a unanimous written resolution signed by or on behalf of all the members of the company or registered society who would be entitled to vote on a special resolution.

(7) In the case of a registered society, 'special resolution' has the meaning given in section 52(3) of the Industrial and Provident Societies Act 1965.

(8) In the case of a company limited by guarantee which makes an application for conversion (whether or not it also has a share capital), the proposed constitution of the

CIO shall (unless subsection (10) applies) provide for the CIO's members to be liable to contribute to its assets if it is wound up, and for the amount up to which they are so liable.

(9) That amount shall not be less than the amount up to which they were liable to contribute to the assets of the company if it was wound up.

(10) If the amount each member of the company is liable to contribute to its assets on its winding up is £10 or less, the guarantee shall be extinguished on the conversion of the company into a CIO, and the requirements of subsections (8) and (9) do not apply.

(11) In subsection (4), and in sections 69H and 69I below, 'the appropriate registrar' means—

    (a)   in the case of an application for conversion by a charitable company, the registrar of companies,

    (b)   in the case of an application for conversion by a registered society, the Financial Services Authority.

(12) In this section, 'charitable company' means a company which is a charity.

Amendment—Charities Act 2006, s 34, Sch 7, Pt 1, para 1.

69H Conversion: consideration of application

(1) The Commission shall consult those to whom it has given notice of an application for conversion under section 69G(4) above about whether the application should be granted.

(2) The Commission shall refuse an application for conversion if—

    (a)   it is not satisfied that the CIO would be a charity at the time it would be registered,

    (b)   the CIO's proposed constitution does not comply with one or more of the requirements of section 69B above and any regulations made under that section, or

    (c)   in the case of an application for conversion made by a company limited by guarantee, the CIO's proposed constitution does not comply with the requirements of subsections (8) and (9) of section 69G above.

(3) The Commission may refuse an application for conversion if—

    (a)   the proposed name of the CIO is the same as, or is in the opinion of the Commission too like, the name of any other charity (whether registered or not),

    (b)   the Commission is of the opinion referred to in any of paragraphs (b) to (e) of section 6(2) above (power of Commission to require change in charity's name) in relation to the proposed name of the CIO (reading paragraph (b) as referring to the proposed purposes of the CIO and to the activities which it is proposed it should carry on), or

    (c)   having considered any representations received from those whom it has consulted under subsection (1), the Commission considers (having regard to any regulations made under subsection (4)) that it would not be appropriate to grant the application.

(4) The Minister may make provision in regulations about circumstances in which it would not be appropriate to grant an application for conversion.

(5) If the Commission refuses an application for conversion, it shall so notify the appropriate registrar (see section 69G(11) above).

Amendment—Charities Act 2006, s 34, Sch 7, Pt 1, para 1.

69I Conversion: supplementary

(1) If the Commission grants an application for conversion, it shall—

    (a)   register the CIO to which the application related in the register of charities, and

    (b)   send to the appropriate registrar (see section 69G(11) above) a copy of each of the resolutions of the converting company or registered society referred to in section 69G(5)(a) and (c) above, and a copy of the entry in the register relating to the CIO.

(2) The registration of the CIO in the register shall be provisional only until the appropriate registrar cancels the registration of the company or registered society as required by subsection (3)(b).

(3) The appropriate registrar shall—

    (a)   register the documents sent to him under subsection (1)(b), and

    (b)   cancel the registration of the company in the register of companies, or of the society in the register of friendly societies,

and shall notify the Commission that he has done so.

(4) When the appropriate registrar cancels the registration of the company or of the registered society, the company or registered society is thereupon converted into a CIO, being a body corporate—

    (a)   whose constitution is that proposed in the application for conversion,

    (b)   whose name is that specified in the constitution, and

    (c)   whose first members are the members of the converting company or society immediately before the moment of conversion.

(5) If the converting company or registered society had a share capital, upon the conversion of the company or registered society all the shares shall by virtue of this subsection be cancelled, and no former holder of any cancelled share shall have any right in respect of it after its cancellation.

(6) Subsection (5) does not affect any right which accrued in respect of a share before its cancellation.

(7) The entry relating to the charity's registration in the register shall include—

    (a)   a note that it is constituted as a CIO,

    (b)   the date on which it became so constituted, and

    (c)   a note of the name of the company or society which was converted into the CIO,

but the matters mentioned in paragraphs (a) and (b) are to be included only when the appropriate registrar has notified the Commission as required by subsection (3).

(8) A copy of the entry in the register shall be sent to the charity at the principal office of the CIO.

(9) The conversion of a charitable company or of a registered society into a CIO does not affect, in particular, any liability to which the company or registered society was subject by virtue of its being a charitable company or registered society.

Amendment—Charities Act 2006, s 34, Sch 7, Pt 1, para 1.

69J Conversion of community interest company

(1) The Minister may by regulations make provision for the conversion of a community interest company into a CIO, and for the CIO's registration as a charity.

(2) The regulations may, in particular, apply, or apply with modifications specified in the regulations, or disapply, anything in sections 53 to 55 of the Companies (Audit, Investigations and Community Enterprise) Act 2004 or in sections 69G to 69I above.

Amendment—Charities Act 2006, s 34, Sch 7, Pt 1, para 1.

69K Amalgamation of CIOs

(1) Any two or more CIOs ('the old CIOs') may, in accordance with this section, apply to the Commission to be amalgamated, and for the incorporation and registration as a charity of a new CIO ('the new CIO') as their successor.

(2) Such an application is referred to in this section and section 69L below as an 'application for amalgamation'.

(3) Subsections (2) to (4) of section 69E above apply in relation to an application for amalgamation as they apply to an application for a CIO to be constituted, but in those subsections—

    (a)   'the applicants' shall be construed as meaning the old CIOs, and
    (b)   references to the CIO are to the new CIO.

(4) In addition to the documents and information referred to in section 69E(2) above, the old CIOs shall supply the Commission with—

    (a)   a copy of a resolution of each of the old CIOs approving the proposed amalgamation, and
    (b)   a copy of a resolution of each of the old CIOs adopting the proposed constitution of the new CIO.

(5) The resolutions referred to in subsection (4) must have been passed—

    (a)   by a 75% majority of those voting at a general meeting of the CIO (including those voting by proxy or by post, if voting that way is permitted), or
    (b)   unanimously by the CIO's members, otherwise than at a general meeting.

(6) The date of passing of such a resolution is—

    (a)   the date of the general meeting at which it was passed, or
    (b)   if it was passed otherwise than at a general meeting, the date on which provision in the CIO's constitution or in regulations made under paragraph 13 of Schedule 5B to this Act deems it to have been passed (but that date may not be earlier than that on which the last member agreed to it).

(7) Each old CIO shall—

    (a)   give notice of the proposed amalgamation in the way (or ways) that in the opinion of its charity trustees will make it most likely to come to the attention of those who would be affected by the amalgamation, and

(b)   send a copy of the notice to the Commission.

(8) The notice shall invite any person who considers that he would be affected by the proposed amalgamation to make written representations to the Commission not later than a date determined by the Commission and specified in the notice.

(9) In addition to being required to refuse it on one of the grounds mentioned in section 69E(3) above as applied by subsection (3) of this section, the Commission shall refuse an application for amalgamation if it considers that there is a serious risk that the new CIO would be unable properly to pursue its purposes.

(10) The Commission may refuse an application for amalgamation if it is not satisfied that the provision in the constitution of the new CIO about the matters mentioned in subsection (11) is the same, or substantially the same, as the provision about those matters in the constitutions of each of the old CIOs.

(11) The matters are—

(a)   the purposes of the CIO,
(b)   the application of property of the CIO on its dissolution, and
(c)   authorisation for any benefit to be obtained by charity trustees or members of the CIO or persons connected with them.

(12) For the purposes of subsection (11)(c)—

(a)   'benefit' means a direct or indirect benefit of any nature, except that it does not include any remuneration (within the meaning of section 73A below) whose receipt may be authorised under that section, and
(b)   the same rules apply for determining whether a person is connected with a charity trustee or member of the CIO as apply, in accordance with section 73B(5) and (6) below, for determining whether a person is connected with a charity trustee for the purposes of section 73A.

Amendment—Charities Act 2006, s 34, Sch 7, Pt 1, para 1.

69L Amalgamation: supplementary

(1) If the Commission grants an application for amalgamation, it shall register the new CIO in the register of charities.

(2) Upon the registration of the new CIO it thereupon becomes by virtue of the registration a body corporate—

(a)   whose constitution is that proposed in the application for amalgamation,
(b)   whose name is that specified in the constitution, and
(c)   whose first members are the members of the old CIOs immediately before the new CIO was registered.

(3) Upon the registration of the new CIO—

(a)   all the property, rights and liabilities of each of the old CIOs shall become by virtue of this subsection the property, rights and liabilities of the new CIO, and
(b)   each of the old CIOs shall be dissolved.

(4) Any gift which—

(a)   is expressed as a gift to one of the old CIOs, and
(b)   takes effect on or after the date of registration of the new CIO,

takes effect as a gift to the new CIO.

(5) The entry relating to the registration in the register of the charity constituted as the new CIO shall include—

(a)   a note that it is constituted as a CIO,

(b)   the date of the charity's registration, and

(c)   a note that the CIO was formed following amalgamation, and of the name of each of the old CIOs.

(6) A copy of the entry in the register shall be sent to the charity at the principal office of the new CIO.

Amendment—Charities Act 2006, s 34, Sch 7, Pt 1, para 1.

69M Transfer of CIO's undertaking

(1) A CIO may resolve that all its property, rights and liabilities should be transferred to another CIO specified in the resolution.

(2) Where a CIO has passed such a resolution, it shall send to the Commission—

(a)   a copy of the resolution, and

(b)   a copy of a resolution of the transferee CIO agreeing to the transfer to it.

(3) Subsections (5) and (6) of section 69K above apply to the resolutions referred to in subsections (1) and (2)(b) as they apply to the resolutions referred to in section 69K(4).

(4) Having received the copy resolutions referred to in subsection (2), the Commission—

(a)   may direct the transferor CIO to give public notice of its resolution in such manner as is specified in the direction, and

(b)   if it gives such a direction, must take into account any representations made to it by persons appearing to it to be interested in the transferor CIO, where those representations are made to it within the period of 28 days beginning with the date when public notice of the resolution is given by the transferor CIO.

(5) The resolution shall not take effect until confirmed by the Commission.

(6) The Commission shall refuse to confirm the resolution if it considers that there is a serious risk that the transferee CIO would be unable properly to pursue the purposes of the transferor CIO.

(7) The Commission may refuse to confirm the resolution if it is not satisfied that the provision in the constitution of the transferee CIO about the matters mentioned in section 69K(11) above is the same, or substantially the same, as the provision about those matters in the constitution of the transferor CIO.

(8) If the Commission does not notify the transferor CIO within the relevant period that it is either confirming or refusing to confirm the resolution, the resolution is to be treated as confirmed by the Commission on the day after the end of that period.

(9) Subject to subsection (10), 'the relevant period' means—

(a)   in a case where the Commission directs the transferor CIO under subsection (4) to give public notice of its resolution, the period of six months beginning with the date when that notice is given, or

(b)   in any other case, the period of six months beginning with the date when both of the copy resolutions referred to in subsection (2) have been received by the Commission.

(10) The Commission may at any time within the period of six months mentioned in subsection (9)(a) or (b) give the transferor CIO a notice extending the relevant period by such period (not exceeding six months) as is specified in the notice.

(11) A notice under subsection (10) must set out the Commission's reasons for the extension.

(12) If the resolution is confirmed (or treated as confirmed) by the Commission—

(a) all the property, rights and liabilities of the transferor CIO shall become by virtue of this subsection the property, rights and liabilities of the transferee CIO in accordance with the resolution, and

(b) the transferor CIO shall be dissolved.

(13) Any gift which—

(a) is expressed as a gift to the transferor CIO, and

(b) takes effect on or after the date on which the resolution is confirmed (or treated as confirmed),

takes effect as a gift to the transferee CIO.

Amendment—Charities Act 2006, s 34, Sch 7, Pt 1, para 1.

Winding up, insolvency and dissolution

69N Regulations about winding up, insolvency and dissolution

(1) The Minister may by regulations make provision about—

(a) the winding up of CIOs,

(b) their insolvency,

(c) their dissolution, and

(d) their revival and restoration to the register following dissolution.

(2) The regulations may, in particular, make provision—

(a) about the transfer on the dissolution of a CIO of its property and rights (including property and rights held on trust for the CIO) to the official custodian or another person or body,

(b) requiring any person in whose name any stocks, funds or securities are standing in trust for a CIO to transfer them into the name of the official custodian or another person or body,

(c) about the disclaiming, by the official custodian or other transferee of a CIO's property, of title to any of that property,

(d) about the application of a CIO's property cy-près,

(e) about circumstances in which charity trustees may be personally liable for contributions to the assets of a CIO or for its debts,

(f) about the reversal on a CIO's revival of anything done on its dissolution.

(3) The regulations may—

(a) apply any enactment which would not otherwise apply, either without modification or with modifications specified in the regulations,

(b) disapply, or modify (in ways specified in the regulations) the application of, any enactment which would otherwise apply.

(4) In subsection (3), 'enactment' includes a provision of subordinate legislation within the meaning of the Interpretation Act 1978.

Amendment—Charities Act 2006, s 34, Sch 7, Pt 1, para 1.

Miscellaneous

69O Power to transfer all property of unincorporated charity to one or more CIOs

Section 74 below (power to transfer all property of unincorporated charity) applies with the omission of paragraph (a) of subsection (1) in relation to a resolution by the charity trustees of a charity to transfer all its property to a CIO or to divide its property between two or more CIOs.

Amendment—Charities Act 2006, s 34, Sch 7, Pt 1, para 1.

69P Further provision about CIOs

The provisions of Schedule 5B to this Act shall have effect with respect to CIOs.

Amendment—Charities Act 2006, s 34, Sch 7, Pt 1, para 1.

69Q Regulations

(1) The Minister may by regulations make further provision about applications for registration of CIOs, the administration of CIOs, the conversion of charitable companies, registered societies and community interest companies into CIOs, the amalgamation of CIOs, and in relation to CIOs generally.

(2) The regulations may, in particular, make provision about—

    (a)   the execution of deeds and documents,

    (b)   the electronic communication of messages or documents relevant to a CIO or to any dealing with the Commission in relation to one,

    (c)   the maintenance of registers of members and of charity trustees,

    (d)   the maintenance of other registers (for example, a register of charges over the CIO's assets).

(3) The regulations may, in relation to charities constituted as CIOs—

    (a)   disapply any of sections 3 to 4 above,

    (b)   modify the application of any of those sections in ways specified in the regulations.

(4) Subsections (3) and (4) of section 69N above apply for the purposes of this section as they apply for the purposes of that.][472]

Amendment—Charities Act 2006, s 34, Sch 7, Pt 1, para 1.

PART IX
MISCELLANEOUS

Powers of investment

70 ...[473]

Amendment—Trustee Act 2000, s 40(1), (3), Sch 2, Pt I, para 2(1), Sch 4, Pt I.

---

[472]   Amendment: Part 8A inserted: Charities Act, s 34, Sch 7, Pt 1, para 1.
[473]   Amendment: Section omitted: Trustee Act 2000, s 40(1), (3), Sch 2, Pt I, para 2(1), Sch 4, Pt I (in Scotland: Charities and Trustee Investment (Scotland) Act 2005, s 95, Sch 3, para 9).

71 ...[474]

Amendment—Trustee Act 2000, s 40(1), (3), Sch 2, Pt I, para 2(1), Sch 4, Pt I.

[Charity trustees][475]

72 Persons disqualified for being trustees of a charity

(1) Subject to the following provisions of this section, a person shall be disqualified for being a charity trustee or trustee for a charity if—

(a) he has been convicted of any offence involving dishonesty or deception;

(b) he has been adjudged bankrupt or sequestration of his estate has been awarded and (in either case) he has not been discharged [or he is the subject of a bankruptcy restrictions order or an interim order][476];

(c) he has made a composition or arrangement with, or granted a trust deed for, his creditors and has not been discharged in respect of it;

(d) he has been removed from the office of charity trustee or trustee for a charity by an order made—

(i) by the [Commission or][477] Commissioners under section 18(2)(i) above, or

(ii) by the Commissioners under section 20(1A)(i) of the Charities Act 1960 (power to act for protection of charities) or under section 20(1)(i) of that Act (as in force before the commencement of section 8 of the Charities Act 1992), or

(iii) by the High Court,

on the grounds of any misconduct or mismanagement in the administration of the charity for which he was responsible or to which he was privy, or which he by his conduct contributed to or facilitated;

(e) he has been removed, under section 7 of the Law Reform (Miscellaneous Provisions) (Scotland) Act 1990 (powers of Court of Session to deal with management of charities)[or section 34(5)(e) of the Charities and Trustee Investment (Scotland) Act 2005 (powers of the Court of Session)][478], from being concerned in the management or control of any body;

(f) he is subject to a disqualification order [or disqualification undertaking][479] under the Company Directors Disqualification Act 1986 [to a disqualification order under Part II of the Companies (Northern Ireland) Order 1989][480] [or disqualification undertaking under the Company Directors Disqualification (Northern Ireland) Order 2002][481] or to an order made under section 429(2)(b) of the Insolvency Act 1986 (failure to pay under county court administration order).

(2) In subsection (1) above—

---

[474] Amendment: Section omitted: Trustee Act 2000, s 40(1), (3), Sch 2, Pt I, para 2(1), Sch 4, Pt I (in Scotland: Charities and Trustee Investment (Scotland) Act 2005, s 95, Sch 3, para 9).

[475] Amendment: Heading substituted: Charities Act 2006, s 75(1), Sch 8, paras 96, 155.

[476] Amendment: Words inserted: The Enterprise Act 2002 (Disqualification from Office: General) Order 2006, SI 2006/1722, art 2(2), Sch 2, Pt 1, para 4(a).

[477] Amendment: Words inserted: Charities Act 2006, s 75(1), Sch 8, paras 96, 156(1), (2).

[478] Amendment: Words inserted: The Charities and Trustee Investment (Scotland) Act 2005 (Consequential Provisions and Modifications) Order 2006, SI 2006/242, art 5, Sch, Pt 1, para 6(1), (2).

[479] Amendment: Words inserted: Insolvency Act 2000, s 8, Sch 4, Pt II, para 18(a).

[480] Amendment: Words inserted: Insolvency Act 2000, s 8, Sch 4, Pt II, para 18(a).

[481] Amendment: Words inserted: The Insolvency Act 2000 (Company Directors Disqualification Undertakings) Order 2004, SI 2004/1941, art 3, Sch, para 5(a).

(a) paragraph (a) applies whether the conviction occurred before or after the commencement of that subsection, but does not apply in relation to any conviction which is a spent conviction for the purposes of the Rehabilitation of Offenders Act 1974;

(b) paragraph (b) applies whether the adjudication of bankruptcy or the sequestration [or the making of a bankruptcy restrictions order or an interim order][482] occurred before or after the commencement of that subsection;

(c) paragraph (c) applies whether the composition or arrangement was made, or the trust deed was granted, before or after the commencement of that subsection; and

(d) paragraphs (d) to (f) apply in relation to orders made and removals effected before or after the commencement of that subsection.

(3) Where (apart from this subsection) a person is disqualified under subsection (1)(b) above for being a charity trustee or trustee for any charity which is a company, he shall not be so disqualified if leave has been granted under section 11 of the Company Directors Disqualification Act 1986 (undischarged bankrupts) for him to act as director of the charity; and similarly a person shall not be disqualified under subsection (1)(f) above for being a charity trustee or trustee for such a charity if—

[(a) in the case of a person subject to a disqualification order or disqualification undertaking under the Company Directors Disqualification Act 1986, leave for the purposes of section 1(1)(a) or 1A(1)(a) of that Act has been granted for him to act as director of the charity,

(aa) in the case of a person subject to a disqualification order under Part II of the Companies (Northern Ireland) Order 1989[or disqualification undertaking under the Company Directors Disqualification (Northern Ireland) Order 2002][483], leave has been granted by the High Court in Northern Ireland for him to act as director of the charity][484]

(b) in the case of a person subject to an order under section 429(2)(b) of the Insolvency Act 1986, leave has been granted by the court which made the order for him to so act.

(4) [The Commission][485] may, on the application of any person disqualified under subsection (1) above, waive his disqualification either generally or in relation to a particular charity or a particular class of charities; but no such waiver may be granted in relation to any charity which is a company if—

(a) the person concerned is for the time being prohibited, by virtue of—
    (i) a disqualification order [or disqualification undertaking][486] under the Company Directors Disqualification Act 1986, or

---

[482] Amendment: Words inserted: The Enterprise Act 2002 (Disqualification from Office: General) Order 2006, SI 2006/1722, art 2(2), Sch 2, Pt 1, para 4(b).

[483] Amendment: Words inserted: The Insolvency Act 2000 (Company Directors Disqualification Undertakings) Order 2004, SI 2004/1941, art 3, Sch, para 5(b).

[484] Amendment: Paragraphs substituted: Insolvency Act 2000, s 8, Sch 4, Pt II, para 18(b).

[485] Amendment: Words substituted: Charities Act 2006, s 75(1), Sch 8, paras 96, 156(1), (3).

[486] Amendment: Words inserted: Insolvency Act 2000, s 8, Sch 4, Pt II, para 18(c)(i).

     (ii)   section 11(1) [12(2)[, 12A or 12B]⁴⁸⁷]⁴⁸⁸ of that Act (undischarged bankrupts; failure to pay under county court administration order[; Northern Irish disqualification orders]⁴⁸⁹)[; Northern Irish disqualification undertakings]⁴⁹⁰,

     from acting as director of the charity; and

  (b)   leave has not been granted for him to act as director of any other company.

[(4A) If—

  (a)   a person disqualified under subsection (1)(d) or (e) makes an application under subsection (4) above five years or more after the date on which his disqualification took effect, and

  (b)   the Commission is not prevented from granting the application by virtue of paragraphs (a) and (b) of subsection (4),

the Commission must grant the application unless satisfied that, by reason of any special circumstances, it should be refused.]⁴⁹¹

(5) Any waiver under subsection (4) above shall be notified in writing to the person concerned.

(6) For the purposes of this section [the Commission]⁴⁹² shall keep, in such manner as [it thinks fit]⁴⁹³, a register of all persons who have been removed from office as mentioned in subsection (1)(d) above either—

  (a)   by an order of [the Commission or]⁴⁹⁴ the Commissioners made before or after the commencement of subsection (1) above, or

  (b)   by an order of the High Court made after the commencement of section 45(1) of the Charities Act 1992;

and, where any person is so removed from office by an order of the High Court, the court shall notify [the Commission]⁴⁹⁵ of his removal.

(7) The entries in the register kept under subsection (6) above shall be available for public inspection in legible form at all reasonable times.

[(8) In this section 'the Commissioners' means the Charity Commissioners for England and Wales.]⁴⁹⁶

Amendments—Insolvency Act 2000, s 8, Sch 4, Pt II, para 18; : The Insolvency Act 2000 (Company Directors Disqualification Undertakings) Order 2004, SI 2004/1941, art 3, Sch, para 5; The Enterprise Act 2002 (Disqualification from Office: General) Order 2006, SI 2006/1722, art 2(2), Sch 2, Pt 1, para 4; The Charities and Trustee Investment (Scotland) Act 2005 (Consequential Provisions and Modifications) Order 2006, SI 2006/242, art 5, Sch 1, Pt 1, para 6(1), (2); Charities Act 2006, ss 35, 75(1), Sch 8, paras 96, 156.

---

⁴⁸⁷   Amendment: Words substituted: The Insolvency Act 2000 (Company Directors Disqualification Undertakings) Order 2004, SI 2004/1941, art 3, Sch, para 5(c).

⁴⁸⁸   Amendment: Words substituted: Insolvency Act 2000, s 8, Sch 4, Pt II, para 18(c)(ii).

⁴⁸⁹   Amendment: Words inserted: Insolvency Act 2000, s 8, Sch 4, Pt II, para 18(c)(ii).

⁴⁹⁰   Amendment: Words inserted: The Insolvency Act 2000 (Company Directors Disqualification Undertakings) Order 2004, SI 2004/1941, art 3, Sch, para 5(c).

⁴⁹¹   Amendment: Subsection inserted: Charities Act 2006, s 35, for transitional provisions see s 75(3), Sch 10, para 11.

⁴⁹²   Amendment: Words substituted: Charities Act 2006, s 75(1), Sch 8, paras 96, 156(1), (4)(a).

⁴⁹³   Amendment: Words substituted: Charities Act 2006, s 75(1), Sch 8, paras 96, 156(1), (4)(b).

⁴⁹⁴   Amendment: Words inserted: Charities Act 2006, s 75(1), Sch 8, paras 96, 156(1), (4)(c).

⁴⁹⁵   Amendment: Words substituted: Charities Act 2006, s 75(1), Sch 8, paras 96, 156(1), (4)(d).

⁴⁹⁶   Amendment: Subsection added: Charities Act 2006, s 75(1), Sch 8, paras 96, 156(1), (5).

73 Person acting as charity trustee while disqualified

(1) Subject to subsection (2) below, any person who acts as a charity trustee or trustee for a charity while he is disqualified for being such a trustee by virtue of section 72 above shall be guilty of an offence and liable—

- (a) on summary conviction, to imprisonment for a term not exceeding six months or to a fine not exceeding the statutory maximum, or both;
- (b) on conviction on indictment, to imprisonment for a term not exceeding two years or to a fine, or both.

(2) Subsection (1) above shall not apply where—

- (a) the charity concerned is a company; and
- (b) the disqualified person is disqualified by virtue only of paragraph (b) or (f) of section 72(1) above.

(3) Any acts done as charity trustee or trustee for a charity by a person disqualified for being such a trustee by virtue of section 72 above shall not be invalid by reason only of that disqualification.

(4) Where [the Commission is][497] satisfied—

- (a) that any person has acted as charity trustee or trustee for a charity ...[498] while disqualified for being such a trustee by virtue of section 72 above, and
- (b) that, while so acting, he has received from the charity any sums by way of remuneration or expenses, or any benefit in kind, in connection with his acting as charity trustee or trustee for the charity,

[the Commission may by order][499] direct him to repay to the charity the whole or part of any such sums, or (as the case may be) to pay to the charity the whole or part of the monetary value [(as determined by the Commission)][500] of any such benefit.

(5) Subsection (4) above does not apply to any sums received by way of remuneration or expenses in respect of any time when the person concerned was not disqualified for being a charity trustee or trustee for the charity.

Amendments—Charities Act 2006, ss 12, 75, Sch 5, para 9, Sch 8, paras 96, 157, Sch 9.

[73A Remuneration of trustees etc providing services to charity

(1) This section applies to remuneration for services provided by a person to or on behalf of a charity where—

- (a) he is a charity trustee or trustee for the charity, or
- (b) he is connected with a charity trustee or trustee for the charity and the remuneration might result in that trustee obtaining any benefit.

This is subject to subsection (7) below.

(2) If conditions A to D are met in relation to remuneration within subsection (1), the person providing the services ('the relevant person') is entitled to receive the remuneration out of the funds of the charity.

(3) Condition A is that the amount or maximum amount of the remuneration—

---

[497] Amendment: Words substituted: Charities Act 2006, s 75(1), Sch 8, paras 96, 157(a).
[498] Amendment: Words omitted: Charities Act 2006, ss 12, 75(2), Sch 5, para 9, Sch 9.
[499] Amendment: Words substituted: Charities Act 2006, s 75(1), Sch 8, paras 96, 157(b).
[500] Amendment: Words substituted: Charities Act 2006, s 75(1), Sch 8, paras 96, 157(c).

(a) is set out in an agreement in writing between—

    (i) the charity or its charity trustees (as the case may be), and

    (ii) the relevant person,

under which the relevant person is to provide the services in question to or on behalf of the charity, and

(b) does not exceed what is reasonable in the circumstances for the provision by that person of the services in question.

(4) Condition B is that, before entering into that agreement, the charity trustees decided that they were satisfied that it would be in the best interests of the charity for the services to be provided by the relevant person to or on behalf of the charity for the amount or maximum amount of remuneration set out in the agreement.

(5) Condition C is that if immediately after the agreement is entered into there is, in the case of the charity, more than one person who is a charity trustee and is—

(a) a person in respect of whom an agreement within subsection (3) above is in force, or

(b) a person who is entitled to receive remuneration out of the funds of the charity otherwise than by virtue of such an agreement, or

(c) a person connected with a person falling within paragraph (a) or (b) above,

the total number of them constitute a minority of the persons for the time being holding office as charity trustees of the charity.

(6) Condition D is that the trusts of the charity do not contain any express provision that prohibits the relevant person from receiving the remuneration.

(7) Nothing in this section applies to—

(a) any remuneration for services provided by a person in his capacity as a charity trustee or trustee for a charity or under a contract of employment, or

(b) any remuneration not within paragraph (a) which a person is entitled to receive out of the funds of a charity by virtue of any provision or order within subsection (8).

(8) The provisions or orders within this subsection are—

(a) any provision contained in the trusts of the charity,

(b) any order of the court or the Commission,

(c) any statutory provision contained in or having effect under an Act of Parliament other than this section.

(9) Section 73B below applies for the purposes of this section.][501]

Amendment—Charities Act 2006, s 36.

73B Supplementary provisions for purposes of section 73A

(1) Before entering into an agreement within section 73A(3) the charity trustees must have regard to any guidance given by the Commission concerning the making of such agreements.

(2) The duty of care in section 1(1) of the Trustee Act 2000 applies to a charity trustee when making such a decision as is mentioned in section 73A(4).

---

[501] Amendment: Section inserted: Charities Act 2006, s 36, for transitional provisions see s 75(3), Sch 10, para 12.

(3) For the purposes of section 73A(5) an agreement within section 73A(3) is in force so long as any obligations under the agreement have not been fully discharged by a party to it.

(4) In section 73A—

> 'benefit' means a direct or indirect benefit of any nature;
> 'maximum amount', in relation to remuneration, means the maximum amount of the remuneration whether specified in or ascertainable under the terms of the agreement in question;
> 'remuneration' includes any benefit in kind (and 'amount' accordingly includes monetary value);
> 'services', in the context of remuneration for services, includes goods that are supplied in connection with the provision of services.

(5) For the purposes of section 73A the following persons are 'connected' with a charity trustee or trustee for a charity—

(a)   a child, parent, grandchild, grandparent, brother or sister of the trustee;
(b)   the spouse or civil partner of the trustee or of any person falling within paragraph (a);
(c)   a person carrying on business in partnership with the trustee or with any person falling within paragraph (a) or (b);
(d)   an institution which is controlled—
    (i)   by the trustee or by any person falling within paragraph (a), (b) or (c), or
    (ii)   by two or more persons falling within sub-paragraph (i), when taken together;
(e)   a body corporate in which—
    (i)   the trustee or any connected person falling within any of paragraphs (a) to (c) has a substantial interest, or
    (ii)   two or more persons falling within sub-paragraph (i), when taken together, have a substantial interest.

(6) Paragraphs 2 to 4 of Schedule 5 to this Act apply for the purposes of subsection (5) above as they apply for the purposes of provisions of that Schedule.][502]

Amendment—Charities Act 2006, s 36.

[73C Disqualification of trustee receiving remuneration under section 73A

(1) This section applies to any charity trustee or trustee for a charity—

(a)   who is or would be entitled to remuneration under an agreement or proposed agreement within section 73A(3) above, or
(b)   who is connected with a person who is or would be so entitled.

(2) The charity trustee or trustee for a charity is disqualified from acting as such in relation to any decision or other matter connected with the agreement.

(3) But any act done by such a person which he is disqualified from doing by virtue of subsection (2) above shall not be invalid by reason only of that disqualification.

(4) Where the Commission is satisfied—

---

[502] Amendment: Section inserted: Charities Act 2006, s 36, for transitional provisions see s 75(3), Sch 10, para 12.

(a) that a person ('the disqualified trustee') has done any act which he was disqualified from doing by virtue of subsection (2) above, and

(b) that the disqualified trustee or a person connected with him has received or is to receive from the charity any remuneration under the agreement in question,

it may make an order under subsection (5) or (6) below (as appropriate).

(5) An order under this subsection is one requiring the disqualified trustee—

(a) to reimburse to the charity the whole or part of the remuneration received as mentioned in subsection (4)(b) above;

(b) to the extent that the remuneration consists of a benefit in kind, to reimburse to the charity the whole or part of the monetary value (as determined by the Commission) of the benefit in kind.

(6) An order under this subsection is one directing that the disqualified trustee or (as the case may be) connected person is not to be paid the whole or part of the remuneration mentioned in subsection (4)(b) above.

(7) If the Commission makes an order under subsection (5) or (6) above, the disqualified trustee or (as the case may be) connected person accordingly ceases to have any entitlement under the agreement to so much of the remuneration (or its monetary value) as the order requires him to reimburse to the charity or (as the case may be) as it directs is not to be paid to him.

(8) Subsections (4) to (6) of section 73B above apply for the purposes of this section as they apply for the purposes of section 73A above.][503]

Amendment—Charities Act 2006, s 37.

[73D Power to relieve trustees, auditors etc from liability for breach of trust or duty

(1) This section applies to a person who is or has been—

(a) a charity trustee or trustee for a charity,

(b) a person appointed to audit a charity's accounts (whether appointed under an enactment or otherwise), or

(c) an independent examiner, reporting accountant or other person appointed to examine or report on a charity's accounts (whether appointed under an enactment or otherwise).

(2) If the Commission considers—

(a) that a person to whom this section applies is or may be personally liable for a breach of trust or breach of duty committed in his capacity as a person within paragraph (a), (b) or (c) of subsection (1) above, but

(b) that he has acted honestly and reasonably and ought fairly to be excused for the breach of trust or duty,

the Commission may make an order relieving him wholly or partly from any such liability.

(3) An order under subsection (2) above may grant the relief on such terms as the Commission thinks fit.

(4) Subsection (2) does not apply in relation to any personal contractual liability of a charity trustee or trustee for a charity.

---

[503] Amendment: Section inserted: Charities Act 2006, s 37.

(5) For the purposes of this section and section 73E below—

(a) subsection (1)(b) above is to be read as including a reference to the Auditor General for Wales acting as auditor under section 43B above, and

(b) subsection (1)(c) above is to be read as including a reference to the Auditor General for Wales acting as examiner under that section;

and in subsection (1)(b) and (c) any reference to a charity's accounts is to be read as including any group accounts prepared by the charity trustees of a charity.

(6) This section does not affect the operation of—

(a) section 61 of the Trustee Act 1925 (power of court to grant relief to trustees),

(b) section 727 of the Companies Act 1985 (power of court to grant relief to officers or auditors of companies), or

(c) section 73E below (which extends section 727 to auditors etc of charities which are not companies).][504]

Amendment—Charities Act 2006, s 38.

[73E Court's power to grant relief to apply to all auditors etc of charities which are not companies

(1) Section 727 of the Companies Act 1985 (power of court to grant relief to officers or auditors of companies) shall have effect in relation to a person to whom this section applies as it has effect in relation to a person employed as an auditor by a company.

(2) This section applies to—

(a) a person acting in a capacity within section 73D(1)(b) or (c) above in a case where, apart from this section, section 727 would not apply in relation to him as a person so acting, and

(b) a charity trustee of a CIO.][505]

Amendment—Charities Act 2006, s 38.

[73F Trustees' indemnity insurance

(1) The charity trustees of a charity may arrange for the purchase, out of the funds of the charity, of insurance designed to indemnify the charity trustees or any trustees for the charity against any personal liability in respect of—

(a) any breach of trust or breach of duty committed by them in their capacity as charity trustees or trustees for the charity, or

(b) any negligence, default, breach of duty or breach of trust committed by them in their capacity as directors or officers of the charity (if it is a body corporate) or of any body corporate carrying on any activities on behalf of the charity.

(2) The terms of such insurance must, however, be so framed as to exclude the provision of any indemnity for a person in respect of—

(a) any liability incurred by him to pay—

(i) a fine imposed in criminal proceedings, or

---

[504] Amendment: Section inserted: Charities Act 2006, s 38, for transitional provisions see s 75(3), Sch 10, para 13.

[505] Amendment: Section inserted: Charities Act 2006, s 38, for transitional provisions see s 75(3), Sch 10, para 13.

      (ii)   a sum payable to a regulatory authority by way of a penalty in respect of non-compliance with any requirement of a regulatory nature (however arising);

(b)   any liability incurred by him in defending any criminal proceedings in which he is convicted of an offence arising out of any fraud or dishonesty, or wilful or reckless misconduct, by him; or

(c)   any liability incurred by him to the charity that arises out of any conduct which he knew (or must reasonably be assumed to have known) was not in the interests of the charity or in the case of which he did not care whether it was in the best interests of the charity or not.

(3) For the purposes of subsection (2)(b) above—

(a)   the reference to any such conviction is a reference to one that has become final;

(b)   a conviction becomes final—

      (i)   if not appealed against, at the end of the period for bringing an appeal, or

      (ii)   if appealed against, at the time when the appeal (or any further appeal) is disposed of; and

(c)   an appeal is disposed of—

      (i)   if it is determined and the period for bringing any further appeal has ended, or

      (ii)   if it is abandoned or otherwise ceases to have effect.

(4) The charity trustees of a charity may not purchase insurance under this section unless they decide that they are satisfied that it is in the best interests of the charity for them to do so.

(5) The duty of care in section 1(1) of the Trustee Act 2000 applies to a charity trustee when making such a decision.

(6) The Minister may by order make such amendments of subsections (2) and (3) above as he considers appropriate.

(7) No order may be made under subsection (6) above unless a draft of the order has been laid before and approved by a resolution of each House of Parliament.

(8) This section—

(a)   does not authorise the purchase of any insurance whose purchase is expressly prohibited by the trusts of the charity, but

(b)   has effect despite any provision prohibiting the charity trustees or trustees for the charity receiving any personal benefit out of the funds of the charity.][506]

Amendment—Charities Act 2006, s 39.

[Miscellaneous powers of charities][507]

[74 Power to transfer all property of unincorporated charity

(1) This section applies to a charity if—

(a)   its gross income in its last financial year did not exceed £10,000,

(b)   it does not hold any designated land, and

(c)   it is not a company or other body corporate.

---

[506]   Amendment: Section inserted: Charities Act 2006, s 39.
[507]   Amendment: Heading substituted: Charities Act 2006, s 75(1), Sch 8, paras 96, 158.

'Designated land' means land held on trusts which stipulate that it is to be used for the purposes, or any particular purposes, of the charity.

(2) The charity trustees of such a charity may resolve for the purposes of this section—

(a) that all the property of the charity should be transferred to another charity specified in the resolution, or

(b) that all the property of the charity should be transferred to two or more charities specified in the resolution in accordance with such division of the property between them as is so specified.

(3) Any charity so specified may be either a registered charity or a charity which is not required to be registered.

(4) But the charity trustees of a charity ('the transferor charity') do not have power to pass a resolution under subsection (2) above unless they are satisfied—

(a) that it is expedient in the interests of furthering the purposes for which the property is held by the transferor charity for the property to be transferred in accordance with the resolution, and

(b) that the purposes (or any of the purposes) of any charity to which property is to be transferred under the resolution are substantially similar to the purposes (or any of the purposes) of the transferor charity.

(5) Any resolution under subsection (2) above must be passed by a majority of not less than two-thirds of the charity trustees who vote on the resolution.

(6) Where charity trustees have passed a resolution under subsection (2), they must send a copy of it to the Commission, together with a statement of their reasons for passing it.

(7) Having received the copy of the resolution, the Commission—

(a) may direct the charity trustees to give public notice of the resolution in such manner as is specified in the direction, and

(b) if it gives such a direction, must take into account any representations made to it by persons appearing to it to be interested in the charity, where those representations are made to it within the period of 28 days beginning with the date when public notice of the resolution is given by the charity trustees.

(8) The Commission may also direct the charity trustees to provide the Commission with additional information or explanations relating to—

(a) the circumstances in and by reference to which they have decided to act under this section, or

(b) their compliance with any obligation imposed on them by or under this section in connection with the resolution.

(9) Subject to the provisions of section 74A below, a resolution under subsection (2) above takes effect at the end of the period of 60 days beginning with the date on which the copy of it was received by the Commission.

(10) Where such a resolution has taken effect, the charity trustees must arrange for all the property of the transferor charity to be transferred in accordance with the resolution, and on terms that any property so transferred—

(a) is to be held by the charity to which it is transferred ('the transferee charity') in accordance with subsection (11) below, but

(b) when so held is nevertheless to be subject to any restrictions on expenditure to which it was subject as property of the transferor charity;

and the charity trustees must arrange for the property to be so transferred by such date after the resolution takes effect as they agree with the charity trustees of the transferee charity or charities concerned.

(11) The charity trustees of any charity to which property is transferred under this section must secure, so far as is reasonably practicable, that the property is applied for such of its purposes as are substantially similar to those of the transferor charity.

But this requirement does not apply if those charity trustees consider that complying with it would not result in a suitable and effective method of applying the property.

(12) For the purpose of enabling any property to be transferred to a charity under this section, the Commission may, at the request of the charity trustees of that charity, make orders vesting any property of the transferor charity—

(a)　in the transferee charity, in its charity trustees or in any trustee for that charity, or

(b)　in any other person nominated by those charity trustees to hold property in trust for that charity.

(13) The Minister may by order amend subsection (1) above by substituting a different sum for the sum for the time being specified there.

(14) In this section references to the transfer of property to a charity are references to its transfer—

(a)　to the charity, or

(b)　to the charity trustees, or

(c)　to any trustee for the charity, or

(d)　to a person nominated by the charity trustees to hold it in trust for the charity,

as the charity trustees may determine.

(15) Where a charity has a permanent endowment, this section has effect in accordance with section 74B.][508]

Amendment—Charities Act 2006, s 40.

[74A Resolution not to take effect or to take effect at later date

(1) This section deals with circumstances in which a resolution under section 74(2) above either—

(a)　does not take effect under section 74(9) above, or

(b)　takes effect at a time later than that mentioned in section 74(9).

(2) A resolution does not take effect under section 74(9) above if before the end of—

(a)　the period of 60 days mentioned in section 74(9) ('the 60-day period'), or

(b)　that period as modified by subsection (3) or (4) below,

the Commission notifies the charity trustees in writing that it objects to the resolution, either on procedural grounds or on the merits of the proposals contained in the resolution.

'On procedural grounds' means on the grounds that any obligation imposed on the charity trustees by or under section 74 above has not been complied with in connection with the resolution.

---

[508]　Amendment: Section substituted: Charities Act 2006, s 40.

(3) If under section 74(7) above the Commission directs the charity trustees to give public notice of a resolution, the running of the 60-day period is suspended by virtue of this subsection—

> (a)   as from the date on which the direction is given to the charity trustees, and
>
> (b)   until the end of the period of 42 days beginning with the date on which public notice of the resolution is given by the charity trustees.

(4) If under section 74(8) above the Commission directs the charity trustees to provide any information or explanations, the running of the 60-day period is suspended by virtue of this subsection—

> (a)   as from the date on which the direction is given to the charity trustees, and
>
> (b)   until the date on which the information or explanations is or are provided to the Commission.

(5) Subsection (6) below applies once the period of time, or the total period of time, during which the 60-day period is suspended by virtue of either or both of subsections (3) and (4) above exceeds 120 days.

(6) At that point the resolution (if not previously objected to by the Commission) is to be treated as if it had never been passed.][509]

Amendment—Charities Act 2006, s 40.

74B Transfer where charity has permanent endowment

(1) This section provides for the operation of section 74 above where a charity within section 74(1) has a permanent endowment (whether or not the charity's trusts contain provision for the termination of the charity).

(2) In such a case section 74 applies as follows—

> (a)   if the charity has both a permanent endowment and other property ('unrestricted property')—
>> (i)   a resolution under section 74(2) must relate to both its permanent endowment and its unrestricted property, and
>>
>> (ii)   that section applies in relation to its unrestricted property in accordance with subsection (3) below and in relation to its permanent endowment in accordance with subsections (4) to (11) below;
>
> (b)   if all of the property of the charity is comprised in its permanent endowment, that section applies in relation to its permanent endowment in accordance with subsections (4) to (11) below.

(3) Section 74 applies in relation to unrestricted property of the charity as if references in that section to all or any of the property of the charity were references to all or any of its unrestricted property.

(4) Section 74 applies in relation to the permanent endowment of the charity with the following modifications.

(5) References in that section to all or any of the property of the charity are references to all or any of the property comprised in its permanent endowment.

(6) If the property comprised in its permanent endowment is to be transferred to a single charity, the charity trustees must (instead of being satisfied as mentioned in

---

[509]   Amendment: Section substituted for s 74: Charities Act 2006, s 40.

section 74(4)(b)) be satisfied that the proposed transferee charity has purposes which are substantially similar to all of the purposes of the transferor charity.

(7) If the property comprised in its permanent endowment is to be transferred to two or more charities, the charity trustees must (instead of being satisfied as mentioned in section 74(4)(b)) be satisfied—

(a) that the proposed transferee charities, taken together, have purposes which are substantially similar to all of the purposes of the transferor charity, and

(b) that each of the proposed transferee charities has purposes which are substantially similar to one or more of the purposes of the transferor charity.

(8) In the case of a transfer to which subsection (7) above applies, the resolution under section 74(2) must provide for the property comprised in the permanent endowment of the charity to be divided between the transferee charities in such a way as to take account of such guidance as may be given by the Commission for the purposes of this section.

(9) The requirement in section 74(11) shall apply in the case of every such transfer, and in complying with that requirement the charity trustees of a transferee charity must secure that the application of property transferred to the charity takes account of any such guidance.

(10) Any guidance given by the Commission for the purposes of this section may take such form and be given in such manner as the Commission considers appropriate.

(11) For the purposes of sections 74 and 74A above, any reference to any obligation imposed on the charity trustees by or under section 74 includes a reference to any obligation imposed on them by virtue of any of subsections (6) to (8) above.

(12) Section 74(14) applies for the purposes of this section as it applies for the purposes of section 74.][510]

Amendment—Charities Act 2006, s 40.

[74C Power to replace purposes of unincorporated charity

(1) This section applies to a charity if—

(a) its gross income in its last financial year did not exceed £10,000,

(b) it does not hold any designated land, and

(c) it is not a company or other body corporate.

'Designated land' means land held on trusts which stipulate that it is to be used for the purposes, or any particular purposes, of the charity.

(2) The charity trustees of such a charity may resolve for the purposes of this section that the trusts of the charity should be modified by replacing all or any of the purposes of the charity with other purposes specified in the resolution.

(3) The other purposes so specified must be charitable purposes.

(4) But the charity trustees of a charity do not have power to pass a resolution under subsection (2) above unless they are satisfied—

(a) that it is expedient in the interests of the charity for the purposes in question to be replaced, and

---

[510] Amendment: Section substituted for s 74: Charities Act 2006, s 40.

(b)   that, so far as is reasonably practicable, the new purposes consist of or include purposes that are similar in character to those that are to be replaced.

(5) Any resolution under subsection (2) above must be passed by a majority of not less than two-thirds of the charity trustees who vote on the resolution.

(6) Where charity trustees have passed a resolution under subsection (2), they must send a copy of it to the Commission, together with a statement of their reasons for passing it.

(7) Having received the copy of the resolution, the Commission—

(a)   may direct the charity trustees to give public notice of the resolution in such manner as is specified in the direction, and

(b)   if it gives such a direction, must take into account any representations made to it by persons appearing to it to be interested in the charity, where those representations are made to it within the period of 28 days beginning with the date when public notice of the resolution is given by the charity trustees.

(8) The Commission may also direct the charity trustees to provide the Commission with additional information or explanations relating to—

(a)   the circumstances in and by reference to which they have decided to act under this section, or

(b)   their compliance with any obligation imposed on them by or under this section in connection with the resolution.

(9) Subject to the provisions of section 74A above (as they apply in accordance with subsection (10) below), a resolution under subsection (2) above takes effect at the end of the period of 60 days beginning with the date on which the copy of it was received by the Commission.

(10) Section 74A above applies to a resolution under subsection (2) of this section as it applies to a resolution under subsection (2) of section 74 above, except that any reference to section 74(7), (8) or (9) is to be read as a reference to subsection (7), (8) or (9) above.

(11) As from the time when a resolution takes effect under subsection (9) above, the trusts of the charity concerned are to be taken to have been modified in accordance with the terms of the resolution.

(12) The Minister may by order amend subsection (1) above by substituting a different sum for the sum for the time being specified there.][511]

Amendment—Charities Act 2006, s 41.

[74D   Power to modify powers or procedures of unincorporated charity

(1) This section applies to any charity which is not a company or other body corporate.

(2) The charity trustees of such a charity may resolve for the purposes of this section that any provision of the trusts of the charity—

(a)   relating to any of the powers exercisable by the charity trustees in the administration of the charity, or

(b)   regulating the procedure to be followed in any respect in connection with its administration,

---

[511]   Amendment: Section inserted: Charities Act 2006, s 41.

should be modified in such manner as is specified in the resolution.

(3) Subsection (4) applies if the charity is an unincorporated association with a body of members distinct from the charity trustees.

(4) Any resolution of the charity trustees under subsection (2) must be approved by a further resolution which is passed at a general meeting of the body either—

(a) by a majority of not less than two-thirds of the members entitled to attend and vote at the meeting who vote on the resolution, or

(b) by a decision taken without a vote and without any expression of dissent in response to the question put to the meeting.

(5) Where—

(a) the charity trustees have passed a resolution under subsection (2), and

(b) (if subsection (4) applies) a further resolution has been passed under that subsection,

the trusts of the charity are to be taken to have been modified in accordance with the terms of the resolution.

(6) The trusts are to be taken to have been so modified as from such date as is specified for this purpose in the resolution under subsection (2), or (if later) the date when any such further resolution was passed under subsection (4).][512]

Amendment—Charities Act 2006, s 42.

[75 Power of unincorporated charities to spend capital: general

(1) This section applies to any available endowment fund of a charity which is not a company or other body corporate.

(2) But this section does not apply to a fund if section 75A below (power of larger charities to spend capital given for particular purpose) applies to it.

(3) Where the condition in subsection (4) below is met in relation to the charity, the charity trustees may resolve for the purposes of this section that the fund, or a portion of it, ought to be freed from the restrictions with respect to expenditure of capital that apply to it.

(4) The condition in this subsection is that the charity trustees are satisfied that the purposes set out in the trusts to which the fund is subject could be carried out more effectively if the capital of the fund, or the relevant portion of the capital, could be expended as well as income accruing to it, rather than just such income.

(5) Once the charity trustees have passed a resolution under subsection (3) above, the fund or portion may by virtue of this section be expended in carrying out the purposes set out in the trusts to which the fund is subject without regard to the restrictions mentioned in that subsection.

(6) The fund or portion may be so expended as from such date as is specified for this purpose in the resolution.

(7) In this section 'available endowment fund', in relation to a charity, means—

(a) the whole of the charity's permanent endowment if it is all subject to the same trusts, or

---

[512] Amendment: Section inserted: Charities Act 2006, s 42.

(b)   any part of its permanent endowment which is subject to any particular trusts that are different from those to which any other part is subject.][513]

Amendment—Charities Act 2006, s 43.

[75A Power of larger unincorporated charities to spend capital given for particular purpose

(1) This section applies to any available endowment fund of a charity which is not a company or other body corporate if—

(a)   the capital of the fund consists entirely of property given—
   (i)   by a particular individual,
   (ii)   by a particular institution (by way of grant or otherwise), or
   (iii)   by two or more individuals or institutions in pursuit of a common purpose, and
(b)   the financial condition in subsection (2) below is met.

(2) The financial condition in this subsection is met if—

(a)   the relevant charity's gross income in its last financial year exceeded £1,000, and
(b)   the market value of the endowment fund exceeds £10,000.

(3) Where the condition in subsection (4) below is met in relation to the charity, the charity trustees may resolve for the purposes of this section that the fund, or a portion of it, ought to be freed from the restrictions with respect to expenditure of capital that apply to it.

(4) The condition in this subsection is that the charity trustees are satisfied that the purposes set out in the trusts to which the fund is subject could be carried out more effectively if the capital of the fund, or the relevant portion of the capital, could be expended as well as income accruing to it, rather than just such income.

(5) The charity trustees—

(a)   must send a copy of any resolution under subsection (3) above to the Commission, together with a statement of their reasons for passing it, and
(b)   may not implement the resolution except in accordance with the following provisions of this section.

(6) Having received the copy of the resolution the Commission may—

(a)   direct the charity trustees to give public notice of the resolution in such manner as is specified in the direction, and
(b)   if it gives such a direction, must take into account any representations made to it by persons appearing to it to be interested in the charity, where those representations are made to it within the period of 28 days beginning with the date when public notice of the resolution is given by the charity trustees.

(7) The Commission may also direct the charity trustees to provide the Commission with additional information or explanations relating to—

(a)   the circumstances in and by reference to which they have decided to act under this section, or

---

[513]   Amendment: Section substituted: Charities Act 2006, s 43.

(b)   their compliance with any obligation imposed on them by or under this section in connection with the resolution.

(8) When considering whether to concur with the resolution the Commission must take into account—

(a)   any evidence available to it as to the wishes of the donor or donors mentioned in subsection (1)(a) above, and

(b)   any changes in the circumstances relating to the charity since the making of the gift or gifts (including, in particular, its financial position, the needs of its beneficiaries, and the social, economic and legal environment in which it operates).

(9) The Commission must not concur with the resolution unless it is satisfied—

(a)   that its implementation would accord with the spirit of the gift or gifts mentioned in subsection (1)(a) above (even though it would be inconsistent with the restrictions mentioned in subsection (3) above), and

(b)   that the charity trustees have complied with the obligations imposed on them by or under this section in connection with the resolution.

(10) Before the end of the period of three months beginning with the relevant date, the Commission must notify the charity trustees in writing either—

(a)   that the Commission concurs with the resolution, or

(b)   that it does not concur with it.

(11) In subsection (10) 'the relevant date' means—

(a)   in a case where the Commission directs the charity trustees under subsection (6) above to give public notice of the resolution, the date when that notice is given, and

(b)   in any other case, the date on which the Commission receives the copy of the resolution in accordance with subsection (5) above.

(12) Where—

(a)   the charity trustees are notified by the Commission that it concurs with the resolution, or

(b)   the period of three months mentioned in subsection (10) above has elapsed without the Commission notifying them that it does not concur with the resolution,

the fund or portion may, by virtue of this section, be expended in carrying out the purposes set out in the trusts to which the fund is subject without regard to the restrictions mentioned in subsection (3).

(13) The Minister may by order amend subsection (2) above by substituting a different sum for any sum specified there.

(14) In this section—

(a)   'available endowment fund' has the same meaning as in section 75 above,

(b)   'market value', in relation to an endowment fund, means—

    (i)   the market value of the fund as recorded in the accounts for the last financial year of the relevant charity, or

    (ii)   if no such value was so recorded, the current market value of the fund as determined on a valuation carried out for the purpose, and

(c)   the reference in subsection (1) to the giving of property by an individual includes his giving it under his will.]⁵¹⁴

Amendment—Charities Act 2006, s 43.

75B Power to spend capital subject to special trusts

(1) This section applies to any available endowment fund of a special trust which, as the result of a direction under section 96(5) below, is to be treated as a separate charity ('the relevant charity') for the purposes of this section.

(2) Where the condition in subsection (3) below is met in relation to the relevant charity, the charity trustees may resolve for the purposes of this section that the fund, or a portion of it, ought to be freed from the restrictions with respect to expenditure of capital that apply to it.

(3) The condition in this subsection is that the charity trustees are satisfied that the purposes set out in the trusts to which the fund is subject could be carried out more effectively if the capital of the fund, or the relevant portion of the capital, could be expended as well as income accruing to it, rather than just such income.

(4) Where the market value of the fund exceeds £10,000 and the capital of the fund consists entirely of property given—

(a)   by a particular individual,
(b)   by a particular institution (by way of grant or otherwise), or
(c)   by two or more individuals or institutions in pursuit of a common purpose,

subsections (5) to (11) of section 75A above apply in relation to the resolution and that gift or gifts as they apply in relation to a resolution under section 75A(3) and the gift or gifts mentioned in section 75A(1)(a).

(5) Where—

(a)   the charity trustees have passed a resolution under subsection (2) above, and
(b)   (in a case where section 75A(5) to (11) above apply in accordance with subsection (4) above) either—
    (i)   the charity trustees are notified by the Commission that it concurs with the resolution, or
    (ii)   the period of three months mentioned in section 75A(10) has elapsed without the Commission notifying them that it does not concur with the resolution,

the fund or portion may, by virtue of this section, be expended in carrying out the purposes set out in the trusts to which the fund is subject without regard to the restrictions mentioned in subsection (2).

(6) The fund or portion may be so expended as from such date as is specified for this purpose in the resolution.

(7) The Minister may by order amend subsection (4) above by substituting a different sum for the sum specified there.

(8) In this section—

(a)   'available endowment fund' has the same meaning as in section 75 above,
(b)   'market value' has the same meaning as in section 75A above, and

---

⁵¹⁴ Amendment: Section substituted for s 75: Charities Act 2006, s 43.

(c) the reference in subsection (4) to the giving of property by an individual includes his giving it under his will.][515]

Amendment—Charities Act 2006, s 43.

[Mergers

75C Register of charity mergers

(1) The Commission shall establish and maintain a register of charity mergers.

(2) The register shall be kept by the Commission in such manner as it thinks fit.

(3) The register shall contain an entry in respect of every relevant charity merger which is notified to the Commission in accordance with subsections (6) to (9) and such procedures as it may determine.

(4) In this section 'relevant charity merger' means—

(a) a merger of two or more charities in connection with which one of them ('the transferee') has transferred to it all the property of the other or others, each of which (a 'transferor') ceases to exist, or is to cease to exist, on or after the transfer of its property to the transferee, or

(b) a merger of two or more charities ('transferors') in connection with which both or all of them cease to exist, or are to cease to exist, on or after the transfer of all of their property to a new charity ('the transferee').

(5) In the case of a merger involving the transfer of property of any charity which has both a permanent endowment and other property ('unrestricted property') and whose trusts do not contain provision for the termination of the charity, subsection (4)(a) or (b) applies in relation to any such charity as if—

(a) the reference to all of its property were a reference to all of its unrestricted property, and

(b) any reference to its ceasing to exist were omitted.

(6) A notification under subsection (3) above may be given in respect of a relevant charity merger at any time after—

(a) the transfer of property involved in the merger has taken place, or

(b) (if more than one transfer of property is so involved) the last of those transfers has taken place.

(7) If a vesting declaration is made in connection with a relevant charity merger, a notification under subsection (3) above must be given in respect of the merger once the transfer, or the last of the transfers, mentioned in subsection (6) above has taken place.

(8) A notification under subsection (3) is to be given by the charity trustees of the transferee and must—

(a) specify the transfer or transfers of property involved in the merger and the date or dates on which it or they took place;

(b) include a statement that appropriate arrangements have been made with respect to the discharge of any liabilities of the transferor charity or charities; and

---

[515] Amendment: Section substituted for s 75: Charities Act 2006, s 43.

(c)   in the case of a notification required by subsection (7), set out the matters mentioned in subsection (9).

(9) The matters are—

(a)   the fact that the vesting declaration in question has been made;
(b)   the date when the declaration was made; and
(c)   the date on which the vesting of title under the declaration took place by virtue of section 75E(2) below.

(10) In this section and section 75D—

(a)   any reference to a transfer of property includes a transfer effected by a vesting declaration; and
(b)   'vesting declaration' means a declaration to which section 75E(2) below applies.

(11) Nothing in this section or section 75E or 75F applies in a case where section 69K (amalgamation of CIOs) or 69M (transfer of CIO's undertaking) applies.][516]

Amendment—Charities Act 2006, s 44.

[75D Register of charity mergers: supplementary

(1) Subsection (2) applies to the entry to be made in the register in respect of a relevant charity merger, as required by section 75C(3) above.

(2) The entry must—

(a)   specify the date when the transfer or transfers of property involved in the merger took place,
(b)   if a vesting declaration was made in connection with the merger, set out the matters mentioned in section 75C(9) above, and
(c)   contain such other particulars of the merger as the Commission thinks fit.

(3) The register shall be open to public inspection at all reasonable times.

(4) Where any information contained in the register is not in documentary form, subsection (3) above shall be construed as requiring the information to be available for public inspection in legible form at all reasonable times.

(5) In this section—

'the register' means the register of charity mergers;
'relevant charity merger' has the same meaning as in section 75C.][517]

Amendment—Charities Act 2006, s 44.

75E Pre-merger vesting declarations

(1) Subsection (2) below applies to a declaration which—

(a)   is made by deed for the purposes of this section by the charity trustees of the transferor,
(b)   is made in connection with a relevant charity merger, and

---

[516]   Amendment: Section inserted: Charities Act 2006, s 44, for transitional provisions see s 75(3), Sch 10, para 14.
[517]   Amendment: Section inserted: Charities Act 2006, s 44.

(c)   is to the effect that (subject to subsections (3) and (4)) all of the transferor's property is to vest in the transferee on such date as is specified in the declaration ('the specified date').

(2) The declaration operates on the specified date to vest the legal title to all of the transferor's property in the transferee, without the need for any further document transferring it.

This is subject to subsections (3) and (4).

(3) Subsection (2) does not apply to—

(a)   any land held by the transferor as security for money subject to the trusts of the transferor (other than land held on trust for securing debentures or debenture stock);

(b)   any land held by the transferor under a lease or agreement which contains any covenant (however described) against assignment of the transferor's interest without the consent of some other person, unless that consent has been obtained before the specified date; or

(c)   any shares, stock, annuity or other property which is only transferable in books kept by a company or other body or in a manner directed by or under any enactment.

(4) In its application to registered land within the meaning of the Land Registration Act 2002, subsection (2) has effect subject to section 27 of that Act (dispositions required to be registered).

(5) In this section 'relevant charity merger' has the same meaning as in section 75C.

(6) In this section—

(a)   any reference to the transferor, in relation to a relevant charity merger, is a reference to the transferor (or one of the transferors) within the meaning of section 75C above, and

(b)   any reference to all of the transferor's property, where the transferor is a charity within section 75C(5), is a reference to all of the transferor's unrestricted property (within the meaning of that provision).

(7) In this section any reference to the transferee, in relation to a relevant charity merger, is a reference to—

(a)   the transferee (within the meaning of section 75C above), if it is a company or other body corporate, and

(b)   otherwise, to the charity trustees of the transferee (within the meaning of that section).]518

Amendment—Charities Act 2006, s 44.

[75F Effect of registering charity merger on gifts to transferor

(1) This section applies where a relevant charity merger is registered in the register of charity mergers.

(2) Any gift which—

(a)   is expressed as a gift to the transferor, and

(b)   takes effect on or after the date of registration of the merger,

---

518   Amendment: Section inserted: Charities Act 2006, s 44.

takes effect as a gift to the transferee, unless it is an excluded gift.

(3) A gift is an 'excluded gift' if—

(a)   the transferor is a charity within section 75C(5), and

(b)   the gift is intended to be held subject to the trusts on which the whole or part of the charity's permanent endowment is held.

(4) In this section—

'relevant charity merger' has the same meaning as in section 75C; and 'transferor' and 'transferee' have the same meanings as in section 75E.][519]

Amendment—Charities Act 2006, s 44.

Local charities

76 Local authority's index of local charities

(1)   The council of a county [or county borough][520] or of a district or London borough and the Common Council of the City of London may maintain an index of local charities or of any class of local charities in the council's area, and may publish information contained in the index, or summaries or extracts taken from it.

(2)   A council proposing to establish or maintaining under this section an index of local charities or of any class of local charities shall, on request, be supplied by [the Commission][521] free of charge with copies of such entries in the register of charities as are relevant to the index or with particulars of any changes in the entries of which copies have been supplied before; and [the Commission][522] may arrange that [it will][523] without further request supply a council with particulars of any such changes.(3)   An index maintained under this section shall be open to public inspection at all reasonable times.

(4)   A council may employ any voluntary organisation as their agent for the purposes of this section, on such terms and within such limits (if any) or in such cases as they may agree; and for this purpose 'voluntary organisation' means any body of which the activities are carried on otherwise than for profit, not being a public or local authority.

(5)   A joint board discharging any of a council's functions shall have the same powers under this section as the council as respects local charities in the council's area which are established for purposes similar or complementary to any services provided by the board.

Amendments—Local Government (Wales) Act 1994, s 66(6), Sch 16, para 101(1); Charities Act 2006, s 75(1), Sch 8, paras 96, 159.

Modification—This section 'shall have effect as if the references to a council for any area included references to a National Park authority and as if the relevant Park were the authority's area', Environment Act 1995, s 70, Sch 9, para 15.

---

[519]   Amendment: Section inserted: Charities Act 2006, s 44.
[520]   Amendment: Words inserted: Local Government (Wales) Act 1994, s 66(6), Sch 16, para 101(1).
[521]   Amendment: Words substituted: Charities Act 2006, s 75(1), Sch 8, paras 96, 159(a).
[522]   Amendment: Words substituted: Charities Act 2006, s 75(1), Sch 8, paras 96, 159(a).
[523]   Amendment: Words substituted: Charities Act 2006, s 75(1), Sch 8, paras 96, 159(b).

77 Reviews of local charities by local authority

(1) The council of a county [or county borough]⁵²⁴ or of a district or London borough and the Common Council of the City of London may, subject to the following provisions of this section, initiate, and carry out in co-operation with the charity trustees, a review of the working of any group of local charities with the same or similar purposes in the council's area, and may make to [the Commission]⁵²⁵ such report on the review and such recommendations arising from it as the council after consultation with the trustees think fit.

(2) A council having power to initiate reviews under this section may co-operate with other persons in any review by them of the working of local charities in the council's area (with or without other charities), or may join with other persons in initiating and carrying out such a review.

(3) No review initiated by a council under this section shall extend to any charity without the consent of the charity trustees, nor to any ecclesiastical charity.

(4) No review initiated under this section by the council of a district shall extend to the working in any county of a local charity established for purposes similar or complementary to any services provided by county councils unless the review so extends with the consent of the council of that county.

[(4A) Subsection (4) above does not apply in relation to Wales.]⁵²⁶

(5) Subsections (4) and (5) of section 76 above shall apply for the purposes of this section as they apply for the purposes of that section.

Amendments—Local Government (Wales) Act 1994, s 66(6), Sch 16, para 101(2); Charities Act 2006, s 75(1), Sch 8, paras 96, 160.

Modification—This section 'shall have effect as if the references to a council for any area included references to a National Park authority and as if the relevant Park were the authority's area', Environment Act 1995, s 70, Sch 9, para 15.

78 Co-operation between charities, and between charities and local authorities

(1) Any local council and any joint board discharging any functions of such a council—

(a) may make, with any charity established for purposes similar or complementary to services provided by the council or board, arrangements for co-ordinating the activities of the council or board and those of the charity in the interests of persons who may benefit from those services or from the charity; and

(b) shall be at liberty to disclose to any such charity in the interests of those persons any information obtained in connection with the services provided by the council or board, whether or not arrangements have been made with the charity under this subsection.

In this subsection 'local council' means[, in relation to England,]⁵²⁷ the council of a county, or of a district, London borough, [or parish]⁵²⁸, and includes also the Common

---

⁵²⁴ Amendment: Words inserted: Local Government (Wales) Act 1994, s 66(6), Sch 16, para 101(2).
⁵²⁵ Amendment: Words substituted: Charities Act 2006, s 75(1), Sch 8, paras 96, 160.
⁵²⁶ Amendment: Words inserted: Local Government (Wales) Act 1994, s 66(6), Sch 16, para 101(2).
⁵²⁷ Amendment: Words inserted: Local Government (Wales) Act 1994, s 66(6), Sch 16, para 101(3)(a).
⁵²⁸ Amendment: Words substituted: Local Government (Wales) Act 1994, s 66(6), Sch 16, para 101(3)(b).

Council of the City of London and the Council of the Isles of Scilly [and, in relation to Wales, the council of a county, county borough or community][529].

(2)   Charity trustees shall, notwithstanding anything in the trusts of the charity, have power by virtue of this subsection to do all or any of the following things, where it appears to them likely to promote or make more effective the work of the charity, and may defray the expense of so doing out of any income or money applicable as income of the charity, that is to say—

   (a)   they may co-operate in any review undertaken under section 77 above or otherwise of the working of charities or any class of charities;

   (b)   they may make arrangements with an authority acting under subsection (1) above or with another charity for co-ordinating their activities and those of the authority or of the other charity;

   (c)   they may publish information of other charities with a view to bringing them to the notice of those for whose benefit they are intended.

Amendments—Local Government (Wales) Act 1994, s 66(6), Sch 16, para 101(3).

Modification—This section 'shall have effect as if the references to a council for any area included references to a National Park authority and as if the relevant Park were the authority's area', Environment Act 1995, s 70, Sch 9, para 15.

79   Parochial charities

(1)   Where trustees hold any property for the purposes of a public recreation ground, or of allotments (whether under inclosure Acts or otherwise), for the benefit of inhabitants of a parish having a parish council, or for other charitable purposes connected with such a parish, except for an ecclesiastical charity, they may with the approval of [the Commission][530] and with the consent of the parish council transfer the property to the parish council or to persons appointed by the parish council; and the council or their appointees shall hold the property on the same trusts and subject to the same conditions as the trustees did.

This subsection shall apply to property held for any public purposes as it applies to property held for charitable purposes.

(2)   Where the charity trustees of a parochial charity in a parish, not being an ecclesiastical charity nor a charity founded within the preceding forty years, do not include persons elected by the local government electors, ratepayers or inhabitants of the parish or appointed by the parish council or parish meeting, the parish council or parish meeting may appoint additional charity trustees, to such number as [the Commission][531] may allow; and if there is a sole charity trustee not elected or appointed as aforesaid of any such charity, the number of the charity trustees may, with the approval of [the Commission][532], be increased to three of whom one may be nominated by the person holding the office of the sole trustee and one by the parish council or parish meeting.

(3)   Where, under the trusts of a charity other than an ecclesiastical charity, the inhabitants of a rural parish (whether in vestry or not) or a select vestry were formerly (in 1894) entitled to appoint charity trustees for, or trustees or beneficiaries of, the charity, then—

---

[529]   Amendment: Words inserted: Local Government (Wales) Act 1994, s 66(6), Sch 16, para 101(3)(c).
[530]   Amendment: Words substituted: Charities Act 2006, s 75(1), Sch 8, paras 96, 161(1), (2).
[531]   Amendment: Words substituted: Charities Act 2006, s 75(1), Sch 8, paras 96, 161(1), (3).
[532]   Amendment: Words substituted: Charities Act 2006, s 75(1), Sch 8, paras 96, 161(1), (3).

(a) in a parish having a parish council, the appointment shall be made by the parish council or, in the case of beneficiaries, by persons appointed by the parish council; and

(b) in a parish not having a parish council, the appointment shall be made by the parish meeting.

(4) Where overseers as such or, except in the case of an ecclesiastical charity, churchwardens as such were formerly (in 1894) charity trustees of or trustees for a parochial charity in a rural parish, either alone or jointly with other persons, then instead of the former overseer or church warden trustees there shall be trustees (to a number not greater than that of the former overseer or churchwarden trustees) appointed by the parish council or, if there is no parish council, by the parish meeting.

(5) Where, outside Greater London (other than the outer London boroughs), overseers of a parish as such were formerly (in 1927) charity trustees of or trustees for any charity, either alone or jointly with other persons, then instead of the former overseer trustees there shall be trustees (to a number not greater than that of the former overseer trustees) appointed by the parish council or, if there is no parish council, by the parish meeting.

(6) In the case of an urban parish existing immediately before the passing of the Local Government Act 1972 which after 1 April 1974 is not comprised in a parish, the power of appointment under subsection (5) above shall be exercisable by the district council.

(7) In the application of the foregoing provisions of this section to Wales—

(a) for references in subsections (1) and (2) to a parish or a parish council there shall be substituted respectively references to a community or a community council;

(b) for references in subsections (3)(a) and (b) to a parish, a parish council or a parish meeting there shall be substituted respectively references to a community, a community council or the [council of the county or (as the case may be) county borough][533];

(c) for references in subsections (4) and (5) to a parish council or a parish meeting there shall be substituted respectively references to a community council or the [council of the county or (as the case may be) county borough][534].

(8) Any appointment of a charity trustee or trustee for a charity which is made by virtue of this section shall be for a term of four years, and a retiring trustee shall be eligible for re-appointment but—

(a) on an appointment under subsection (2) above, where no previous appointments have been made by virtue of that subsection or of the corresponding provision of the Local Government Act 1894 or the Charities Act 1960, and more than one trustee is appointed, half of those appointed (or as nearly as may be) shall be appointed for a term of two years; and

(b) an appointment made to fill a casual vacancy shall be for the remainder of the term of the previous appointment.

[(9) This section shall not affect the trusteeship, control or management of any [foundation or voluntary school within the meaning of the School Standards and Framework Act 1998.][535]][536]

---

[533] Amendment: Words inserted: Local Government (Wales) Act 1994, s 66(6), Sch 16, para 101(4).
[534] Amendment: Words inserted: Local Government (Wales) Act 1994, s 66(6), Sch 16, para 101(4).
[535] Amendment: Words substituted: School Standards and Framework Act 1998, s 140(1), Sch 30, para 49.
[536] Amendment: Subsection substituted: Education Act 1996, s 582(1), Sch 37, para 119.

(10)   The provisions of this section shall not extend to the Isles of Scilly, and shall have effect subject to any order (including any future order) made under any enactment relating to local government with respect to local government areas or the powers of local authorities.

(11)   In this section the expression 'formerly (in 1894)' relates to the period immediately before the passing of the Local Government Act 1894, and the expression 'formerly (in 1927)' to the period immediately before 1 April 1927; and the word 'former' shall be construed accordingly.

Amendments—Local Government (Wales) Act 1994, s 66(6), Sch 16, para 101(4); Education Act 1996, s 582(1), Sch 37, para 119; School Standards and Framework Act, s 140(10, Sch 30, para 49; Charities Act 2006, s 75(1), Sch 8, paras 96, 161.

Scottish charities

80 Supervision by [Commission][537] of certain Scottish charities

(1)   The following provisions of this Act, namely—

(a)   sections 8 and 9,
(b)   section 18 (except subsection (2)(ii)),
[(c)   sections 19 to 19C, and
(d)   section 31A,][538]

shall have effect in relation to any recognised body which is managed or controlled wholly or mainly in or from England or Wales as they have effect in relation to a charity.

(2)   Where—

(a)   a recognised body is managed or controlled wholly or mainly in or from Scotland, but
(b)   any person in England and Wales holds any property on behalf of the body or of any person concerned in its management or control,

then, if [the Commission is satisfied][539] as to the matters mentioned in subsection (3) below, [it may make][540] an order requiring the person holding the property not to part with it without [the Commission's approval][541].

(3)   The matters referred to in subsection (2) above are—

(a)   that there has been any misconduct or mismanagement in the administration of the body; and
(b)   that it is necessary or desirable to make an order under that subsection for the purpose of protecting the property of the body or securing a proper application of such property for the purposes of the body;

and the reference in that subsection to [the Commission][542] being satisfied as to those matters is a reference to [the Commission being][543] so satisfied on the basis of such information as may be [supplied to it][544] by the [Scottish Charity Regulator][545].

---

[537]   Amendment: Word substituted: Charities Act 2006, s 75(1), Sch 8, paras 96, 162(1), (7).
[538]   Amendment: Paragraphs substituted: Charities Act 2006, s 75(1), Sch 8, paras 96, 162(1), (2).
[539]   Amendment: Words substituted: Charities Act 2006, s 75(1), Sch 8, paras 96, 162(1), (3)(a).
[540]   Amendment: Words substituted: Charities Act 2006, s 75(1), Sch 8, paras 96, 162(1), (3)(b).
[541]   Amendment: Words substituted: Charities Act 2006, s 75(1), Sch 8, paras 96, 162(1), (3)(c).
[542]   Amendment: Words substituted: Charities Act 2006, s 75(1), Sch 8, paras 96, 162(1), (4)(a).
[543]   Amendment: Words substituted: Charities Act 2006, s 75(1), Sch 8, paras 96, 162(1), (4)(b).
[544]   Amendment: Words substituted: Charities Act 2006, s 75(1), Sch 8, paras 96, 162(1), (4)(c).

(4) Where—

    (a)   any person in England and Wales holds any property on behalf of a recognised body or of any person concerned in the management or control of such a body, and

    (b)   [the Commission is satisfied][546] (whether on the basis of such information as may be [supplied to it][547] by the [Scottish Charity Regulator][548] or otherwise)—

        (i)   that there has been any misconduct or mismanagement in the administration of the body, and

        (ii)   that it is necessary or desirable to make an order under this subsection for the purpose of protecting the property of the body or securing a proper application of such property for the purposes of the body,

[the Commission][549] may by order vest the property in such recognised body or charity as is specified in the order in accordance with subsection (5) below, or require any persons in whom the property is vested to transfer it to any such body or charity, or appoint any person to transfer the property to any such body or charity.

(5) The [Commission][550] may specify in an order under subsection (4) above such other recognised body or such charity as [it considers][551] appropriate, being a body or charity whose purposes are, in the opinion of the [Commission][552], as similar in character to those of the body referred to in paragraph (a) of that subsection as is reasonably practicable; but the [Commission][553] shall not so specify any body or charity unless [it has received][554]—

    (a)   from the persons concerned in the management or control of the body, or

    (b)   from the charity trustees of the charity,

as the case may be, written confirmation that they are willing to accept the property.

(6) In this section 'recognised body' [means a body entered in the Scottish Charity Register][555].

Amendments—The Charities and Trustee Investment (Scotland) Act 2005 (Consequential Provisions and Modifications) Order 2006, SI 2006/242, art 5, Sch, Pt 1, para 6(1), (3); Charities Act 2006, s 75(1), Sch 8, paras 96, 162.

Administrative provisions about charities

81 Manner of giving notice of charity meetings etc

(1) All notices which are required or authorised by the trusts of a charity to be given to a charity trustee, member or subscriber may be sent by post, and, if sent by post, may be

---

[545]   Amendment: Words substituted: The Charities and Trustee Investment (Scotland) Act 2005 (Consequential Provisions and Modifications) Order 2006, SI 2006/242, art 5, Sch, Pt 1, para 6(1), (3)(a).

[546]   Amendment: Words substituted: Charities Act 2006, s 75(1), Sch 8, paras 96, 162(1), (5)(a).

[547]   Amendment: Words substituted: Charities Act 2006, s 75(1), Sch 8, paras 96, 162(1), (5)(b).

[548]   Amendment: Words substituted: The Charities and Trustee Investment (Scotland) Act 2005 (Consequential Provisions and Modifications) Order 2006, SI 2006/242, art 5, Sch, Pt 1, para 6(1), (3)(a).

[549]   Amendment: Words substituted: Charities Act 2006, s 75(1), Sch 8, paras 96, 162(1), (5)(c).

[550]   Amendment: Word substituted: Charities Act 2006, s 75(1), Sch 8, paras 96, 162(1), (6)(a).

[551]   Amendment: Words substituted: Charities Act 2006, s 75(1), Sch 8, paras 96, 162(1), (6)(b).

[552]   Amendment: Word substituted: Charities Act 2006, s 75(1), Sch 8, paras 96, 162(1), (6)(a).

[553]   Amendment: Word substituted: Charities Act 2006, s 75(1), Sch 8, paras 96, 162(1), (6)(a).

[554]   Amendment: Words substituted: Charities Act 2006, s 75(1), Sch 8, paras 96, 162(1), (6)(c).

[555]   Amendment: Words substituted: The Charities and Trustee Investment (Scotland) Act 2005 (Consequential Provisions and Modifications) Order 2006, SI 2006/242, art 5, Sch, Pt 1, para 6(1), (3)(b).

addressed to any address given as his in the list of charity trustees, members or subscribers for the time being in use at the office or principal office of the charity.

(2)   Where any such notice required to be given as aforesaid is given by post, it shall be deemed to have been given by the time at which the letter containing it would be delivered in the ordinary course of post.

(3)   No notice required to be given as aforesaid of any meeting or election need be given to any charity trustee, member or subscriber, if in the list above mentioned he has no address in the United Kingdom.

82 Manner of executing instruments

(1)   Charity trustees may, subject to the trusts of the charity, confer on any of their body (not being less than two in number) a general authority, or an authority limited in such manner as the trustees think fit, to execute in the names and on behalf of the trustees assurances or other deeds or instruments for giving effect to transactions to which the trustees are a party; and any deed or instrument executed in pursuance of an authority so given shall be of the same effect as if executed by the whole body.

(2)   An authority under subsection (1) above—

    (a)   shall suffice for any deed or instrument if it is given in writing or by resolution of a meeting of the trustees, notwithstanding the want of any formality that would be required in giving an authority apart from that subsection;

    (b)   may be given so as to make the powers conferred exercisable by any of the trustees, or may be restricted to named persons or in any other way;

    (c)   subject to any such restriction, and until it is revoked, shall, notwithstanding any change in the charity trustees, have effect as a continuing authority given by the charity trustees from time to time of the charity and exercisable by such trustees.

(3)   In any authority under this section to execute a deed or instrument in the names and on behalf of charity trustees there shall, unless the contrary intention appears, be implied authority also to execute it for them in the name and on behalf of the official custodian or of any other person, in any case in which the charity trustees could do so.

(4)   Where a deed or instrument purports to be executed in pursuance of this section, then in favour of a person who (then or afterwards) in good faith acquires for money or money's worth an interest in or charge on property or the benefit of any covenant or agreement expressed to be entered into by the charity trustees, it shall be conclusively presumed to have been duly executed by virtue of this section.

(5)   The powers conferred by this section shall be in addition to and not in derogation of any other powers.

83 Transfer and evidence of title to property vested in trustees

(1)   Where, under the trusts of a charity, trustees of property held for the purposes of the charity may be appointed or discharged by resolution of a meeting of the charity trustees, members or other persons, a memorandum declaring a trustee to have been so appointed or discharged shall be sufficient evidence of that fact if the memorandum is signed either at the meeting by the person presiding or in some other manner directed by the meeting and is attested by two persons present at the meeting.

(2)   A memorandum evidencing the appointment or discharge of a trustee under subsection (1) above, if executed as a deed, shall have the like operation under section 40

of the Trustee Act 1925 (which relates to vesting declarations as respects trust property in deeds appointing or discharging trustees) as if the appointment or discharge were effected by the deed.

(3) For the purposes of this section, where a document purports to have been signed and attested as mentioned in subsection (1) above, then on proof (whether by evidence or as a matter of presumption) of the signature the document shall be presumed to have been so signed and attested, unless the contrary is shown.

(4) This section shall apply to a memorandum made at any time, except that subsection (2) shall apply only to those made after the commencement of the Charities Act 1960.

(5) This section shall apply in relation to any institution to which the Literary and Scientific Institutions Act 1854 applies as it applies in relation to a charity.

PART X
SUPPLEMENTARY

84 Supply by [Commission][556] of copies of documents open to public inspection

[The Commission][557] shall, at the request of any person, furnish him with copies of, or extracts from, any document in [the Commission's possession][558] which is for the time being open to inspection under Parts II to VI of this Act [or section 75D][559].

Amendments—Charities Act 2006, s 75(1), Sch 8, paras 96, 163.

85 Fees and other amounts payable to [Commission][560]

(1) The Secretary of State may by regulations require the payment to [the Commission][561] of such fees as may be prescribed by the regulations in respect of—

(a)   the discharge by [the Commission][562] of such functions under the enactments relating to charities as may be so prescribed;
(b)   the inspection of the register of charities or of other material [kept by the Commission][563] under those enactments, or the furnishing of copies of or extracts from documents so kept.

(2) Regulations under this section may—

(a)   confer, or provide for the conferring of, exemptions from liability to pay a prescribed fee;
(b)   provide for the remission or refunding of a prescribed fee (in whole or in part) in circumstances prescribed by the regulations.

(3) Any regulations under this section which require the payment of a fee in respect of any matter for which no fee was previously payable shall not be made unless a draft of the regulations has been laid before and approved by a resolution of each House of Parliament.

---

[556]   Amendment: Word substituted: Charities Act 2006, s 75(1), Sch 8, paras 96, 163(1), (5).
[557]   Amendment: Words substituted: Charities Act 2006, s 75(1), Sch 8, paras 96, 163(1), (2).
[558]   Amendment: Words substituted: Charities Act 2006, s 75(1), Sch 8, paras 96, 163(1), (3).
[559]   Amendment: Words added: Charities Act 2006, s 75(1), Sch 8, paras 96, 163(1), (4).
[560]   Amendment: Word substituted: Charities Act 2006, s 75(1), Sch 8, paras 96, 164(1), (5).
[561]   Amendment: Words substituted: Charities Act 2006, s 75(1), Sch 8, paras 96, 164(1), (2)(a).
[562]   Amendment: Words substituted: Charities Act 2006, s 75(1), Sch 8, paras 96, 164(1), (2)(a).
[563]   Amendment: Words substituted: Charities Act 2006, s 75(1), Sch 8, paras 96, 164(1), (2)(b).

(4) [The Commission][564] may impose charges of such amounts as [it considers][565] reasonable in respect of the supply of any publications produced [by it][566].

(5) Any fees and other payments received by [the Commission][567] by virtue of this section shall be paid into the Consolidated Fund.

Amendments—Charities Act 2006, s 75(1), Sch 8, paras 96, 164.

86 Regulations and orders

(1) Any regulations or order of the Secretary of State under this Act—

    (a)   shall be made by statutory instrument; and

    (b)   (subject to subsection (2) below) shall be subject to annulment in pursuance of a resolution of either House of Parliament.

(2) Subsection (1)(b) above does not apply—

    (a)   to an order under section 17(2), ...[568] [73F(6)][569] or 99(2) [or paragraph 6 of Schedule 1C][570]; [or][571]

    [(aa)   to regulations under section 69N above; and no regulations shall be made under that section unless a draft of the regulations has been laid before and approved by a resolution of each House of Parliament; or][572]

    (b)   ...[573]

    (c)   to any regulations to which section 85(3) applies.

(3) Any regulations of the Secretary of State or [the Commission][574] and any order of the Secretary of State under this Act may make—

    (a)   different provision for different cases; and

    (b)   such supplemental, incidental, consequential or transitional provision or savings as the Secretary of State or, as the case may be, [the Commission considers][575] appropriate.

(4) Before making any regulations under section 42, 44[, 45, 69N or 69Q][576] above [or Schedule 5A][577] the Secretary of State shall consult such persons or bodies of persons as he considers appropriate.

Amendments—Trustee Act 2000, s 40(1), (3), Sch 2, Pt I, para 2, Sch 4, Pt I; Charities Act 2006, ss 34, 75(1), Sch 7, Pt 2, paras 3, 6, Sch 8, paras 96, 165.

---

[564] Amendment: Words substituted: Charities Act 2006, s 75(1), Sch 8, paras 96, 164(1), (3)(a).

[565] Amendment: Words substituted: Charities Act 2006, s 75(1), Sch 8, paras 96, 164(1), (3)(b).

[566] Amendment: Words substituted: Charities Act 2006, s 75(1), Sch 8, paras 96, 164(1), (3)(c).

[567] Amendment: Words substituted: Charities Act 2006, s 75(1), Sch 8, paras 96, 164(1), (4).

[568] Amendment: Words omitted: Trustee Act 2000, s 40(1), (3), Sch 2, Pt I, para 2(2)(a), Sch 4, Pt I (in Scotland: Charities and Trustee Investment (Scotland) Act 2005, s 95, Sch 3, para 9).

[569] Amendment: Number inserted: Charities Act 2006, s 75(1), Sch 8, paras 96, 165(1), (2)(a).

[570] Amendment: Words inserted: Charities Act 2006, s 75(1), Sch 8, paras 96, 165(1), (2)(b).

[571] Amendment: Word inserted: Trustee Act 2000, s 40(1), (3), Sch 2, Pt I, para 2(2)(b).

[572] Amendment: Paragraph inserted: Charities Act 2006, s 34, Sch 7, Pt 2, paras 3, 6(a).

[573] Amendment: Paragraph omitted: Trustee Act 2000, s 40(1), (3), Sch 2, Pt I, para 2(3), Sch 4, Pt I (in Scotland: Charities and Trustee Investment (Scotland) Act 2005, s 95, Sch 3, para 9).

[574] Amendment: Words substituted: Charities Act 2006, s 75(1), Sch 8, paras 96, 165(1), (3)(a).

[575] Amendment: Words substituted: Charities Act 2006, s 75(1), Sch 8, paras 96, 165(1), (3)(b).

[576] Amendment: Words substituted: Charities Act 2006, s 34, Sch 7, Pt 2, paras 3, 6(b).

[577] Amendment: Words inserted: Charities Act 2006, s 75(1), Sch 8, paras 96, 165(1), (4).

[86A Consultation by Commission before exercising powers in relation to exempt charity

Before exercising in relation to an exempt charity any specific power exercisable by it in relation to the charity, the Commission must consult the charity's principal regulator.][578]

Amendment—Charities Act 2006, s 14.

87 Enforcement of requirements by order of [Commission][579]

(1)   If a person fails to comply with any requirement imposed by or under this Act then (subject to subsection (2) below) [the Commission][580] may by order give him such directions as [it considers][581] appropriate for securing that the default is made good.

(2)   Subsection (1) above does not apply to any such requirement if—

(a)   a person who fails to comply with, or is persistently in default in relation to, the requirement is liable to any criminal penalty; or

(b)   the requirement is imposed—

(i)   by an order of [the Commission][582] to which section 88 below applies, or

(ii)   by a direction of [the Commission][583] to which that section applies by virtue of section 90(2) below.

Amendments—Charities Act 2006, s 75(1), Sch 8, paras 96, 166.

88 Enforcement of orders of [Commission][584]

A person guilty of disobedience—

[(a)   to an order of the Commission under section 9(1), 19A, 19B, 44(2), 61, 73, 73C or 80 above; or][585]

(b)   to an order of [the Commission][586] under section 16 or 18 above requiring a transfer of property or payment to be called for or made; or

(c)   to an order of [the Commission][587] requiring a default under this Act to be made good;

may on the application of [the Commission to][588] the High Court be dealt with as for disobedience to an order of the High Court.

Amendments—Charities Act 2006, s 75(1), Sch 8, paras 96, 167.

89 Other provisions as to orders of [Commission][589]

(1)   Any order made by [the Commission][590] under this Act may include such incidental or supplementary provisions as [the Commission thinks][591] expedient for carrying into

---

[578]   Amendment: Section inserted: Charities Act 2006, s 14.
[579]   Amendment: Word substituted: Charities Act 2006, s 75(1), Sch 8, paras 96, 166(1), (4).
[580]   Amendment: Words substituted: Charities Act 2006, s 75(1), Sch 8, paras 96, 166(1), (2)(a).
[581]   Amendment: Words substituted: Charities Act 2006, s 75(1), Sch 8, paras 96, 166(1), (2)(b).
[582]   Amendment: Words substituted: Charities Act 2006, s 75(1), Sch 8, paras 96, 166(1), (3).
[583]   Amendment: Words substituted: Charities Act 2006, s 75(1), Sch 8, paras 96, 166(1), (3).
[584]   Amendment: Word substituted: Charities Act 2006, s 75(1), Sch 8, paras 96, 167(1), (5).
[585]   Amendment: Paragraph substituted: Charities Act 2006, s 75(1), Sch 8, paras 96, 167(1), (2).
[586]   Amendment: Words substituted: Charities Act 2006, s 75(1), Sch 8, paras 96, 167(1), (3).
[587]   Amendment: Words substituted: Charities Act 2006, s 75(1), Sch 8, paras 96, 167(1), (3).
[588]   Amendment: Words substituted: Charities Act 2006, s 75(1), Sch 8, paras 96, 167(1), (4).
[589]   Amendment: Word substituted: Charities Act 2006, s 75(1), Sch 8, paras 96, 168(1), (7).
[590]   Amendment: Words substituted: Charities Act 2006, s 75(1), Sch 8, paras 96, 168(1), (2)(a).
[591]   Amendment: Words substituted: Charities Act 2006, s 75(1), Sch 8, paras 96, 168(1), (2)(b).

effect the objects of the order, and where [the Commission exercises][592] any jurisdiction to make such an order on an application or reference [to it, it may][593] insert any such provisions in the order notwithstanding that the application or reference does not propose their insertion.

(2)   Where [the Commission makes][594] an order under this Act, then (without prejudice to the requirements of this Act where the order is subject to appeal) [the Commission may itself][595] give such public notice as [it thinks fit][596] of the making or contents of the order, or may require it to be given by any person on whose application the order is made or by any charity affected by the order.

(3)   [The Commission][597] at any time within twelve months after [it has][598] made an order under any provision of this Act other than section 61 if [it is][599] satisfied that the order was made by mistake or on misrepresentation or otherwise than in conformity with this Act, may with or without any application or reference [to it][600] discharge the order in whole or in part, and subject or not to any savings or other transitional provisions.

(4)   Except for the purposes of subsection (3) above or of an appeal under this Act, an order made by [the Commission][601] under this Act shall be deemed to have been duly and formally made and not be called in question on the ground only of irregularity or informality, but (subject to any further order) have effect according to its tenor.

[(5)   Any order made by the Commission under any provision of this Act may be varied or revoked by a subsequent order so made.][602]

Amendments—Charities Act 2006, s 75(1), Sch 8, paras 96, 168.

90 Directions of [the Commission][603]

(1)   Any direction given by [the Commission][604] under any provision contained in this Act—

    (a)   may be varied or revoked by a further direction given under that provision; and

    (b)   shall be given in writing.

(2)   Sections 88 and 89(1), (2) and (4) above shall apply to any such directions as they apply to an order of [the Commission][605].

(3)   In subsection (1) above the reference to [the Commission][606] includes, in relation to a direction under subsection (3) of section 8 above, a reference to any person conducting an inquiry under that section.

---

[592]   Amendment: Words substituted: Charities Act 2006, s 75(1), Sch 8, paras 96, 168(1), (2)(c).
[593]   Amendment: Words substituted: Charities Act 2006, s 75(1), Sch 8, paras 96, 168(1), (2)(d).
[594]   Amendment: Words substituted: Charities Act 2006, s 75(1), Sch 8, paras 96, 168(1), (3)(a).
[595]   Amendment: Words substituted: Charities Act 2006, s 75(1), Sch 8, paras 96, 168(1), (3)(b).
[596]   Amendment: Words substituted: Charities Act 2006, s 75(1), Sch 8, paras 96, 168(1), (3)(c).
[597]   Amendment: Words substituted: Charities Act 2006, s 75(1), Sch 8, paras 96, 168(1), (4)(a).
[598]   Amendment: Words substituted: Charities Act 2006, s 75(1), Sch 8, paras 96, 168(1), (4)(b).
[599]   Amendment: Words substituted: Charities Act 2006, s 75(1), Sch 8, paras 96, 168(1), (4)(c).
[600]   Amendment: Words substituted: Charities Act 2006, s 75(1), Sch 8, paras 96, 168(1), (4)(d).
[601]   Amendment: Words substituted: Charities Act 2006, s 75(1), Sch 8, paras 96, 168(1), (5).
[602]   Amendment: Subsection added: Charities Act 2006, s 75(1), Sch 8, paras 96, 168(1), (6).
[603]   Amendment: Words substituted: Charities Act 2006, s 75(1), Sch 8, paras 96, 169.
[604]   Amendment: Words substituted: Charities Act 2006, s 75(1), Sch 8, paras 96, 169.
[605]   Amendment: Words substituted: Charities Act 2006, s 75(1), Sch 8, paras 96, 169.
[606]   Amendment: Words substituted: Charities Act 2006, s 75(1), Sch 8, paras 96, 169.

(4)   Nothing in this section shall be read as applying to any directions contained in an order made by [the Commission][607] under section 87(1) above.

Amendments—Charities Act 2006, s 75(1), Sch 8, paras 96, 169.

91 Service of orders and directions

(1)   This section applies to any order or direction made or given by [the Commission][608] under this Act.

(2)   An order or direction to which this section applies may be served on a person (other than a body corporate)—

(a)   by delivering it to that person;
(b)   by leaving it at his last known address in the United Kingdom; or
(c)   by sending it by post to him at that address.

(3)   An order or direction to which this section applies may be served on a body corporate by delivering it or sending it by post—

(a)   to the registered or principal office of the body in the United Kingdom, or
(b)   if it has no such office in the United Kingdom, to any place in the United Kingdom where it carries on business or conducts its activities (as the case may be).

(4)   Any such order or direction may also be served on a person (including a body corporate) by sending it by post to that person at an address notified by that person to [the Commission][609] for the purposes of this subsection.

(5)   In this section any reference to [the Commission][610] includes, in relation to a direction given under subsection (3) of section 8 above, a reference to any person conducting an inquiry under that section.

Amendments—Charities Act 2006, s 75(1), Sch 8, paras 96, 170.

92 ...[611]

Amendments—Charities Act 2006, s 75, Sch 8, paras 96, 171, Sch 9.

93 Miscellaneous provisions as to evidence

(1)   Where, in any proceedings to recover or compel payment of any rentcharge or other periodical payment claimed by or on behalf of a charity out of land or of the rents, profits or other income of land, otherwise than as rent incident to a reversion, it is shown that the rentcharge or other periodical payment has at any time been paid for twelve consecutive years to or for the benefit of the charity, that shall be prima facie evidence of the perpetual liability to it of the land or income, and no proof of its origin shall be necessary.

(2)   In any proceedings, the following documents, that is to say,—

---

[607]   Amendment: Words substituted: Charities Act 2006, s 75(1), Sch 8, paras 96, 169.
[608]   Amendment: Words substituted: Charities Act 2006, s 75(1), Sch 8, paras 96, 170.
[609]   Amendment: Words substituted: Charities Act 2006, s 75(1), Sch 8, paras 96, 170.
[610]   Amendment: Words substituted: Charities Act 2006, s 75(1), Sch 8, paras 96, 170.
[611]   Amendment: Section omitted: Charities Act 2006, s 75, Sch 8, paras 96, 171, Sch 9, for transitional provisions see s 75(3), Sch 10, para 18.

(a) the printed copies of the reports of the Commissioners for enquiring concerning charities, 1818 to 1837, who were appointed under the Act 58 Geo. 3. c. 91 and subsequent Acts; and

(b) the printed copies of the reports which were made for various counties and county boroughs to the Charity Commissioners by their assistant commissioners and presented to the House of Commons as returns to orders of various dates beginning with 8th December 1890, and ending with 9th September 1909,

shall be admissible as evidence of the documents and facts stated in them.

[(3) Evidence of any order, certificate or other document issued by the Commission may be given by means of a copy which it retained, or which is taken from a copy so retained, and evidence of an entry in any register kept by it may be given by means of a copy of the entry, if (in each case) the copy is certified in accordance with subsection (4).

(4) The copy shall be certified to be a true copy by any member of the staff of the Commission generally or specially authorised by the Commission to act for that purpose.

(5) A document purporting to be such a copy shall be received in evidence without proof of the official position, authority or handwriting of the person certifying it.

(6) In subsection (3) above 'the Commission' includes the Charity Commissioners for England and Wales.][612]

Amendment—Charities Act 2006, s 75(1), Sch 8, paras 96, 172.

94 Restriction on institution of proceedings for certain offences

(1) No proceedings for an offence under this Act to which this section applies shall be instituted except by or with the consent of the Director of Public Prosecutions.

(2) This section applies to any offence under—

(a) section 5;
(b) section 11;
(c) section 18(14);
(d) section 49; or
(e) section 73(1).

95 Offences by bodies corporate

Where any offence under this Act is committed by a body corporate and is proved to have been committed with the consent or connivance of, or to be attributable to any neglect on the part of, any director, manager, secretary or other similar officer of the body corporate, or any person who was purporting to act in any such capacity, he as well as the body corporate shall be guilty of that offence and shall be liable to be proceeded against and punished accordingly. In relation to a body corporate whose affairs are managed by its members, 'director' means a member of the body corporate.

---

[612] Amendment: Subsections substituted for subsection (3): Charities Act 2006, s 75(1), Sch 8, paras 96, 172.

96 Construction of references to a 'charity' or to particular classes of charity

(1)   In this Act, except in so far as the context otherwise requires—

['charity' has the meaning given by section 1(1) of the Charities Act 2006;][613]
'ecclesiastical charity' has the same meaning as in the Local Government Act 1894;
'exempt charity' means ...[614] a charity comprised in Schedule 2 to this Act;
'local charity' means, in relation to any area, a charity established for purposes which are by their nature or by the trusts of the charity directed wholly or mainly to the benefit of that area or of part of it;
'parochial charity' means, in relation to any parish or (in Wales) community, a charity the benefits of which are, or the separate distribution of the benefits of which is, confined to inhabitants of the parish or community, or of a single ancient ecclesiastical parish which included that parish or community or part of it, or of an area consisting of that parish or community with not more than four neighbouring parishes or communities.

(2)   The expression 'charity' is not in this Act applicable—

(a)   to any ecclesiastical corporation (that is to say, any corporation in the Church of England, whether sole or aggregate, which is established for spiritual purposes) in respect of the corporate property of the corporation, except to a corporation aggregate having some purposes which are not ecclesiastical in respect of its corporate property held for those purposes; or

(b)   to any Diocesan Board of Finance [(or any subsidiary thereof)][615] within the meaning of the Endowments and Glebe Measure 1976 for any diocese in respect of the diocesan glebe land of that diocese within the meaning of that Measure; or

(c)   to any trust of property for purposes for which the property has been consecrated.

(3)   A charity shall be deemed for the purposes of this Act to have a permanent endowment unless all property held for the purposes of the charity may be expended for those purposes without distinction between capital and income, and in this Act 'permanent endowment' means, in relation to any charity, property held subject to a restriction on its being expended for the purposes of the charity.

(4)   ...[616]

(5)   [The Commission][617] may direct that for all or any of the purposes of this Act an institution established for any special purposes of or in connection with a charity (being charitable purposes) shall be treated as forming part of that charity or as forming a distinct charity.

[(6)   [The Commission][618] may direct that for all or any of the purposes of this Act two or more charities having the same charity trustees shall be treated as a single charity.][619]

Amendments—Charities (Amendment) Act 1995, s 1; Church of England (Miscellaneous Provisions) Measure 2000, s 11; Charities Act 2006, s 75, Sch 8, paras 96, 173, Sch 9.

---

[613]   Amendment: Definition substituted: Charities Act 2006, s 75(1), Sch 8, paras 96, 173(1), (2).
[614]   Amendment: Words omitted: Charities Act 2006, s 75, Sch 8, paras 96, 173(1), (3)(a), Sch 9.
[615]   Amendment: Words inserted: Church of England (Miscellaneous Provisions) Measure 2000, s 11.
[616]   Amendment: Subsection omitted: Charities Act 2006, s 75, Sch 8, paras 96, 173(1), (3)(b), Sch 9.
[617]   Amendment: Words substituted: Charities Act 2006, s 75(1), Sch 8, paras 96, 173(1), (4).
[618]   Amendment: Words substituted: Charities Act 2006, s 75(1), Sch 8, paras 96, 173(1), (4).
[619]   Amendment: Subsection inserted: Charities (Amendment) Act 1995, s 1.

97 General interpretation

(1)　In this Act, except in so far as the context otherwise requires—

'charitable purposes' means purposes which are exclusively [charitable purposes as defined by section 2(1) of the Charities Act 2006;][620]

'charity trustees' means the persons having the general control and management of the administration of a charity;

['CIO' means charitable incorporated organisation;][621]

['the Commission' means the Charity Commission;][622]

'company' means a company formed and registered under the Companies Act 1985 or to which the provisions of that Act apply as they apply to such a company;

'the court' means the High Court and, within the limits of its jurisdiction, any other court in England and Wales having a jurisdiction in respect of charities concurrent (within any limit of area or amount) with that of the High Court, and includes any judge or officer of the court exercising the jurisdiction of the court;

'financial year'—

(a)　in relation to a charity which is a company, shall be construed in accordance with section 223 of the Companies Act 1985; and

(b)　in relation to any other charity, shall be construed in accordance with regulations made by virtue of section 42(2) above;

but this definition is subject to the transitional provisions in section 99(4) below and Part II of Schedule 8 to this Act;

'gross income', in relation to charity, means its gross recorded income from all sources including special trusts;

'independent examiner', in relation to a charity, means such a person as is mentioned in section 43(3)(a) above;

'institution' [means an institution whether incorporated or not, and][623] includes any trust or undertaking;

['members', in relation to a charity with a body of members distinct from the charity trustees, means any of those members;][624]

['the Minister' means the Minister for the Cabinet Office;][625]

'the official custodian' means the official custodian for charities;

'permanent endowment' shall be construed in accordance with section 96(3) above;

['principal regulator', in relation to an exempt charity, means the charity's principal regulator within the meaning of section 13 of the Charities Act 2006;][626]

'the register' means the register of charities kept under section 3 above and 'registered' shall be construed accordingly;

'special trust' means property which is held and administered by or on behalf of a charity for any special purposes of the charity, and is so held and administered on separate trusts relating only to that property but a special trust shall not, by itself, constitute a charity for the purposes of Part VI of this Act;

['the Tribunal' means the Charity Tribunal;][627]

---

[620]　Amendment: Words substituted: Charities Act 2006, s 75(1), Sch 8, paras 96, 174(a).
[621]　Amendment: Definition inserted: Charities Act 2006, s 34, Sch 7, Pt 2, paras 3, 7.
[622]　Amendment: Definition substituted: Charities Act 2006, s 75(1), Sch 8, paras 96, 174(b).
[623]　Amendment: Words inserted: Charities Act 2006, s 75(1), Sch 8, paras 96, 174(c).
[624]　Amendment: Definition inserted: Charities Act 2006, s 75(1), Sch 8, paras 96, 174(d).
[625]　Amendment: Definition inserted: Charities Act 2006, s 75(1), Sch 8, paras 96, 174(d).
[626]　Amendment: Definition inserted: Charities Act 2006, s 75(1), Sch 8, paras 96, 174(d).
[627]　Amendment: Definition inserted: Charities Act 2006, s 75(1), Sch 8, paras 96, 174(d).

'trusts' in relation to a charity, means the provisions establishing it as a charity and regulating its purposes and administration, whether those provisions take effect by way of trust or not, and in relation to other institutions has a corresponding meaning.

(2) In this Act, except in so far as the context otherwise requires, 'document' includes information recorded in any form, and, in relation to information recorded otherwise than in legible form—

(a) any reference to its production shall be construed as a reference to the furnishing of a copy of it in legible form; and

(b) any reference to the furnishing of a copy of, or extract from, it shall accordingly be construed as a reference to the furnishing of a copy of, or extract from, it in legible form.

(3) No vesting or transfer of any property in pursuance of any provision of [Part 4, 7, 8A or 9][628] of this Act shall operate as a breach of a covenant or condition against alienation or give rise to a forfeiture.

Amendments—Charities Act 2006, ss 34, 75(1), Sch 7, Pt 2, paras 3, 7, Sch 8, paras 96, 174, 175.

98 Consequential amendments and repeals

(1) The enactments mentioned in Schedule 6 to this Act shall be amended as provided in that Schedule.

(2) The enactments mentioned in Schedule 7 to this Act are hereby repealed to the extent specified in the third column of the Schedule.

99 ...[629]

Amendment—Statute Law (Repeals) Act 2004.

100 Short title and extent

(1) This Act may be cited as the Charities Act 1993.

(2) Subject to subsection (3) to (6) below, this Act extends only to England and Wales.

(3) [Sections 10 to 10C][630] above and this section extend to the whole of the United Kingdom.

(4) Section 15(2) [and sections 24 to 25A extend][631] also to Northern Ireland.

(5) ...[632]

(6) The amendments in Schedule 6 and the repeals in Schedule 7 have the same extent as the enactments to which they refer and section 98 above extends accordingly.

Amendments—Charities and Trustee Investment (Scotland) Act 2005, s 95, Sch 3, para 9; Charities Act 2006, ss 23(5), 75(1), Sch 8, paras 96, 176.

---

[628] Amendment: Words substituted: Charities Act 2006, s 75(1), Sch 8, paras 96, 175.
[629] Amendment: Section repealed: Statute Law (Repeals) Act 2004.
[630] Amendment: Words substituted: Charities Act 2006, s 75(1), Sch 8, paras 96, 176.
[631] Amendment: Words substituted: Charities Act 2006, s 23(5).
[632] Amendment: Subsection repealed: Charities and Trustee Investment (Scotland) Act 2005, s 95, Sch 3, para 9.

Schedules

Schedule 1

...⁶³³

Amendment—Charities Act 2006, ss 6(6), 75(2), Sch 9.

[Schedule 1A
The Charity Commission

SECTION 1A

Membership

1

(1) The Commission shall consist of a chairman and at least four, but not more than eight, other members.

(2) The members shall be appointed by the Minister.

(3) The Minister shall exercise the power in sub-paragraph (2) so as to secure that—

(a) the knowledge and experience of the members of the Commission (taken together) includes knowledge and experience of the matters mentioned in sub-paragraph (4),
(b) at least two members have a seven year general qualification within the meaning of section 71 of the Courts and Legal Services Act 1990, and
(c) at least one member knows about conditions in Wales and has been appointed following consultation with the National Assembly for Wales.

(4) The matters mentioned in this sub-paragraph are—

(a) the law relating to charities,
(b) charity accounts and the financing of charities, and
(c) the operation and regulation of charities of different sizes and descriptions.

(5) In sub-paragraph (3)(c) 'member' does not include the chairman of the Commission.

Terms of appointment and remuneration

2

The members of the Commission shall hold and vacate office as such in accordance with the terms of their respective appointments.

3

(1) An appointment of a person to hold office as a member of the Commission shall be for a term not exceeding three years.

(2) A person holding office as a member of the Commission—

(a) may resign that office by giving notice in writing to the Minister, and

---

⁶³³ Amendment: Schedule repealed: Charities Act 2006, ss 6(6), 75(2), Sch 9.

(b)   may be removed from office by the Minister on the ground of incapacity or misbehaviour.

(3) Before removing a member of the Commission the Minister shall consult—

(a)   the Commission, and
(b)   if the member was appointed following consultation with the National Assembly for Wales, the Assembly.

(4) No person may hold office as a member of the Commission for more than ten years in total.

(5) For the purposes of sub-paragraph (4), time spent holding office as a Charity Commissioner for England and Wales shall be counted as time spent holding office as a member of the Commission.

4

(1) The Commission shall pay to its members such remuneration, and such other allowances, as may be determined by the Minister.

(2) The Commission shall, if required to do so by the Minister—

(a)   pay such pension, allowances or gratuities as may be determined by the Minister to or in respect of a person who is or has been a member of the Commission, or
(b)   make such payments as may be so determined towards provision for the payment of a pension, allowances or gratuities to or in respect of such a person.

(3) If the Minister determines that there are special circumstances which make it right for a person ceasing to hold office as a member of the Commission to receive compensation, the Commission shall pay to him a sum by way of compensation of such amount as may be determined by the Minister.

Staff

5

(1) The Commission—

(a)   shall appoint a chief executive, and
(b)   may appoint such other staff as it may determine.

(2) The terms and conditions of service of persons appointed under sub-paragraph (1) are to be such as the Commission may determine with the approval of the Minister for the Civil Service.

Committees

6

(1) The Commission may establish committees and any committee of the Commission may establish sub-committees.

(2) The members of a committee of the Commission may include persons who are not members of the Commission (and the members of a sub-committee may include persons who are not members of the committee or of the Commission).

Procedure etc

7

(1) The Commission may regulate its own procedure (including quorum).

(2) The validity of anything done by the Commission is not affected by a vacancy among its members or by a defect in the appointment of a member.

Performance of functions

8

Anything authorised or required to be done by the Commission may be done by—

    (a)   any member or member of staff of the Commission who is authorised for that purpose by the Commission, whether generally or specially;

    (b)   any committee of the Commission which has been so authorised.

Evidence

9

The Documentary Evidence Act 1868 shall have effect as if—

    (a)   the Commission were mentioned in the first column of the Schedule to that Act,

    (b)   any member or member of staff of the Commission authorised to act on behalf of the Commission were specified in the second column of that Schedule in connection with the Commission, and

    (c)   the regulations referred to in that Act included any document issued by or under the authority of the Commission.

Execution of documents

10

(1) A document is executed by the Commission by the fixing of its common seal to the document.

(2) But the fixing of that seal to a document must be authenticated by the signature of—

    (a)   any member of the Commission, or

    (b)   any member of its staff,

who is authorised for the purpose by the Commission.

(3) A document which is expressed (in whatever form of words) to be executed by the Commission and is signed by—

    (a)   any member of the Commission, or

    (b)   any member of its staff,

who is authorised for the purpose by the Commission has the same effect as if executed in accordance with sub-paragraphs (1) and (2).

(4) A document executed by the Commission which makes it clear on its face that it is intended to be a deed has effect, upon delivery, as a deed; and it is to be presumed (unless a contrary intention is proved) to be delivered upon its being executed.

(5) In favour of a purchaser a document is to be deemed to have been duly executed by the Commission if it purports to be signed on its behalf by—

(a)   any member of the Commission, or

(b)   any member of its staff;

and, where it makes it clear on its face that it is intended to be a deed, it is to be deemed to have been delivered upon its being executed.

(6) For the purposes of this paragraph—

'authorised' means authorised whether generally or specially; and

'purchaser' means a purchaser in good faith for valuable consideration and includes a lessee, mortgagee or other person who for valuable consideration acquired an interest in property.

Annual report

11

(1) As soon as practicable after the end of each financial year the Commission shall publish a report on—

(a)   the discharge of its functions,

(b)   the extent to which, in its opinion, its objectives (see section 1B of this Act) have been met,

(c)   the performance of its general duties (see section 1D of this Act), and

(d)   the management of its affairs,

during that year.

(2) The Commission shall lay a copy of each such report before Parliament.

(3) In sub-paragraph (1) above, 'financial year' means—

(a)   the period beginning with the date on which the Commission is established and ending with the next 31 March following that date, and

(b)   each successive period of 12 months ending with 31 March.

Annual public meeting

12

(1) The Commission shall hold a public meeting ('the annual meeting') for the purpose of enabling a report under paragraph 11 above to be considered.

(2) The annual meeting shall be held within the period of three months beginning with the day on which the report is published.

(3) The Commission shall organise the annual meeting so as to allow—

(a)   a general discussion of the contents of the report which is being considered, and

(b)   a reasonable opportunity for those attending the meeting to put questions to the Commission about matters to which the report relates.

(4) But subject to sub-paragraph (3) above the annual meeting is to be organised and conducted in such a way as the Commission considers appropriate.

(5) The Commission shall—

(a)   take such steps as are reasonable in the circumstances to ensure that notice of the annual meeting is given to every registered charity, and

(b)   publish notice of the annual meeting in the way appearing to it to be best calculated to bring it to the attention of members of the public.

(6) Each such notice shall—

(a)   give details of the time and place at which the meeting is to be held,

(b)   set out the proposed agenda for the meeting,

(c)   indicate the proposed duration of the meeting, and

(d)   give details of the Commission's arrangements for enabling persons to attend.

(7) If the Commission proposes to alter any of the arrangements which have been included in notices given or published under sub-paragraph (5) above it shall—

(a)   give reasonable notice of the alteration, and

(b)   publish the notice in the way appearing to it to be best calculated to bring it to the attention of registered charities and members of the public.][634]

Amendment—Charities Act 2006, s 6(2), Sch 1, para 1.

[Schedule 1B
The Charity Tribunal

SECTION 2A(3)

Membership

(1) The Tribunal shall consist of the President and its other members.

(2) The Lord Chancellor shall appoint—

(a)   a President of the Tribunal,

(b)   legal members of the Tribunal, and

(c)   ordinary members of the Tribunal.

(3) A person may be appointed as the President or a legal member of the Tribunal only if he has a seven year general qualification within the meaning of section 71 of the Courts and Legal Services Act 1990.

(4) A person may be appointed as an ordinary member of the Tribunal only if he appears to the Lord Chancellor to have appropriate knowledge or experience relating to charities.

Deputy President

2

(1) The Lord Chancellor may appoint a legal member as deputy President of the Tribunal.

---

[634]   Amendment: Schedule inserted: Charities Act 2006, s 6(2), Sch 1, para 1. For supplementary provisions relating to the establishment of the Charity Commission see Charities Act 2006, s 6, Sch 2.

(2) The deputy President—

    (a)   may act for the President when he is unable to act or unavailable, and

    (b)   shall perform such other functions as the President may delegate or assign to him.

Terms of appointment

3

(1) The members of the Tribunal shall hold and vacate office as such in accordance with the terms of their respective appointments.

(2) A person holding office as a member of the Tribunal—

    (a)   may resign that office by giving notice in writing to the Lord Chancellor, and

    (b)   may be removed from office by the Lord Chancellor on the ground of incapacity or misbehaviour.

(3) A previous appointment of a person as a member of the Tribunal does not affect his eligibility for re-appointment as a member of the Tribunal.

Retirement etc

4

(1) A person shall not hold office as a member of the Tribunal after reaching the age of 70.

(2) Section 26(5) and (6) of the Judicial Pensions and Retirement Act 1993 (extension to age 75) apply in relation to a member of the Tribunal as they apply in relation to a holder of a relevant office.

Remuneration etc

5

(1) The Lord Chancellor may pay to the members of the Tribunal such remuneration, and such other allowances, as he may determine.

(2) The Lord Chancellor may—

    (a)   pay such pension, allowances or gratuities as he may determine to or in respect of a person who is or has been a member of the Tribunal, or

    (b)   make such payments as he may determine towards provision for the payment of a pension, allowances or gratuities to or in respect of such a person.

(3) If the Lord Chancellor determines that there are special circumstances which make it right for a person ceasing to hold office as a member of the Tribunal to receive compensation, the Lord Chancellor may pay to him a sum by way of compensation of such amount as may be determined by the Lord Chancellor.

Staff and facilities

6

The Lord Chancellor may make staff and facilities available to the Tribunal.

Panels

7

(1) The functions of the Tribunal shall be exercised by panels of the Tribunal.

(2) Panels of the Tribunal shall sit at such times and in such places as the President may direct.

(3) Before giving a direction under sub-paragraph (2) above the President shall consult the Lord Chancellor.

(4) More than one panel may sit at a time.

8

(1) The President shall make arrangements for determining which of the members of the Tribunal are to constitute a panel of the Tribunal in relation to the exercise of any function.

(2) Those arrangements shall, in particular, ensure that each panel is constituted in one of the following ways—

    (a)   as the President sitting alone,
    (b)   as a legal member sitting alone,
    (c)   as the President sitting with two other members,
    (d)   as a legal member sitting with two other members,
    (e)   as the President sitting with one other member,
    (f)   as a legal member sitting with one other member,

(and references in paragraphs (d) and (f) to other members do not include the President).

(3) The President shall publish arrangements made under this paragraph.

Practice and procedure

9

(1) Decisions of the Tribunal may be taken by majority vote.

(2) In the case of a panel constituted in accordance with paragraph 8(2)(e), the President shall have a casting vote.

(3) In the case of a panel constituted in accordance with paragraph 8(2)(f) which consists of a legal member and an ordinary member, the legal member shall have a casting vote.

(4) The President shall make and publish arrangements as to who is to have a casting vote in the case of a panel constituted in accordance with paragraph 8(2)(f) which consists of two legal members.

10

The President may, subject to rules under section 2B of this Act, give directions about the practice and procedure of the Tribunal.][635]

---

[635] Amendment: Schedule inserted: Charities Act 2006, s 8(2), Sch 3, para 1.

Amendment—Charities Act 2006, s 8(2), Sch 3, para 1.

[Schedule 1C
Appeals and Applications to Charity Tribunal

SECTION 2A(4)

Appeals: general

1

(1) Except in the case of a reviewable matter (see paragraph 3) an appeal may be brought to the Tribunal against any decision, direction or order mentioned in column 1 of the Table.

(2) Such an appeal may be brought by—

    (a)   the Attorney General, or

    (b)   any person specified in the corresponding entry in column 2 of the Table.

(3) The Commission shall be the respondent to such an appeal.

(4) In determining such an appeal the Tribunal—

    (a)   shall consider afresh the decision, direction or order appealed against, and

    (b)   may take into account evidence which was not available to the Commission.

(5) The Tribunal may—

    (a)   dismiss the appeal, or

    (b)   if it allows the appeal, exercise any power specified in the corresponding entry in column 3 of the Table.

Appeals: orders under section 9

2

(1) Paragraph 1(4)(a) above does not apply in relation to an appeal against an order made under section 9 of this Act.

(2) On such an appeal the Tribunal shall consider whether the information or document in question—

    (a)   relates to a charity;

    (b)   is relevant to the discharge of the functions of the Commission or the official custodian.

(3) The Tribunal may allow such an appeal only if it is satisfied that the information or document in question does not fall within either paragraph (a) or paragraph (b) of sub-paragraph (2) above.

Reviewable matters

3

(1) In this Schedule references to 'reviewable matters' are to—

    (a)   decisions to which sub-paragraph (2) applies, and

    (b)   orders to which sub-paragraph (3) applies.

(2) This sub-paragraph applies to decisions of the Commission—

(a)   to institute an inquiry under section 8 of this Act with regard to a particular institution,

(b)   to institute an inquiry under section 8 of this Act with regard to a class of institutions,

(c)   not to make a common investment scheme under section 24 of this Act,

(d)   not to make a common deposit scheme under section 25 of this Act,

(e)   not to make an order under section 26 of this Act in relation to a charity,

(f)   not to make an order under section 36 of this Act in relation to land held by or in trust for a charity,

(g)   not to make an order under section 38 of this Act in relation to a mortgage of land held by or in trust for a charity.

(3) This sub-paragraph applies to an order made by the Commission under section 69(1) of this Act in relation to a company which is a charity.

Reviews

4

(1) An application may be made to the Tribunal for the review of a reviewable matter.

(2) Such an application may be made by—

(a)   the Attorney General, or

(b)   any person mentioned in the entry in column 2 of the Table which corresponds to the entry in column 1 which relates to the reviewable matter.

(3) The Commission shall be the respondent to such an application.

(4) In determining such an application the Tribunal shall apply the principles which would be applied by the High Court on an application for judicial review.

(5) The Tribunal may—

(a)   dismiss the application, or

(b)   if it allows the application, exercise any power mentioned in the entry in column 3 of the Table which corresponds to the entry in column 1 which relates to the reviewable matter.

Interpretation: remission of matters to Commission

5

References in column 3 of the Table to the power to remit a matter to the Commission are to the power to remit the matter either—

(a)   generally, or

(b)   for determination in accordance with a finding made or direction given by the Tribunal.

TABLE		
1	2	3
Decision of the Commission under section 3 or 3A of this Act— (a) to enter or not to enter an institution in the register of charities, or (b) to remove or not to remove an institution from the register.	The persons are— (a) the persons who are or claim to be the charity trustees of the institution, (b) (if a body corporate) the institution itself, and (c) any other person who is or may be affected by the decision.	Power to quash the decision and (if appropriate)— (a) remit the matter to the Commission, (b) direct the Commission to rectify the register.
Decision of the Commission not to make a determination under section 3(9) of this Act in relation to particular information contained in the register.	The persons are— (a) the charity trustees of the charity to which the information relates, (b) (if a body corporate) the charity itself, and (c) any other person who is or may be affected by the decision.	Power to quash the decision and (if appropriate) remit the matter to the Commission.
Direction given by the Commission under section 6 of this Act requiring the name of a charity to be changed.	The persons are— (a) the charity trustees of the charity to which the direction relates, (b) (if a body corporate) the charity itself, and (c) any other person who is or may be affected by the direction.	Power to— (a) quash the direction and (if appropriate) remit the matter to the Commission, (b) substitute for the direction any other direction which could have been given by the Commission.
Decision of the Commission to institute an inquiry under section 8 of this Act with regard to a particular institution.	The persons are— (a) the persons who have control or management of the institution, and (b) (if a body corporate) the institution itself.	Power to direct the Commission to end the inquiry.
Decision of the Commission to institute an inquiry under section 8 of this Act with regard to a class of institutions.	The persons are— (a) the persons who have control or management of any institution which is a member of the class of institutions, and (b) (if a body corporate) any such institution.	Power to— (a) direct the Commission that the inquiry should not consider a particular institution, (b) direct the Commission to end the inquiry.

TABLE		
1	2	3
Order made by the Commission under section 9 of this Act requiring a person to supply information or a document	The persons are any person who is required to supply the information or document.	Power to— (a) quash the order, (b) substitute for all or part of the order any other order which could have been made by the Commission.
Order made by the Commission under section 16(1) of this Act (including such an order made by virtue of section 23(1)).	The persons are— (a) in a section 16(1)(a) case, the charity trustees of the charity to which the order relates or (if a body corporate) the charity itself, (b) in a section 16(1)(b) case, any person discharged or removed by the order, and (c) any other person who is or may be affected by the order.	Power to— (a) quash the order in whole or in part and (if appropriate) remit the matter to the Commission, (b) substitute for all or part of the order any other order which could have been made by the Commission, (c) add to the order anything which could have been contained in an order made by the Commission.
Order made by the Commission under section 18(1) of this Act in relation to a charity.	The persons are— (a) the charity trustees of the charity, (b) (if a body corporate) the charity itself, (c) in a section 18(1)(i) case, any person suspended by the order, and (d) any other person who is or may be affected by the order.	Power to— (a) quash the order in whole or in part and (if appropriate) remit the matter to the Commission, (b) substitute for all or part of the order any other order which could have been made by the Commission, (c) add to the order anything which could have been contained in an order made by the Commission.

TABLE		
1	2	3
Order made by the Commission under section 18(2) of this Act in relation to a charity.	The persons are— (a) the charity trustees of the charity, (b) (if a body corporate) the charity itself, (c) in a section 18(2)(i) case, any person removed by the order, and (d) any other person who is or may be affected by the order.	Power to— (a) quash the order in whole or in part and (if appropriate) remit the matter to the Commission, (b) substitute for all or part of the order any other order which could have been made by the Commission, (c) add to the order anything which could have been contained in an order made by the Commission.
Order made by the Commission under section 18(4) of this Act removing a charity trustee.	The persons are— (a) the charity trustee, (b) the remaining charity trustees of the charity of which he was a charity trustee, (c) (if a body corporate) the charity itself, and (d) any other person who is or may be affected by the order.	Power to— (a) quash the order in whole or in part and (if appropriate) remit the matter to the Commission, (b) substitute for all or part of the order any other order which could have been made by the Commission, (c) add to the order anything which could have been contained in an order made by the Commission.

TABLE		
1	2	3
Order made by the Commission under section 18(5) of this Act appointing a charity trustee	The persons are— (a) the other charity trustees of the charity, (b) (if a body corporate) the charity itself, and (c) any other person who is or may be affected by the order.	Power to— (a) quash the order in whole or in part and (if appropriate) remit the matter to the Commission, (b) substitute for all or part of the order any other order which could have been made by the Commission, (c) add to the order anything which could have been contained in an order made by the Commission.
Decision of the Commission— (a) to discharge an order following a review under section 18(13) of this Act, or (b) not to discharge an order following such a review.	The persons are— (a) the charity trustees of the charity to which the order relates, (b) (if a body corporate) the charity itself, (c) if the order in question was made under section 18(1)(i), any person suspended by it, and (d) any other person who is or may be affected by the order.	Power to— (a) quash the decision and (if appropriate) remit the matter to the Commission, (b) make the discharge of the order subject to savings or other transitional provisions, (c) remove any savings or other transitional provisions to which the discharge of the order was subject, (d) discharge the order in whole or in part (whether subject to any savings or other transitional provisions or not).
Order made by the Commission under section 18A(2) of this Act which suspends a person's membership of a charity.	The persons are— (a) the person whose membership is suspended by the order, and (b) any other person who is or may be affected by the order.	Power to quash the order and (if appropriate) remit the matter to the Commission.

TABLE		
1	2	3
Order made by the Commission under section 19A(2) of this Act which directs a person to take action specified in the order.	The persons are any person who is directed by the order to take the specified action.	Power to quash the order and (if appropriate) remit the matter to the Commission.
Order made by the Commission under section 19B(2) of this Act which directs a person to apply property in a specified manner.	The persons are any person who is directed by the order to apply the property in the specified manner.	Power to quash the order and (if appropriate) remit the matter to the Commission.
Order made by the Commission under section 23(2) of this Act in relation to any land vested in the official custodian in trust for a charity.	The persons are— (a) the charity trustees of the charity, (b) (if a body corporate) the charity itself, and (c) any other person who is or may be affected by the order.	Power to— (a) quash the order and (if appropriate) remit the matter to the Commission, (b) substitute for the order any other order which could have been made by the Commission, (c) add to the order anything which could have been contained in an order made by the Commission.
Decision of the Commission not to make a common investment scheme under section 24 of this Act.	The persons are— (a) the charity trustees of a charity which applied to the Commission for the scheme, (b) (if a body corporate) the charity itself, and (c) any other person who is or may be affected by the decision.	Power to quash the decision and (if appropriate) remit the matter to the Commission.

TABLE		
1	2	3
Decision of the Commission not to make a common deposit scheme under section 25 of this Act.	The persons are— (a) the charity trustees of a charity which applied to the Commission for the scheme, (b) (if a body corporate) the charity itself, and (c) any other person who is or may be affected by the decision.	Power to quash the decision and (if appropriate) remit the matter to the Commission.
Decision by the Commission not to make an order under section 26 of this Act in relation to a charity.	The persons are— (a) the charity trustees of the charity, and (b) (if a body corporate) the charity itself.	Power to quash the decision and (if appropriate) remit the matter to the Commission.
Direction given by the Commission under section 28 of this Act in relation to an account held in the name of or on behalf of a charity.	The persons are— (a) the charity trustees of the charity, (b) (if a body corporate) the charity itself, and (c) any other person who is or may be affected by the order.	Power to— (a) quash the direction and (if appropriate) remit the matter to the Commission, (b) substitute for the direction any other direction which could have been given by the Commission, (c) add to the direction anything which could have been contained in a direction given by the Commission.
Order made by the Commission under section 31 of this Act for the taxation of a solicitor's bill.	The persons are— (a) the solicitor, (b) any person for whom the work was done by the solicitor, and (c) any other person who is or may be affected by the order.	Power to— (a) quash the order, (b) substitute for the order any other order which could have been made by the Commission, (c) add to the order anything which could have been contained in an order made by the Commission.

TABLE		
1	2	3
Decision of the Commission not to make an order under section 36 of this Act in relation to land held by or in trust for a charity.	The persons are— (a) the charity trustees of the charity, (b) (if a body corporate) the charity itself, and (c) any other person who is or may be affected by the decision.	Power to quash the decision and (if appropriate) remit the matter to the Commission.
Decision of the commission not to make an order under section 38 of this Act in relation to a mortgage of land held by or in trust for a charity.	The persons are— (a) the charity trustees of the charity, (b) (if a body corporate) the charity itself, and (c) any other person who is or may be affected by the decision.	Power to quash the decision and (if appropriate) remit the matter to the Commission.
Order made by the Commission under section 43(4) of this Act requiring the accounts of a charity to be audited.	The persons are— (a) the charity trustees of the charity, (b) (if a body corporate) the charity itself, and (c) any other person who is or may be affected by the order.	Power to— (a) quash the order, (b) substitute for the order any other order which could have been made by the Commission, (c) add to the order anything which could have been contained in an order made by the Commission.
Order made by the Commission under section 44(2) of this Act in relation to a charity, or a decision of the Commission not to make such an order in relation to a charity.	The persons are— (a) the charity trustees of the charity, (b) (if a body corporate) the charity itself, (c) in the case of a decision not to make an order, the auditor, independent examiner or examiner, and (d) any other person who is or may be affected by the order or the decision.	Power to— (a) quash the order or decision and (if appropriate) remit the matter to the Commission, (b) substitute for the order any other order of a kind the Commission could have made, (c) make any order which the Commission could have made.

TABLE		
1	2	3
Decision of the Commission under section 46(5) of this Act to request charity trustees to prepare an annual report for a charity.	The persons are— (a) the charity trustees, and (b) (if a body corporate) the charity itself.	Power to quash the decision and (if appropriate) remit the matter to the Commission.
Decision of the Commission not to dispense with the requirements of section 48(1) in relation to a charity or class of charities.	The persons are the charity trustees of any charity affected by the decision.	Power to quash the decision and (if appropriate) remit the matter to the Commission.
Decision of the Commission— (a) to grant a certificate of incorporation under section 50(1) of this Act to the trustees of a charity, or (b) not to grant such a certificate.	The persons are— (a) the trustees of the charity, and (b) any other person who is or may be affected by the decision.	Power to quash— (a) the decision, (b) any conditions or directions inserted in the certificate, and (if appropriate) remit the matter to the Commission.
Decision of the Commission to amend a certificate of incorporation of a charity under section 56(4) of this Act.	The persons are— (a) the trustees of the charity, and (b) any other person who is or may be affected by the amended certificate of incorporation.	Power to quash the decision and (if appropriate) remit the matter to the Commission.
Decision of the Commission not to amend a certificate of incorporation under section 56(4) of this Act.	The persons are— (a) the trustees of the charity, and (b) any other person who is or may be affected by the decision not to amend the certificate of incorporation.	Power to— (a) quash the decision and (if appropriate) remit the matter to the Commission, (b) make any order the Commission could have made under section 56(4).

TABLE		
1	2	3
Order of the Commission under section 61(1) or (2) of this Act which dissolves a charity which is an incorporated body.	The persons are— (a) the trustees of the charity, (b) the charity itself, and (c) any other person who is or may be affected by the order.	Power to— (a) quash the order and (if appropriate) remit the matter to the Commission, (b) substitute for the order any other order which could have been made by the Commission, (c) add to the order anything which could have been contained in an order made by the Commission.
Decision of the Commission to give, or withhold, consent under section 64(2), 65(4) or 66(1) of this Act in relation to a body corporate which is a charity.	The persons are— (a) the charity trustees of the charity, (b) the body corporate itself, and (c) any other person who is or may be affected by the decision.	Power to quash the decision and (if appropriate) remit the matter to the Commission.
Order made by the Commission under section 69(1) of this Act in relation to a company which is a charity.	The persons are— (a) the directors of the company, (b) the company itself, and (c) any other person who is or may be affected by the order.	Power to— (a) quash the order and (if appropriate) remit the matter to the Commission, (b) substitute for the order any other order which could have been made by the Commission, (c) add to the order anything which could have been contained in an order made by the Commission.

TABLE		
1	2	3
Order made by the Commission under section 69(4) of this Act which gives directions to a person or to charity trustees.	The persons are— (a) in the case of directions given to a person, that person, (b) in the case of directions given to charity trustees, those charity trustees and (if a body corporate) the charity of which they are charity trustees, and (c) any other person who is or may be affected by the directions.	Power to— (a) quash the order, (b) substitute for the order any other order which could have been made by the Commission, (c) add to the order anything which could have been contained in an order made by the Commission.
Decision of the Commission under section 69E of this Act to grant an application for the constitution of a CIO and its registration as a charity.	The persons are any person (other than the persons who made the application) who is or may be affected by the decision.	Power to quash the decision and (if appropriate)— (a) remit the matter to the Commission, (b) direct the Commission to rectify the register of charities.
Decision of the Commission under section 69E of this Act not to grant an application for the constitution of a CIO and its registration as a charity.	The persons are— (a) the persons who made the application, and (b) any other person who is or may be affected by the decision.	Power to— (a) quash the decision and (if appropriate) remit the matter to the Commission, (b) direct the Commission to grant the application.
Decision of the Commission under section 69H of this Act not to grant an application for the conversion of a charitable company or a registered society into a CIO and the CIO's registration as a charity.	The persons are— (a) the charity which made the application, (b) the charity trustees of the charity, and (c) any other person who is or may be affected by the decision.	Power to— (a) quash the decision and (if appropriate) remit the matter to the Commission, (b) direct the Commission to grant the application.

TABLE		
1	2	3
Decision of the Commission under section 69K of this Act to grant an application for the amalgamation of two or more CIOs and the incorporation and registration as a charity of a new CIO as their successor.	The persons are any creditor of any of the CIOs being amalgamated.	Power to quash the decision and (if appropriate) remit the matter to the Commission.
Decision of the Commission under section 69K of this Act not to grant an application for the amalgamation of two or more CIOs and the incorporation and registration as a charity of a new CIO as their successor.	The persons are— (a) the CIOs which applied for the amalgamation, (b) the charity trustees of the CIOs, and (c) any other person who is or may be affected by the decision.	Power to— (a) quash the decision and (if appropriate) remit the matter to the Commission, (b) direct the Commission to grant the application.
Decision of the Commission to confirm a resolution passed by a CIO under section 69M(1) of this Act.	The persons are any creditor of the CIO.	Power to quash the decision and (if appropriate) remit the matter to the Commission.
Decision of the Commission not to confirm a resolution passed by a CIO under section 69M(1) of this Act.	The persons are— (a) the CIO, (b) the charity trustees of the CIO, and (c) any other person who is or may be affected by the decision.	Power to— (a) quash the decision and (if appropriate) remit the matter to the Commission, (b) direct the Commission to confirm the resolution.
Decision of the Commission under section 72(4) of this Act to waive, or not to waive, a person's disqualification.	The persons are— (a) the person who applied for the waiver, and (b) any other person who is or may be affected by the decision.	Power to— (a) quash the decision and (if appropriate) remit the matter to the Commission, (b) substitute for the decision any other decision of a kind which could have been made by the Commission.

TABLE		
1	2	3
Order made by the Commission under section 73(4) of this Act in relation to a person who has acted as charity trustee or trustee for a charity.	The persons are— (a) the person subject to the order, and (b) any other person who is or may be affected by the order.	Power to— (a) quash the order and (if appropriate) remit the matter to the Commission, (b) substitute for the order any other order which could have been made by the Commission.
Order made by the Commission under section 73C(5) or (6) of this Act requiring a trustee or connected person to repay, or not to receive, remuneration.	The persons are— (a) the trustee or connected person, (b) the other charity trustees of the charity concerned, and (c) any other person who is or may be affected by the order.	Power to— (a) quash the order and (if appropriate) remit the matter to the Commission, (b) substitute for the order any other order which could have been made by the Commission.
Decision of the Commission to notify charity trustees under section 74A(2) of this Act that it objects to a resolution of the charity trustees under section 74(2) or 74C(2).	The persons are— (a) the charity trustees, and (b) any other person who is or may be affected by the decision.	Power to quash the decision.
Decision of the Commission not to concur under section 75A of this Act with a resolution of charity trustees under section 75A(3) or 75B(2).	The persons are— (a) the charity trustees, (b) (if a body corporate) the charity itself, and (c) any other person who is or may be affected by the decision.	Power to quash the decision and (if appropriate) remit the matter to the Commission.
Decision of the Commission to withhold approval for the transfer of property from trustees to a parish council under section 79(1) of this Act.	The persons are— (a) the trustees, (b) the parish council, and (c) any other person who is or may be affected by the decision.	Power to quash the decision and (if appropriate) remit the matter to the Commission

TABLE		
1	2	3
Order made by the Commission under section 80(2) of this Act in relation to a person holding property on behalf of a recognised body or of any person concerned in its management or control.	The persons are— (a) the person holding the property in question, and (b) any other person who is or may be affected by the order.	Power to quash the order and (if appropriate) remit the matter to the Commission.
Decision of the Commission not to give a direction under section 96(5) or (6) of this Act in relation to an institution or a charity.	The persons are the trustees of the institution or charity concerned.	Power to quash the decision and (if appropriate) remit the matter to the Commission.
Decision of the Commission under paragraph 15 of Schedule 5B to this Act to refuse to register an amendment to the constitution of a CIO.	The persons are— (a) the CIO, (b) the charity trustees of the CIO, and (c) any other person who is or may be affected by the decision.	Power to quash the decision and (if appropriate)— (a) remit the matter to the Commission, (b) direct the Commission to register the amendment.

Power to amend Table etc

6

(1) The Minister may by order—

    (a)   amend or otherwise modify an entry in the Table,

    (b)   add an entry to the Table, or

    (c)   remove an entry from the Table.

(2) An order under sub-paragraph (1) may make such amendments, repeals or other modifications of paragraphs 1 to 5 of this Schedule, or of an enactment which applies this Schedule, as the Minister considers appropriate in consequence of any change in the Table made by the order.

(3) No order shall be made under this paragraph unless a draft of the order has been laid before and approved by a resolution of each House of Parliament.

7

Paragraph 6 above applies (with the necessary modifications) in relation to section 57 of the Charities Act 2006 as if—

    (a)   the provisions of that section were contained in this Schedule, and

(b)   the reference in that paragraph to paragraphs 1 to 5 of this Schedule included a reference to any other provision relating to appeals to the Tribunal which is contained in Chapter 1 of Part 3 of the Charities Act 2006.][636]

Amendment—Charities Act 2006, s 8(3), Sch 4.

[Schedule 1D
References to Charity Tribunal

SECTION 2A(4)

References by Commission

1

(1) A question which—

(a)   has arisen in connection with the exercise by the Commission of any of its functions, and

(b)   involves either the operation of charity law in any respect or its application to a particular state of affairs,

may be referred to the Tribunal by the Commission if the Commission considers it desirable to refer the question to the Tribunal.

(2) The Commission may make such a reference only with the consent of the Attorney General.

(3) The Commission shall be a party to proceedings before the Tribunal on the reference.

(4) The following shall be entitled to be parties to proceedings before the Tribunal on the reference—

(a)   the Attorney General, and

(b)   with the Tribunal's permission—

(i)   the charity trustees of any charity which is likely to be affected by the Tribunal's decision on the reference,

(ii)   any such charity which is a body corporate, and

(iii) any other person who is likely to be so affected.

References by Attorney General

2

(1) A question which involves either—

(a)   the operation of charity law in any respect, or

(b)   the application of charity law to a particular state of affairs,

may be referred to the Tribunal by the Attorney General if the Attorney General considers it desirable to refer the question to the Tribunal.

(2) The Attorney General shall be a party to proceedings before the Tribunal on the reference.

---

[636]   Amendment: Schedule inserted: Charities Act 2006, s 8(3), Sch 4.

(3) The following shall be entitled to be parties to proceedings before the Tribunal on the reference—

    (a)   the Commission, and

    (b)   with the Tribunal's permission—

        (i)   the charity trustees of any charity which is likely to be affected by the Tribunal's decision on the reference,

        (ii)   any such charity which is a body corporate, and

        (iii)   any other person who is likely to be so affected.

Powers of Commission in relation to matters referred to Tribunal

3

(1) This paragraph applies where a question which involves the application of charity law to a particular state of affairs has been referred to the Tribunal under paragraph 1 or 2 above.

(2) The Commission shall not take any steps in reliance on any view as to the application of charity law to that state of affairs until—

    (a)   proceedings on the reference (including any proceedings on appeal) have been concluded, and

    (b)   any period during which an appeal (or further appeal) may ordinarily be made has ended.

(3) Where—

    (a)   paragraphs (a) and (b) of sub-paragraph (2) above are satisfied, and

    (b)   the question has been decided in proceedings on the reference,

the Commission shall give effect to that decision when dealing with the particular state of affairs to which the reference related.

Suspension of time limits while reference in progress

4

(1) Sub-paragraph (2) below applies if—

    (a)   paragraph 3(2) above prevents the Commission from taking any steps which it would otherwise be permitted or required to take, and

    (b)   the steps in question may be taken only during a period specified in an enactment ('the specified period').

(2) The running of the specified period is suspended for the period which—

    (a)   begins with the date on which the question is referred to the Tribunal, and

    (b)   ends with the date on which paragraphs (a) and (b) of paragraph 3(2) above are satisfied.

(3) Nothing in this paragraph or section 74A of this Act prevents the specified period being suspended concurrently by virtue of subparagraph (2) above and that section.

Agreement for Commission to act while reference in progress

5

(1) Paragraph 3(2) above does not apply in relation to any steps taken by the Commission with the agreement of—

    (a)   the persons who are parties to the proceedings on the reference at the time when those steps are taken, and

    (b)   (if not within paragraph (a) above) the charity trustees of any charity which—

        (i)   is likely to be directly affected by the taking of those steps, and

        (ii)   is not a party to the proceedings at that time.

(2) The Commission may take those steps despite the suspension in accordance with paragraph 4(2) above of any period during which it would otherwise be permitted or required to take them.

(3) Paragraph 3(3) above does not require the Commission to give effect to a decision as to the application of charity law to a particular state of affairs to the extent that the decision is inconsistent with any steps already taken by the Commission in relation to that state of affairs in accordance with this paragraph.

Appeals and applications in respect of matters determined on references

6

(1) No appeal or application may be made to the Tribunal by a person to whom sub-paragraph (2) below applies in respect of an order or decision made, or direction given, by the Commission in accordance with paragraph 3(3) above.

(2) This sub-paragraph applies to a person who was at any stage a party to the proceedings in which the question referred to the Tribunal was decided.

(3) Rules under section 2B(1) of this Act may include provision as to who is to be treated for the purposes of sub-paragraph (2) above as being (or not being) a party to the proceedings.

(4) Any enactment (including one contained in this Act) which provides for an appeal or application to be made to the Tribunal has effect subject to sub-paragraph (1) above.

Interpretation

7

(1) In this Schedule—

    'charity law' means—

        (a)   any enactment contained in, or made under, this Act or the Charities Act 2006,

        (b)   any other enactment specified in regulations made by the Minister, and

        (c)   any rule of law which relates to charities, and

    'enactment' includes an enactment comprised in subordinate legislation (within the meaning of the Interpretation Act 1978), and includes an enactment whenever passed or made.

(2) The exclusions contained in section 96(2) of this Act (ecclesiastical corporations etc) do not have effect for the purposes of this Schedule.][637]

Amendment—Charities Act 2006, s 8(3), Sch 4.

Schedule 2
Exempt Charities

SECTIONS 3 AND 96

The following institutions, so far as they are charities, are exempt charities within the meaning of this Act, that is to say—

(a) any institution which, if the Charities Act 1960 had not been passed, would be exempted from the powers and jurisdiction, under the Charitable Trusts Acts 1853 to 1939, of [the Charity Commissioners for England and Wales][638] or Minister of Education (apart from any power of the Commissioners or Minister to apply those Acts in whole or in part to charities otherwise exempt) by the terms of any enactment not contained in those Acts other than section 9 of the Places of Worship Registration Act 1855 [*(but see Note 1)*]][639];

(b) the universities of Oxford, Cambridge, London, Durham and Newcastle, the colleges and halls in the universities of Oxford, Cambridge, Durham and Newcastle, [and][640] Queen Mary and Westfield College in the University of London...[641];

(c) any university, university college, or institution connected with a university or university college, which Her Majesty declares by Order in Council to be an exempt charity for the purposes of this Act;

(d) ...[642]

[(da) the Qualifications and Curriculum Authority;][643]

(e) ...[644]

(f) ...[645]

(g) ...[646]

[(h) a higher education corporation;][647]

(i) a successor company to a higher education corporation (within the meaning of section 129(5) of the Education Reform Act 1988) at a time when an institution conducted by the company is for the time being designated under that section;

[(j) a further education corporation;][648]

(k) the Board of Trustees of the Victoria and Albert Museum;

---

[637] Amendment: Schedule inserted: Charities Act 2006, s 8(3), Sch 4.

[638] Amendment: Words substituted: Charities Act 2006, s 75(1), Sch 8, paras 96, 177.

[639] Amendment: Words inserted: Charities Act 2006, s 11(1), (2).

[640] Amendment: Words inserted: Charities Act 2006, s 11(1), (3)(a).

[641] Amendment: Words omitted: Charities Act 2006, ss 11(1), (3)(b), 75(2), Sch 9.

[642] Amendment: Paragraph repealed: School Standards and Framework Act 1998, s 140(3), Sch 31.

[643] Amendment: Paragraph substituted: Education Act 1997, s 57 (1), Sch 7, para 7(a), for saving see The Education Act 1997 (Commencement No. 2 and Transitional Provisions) Order 1997, SI 1997/1468, Sch 2, Pt II.

[644] Amendment: Paragraph repealed: Education Act 1996, s 582(2), Sch 38, Pt I.

[645] Amendment: Paragraph repealed: The Qualifications, Curriculum and Assessment Authority for Wales (Transfer of Functions to the National Assembly for Wales and Abolition) Order 2005, SI 2005/3239, art 9(1), Sch 1, para 4, for transitional provisions see art 7 thereof.

[646] Amendment: Paragraph repealed: Education Act 1996, s 582(2), Sch 38, Pt I.

[647] Amendment: Paragraph inserted: Charities Act 2006, s 11(1), (4).

[648] Amendment: Paragraph inserted: Charities Act 2006, s 11(1), (5).

(l)   the Board of Trustees of the Science Museum;

(m)   the Board of Trustees of the Armouries;

(n)   the Board of Trustees of the Royal Botanic Gardens, Kew;

(o)   the Board of Trustees of the National Museums and Galleries on Merseyside;

(p)   the trustees of the British Museum and the trustees of the Natural History Museum;

(q)   the Board of Trustees of the National Gallery;

(r)   the Board of Trustees of the Tate Gallery ;

(s)   the Board of Trustees of the National Portrait Gallery;

(t)   the Board of Trustees of the Wallace Collection;

(u)   the Trustees of the Imperial War Museum;

(v)   the Trustees of the National Maritime Museum;

(w)   any institution which is administered by or on behalf of an institution included above and is established for the general purposes of, or for any special purpose of or in connection with, the last-mentioned institution [*(but see Note 2)*][649];

(x)   ...[650]

(y)   any registered society within the meaning of the Industrial and Provident Societies Act 1965 [and which is also registered in the register of social landlords under Part 1 of the Housing Act 1996;][651]

(z)   the Board of Governors of the Museum of London;

(za)   the British Library Board.

[(zb)   the National Lottery Charities Board][652]

[*Notes*

1. Paragraph (a) above does not include—

(a)   any Investment Fund or Deposit Fund within the meaning of the Church Funds Investment Measure 1958,

(b)   any investment fund or deposit fund within the meaning of the Methodist Church Funds Act 1960, or

(c)   the representative body of the Welsh Church or property administered by it.

2. Paragraph (w) above does not include any students' union.][653]

Amendments—National Lottery etc Act 1993, s 37, Sch 5, para 12; Education Act 1996, s 582(2), Sch 38, Pt I; Education Act 1997, s 57 (1), Sch 7, para 7; School Standards and Framework Act 1998, s 140(3), Sch 31; Teaching and Higher Education Act 1998, s 44(2), Sch 4; The Qualifications, Curriculum and Assessment Authority for Wales (Transfer of Functions to the National Assembly for Wales and Abolition) Order 2005, SI 2005/3239, art 9(1), Sch 1, para 4; Lottery Act 2006, s 21, Sch 3; Charities Act 2006, ss 11(1)–(9), 75, Sch 8, paras 96, 177, Sch 9.

---

[649] Amendment: Words inserted: Charities Act 2006, s 11(1)(6).

[650] Amendment: Paragraph omitted: Charities Act 2006, ss 11(1), (7), 75(2), Sch 9.

[651] Amendment: Words substituted: Charities Act 2006, s 11(1), (8).

[652] Amendment: Paragraph inserted: National Lottery etc Act 1993, s 37, Sch 5, para 12; Prospective amendment: paragraph repealed: Lottery Act 2006, s 21, Sch 3 as from a date to be appointed.

[653] Amendment: Notes inserted: Charities Act 2006, s 11(1), (9).

Schedule 3
Enlargement of Areas of Local Charities

SECTION 13

Existing area	Permissible enlargement
1. Greater London	Any area comprising Greater London.
2. Any area in Greater London and not in, or partly in, the City of London.	(i) Any area in Greater London and not in, or partly in, the City of London;
	(ii) the area of Greater London exclusive of the City of London;
	(iii) any area comprising the area of Greater London, exclusive of the City of London;
	(iv) any area partly in Greater London and partly in any adjacent parish or parishes (civil or ecclesiastical), and not partly in the City of London.
3. A district	Any area comprising the district
[3A. A Welsh county or county borough	Any area comprising that county or county borough.]*
4. Any area in a district	(i) Any area in the district;
	(ii) the district;
	(iii) any area comprising the district;
	(iv) any area partly in the district and partly in any adjacent district [or in any adjacent Welsh county or county borough]**.
[4A. Any area in a Welsh county or county borough	(i) Any area in the county or county borough;
	(ii) the county or county borough;
	(iii) any area comprising the county or county borough;
	(iv) any area partly in the county or county borough and partly in any adjacent Welsh county or county borough or in any adjacent district.]***

Existing area	Permissible enlargement
5. A parish (civil or ecclesiastical), or two or more parishes, or an area in a parish, or partly in each of two or more parishes.	Any area not extending beyond the parish or parishes comprising or adjacent to the area in column 1.
6. In Wales, a community, or two or more communities, or an area in a community, or partly in each of two or more communities.	Any area not extending beyond the community or communities comprising or adjacent to the area in column 1.

Amendments—Local Government (Wales) Act 1994, s 66(6), Sch 16, para 101(5), (6). *Paragraph inserted: Local Government (Wales) Act 1994, s 66(6), Sch 16, para 101(5). **Words inserted: Local Government (Wales) Act 1994, s 66(6), Sch 16, para 101(6). ***Paragraph inserted: Local Government (Wales) Act 1994, s 66(6), Sch 16, para 101(6).

Schedule 4
Court's Jurisdiction Over Certain Charities Governed by or Under Statute

SECTION 15

1

The court may by virtue of section 15(3) of this Act exercise its jurisdiction with respect to charities—

- (a) in relation to charities established or regulated by any provision of the Seamen's Fund Winding-up Act 1851 which is repealed by the Charities Act 1960;
- (b) in relation to charities established or regulated by schemes under the Endowed Schools Act 1869 to 1948, or section 75 of the Elementary Education Act 1870 or by schemes given effect under section 2 of the Education Act 1973 [or section 554 of the Education Act 1996][654];
- (c) ...[655]
- (d) in relation to fuel allotments, that is to say, land which, by any enactment relating to inclosure or any instrument having effect under such an enactment, is vested in trustees upon trust that the land or the rents and profits of the land shall be used for the purpose of providing poor persons with fuel;
- (e) in relation to charities established or regulated by any provision of the Municipal Corporations Act 1883 which is repealed by the Charities Act 1960 or by any scheme having effect under any such provision;
- (f) in relation to charities regulated by schemes under the London Government Act 1899;
- (g) in relation to charities established or regulated by orders or regulations under section 2 of the Regimental Charitable Funds Act 1935;
- (h) in relation to charities regulated by section 79 of this Act, or by any such order as is mentioned in that section.

---

[654] Amendment: Words inserted: Education Act 1996, s 582(1), Sch 37, para 121.
[655] Amendment: Subparagraph repealed: Statute Law (Repeals) Act 1993.

2

Notwithstanding anything in section 19 of the Commons Act 1876 a scheme for the administration of a fuel allotment (within the meaning of the foregoing paragraph) may provide—

(a) for the sale or letting of the allotment or any part thereof, for the discharge of the land sold or let from any restrictions as to the use thereof imposed by or under any enactment relating to inclosure and for the application of the sums payable to the trustees of the allotment in respect of the sale or lease; or

(b) for the exchange of the allotment or any part thereof for other land, for the discharge as aforesaid of the land given in exchange by the said trustees, and for the application of any money payable to the said trustees for equality of exchange; or

(c) for the use of the allotment or any part thereof for any purposes specified in the scheme.

Amendments—Statute Law (Repeals) Act 1993; Education Act 1996, s 582(1), Sch 37, para 121.

Schedule 5
Meaning of 'Connected Person' for Purposes of Section 36(2)

SECTION 36(2)

1

[(1) In section 36(2) of this Act 'connected person', in relation to a charity, means any person who falls within sub-paragraph (2)—

(a) at the time of the disposition in question, or
(b) at the time of any contract for the disposition in question.

(2) The persons falling within this sub-paragraph are –][656]

(a) a charity trustee or trustee for the charity;
(b) a person who is the donor of any land to the charity (whether the gift was made on or after the establishment of the charity);
(c) a child, parent, grandchild, grandparent, brother or sister of any such trustee or donor;
(d) an officer, agent or employee of the charity;
(e) the spouse [or civil partner][657] of any person falling within any of sub-paragraphs (a) to (d) above;
[(ea) a person carrying on business in partnership with any person falling within any of sub-paragraphs (a) to (e) above;][658]
(f) an institution which is controlled—
  (i) by any person falling within any of sub-paragraphs (a) to [(ea)][659] above, or
  (ii) by two or more such persons taken together; or
(g) a body corporate in which—
  (i) any connected person falling within any of sub-paragraphs (a) to (f) above has a substantial interest, or

---

[656] Amendment: Subparagraphs substituted: Charities Act 2006, s 75(1), Sch 8, paras 96, 178(1), (2).
[657] Amendment: Words inserted: Civil Partnership Act 2004, s 261(1), Sch 27, para 147.
[658] Amendment: Subparagraph inserted: Charities Act 2006, s 75(1), Sch 8, paras 96, 178(1), (4).
[659] Amendment: Word substituted: Charities Act 2006, s 75(1), Sch 8, paras 96, 178(1), (4).

(ii)   two or more such persons, taken together, have a substantial interest.

2

(1) In paragraph [1(2)(c)][660] above 'child' includes a stepchild and an illegitimate child.

(2) For the purposes of paragraph [1(2)(e)][661] above a person living with another as that person's husband or wife shall be treated as that person's spouse.

[(3) Where two persons of the same sex are not civil partners but live together as if they were, each of them shall be treated for those purposes as the civil partner of the other.][662]

3

For the purposes of paragraph [1(2)(f)][663] above a person controls an institution if he is able to secure that the affairs of the institution are conducted in accordance with his wishes.

4

(1) For the purposes of paragraph [1(2)(g)][664] above any such connected person as is there mentioned has a substantial interest in a body corporate if the person or institution in question—

(a)   is interested in shares comprised in the equity share capital of that body of a nominal value of more than one-fifth of that share capital, or

(b)   is entitled to exercise, or control the exercise of, more than one-fifth of the voting power at any general meeting of that body.

(2) The rules set out in Part I of Schedule 13 to the Companies Act 1985 (rules for interpretation of certain provisions of that Act) shall apply for the purposes of sub-paragraph (1) above as they apply for the purposes of section 346(4) of that Act ('connected persons' etc).

(3) In this paragraph 'equity share capital' and 'share' have the same meaning as in that Act.

Amendments—Civil Partnership Act 2004, s 261(1), Sch 27, para 147; Charities Act 2006, s 75(1), Sch 8, paras 96, 178.

---

[660]   Amendment: Paragraph number substituted: Charities Act 2006, s 75(1), Sch 8, paras 96, 178(1), (5)(a).
[661]   Amendment: Paragraph number substituted: Charities Act 2006, s 75(1), Sch 8, paras 96, 178(1), (5)(b).
[662]   Amendment: Subparagraph added: Charities Act 2006, s 75(1), Sch 8, paras 96, 178(1), (5)(c).
[663]   Amendment: Paragraph number substituted: Charities Act 2006, s 75(1), Sch 8, paras 96, 178(1), (6).
[664]   Amendment: Paragraph number substituted: Charities Act 2006, s 75(1), Sch 8, paras 96, 178(1), (7).

[Schedule 5A
Group Accounts

SECTION 49A

Interpretation

1

(1) This paragraph applies for the purposes of this Schedule.

(2) A charity is a 'parent charity' if—

(a) it is (or is to be treated as) a parent undertaking in relation to one or more other undertakings in accordance with the provisions of section 258 of, and Schedule 10A to, the Companies Act 1985, and

(b) it is not a company.

(3) Each undertaking in relation to which a parent charity is (or is to be treated as) a parent undertaking in accordance with those provisions is a 'subsidiary undertaking' in relation to the parent charity.

(4) But sub-paragraph (3) does not have the result that any of the following is a 'subsidiary undertaking'—

(a) any special trusts of a charity,

(b) any institution which, by virtue of a direction under section 96(5) of this Act, is to be treated as forming part of a charity for the purposes of this Part of this Act, or

(c) any charity to which a direction under section 96(6) of this Act applies for those purposes.

(5) 'The group', in relation to a parent charity, means that charity and its subsidiary undertaking or undertakings, and any reference to the members of the group is to be construed accordingly.

(6) For the purposes of—

(a) this paragraph, and

(b) the operation of the provisions mentioned in subparagraph (2) above for the purposes of this paragraph,

'undertaking' has the meaning given by sub-paragraph (7) below.

(7) For those purposes 'undertaking' means—

(a) an undertaking as defined by section 259(1) of the Companies Act 1985, or

(b) a charity which is not an undertaking as so defined.

Accounting records

2

(1) The charity trustees—

(a) of a parent charity, or

(b) of any charity which is a subsidiary undertaking,

must ensure that the accounting records kept in respect of the charity under section 41(1) of this Act not only comply with the requirements of that provision but also are such as to enable the charity trustees of the parent charity to ensure that, where any group accounts are prepared by them under paragraph 3(2), those accounts comply with the relevant requirements.

(2) If a parent charity has a subsidiary undertaking in relation to which the requirements of section 41(1) of this Act do not apply, the charity trustees of the parent charity must take reasonable steps to secure that the undertaking keeps such accounting records as to enable the trustees to ensure that, where any group accounts are prepared by them under paragraph 3(2), those accounts comply with the relevant requirements.

(3) In this paragraph 'the relevant requirements' means the requirements of regulations under paragraph 3.

Preparation of group accounts

3

(1) This paragraph applies in relation to a financial year of a charity if it is a parent charity at the end of that year.

(2) The charity trustees of the parent charity must prepare group accounts in respect of that year.

(3) 'Group accounts' means consolidated accounts—

    (a)   relating to the group, and
    (b)   complying with such requirements as to their form and contents as may be prescribed by regulations made by the Minister.

(4) Without prejudice to the generality of sub-paragraph (3), regulations under that sub-paragraph may make provision—

    (a)   for any such accounts to be prepared in accordance with such methods and principles as are specified or referred to in the regulations;
    (b)   for dealing with cases where the financial years of the members of the group do not all coincide;
    (c)   as to any information to be provided by way of notes to the accounts.

(5) Regulations under that sub-paragraph may also make provision—

    (a)   for determining the financial years of subsidiary undertakings for the purposes of this Schedule;
    (b)   for imposing on the charity trustees of a parent charity requirements with respect to securing that such financial years coincide with that of the charity.

(6) If the requirement in sub-paragraph (2) applies to the charity trustees of a parent charity in relation to a financial year—

    (a)   that requirement so applies in addition to the requirement in section 42(1) of this Act, and
    (b)   the option of preparing the documents mentioned in section 42(3) of this Act is not available in relation to that year (whatever the amount of the charity's gross income for that year).

(7) Sub-paragraph (2) has effect subject to paragraph 4.

Note—For transitional provisions in relation to para 3(2), see s 75(3), Sch 10, para 17.

Exceptions relating to requirement to prepare group accounts

4

(1) The requirement in paragraph 3(2) does not apply to the charity trustees of a parent charity in relation to a financial year if at the end of that year it is itself a subsidiary undertaking in relation to another charity.

(2) The requirement in paragraph 3(2) does not apply to the charity trustees of a parent charity in relation to a financial year if the aggregate gross income of the group for that year does not exceed such sum as is specified in regulations made by the Minister.

(3) Regulations made by the Minister may prescribe circumstances in which a subsidiary undertaking may or (as the case may be) must be excluded from group accounts required to be prepared under paragraph 3(2) for a financial year.

(4) Where, by virtue of such regulations, each of the subsidiary undertakings which are members of a group is either permitted or required to be excluded from any such group accounts for a financial year, the requirement in paragraph 3(2) does not apply to the charity trustees of the parent charity in relation to that year.

Preservation of group accounts

5

(1) The charity trustees of a charity shall preserve any group accounts prepared by them under paragraph 3(2) for at least six years from the end of the financial year to which the accounts relate.

(2) Subsection (4) of section 41 of this Act shall apply in relation to the preservation of any such accounts as it applies in relation to the preservation of any accounting records (the references to subsection (3) of that section being construed as references to subparagraph (1) above).

Audit of accounts of larger groups

6

(1) This paragraph applies where group accounts are prepared for a financial year of a parent charity under paragraph 3(2) and—

(a)   the aggregate gross income of the group in that year exceeds the relevant income threshold, or

(b)   the aggregate gross income of the group in that year exceeds the relevant income threshold and at the end of the year the aggregate value of the assets of the group (before deduction of liabilities) exceeds the relevant assets threshold.

(2) In sub-paragraph (1)—

(a)   the reference in paragraph (a) or (b) to the relevant income threshold is a reference to the sum prescribed as the relevant income threshold for the purposes of that paragraph, and

(b)   the reference in paragraph (b) to the relevant assets threshold is a reference to the sum prescribed as the relevant assets threshold for the purposes of that paragraph.

'Prescribed' means prescribed by regulations made by the Minister.

(3) This paragraph also applies where group accounts are prepared for a financial year of a parent charity under paragraph 3(2) and the appropriate audit provision applies in relation to the parent charity's own accounts for that year.

(4) If this paragraph applies in relation to a financial year of a parent charity by virtue of sub-paragraph (1) or (3), the group accounts for that year shall be audited—

- (a) (subject to paragraph (b) or (c) below) by a person within section 43(2)(a) or (b) of this Act;
- (b) if section 43A of this Act applies in relation to that year, by a person appointed by the Audit Commission (see section 43A(7));
- (c) if section 43B of this Act applies in relation to that year, by the Auditor General for Wales.

(5) Where it appears to the Commission that sub-paragraph (4)(a) above has not been complied with in relation to that year within ten months from the end of that year—

- (a) the Commission may by order require the group accounts for that year to be audited by a person within section 43(2)(a) or (b) of this Act, and
- (b) if it so orders, the auditor shall be a person appointed by the Commission.

(6) Section 43(6) of this Act shall apply in relation to any such audit as it applies in relation to an audit carried out by an auditor appointed under section 43(5) (reading the reference to the funds of the charity as a reference to the funds of the parent charity).

(7) Section 43A(4) and (6) of this Act apply in relation to any appointment under sub-paragraph (4)(b) above as they apply in relation to an appointment under section 43A(2).

(8) If this paragraph applies in relation to a financial year of a parent charity by virtue of sub-paragraph (1), the appropriate audit provision shall apply in relation to the parent charity's own accounts for that year (whether or not it would otherwise so apply).

(9) In this paragraph 'the appropriate audit provision', in relation to a financial year of a parent charity, means—

- (a) (subject to paragraph (b) or (c) below) section 43(2) of this Act;
- (b) if section 43A of this Act applies in relation to that year, section 43A(2);
- (c) if section 43B of this Act applies in relation to that year, section 43B(2).

Examination of accounts of smaller groups

7

(1) This paragraph applies where—

- (a) group accounts are prepared for a financial year of a parent charity under paragraph 3(2), and
- (b) paragraph 6 does not apply in relation to that year.

(2) If—

- (a) this paragraph applies in relation to a financial year of a parent charity, and
- (b) sub-paragraph (4) or (5) below does not apply in relation to it,

subsections (3) to (7) of section 43 of this Act shall apply in relation to the group accounts for that year as they apply in relation to the accounts of a charity for a financial year in relation to which subsection (2) of that section does not apply, but subject to the modifications in sub-paragraph (3) below.

(3) The modifications are—

 (a) any reference to the charity trustees of the charity is to be construed as a reference to the charity trustees of the parent charity;

 (b) any reference to the charity's gross income in the financial year in question is to be construed as a reference to the aggregate gross income of the group in that year; and

 (c) any reference to the funds of the charity is to be construed as a reference to the funds of the parent charity.

(4) If—

 (a) this paragraph applies in relation to a financial year of a parent charity, and

 (b) section 43A of this Act also applies in relation to that year,

subsections (3) to (6) of that section shall apply in relation to the group accounts for that year as they apply in relation to the accounts of a charity for a financial year in relation to which subsection (2) of that section does not apply.

(5) If—

 (a) this paragraph applies in relation to a financial year of a parent charity, and

 (b) section 43B of this Act also applies in relation to that year,

subsection (3) of that section shall apply in relation to the group accounts for that year as they apply in relation to the accounts of a charity for a financial year in relation to which subsection (2) of that section does not apply.

(6) If the group accounts for a financial year of a parent charity are to be examined or audited in accordance with section 43(3) of this Act (as applied by sub-paragraph (2) above), section 43(3) shall apply in relation to the parent charity's own accounts for that year (whether or not it would otherwise so apply).

(7) Nothing in sub-paragraph (4) or (5) above affects the operation of section 43A(3) to (6) or (as the case may be) section 43B(3) in relation to the parent charity's own accounts for the financial year in question.

Supplementary provisions relating to audits etc

8

(1) Section 44(1) of this Act shall apply in relation to audits and examinations carried out under or by virtue of paragraph 6 or 7, but subject to the modifications in sub-paragraph (2) below.

(2) The modifications are—

 (a) in paragraph (b), the reference to section 43, 43A or 43B of this Act is to be construed as a reference to paragraph 6 above or to any of those sections as applied by paragraph 7 above;

 (b) also in paragraph (b), the reference to any such statement of accounts as is mentioned in sub-paragraph (i) of that paragraph is to be construed as a reference to group accounts prepared for a financial year under paragraph 3(2) above;

 (c) in paragraph (c), any reference to section 43, 43A or 43B of this Act is to be construed as a reference to that section as applied by paragraph 7 above;

 (d) in paragraphs (d) and (e), any reference to the charity concerned or a charity is to be construed as a reference to any member of the group; and

(e)   in paragraph (f), the reference to the requirements of section 43(2) or (3) of this Act is to be construed as a reference to the requirements of paragraph 6(4)(a) or those applied by paragraph 7(2) above.

(3) Without prejudice to the generality of section 44(1)(e), as modified by sub-paragraph (2)(d) above, regulations made under that provision may make provision corresponding or similar to any provision made by section 389A of the Companies Act 1985 (c 6) in connection with the rights exercisable by an auditor of a company in relation to a subsidiary undertaking of the company.

(4) In section 44(2) of this Act the reference to section 44(1)(d) or (e) includes a reference to that provision as it applies in accordance with this paragraph.

Duty of auditors etc to report matters to Commission

9

(1) Section 44A(2) to (5) and (7) of this Act shall apply in relation to a person appointed to audit, or report on, any group accounts under or by virtue of paragraph 6 or 7 above as they apply in relation to a person such as is mentioned in section 44A(1).

(2) In section 44A(2)(a), as it applies in accordance with subparagraph (1) above, the reference to the charity or any connected institution or body is to be construed as a reference to the parent charity or any of its subsidiary undertakings.

Annual reports

10

(1) This paragraph applies where group accounts are prepared for a financial year of a parent charity under paragraph 3(2).

(2) The annual report prepared by the charity trustees of the parent charity in respect of that year under section 45 of this Act shall include—

(a)   such a report by the trustees on the activities of the charity's subsidiary undertakings during that year, and

(b)   such other information relating to any of those undertakings,

as may be prescribed by regulations made by the Minister.

(3) Without prejudice to the generality of sub-paragraph (2), regulations under that sub-paragraph may make provision—

(a)   for any such report as is mentioned in paragraph (a) of that sub-paragraph to be prepared in accordance with such principles as are specified or referred to in the regulations;

(b)   enabling the Commission to dispense with any requirement prescribed by virtue of sub-paragraph (2)(b) in the case of a particular subsidiary undertaking or a particular class of subsidiary undertaking.

(4) Section 45(3) to (3B) shall apply in relation to the annual report referred to in sub-paragraph (2) above as if any reference to the charity's gross income in the financial year in question were a reference to the aggregate gross income of the group in that year.

(5) When transmitted to the Commission in accordance with subparagraph (4) above, the copy of the annual report shall have attached to it both a copy of the group accounts prepared for that year under paragraph 3(2) and—

(a)   a copy of the report made by the auditor on those accounts; or

(b)   where those accounts have been examined under section 43, 43A or 43B of this Act (as applied by paragraph 7 above), a copy of the report made by the person carrying out the examination.

(6) The requirements in this paragraph are in addition to those in section 45 of this Act.

Excepted charities

11

(1) This paragraph applies where—

(a)   a charity is required to prepare an annual report in respect of a financial year by virtue of section 46(5) of this Act,

(b)   the charity is a parent charity at the end of the year, and

(c)   group accounts are prepared for that year under paragraph 3(2) by the charity trustees of the charity.

(2) When transmitted to the Commission in accordance with section 46(7) of this Act, the copy of the annual report shall have attached to it both a copy of the group accounts and—

(a)   a copy of the report made by the auditor on those accounts; or

(b)   where those accounts have been examined under section 43, 43A or 43B of this Act (as applied by paragraph 7 above), a copy of the report made by the person carrying out the examination.

(3) The requirement in sub-paragraph (2) is in addition to that in section 46(6) of this Act.

Exempt charities

12

Nothing in the preceding provisions of this Schedule applies to an exempt charity.

Public inspection of annual reports etc

13

In section 47(2) of this Act, the reference to a charity's most recent accounts includes, in relation to a charity whose charity trustees have prepared any group accounts under paragraph 3(2), the group accounts most recently prepared by them.

Offences

14

(1) Section 49(1) of this Act applies in relation to a requirement within sub-paragraph (2) as it applies in relation to a requirement within section 49(1)(a).

(2) A requirement is within this sub-paragraph where it is imposed by section 45(3) or (3A) of this Act, taken with—

(a)   section 45(3B), (4) and (5), and

(b)   paragraph 10(5) or 11(2) above,

as applicable.

(3) In sub-paragraph (2) any reference to section 45(3), (3A) or (3B) of this Act is a reference to that provision as applied by paragraph 10(4) above.

(4) In section 49(1)(b) the reference to section 47(2) of this Act includes a reference to that provision as extended by paragraph 13 above.

Aggregate gross income

15

The Minister may by regulations make provision for determining for the purposes of this Schedule the amount of the aggregate gross income for a financial year of a group consisting of a parent charity and its subsidiary undertaking or undertakings.][665]

Amendment—Charities Act 2006, s 30(2), Sch 6.

[Schedule 5B
Further Provision about Charitable Incorporated Organisations

SECTION 69P

Powers

1

(1) Subject to anything in its constitution, a CIO has power to do anything which is calculated to further its purposes or is conducive or incidental to doing so.

(2) The CIO's charity trustees shall manage the affairs of the CIO and may for that purpose exercise all the powers of the CIO.

Constitutional requirements

2

A CIO shall use and apply its property in furtherance of its purposes and in accordance with its constitution.

3

If the CIO is one whose members are liable to contribute to its assets if it is wound up, its constitution binds the CIO and its members for the time being to the same extent as if its provisions were contained in a contract—

    (a)   to which the CIO and each of its members was a party, and

    (b)   which contained obligations on the part of the CIO and each member to observe all the provisions of the constitution.

4

Money payable by a member to the CIO under the constitution is a debt due from him to the CIO, and is of the nature of a specialty debt.

---

[665] Amendment: Schedule inserted: Charities Act 2006, s 30(2), Sch 6, for transitional provisions relating to para 3(2), see s 75(3), Sch 10, para 17.

Third parties

5

(1) Sub-paragraphs (2) and (3) are subject to sub-paragraph (4).

(2) The validity of an act done (or purportedly done) by a CIO shall not be called into question on the ground that it lacked constitutional capacity.

(3) The power of the charity trustees of a CIO to act so as to bind the CIO (or authorise others to do so) shall not be called into question on the ground of any constitutional limitations on their powers.

(4) But sub-paragraphs (2) and (3) apply only in favour of a person who gives full consideration in money or money's worth in relation to the act in question, and does not know—

    (a)   in a sub-paragraph (2) case, that the act is beyond the CIO's constitutional capacity, or
    (b)   in a sub-paragraph (3) case, that the act is beyond the constitutional powers of its charity trustees,

and (in addition) sub-paragraph (3) applies only if the person dealt with the CIO in good faith (which he shall be presumed to have done unless the contrary is proved).

(5) A party to an arrangement or transaction with a CIO is not bound to inquire—

    (a)   whether it is within the CIO's constitutional capacity, or
    (b)   as to any constitutional limitations on the powers of its charity trustees to bind the CIO or authorise others to do so.

(6) If a CIO purports to transfer or grant an interest in property, the fact that the act was beyond its constitutional capacity, or that its charity trustees in connection with the act exceeded their constitutional powers, does not affect the title of a person who subsequently acquires the property or any interest in it for full consideration without actual notice of any such circumstances affecting the validity of the CIO's act.

(7) In any proceedings arising out of sub-paragraphs (2) to (4), the burden of proving that a person knew that an act—

    (a)   was beyond the CIO's constitutional capacity, or
    (b)   was beyond the constitutional powers of its charity trustees,

lies on the person making that allegation.

(8) In this paragraph and paragraphs 6 to 8—

    (a)   references to a CIO's lack of 'constitutional capacity' are to lack of capacity because of anything in its constitution, and
    (b)   references to 'constitutional limitations' on the powers of a CIO's charity trustees are to limitations on their powers under its constitution, including limitations deriving from a resolution of the CIO in general meeting, or from an agreement between the CIO's members, and 'constitutional powers' is to be construed accordingly.

6

(1) Nothing in paragraph 5 prevents a person from bringing proceedings to restrain the doing of an act which would be—

(a)　　beyond the CIO's constitutional capacity, or

(b)　　beyond the constitutional powers of the CIO's charity trustees.

(2) But no such proceedings may be brought in respect of an act to be done in fulfilment of a legal obligation arising from a previous act of the CIO.

(3) Sub-paragraph (2) does not prevent the Commission from exercising any of its powers.

7

Nothing in paragraph 5(3) affects any liability incurred by the CIO's charity trustees (or any one of them) for acting beyond his or their constitutional powers.

8

Nothing in paragraph 5 absolves the CIO's charity trustees from their duty to act within the CIO's constitution and in accordance with any constitutional limitations on their powers.

Duties

9

It is the duty of—

(a)　　each member of a CIO, and

(b)　　each charity trustee of a CIO,

to exercise his powers, and (in the case of a charity trustee) to perform his functions, in his capacity as such, in the way he decides, in good faith, would be most likely to further the purposes of the CIO.

10

(1) Subject to any provision of a CIO's constitution permitted by virtue of regulations made under sub-paragraph (2), each charity trustee of a CIO shall in the performance of his functions in that capacity exercise such care and skill as is reasonable in the circumstances, having regard in particular—

(a)　　to any special knowledge or experience that he has or holds himself out as having, and

(b)　　if he acts as a charity trustee in the course of a business or profession, to any special knowledge or experience that it is reasonable to expect of a person acting in the course of that kind of business or profession.

(2) The Minister may make regulations permitting a CIO's constitution to provide that the duty in sub-paragraph (1) does not apply, or does not apply in so far as is specified in the constitution.

(3) Regulations under sub-paragraph (2) may provide for limits on the extent to which, or the cases in which, a CIO's constitution may disapply the duty in sub-paragraph (1).

Personal benefit and payments

11

(1) A charity trustee of a CIO may not benefit personally from any arrangement or transaction entered into by the CIO if, before the arrangement or transaction was entered into, he did not disclose to all the charity trustees of the CIO any material interest of his in it or in any other person or body party to it (whether that interest is direct or indirect).

(2) Nothing in sub-paragraph (1) confers authority for a charity trustee of a CIO to benefit personally from any arrangement or transaction entered into by the CIO.

12

A charity trustee of a CIO—

    (a)   is entitled to be reimbursed by the CIO, or
    (b)   may pay out of the CIO's funds,

expenses properly incurred by him in the performance of his functions as such.

Procedure

13

(1) The Minister may by regulations make provision about the procedure of CIOs.

(2) Subject to—

    (a)   any such regulations,
    (b)   any other requirement imposed by or by virtue of this Act or any other enactment, and
    (c)   anything in the CIO's constitution,

a CIO may regulate its own procedure.

(3) But a CIO's procedure shall include provision for the holding of a general meeting of its members, and the regulations referred to in sub-paragraph (1) may in particular make provision about such meetings.

Amendment of constitution

14

(1) A CIO may by resolution of its members amend its constitution (and a single resolution may provide for more than one amendment).

(2) Such a resolution must be passed—

    (a)   by a 75% majority of those voting at a general meeting of the CIO (including those voting by proxy or by post, if voting that way is permitted), or
    (b)   unanimously by the CIO's members, otherwise than at a general meeting.

(3) The date of passing of such a resolution is—

    (a)   the date of the general meeting at which it was passed, or

(b)   if it was passed otherwise than at a general meeting, the date on which provision in the CIO's constitution or in regulations made under paragraph 13 deems it to have been passed (but that date may not be earlier than that on which the last member agreed to it).

(4) The power of a CIO to amend its constitution is not exercisable in any way which would result in the CIO's ceasing to be a charity.

(5) Subject to paragraph 15(5) below, a resolution containing an amendment which would make any regulated alteration is to that extent ineffective unless the prior written consent of the Commission has been obtained to the making of the amendment.

(6) The following are regulated alterations—

(a)   any alteration of the CIO's purposes,
(b)   any alteration of any provision of the CIO's constitution directing the application of property of the CIO on its dissolution,
(c)   any alteration of any provision of the CIO's constitution where the alteration would provide authorisation for any benefit to be obtained by charity trustees or members of the CIO or persons connected with them.

(7) For the purposes of sub-paragraph (6)(c)—

(a)   'benefit' means a direct or indirect benefit of any nature, except that it does not include any remuneration (within the meaning of section 73A of this Act) whose receipt may be authorised under that section, and
(b)   the same rules apply for determining whether a person is connected with a charity trustee or member of the CIO as apply, in accordance with section 73B(5) and (6) of this Act, for determining whether a person is connected with a charity trustee for the purposes of section 73A.

Registration and coming into effect of amendments

15

(1) A CIO shall send to the Commission a copy of a resolution containing an amendment to its constitution, together with—

(a)   a copy of the constitution as amended, and
(b)   such other documents and information as the Commission may require,

by the end of the period of 15 days beginning with the date of passing of the resolution (see paragraph 14(3)).

(2) An amendment to a CIO's constitution does not take effect until it has been registered.

(3) The Commission shall refuse to register an amendment if—

(a)   in the opinion of the Commission the CIO had no power to make it (for example, because the effect of making it would be that the CIO ceased to be a charity, or that the CIO or its constitution did not comply with any requirement imposed by or by virtue of this Act or any other enactment), or
(b)   the amendment would change the name of the CIO, and the Commission could have refused an application under section 69E of this Act for the constitution and registration of a CIO with the name specified in the amendment on a ground set out in subsection (4) of that section.

(4) The Commission may refuse to register an amendment if the amendment would make a regulated alteration and the consent referred to in paragraph 14(5) had not been obtained.

(5) But if the Commission does register such an amendment, paragraph 14(5) does not apply.][666]

Amendment—Charities Act 2006, s 34, Sch 7, Pt 1, para 2.

Schedule 6
Consequential Amendments

Not reproduced.

Schedule 7
Repeals

Not reproduced.

Schedule 8
Transitional Provisions

...[667]

Amendment—Statute Law (Repeals) Act 2004.

Table of derivations

Note: The following abbreviations are used in this Table—

1872 – The Charitable Trustees Incorporation Act 1872 (c 24)

1960 – The Charities Act 1960 (c 58)

1992 – The Charities Act 1992 (c 41)

Provision	Derivation
1	1960, s 1; 1992, Sch 3, para 1.
2	1960, s 3.
3	1960, ss 4, 43(1), 45(6); 1992, s 2, Sch 1
4	1960, ss 5, 43(1).
5	1992, s 3.
6	1992, s 4.
7	1992, s 5.
8	1960, s 6; 1992, s 6.

---

[666] Amendment: Schedule inserted: Charities Act 2006, s 34, Sch 7, Pt 1, para 2.
[667] Amendment: Schedule 8 repealed: Statute Law (Repeals) Act 2004.

Provision	Derivation
9	1960, s 7; 1992, s 7.
10	1992, s 52.
11	1992, s 54.
12	1992, s 53.
13	1960, s 13.
14	1960, s 14; 1992, s 15.
15	1960, s 15; Northern Ireland (Temporary Provisions) Act 1972 (c 22), s 1(3); Northern Ireland Constitution Act 1973 (c 36), Sch 5, para 1; Northern Ireland Act 1974 (c 28), Sch 1, para 1(7).
16	1960, s 18; Local Government Act 1972 (c 70), s 179(1)(4); 1992, s 13, Sch 3, para 6.
17	1960, s 19; 1992, Sch 3, para 7.
18	1960, s 20; 1992, s 8, Sch 1.
19	1960, ss 20A, 43(1); 1992, s 9.
20	1960, s 21; Local Government Act 1972 (c 70), s 179(1)(4); 1992, Sch 3, para 8.
21	1960, s 16; 1992, Sch 3, para 4.
22	1960, s 17; 1992, Sch 3, para 5.
23	1992, s 31.
24	1960, s 22.
25	1960, s 22A; 1992, s 16.
26	1960, s 23.
27	1960, s 23A; 1992, s 17.
28	1992, s 18; Banking Coordination (Second Council Directive) Regulations 1992 (SI 1992/3218), Sch 10, para 33.
29	1960, s 24.
30	1960, ss 25, 43(1).
31	1960, s 26.
32	1960, s 26A; 1992, s 28.

Provision	Derivation
33	1960, s 28(1) to (8); 1992, Sch 3, para 10.
34	1960, s 28A; 1992, s 11.
35	1960, s 21A; 1992, s 14.
36	1992, s 32.
37	1992, s 33.
38	1992, s 34.
39	1992, s 35.
40	1992, s 37(1) to (4).
41	1992, s 19.
42	1992, s 20.
43	1992, s 21.
44	1992, s 22.
45	1992, s 23.
46	1960, s 32(1)(2); 1992, s 24, Sch 3, para 13.
47	1992, s 25.
48	1992, s 26.
49	1992, s 27.
50	1872, s 1; 1992, Sch 4, para 1.
51	1872, s 2; 1992, Sch 4, para 2.
52	1872, s 3; 1992, Sch 4, para 3.
53	1872, s 4; 1992, Sch 4, para 4.
54	1872, s 5; 1992, Sch 4, para 5.
55	1872, s 6.
56	1872, s 6A; 1992, Sch 4, para 6.
57	1872, s 7; 1992, Sch 4, para 7.
58	1872, s 8; 1992, Sch 4, para 8.
59	1872, s 10.

Provision	Derivation
60	1872, s 12; 1992, Sch 4, para 9 (part).
61	1872, s 12A; 1992, Sch 4, para 9 (part).
62	1872, s 14; 1992, Sch 4, para 10.
63	1960, s 30; Companies Act 1989 (c 40), s 111(1); 1992, s 10.
64	1960, s 30A; Companies Act 1989 (c 40) s 111(1); 1992, s 40.
65	1960, s 30B; Companies Act 1989 (c 40), s 111(1).
66	1960, s 30BA; 1992, s 41.
67	1960, s 30BB; 1992, s 42.
68	1960, s 30C; Companies Act 1989 (c 40), s 111(1); 1992, Sch 3, para 11.
69	1960, s 8; 1992, Sch 3, para 2; Companies Act 1989 (Eligibility for Appointment as Company Auditor) (Consequential Amendments) Regulations 1991 (SI 1991/1997).
70	1992, s 38.
71	1992, s 39.
72	1992, s 45.
73	1992, s 46.
74	1992, s 43.
75	1992, s 44.
76	1960, s 10; London Government Act 1963 (c 33), s 81(9)(b); Local Government Act 1972 (c 70), s 210(9)(a).
77	1960, s 11; London Government Act 1963 (c 33), s 81(9)(b); Local Government Act 1972 (c 70), s 210(9)(b).
78	1960, s 12; Local Government Act 1972 (c 70), ss 179(1)(4), 210(9)(c).
79	1960, s 37; London Government Act 1963 (c 33), s 4(4); Local Government Act 1972 (c 70), ss 179(1)(4), 210(9)(e); Education Reform Act 1988 (c 40), Sch 12, para 9.
80	1992, s 12.
81	1960, s 33.

Provision	Derivation
82	1960, s 34; 1992, Sch 3, para 14.
83	1960, s 35.
84	1960, s 9; 1992, s 25(2), Sch 3, para 3.
85	1992, s 51.
86	1960, ss 4(8B), 18(14), 43(2A)(3); Education Act 1973 (c 16), Sch 1, para 1(1); 1992, ss 2(7), 13(6), 77, Sch 3, para 17.
87	1992, s 56(1)(2)(6).
88	1960, s 41; 1992, s 56(3)(6), Sch 3, para 16.
89	1960, s 40; 1992, s 56(4)(5)(6).
90	1992, s 57.
91	1960, s 40A; 1992, s 76, Sch 3, para 15.
92	1960, s 42.
93	1960, s 36.
94	1992, s 55.
95	1992, s 75.
96	1960, s 45(1) to (5); Local Government Act 1972 (c 70), s 179(1)(4); 1992, s 1(2), Sch 3, para 18; Endowments and Glebe Measure 1976 (No 4), s 44.
97	1960, ss 16(5) (part), 46; Companies Act 1989 (c 40), s 111(2); 1992, s 1(1) to (4).
98	
99	
100	1960, s 49(2)(c); 1992, s 79(3)(4)(5).
Sch 1	1960, Sch 1; Courts and Legal Services Act 1990 (c 41), Sch 10, para 14; 1992, s 12(1), Sch 3, paras 20, 21.
Sch 2	
para (a)	1960, Sch 2, para (a).
para (b)	1960, Sch 2, para (b); Universities of Durham and Newcastle-upon-Tyne Act 1963 (c xi), s 18; Queen Mary and Westfield College Act 1989 (c xiii), s 10.

Provision	Derivation
para (c)	1960, Sch 2, para (c).
paras (d) to (i)	Education Reform Act 1988 (c 40), Sch 12, paras 10, 63, 64.
para (j)	Further and Higher Education Act 1992 (c 13), Sch 8, para 69.
paras (k) to (n)	1960, Sch 2, paras (ca) to (cd); National Heritage Act 1983 (c 47), Sch 5, para 4.
para (o)	Local Government Reorganisation (Miscellaneous Provisions) Order 1990 (SI 1990/1765), art 3(1)(b).
para (p)	1960, Sch 2, para (d); Museums and Galleries Act 1992 (c 44), Sch 8, para 4.
paras (q) to (t)	1960, Sch 2, paras (ce) to (ch); Museums and Galleries Act 1992 (c 44), Sch 8, para 10.
para (u)	Imperial War Museum Act 1920 (c 16), s 5.
para (v)	National Maritime Museum Act 1934 (c 43), s 7.
para (w)	1960, Sch 2, para (e); Education Reform Act 1988 (c 40), Sch 12, paras 10, 63, 64; Further and Higher Education Act 1992 (c 13), Sch 8, para 69.
para (x)(y)	1960, Sch 2, paras (f)(g).
para (z)	1960, Sch 2, para (h); Museum of London Act 1965 (c 17), s 11.
para (za)	1960, Sch 2, para (i); British Library Act 1972 (c 54), s 4(2).
Sch 3	1960, Sch 3; London Government Act 1963 (c 33), s 81(9)(c); Local Government Act 1972 (c 70), ss 179(1)(4), 210(9)(f).
Sch 4	1960, Sch 4; Education Act 1973 (c 16), s 2(7).
Sch 5	1992, Sch 2.
Sch 6	1960, s 40(5) (as to, paras 1(3), 2, 3(3)) and 1992, ss 54(1)(b)(3), 56(4)(5) (as to, para 29 (7)(8)).
Sch 7	
Sch 8	

INDEX

References are to paragraph numbers.